ALSO BY ELLIS AMBURN

Buddy Holly: A Biography

Pearl: The Obsessions and Passions of Janis Joplin

Dark Star: The Roy Orbison Story

SUBTERRANEAN KEROUAC

SUBTERRANEAN KEROUAC

THE HIDDEN LIFE OF JACK KEROUAC

ELLIS AMBURN

ST. MARTIN'S PRESS   NEW YORK

Design by Bryanna Millis

Library of Congress Cataloging-in-Publication Data

Amburn, Ellis.
    Subterranean Kerouac : the hidden life of Jack Kerouac / Ellis
Amburn. — 1st ed.
        p.   cm.
    Includes bibliographical references and index.
    ISBN 0-312-14531-4
    1. Kerouac, Jack, 1922–1969—Biography.   2. Authors,
American—20th century—Biography.   3. Beat generation—Biography.
I. Title.
PS3521.E735Z54   1998
813'.54—dc21   98-14324
[B]   CIP

First Edition: August 1998

10 9 8 7 6 5 4 3 2 1

To the memory of
F. W. Dupee
and
Lionel Trilling,
my Columbia mentors
who set me on my life's course

"I was torn between Carolyn and Neal, and I married Stella because she's Sammy's sister. Figure that out and you've got the secret to my life and work."

—Jack Kerouac to the author, 1967

CONTENTS

PREFACE

Why a new book on Jack Kerouac, who has been the subject of more biographies in recent years than almost any other modern writer? There are several good reasons: I was Kerouac's editor in the 1960s, and I shared the dedication page of his last novel, *Vanity of Duluoz*, with his wife Stella. As the editor of two of his novels, *Desolation Angels* and *Vanity of Duluoz*, I saw a side of Kerouac that no one else knew or has written about—the man I call the "hidden Jack Kerouac." I believe that the fears and concerns he shared with me shed new light on his work, his sexuality, and the paradoxical world in which he existed, a world not unlike our own, where increasingly twisted values and ingrained prejudices still warp human nature.

During the years I was personally involved with Kerouac, 1964–1969, I gradually came to realize that his drinking was destroying him, and that this was somehow connected with his troubled sexuality. Years later, writing this book, I saw his life as a Greek tragedy in which a great and talented human being is destroyed by his fatal flaws. I have tried to show the enormous impact of his sex conflict, his desperate attempt to escape his own nature with compulsive heterosexuality. And I have tried to show, as well, the devastating effect of alcoholic insanity.

As a result, this biography focuses on Kerouac and the world that would inspire his novels, as opposed to being a work that examines his *oeuvre* from a more literary basis. I leave that formidable task to scholars.

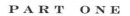

CLIMAX RUNNER

ONE

THE AGONIZED COCK OF THE MATTER

Jack Kerouac's childhood and adolescence were lived at a pitch of romantic intensity and fulfillment rarely equaled in his adulthood, when he became tormented, and often paralyzed, by conflicting sexual passions. After becoming a writer, he addressed the sublimity and lewdness of what he called "the littleboy loves of puberty" and "the kick of sex and adolescent lacerated love" with perhaps unprecedented depth and insight, both in the four "Lowell novels" about his youth—*The Town and the City, Dr. Sax, Maggie Cassidy*, and *Visions of Gerard*—and in a newly published 1950 letter to his friend Neal Cassady.

The letter marked Kerouac's first attempt to write in a totally honest, spontaneous, confessional way, a style that became the foundational rock for *On the Road* and all the books that followed. Jack sensed that he and Cassady were to be the architects of a dawning American literary renaissance, but first he had to empty his heart to Cassady. The "agonized cock of the matter," he wrote Neal, led straight to his childhood, and his choice of words clearly shows that Kerouac saw his life as a sexual drama, as indeed it would prove to be, as he moved restlessly from homoerotic to bisexual and heterosexual liaisons.

Until high school, he expressed his sexuality, as do many boys, almost entirely in homoerotic terms. These early emotions were recounted with lyricism and obsessiveness in Kerouac's correspondence with Cassady and later in *Dr. Sax, Maggie Cassidy*, and *Visions of Gerard*. In Kerouac's world, children not only fall passionately in love, but "love each other like lovers," as he wrote in *Maggie Cassidy*. His account of his nine-year-old brother Gerard's passion for Lajoie, a grade-school friend, was confined, in

Visions of Gerard, to voyeurism and genital fondling, but Kerouac went much further as a child, he confessed in a 1951 letter to Cassady. At five, he enjoyed masturbatory "pissadventures" with two other five-year-olds, Ovila "Banana" Marchand and Ovila's twin brother, Robert. Though the exciting episode with the twins stimulated Kerouac's curiosity about girls, it also led to his "dream-fear of homosexuality," he admitted to Cassady. In his teen years, though other biographies fail to mention it, there occurred an extraordinary, protracted French kiss between Jack and one of his adolescent buddies, in front of his parents and a number of friends, which is unflinchingly described in *Maggie Cassidy*, as is a full-fledged "juvenile homosexual ball" in *Dr. Sax*. The incredibly varied emotional reality of his childhood and youth provided the groundwork for the magnificently complex web of relationships that sparked Kerouac's novels, even while they turned his personal life into a battleground.

The publication of his *Selected Letters* in 1995 went a long way toward confirming the autobiographical nature of Kerouac's novels, but during his lifetime he told many people, including myself, that "every word I write is true." In the preface to *Big Sur*, he wrote, "My work comprises one vast book like Proust's . . . seen through the eyes of poor Ti Jean (me), otherwise known as Jack Duluoz." The commonly held assumption of all Kerouac scholars and aficionados is that his works are thinly veiled accounts of real people and actual events. In this book as in other biographies, stories are recounted with real people's names as accurate accounts of real events. Throughout, I have relied on the well-researched character key put together by pioneering Kerouac scholar Ann Charters and expanded by Barry Gifford, Lawrence Lee, and Dave Moore, and by others such as Gore Vidal, who in their memoirs have acknowledged their part in Kerouac's life. Because of these character keys, I, like other Kerouac biographers, have been able to rely on fictional works as primary nonfiction sources. The presumption of every Kerouac scholar, for example, is that the character "Japhy Ryder" in *The Dharma Bums* is Gary Snyder, that "Cody Pomeray" in *Visions of Cody* is Neal Cassady, and that "Mary Lou" in *On the Road* is LuAnne Henderson. Such attribution has not been signaled in the text in every instance but has been indicated in the notes section. As Kerouac's biographer, I have attempted to cross-check everything in his novels, using not only his letters, but also interviews and numerous other primary and secondary sources. The greatest help, of course, was having been his editor at Coward-McCann, Inc. for some of his most important work. Even prior to contract negotiations for *Vanity of Duluoz*, Kerouac assured me that his fiction was entirely factual, and that he hoped future biographers, if there were any, would regard his *oeuvre* as his truthful autobiography.[1]

During the time I knew him, Kerouac attempted to trace his "agonized cock" even further back than childhood, digging deeply into his family's roots. I vividly remember the day in the 1960s when he rang my office at 200 Madison Avenue. A former English major, just turning thirty and in my first publishing job, I still got cold chills every time my secretary, Ann Sheldon, came to my door or buzzed me on the intercom and said Jack Kerouac was calling. Though his books weren't selling well any more, everyone remembered him as the wild rebel who'd shaken up the world a few years previously with the groundbreaking, best-selling *On the Road*. On the phone, in a voice that was still bright and boyish, he told me he was going to France to discover his roots. Convinced he was the scion of Louis Alexandre Lebris de Kerouac, a noble Breton, he was off to do genealogical research in the Paris libraries and then to locate his ancestor's hometown in Brittany. When he returned a few weeks later, he told me that he'd given up his search in Brest. I didn't take his pretensions to aristocratic birth seriously, believing, along with James Joyce's biographer Richard Ellmann, that "the best dreams of noble ancestors occur on straw beds."

Kerouac, who began life as a poor mill-town boy in Lowell, Massachusetts, unfortunately never lived long enough to see his aristocratic claims borne out. In 1990, twenty-one years after Kerouac's death in 1969, a distant Canadian relative, Colette Bachand Wood, discovered the family's ancestral home not far from Brest. The elegant gray stone Chateau de Kerouartz (one of the many spellings of the clan's name) sits on a hill in Brittany, France, near the town of Lannilis. Throughout Kerouac's novels and in other biographies, the family's coat of arms is reported to bear the inscription, "*Aimer, Travailler, et Souffrir*" ("Love, Work, and Suffer"), but when Ms. Wood came upon the coat of arms at Chateau de Kerouartz, she discovered a silver sable, three iron crosses, and the motto, "*Tout en l'honneur de Dieu*" ("All in the name of God").[2]

Taken together, the two inscriptions sum up Kerouac's brief but fascinating life, which was passionate, productive, painful, and pious. But neither begins to suggest the transformative effect that Kerouac had on modern society. Only in the 1990s, nearly forty years after the publication of *On the Road*, would he come to be recognized as one of the major novelists of the twentieth century. The critical revaluation that greeted the long-anticipated release of his *Selected Letters* in 1995 reflected a popularity that had been growing for some time. Unfortunately, when I knew him in his last years, he was unread and forgotten.

At some point in their illustrious history, Kerouac's ancestors emigrated from France to Canada. Then, in 1890, tired of scratching potatoes from the frozen soil of Quebec, they drifted to New England and found work in the mill towns along the Concord and Merrimack Rivers, where the Industrial Revolution had begun earlier in the nineteenth century. Jack's grandfather, Jean-Baptiste, built a home at 16 Pierce Street, in Nashua, New Hampshire, forty miles north of Boston.

The French Canadians were called Canucks, and spoke a crude patois, *joual*, which led to their being scorned as outsiders. They lived in ghettos called "Little Canadas," intermarried, and regarded everyone outside their tight little community with a suspicion bordering on paranoia. Unfortunately, their narrow-mindedness and racism found their way into Kerouac's novels, but their unity and bravery are also woven into his life and work. For the despised Canucks, survival became a mystique. They called it *"la survivance."*

Drinking was one method of survival, and alcoholism ran in the Kerouac family. Jean-Baptiste loved vodka, and made it from potato peels. His son, Leo, Jack Kerouac's father, born in 1889, was also a drunk. Leo was blue-eyed, black-haired, and handsome — five-foot-seven and two hundred pounds of solid muscle, including a neck worthy of Atlas, and thick eyebrows that darted straight across his nose. True to his fiery astrological namesake, Leo was both a moody, philosophical man and a notorious good-time Charley who bounced between pessimistic resignation and a raging ambition for money and prestige. On the basketball court at the local Y, he was a fierce competitor, and his powerful legs seemed inexhaustible. In Leo's late teens, he maneuvered himself out of the sawmills and into a job at the *Nashua Telegraph* as an apprentice printer. Later, he worked as a reporter and type-setter at the French newspaper *L'Impartial*. Then, around 1912, the owner sent him fourteen miles down the Merrimack River to Lowell, Massachusetts, a rough textile and tenement town, to work on another of his newspapers, *L'Étoile.*

Leo's relatives in Lowell noticed that he liked his whiskey but couldn't hold it. On dates, he often ended up "breaking the furniture, in uncontrol-lable fury," his relative Cecile Plaud recalled in 1981. She also remembered Leo's "beautiful black hair and deep-set eyes," assets that no doubt attracted pretty Gabrielle Ange L'Evesque, his future wife.[3] Alcohol flowed freely in Gabrielle's family, too. Her father had been a bartender and tavern owner in Nashua. Both parents died early, leaving her an orphan at sixteen. She worked as a housemaid for aunts and uncles, and then went into the New England shoe factories, where her work as a skiving machine operator left her fingers permanently stained by black dye. At twenty, Gabrielle was a short, stocky, rosy-cheeked young woman with large blue eyes, coal-black hair, and a sunny disposition. She met Leo in Nashua and married him shortly thereafter, on October 15, 1915, not because she found him sexually appealing but because she thought he would save her from a life of servitude. A man's man, a heavy smoker, a reckless gambler, and a hard drinker, Leo provided Jack Kerouac's ideal of masculinity. It was ironic that Jack admired Leo's "virility," because according to novelist Gore Vidal, later one of Jack's sex partners, Leo was a "pansy." In *Visions of Cody*, Jack wrote that his father often appeared as a woman in his dreams, as "one-legged," and as "Louise," the name of a handicapped aunt — all suggesting that Jack not only sensed his father's homoeroticism, but, true to the mores of his time, considered it a crippling drawback rather than a natural form of sexual expression.

Though Gabrielle appeared to be strong, she was as emotionally vulner-able and prone to alcoholism as Leo was. Devout, volatile, insecure, suspicious, and almost pathologically stubborn, she refused to learn English, and continued speaking bastardized French, or *joual*, throughout her life. Jack Kerouac understood no English until he was six and spoke halting English until he was eighteen. His feeling that his life was tragic began with his difficult birth as a blue baby, and was exacerbated by a traumatic experience involving his older brother, Gerard, which he later described in his autobiographical letters to Cassady.[4]

Jack, or "Ti Jean" ("Little John"), as he was known, was born on March 12, 1922, at 9 Lupine Road, in the upstairs apartment of a shabby duplex building in a Lowell slum called Centralville. He was delivered at home by Dr. Victor Rochette, whom Kerouac later described as a lonely, desolate man, unwanted and unloved. According to a neighbor, Reginald Ouellette, Dr. Rochette's wife had died in childbirth and he'd never remarried, which struck Jack, who grew up in a close-knit family that spoiled him, as tragic. In a December 28, 1950, letter to Cassady, Kerouac disclosed that his birth occurred at 5 P.M. and that Gabrielle later gave him a blow-by-blow account of his delivery. As Jack was born, his mother could hear Pawtucket Falls a mile away, crashing into the Merrimack River, heavy with spring-thaw snow and ice. Her lurid description of the way he was forcibly dragged from her body, and then yelled at and spanked into life, led to his belief that birth was the beginning of the tragedy of consciousness, the dance of life that ends in death. The processes of nature, which most writers extol as symbols of renewal and eternal life, were always seen darkly by Kerouac.

According to Jack Kerouac's certificate of baptism, Rev. D. W. Boisvert baptized him as Jean Louis Kirouac on March 19, 1922, at the Parish of Saint Louis-de-France, in Centralville. This odd-looking subterranean church was originally the basement of what had been planned as a grand cathedral, but the poor Franco-Americans of Centralville had never been able to complete it. As a result, one walks down to the auditorium, rather than up, as if entering hell rather than heaven. The infant's godfather was an uncle from Nashua named Jean-Baptiste Kirouac Jr., whose wife, Rosanna Dumais Kirouac, was also present as a sponsor. Ti Jean was the youngest of Leo and Gabrielle's three children. Francois Gerard had been born August 23, 1916, and Caroline ("Nin") on October 25, 1918.

The family constantly moved around town, in and out of apartments and tenements, as Leo squandered his salary on gambling and booze and ran from landlords and other debtors, according to their neighbors in Lowell. Altogether, they made twenty moves in twenty years. But Ti Jean quickly blossomed into a chubby, healthy baby. His description of Gabrielle Kerouac in a letter to Cassady makes her sound like the mother of every child's dreams, a woman born to nurture and comfort. Even in the Great Depression, when some neighbors were subsisting on lard sandwiches, she set a table groaning with delectables: crêpes with maple syrup, sausage, and chocolate milk; pork meatball stew with onions, carrots, and potatoes; and home-cooked hot cherry pie with whipped cream. Ti Jean felt secure in her arms, resting his cheek against her smooth brown Art Deco bathrobe as she rocked him and sang French songs. He never denied the sexual nature of his love for his mother, and proudly told Cassady in a 1951 letter that, as a small child, he'd permitted her to fondle his anus. She'd taken him along to a sewing bee at the home of one of Leo's business associates, and as the women sat around the table, she took Jack's clothes off, placed him across her lap, and started pulling tapeworms, or some form of parasite, from his "ass-hole," he wrote. Though he insisted that all French-Canadian mothers enjoyed picking at their offspring, there could be little doubt that something had gone seriously awry in this household.[5]

Uncritically portrayed in other biographies, Ti Jean's brother, Gerard Kerouac, could at times be a rather nasty brat who slapped Ti Jean around without mercy, but he was also capable of great kindness and generosity. Gabrielle made no secret that Gerard was her favorite, and no doubt one of the reasons she indulged him was that he suffered from rheumatic fever, a disease that was carrying away children by the thousands in the 1920s, before the advent of penicillin and heart-valve transplants. His condition was exacerbated by the toxic, sometimes violent atmosphere at home. Both parents were combative drunks, forever fighting over Leo's gambling, chronic impecuniousness, and whoring. In *Visions of Gerard*, a tenement wife shouts at her husband, "They always told me not to marry you, you were a drunkard at sixteen," and her husband retorts, "Aw shut ya big ga dam mouth. I gave you your money, I'm goin to work, I'll be gone all night, you oughta be satisfied, ya cow." In such a household, cringing, innocent children catch the disease of alcoholism years before they take their first drink.

The frail, neurotic Gerard attended Saint Louis-de-France Elementary School, where he impressed the priests and nuns with his precocious spirituality, but he was also an earthy, lusty boy, obsessed with the "little ding-dong" ("*sa tite gidigne*") of Lajoie, a classmate who stood next to him at the urinals during recess. When Gerard and Lajoie finished peeing, they went into a corner and became engrossed with each other's genitals. It would have remained a typical childhood incident of no particular significance had it not been for a later episode that left Ti Jean frightened and traumatized. Kerouac wrote Cassady that he dreaded Gerard and privately suspected that Gerard despised him. Gabrielle was convinced that Gerard was a saint, and was so successful in polluting Ti Jean's head with this fanatical notion that Kerouac was still talking about it in the mid-1960s, when he told his Florida friend, Ron Lowe, "*I swear to God*, small birds would even light on Gerard's outstretched hands as he stood at the window."

The pressure of being the "brother of Jesus" carried too high a price, and Ti Jean came to view Gerard with a mixture of love and loathing. Gerard absolutely doted on Ti Jean, turning him into a helpless emotional hostage. Ti Jean was so comfortable cuddling in bed with Gerard in the morning that he never wanted to get up. Gerard was convinced that the Virgin Mary herself had appointed him Ti Jean's protector. He deliberately frightened Ti Jean with ghost stories so that he could rush to the terrified child's rescue. Even at three years old, Ti Jean had erotic feelings for Gerard, and that was the "agonized cock of the matter," Jack wrote in a 1950 letter to Cassady. And Kerouac's 1956 novel, *Visions of Gerard*, swarms with erotic references such as "kissable Gerard," whose breath was "like crushed flowers." To kiss Gerard, Kerouac recalled, was like "kissing a lamb in the belly or an angel in her wing."

At the urinals in school, Gerard finally became so enamored of Lajoie that he confessed everything to a priest, who made him say fifteen Hail Marys. Around the same time, Ti Jean received a weird midnight visitation from Gerard as he lay in his crib. He awoke to see Gerard hovering over him, looking "implacable" (defined in *American Heritage Dictionary* as "grim, inexorable, merciless, remorseless, unrelenting, unyielding, intransigent, unbending"). Kerouac later confirmed to Cassady that Gerard seemed to be "intent on me with hate" that night. After the incident, Ti Jean became so shy that he refused to let anyone see him naked. At Salisbury Beach, someone offered him five dollars if he'd put on his bathing trunks, but he absolutely refused. "Nobody was going to see me part naked in those days," he recalled. The emotional difficulties Jack experienced in adulthood seem to have stemmed in part from the trauma with Gerard, which he defined in his letter to Neal as the root of all his "mysteries."

Gerard's own emotional deformities sprang largely from the unnatural role thrust upon him as the oldest son in a troubled, alcoholic home. Sometimes Leo staggered in at 10 A.M., his poker games having lasted all night or even through an entire weekend. He also played the horses and spent eight hours a day in a bookie joint. "You no good basted," yells a beleaguered mill-town wife in Kerouac's *The Town and the City*, possibly echoing Gabrielle. "I haven't got enough money to buy a dress, I have to wait here while you go drinkin' and whorin' all over the country." Witnessing the scene, young Joe Martin feels a deep sense of shame, which is typical of children of alcoholic parents. In Leo's absence, nine-year-old Gerard, even in his weakened condition, took on the role of surrogate husband to Gabrielle and father to Ti Jean and Nin, doing his best to hold the shattered household together. One night, Gabrielle lay "flopped in despair" on the couch, racked by a splitting headache, while Leo was away at a poker game. Even though it was freezing outside, Gerard offered to go to the pharmacy for a bottle of aspirin, and Gabrielle permitted him to do so, calling him "my golden."⁶

Despite his dissolute lifestyle, Leo prospered as a businessman during Ti Jean's first years. He moved up from *L'Étoile* to become an insurance salesman, and then went into business for himself, establishing Spotlite Print at 463 Market Street, near a canal in downtown Lowell. He published weekly programs for local movie and burlesque houses, as well as the *Lowell Spotlite*, a theatrical newspaper featuring humorous reviews of vaudeville and movie attractions. Driven to succeed, Leo also worked as *L'Étoile*'s advertising manager at 26 Prince Street, and even tried his hand at political commentary, contributing a controversial column to another small paper, the *Focus*. He took intemperate potshots at officials in City Hall and began to make enemies in high places. But Kerouac would remember him, in a letter to Neal, as a dynamic, jovial young hustler. With Leo's rare combination of editorial acumen and business know-how, he might have become a publishing giant had he not permitted his drinking and gambling to hold him back. "I see now his true soul, which is like mine — life means nothing to him," Jack once observed. In the Kerouacs' divided household, Jack sided with his mother against his father, accepting her judgment that Leo was "a drunkard and didn't . . . give a shit." Cecile Plaud once commented on the striking physical resemblance between Jack and his father, citing their black hair, pensive expressions, and "beautifully cut" features. Realizing that Jack was a "star-crossed victim of heredity" filled her with a feeling of "tragic déjà vu." She feared that a hard life was ahead for Jack as the son of an alcoholic.

Gabrielle was also a heavy drinker, and the Kerouac home was often the scene of boisterous celebrations, especially after the move from Lupine Road to Maiden Lane. On New Year's Eve in 1924, at the stroke of midnight, Ti Jean awoke from a deep sleep as his room filled with drunks wearing party hats. Laughing and yelling, the revelers swarmed all over the children, kissing and slobbering.

Years later, research into the lives of children of alcoholic parents revealed that such children hate themselves, their parents, and life in general. As Kerouac grew up, he came to blame himself for his parents' drinking, his mother's unhappiness, his father's joblessness, and even his brother's death. In a letter to Cassady, Kerouac revealed that William S. Burroughs had once subjected him to lay analysis and had concluded that Kerouac wanted Gerard to die. At the same time, Ti Jean was fiercely possessive of his brother. "Jack was jealous and didn't like the idea of anyone else being there with Gerard," recalled Roger Ouellette, Reginald's brother and a childhood neighbor of the Kerouacs. "I was asked to leave without staying there too long," he added.

Ouellette's sister, Pauline, saw Gerard in the spring of 1926, sitting in the backyard on Beaulieu Street swathed in blankets, though the day was warm and sunny. She described him as looking "sickly, very pale, and light-haired. His mother hovered over him. There was nothing exceptional about him. He was like any other kid, [but] if you've ever lost a child, you would understand." Gabrielle eventually crumbled under the strain, suffering a nervous breakdown at the age of twenty-nine. Kerouac was four years old in 1926 when his family went "crazy," he later wrote in the "88th Chorus" of *Mexico City Blues*. That was the year that Gerard died, at nine years of age, and the strange experiences of his last days, conveyed to Kerouac over the years by his mother, had an enormous impact on Kerouac's work and marked the beginning of what he called his "immortal *idealism*."[7]

Just before the end, Gerard said he'd seen a vision while sitting in catcchism class at Saint Louis-de-France. The Virgin Mary appeared to him, her robes billowing behind her, held aloft by thousands of bluebirds. Then he saw himself ascending to heaven in a white wagon pulled by snowy lambs. Coming out of his trance, he told a startled nun that she should never again be afraid of anything, because everyone was already in heaven, though no one knew it. "All is well," he added. "Practice kindness. Heaven is nigh."

His death was gruesome. The specific cause, as diagnosed by Dr. Nathan Pulsifer, was "purpura hemorragica," bleeding of such furious and uncontrollable intensity that his skin turned purple and he choked to death on his own blood, screaming, suffocating, and writhing in agony. Convinced he was a saint, nuns from school hovered about his bed and recorded his dying words, which concerned "the unreality of death (and life too) . . . the calm hand of God everywhere slowly benedicting." Gerard's "visions," as filtered through Gabrielle's superstitious Canuck mind, became the bedrock of Kerouac's adult philosophy, bolstered by his discovery of Buddhism and his continuing faith in what he called "my sweet Christ."

From these ethical systems and from his own wrenching experience, Jack forged his belief that the ultimate answer is to be found in the shimmering golden emptiness of the here and now, a concept in which eternity and the present moment are one and the same. In the 1960s, as Kerouac evolved into the spiritual leader of the Beat Generation (along with Allen Ginsberg), he returned again and again to Gerard, his childhood inspiration. "I marvel at my love for him," he wrote thirty years after his brother's death. According to Gerard's death certificate, he expired at 11:45 P.M. on June 2, 1926. It was a significant date in American letters, for Gerard would haunt the life and work of Jack Kerouac, sending him on a passionate search for male companions to replace his lost brother — a search that culminated with Neal Cassady and On the Road — and also inspiring the luminous Visions of Gerard, a novel of magical grace and the author's personal favorite.

Gerard was buried in Nashua, New Hampshire, in the St. Louis de Gonzague Cemetery, named after the patron saint of Catholic youth.[8] Kerouac's often-quoted statement that he had a "beautiful" childhood, originally written on a Viking Press publicity questionnaire, misled many of his biographers. Though his later boyhood in Pawtucketville was indeed gleeful, his earliest years in Centralville, following Gerard's death, were spent in abject terror. Only his imagination saved him. His first artistic creations were but visualized fears that he once described as "fantastic flights of beauty into a world populated by saints and incredible monsters." He somehow convinced himself that a movie was being made of his life and that cameramen were following him everywhere. He even made up a title for the film: The Complete Life of a Parochial School Boy. In Mexico City Blues, he touchingly wrote that he was the "first crazy person" he'd ever known. His parents became concerned about his loneliness and isolation after Gerard's death and introduced him to two new playmates, never suspecting they would become his first sex partners. They were five-year-old, orphaned twin boys, Ovila ("Banana") and Robert, who lived in a ramshackle Victorian house on Hildreth Ridge, where they were being raised by an aunt. Ti Jean climbed under the porch with them, and they urinated together and then left their penises exposed, only pretending to pee. To Ti Jean, it was a highly satisfying erotic "game," he later wrote Cassady, describing his "masturbatory world." The thrilling "kick" of unlimited voyeurism and sex with Banana and Robert, Kerouac confessed, brought about his lifelong fear of being gay. In his 1950–1952 letters to Cassady, written when Jack was in his late twenties and hopelessly smitten with Neal, he composed both a thumbnail autobiography and a plea for love. The duality of Kerouac's nature was such that, even as he sought homoerotic fulfillment through Cassady, he implored Cassady to make him an acceptable, stereotypical male — a "wrangler" out of the Old West — and save him from the horrors of Lowell, the scene of his crippling childhood trauma. His January 10, 1951, letter ended in a *cri de coeur*, as Kerouac begged Cassady to recognize how "strangely connected" they were. He was seeking the closeness he'd known with Gerard, and as Neal would discover, being Kerouac's brother was a tall order indeed.[9]

In 1928, Ti Jean, now six years old, enrolled in the "baby grade" at Saint Louis-de-France parochial school. The sonorous language of the Catholic liturgy — the Apostles' Creed, the Hail Mary, the rosary — gave him his first taste of great writing. On May 17, 1928, dressed in a white suit and holding a rosary and a golden crucifix, Ti Jean went to confession prior to taking his first communion. "You played with your little *gidigne?*" the priest asked. "Yes, *mon pere*," he replied, and he had to say the entire rosary, ten *Our Fathers*, and ten *Hail Marys*. As he prayed, he imagined that he could hear God telling him that he had a good soul, but would suffer and die in pain and terror; ultimately, however, he would be saved. Four months later, he enrolled in the first grade at Saint Louis-de-France, "a harrowing experience," according to his later friend, poet Philip Whalen, who reflected, "American Catholicism . . . takes this tough line about how the body is evil. . . . So he had this trip about 'dirty me.' . . . This helped complicate his life."

Just over a year later, in October 1929, the Great Depression hit, and although Leo managed to hold onto his print shop, the family went into a downward spiral that landed them in less desirable neighborhoods with each successive move. For little children, frequent moves constitute "a real and unnameable tragedy . . . a catastrophe of their hearts," Kerouac wrote. Though he would grow up to become a homeless wanderer for much of his life, he never overcame the fear and sense of doom that characterized his rootless childhood.

In 1930, the impulsive Leo destroyed the only chance he would ever have to become a man of importance. Impressed with Leo's exposés of graft at City Hall, a group of powerful citizens offered to back him if he'd run for mayor. "Sure," he blurted, "I'll run for mayor, but if I win I'll have to throw every crook out of Lowell, and there'll be nobody left in town." The offer was never repeated. At forty-one, Leo was washed up in Lowell. In his perceptive article, "Ti Jean and Papa Leo: Jack Kerouac's Relationship with His French-Canadian Father," Richard S. Morrell wrote that Leo viewed the world as a "pigsty" and was "forever complaining about those in Lowell who had done him wrong." Kerouac acknowledged, in *Visions of Cody*, that his father was indeed "an angry, a *hating* man," but he always gave Leo credit for being brave and determined. "Whenever somebody gave him some gaff, he let em have it," Jack wrote.[10] Despite ruinous setbacks, Leo continued to try his luck in various fields, and at one point he became a fight promoter, managing a gym in Centralville.

Ti Jean, who was about nine, became infatuated with one of Leo's wrestlers, Armand Gauthier, and when Leo invited Armand home for supper, Ti Jean "beseeched him to show us his muscles. Nin [who was ten years old] would hang from one biceps and I hung from the other, whee . . . what a build! Like Mister America." Ti Jean also cruised the urinals at school, as Gerard had done before him, and stared at other boys' penises. He told a priest about it, and the priest became excited, asking for full details including size. Later, while prowling around the grotto, a religious shrine that Gerard had introduced him to, Ti Jean happened upon some boys from parochial school playing with their penises, and joined in. When he confessed this to a priest, he was told to recite the entire rosary.

Sometimes he spent the night with a tough, likable neighborhood friend, and this inevitably led to pubescent sex play. Kerouac estimated their ages at the time to be eight or nine years old. His friend lived in a large old Victorian house, and Jack's parents often went there to drink moonshine with a group known as the "Jolly Fourteen." Ti Jean's friend, a daring and fearless forerunner of Neal Cassady, became the first of Kerouac's "littleboy loves of puberty." He was the opposite of Ti Jean, who still believed in ghosts and imagined goblins lurking in every shadow. Nothing scared his friend, despite the turrets, attics, and spooky dark nooks in his house. In bed with his friend, Ti Jean "could feel the goose pimples of his cold legs or the leather of his tar black heel, as we lay in dank barns and attics of his various homes," Kerouac wrote in *Dr. Sax*. By day, they hiked along the banks of the Merrimack and explored deserted houses. Stopping to take a leak, they stood next to each other and looked at "drawings of great cocks of the length of snakes, with dumb venom spittles." As always, "pissing was a thrill." On summer nights, with the Jolly Fourteen rioting downstairs, Ti Jean and his friend fondled each other "in pissy mattresses . . . playing with our ding dongs . . . old buddies of the lifetime of boyhood." Soon, they graduated to more definitive sex. After watching a man and woman make love in the riverside litter by the Boott Mills, "dimpled lady legs and hairy manlegs" all atangle, the boys went to bed together, and were "darker, wilder, sexualler, with flash-lights, dirty magazines, jiggling hands, sucks." At ten, they ran away together, but their frantic families found them the following day under a bridge in Tyngsboro, New Hampshire, taking a break prior to heading north. It was probably his childhood eroticism that grounded Ti Jean in reality and kept him sane, despite a pathological home environment. When Gabrielle permitted him to sleep with her, he wound his legs around her and dreamed that she rubbed her pink thigh in his groin.

The most intense relationship of his childhood was with a bright school-boy from a socially prominent family, whom he met at St. Joseph's Parochial when he was still ten. Ti Jean by now had glossy dark hair and serious blue eyes, and was a favorite of the Marist Brothers, who were grooming him to be an altar boy at the prestigious St. Jean Baptiste Cathedral. They urged him to prepare for the priesthood, but Ti Jean was swept away by his obses-sion with the schoolboy, doting on him during class and in the playground during recess. Years later, Kerouac described the boy as being "more beautiful than any of the girls in school, had redder cheeks, whiter teeth, and angelic eyes." In both *Dr. Sax* and *Maggie Cassidy*, Kerouac portrayed him as the love of his young life. He came from an upper-class section of town and was driven to school each day by his father, who was powerful in local politics. Though the boys lived on opposite sides of the tracks, Ti Jean was often a guest in his friend's home, where he first discovered the world of books in the family's extensive library. Afterward, Ti Jean would be driven back to Pawtucketville in the family's expensive sedan. At home, standing in front of a portrait of Gerard, Ti Jean prayed for his friend to fall in love with him. He wanted to hold hands with him, and he asked Gerard to make his friend declare his love and to arrange for them to run away to Africa together. The following year, his obsession only increased, and in *Dr. Sax*, he described it as "a real love affair at eleven." It ended when Jack was graduated early from St. Joseph's, and his friend remained at the school. Jack later speculated that zoning laws may have been responsible for his premature removal from the school, but this seems unlikely, since Jack lived within walking distance of St. Joseph's, while his friend lived several miles away. Leo blamed the boy's family, pointing out that Jack and his friend were archrivals as the school's top honor students, and Jack was deemed to be too "challenging." Jack later dismissed his friend with the remark, "He became a sour Yankee with dreams of small editorships in Vermont."[11]

At Christmas 1932, Gabrielle scurried about the kitchen on Phebe Ave-nue, peering into the oven while Leo relaxed by the radio, smoking his cigar and reading the funnies. The fact that Nin shoveled snow while Ti Jean went hiking reveals how spoiled he was by a family that adored and pampered him. When he returned from his hike, he looked through the window before going inside. "My heart breaks," he later wrote, "to see they're moving so slowly, with such dear innocence within, they don't realize time and death will catch them." As an altar boy, Ti Jean served Mass at the main altar at St. Jean Baptiste, and on June 8, 1933, Francis Spellman, the future cardinal and archbishop of New York, who became one of the world's most powerful religious leaders, officiated at Ti Jean's confirmation. Lowell was in the Archdiocese of Boston, and at the time Spellman was auxiliary bishop to Lowell-born William Cardinal O'Connell. As Ti Jean stood before him, Spellman anointed his head with chrism, a consecrated mixture of oil and balsam, and lightly slapped his cheek, a ritual reminding the confirmant that he must show courage as a "soldier in the army of Christ," a defender of the Catholic faith. During the same month, Ti Jean graduated from St. Joseph's, marking the end of his French-oriented education.

The following September, at the age of eleven, he entered the seventh grade at Bartlett Junior High, walking a mile and a half from Pawtucketville. For the first time, he entered a world that was not exclusively French. The school was located in a predominantly Greek and Irish section called The Acre, and to his tough new friends, Kerouac was no longer Ti Jean or Jean Louis, the names he would continue to be called at home — he was now Jackie Kerouac. Walking home one day with Billy Chandler, who later appeared as "Dicky Hampshire" in *Dr. Sax*, Billy flattered him by scrawling "Jack is a big punk" on an alley fence off Salem Street. Billy Chandler, destined to die in combat on Bataan in World War II, was at Kerouac's side when he made his earliest foray into narrative as well as graphic art. On long afternoons in their Pawtucketville bedrooms, they drew cartoons together and eventually created an elaborate tale of jungle adventures in Guatemala, where Billy's brother was going.

When alone in his room, Jackie acted out many other fantasies, inching his way into a life of authorship. One of his most elaborate fantasies was inspired by the popular pulp magazine of the 1930s, *The Shadow*, which featured a ghostly detective who could render himself invisible at will. Jackie bought the pulps at a store run by a dirty old man who sometimes lured neighborhood kids into the back room, using candy or pennies as bait, and played with their "dingdangs." Emboldened by his readings in *The Shadow*, Ti Jean dressed up in Leo's slouch hat and Nin's cape, and swooped around Pawtucketville, stealing small items from neighbors and leaving cryptic notes, wadded in cans, warning, "The Silver Tin Can Will Visit You Tomorrow." These exercises in imagination and incipient juvenile delinquency soon gave way to an overweening interest in sports, which began when Leo took Jackie to Red Sox baseball games in Boston, and to the horse races at Rockingham, Suffolk Downs, and Narragansett. From that point on, athletics and esthetics were inextricably linked in Kerouac's life and shaped the kind of artist he would become.

In a profound sense, it was sports, more than anything else, that galvanized Kerouac as a writer. At home, in his grandest imaginative flight to date, he invented his own intricate athletic games. Using a rock, he would draw a baseball diamond in the mud of the backyard and play out whole seasons, using a nail as a baseball bat and a ball bearing as the baseball. Up in his room, on rainy days, he amused himself by inventing a horse race, using marbles for horses. First he would dry-mop the flowery linoleum floor, creating a smooth, clean track. Then, after placing bets, he would release the marbles from under a ruler barrier, and let them slide down a folded Parcheesi board, propped at an incline on a stack of books. As the marbles raced across the floor, he made bugle sounds through his fist and imagined a roaring crowd in the grandstand. In time, he created a whole world of horse racing, and even handprinted a newspaper to write up the races.

These games, though still unconsciously, had the effect of honing his skills in the fictional saga form. Each of his imaginary horses had its own name, personality, and history—Don Pablo, Flying Doodad, Rownomore, a-Remonade Girl, and Old Mate. Don Pablo was the most chipped because he'd long been a heroic turf champion. Jackie invented trainer Ben Smith, the owners, the president of the racing association, and even the bettors in the stands, giving them all distinctive personalities, especially jockey Jack Lewis, who bore the American version of Kerouac's given name, Jean Louis. Kerouac made up the Turf, the Graw Futurity, and the Mohican Futurity, and sometimes even rigged races so that two of the fans, based on Leo and Jackie, an impoverished father and son from the South, could win. Jackie assumed various roles, from track handicapper to racing forum publisher, but usually he was Jack Lewis, who owned and rode mighty Repulsion, a solid steel ball bearing that usually came out ahead of the other marbles. This imagined world included upsets—Mate became the Turf's first winner, and then despite incredible complications, Don Pablo, though chipped and battered, proved to be the toughest horse of all, and won the Turf in an 18–1 upset. The excitement in all this competition gave Kerouac his first sense of dramatic form, and his epic accounts of the races in his homemade newspaper foreshadowed his multiple-volume life work, "The Duluoz Legend."

He went on to invent a baseball playing-card game that was amazing in its complexity, comparable to the later game in Robert Coover's *The Universal Baseball Association*. Kerouac continued to play his game of baseball solitaire throughout his life. He created statistics, box scores, and fleshed-out baseball players who reappeared from game to game, and season to season, like the characters in a Faulkner Yoknapatawpha County novel. Among his mythic athletes were Francis X. Cudley, a Boston Irishman who stood at the plate as erect as a Jesuit priest; Pictorial Review Jackson, known as "Pic," the best pitcher in the league, who acquired his name from his love of reading the Sunday newspaper supplements; and Roddy Delaney, who began as a rookie and ended up as a veteran pitcher. In the end, Kerouac created a whole cosmology, unwittingly practicing some of the most exacting tasks of the novelist. There was a more immediate reason for creating an alternative world. He was still struggling to break free from the "ghosts of the Pawtucketville night," the legacy of a childhood marred by fear, superstition, and death.[12]

Again, Gabrielle worried that he was spending too much time alone and urged him to go outside and play. This led to his involvement in real sports, particularly football, which came to dominate his life for the next decade. He connected with a robust gang of Pawtucketville boys, and developed formidable athletic skills during long summer afternoons of sandlot football and "scrub," an abbreviated form of baseball. From ages eleven through sixteen, Jackie and his new friends converged on the "wrinkly tar" corners of Pawtucketville for bull sessions, and then spread out to the various playgrounds around Lowell: the cowfield near St. Rita's church, Bartlett Junior High, Dracut, and Textile field. Organizing themselves as the Dracut Tigers, they became the nucleus of what would later be the Lowell High School varsity football team. Jackie was about twelve years old when he developed a serious case of hero worship on a superb sandlot athlete who spat with exquisite disdain as he wound up on the mound.

While baseball was fun, Jackie soon discovered his true métier was football. One teammate called Kerouac "a great athlete. When I tackled him, or tried to . . . I saw stars. He plowed right through me." His friends nicknamed him "Zagg" after a neighborhood drunk who zigzagged when he stumbled down the street, but one buddy attributed the nickname to Jackie's awesome maneuvers in the backfield. Admired by all, he soon became the leader of the pack. "Jack had everything," a member of the gang recalled, and it was true: as an adolescent, he was handsome, intelligent, funny, strong, quick, and agile, everything most boys dream of being. As he grew up, his facial features took on the dark, chiseled majesty of Gabrielle's half-Indian grandmother, and he'd also inherited Leo's muscular physique. He felt like a god, and everybody treated him like one.

Sensing his potential, Jack's status-conscious parents urged him to seek a better class of friends than his Pawtucketville running mates. They pointed out that one of the boys was poor and had no father, and another was a Greek, which automatically made him a sex fiend in their estimation. They perhaps suspected the strong homoerotic element in Jackie, who marveled at one buddy's giant penis; the boy would lay it out on a table and challenge "anyman to have a bigger one," Kerouac wrote in *Maggie Cassidy*. As the organ became erect, the boy would "shove seven or eight or nine or ten quarters off a table with his piece."

One day Jackie tried to tell a special friend in the gang that he loved him, and only him, but he choked on the words. His friend's unusual combination of sensitivity and brawn also characterized Jackie, but these attributes did not seem to be at war in his friend the way they were in Kerouac. Before he met Neal Cassady the following decade, he idealized this youth as a sort of superman, who was both intellectual and manly.

As Kerouac entered his teens, these aspects of his own nature remained unreconciled. He had to conceal the homoerotic side of his personality in order to retain his status among his straight Pawtucketville buddies. Repressing this fact of his identity, he would become increasingly frantic as he grew older. Sensing his true self slipping away from him, he was left with nothing but the ghost of an unlived life. He idolized his friends for their honesty, naturalness, and spontaneity, but he could never permit himself the same openness, trapped as he was in a judgmental heterosexual world that was often at odds with his complex nature. The horseplay of the Pawtucketville gang was loaded with sexual overtones, such as grabbing and squeezing each other's testicles. In *Dr. Sax*, Kerouac wrote that he held one boy's "balls, hanging helplessly in my grip" until the boy took a bite out of his backside. While Kerouac's friends regarded him as "a hard-nosed backfield man . . . a real speeder," he doted on the matinee-idol allure of one youth who resembled Tyrone Power. In *Maggie Cassidy* Kerouac referred to this boy's "conscious perfect good looks . . . thin as a razor, sharply handsome, cut with a fingernail file," and his wiry body that "swiveled on inexistent [sic] hips." A favorite pastime was "basking nekkid in the sun" at Beaver Brook, known as "Bareass Beach" in Kerouac's Lowell novels.

Though the boys didn't consider their behavior to be homoerotic, many experts would call it homosexual, as did Kerouac himself, who depicted one of their sex orgies in *Dr. Sax* as "a juvenile homosexual ball." The boys had cultivated a handsome but retarded nineteen-year-old Franco-American named Zaza, who masturbated for them on demand, "spermatazoing in all directions." He would do it as many times as they asked him to — "thirteen times last Monday — he came each time exactly, no lie — Zaza has an endless supply of come." Zaza was also adept at "jacking off dogs and worst of all sucking off dogs." Later, even as young men of seventeen, they continued to fool around with Zaza, who was still "always masturbating in front of the others." Eventually, the gang forswore these "childlike pursuits haunted by darkness and goofs," and thereafter they "hung themselves" on "lacerated" relationships with girls, beginning with a two-hundred-pound prostitute, who would sit in a rocking chair and occasionally flash her vagina. Leo was one of her regular customers.[13]

By 1935, it was obvious to everyone that Jackie was the best athlete in the gang and destined for some kind of stardom. Leo had once been built like a fireplug, squat and muscular, and the description also fit Jackie. "He was good at *everything*," commented a Lowell admirer years later in *Sports Illustrated*. Still others recalled that Kerouac was "strong as a goddam bull . . . Right here, right in his thighs, that's where he had it. . . . What a build." Determined to become a great runner, Jackie devised his own stopwatch using an old phonograph turntable. Soon he impressed onlookers at Textile Institute's cinder track, charging across the finish line ahead of everyone else. He played his first serious sandlot football game in October 1935 at a cow pasture in Dracut. Though Kerouac was the youngest player, he scored nine touchdowns, and his team, the Dracut Tigers, clobbered Rosemont 60–0. "*Nine* touchdowns," recalled Sam Samaras in *Sports Illustrated*. "You had to hit him early, because once he got out of the backfield he was gone. Couldn't catch him. He was *dangerous*." Overnight, Kerouac became a "local sandlot sensation."

His teachers at Bartlett Junior High thought him as gifted intellectually as he was physically. According to a teacher always referred to simply as Miss Dineen, he liked Walt Whitman's "O Captain! My Captain!" and the New England poet John Greenleaf Whittier, who was born just twenty miles northeast of Lowell in 1807 and who for many generations was one of the most popular poets taught in U.S. schools. Whittier's "Evangeline" and "Snowbound" focused Kerouac's attention on the "tragedies of family life," recalled Miss Dineen, and Whittier also helped him appreciate "God's Infinite Beauty reflected in all creation." Another teacher, Miss Mansfield, encouraged all her students to read the *Iliad*. One day, she asked a student named Mickey O'Brien, "Who was Agamemnon?" Mickey said, "He was a Greek." Miss Mansfield said, "Elucidate." Mickey said, "He was a Greek, too."

In 1934, under the influence of dedicated teachers like Miss Dineen and Miss Mansfield, Jackie launched himself into his lifelong occupation and started chronicling his "history of myself." After reading Mark Twain's *Huckleberry Finn*, he handprinted in a nickel notebook a novel entitled *Mike Explores the Merrimack*, which established the basic plotline that his mature fiction would follow: going forth into the world for adventure and then returning home. After reading Jack London, he wrote a story about an engineer tramping the Rocky Mountains, and it was fully stocked with all the Jack London trappings—jodhpurs, boots, a jacket with many pockets, a brave German shepherd, a Turkish wood pipe, and a barful of imported Scotch. Miss Mansfield pronounced it excellent.

The most intellectually stimulating person Jackie met at Bartlett was Sebastian "Sammy" Sampas, who was the same age as Jackie but one grade below him. The importance of Sammy Sampas in the life of Jack Kerouac, from both an artistic and personal standpoint, cannot be overstated, for as Kerouac wrote in the introduction to *Lonesome Traveler*, he "decided to become a writer at age 17 under influence of Sebastian Sampas." As a pivotal character in some of Kerouac's most important works, Sammy appears as "Alexander Panos" in *The Town and the City*, "Sebastian" in *Visions of Cody*, "Savas" in *Visions of Gerard*, and "Sabbas 'Sabby' Savakis" in *Vanity of Duluoz*. Their relationship began one day in junior high when Jackie defended Sammy against a gang of bullies. According to Kerouac, Sammy idolized him from then on. The curly-haired Sammy's romantic Victor Mature–like visage appealed to Jackie, but his friends considered Sammy to be a "sissy more than anything else," G. J. Apostolos recalled. The word *sissy* was, and remains, the most common American euphemism for homosexual, and it also denotes a coward. Sammy was certainly no coward. In a 1995 interview, Billy Koumantzelis, the younger brother of Lowell High varsity track star Johnny Koumantzelis, said that Sammy "was surrounded by some tough guys, but I think Sammy could have held his own with any one of them. He had guts. The Sampas family has guts." Charles Jarvis, who attended Greek Parochial School with Sammy, described him as a crybaby with a pretty face who became the butt of childish pranks. But even Jarvis wouldn't call him a sissy. He once saw Sammy attack a bully who was tormenting a smaller boy. Sammy bravely exchanged punches with the bully until a teacher broke them up.

Fifteen years later, in *Visions of Cody*, Kerouac defined the nature of his relationship with Sammy, comparing it with the gay love affair of the nineteenth-century French poets Arthur Rimbaud and Paul Marie Verlaine. Like Rimbaud, Kerouac required a gay muse, and Sammy became his Verlaine. In the same passage, he wrote that Neal Cassady had also required a homoerotic muse, and Allen Ginsberg had fulfilled that role. Even Kerouac's friend, Lucien Carr, who killed his gay suitor, David Kammerer, had needed Kammerer the same way a flower needs the sun to unfold. In each case, the love of another man was required for validation as a human being and artist. In his pioneering study, *Jack Kerouac*, Warren French remarked on the "homoerotic element in [Kerouac's] relationship with Sebastian . . . suggest [ing] a stronger feeling than customary male bonding." Kerouac's account of their relationship was couched in romantic terms in his novels, which included anguished lovers' partings in train stations and a skinny-dipping scene in which the Sammy character reads aloud from "Ode on a Grecian Urn," Keats's classic of ambivalent love ("Bold lover, never, never canst thou kiss, though winning near the goal"). Kerouac's parents disapproved of Sammy, and Leo called him "Garbo." But Kerouac always saw Sammy in heroic terms and referred to him, in one of his letters, as "a tawny lusty youth." Like Rimbaud, Neal, and Lucien, Jack had to be in touch with the honest truth about himself, even if it was at odds with society's notion of masculinity, before his power could be released. Love, supplied by Sebastian, was the key.

The Pawtucketville gang was appalled by Sammy's histrionics—he wore a laurel wreath in his hair on the streets of Lowell—but Sammy made Kerouac believe in himself as a writer, and their friendship "opened up into a springtime of wonder and knowledge," Kerouac wrote. Sammy managed to get Jackie accepted into an elite group of student writers at Bartlett called the Scribbler's Club, and Jackie's short story, "The Cop on the Beat," was praised by Miss Mansfield for its descriptive power. Sammy was the moving spirit behind "The Young Prometheans," an intellectual discussion round table, and interested Jackie in joining the group. The Young Prometheans frequently convened at the Sampas house at 2 Stevens Street to debate literary, social, and political issues.

Sammy's sister, petite, five-foot-one-inch Stella, was attracted to Jackie, and Jackie was drawn to her, especially when he heard that Stella, though only a teenager, had helped raise and support the younger children in the large Sampas family. A brunette with flashing brown eyes, Stella was modest, quiet, and soft-spoken. Somewhat older than Kerouac, having been born on Armistice Day 1918, she had worked as a stitcher since 1932, when she was a fourteen-year-old in the eighth grade. Self-sacrifice was expected of the eldest daughter in a traditional Greek family, and Stella carried out her burden in her characteristically kind and easygoing fashion. "Sebastian was a poet," Stella said years later. "He had the potential to become a truly great man." When Kerouac began to visit the Sampas home, she was secretly ecstatic. "Stella was in love with Jack from the beginning," Betty Watley, a later friend of Stella's, recalled. "She was willing to wait forever for him, if necessary." Stella was aware, through Sammy, of Jackie's popularity and athletic prowess. "Stella had a crush on Jack Kerouac since they were kids, though Jack was not aware of it," said her brother John. "She always treated him like a kid brother, just like Sebastian." The lives of the three friends—Jack, Sammy, and Stella—would be intertwined forever, and even today, they lie next to each other in a quiet, leafy cemetery in Lowell.[14]

In the spring of 1936, a terrible disaster hit the Lowell valley, affecting the lives of most of the city's inhabitants, including the Kerouac and Sampas families. The flood of 1936, later described by Kerouac as "a great colossus dominating our lives," destroyed Leo's print shop, inundating it in six feet of water and wrecking his career as an independent businessman. Afterward, he became an itinerant Linotype operator, and also ran the bowling-alley concession at the Pawtucketville Social Club. Hilly Pawtucketville was spared the ravages of the flood, and the Kerouacs' Sarah Street residence was safe, but by 1938 they were unable to meet the rent, and moved into a grim tenement over a greasy spoon called Textile Lunch at 736 Moody Street. The Sampases were even harder hit by the flood: Their house in Rosemont was under water, and Sammy's mother Maria had to be evacuated by boat. Miss Mansfield was also wiped out; Jackie and G. J. Apostolos stood watching helplessly as the Merrimack River roared over twenty-foot-high sandbags and poured through her windows. Years later, when Kerouac described the flood in *Dr. Sax* as "the huge mountain of ugly sinister waters lunging around Lowell like a beast dragon," Miss Mansfield said his description was "extremely accurate." After her home was destroyed, the Scribbler's Club was disbanded. The Sampas family moved across the river from Jackie to a section called Highlands, and for a while he and Sammy saw less of each other. As Kerouac later wrote in *Dr. Sax*, the flood had been "an unforgettable flow of evil and of wrath and of Satan barging thru my hometown."

Sports absorbed Jackie almost exclusively for the next few years. In 1936, he and Scotcho Beaulieu formed the Pawtucketville baseball team and fought successfully to get it accepted in the new W.P.A. league. Jackie amassed the highest batting average, led in home runs, and on one occasion struck the ball so hard that it bounced off a mill wall eighty-five yards away. Pawtucketville, the only team in the league without a playing field, almost won the city championship. These were Kerouac's happiest days as an athlete, before he entered the world of institutionalized sports. All that mattered on the sandlot were the skill and bravery of the individual player. There were no politics, just the joy of sport. All that would change when he entered high school in the fall.

He'd been Ti Jean in grade school, Jackie in junior high, and now at fourteen, upon entering Lowell High, he became Jack Kerouac. One of his first discoveries when he went out for sports was that ability mattered less than that he was poor, French-Canadian, and came from Pawtucketville instead of Belvidere or Highlands. The students were largely made up of Irish and Canuck offspring of mill workers, and as soon as word got around that Jack wanted to be a writer, they started calling him a sissy. His understanding of the word came from his father. "A sissy . . . likes boys better than girls," says George Martin, the character based on Leo in *The Town and the City*, "two big boys playing with each other like those morons who hang around men's rooms in the subway." In *Visions of Gerard*, when Ti Jean tells his father, "I wanta write—I'm an *artist*," his father snaps, "Artist shmartist, ya can't be supported all ya life." In desperation, Jack went to his church, St. Jean Baptiste, and sought out a priest. Years later, in "A Catholic's View of Kerouac," Rev. Armand "Spike" Morissette recalled that Kerouac appeared to be agitated and deeply disturbed, "shy and delicate but a ticking bomb."

"What's the matter with you?" Spike asked. "You look so upset."

"Everybody's laughing at me," Jack replied. "I want to be a writer and a poet and they all make fun of me. They say I'm a sissy."

"*I'm* not laughing," Spike said. As he later recalled, Kerouac could have been "a Napoleon or a movie star," but he chose to be a writer, and the young priest found that very touching. He told Jack that worldly criticism was never of any importance, that one's opinion of oneself was all that mattered, and that authorship was a sacred calling because writers "influence countless people."

"I'm going to write," Jack said. "I'm going to write books and poems and I'm going to tell the world what I think." Spike told him to go to New York, get an education, and meet publishers and other writers, but Jack said he was too poor.

"Try for a scholarship," Spike said. He recalled years later, "to be a writer he would have to go to the university, and his parents had not much money."

"Well, I'll play football," Jack said. "I'll get a scholarship. And I'll show them I'm not a sissy."

To Spike, Kerouac seemed to be consumed with ambition, but also "infinitely rich spiritually." Before Jack left the rectory, they spoke about religion, and Spike found him to be "profoundly religious . . . truly exalted by his visions," but also critical of the Catholic Church for "enslaving people, giving them a sense of guilt. . . . He was such a good person, so deep. . . . He hated hypocrisy."[15]

Jack immediately followed Spike's advice and went out for football at Lowell High. Because he had skipped a grade in parochial school he was younger and smaller than the other players, and couldn't even make it through calisthenics the first day of practice, collapsing on the field and vomiting in front of the other players. Coach Tom Keady sized him up as a child who was still growing, but according to Billy Koumantzelis, politics was the reason that Jack had difficulty making the varsity. Leo's controversial reputation proved to be Jack's albatross. As *Sporting News* writer Glenn Stout explained at a 1996 Lowell seminar on Kerouac as an athlete, small-town gossip, rivalries, and resentments all had an impact on the high-school athletic program, and the battles of the parents were often carried into the public arena by the coaches and players. Despite his humiliation, Jack was back at practice the next day. Leo watched from the stands, shaking his head, convinced that Ti Jean would never survive the rough game or even strike a sufficiently cocky attitude to catch the coach's eye.

Though Jack was only five-foot-seven and weighed one hundred and fifty pounds, he had the most powerful set of legs on the team. One magic day, his prospects at last began to improve when an assistant coach glanced down at his muscular thighs and called him in as a replacement. He threw himself into the scrimmage with a determination that was almost suicidal. Charged by a famous Lowell end, he bent down and butted him with his head. The bone-crushing collision knocked Jack to the ground, almost unconscious, but he made it back to the huddle. Keady was impressed that he'd had the guts to lead with his head, and called him back for the same play. Once again, Jack ran at the Lowell end as hard as he could, but this time he used his shoulder and rammed the larger boy to the ground. One of the assistant coaches yelled at Jack, "Hey, nice block!" On the next play, Keady himself joined the huddle and said, "Let Kerouac carry the ball." Jack took the snapback, zigzagged around his own blockers, and streaked down the sidelines. Suddenly, the coach blew his whistle and ended the play, but the spiteful Lowell end charged at Jack, knocking him into the buckets on the sidelines. Feeling foolish, Jack disentangled himself, but Keady clapped him on the shoulder and said, "That was some sprint, kid."

On subsequent plays, the Lowell end kept harassing him, until Jack finally devised a highly deceptive—and nearly lethal—ploy. He coyly dodged a flying tackle, but the next time, he surprised the Lowell end and charged him with a force that he'd always known was his, but had never dared to use. There was a cracking sound, and everyone stopped. Jack was still standing, but the tall kid was on his knees, holding onto Jack's hips. "My neck is broken," he croaked. Still holding the ball, Kerouac felt a moment of fear followed by a surge of satisfaction. "Almost killing someone feels good," he later told me, as we edited the football scenes in *Vanity of Duluoz*. "Victory is sweet," he added, "but to win is also to destroy." The boy's neck wasn't broken after all, but he left the field a litter case. Jack's performance that day at last caught the coaching staff's attention, and they realized they had a player who'd do anything to win, even maim and kill.

In the locker room, starters who'd previously snubbed him came over to "fondle my butt, as if we'd always been asshole buddies," he said. Having injured his leg during practice that day, he hobbled out of the shower. An assistant handed him a bright new regulation Red and Gray football uniform, with a big "35" on the jersey, and two new pairs of glossy backfield shoes. He had made the varsity and was now on the second-ranked team of one of the most famous prep leagues in the nation. A photographer from the *Sun* snapped his picture, and he went home in a state of dazed disbelief.

Jack continued to excel in practice sessions in his junior year and was mentioned in the local press, though the reporters could never get his name right, even when he scored a touchdown. After a B-squad game in which he knifed his way to a four-yard score, the *Sun* said, "Leo Kerouac seems to be well on the way to becoming an excellent ball carrier." Nevertheless, Jack developed into a fleet and savvy halfback, and the nickname "Zagg" caught on again as he shifted his way through would-be tacklers. His astonished father now watched him at practice three times a week. Unfortunately, Jack soon discovered that making the varsity did not guarantee playing time, nor did it prevent a certain amount of hazing from senior teammates, such as Henry Mazur, who threw Jack out of the shower room. Jock protocol excluded rookies from the showers until all the veteran players had finished. Kerouac never forgave Mazur, who went on to play for Army. Interviewed in 1973, Mazur, a retired army colonel, did not recall the locker-room altercation.

The question of why coach Keady used Kerouac so rarely in his junior year continued to baffle Kerouac throughout his life. Duke Chiungos, who was in the starting lineup, later explained that Kerouac was only a substitute and that the eleven starters played the entire sixty minutes. "You could have a half-broken leg but if you were the starter, you played," Duke said. But Kerouac felt differently. It seemed to him that the coaches were cruising him. Convinced that they would use him more if he surrendered to them sexually, he compared himself to Melville's Billy Budd, who was destroyed by a repressed homosexual, John Claggart. "It was my fate," he said, "to always have a Claggart for a football coach."

While it's possible that Kerouac was discriminated against, it's also true that he faced stiff competition in the starter at halfback, Peter Kouchalakos, who'd overcome his relatively small size (155 pounds, 5' 7½") to become widely regarded as the best athlete in Massachusetts. "Kouch" was a triple-threat halfback who could kick, run, and pass, and as an added advantage, he didn't have Jack's tendency to fumble the ball. In *Vanity of Duluoz*, Kerouac confessed that he was a notorious fumbler, carrying the ball with one hand in order to keep the other free for the balance he needed in his sharp, "jackoff" turns. Many of his teammates excelled both offensively and defensively, but Jack lacked both the size and endurance for two-way football. Neither a great passer nor punter, he was rather monodimensional as a grid-iron competitor. But Mike D'Orso argued in *Sports Illustrated* that Kerouac more than compensated for his limitations by being an innovative player. "Jack was just ahead of his time," Duke Chiungos said. "All we had were these moth-eaten plays . . . bulling through the line for four or five yards . . . Jack was a breakaway player, and they weren't used to that." If he was resented, it was for the same reason that he later enraged the literary establishment: His dazzling performances disconcerted the other players in an antiquated game.[16]

Academically, he was just managing to stay afloat. His junior-year average was 84, despite the fact that, as Chiungos put it, "I never saw him take a book home." He was absent 32 out of a total of 178 school days, but much of that time he spent in the Pollard Memorial Library at 401 Merrimack Street, hiding out in the children's department and consuming books voraciously. In 1995, the publication of *Selected Letters* at last revealed that Kerouac was keenly aware of the grand literary tradition of his native New England. Ralph Waldo Emerson and Henry David Thoreau had lived a stone's throw from Lowell, and from Nathaniel Hawthorne in nearby Salem and Emily Dickinson in Amherst, and Melville had written *Moby-Dick* in Pittsfield, just across the Berkshires.

In *Vanity of Duluoz*, Kerouac listed his high-school literary enthusiasms as Victor Hugo, Goethe, H. G. Wells, and the *Encyclopaedia Britannica*, leading biographers to place him in a European tradition. But *Selected Letters* demonstrates the more significant influence of Emerson, Thoreau, Dickinson, and Melville. Kerouac related to Emerson's mysticism, Thoreau's individualism, and the strong homoerotic strain in Melville, Whitman, and Dickinson. His high-school English teacher, Joe Pine, was praised by Kerouac in a 1961 letter to Bernice Lemire as one of the two best English teachers he ever had (the other, unnamed, was also at Lowell High). He was particularly grateful to Pine for encouraging his love of Emily Dickinson and other American poets. Dickinson's erotic feelings for her own sex were revealed in her love poem to Susan Huntington Gilbert, in which she wrote, "One sister have I in our house, and one, a hedge away. . . . I chose this single star from out the wide night's numbers — Sue — forevermore!" In a 1955 letter to Ginsberg, Kerouac listed Dickinson among his top three favorite authors, along with Thoreau and William Blake, and Kerouac once told me that two of his favorite lines from Dickinson were: "Much madness is divinest sense" and "Good morning, midnight."[17] Thoreau immortalized the river that runs through Jack's hometown in *A Week on the Concord and Merrimack Rivers*. And from Blake, Jack gained a lifelong affinity for visionary experience.

In high school, he at last became keenly aware of girls and realized that they were peering into his "blue windows for romance." To girls in class, he appeared to be daydreaming, and they assumed he was in love, but actually he was thinking of his mother's hot date pie with whipped cream. Years later, Stella Sampas said she had not been popular like Jack, but he quickly corrected her, pointing out that he was resented by most people in high school, either for being attractive and well-built or for "trying to outdo everybody in everything." When at last he began to attend high-school dances, he was proud to be the best-looking boy in the room and the most sought-after, but he didn't know how to dance, and he couldn't talk to a girl without blushing and stammering. What interested him chiefly at the dances was the big-band swing music, which was now beginning to sweep the land. Swing became a lifelong passion, and the music lent to his writing its distinctive rhythm.

In the spring of 1938, Jack went out for track and made a lasting friendship with Lowell's leading runner, Johnny Koumantzelis. Jack went all the way to the state meet in Boston, winning the three-hundred-yard dash, and came to the attention of Frank Leahy, later Notre Dame's legendary football coach, but still at Boston College at the time. Leahy decided to watch Kerouac closely during his senior year, and told BC sports publicist Billy Sullivan, "We'll offer him a scholarship in November."

After Kerouac's track victories, Leo and Gabrielle sacrificed everything for him, convinced that he would eventually become a successful insurance salesman and support them in their old age. The 1938 football season began and Kerouac, confident of winning a scholarship, switched from the commercial to the college curriculum, hoping to meet Ivy League entrance requirements. At the tenement on Moody Street, in his corner-bedroom aerie four floors above Textile Lunch, he slept with his cat and kept his football beside the bed where he could touch it for good luck. On cold autumn mornings, he'd place his socks on the oil stove to warm and then go over to his "tragic closet," cluttered with handwritten manuscript pages, jockstraps, bats, and gloves. After dressing, he'd devour a breakfast of toast and gruel. At football practice, the coaches noticed that he was brawnier, at five-foot-nine and 165 pounds, but still smaller than regulars like Joe Sorota, who was five-eleven and 173 pounds, and Chester Lipka, who was six-two and 195 pounds.

Without Jack's being aware of it, Keady had plans to put him into games late in the play as Lowell's secret weapon after the regulars had exhausted themselves. According to Glenn Stout, "He was fast, shifty, good in the open field, and surprisingly strong when faced one-on-one. It was that singular ability that allowed him to vault over some players who were more skilled than he, and challenge them for a starting position." Keady set out at once to correct some of Kerouac's deficiencies. Since Jack didn't know how to punt, Keady assigned his best kicker, Sorota, to give Jack special lessons. In an interview fifty-seven years later, Sorota recalled that Keady told him, "Try to show 'his highness' how to kick a ball." When asked what kind of a teammate Kerouac was, Sorota replied, "Jack was all right to play with. He pulled his load. Jack wasn't too tall but he could run."

Kerouac knew that if he didn't play brilliantly during his senior year, he would never go to college and would end up a mill rat. Fortunately, he was able to start in the first major scrimmage, on September 15, against Melrose. Kouchalakos, the star of the team, couldn't play due to a sprained ankle, an injury that would plague him throughout the season. Though the team was considered to be light, green, and lacking in veterans, they creamed Greenfield High in the season opener, 26–0. Kerouac scored two touchdowns that were called back. "Young Kerouac has the legs and the style," noted the *Sun*'s reporter, but then added, in what Kerouac considered to be an insulting understatement, "he looks like a football player." Certainly, the near-perfect game that Kerouac played against Greenfield entitled him to a place in the starting lineup, but it was withheld, and he began to realize that although he still loved football, he was too much of an individual ever to fit into the team.

Kouchalakos returned to the lineup in the game against Gardner, and Kerouac played only the last two minutes. Lowell won, 18–0, and continued its winning streak a week later, when Kerouac scored a trio of touchdowns in the game against Worcester Classical. This was the game that got not only Keady's attention, but the whole town's. People Jack didn't even know, teachers and students alike, thanked him for helping to smear Worcester, 43–0. Pretty girls winked and said, "I can't *wait* till Saturday," referring both to the upcoming game with Manchester Central and possibly their anticipated deflowering by Kerouac. "It's the greatest feeling in the world to walk into a room and know you can have anybody you want, man, woman, or child," Kerouac told me as we worked on his account of Worcester Classical in *Vanity of Duluoz*. "Just knowing this gives you a hard-on, and people see the hard-on, or sense it, and think you're superman. There is nothing like being a football star, not even publishing your first novel."

During the next game, he never left the bench. In the stands, his fans chanted, "*We want Kerouac. . . . We want Kerouac.*" "I was better than Kouchalakos, yet I had to sit on the sidelines and watch him play like an old heifer," Jack recalled. "And then Kouchalakos limped off the field with a minor injury that I would have played right through, and removed his helmet so everyone could see who he was." His teammates managed to stomp Manchester Central 20–0 without any help from Kerouac. Ecstatic over another shutout, the football-crazed citizens of Lowell began to dream of the state championship. The Red and Gray had rolled up 107 points and was still unscored on after four games. But Jack panicked after he was ignored in the Manchester Central match. He had his heart set on going to Columbia College, but his chances at this point in the season were nil. What he did not know was that he was being held in reserve for crucial upcoming games. All of Lowell's remaining opponents for the season — Malden, Lynn, Lynn Classical, and New Britain — sent scouts to the Manchester Central contest, and Kerouac was deliberately kept off the field so that Keady could spring him as a surprise in future games. At the moment, Lowell was undefeated, but there were some tough games ahead, and Kerouac's speed and daring could be the deciding factor.

Just before Lowell played Keith Academy, which was also undefeated and unscored upon, the *Sun* announced, "Jack Kerouac, Lowell's speed-king, will be used as a 'situation' ball carrier. . . . One of the fastest schoolboy backs in the state is expected to play a major part in Lowell's offense tomorrow." Reporter Bill McNiskin dubbed Kerouac "the speed merchant," and *Lowell Union Leader* columnist Billy Sullivan observed, "Figures don't lie," referring to Jack's record as one of the team's top scorers. When the Red and Gray faced Keith's Blue and Gray at Alumni Field, Kerouac played like a wild animal thirsting for blood. He scored two touchdowns, and in a *Sun* photo the following day he was shown grimacing with fierce determination as he raced toward the goalpost. The caption read: "Lowell's situation back . . . breaking off his tackle for thirteen yards and the score." The final tally was Lowell 53, Keith Academy 0. Kerouac later told me that he'd actually scored three touchdowns, but one was called back, and he complained that Keady had only let him play one quarter.

With a record of 5–0, the Lowell team was written up all over New England, and one Boston daily headlined, "John Kerouac, Climax Runner, 12th Man of Unbeaten, Unscored Upon 11." The reporter wrote, "At opportune moments when the stage is nicely tidied up and ready for a hurricane, in frolics Kerouac to go to town." Jack and I discussed the story when he was writing *Vanity of Duluoz*, debating how much of it to use. He loved the clause, "in frolics Kerouac," but for some reason didn't use it. He wasn't sure readers would know what "climax runner" meant and left it out, although he used the portion of the headline that made it clear he belonged in the starting lineup.

"Climax runner" is not a phrase currently in use in football, but the mystery was cleared up in 1996 when Glenn Stout interviewed Charley O'Rourke, a Boston College quarterback of the 1940s. Coaches couldn't substitute at will in the thirties, O'Rourke explained, because of the one-platoon style of football. However, substitutions could go in at the end of a quarter or the end of a half. "A lot of teams had a back like Jack Kerouac, who was called a climax runner—a player who they kept out of the game early," Stout said. "In the second quarter or second half, when the other players were getting tired, boom, let's put in [the climax runner]. . . . Kerouac . . . would return punts sixty yards, go for those long broken field runs, drawing attention from the main player—Kouchalakos in Lowell's case—that the defense was focused on."[18]

As Kerouac's fame spread throughout high-school and intercollegiate football circles, so did his ego; in *Maggie Cassidy* he described his "ivory white face . . . noble . . . neck . . . slope-muscled shoulders . . . eyes hard and steely . . . like Mickey Mantle at nineteen." He cultivated an enigmatic, Mona Lisa look, gazing at people from under a crown of "curly black locks." Girls were his for the taking, but he wasn't sure he wanted them. As he later wrote in *Book of Dreams*, he had a nightmare in which the police accused him of being a sex pervert, citing him for taking off his pants in front of high-school students of both sexes. He portrayed himself in the dream as a "queer saint" with a "hardon." A girl exposed her crotch to him, but instead of a vagina she had "a tiny cock." He took out his penis, but it was so small that he hid it in embarrassment. In *The Town and the City*, when the autobiographical protagonist Peter Martin finds himself the object of feminine desire, he feels threatened, and to avoid girls, he hurries home from school and buries himself in books, reading through the entire shelf of "Harvard Classics."

Despite similar qualms, Kerouac was so eager to be envied by other men and to have them drooling over his girls, that he finally decided to start dating. He had no idea how to go about this, but one night, on his way to a banquet for the football players, he stopped to look in on the Girl Officers' Prom at the high school. Lowell High offered a military-type alternative to gym classes for boys and girls who had no interest in sports, and each year the Girl Officers sponsored a dance, asking boys for dates. Kerouac arrived stag and right away spotted Joe Sorota, who was talking with Margaret Coffey, Joe's next-door neighbor in Centralville. "We were just friends," Sorota recalled. "Margaret was a good singer, and she was planning to sing with Tommy Cotten's orchestra that night, sort of between sets." Margaret had dark hair and a figure that was terrific but only "up to a certain point," Sorota noted. "She was bowlegged. She wasn't too happy with her legs. Good upper body, and beautiful big green eyes. Boy, could she do tricks with them. She looked good in her Girl Officers uniform—navy blue with gold trim. Chet Lipka was there, Johnny Varoski; everybody went by and said, 'Hello, Joe.' Jack Kerouac went by, and Margaret said, 'Who's that?'

" 'Jack Kerouac,' I said.

" 'Why don't you stop him and introduce me?'

" 'Margaret, I can't grab him by the shoulders and hold him here. You'll have to wait, that's all there is to it.' "

When the break came at 11 P.M., Margaret again asked, "Is Jack Kerouac here? Tommy has asked me to come up and do a song." As she sang that night, she saw Jack in the crowd and started flirting brazenly. "She embarrassed the hell out of me, just by lookin' at him, movin' her eyes up and down, sideways," Joe Sorota said. "She kept looking right at him. He was tryin' to hide behind people. The more he'd hide, the more people would watch him. He got embarrassed. Oh God. After she got off the stage, she hit me in the ribs and said, 'I want you to introduce me to Jack.'

" 'Okay,' I said, 'as soon as I see him.'

" 'I know where he is,' she said, and brought me right over to Jack. Oh boy, what a night that was. She got Jack to take her out. It was funny—me, I didn't care because I wasn't goin' out with Margaret. We were like brother and sister, but she could get me in an awful lot of trouble. She was like a tomboy. She wanted to learn how to play tennis, and we'd go down and play tennis, baseball, and everything. She was a son-of-a-gun. She made Jack look like a damn fool that night."

Margaret Coffey as she appears as "Pauline (Moe) Cole" in *Maggie Cassidy* boldly told Jack that she liked his beguiling combination of bashfulness and animal magnetism. He had been anxiously hoping for the prom to end, waiting around only because he had plans to attend a banquet later with the other football players. In a reversal of the usual male-female routine, Margaret led him onto the dance floor and squeezed him provocatively. Later, he took her home, and though she had threatened to kiss him at the dance, he stood in her doorway, uncertain how to kiss a woman. He let her make all the moves, and when they finally kissed, Margaret initiated it.

Kerouac subsequently described the kiss in *Maggie Cassidy*, but skimmed over it to get to what really interested him, which was how he demonstrated the kiss to a male friend. When Kerouac bragged about his and Margaret's marathon kiss, his buddy asked him to repeat it and offered his lips. "We did it, too," Kerouac wrote. Several members of the Pawtucketville gang were present, and so were Gabrielle and Leo, but they took no notice. During the boys' long, passionate kiss, "the others didn't even stop talking," Kerouac wrote. Later, he told Margaret that he had kissed his friend, and she in turn told the friend that she knew something naughty about him and he ought to be mortified. The young man then described how Jack had kissed him, and later shared this with Jack, bringing the curious episode full circle. Jack felt his friend's "love . . . man to man, boy to boy," he wrote. In *Maggie Cassidy*, the encounter between the two men ends with Jack's friend going home to fantasize about him and have wet dreams.

A few days after Sorota introduced Jack and Margaret, he saw them together on Margaret's front porch. The following day, Jack asked Joe, "Do you mind if I go out with Margaret?"

"Hell, no," Joe said. "Go ahead. We're not goin' anywhere. I have no plans anyway." After that, Jack and Margaret dated "pretty steady," Joe said. "Margaret became his girlfriend. They were alike in a way. She was kind of fickle when it came to men; he was fickle about girls. They made hay for a little while anyway."

The round-robin kiss in *Maggie Cassidy* powerfully demonstrates that rigid divisions such as hetero-, bi-, and homosexuality do not fit reality, certainly not Kerouac's, and should not be used to label him. Though everyone seems to have a genetic inclination in one direction or the other, it is dangerous to use sex to define anyone. As Gore Vidal has written, "Most people are a mixture of impulses if not practices, and what anyone does with a willing partner is of no social or cosmic significance." Like George Martin in *The Town and the City*, Kerouac's father appeared to believe that it was all right for thirteen-year-old boys to have sex with each other, as long as they outgrew it by the age of fifteen and started dating girls. Otherwise, he warned, America "was going straight to hell," and he later lumped together "Alexander Panos," the character based on Sammy, and "Leon Levinsky," the Ginsberg-inspired character, as "screwballs." According to Duke Chiungos, Jack Lang, and other former Lowell athletes, Leo began to be rougher with Jack and put him under constant pressure to excel as an athlete.[19]

Leo was not happy when Jack and Sammy's relationship as members of the Young Prometheans intensified. Sammy was not athletic, but he attained the rank of major as a Boy Officer. At Young Promethean meetings, Kerouac also saw Stella, who was "hungry for knowledge," *Sun* reporter Edward Manzi later wrote. Stella hovered about the group, mostly so she could look at Jack, but also "serving the boys coffee — and helping herself to their knowl-

edge." Politics and current events were fervently debated. A former Promethean, George Constantinedes, recalled, "Sam said Prometheus represented
altruism, imparting knowledge to mankind and being of service. . . . He believed that if mankind is to progress, it would be through politics." Both
Sammy and Jack flirted with Communism, and Jack longed to go to the
U.S.S.R., commune with his Russian comrades, and bring back a white tunic
for Sammy.

But Kerouac was never serious about politics, and though he was moved
by Sammy's concept of universal brotherhood, the tenor of their relationship
remained lighthearted and increasingly romantic. Sammy sang love songs to
him, like Cole Porter's "Begin the Beguine," and recited Lord Byron's se-
ductive lines, "The night was made for loving, and the day returns too soon."
One evening, as Sammy waited for Jack on the library steps, he started reciting poetry to some Greek boys from the neighborhood. He chose Byron's
salute to Greece's lesbian poet laureate, Sappho, and declaimed, " 'The isles
of Greece, the isles of Greece! Where burning Sappho loved and sung.' "
Charles Jarvis was present that night, and recalled that the boys began to
heckle Sammy, one yelling that Byron "must have had a wang as big as a
buffalo's." Undaunted, Sammy lectured them on Byron's role in freeing their
parents' native Greece from Turkish tyranny. Suddenly, Kerouac emerged
from the library and he and Sammy went off into the night together, leaving
the other boys behind.

One of the toughs called Kerouac "Sammy's soulmate," adding that the
two boys often took lengthy strolls together and talked about "stuff" like
writing and art. "Bullshit," said another boy, defending Kerouac as a football
player and member of the high-school track team. Then, remembering he'd
just seen Jack leave with Sammy, he conceded that Jack must be "strange."
At school, when Jack's varsity teammates teased him about Sammy, he realized that his status as a "big athlete" was in jeopardy, and he later told
Jarvis that he began to ponder why "the hell" he was "hanging around with
this guy." But he couldn't give up Sammy; their association was the most
joyous of his life, and Sammy was the only person in Lowell who could show
him how to become what he wanted to be: "a scholar, a creative person."
In *The Town and the City*, Kerouac portrayed himself, as "Peter Martin," as
wanting to reach out and take the hand of "Alexander," the Sammy-based
character, but he held back and then wondered "mournfully" why he was
afraid to touch his dearest friend.[20]

Just a week after the Boston paper crowned Kerouac Lowell's climax
runner, he played before twelve thousand people in Malden High's stadium,
five miles north of Boston. The Malden team was a terror, and the game was
expected to determine the front runner for the state championship. Malden's
passing attack during the 1939 season had been "nothing short of sensational," one sports reporter wrote, but he added that most observers favored
Lowell, "with such tricky running backs as Christy Zoukis, Pete Kouchalakos,
Jack Kerouac, and Warren 'Lefty' Arsenault." For days before the game, area

sports commentators speculated on whether Keady would use Kerouac. Sorota had injured his knee, and the *Sun*'s Frank Moran predicted that Jack
might replace him in the Lowell backfield, but only "at the eleventh
hour." McNiskin observed, "If Sorota does not start . . . Jack Kerouac will
be getting the chance he has deserved for the past three weeks." Sorota
and Kerouac remained good friends, despite competition in sports and
love. "Me and Jack would hang around down in [Donald R.] McIntyre's
office a little bit," Sorota recalled. "McIntyre was the athletic director, over
the coach. He took care of all the arrangements for all the teams to play
here and there, goin' down to Boston, bookin'." On the eve of the game,
Sorota's knee improved dramatically, and he was expected to take his position in the starting backfield. But Keady told the press that he intended
to use Kerouac anyway. "Jack Kerouac, Lowell's 'situation' back, is primed
and ready for heavy duty tomorrow and will see much action against Malden," the *Sun* reported.

Going into the game, the undefeated teams were almost evenly matched.
Lowell had five wins over Malden's four wins and one tie. "The press of
New England was aroused to the unprecedented enthusiasm of calling Lowell High of '38 the greatest schoolboy team in Lowell's history," wrote columnist John Kenney. To Kerouac, the game represented a clash of the giants
of Massachusetts football, and he was frankly afraid of Malden's gorilla-like
players, who reminded him of Iroquois warriors. As usual, he didn't start, but
Keady brought him into the game in the second half. "It was an exciting
game," said Duke Chiungos, who explained that Lowell beat back Malden's
seven goal-line attempts to score touchdowns. Kerouac at last came on the
field after a Lowell quarterback sustained a fractured shoulder. Kerouac broke
away and raced for sixty-five yards. "Someone came across the field and
nailed him at the fifteen-yard line," said Chiungos. "Otherwise, Jack would
have been the real hero there." But the giants exhausted each other, and
neither Lowell nor Malden emerged the winner, tying 0–0. The game took
a ruinous toll on Lowell's starters. "We were all burnt out, everyone on that
team," Duke said.

With the first-stringers reduced to physical wrecks, Kerouac now stood
at the threshold of the greatest opportunity of his life. He was used almost
constantly in the next game against Lynn Classical, an underdog team that
hoped to redeem its mediocre record by trouncing vaunted Lowell. "I
flubbed it," he said, when he read chapter six of book one of *Vanity of
Duluoz* aloud to me one day. "Zoukis threw me a pass and I dropped it—
my only real fuck-up of the season." Played on an alien field, the Manning
Bowl gridiron, the contest was the most violent of the season, with Kerouac
in action from start to finish. One observer wrote, "The players continually
'slugged,' that is, punched, kicked, mauled, and piled. . . . Any efficiency on
the part of the officials in charge of the game would have resulted in this
type of play being quelled immediately. . . . The 'slugging' was clearly spotted
from the press box . . . with both the Lowell and Classical players involved."

A Lynn Classical lineman suffered a concussion in a massive pileup. Kerouac was tough enough to survive the physical punishment, but the game turned into a humiliating 6–0 defeat for Lowell and brought Kerouac embarrassing press notices. McNiskin wrote, "Jack Kerouac caused the fans to gulp by getting clear for a toss from Zoukis but his over-anxiety caused him to lose the pellet." The *Sun*, which rarely noted Kerouac's triumphs, was always quick to spotlight his mistakes, reporting: "Zoukis passed to Kerouac who fumbled the ball with a touchdown in view. He was alone and could have raced over to tie the score easily." The story was headlined, "Defeat by Lynn Classical Leaves Fandom Shocked; Red and Gray 'Just Another Team' Now."

Sorota, who fought Lynn Classical on a bad knee and ankle, recalled that "Kerouac fell on his can. . . . That was the game we all could have killed him. He dropped two balls, and nobody near him. Within twenty yards of a touchdown, he could have walked it. He took his eye off the ball both times. He doesn't talk about that in the books. But, once in a while, he had a lapse of memory when it came to catchin' balls. His concentration was someplace else all the time." Added Sorota, "When it came to women it was a different story. He perked right up."

Kerouac later wrote in *Maggie Cassidy* that he first became seriously interested in girls during his senior year, and the experience plunged him into confusion and despair, which may explain why his game was off. The night before the New Britain, Connecticut, match, Jack was disgusted with many of his teammates for breaking practice and slipping out of their hotel to attend a dance. Even worse, as he charged in *Vanity of Duluoz*, the players who remained in their rooms spent the night making so much noise that he couldn't sleep, and he was exhausted by game time the following day. Two of his teammates later challenged Kerouac's account. Chiungos said, "We were all back where we belonged by nine-thirty or ten o'clock. If we stepped out of line, we were monitored pretty close. The only ones who weren't monitored were the coaches." Sorota recalled, "We were down in New Britain, and Jack met a girl down there and when we got back he was ready to quit school and move down there. He fell in love with women like nuthin', at the drop of a hat. Oh, God, and how, always havin' a crush. He almost left school on account of it. He bought the young woman in New Britain a friendship ring and everything. I said, 'You've got to be crazy, Jack.' I guess he must have talked to a few other people down there because he didn't make it, he stayed. He finished off high school and that was it. He went all out for women, there was no gettin' away from it."

He could no longer complain that Keady wasn't using him; he carried the ball throughout the New Britain game, ending up bloody, bruised, haggard, and disillusioned. Lowell suffered a 20–0 defeat. Later, in the locker room, coaches, reporters, and dedicated camp followers glowered at the Lowell athletes as they undressed, showered, and wearily donned their street clothes. But Kerouac had ample reason to rejoice. Keady alerted the junior men on the team that they were about to get their chance; the senior players had disappointed him in recent weeks and he was benching many of them. According to sportswriter Glenn Stout, "At this point, Kerouac was the star of the team."[21]

In the next game, Nashua, Leo and Gabrielle's hometown, everything was on Jack's shoulders, and he played his most heroic game in mud and driving rain. Though Lowell lost, 13–19, he would always regard Nashua as the high point of his football career. Too many of the regulars were permitted to skip the game, leaving Kerouac nothing but rookies to play with, and Kenney wrote that Lowell unaccountably "fell flat against an inferior Nashua invader." Kerouac suspected the game was fixed—that the veteran players were deliberately kept off the field so that Lowell would lose, thus raising the odds for the climactic game of the season, the Thanksgiving Day grudge match with Lawrence. The only pastime in Lowell more popular than football was gambling, and the two often went hand in hand. Kerouac faced the powerful Nashua team virtually alone, ran for a fifteen-yard touchdown, and accounted for 130 out of 149 total yards for Lowell. In a grueling sixty-yard dash, he was transformed into a muddy apparition that no longer looked human. He also made his share of mistakes that day according to the *Nashua Telegraph*, which reported, "With a touchdown seemingly a sure thing, Kerouac fumbled." But the game paid off handsomely for Jack. Scouts from Duke, B.C., and Columbia caught his rugged performance and immediately recommended him for scholarships. He had accomplished the goal he and Spike had dreamed of, and his future was assured.

When he returned to the Rex, the team's hotel in Nashua, he was offended to find the regulars luxuriating in Turkish baths. Back home, in his bed on Moody Street, he woke up screaming in the middle of the night, his muscles locked in tortuous charley horses. Later, he limped into Frank Sargent's office at the *Courier-Citizen* and requested better coverage in the paper's sports pages for his gridiron performances. When rumors of his visit circulated around town, some were amused, while others found him to be a "very forward kid," as one Lowell businessman put it. Jack would never receive the glowing notices regularly accorded Kouchalakos, the darling of the press, even when Jack's feats far outstripped Kouch's.

Despite their recent losses, the Lowell Red and Gray was the number one topic of conversation during the Thanksgiving holidays. As Lowell was blanketed with a record November snowfall, everyone looked forward to the Lawrence game, the most anticipated local event of the year and the final game of the season. *Sun* columnist Charles G. Sampas, Sammy's brother, wrote on November 23, 1938, "Be thankful for football heroes." John Kenney warned, "To blow this one would cover the whole season with the shroud of failure." Conversely, he said, a Lowell victory would completely erase the shame of their recent string of defeats. The statistics favored Lowell. Only one man on the Lawrence squad, Leo Ouellette, had scored more touchdowns than had Kerouac.

Early on Thanksgiving morning, the people of Lowell awoke to an icy, gray day, according to Sullivan's account in the *Union Leader*. Shortly after 9 A.M., the town virtually emptied as hordes of people drove the dozen miles up along the Merrimack River to Lawrence's Memorial Stadium. A record crowd of fourteen thousand assembled in the stands. Spike located his seat, proud to be a friend of the star of the day. Leo and Gabrielle attended with a bevy of relatives, and at some point in the game Leo spotted Leahy and invited him for Thanksgiving dinner. Outside the stadium, Billy Koumantzelis, Johnny's younger brother, got into a fight. "There was always a big rivalry between Lowell and Lawrence, and there's always a brawl connected with the Lowell-Lawrence game," Billy recalled. Lowell's band marched across the field playing "Alexander's Ragtime Band," followed by a battery of baton twirlers. Below the stands, in the bowels of the stadium, Kerouac sat on a bench tensely awaiting another bloody gladiatorial. The air in the cold, gloomy locker room was thick with fear, bordering on panic, and as Jack changed into his uniform, he felt faint. Keady sensed the team's vulnerability and goaded them with insults, hoping to provoke their anger and courage. Suddenly, an official burst in and announced there were two minutes to kickoff. A hush fell over the players as Keady reminded them that they'd dreamed of making the varsity and whipping Lawrence since boyhood — and now was their chance. His words activated Jack's killer instincts. The team broke into cheers for the coach and then stormed onto the field, ready for anything Lawrence could dish out. An official blew his whistle, the throngs in the stands grew quiet, and the forty-second "Turkey-day classic" began.

Lawrence dominated the play throughout the first half, banging off four first downs to Lowell's one. Jack started, but was replaced by Kouch in the second quarter. The first half ended with both teams scoreless. The players on both sides were afraid of bone-snapping falls on the hard, frozen ground. At halftime, Keady exploded in the locker room, calling the players a bunch of sissies and suggesting they strap pillows to their bottoms. In the second half, Lowell pulled ahead by 2–0 in the third quarter, capitalizing on a bad kick. The game was nearly over. Zoukis and Kerouac gained enough yardage to give Lowell a first down on the Lawrence seventeen-yard line. Zoukis faded back to the twenty-one-yard line and tossed a screen pass to Kerouac, who was running down the sideline. He reached for the ball, but a Lawrence man tipped it, and it started to fall incomplete. Jack reversed field, scooped the ball inches from the turf and sprang toward the goal line with a pack of opponents at his ankles. Five yards from a touchdown, two Lawrence players appeared in front of him. He dropped his shoulder, smashed through them with brain-jarring force, and scored the only touchdown of the day. Seconds later, the game ended, and Kerouac became a Lowell football legend. "*He did it!*" Leo howled, while polishing off a quart of whiskey. Gabrielle snatched a flag from the hands of a relative and waved it frantically, raving about Jackie's "touchball." Though Spike had guided Kerouac to this triumph, the priest smiled quietly and thanked God. "Oh, boy, I mean he was the *hero*," he told *Sports Illustrated* fifty years later. "Lots of headlines. Just like Doug Flutie, you know?" Spike was referring to Boston College quarterback Doug Flutie, who, in an important game with Miami, threw a 48-yard pass, later known as a "Hail Mary pass," as time was running out in the last quarter, and became another "last second" hero like Kerouac.

In the visitors' locker room, the Lowell team showered and "danced on pink feet," Kerouac recalled, but even in victory he was made to feel like an outsider. Resenting that a substitute instead of a first-string player had scored the only touchdown, Kouch threw down his helmet—a gesture of defeat rather than victory. Jack tried to avoid well-wishers, and when the bus dropped him at school, he walked home alone along the canals in the shadows of the mills. He somehow knew that he would be quickly forgotten and preferred his private fantasies to public acclaim. In his mind, he was a "prince disguised as a pauper, Orestes returned from distant heroisms and hiding within the land." It was only after he crossed the bridge and entered the Pawtucketville slum that he began to feel good. Neighbors rushed into the streets or yelled from tenement windows in a sudden shower of love and adoration. His refracted glory ennobled the ghetto, if only for a day. *Sports Illustrated* later observed, "It also made him the kind of local hero that his literary career never could." At the same time, he had an odd feeling that his fame was a betrayal of his roots. Emotionally, he was living untruthfully at such a deep level that he felt phony about everything.

The signature moment of Kerouac's football career also marked the beginning of his protracted downfall. For those afflicted with the disease of alcoholism, as Jack was, the worst drink is the first one, for after that they can never get enough. A lifetime of alcoholism began over Thanksgiving dinner in 1938. A drunken Leo insisted that his son take a drink and practically forced liquor down Jack's throat. Throughout the meal, Leo kept urging wine on Jack and even poked a cigar in his mouth, telling him to act like a man. *Boston College Magazine* later reported that the Kerouac family's "Thanksgiving dinner table was set for the family and two guests: Billy Sullivan and Frank Leahy." In *Vanity of Duluoz*, Kerouac added that Columbia's head coach, the legendary Lou Little, arrived within several days. Lou Little was known as the man who created All-Americans.

Colleges like Columbia, Duke, and B.C. were engaged in a recruiting war at the time, and all of them vied for Kerouac, not so much for his fantastic performance that day as for the ability he'd displayed throughout the season as a climax runner. While major-league schools offered Jack scholarships, Kouchalakos had to settle for an obscure backwater college. As an additional inducement, Leahy promised to take Jack with him to Notre Dame. But it was Jack's Columbia offer that became the talk of Lowell. Recalled Charlie Kirklies, a track teammate, "Who ever heard of one of *us* going to Columbia? We thought it couldn't happen to a nicer guy."

Despite Kerouac's efforts to get better press coverage for himself, the newspaper reporters claimed a team victory and failed to single out Kerouac as the obvious hero of the Lowell-Lawrence game. Frank Moran managed to write an entire lead without even mentioning Kerouac, referring anonymously to "a touchdown pass." But pictures don't lie, and Jack's spectacular dive over the goal line was captured in a dramatic front-page photo in both the *Sun* and the *Courier-Citizen*. The *Sun's* simple, eloquent caption stated, "Here's the hero, caught by the *Sun* staff cameraman in perfect action." As an athlete, Jack was an example of nature perfecting itself, and these were indeed his glory days.[22]

Throughout the winter months following his success, he pondered various scholarship offers and finally in the spring of 1939 decided on Columbia. There were unfortunate repercussions. B. C.'s Leahy was furious and used his connections to have Leo fired from Sullivan Printers. Billy Sullivan, whose uncle managed the company, did not deny that Leo was fired, but claimed that "Leo Kerouac was a poor employee who already had been kept on the payroll too long." Following the classic pattern of children of alcoholics, Jack took full blame for his father's misfortune, and the thrill of his scholarship was spoiled by guilt. Nothing, however, could diminish the pleasure he took in his varsity-letter sweater, with its big "$\mathcal{L}$", though he felt uncomfortably warm in it. He also made "All–Massachusetts State."

In the heady afterglow, Kerouac first conceived his ambition to become a leader of multitudes, a founder of philosophies and lifestyles, an avatar who would define the needs of society, stage revolutions, and set up new governments—a fabulous "life-changing prophetic artist," as he later put it in a letter to Cassady. Though he did not yet know what his message would be, he already foresaw that he would be destroyed in the act of making it public. He would seize the headlines, shake up the establishment, and then mysteriously fade from view, disappearing into the mists of his own imagination. But in the first lap of his march to sainthood, he intended to wow everyone, "impressing the women, amazing the men." Such lofty ambitions were completely at odds with the blistering love affair that started on January 1, 1939, one that threatened to consign him to mill-town drudgery for the rest of his life.[23]

Kerouac was sixteen, still in his senior year, when he fell in love with a ravishing Irish beauty named Mary Carney. Reminiscing about her years later in an October 12, 1952, letter to novelist John Clellon Holmes, he revealed that he'd wanted to make her his wife, settle down, and work as a brakeman for the Boston & Maine Railroad. He loved her sultry, tragic aura, he told Holmes, and regretted that he'd ever let an "asshole" such as Neal Cassady drag him into vagrancy and "sexfiend" behavior. Mary seemed to be his one chance for a normal, happy life, but she wanted him to give up college and his dream of becoming a writer, and this he would never do.

Internal evidence in *Maggie Cassidy*, the novel he wrote in 1953, suggests deeper, psychological reasons for their conflicts. Jack called himself "Jack Duluoz" and set the story in Lowell, portraying himself as "the beloved youth"—football and track star, budding genius, gorgeous Adonis, desired by all, and possessed by none. Though Jack Duluoz already has sexy Pauline

Cole/Margaret Coffey waiting for him under the clock every day at school, he becomes obsessed with Maggie, daughter of a railroad man, when they meet at a New Year's dance in the Rex Ballroom. To Jack—both the character and the author—Maggie represents eternal woman, part-Carmen and part–Virgin Mary. Pauline jealously warns him that Maggie, a junior-high-school dropout, only wants him to prove to herself that she can ensnare a star athlete.

Kerouac found himself uncomfortable in the role of sex object, and later wrote in the "32nd Chorus" of *San Francisco Blues* that pretty girls have it easy, but handsome men truly "suffer."[24] The misery he underwent as an unwilling Don Juan is graphically, relentlessly portrayed both in *Maggie Cassidy* and *The Town and the City*, as is the torment of the girls innocently drawn into the chaos of a young man at war with himself. "Kiss me, you're an awful *tease*," begs Mary Gilhooley in *The Town and the City*. "Other fellows always want to neck," she says. "All you want to do is look at my eyes." He will let a girl kiss him but go no further, and with the insatiable Maggie Cassidy, the result is thirty-five-minute kisses that leave them both with bleeding, blistered lips.

The reason he volunteers for such torture gradually emerges in the story—it's important to him to have girls fawning over him, preferably in public, so the world will know he's a virile, bona fide male. His good looks and heroic status assure the pick of beauties, but then he doesn't know what to do with them, fearing "unknown suicides of weddings and honeymoons." He ends up hating women. His fundamental misogyny, which bursts out in his description of Maggie's "loose ugly grin of self-satisfied womanly idiocy-flesh," is part and parcel of his not being true to his own sexuality. Participating in sex play with a woman just to prove he's not gay, he projects his self-loathing onto women, something only a man uncomfortable with his sexuality would do. In a clench with Maggie, he suddenly wants "to rip her mouth out and murder her." Finally, acting as a weird kind of pimp, he fobs her off on a friend. With both of the girls in the book, Pauline and Maggie, he behaves like a male counterpart of the stereotypical female "prick tease," taking an almost sadistic satisfaction in the frustration he sows.

How authentic Kerouac's feelings were for Mary Carney is still difficult to ascertain, despite considerable documentation. The Kerouac archive in Lowell contains "eight to ten" letters from Mary to Jack, and they deal with "not seeing each other and missing each other," according to John Sampas. In Kerouac's letters to Stella, Neal and Carolyn Cassady, John Clellon Holmes, and John MacDonald, he wrote that he loved Mary, but in the MacDonald letter, in which he claimed to be "madly" enamored, he called her a "wench," which leaves his sincerity open to question. Kerouac's "sexual intercourse" list, stored at the archive, reveals that he and Mary Carney never consummated their affair. His varsity teammates, Joe Sorota and Jack Lang, both insisted in 1995 that Jack had been more serious about Margaret Coffey, and indeed Kerouac's sex list indicates he and Margaret made love twenty times. According to Duke Chiungos, Kerouac never spoke of Mary, but raved about Margaret. Nor did Kerouac's Pawtucketville intimate and confidant Albert "Lousy" Blazon remember Mary. G. J. Apostolos, who sometimes saw Jack and Mary together, dismissed Jack's love for her as a figment of his imagination, explaining, "Every time I'd ask Jack, 'D'you get in?' the answer was in the negative." When advised in 1996 of G. J.'s remark, John Sampas said, "Maybe Jack didn't tell G. J. how much they were seeing of each other." Mary Carney, who rarely granted interviews, told Gifford and Lee (1978) that "there was something deep between Jack and me." She did not elaborate beyond saying that Jack was "sensitive" and had confided in her. In 1962, she told Bernice Lemire, Kerouac's first biographer, that *Maggie Cassidy* was "almost all true, three-quarters of it at least," but after the interview, Lemire concluded that Kerouac's portrayal of Mary as the love of his life was pure "illusion," and that he had only used her in the novel as a convenient symbol for the Lowell of his youth.

There can be no question that the feelings expressed in the novel are powerful, but the total evidence strongly suggests that these feelings stemmed from other relationships Jack was having, both in high school and later, in 1953, when he wrote *Maggie Cassidy*. The most authentic emotions he had in his youth were focused on Sammy Sampas—"*amour*," as Kerouac summed them up in a 1944 letter to Sammy—but in the climate of the time, they could hardly be expressed, either in his life or in his work. By the time he wrote *Maggie Cassidy*, he was embroiled in a tangled triangle with Neal and Carolyn Cassady, and this was equally taboo. The similarity of the name *Cassady* and the title *Maggie Cassidy* suggests an obvious connection, and I pointed it out to Carolyn in 1996. "It's odd now that I think of it," she replied. "I never had the vanity? nerve? fear of the answer? to ask Jack if there was any connection in his mind with me in the title *Maggie Cassidy* or, which other people tell me must have been the case, 'St. Carolyn by the Sea.' (His sister's name was 'Caroline,' as you know.)" It seems likely that Kerouac was displacing other relationships onto Mary Carney when he wrote *Maggie Cassidy*.

Two early 1950s letters to Carolyn Cassady hint at Kerouac's continuing confusion over his feelings for Mary Carney. In one letter, he stated that he was writing a novel based on his romance with Mary, and in the other, he called the story "Proustian." Just how Proustian it was can be seen in an erotic dream Kerouac had about Neal and Maggie Cassidy. In the dream, a woman asks Jack to make love to her. He recoils in horror, then suddenly a Neal-type sailor comes along—"goodlooking, muscles, strange long arms"— and slams the girl "back to wall, thug to cunt." After the sailor finishes, Jack tries having sex with her, but she rejects him. The divisive feelings that dominate the dream also pervade *Maggie Cassidy*. Though drawn to women, he wrote in *Visions of Cody* that they were "impractical" for him. He was uncomfortable with them because of his inability to achieve true intimacy. He could be sexual—"I like girls," he wrote in *Some of the Dharma*—but this was not the same thing as being intimate. He was going against his nature and then blaming women for his self-deception and unhappiness. According to critic Warren French, Kerouac "lacked the courage to resolve his emotional problems heroically. He didn't have the guts to be gay and hated himself for it."[25]

Despite the trenchancy of Warren French's analysis, what he fails to consider is that no one had that kind of guts in 1939. Even at a 1995 seminar on Kerouac and Sammy Sampas at the University of Massachusetts–Lowell, a classmate of theirs coldly observed in front of a dozen members of the Sampas family, "I knew both Kerouac and Sammy in high school. To me, Kerouac was a track star and a football player. Sam was different, theatrical, the way he talked, the way he walked, the way he waved his arms. He called attention to himself by his speech and his thoughts. He recited his poetry to us, and we didn't take to it very well then." Such intolerance explains almost all the misery there is in the world.

Though Jack loved Sammy, he enjoyed his hard-won status as a champion athlete too much to risk it for love. Their relationship became an emotional quagmire, and in *The Town and the City* Kerouac represented it as having a dark sense of incompleteness, leaving Peter Martin, the Kerouac character, so depressed that he is "saddened by the mere sight of life." When Alexander, the Sammy character, calls Peter "the last of the human beings on earth for me," Peter backs away from him, afraid to unleash his feelings or even admit them. Alexander cries, "Everything seems gone! I know I will die young, before I'm twenty-three. What blackness is closing in on me!" Kerouac also considered suicide, he later revealed, both in an article in *Life* magazine and in a draft of *The Town and the City*.

He graduated from high school on June 28, 1939, at City Auditorium, where Mayor Archambault handed him his diploma, awarded despite his record of flagrant absenteeism and scholastic deficiencies. The latter unfortunately blocked Jack's admittance to Columbia.[26] He couldn't pass French, though *joual* was his native tongue, and he would have to make up credits in French as well as in math, another subject he neglected in high school. The Columbia scholarship proved to be inadequate to his needs, and he'd probably have been better off going to B.C. or Duke. Before Columbia College would admit him, he had to attend high-school-level courses for a year at a Bronx prep school, Horace Mann School for Boys, for which only part of his expenses were paid. Columbia made no provision for his room and board, and Gabrielle had to prevail on her stepmother, who lived in Brooklyn, to put him up.

On his last night in Lowell, Jack Kerouac dreaded leaving the security of home, but felt the inexorable pull of a world he had not even begun to imagine.

MAD ABOUT THE BOY

In September 1939, aboard a Greyhound bus, Jack Kerouac came rolling down from New England and entered Manhattan by way of Port Chester and New Rochelle, suburban gateways to the sprawling metropolis. That evening, he stood at the window of his room in his step-grandmother's boardinghouse near the Fulton Street IRT subway stop and looked out over the same Brooklyn where Thomas Wolfe, one of his favorite authors, wrote *Of Time and the River* and *From Death to Morning*. Despite exciting new surroundings, he was hounded by all the emotional baggage he'd brought from Lowell. Like the autobiographical character in *The Town and the City* whose divided nature Kerouac described as "vast, false, complex, shifting, treacherous," he sensed that he was not being true to himself and that a dishonest life was not worth living.

After only one day at Horace Mann he reverted to his habit of truancy and hopped off the subway at Times Square, where he discovered a world of hookers, con men, and dope addicts, the lost of the earth whose poet laureate he would soon become. Feeling more confident now that he had found his niche, he picked up a red-haired prostitute and banged her in a dingy side-street hotel. Though one biographer later wrote that it was a pleasant experience, Kerouac himself recalled in *Maggie Cassidy* that he was absolutely terrified, thinking of nothing but "sins [and] syphilis." When Maggie/Mary subsequently asked him to show her what he'd done to the girls in Manhattan, he flatly refused. Kerouac usually preferred oral sex to intercourse so that he could fantasize anything he wanted to while giving or receiving pleasure. "He liked to eat girls," Allen Ginsberg wrote. "That's what really

excited him." Kerouac also enjoyed "beautiful boys," Ginsberg added, noting
that he was "very mixed sexually." Ginsberg said he "blew" Kerouac and that
Kerouac "blew" him, but Kerouac felt it was morally improper for him to
"participate in the erotic." Ginsberg blamed such negativity on Jack's prudish,
snoopy mother, but a more obvious cause was society itself, which opposed
homoeroticism with laws, social stigma, and dire religious proscriptions. In
1950, for example, a Senate subcommittee published a report on the threat
of gays in government, and many magazines and psychological "experts"
analyzed homosexuality as a flight from masculinity and maturity.

Kerouac later described his first days in New York City in *Vanity of
Duluoz*, and when I worked with him on the novel, he said, "Let's call it
'An Adventurous Education, 1935–1946.'" He added that being an autodidact "won't get you on the honor roll, but gives you plenty to write about."
When he finally made it to class at Horace Mann, he found himself surrounded by rich boys who were eager to share their turkey sandwiches, napoleons, and chocolate milk with him. The other athletes criticized him for
wearing nothing but a jockstrap while wrestling with one of his admirers.
Like most of the wealthy students at Horace Mann, Jack's wrestling partner
was Jewish and was delivered to school in a chauffeured limousine. Soon he
invited Jack to spend weekends in his father's opulent Manhattan apartment
and introduced him to the novels of Ernest Hemingway, whose "pearls of
words on a white page," Jack once said, provide "an exact picture" of reality.
Though Kerouac attempted to imitate "Papa's" pristine, mannered style, he
preferred the free-flowing prose poems of Thomas Wolfe, "a torrent of American heaven and hell that opened my eyes to America as a subject in itself."
His intellectually eclectic friend also introduced Jack to Dixieland jazz and
art cinema. Though the Waspish football team continued to chide Jack for
associating with nonathletes, and Jewish ones at that, he cultivated them
assiduously, especially after he discovered a way to get at their cash. For two
dollars, he ghosted term papers for these well-heeled schoolmates, whom he
later characterized as "J. D. Salinger middle-class Jewish"—bright, sensitive,
and smart-alecky. Another new friend, described by Jack as a "silent slender
lad," was William F. Buckley, Jr., future author, publisher of the conservative
National Review, and television talk-show host.

Two Horace Mann classmates became Jack's lifelong friends. Henri Cru
was a rebellious, six-foot-three French boy whose parents had brought him
to the United States to attend private schools. During recess, he ran a flourishing business in the toilets selling daggers to tiny fourth-formers at ten
dollars each. Kerouac lacked the nerve to defy convention himself and depended on "madmen" like Cru, and later Neal, to lead him into adventure.
Cru appears as "Remi Boncoeur," one of the original Beats, in *On the Road*
and as "Deni Bleu," in *Visions of Cody, Desolation Angels, Vanity of Duluoz*,
and *Lonesome Traveler*.

The student who would have the most transformative and far-reaching
impact on Kerouac was Seymour Wyse, later portrayed in *Vanity of Duluoz*

as "Lionel Smart," Jack's "really best friend," a Liverpool Jew whose parents had sent him to America to avoid the blitz (Seymour offered a tactful correction in an article entitled "My Really Best Friend," writing that he was born in London in 1923 and had no connection with Liverpool). In one of the watershed moments of Kerouac's life, Seymour introduced him to the glories of jazz. At Kelly's Stable in Harlem, Jack lit up his first joint and listened to Roy Eldridge blow the wildest trumpet since Louis Armstrong and Dizzy Gillespie. As pot dissolved the linear blockades of perception, Kerouac discovered the art of spontaneity and improvisation, on which he would later found a new prose esthetic.

When Kerouac deigned to look in on his classes, he discovered that Horace Mann was one of the best and most rigorous educational institutions in the world. Named after the pioneering proponent of free public education, the school was an extension of Columbia University Teachers College and was overseen by Nicholas Murray Butler, whose epic reign as president of Columbia extended from 1889 until General Dwight D. Eisenhower replaced him in 1946. Jack managed to achieve a 92 average. He became an instant football star when the big-city coaches, immediately appreciating his speed and daring, started him in every game. Horace Mann played Columbia College's freshmen in a torrential downpour, and Jack scored a touchdown as his team clobbered Columbia, 20–2. Word quickly spread to Columbia's Lou Little—and to sports fans in the metropolitan area—that Horace Mann was the team to watch in 1939.

Leo came down from Lowell for the Garden City game, and invaded the locker room as Jack and his teammates changed into their uniforms. No other fathers were present, and Jack was embarrassed until he realized that the coaches and players seemed to find Leo delightful. During the game, Jack scored three touchdowns and hit a rival runner so hard that the unfortunate boy was knocked ten feet and had to be carried from the field on a stretcher. Though Jack led Horace Mann to a 27–0 victory, he began to feel bad about dealing out so much physical punishment. War was on everyone's mind that fall as Hitler's blitzkrieg swept through Europe, and Jack at last recognized that gratuitous violence was evil, whether practiced on the battlefield or the gridiron. Football had served its purpose in his life, and it would be increasingly difficult for him to continue playing the game.

He preferred going around Manhattan like a latter-day Jay Gatsby, hanging out with rich friends in the Palm Court of the Plaza Hotel and sipping crème de menthe. During Kerouac's first year in New York, F. Scott Fitzgerald, chronicler of the "Lost Generation" and spokesman for the insurgent youth of the jazz age, died of a heart attack on December 21, 1940, at the age of forty-four. Because of his drinking, Fitzgerald had always known he was going to die young—but not that alcohol would stop working for him so long before the end. He told his editor at Scribner's, Maxwell Perkins, that he'd get together with a few old friends and drink himself to death if he weren't so completely burnt out on "life, liquor and literature." Though

Kerouac would follow in Fitzgerald's alcoholic footsteps, he was never a devotee of Fitzgerald's novels, referring to him as "sweetly unnecessary." His literary judgment was usually more astute.

In the final game of the season with Tome, an undefeated Maryland team, Jack scored the only touchdown, making Horace Mann the number one high-school team in New York City. Years later, when he read his account of the Tome game to me on the phone, which was the way we edited *Vanity of Duluoz* together, I queried his use of the term *jack off*, as in *"jack off* to the left." He explained, *"Reverse* is what I mean, but it doesn't capture the speed of what I was doing that day. The reader will get it—I mean, who's gonna stop to masturbate during a touchdown run?" Nonetheless, he inserted a few words of clarification in the final manuscript.

The Tome victory made him the darling of the New York press, something he would never be later on as an author. The Lowell sportswriters had taken him for granted, but the *New York Times* singled out his sixty-five-yard run, his surprise punt that rolled to within inches of the Tome goal line, and his forward pass to Quinn that brought Horace Mann a first down. The whole game, according to the *New York Herald Tribune*, was nothing more than "a vague background for the brilliant running of Kerouac. His touchdown was the highlight of the game." The editors of the *Horace Mann Yearbook* wrote that "Kerouac turned in one of the most remarkable individual performances ever seen on the Maroon and White gridiron." *Sports Illustrated* noted years later that Kerouac "achieved his Bing Crosby dream" at Horace Mann. "I loved being a BMOC," he told me, using a popular collegiate phrase denoting "big man on campus." He confided in his notebook that his football triumphs were responsible for his being able at last to break into print. The following spring he found himself the star of the school's literary magazine. The caption under his yearbook photo offers substantial evidence that he was the king of his class at Horace Mann: "Brain and brawn found a happy combination in Jack, a newcomer to school this year. A brilliant back in football, he also won his spurs as a *Record* reporter and a leading *Quarterly* contributor. Was an outfielder on the Varsity baseball nine."[1]

His first published writings focused on jazz. In an article in the *Horace Mann Record* entitled "Count Basie's Band Best in Land," the fledgling jazz critic demonstrated a keen analytical skill as well as uncanny foresight into the future of the rapidly evolving music. His reference to Lester Young's "enormous store of ideas" showed that he understood jazz as a form of personal expression. He quickly grasped how Basie's band functioned: A swing ensemble, it was fundamentally a big band performing for dancers and adhering to rehearsed arrangements, but at intervals soloists would erupt in improvised melodies and the listener would be treated to an all-but-unprecedented glimpse of the creative process in action. Although Basie's swing might be more restrained than that of many other big bands, it packed "more drive, more power, and more thrill than the loudest gang of corn artists can acquire by blowing their horns apart," he wrote. Though colorful,

Jack's pre–Neal Cassady style was still conventionally reportorial and one-dimensional. Even at this early stage — he turned eighteen in 1940 — he could appreciate Lester Young's incomparable phrasing and correctly predict that Young would transform the heretofore obscure tenor sax into the preeminent instrument of jazz. The subsequent evolution of jazz and the emergence of tenor sax stars such as Stan Getz bear out the accuracy of Kerouac's vision. As a beginning writer, he envied the suppleness and power that enabled Lester Young to articulate beautifully cadenced ideas and project nuanced emotions. That Young's most daring and innovative riffs sometimes came from a single exhalation of breath was not lost on Kerouac, who would later maintain that one should write in the same kind of nonstop, unedited bursts of thought.

In March 1940, Kerouac interviewed Glenn Miller at the Paramount in Times Square. With a string of hit records, such as "Moonlight Serenade" and "In the Mood," the thirty-six-year-old trombonist had emerged the previous year as swing's sophisticated master of musical moods and contrasts. Though Kerouac preferred Basie's raw improvisational genius, he later told me, "Glenn Miller and I had a lot in common. We both played football and both cut class." His article ran in the *Horace Mann Record* under the headline, "Glenn Miller Skipped School to Play Trombone, Now Is Nation's Most Popular Band Leader." During the interview, Miller diligently answered Kerouac's questions but seemed edgy and at one point snapped, glared at an assistant, and said, "Shit." When Jack asked Miller what he thought about his new fame, he replied, "It's murder. So many people are asking me to do so many things . . . I just don't know I have the time." Exhausted from overbooking, Miller had already collapsed once during his Paramount run, and Gene Krupa and Tommy Dorsey had substituted for him while he'd recovered at Mount Sinai Hospital. Against doctors' orders, he'd returned to the Paramount just before Kerouac's interview. Four years later, Glenn Miller died while serving as a captain in the army in WWII. His most famous wartime recording was drummer Ray McKinley's swinging martial arrangement, "St. Louis Blues March," which survived into the postwar years as a gridiron halftime favorite.

The most important development that occurred in the jazz world while Kerouac was covering it in the early 1940s was the decline of swing and the rise of a new style called "bebop" — or simply "bop" after Helen Humes scored her hit record "Hey Baba Ree Bop" in the mid-1940s. In Kerouac's 1959 *Escapade* essay, "The Beginning of Bop," he called it the music of "America's inevitable Africa." Spearheaded by Charlie Parker, Thelonious Monk, and Dizzy Gillespie, bop launched the second jazz age — the sound of the 1940s and 1950s — and provided both the creative impetus and the recreational background music for the Beat Generation.

In the new music, African American culture became the archetype of the loneliness and alienation of modern man, a central theme of Beat philosophy and writing. Though in 1940 the hipster style was still five years away, there were already signs of it in Harlem in the early forties. Kerouac absorbed it from both the music and the demeanor of Charlie "Yardbird" Parker, whose cool-cat, unflappable style had been acquired on Kansas City street corners and from jam-session etiquette. Thelonious Sphere Monk, a big, bearlike man, sported one of the first goatees seen in a jazz joint and always wore shades, even indoors, introducing the signature look of the Beats. When Monk attacked the piano, which Kerouac called "the big masterbox," it sounded like "anvils in Petrograd." And in Charlie Parker's hands, the alto sax, still a relatively new invention in the 1940s, was the most expressive and versatile instrument Kerouac had ever heard, especially in Parker's scintillating bop reinventions of standards such as "I Got Rhythm," "What Is This Thing Called Love?" "Don't Blame Me," and "How High the Moon." Working with nothing but his instrument and a column of air, Parker could turn a note into a thing of incredible plasticity, shaping it, bending it, and varying the pitch in a continual search for wild ideas. *That* was how Kerouac wanted to write. "Bring it up out of the gut," Parker said, explaining the source of his seemingly endless supply of breath. "You got to use a lot of diaphragm. There's got to be a foundation. It's got to come from the bottom. After you get the wind up in your throat and mouth you can shape the sound any way you want, make it pretty or loud or soft, but first you got to have the foundation. It's got to come out of the gut."

In Kerouac's 1959 manifesto, "Belief and Technique for Modern Prose," published in *Evergreen Review*, he would echo Parker's advice, telling writers to "blow as deep as you want. . . . Sketch the flow that already exists intact in mind . . . crazier the better." And in "Essentials of Spontaneous Prose," published in the *Black Mountain Review* in 1957, he emphasized that the writer should permit language to stream from the brain without interruption, laying bare the secrets of the mind as freely as a jazz saxophonist blows a riff. In that way a writer could discover his own unique voice — the only sound that would take him to greatness. In Kerouac's opinion, a writer could no more rehearse or revise his prose than a jazz musician could edit his riffs. When beginning to write a passage, an author should clear his mind of outlines, themes, and plots, and focus instead on the "jewel center" of his obsession, letting the words flow out in a "sea of language." The crucial component in the creative process is the "moment of writing." "*Blow! — now!*" he urged. "Tap . . . the song of yourself."

The natural music of the mind was what he was after. Kerouac would tell a Tampa friend in 1968, "I got every record Charlie Parker ever made." To Kerouac, Parker was the sound of God ("Eternal Slowdown") and the ideal he sought to emulate. Many believe Kerouac succeeded. As Jim Christy wrote, "When he let loose with one of his pages-long improvisations, it was like a tenor man stepping out of a section and blowing chorus after rolling chorus."

Though just a preppie on a student newspaper in 1940, Kerouac was one of the few New York journalists to recognize and praise the new bop musicians. Columnist Jimmy Cannon wrote that Parker and Gillespie sounded "like a hardware store in an earthquake," and even fellow musician Tommy Dorsey complained, "Bebop has set music back twenty years." But somewhere in the mysterious, primal forces suggested by Parker's flow of musical ideas lay the source of the spurting genital style of Jack Kerouac.[2]

That style was still a decade away. His first published fiction, "The Brothers," appeared in the *Horace Mann Quarterly*. In this spare, realistic detective story, a team of sleuths solves a case in which the villain, Elmo, attempts to murder his own brother. Though it bears little stylistic resemblance to Kerouac's mature work, "The Brothers" is his first "buddy" story, a genre that would culminate in *On the Road*. One of the detectives admires the other's superior composure and competence, anticipating Sal Paradise's veneration of Dean Moriarty in *On the Road*. Of biographical significance is the story's attempted fratricide, which may have sprung from Kerouac's memory of Gerard and the midnight crib trauma. In the narrative, the victim lies in his bed, "sleeping calmly, oblivious . . . of the silent menace." Later, when detective Browne thwarts Elmo's plot to kill his brother, Browne comments, ruefully, "Brotherly love . . . Elmo was one of those brothers who believe in the process of elimination." In another autobiographical parallel, the detective's name is Brown—the same as the color of Gabrielle's robe—which for Kerouac signified security and safety. The mystery genre would continue to appeal to Kerouac, and in a few years, he and Burroughs would collaborate on a crime novel.

Another of his Horace Mann stories, "*Une Veille de Noel*," introduces two of Kerouac's most abiding concerns: alcoholism and spirituality. The story is set in a Greenwich Village bar on a snowy night. The drinkers include a middle-aged alcoholic who has wasted his life, and several college students who are at the beginning of their drinking careers but already on the way to alcoholism. The door suddenly opens, and from out of the snowy mists, Jesus Christ appears in the form of a mysterious stranger. He wishes everyone Merry Christmas, but when the bartender tries to take his order, Christ says, "I don't drink." The students immediately put aside their drinks, pay their bill, and clear out. When the middle-aged drunk's son Joey arrives to take him home, the boy says he's just seen an angel. The terse parable makes a definite impression, but it's chiefly of interest for the light it sheds on Kerouac's attitude toward alcohol. He seemed powerfully aware, even at this early stage, that drinking destroys lives, and even goes against God's will. The drunken father and his son Joey seem to represent Leo and Jack; like young Joey, who leads his father from the bar, Jack was constantly trying to redeem his father through feats of glory on the football field.[3]

Kerouac evidently had some sort of flirtation with Cole Porter around 1940, as suggested in *Duluoz*. The composer of "Night and Day" was a well-known homosexual, though married to a rich, older woman, Linda Lee Thomas. Due to his infidelities, Linda decided to divorce Cole, but after a horseback riding accident left him crippled and helpless, she remained with him, explaining, "You don't desert a sinking ship." In *Duluoz*, Kerouac wrote of encountering a man in a wheelchair on lower Fifth Avenue one evening, who was, he speculated, "Cole Porter on a secret spree?" For Porter, despite his accident two years previously, adventure was a basic necessity of life. The "small paralyzed man," as Kerouac described him, permitted Jack to sweep him up in his arms and go running "pellmell" down the middle of Fifth Avenue. Finally, Kerouac hailed a cab and lifted him into the backseat, carefully folding up his wheelchair. "Thanks," the man said, "that was a great run! I'm a music publisher, my name is Porter."

When I came to this passage while editing *Duluoz*, I asked Kerouac to "elaborate" and "clarify." He said it was clear enough already, and referred me to a specific line in the same chapter: "casual love affairs (?) (no such thing)." No one would "get it," I said, but he replied jokingly, "It was just one of those flings." Porter had many casual relationships, according to Truman Capote, who was a mutual acquaintance of both Porter and Kerouac. According to Capote, one of Porter's sex partners, singing star Jack Cassidy, made Cole crawl across the floor of his bedroom in the Waldorf Towers, while Cassidy undressed and said, "Do you want this cock? Then come and get it!" Porter was the composer of some of the most popular tunes of the era, such as "I'm a Gigolo," "Anything Goes," and "Blow, Gabriel, Blow," which were rife with sexual innuendoes, as well as "Begin the Beguine," one of Sammy Sampas's favorite songs.

The episode in *Duluoz* exposed a little-known side of Kerouac's personality, though not an uncharacteristic one, according to Allen Ginsberg. He described Kerouac's "appreciation of older queens . . . which was like a sharing of common humanity . . . even a sharing of the erotic." In *Palimpsest: A Memoir*, Gore Vidal disclosed that a well-known writer used Jack as a hustler. "Jack was bisexual," Vidal explained in Gifford and Lee's oral history of Kerouac, and added that Jack employed his "physical charms . . . to advance his career as a writer."

Kerouac's reference to the wheelchair-bound Porter in *Duluoz* echoed a similar though nonsexual experience in *The Town and the City*, in which a prep-school student is paid fifteen cents a night to take a nonagenarian outside for his daily exercise. As a youth of no means, Kerouac would often have had nothing but his physical assets to go on, and he learned early to capitalize on them. In *Mexico City Blues*, in the "37th Chorus," he quoted a line from Noel Coward, " 'Mad about the Boy.' " The Coward song described a youth who seemed rather sad despite his "gay appeal."[4] Similarly, Kerouac's dashing athletic persona concealed a timid soul inside, who was afraid to live and who, to paraphrase Edith Wharton, would only occasionally catch glimpses of the full life, like the scent of land that one sometimes smells on an ocean liner far out at sea.

The summer after graduation from prep school, he returned to his old friends in Lowell, particularly to Sammy, and began to nurse a lifelong grudge against his rich Horace Mann friends, who dropped him the moment he reverted from Mr. Touchdown U.S.A. to lower-class mill-town untouchable. In a coruscating, anti-Semitic letter addressed to Ginsberg a decade later, Kerouac bitterly denounced them as "millionaire jews." In Lowell, he felt even more acutely than before a conflict between his homoerotically inclined life with Sammy and the blustering masculinity he affected with his rowdier Pawtucketville crowd. Though he enjoyed watching his buddies' heterosexual gang bangs, he refrained from participating in them. However, he relished the all-male pastime of sunbathing at Bareass Beach. To assuage the pain of repressed emotions, Jack and Sammy got drunk together. In a letter the following year, Jack begged Sammy not to embarrass him in front of G. J. and Salvey, and to desist from discussing literature and other matters that were over their heads. He professed to hate intellectual discussions, but in fact there were few pleasures he appreciated more than reviewing the summer's reading matter with Sammy—Thomas Hardy, Thoreau, Dickinson, and Jack London. Sammy had just graduated from Lowell High and was going to Emerson College in Boston in the fall to major in drama. "Sammy came to Emerson with a dream," one of his classmates recalled in 1995. "He wanted to be an actor, a writer. He especially admired Thomas Wolfe and Walt Whitman." Kerouac was often in Sammy's home, where he experienced an almost mystical rapport with Sammy's mother Maria, whom he called "Ya-Ya." He also grew very fond of Stella. "Stella was in love with Jack years and years and years before they ever got married," Betty Watley recalled. "When he was a boy running around with Sammy, she was in love with Jack then. She waited all that time, over twenty years, for him."

According to one biographer, Kerouac drank his first beer that summer at Barrett's Cafe on Moody Street, but Kerouac himself placed the event somewhat earlier, writing in *Maggie* that he was already drinking heavily at Horace Mann. In fact, he'd been drinking alcoholically—that is, to get drunk—ever since Leo forced liquor on him in 1938. It was perhaps impossible for him to live otherwise, because of the unbearable polarities of his divided nature, and the deliberate fallacy he'd trapped himself in. He equated intelligence (art, spirituality, Sammy) with being a sissy, and action (heterosexual Pawtucketville buddies and later Cassady-type wranglers) with being a man. Unless and until he was willing to look at his sexuality, his alcoholism would not stand a chance of being approached honestly and effectively. His alcohol and sex issues, though separate problems, were symbiotic in a sense, running parallel courses and feeding off each other. Temperamentally and psychologically, he was already firmly entrenched in the mainstream of mid-century American writers, such as Nobel laureates Ernest Hemingway and William Faulkner, who felt that writing was not a red-blooded masculine pursuit and who were both alcoholics. They typified an American era that was uncertain about sexuality, obsessed with ambition, morbid about religion, and incurably alcoholic.[5]

Jack enrolled in Columbia College in September 1940. Leo, now bloated by alcohol to 350 pounds, tagged along and begged coach Lou Little to find him a job. According to sportswriter Glenn Stout, "Jack got on Lou Little's bad side and was out of the lineup." He settled in room 209, Livingston Hall, which commanded a magnificent view of the Van Am Quadrangle, a vast expanse of green lawn and red-brick promenades at the center of the campus. Unfortunately, his workload was too heavy for him to derive much benefit or pleasure from his Columbia years. In addition to daily football practice, he had a full class schedule and was required to wash dishes to pay for his meals. The classical curriculum also left him cold, and he grouched to Sammy that he missed the kinds of books they read together in Lowell, such as James Joyce's A *Portrait of the Artist as a Young Man.* Joyce's novel about a youth's growing self-awareness as an artist had a seismic impact on Kerouac, who, like Joyce, was a renegade Catholic and stylistic innovator. In 1940, Joyce, the fifty-eight-year-old author of *Ulysses,* widely regarded as the greatest novel of the twentieth century, was in great peril. Having exiled himself from his native Ireland, he was living in France when it fell to the Nazis. Alcoholic, almost blind, and desperately ill, he fled to Zurich, where he died of uremic poisoning on January 10, 1941, after surgery for a malignant duodenal ulcer. Joyce had been shattered by the commercial and critical failure of his final novel, *Finnegans Wake,* which would later influence one aspect of Kerouac's style—his playful use of language as pure sound.[6]

On October 12, 1940, Columbia's freshman football team played its first game of the season against Rutgers in New Brunswick, New Jersey. Jack wasn't put in until the second half. He played brilliantly, but it was too late; Rutgers won, 18–7. The *Columbia Spectator* called Jack "probably the best back on the field," and Lou Little decided to use him in the next game against St. Benedict's Prep. At one point, when Jack had just caught a punt and tacklers had his ankles in a viselike grip, he made an unwise decision. Trying to twist loose, he broke his leg. The *Spectator* reported that Columbia's "star back will be out with a leg injury for the rest of the season. . . . The loss of Kerouac, fleet-footed backfield ace, is a blow to the Yearlings' chances of breaking into the victory column." A quarter of a century later, his leg still hurt him on damp days.

"I met Jack on crutches in 1940," his future wife, Frankie Edith "Edie" Parker, recalled. "I was engaged to Henri Cru, then fell in love with Jack." Originally from Grosse Pointe, Michigan, Edie arrived in New York at nineteen to stay with her grandmother and study art but was far more interested in having a good time. She met Cru in the elevator of her building at 116th Street, near the Columbia campus. He was exactly the kind of party boy she was looking for. Cru introduced her to Kerouac, who sized her up as an uninhibited bohemian who would make a good drinking buddy and bedmate. A brunette when they first met, she later peroxided her hair, and Kerouac would subsequently compare her with the 1950s blond bombshell Mamie Van Doren. He called her "Johnnie," after the barroom song "Frankie and Johnnie." An incorrigible barfly, Edie counted the West End Bar's Johnny, the bartender, as one of her best friends.

While Edie and Jack grew closer, he kept up a steady stream of cards to Sammy at Emerson College, but cautioned him on February 26, 1941, to hide them from Stella. He was "being boyish," he wrote. Confiding that he no longer bothered to study, he added that he preferred to roam the fabulously varied "web" of New York City on a nightly basis. He was reading Thomas Wolfe until four in the morning, and Wolfe's influence was increasingly obvious in Kerouac's language. In *The Web and the Rock*, Wolfe defined Manhattan as "the Rock," while "the Web" was the intricate network of relationships stretching all the way back to Asheville, the North Carolina town of his birth. Jack's correspondence with Sammy reveals that like many idealistic young people of the thirties and forties, they took their Communism seriously, and they even made romantic plans to meet in Russia in five years, where they would toast each other with vodka and gaze at the rooftops of Moscow from their hotel room. In his March 25 letter, Jack grew sentimental, admitting that he cried every time he heard songs like "I'll See You Again," "The Man I Love," and "You Go to My Head." Obviously, he was in love with Sammy but unable to admit it.

At the same time he was writing daily cards to Sammy, Jack was hotly pursuing a Barnard girl named Norma Blickfelt. Barnard College for Women is Columbia's sister school, located just across Broadway from the Columbia campus. In April 1941, Jack and Norma had a twelve-hour date that he later recounted, in a letter to her, in ecstatic terms. A blue-eyed Nordic beauty, Norma was of Norwegian lineage, and her body excited him. Though according to Jack she had already given her class ring to another Columbia boy, she and Jack enjoyed a tryst in a Third Avenue penthouse. He told her about Thomas Wolfe and William Saroyan, and she told him about Thomas Mann, later serenading Jack with German lieder. They strolled through Union Square and the Bowery and dined in a basement restaurant in Chinatown. Later, they took the Staten Island ferry, and as they stood on the deck he admired her "straw-colored" hair, billowing in the breeze. She planned to work as a counselor at a children's camp near Poughkeepsie the following summer, and she was especially interested in working with blind children. Wanting to see more of her, Jack found it unsettling when she revealed she was already involved with another boy. She thought like a man, he told her, but she had the voluptuous shape and compassionate heart of a woman—a tragic and passionate Helen. He was sounding more and more like Thomas Wolfe, who idolized women as Hellenic goddesses when he wasn't abusing them, but Kerouac had also been reading Budd Schulberg's hard-bitten Hollywood novel, *What Makes Sammy Run?*, one of the year's best-sellers, and agreed with Schulberg's sexist contention that intelligent women have masculine minds.

Later, following Norma's advice, Kerouac read Thomas Mann, and he even had a brief encounter with the Nobel laureate when Mann visited the Columbia campus after fleeing Nazi Germany. Kerouac had shed his plaster leg cast and was working as a waiter in the John Jay dining hall. When he served the sixty-five-year-old Thomas Mann his coffee that day, Kerouac was just nineteen years old, the same age as Franz Westermeier, the Bavarian waiter with whom the bisexual Mann would fall in love in 1950. "Young men are my suffering and my delight," Mann said, according to his biographer, Anthony Heilbut. Kerouac found Mann to be a noble "humanist," he wrote Norma, and he compared Mann's ideas with those of Sammy's Young Prometheans. In the same letter, he acknowledged that he owed much of his intellectual development to the Prometheans. He was in love with Norma but continued to play the field, and when G. J. came to the city on a weekend visit, they had sex with several girls, he boasted in an April 15, 1941, letter to Sammy. Jack apologized for neglecting Sammy, who'd been in New York at the same time, but urged him to return for a New York "interlude."[7]

By the end of his freshman year, Jack was one of the most popular undergraduates at Columbia, largely as a result of his headline-grabbing play in the Rutgers game, his subsequent injury, and his distinctive leg cast, which he had flaunted like a badge of courage, hobbling into the Lion's Den on crutches and taking his favorite chair by the fire. In the spring of 1941 he was elected vice president of the sophomore class for the forthcoming academic year, 1941–1942. The men of Phi Gamma Delta invited him to join, and he accepted with the provision that he'd never have to wear the blue pledge skullcap. But there was one frat ritual he adored: getting drunk during the initiation event known as the "beer barrel." The pledge was expected to gulp an entire keg, which posed no difficulty for Kerouac, who happily "drained it of its dregs" and asked for more, though dawn was breaking over Morningside Heights.

His drinking soon turned him into the kind of bully he'd always hated. He went on a drunken gay-bashing binge in Greenwich Village with some other football players, and participated in a brutal assault on an innocent man later identified as a gay violinist. With this crime, committed out of fear and self-loathing, Kerouac joined the ranks of perhaps the least enviable of human anomalies, the homophobic homoerotic. Though he later denounced his jock buddies as "a bunch of jerks," his own culpability would haunt him forever, almost as if he had brought down on himself the ancient karmic curse, "Ye who inflict pain and suffering on your own kind shall inherit the wind." Remorsefully, he admitted in *The Subterraneans* that he was a "nannybeater" and that even hipsters, including those who regarded him as a "crazy saint," began to avoid him. "They're afraid I'll suddenly become a hoodlum," he wrote. Sadly, the transformation was already complete; he now qualified as a genuine thug. His shame was evident in his masochistic reply to a gay man who sat down next to him on a bench in Riverside Park one day and began to cruise him.

"How you hung?" the man inquired.

"By the neck, I hope," he said.

Feeling like an outcast, Jack began to isolate himself in the frat house on 114th Street. While his Phi Gamma Delta brothers went out on dates,

Jack sat in an easy chair in the lounge and played Glenn Miller records. Another record he liked was the Frank Sinatra–Tommy Dorsey hit "The One I Love (Belongs to Somebody Else)," which epitomized the star-crossed nature of most of his relationships. An exception was Maria Livornese, the sister of Jack's Columbia classmate Tom Livornese. When Jack arrived at her house in Lynbrook, Long Island, to take her to a prom, he told her, "How beautiful you are," speaking in French. It was an exhilarating, windswept evening, and they "danced and kissed — all night long," she added. Later, on double dates, they drove to Jones Beach in a convertible and parked. "We would just lie on the beach on our blankets and look at the stars," she remembered. When the temperature would drop in the early morning hours, they'd climb in the Buick and use the canvas top as an extra blanket. They continued to see each other off and on until 1953. "You never knew when Jack was going to turn up," she recalled.

Back in Lowell in the summer of 1941, it was "one goddamn crisis after a friggin other," he wrote in *Vanity of Duluoz*. He got into trouble almost every time he drank, one of the surest signs of alcoholism. During one bender with Sammy and G. J., he dove twenty feet into a Vermont quarry and would have drowned had Sammy not jumped in and saved him. They were supposed to have dates with Manchester girls, but by the time they drove into town they were scarcely ambulatory. Jack's girl, a bright, dynamic coed from North Adams, took one look at them and called everything off. He became depressed when he realized his drinking had ruined a promising new relationship, but G. J. insisted they'd done nothing wrong. Sammy knew better and wept. On the long drive home, Jack slept "on Sabby's lap all the way, as he cried, then dozed, all night," Jack wrote, using the fictional name "Sabby Savakis" for Sammy in *Vanity of Duluoz*. Predictably, they almost had a fatal accident. Due to a serious car wreck the previous year on another drunken spree in Vermont, Jack developed a phobia and would never be able to drive an automobile with any degree of confidence or proficiency. "He never learned to drive," Maria Livornese recalled. "He loved me to drive him around New York. 'Jesus,' he'd say, 'you drive just like a taxicab driver.' "

While women were convenient, it was male bonding that nourished Kerouac's spirit and emotions, as he revealed in a letter to Cornelius ("Connie") Murphy, one of the Young Prometheans. His dalliances with "wenches" were nothing compared with the "glory" of male companionship, he told Murphy, adding that he preferred the love of men. Having admitted all this, he still thought it was "folly" for anyone to suggest that his behavior suggested either schizophrenia or unconventional sexuality. Despite his condescending attitude toward women, he boasted to Connie that he kept mistresses. His total copulations with girls during the war years came to 250, he related in a 1965 letter to Seymour Krim. His steady date that summer was the talented and attractive Margaret Coffey, who would shortly do a stint as Benny Goodman's vocalist. Margaret was alluring in her skimpy red dress and high-heeled slippers. Almost every Friday night in the summer of 1941, Margaret and Jack would sit under an apple tree in Centralville and sing Broadway show tunes, like Oscar Hammerstein and Jerome Kern's poignant ode to the recent fall of France, "The Last Time I Saw Paris."[8]

In July 1941, Sammy's fifty-two-year-old father, George, got into a fight with Peter Apostalakos, a man who's been stalking him, and shot him dead in the middle of Market Street. From his Lowell jail cell, Sampas explained that he and Apostalakos had been squabbling ever since 1920. Within minutes of the shooting, the Greek colony in Lowell was in an uproar, plotting reprisals. Concerned for the safety of his ten children, George begged the police to protect them. Sammy and his brothers and sisters emerged from the crisis traumatized by their father's ordeal but physically unharmed. The following December, George pleaded guilty to manslaughter and was sentenced to twelve to twenty years in prison. "My father had led strikes against local mills for better conditions, and this was used against him," John Sampas said. Despite Sammy's abhorrence of violence, he remained loyal to his father. "The only job my father knew was in the shoe shop," he wrote, according to his nephew Tony. Sammy had once looked in on his father at work and stood watching as George sweated and tugged at the tough, unyielding leather, sweat streaming from his brow. Afterward, Sammy appreciated the hard labor required to feed a large growing family. "I loved and respected that man pulling at a shoe," he wrote. Feelings for his father also infused Sammy's poem, "Summer in the Mill Town," in which he portrayed the heinous conditions in Lowell's factories. The summer heat turned the workrooms into ovens as French, Greek, and Polish workers pulled velvet cloth through toxic dyes, cloth that would soon cover a rich man's treasure chest—"or a casket." A century before, in *A Week on the Concord and Merrimack Rivers*, Thoreau had extolled the area's natural beauty, but to Sammy, son of a mill worker, the Merrimack was a river of sweat and blood.[9]

In the fall before returning to Columbia, Jack helped his family move to West Haven, Connecticut, where they found a seaside cottage at 5 Bradley Point for forty dollars a month. Jack wrote a heartbreaking letter to Nin, who had remarried and moved away, describing the family crisis. No longer able to find work in Lowell, Leo was operating a hot-lead Linotype machine in New Haven while Gabrielle cleaned tables in a hash joint. His parents were still willing to indulge Jack as long as he stayed in college and made them proud of him, and he admitted to Nin that he was enjoying himself at the seashore, going swimming, rowing, and living like a "millionaire." He begged Nin to come back and look after their parents, who struck him as helpless and abandoned, but he failed to see that their problem was excessive drinking. In 1941, Leo was only fifty-two and Gabrielle just forty-seven, but Jack wrote of them as if they were old people in their death throes.

Back at Columbia, he clashed almost immediately with Lou Little, who complained that Jack was no longer fast enough for the starting lineup. In a 1961 interview, Little said that he'd found Kerouac promising but "headstrong." Furious over the prospect of another season on the bench, Jack stalked off the playing field and dropped out of Columbia the following day, making what he later called the most significant move of his life up until that time. The only clue he had to his destiny was a vague impulse to follow the footsteps of Thomas Wolfe and head south. On a bus to Washington, D.C., he reflected on the momentous step he'd taken. "I was on the road for the first time," he later wrote, and he loved the taste of freedom. By his defection, he was demonstrating that he would no longer enslave himself to the dreams of his parents, the ambitions of his coach, or the demands of his professors. In effect, he was telling these representatives of the establishment "to go jump in the big fat ocean of their own folly." On September 26, the *New York Times* carried a cryptic item on the sports page noting that "Jack Kerouac, Sophomore wingback, will not be available this fall."

First published in 1996, Kerouac's story, "Washington in 1941," which Tony Sampas discovered among Sammy's papers, tells of Kerouac's first road trip. Arriving in the nation's capital, he deposited his bag in his squalid room and went out to roam the city, eager for a glimpse of Franklin D. Roosevelt or at least of Henry Wallace. Instead, he became fascinated by the Negroes hanging around the hotel and stood listening to their jive. Finally, he moved on and found relief from the heat of the day in the "cool and crypt-like" atmosphere of the Capitol. Proceeding to the National Gallery, he admired the Rembrandts and later visited the FBI and Department of Justice buildings. Finally, he gave up all hope of spotting a famous politician and took in a movie, *Dive Bomber*. In the darkness of the auditorium, he was overcome with loneliness and began to weep. Back at the hotel, he discovered that his bed was sticky and bug-infested.

At last the magnitude of what he had done hit him. After having clawed his way from the ghetto to the Ivy League, he'd sacrificed it all for mere hurt pride. "It was one of the worst moments of my life," he recalled. Unable to sleep, he wrote a letter to Sammy that he later called his best composition. It was devoid of artifice because he was too desperate to do anything but spew out his true feelings. In a burst of characteristic narcissism, he portrayed himself as the spokesman for every solitary writer who'd ever lived—sick, lonely, and helpless. The next morning he went to a bookstore and bought Emerson's *Essays*. The Emersonian concepts of self-reliance and nonconformity gave him the validation he needed for the radically individualistic turn his life had taken. "Trust thyself," Emerson wrote, "Whoso would be a man must be a nonconformist." Already, Kerouac was assembling the ideas for the revolution he would foment the following decade. The environment of conformity that he challenged in the 1950s, epitomized by William Whyte's *Organization Man* and David Reisman's *Lonely Crowd*, was the bane of the Beats, especially of the Zen lunatics in *The Dharma Bums*, whose poetic and spiritual breakthroughs would give "visions of eternal freedom to everybody and to all living creatures."

But at nineteen, nearly broke, still afraid to hitchhike, and with only enough money for bus fare home, he retreated to his parents in West Haven and threw himself upon their mercy. Returning home when it got rough would become a habit, leading to further doubts about his ruggedness. Leo was tired of supporting him. Hinting that Jack was no longer welcome at home, Leo suggested he look up his childhood friend Mike Fournier, who might help him find a job as a gas-station attendant in East Hartford, Connecticut. In a late September 1941 letter to Sammy, Jack described how he glided out of New Haven aboard a train bound for Hartford, the autumn air pregnant with the enchanting and numinous feel of his favorite month, October. He urged Sammy to read *Of Time and the River*, Wolfe's autobiographical saga of a young man's search for fulfillment in which Wolfe wrote, "All things on earth point home in old October: sailors to sea, travelers to walls and fences . . . the lover to the love he has forsaken." The novel's mysterious refrain, "of wandering forever and the earth again," appealed strongly to the future author of *On the Road*, and the homoerotically charged relationship between Wolfe's protagonist, Eugene Gant, and his gay Harvard classmate, Francis Starwick, was similar in many respects to that of Kerouac and Sampas. To Eugene, Starwick represents "a life forever good, forever warm and beautiful, forever flashing with the fires of passion, poetry and joy." Kerouac called Wolfe the first of his many literary angels.[10]

In Hartford that fall, Kerouac undertook his first large-scale effort as a writer, working on novels and completing numerous short stories, but at first literary matters gave way to more pressing priorities, such as earning a living for the first time in his life. He worked at a gas station in East Hartford and subsequently at another in Manchester, and somehow managed to hold his own as a mechanic, wielding a tire iron, grease-gun, and monkey wrench. On his salary of $27.50 a week, he lived in a succession of rooming houses, writing Sammy in October that he was conducting an in-depth study of his roommate, "old Mike," in order to understand human nature and the suffering of mankind. He was reading Wolfe, Saroyan, John Dos Passos, and William James and toying with the idea of transferring from Columbia to Notre Dame on a football scholarship. After seeing Orson Welles's *Citizen Kane*, he dashed off a screen treatment entitled *Oktober*, but Hollywood promptly bounced it back to him. He also wrote a manuscript that he referred to only as *FSSFMT* and sent it off to Harper's. The archive contains no record of either Welles's or Harper's reactions to these submissions.

His sex life had never been better, but from the way he described it to Cassady in a letter dated January 10, 1951, it appeared to have been conducted primarily as a way of convincing his fellow grease monkeys that he was a real cocksman and not just another Ivy League sissy. His treatment of a high-school girl named Kitty, whom he lured into the bushes outside Pratt & Whitney Aircraft, was "ghastly," he confessed. They emerged from their lovemaking just as the factory was letting out for the day and were jeered by the entire work force. Later, he succeeded in penetrating the girl "hard and fast," and boasted of having ejaculated in sixty seconds. Like many men, he considered a speedy climax to be a sign of virility rather than what it was—proof of selfishness and ignorance. Kitty's lace panties excited him more than Kitty herself did, and he kept his "saggy" condom as evidence of his conquest, later displaying it on the pump island of the gas station, where, to his chagrin, it was ignored. In Manchester, at the Atlantic Whiteflash gas station, he again postured in front of the mechanics, showily fondling his "genitaliae [sic]." His sexual banter at Atlantic Whiteflash was so persuasive that his boss called him a "cuntlapper." One day, Jack and two other mechanics took a pair of girls out in a car, and Jack started making out with one of them, Agnes, though he'd been warned she had VD. Even before the driver could get the car in high gear, he was cupping her juicy "vaginal heart" in his hand and was about to explode. No sooner had they parked in the woods than he was inside her. Although he considered himself to be a "cockmaster," he was at first too nervous to have an orgasm, and compared himself with Captain Ahab in *Moby-Dick*, who was petrified when he at last confronted the leviathan. Finally, after the car bumped up and down for twenty minutes, Kerouac came once and Agnes came four times. He had very nearly "fucked" her to death, Agnes said, though she was eager for more. He tossed his condom out the window and relinquished her to the others.[11]

That night, Jack reclaimed his typewriter from an army of cockroaches and knocked off a short story. Eventually, according to his estate, he would have twenty to thirty stories, enough for a collection entitled *Atop an Underwood*, but he admitted that they were imitative of Saroyan, Hemingway, and Wolfe and were not worth printing. He was also writing a Joycean novel in which he portrayed himself as a Dedalus-like character named Duluoz, and another novel entitled *La Nuit Est Ma Femme (The Night Is My Woman)*.

At Thanksgiving 1941, Jack yearned for his mother's home cooking but had to work for five hours at the gas pumps. Later, in his rented room, he was swatting cockroaches when Sammy burst in on him. Seeing Jack in greasy coveralls, Sammy's eyes filled with tears as he gauged his friend's fall from Ivy League glory to working-class squalor. Was Jack sure he'd made the right decision in leaving Columbia? inquired Sammy, and Jack happily replied that he was brimming with creativity. "You and I alone in this room," Sammy said, according to Kerouac's account of their visit in *Vanity of Duluoz*. When Kerouac read this passage to me as we worked on the manuscript in 1967, I asked him to explain Sammy's remark. "I think it's clear enough that Sammy loved me," he said, and continued reading. Eventually they went out to eat and ordered the turkey blue-plate special at a luncheonette. Jack asked Sammy to write him a poem, and Sammy recited one on the spot—a celebration of shared experiences, sunsets they'd seen together, books they'd read, leisurely swims, "long ago" laughter in misty New England. They couldn't agree on a movie, so Jack went alone to see *I Wake Up Screaming*, a moody thriller starring Victor Mature and Betty Grable, but he kept thinking about Sammy because of his striking resemblance to Mature.

Later that month, Jack moved back to Lowell with his family, and they settled again in Pawtucketville, on the first floor of a two-family dwelling on Crawford Street. He trudged the icy sidewalks looking for menial work, wishing he was back in glittery Manhattan as the tweedy vice president of Columbia's sophomore class. In the last few days before Pearl Harbor, he went into a depression. The book he was reading, Dostoyevsky's *Notes From Underground*, held out little hope for humanity, and on December 7, 1941, as if to confirm Dostoyevsky's gloomy prognosis, the world entered the most bloody and destructive war in history. Several days after the Japanese virtually bombed the American navy out of existence, Germany and Italy declared war on the United States. World War II raged for the next four years, and its effect on a generation of major American writers then coming of age— Kerouac, Norman Mailer, James Jones, and J. D. Salinger, all of whom served in the armed forces—would forever alter their lives and leave an indelible stamp on twentieth-century literature.

Meanwhile Kerouac continued to search for odd jobs around Lowell. When he applied for a delivery job at the *Sun*, sportswriter Frank Moran recognized him as the hero of the Lowell-Lawrence game and hired him as a sports reporter at fifteen dollars a week. Copy editor Clare Foye found Kerouac to be "a real gentleman. It didn't surprise me at all that he became a literary great," she later said. Occasionally Leo, who worked part-time at the paper, found himself setting Jack's articles in type. The *Sun* still couldn't spell Jack's name right, printing it as "Jack Korouac" on his only bylined story, "Lowell Stages Second Half Rally to Beat Lawrence in Hoop Series Opener," published on February 19, 1942.

More accustomed to starring in athletic events than chronicling them, Jack soon tired of sports reporting and spent his time at the *Sun* writing the first version of *Vanity of Duluoz* on company time. He would not complete the novel until a quarter of a century later when I, as his editor at Coward-McCann, paid him to do so. Kerouac described the first draft, which was markedly different from the final one I edited, as "an attempt to delineate all of Lowell as Joyce had done for Dublin." In the preface to his posthumously published collection, *Heaven and Other Poems*, he made another reference to this early version, comparing it with *Ulysses*. He showed some of the first pages to his Young Promethean friend John MacDonald, who pronounced them powerful and promising. John Sampas explained in 1995 how Kerouac had come up with the title *Vanity of Duluoz*. "Jack saw the name Daoulas in the newspaper one day when he was working at the *Sun* in 1942," John said. "When he wrote *The Town and the City* in the late 1940s, he had three different names for the Martin family, which earlier was the Daoulas family. At some point, he changed Daoulas to Duluoz to Frenchify it." As I dined with the Sampas family one night in 1995 at La Boniche Restaurant (formerly Nicky's Bar, one of Jack's favorite watering holes in Lowell), John spotted Mr. Daoulas at another table and introduced us. A friendly man, Daoulas smiled when we told him that Kerouac had named a novel after him, and related that he'd once known Jack's family. Jack himself claimed that Duluoz was an old Gaelic name.

At home, while his parents were working, Jack and an old girl friend made love on the couch—sometimes with her on top and sometimes with him on top, he revealed in *Duluoz*—but he was bored in Lowell and soon drifted back to New York. He caught Sinatra's show at the Paramount and fell in briefly with the Columbia crowd. In a letter to Norma Blickfelt, he wrote that he went to Washington, D.C., in the spring of 1942 and continued studying the American South as possible material for fiction. He earned sixty dollars per week as a construction worker on the Pentagon, which was then going up in Arlington, Virginia. When completed, at a cost of $49.6 million, the Pentagon was the largest office building in the world, consolidating all the scattered offices of the War Department, as it was called then. Designed to house twenty-five thousand workers, the Pentagon's Chinese-box design— five interlocking rings, one smaller than the next, around a five-acre court called "Ground Zero"—would later be ridiculed by architecture critics as "Puzzle Palace" and "Fort Fumble." Kerouac called it "the new Gethsem-ane" and would have agreed with *New York Times* political reporter Allen Drury, who wrote, "Its real business is Death." In a letter to Norma, Jack admitted playing hooky from his job in order to hike through the Virginia countryside, returning to the Pentagon just in time to punch his card. In Washington, he stayed in a rented room with G. J. Apostolos, who had taken a wartime job in a government office.

G. J. noticed that Jack had changed radically, and not for the better. His excessive drinking shocked G. J., as did the fact that he was packing a gun. He drank at work and hid out in an excavation on the gargantuan five-mile construction site. In an act of public lewdness, which could easily have landed him in jail, he took out his penis in front of the Capitol and waved it at a flag. Like Sammy, Kerouac was convinced he was going to die soon. So were many young men in World War II, but Kerouac's reason was different: he hated the fundamental dishonesty of his life. Predictably, he was fired from the Pentagon when the field boss discovered him loafing.

For a while, he worked as a short-order cook and soda jerk at a lunch counter in northwest Washington. One day, a brash brunette from Georgia sat down at the counter, gave him a pack of pornographic playing cards, and offered to keep him if he would regularly make love to her and walk her poodle. His specialty as a lover was stamina, he later boasted, and the brunette moaned that he was screwing her "to dayeth." She left him for a one-armed cabdriver. He described his life as interesting and exciting in a letter to Norma, but soon he left Washington and wandered from town to town in the South, hopping freight trains and listening to blacks sing blues songs. He wanted to visit Thomas Wolfe's "Old Kentucky Home" in North Carolina but grew road-weary halfway through the state of Virginia, turned around, and headed north. He resolved to get a job and save money in order to return to New York and Columbia.[12]

According to Edie Parker, after Jack showed up in Manhattan she met him on the Columbia campus at the Lion's Den, where she saw him standing in the doorway, a cigarette dangling from his lips, looking blasé in his black pants and lumberjack shirt. When she approached him, he embraced her with one arm only and continued to hold her that way. "He smelled so good," she recalled, and he was "oh! so handsome!" Picking up his suitcase, he led her across Broadway to the West End where they settled in their favorite booth, ordered beers, and held hands across the table. Their desire for each other was "choking" them, Edie said, and they "desperately" wanted to make love. Finishing their drinks, they went to her apartment, which she shared with the future wife of William S. Burroughs, Joan Vollmer Adams, a Barnard student whose current husband, Paul, a former Columbia law student, was in the infantry. Though there was a mattress and plenty of candles, neither comfort nor a romantic setting mattered as Jack and Edie devoured each other on the bare floor. From then on, Edie considered herself to be Jack's "pretend" bride.

Returning once again to Lowell, Jack exchanged letters with Lou Little, who arranged for him to enroll in Columbia in the fall. But he'd lost his scholarship status due to an *F* in freshman chemistry and needed four hundred dollars to cover his expenses until the scholarship was restored. The U.S. Merchant Marine seemed to offer a solution. To Kerouac and to many others, the merchant marine was the unsung hero of World War II, defying Nazi U-boats to carry supplies to America's overseas allies. While he was opposed to war and killing, he wanted to join his American and Russian "brothers" at sea, he wrote Norma. He was also looking for adventure, fellowship, and material for the kind of war stories *Esquire*'s Chicago editors advised him they were currently buying. He already knew that he was "a great writer," and did not hesitate to tell Norma so.

Although his long-range plans included reenrolling in Columbia in January 1943 for the second semester, he seemed to be in a headlong flight from the wreckage of his past and eager to cast off entangling relationships. Full of resolve, he hitchhiked to Boston, applied for a passport, joined the National Maritime Union, and obtained a U.S. Coast Guard sailing pass. Sammy offered to join the merchant marine and go to sea with him, but Jack wanted no reminders of the mess he'd made of his life and did not encourage Sammy. Waiting for a merchant ship, he finally lost his patience and impulsively enlisted in the U.S. Marines. Then, in mid-July, he got drunk with some sailors in Scollay Square and staggered into the National Maritime Union hall. He learned that a job as a scullion, washing pots and pans, was available on the SS *Dorchester*, which was bound for Murmansk. He signed on with the merchant marine, completely disregarding, as did the Marine Corps, his marine commitment. Sammy angrily accused Jack of running away from him, and Jack admitted that he needed to escape everyone and everything—his parents, emotional conflicts, and the Columbia debacle. Sammy at last relinquished all hope of an honest expression of feelings between them. Jack tried to persuade him to return the following day to see him off, but Sammy's eyes glazed over and he turned and walked away without saying goodbye, marking the first time that Sammy had parted from Jack without a warm farewell.

Before sailing, Jack went on a binge in South Boston with some of his shipmates and ended up on his knees in the toilet of a Scollay Square dive. Hugging a commode, he "got pissed and puked on all night long by a thousand sailors and seamen," he wrote in *Vanity of Duluoz*. Years later, as I edited the novel, I asked Kerouac if he meant the sentence to be taken literally. He replied, "It *looked* like a thousand guys pissed, puked, *and* shit on me, I was so dirty, but, sure, it was probably more like forty, fifty. But leave it a thousand—the reader will get it." I explained that it was not the number of sailors involved, but what he'd permitted them to do to him that seemed so unusual and required explanation. "Permitted?" he said. "I was comatose, but after the first piss, you sort of get into it." The remark was contradictory, but he refused to elaborate or to amend the passage. After the novel was published in 1968, he became irate when Charles E. Jarvis cited the toilet scene as an obvious example of self-abasement. Instantly on the defensive, Kerouac snapped, "I have never practiced self-abasement. From the time I was a little kid, I wanted to excel—and I did." But on the morning of July 18, 1942, when he woke up with his head in excrement, he ran to the harbor and jumped into the ocean to wash himself clean.

Later, aboard the *Dorchester*, he set out for Greenland, one of the most strategic ports in the Battle of the Atlantic. Though he was heading into waters infested with German U-boat "wolf packs," he was convinced that "the Germans should not have been our 'enemies.'" Like his father, he regarded the Germans as "our allies," but Jack's pro-Nazi sympathies were not only anti-Semitically based like Leo's, they were also sexual. He wrote adulatingly of "the German Blond Boy Waste of This World," despite U-boat attacks that later mutilated, burned, and drowned many of his shipmates. Even in 1967, in *Vanity of Duluoz*, he still refused to acknowledge Germany as the aggressor in World War II, and instead identified the threat to the *Dorchester* as the mighty forces of nature. One morning in 1942, he was preparing breakfast for the crew when the *Dorch* dropped a depth charge and destroyed a U-boat. He did not join in the celebration but mourned the deaths of "sweet blond German Billy Budd[s]." I found such passages abhorrent when he read them aloud to me on the phone during the writing and editing of *Vanity of Duluoz*, and finally objected to the line, "High Germanic Nordic Aryans you brutes of my heart...Kill me!...Crucify me!" I told him frankly that it sounded like a sadomasochistic sexual invitation. "It is," he said, and went on reading. The line remained unchanged.

Some people in Lowell still talk about the night during the 1960s when Kerouac scandalized the diners at the upscale Spear steak house, bragging in earshot of nearby tables, "I was buggered by sailors halfway across the Atlantic." In *Vanity of Duluoz*, he wrote that he "pleased" one of the gay cooks, who expressed his appreciation by giving Jack a leather jacket, an item known among homosexuals as "the gay mink." In a 1967 interview, Kerouac admitted that a heavyset cook on the *Dorch* "deflowered" him. His terminology—"I got buggered. . . . I was corn holed"—made it unmistakably clear that Kerouac had been the submissive partner in anal intercourse. "There *was* buggery on the SS *Dorchester*," he said, adding, "Nobody has ever been raped on the high seas." During the interview, he got drunk, blacked out, became confused, and started contradicting himself. "They couldn't corner me," he said. "I ain't no Greek. . . . Sodomy is a sin." On another occasion, he confided to a Lowell friend that he indulged in homosexual acts in the merchant marine and that the ship was a hotbed of sexual activity throughout the voyage. Homoeroticism wasn't his first preference when it came to sex, he asserted, but when he was horny he would gladly embrace it, and he told Sammy in a November 1942 letter that Sammy ought to write a novel entitled *A Seaman's Semen*. In describing how much he missed Sammy, he echoed Emily Dickinson's line about her beloved Sue being only "a hedge away"; Kerouac wrote that Sammy was almost two thousand miles away but a mere "2 feet asoul."[13]

The *Dorch* pulled into Greenland just as the United States took over the country from Denmark for the duration of the war, routing the German soldiers who'd been manning Wehrmacht weather stations. The ship remained in Greenland for four months while its construction gang built an airfield, barracks, kitchens, and mess halls. One day Kerouac went ashore and scaled a four-thousand-foot peak with a haggard, haunted young man named Duke Ford. They dislodged a boulder from a ledge where it had sat for millions of years and watched it go thundering into ravines and crashing into icebergs. In the Arctic, he felt he had penetrated at last to "the fantastic North of men's souls" and was ready to write a big sea novel, which he referred to in a letter to G. J. as *The Sea Is My Brother*. On August 25, he wrote Norma that he'd soon be coming home. During the return voyage, the *Dorch* steamed into Sydney, Nova Scotia, in September, and Jack went on a bender. He had sex three times with a prostitute in the shadows of the collieries, blacked out, was fired at by the shore patrol, jailed, and fined for going AWOL. He had problems enough sober, but when drunk he became uncontrollable, a serious threat to himself.

In going to sea, he had tried to escape the confusion of his life, but his drinking had plunged him even deeper into chaos. Emerging from a horrendous hangover in Nova Scotia, he experienced a rare moment of clarity and realized that a life with Sammy Sampas was the answer after all. On September 26, he wrote Sammy from Sydney and proposed setting up housekeeping together in Greenwich Village. He envisaged their life together as merchant seamen, regularly checking in at the union hall downtown and shipping out in tandem to exotic ports such as the West Indies, Russia, and the Far East. He also was eager to have long talks with Sammy about his latest enthusiasms, including Picasso, Corot, modern dance, and of course, Prometheanism.

Sammy was waiting for him at the dock when the *Dorchester* hove to in late October 1942. G. J. was also there, wearing a U.S. Coast Guard uniform. G. J. handed Jack his pay envelope, which contained $470. Sammy wanted to ride back to Lowell on the train, and as usual Jack felt torn between G. J. and Sammy, but eventually left with Sammy.

He later wrote G. J. a painful letter, explaining that he was under *"tremendous"* coercion from intellectual friends such as Sammy to renounce G. J. as a yokel and a ruffian. G. J. and Sammy represented the opposing sides of Kerouac's divided nature: Sammy stood for his sensitive, artistic self, which Jack saw as unhealthy and unmanly, while G. J. represented normality, which Jack equated with being a football star, whoremonger, heavy drinker, sailor, and jazz buff. He was exhausted from the effort of trying to reconcile what he mistook to be opposing selves, not realizing that the solution lay in acceptance of his homoerotic self as wholesome and natural.

Like many men, then as now, he was tyrannized by a masculine stereotype that excluded the full range of human emotions and absolutely outlawed anything but regulation heterosexuality. As long as he continued to feel that it was unmanly to be an artist and homoerotically inclined, he would never succeed in integrating his personality. He confessed in his letter to G. J. that the tension of this perceived duality was destroying him, even as it supplied him with what would become the major theme of his fiction. His ultimate expression of what he called his "dual mind" was personified in Sal Paradise, the brooding New York writer, and Dean Moriarty, the rugged Denver wrangler, in *On the Road*. Though unarticulated by Kerouac, the schism was also sexual: G. J. signified the macho proletarian he-man Jack wanted to be in order to impress the world, and Sammy was man at his ethical best, as well as the person Kerouac wanted to spend the rest of his life with, as the ardent proposals in his recently published correspondence demonstrate. He always felt free to be himself in his letters to Sammy, which had a light, contented, natural tone. In one, he told Sammy he felt profoundly "Sebastianish," which he defined as "gay." But his letters to G. J. and Neal, though brilliant, are tortured, agonizingly analytical, striving, and dissatisfied.

In Lowell, Jack greeted his parents and then read a telegram from Lou Little: YOU CAN COME BACK ON THE TEAM IF YOU WANT TO TAKE THE BULL BY THE HORNS. The advent of war had radically changed American collegiate football. Many of the best players were in the service, and the caliber of the game suffered—except at the two service academies, West Point and Annapolis, which offered exemptions and could therefore attract the best players, such as Doc Blanchard and Glenn Davis. Lou Little's own football squad had been decimated by the draft, and a player of Kerouac's reputation was now a rare catch. The following day he took the train to New York and once again matriculated at Columbia.[14]

The undergraduate college's most famous and beloved teacher, Mark Van Doren, had given Kerouac an A in his freshman year, and now Kerouac signed up for Van Doren's Shakespeare class. The rather boyish-looking, clean-cut Van Doren was drawn to renegades such as Kerouac and Thomas Merton, who had preceded Kerouac at Columbia by a few years. Merton's biographer, Michael Mott, wrote, "Van Doren appeared to find his gifted students among unsociable eccentrics or among the 'barbarians,' the throwers of water bombs from the windows of John Jay, the 'Columbia bums.'" As Merton wrote in *The Seven Storey Mountain*, Van Doren "purified and educated the perceptions" of his students, "educing" from them "excellent things that you did not know you knew, and that you had not, in fact, known before. . . . [He] made your mind produce its own explicit ideas."

While Kerouac treasured Van Doren's wisdom and humility, he despised Lou Little's abrasiveness, once again clashing with the coach even before football practice. They ran into each other on Amsterdam Avenue, and Little made no secret of his disappointment that Jack had lost weight at sea. At 155 pounds, Jack would be useless as a guard, Little griped. Nor could it have helped Jack's prospects that Leo was again trying to extort a job out of Little, as well as criticizing the coach for keeping Jack on the bench. One day, as Jack waited outside Little's office, he could hear his father and the coach screaming at each other. Finally, Leo came stomping out and told Jack, "Come on home, these wops are just cheating you and me both." Leo's all-encompassing racism included even Little, an Italian who had anglicized his name in order to pass muster in the Waspish Ivy League. Both Jack and Leo suspected that Little played favorites and was stuck on an Italian boy whom Jack referred to as "the Roman hero." Thus, Lou Little was seen as yet another in a long line of lecherous Claggarts on the make for Jack, though Jack offered no hard evidence for this contention. Jack spent the important Columbia-Army game on the bench, fuming. From Little's point of view, Kerouac was "tired," but sportswriter Glenn Stout suggested in 1996 that Kerouac would have made all-American had he not been "slighted by Lou Little." Cornell coach Ed McKeever told Frank Leahy that Kerouac was the world's "best halfback," Kerouac claimed in a 1949 letter to Neal Cassady. In all probability, Kerouac would have played brilliantly against Army if only to avenge himself on Army star Henry Mazur, who'd once clobbered Kerouac in the showers at Lowell High.

Two days after the Army game, Kerouac refused to report for practice, dropped out of Columbia again, and eventually returned to Lowell. No matter how hard he tried, however, he could not cut loose from Columbia. For good or ill, the college was his emotional and intellectual umbilical cord and would supply him with friends and lovers as well as ideas for years to come. No sooner had he left Columbia for the second time than he began to devise a circuitous scheme for a respectable return to college, which involved enlisting in the U.S. Naval Air Force. If he took the navy exam in Boston and passed it, he could enroll in the collegiate V-12 program and become an officer. As he waited in Lowell to be called for the exam, he came down with German measles, and Gabrielle put him to bed. When he finally received a call from the navy, he was still sick and had to request a postponement, which was granted. He used the time to handprint his novel *The Sea Is My Brother* while listening to Shostakovich's Fifth Symphony. In January 1943, he described the novel as an immense "saga" in a letter to Bill Ryan, an engineering student at Boston College. The Ryan letter, which Jack never mailed, was made public for the first time in 1995 and at last established the importance of this novel in Kerouac's overall development.

The Sea Is My Brother was a generational epic covering not only life at sea but the tumultuous fortunes of an American family, the Martins; included were love stories, wartime exploits, foreign travel, and a young man's coming of age in New York City. In a letter to Sammy dated March 15, 1943, Jack defined the subject matter of *The Sea Is My Brother* as both the merchant marine and a panoramic portrait of life in the United States. Whatever its literary quality, clearly the novel was a dry run for his ambitious family saga of a decade later, *The Town and the City*. The Martin brothers of that novel made their first appearance in *The Sea Is My Brother*, one of them by the same name, Peter, and the others as Wesley and "Big Slim." *The Sea Is My Brother* was not intended as a "slick" novel but as a work of profound esthetic and spiritual import. When Connie Murphy read it, he called it "superb," according to Jack, and another fellow Promethean, John MacDonald, said it was precocious as well as energetic and gutsy. Years later, in *Book of Dreams*, Kerouac dismissed it as "a dreary attempt at Naturalism with a sea background," and he once told me when we were working on *Vanity of Duluoz* that it was "a crock of shit." In a 1978 interview, Ginsberg recalled it as "just a lot of reverie prose," but the publication in 1995 of Jack's letter to Bill Ryan made it clear that *The Sea Is My Brother* is significant as the author's first adult attempt at the epic narrative form, which would characterize so much of his later work, from his first published novel, *The Town and the City*, to his last, *Vanity of Duluoz*. The Kerouac estate indicated in 1997 that the novel would eventually be published.

In February 1943, Jack wrote long, thoughtful letters to Sammy, who had joined the army and was in training at boot camp in Camp Lee, Virginia, to be a frontline medic. Sammy felt that the war had robbed him and other young men of their lives, but saw the larger issue that Kerouac always missed: the lights of freedom were going out in the world, one by one, as Hitler took over civilized countries and instituted a reign of terror. Sammy volunteered for one of the war's most hazardous jobs—going under fire to save the wounded—and his training as a medic sometimes proved as dangerous as combat itself. He injured his jaw and bled so profusely that he suspected he might have hemophilia. Afraid that Sammy might die, Jack wondered, in a February letter, whether he would be able to go on "alone" without Sammy by his side. It was not only a declaration of love but a last-ditch cry for help.

Yearning to break out and live honestly and fully, yet determined to destroy the part of his nature that was artistic and homoerotic, Jack was pushing himself toward a nervous breakdown. Gabrielle noticed his hands shaking every time he tried to drink a cup of coffee. On March 12, 1943, he turned twenty-one and wrote Sammy a tipsily affectionate letter fraught with his usual contradictions. Insane "with ardor" for Sammy but saving himself sexually for Norma, ultimately he'd lose them both. From Virginia, Sammy sent back a leaf pressed between the pages of a letter, a token of their common love of Thomas Wolfe, whose *Look Homeward, Angel* opens with the words, "a stone, a leaf, an unfound door," signifying man's search for "the lost lane-end into heaven." In his letter, Sammy proposed setting up a commune, which sounded rather like Brook Farm, the nineteenth-century transcendentalist commune established by Nathaniel Hawthorne and Margaret Fuller. Kerouac expressed skepticism about the Promethean farm, stating that as an artist he preferred to immerse himself in experience rather than cloister himself in an elite environment. Sammy was furious and scolded him for threatening the unity of the Young Prometheans at a vulnerable time when the war had already driven them apart geographically. How could they improve the world with dissension at the helm? But Sammy admitted he wasn't sure of his own participation in the Promethean commune, since his postwar life might well take him to Greenwich Village or Hollywood or to the high seas as a steward on a cruise ship.

Kerouac told Sammy that sending the pressed leaf had been a "beautiful" gesture, but he still wanted to marry Norma. Then, in the same letter, he thought better of it and decided to put the marriage off until he was ten, fifteen, or twenty years older, or "perhaps 45" — the further the better. His wish to conceive with Norma what he called a passel of "brats" sounded more ego- than desire-driven, for he added that he wanted all of his children to be important authors, wits, philosophers, reviewers, poets, and playwrights — and of course, Communists. But the chances of a Barnard girl marrying a roving "revolutionist" were so slim that he could relax and feel safe. It was curious of Jack to say that he wanted his offspring to become critics, for in the same breath he said he loathed all critics. He had been reading Alfred Kazin's *On Native Grounds*, a critical study that traced the development of American prose from William Dean Howells to the present. Kerouac was enraged that Kazin dismissed Wolfe as a man-child who could write nothing but autobiography. Scorning Kazin as a writer with no viewpoint of his own, Kerouac made the assumption that Kazin was a failed creative artist. He would later revise this opinion after meeting Kazin. A reviewer named Louise Levitas also drew Jack's ire because she'd poked fun at Orson Welles. Levitas was obviously envious of Welles, Jack charged, and called critics "art-killer[s]." Even worse, and here his misogyny resurfaced, Levitas was a woman, a lecherous "Bitch." Curiously, despite his aversion to critics, he would not hesitate in the coming decade to court them shamelessly — including Kazin himself — when he discovered how useful they could be in recommending him for grants and introducing him to editors.[15]

Kerouac finally joined the U.S. Navy in 1943. The pressures of his conflicted, divided nature, which had already brought him close to a crack-up, now pushed him over the edge.

THREE

MACHO MANSLAUGHTER

Perhaps more than any other single factor, it was Kerouac's failure to be accepted for officer's training that precipitated his first mental crack-up, his subsequent alienation from society, and ultimately his fame as "King of the Beats." There were deeper underlying reasons, but accustomed as he was to being regarded as a star—whether at home, on the gridiron, as vice president of his class at Columbia, or as the Adonis everyone wanted to have sex with—he found it hard to believe that the U.S. Naval Air Force officer program didn't want him. He flunked the mechanical aptitude test and was consigned to boot camp at the naval base in Newport, Rhode Island, in March 1943. Along with Nin, who was a private in the Women's Army Corps (WAC), he joined the ranks of sixteen million American men and women who served in uniform in World War II.

A letter from Jack's mother published in 1995 revealed for the first time that Jack initially loved being in the navy. On March 24, 1943, Gabrielle admitted she'd been worried about him but was relieved to know he was enjoying boot camp. Gabrielle then gave him all the news from home. Nin too was happy in the military. Leo was on the road, working again as an itinerant printer, and Gabrielle was selling all their possessions, preparing for a move to Brooklyn. "Jack's mother held a yard sale," recalled a neighbor, Gertrude Maher. "They were always moving around, and every time they did, Mrs. Kerouac put on a bazaar." Whatever pleasure Jack took in the navy evaporated the day he pulled his first KP—kitchen patrol—and realized that instead of "seeing the world," as the navy's recruitment poster promised, he was looking at more scullion slops, no different from the drudgery he'd known aboard the *Dorchester*. In a March 25 letter to Sammy, he complained that KP details were nothing but "slave" duty. Prisoners of war had it easier than trainees, he wrote, pointing out that the armed forces should hire civilian labor instead of abusing warriors by forcing them to perform tasks that had nothing to do with battle. The U.S. military's labor policies, he maintained, were identical to those of the Nazi party. Less onerous, he told Sammy, was pulling "watch," or guard duty. Uniformed in his peacoat, pants, white belt, leggings, and bowcap, and swinging a billy club, he enjoyed strolling through the barracks, supposedly inspecting the troops and enforcing regulations but in reality giving everyone a break. As far as he was concerned, the troops could expose "their peckers," and he'd never report them.

Sammy too was in conflict with the military and wrote from Camp Lee that he found it increasingly difficult to reconcile duty with honor. He was a guard in the stockade, and one day a prisoner looked accusingly at him and said the only "prisoner" was the guard, not the man behind the bars. Sammy was able to draw strength from his belief in God and ultimately adjusted to the war and military life, writing a friend that God brought him through every conceivable calamity and kept him strong and serene even in bloody combat. Though Sammy wasn't sure that God existed, he prayed anyway and seemed to get the power he needed. Jack no longer had access to such help. The sexual turmoil overwhelming him in adulthood had left him convinced that God was insane. As Leo often said, he was on his own in a fundamentally hostile world, and Jack would be even more pessimistic in *The Town and the City*, in which one of the characters says that God created man as shark food. For both Leo and Jack, alcohol had replaced God. "Here's the chalice," Jack wrote in the cynical last line of *Duluoz*. "Be sure there's wine in it."

But as a young man in 1943, Jack still held onto some hope, and he was not yet ready to surrender in any way to a world that he found to be wretched and evil. In a sense, the positive social changes of the 1960s began with Kerouac's inability in 1943 to accept life on life's terms. Depending on one's viewpoint, he was either incredibly foolhardy or heroically brave to stage his one-man rebellion against the system as represented by the U.S. Navy. Finally fed up with the menial chores of boot camp, he announced in a letter to Sammy that he intended to resist any further "crap," such as KP and picking up cigarette butts. He began to have headaches, and at first he attempted to conceal them, as he wrote his mother on March 30, but when he repeatedly went to the infirmary to ask for aspirin, the authorities took note. He had other disturbing symptoms, such as trembling hands, which Gabrielle had previously noticed. The trembling might be due, Kerouac suspected, to the car accident he'd had in Vermont or to years of head-on collisions in the brutal game of football. An obvious source of his shakes, though one that didn't occur to him, was alcohol withdrawal. His final showdown with the navy started with his refusal to carry out orders given to him by superiors; borrowing a line from Melville's "Bartleby the Scrivener," he simply said, "I'd prefer not to."

One day during drill, he threw his gun down, told everyone to go to hell, broke formation, and went to the base library to read. When he was apprehended, he appeared to be deranged, explaining with a perfectly straight face that he was a "field marshal" and wanted to be confined with the "other nuts." His wish was granted, and he was locked up in 0-7 Sick Bay, U.S. Naval Training Station, where day after day he sat in the lounge, chain-smoking and wondering what was going to happen to him. On March 30, 1943, he relayed to his mother the sinister-sounding news that he was "under observation" like a laboratory specimen, and added that his eyes were hurting him. In early April, his letters from 0-7 Sick Bay were even more ominous: he wrote John MacDonald that he was schizophrenic, was spending his days staring into space, and felt that the world was to blame for his woes. However, he was still determined to get in as much screwing and hell-raising as possible. He wanted to see his girlfriend Norma, though he suspected she no longer cared for him. No matter, he wrote, brushing her off—she couldn't break his heart since he'd never really been serious about her. In fact, he added, after Mary Carney, he'd sworn off fiery romances.

On April 7, still confined in the Newport mental ward, he wrote G. J. that the split in his "malleable personality"—between the sensitivity required by art and the rugged show of masculinity demanded by society—was what had driven him to a "schizoid" crack-up. Initially, he accepted his doctors' diagnosis that he was insane, a victim of schizophrenia, but in the pecking order of the asylum no one wants to be called crazy, and Kerouac soon changed his tune. By the time he wrote Connie Murphy—the letter was dated only "Wednesday morning" and apparently was never sent—he decided that the diagnosis of insanity was a joke. He was merely neurotic, not psychotic, and just experiencing a temporary adjustment problem. Though the insanity label was humiliating, he went to great lengths to convince the navy doctors that he was crazy, gay, alcoholic, and suicidal—anything that would get him out of the military. As he later pointed out in *The Town and the City*, it was merely academic whether he was actually crazy or just pretending to be. "In any case it's a withdrawal," observes the doctor in the novel, "and it reveals a basic neurotic tendency."

Gabrielle wrote on May 3, 1943, full of anguish over his mental condition but even more concerned over the disgrace of a possible dishonorable discharge, which would "mark" him for life, she warned. Although she shamed him for refusing to defend his country in time of war, she remained steadfast in her loyalty, assuring him of her love, and she even kidded him for landing in the "Hoose Gow." As a German sympathizer, Leo was so proud of Jack for declining to fight in what he regarded as "a war for the Marxist Communist Jews" that he rushed to Jack's side, making the arduous 150-mile train trip from New York. Sammy was another visitor, appearing one day in the mental ward, looking sharp in his U.S. Army uniform and a fresh crew cut. Later, in *Duluoz*, Kerouac represented Sammy as looking at him with compassion and saying, "I have remembered, Jack, I have kept faith."

Sammy was about to be shipped to a port of embarkation and then to the European front. As they chatted, Jack reminded Sammy of the day they'd parted years ago when Sammy had chased his train, singing, "I'll See You Again." Sammy was going into battle at the worst possible time, as the Allies prepared their massive invasions, the famous "end runs" through Europe and the Pacific. World War II was "getting so tough," Gabrielle had written in her May letter, and indeed almost everyone in the United States by then had lost a family member, relative, or friend in combat. Now, Jack was letting the only person he'd ever truly loved slip away from him. Though his and Sammy's relationship was rich in many ways, it represented a travesty of life in its emotional dishonesty and wastefulness, and it ended, perhaps appropriately, in the latrine of a navy mental ward as drooling lunatics lunged at them.

One of Sammy's last letters to Jack was dated May 26, 1943. Prior to the publication of Kerouac's *Selected Letters* in 1995, Kerouac scholarship had reached a standstill. Sammy's May 26 letter was included in the volume, and it cast a startling new light on the origins of many of Kerouac's ideas. In his letter, Sammy rejected Western material and scientific progress as empty Faustian vanity and stated that personal ambition, the mainstay of American life, was pitiful. Western civilization had gone as far as it could and was now at a dead end. Most contemporary writers were spiritually bankrupt. Then, quoting Thomas Wolfe, Sammy sounded a ringing challenge for Kerouac. "A wind is rising," he wrote. The United States of America was ready to give birth to "a new soul," and modern life was about to change for the better. Finally, in an extraordinary presentiment of Kerouac, the Beat Generation, and the counterculture that followed it in the sixties, Sammy defined the new cultural paradigm: a noble savage, "crude, raw, unfinished," would rise from the devastation of World War II and mold the future, destroying old forms and creating a freer civilization. In the new order, people would connect with the Emersonian Oversoul, values would shift from rugged individualism to compassionate concern for one's fellow beings, and people would move from the crowded cities and rediscover the wide open spaces. As society gradually renewed itself, spirituality would flourish as never before, and art, "livingly created" in a revitalized vernacular, would be reclaimed from the academicians and given back to the common man. As a parting gift, Sammy's May 26 letter virtually handed Kerouac an ideological blueprint for his life's work.[1]

Then, abruptly, Sammy vanished into the chaos of war. He was headed for the Anzio beachhead, one of the bloodiest engagements of World War II. Meanwhile, Kerouac's mental condition continued to deteriorate. One day, his delusions took on a frightening reality: he could see into people's heads. When one of the patients shot himself in the head and somehow survived, Kerouac looked at him and could see the "corridor in the brain" that had been blasted out by the bullet. New friends helped him hold onto his sanity. One of them was William Holmes ("Big Slim") Hubbard, the first of his beloved hoboes and the prototype of Kerouac's later study, "The Vanishing America Hobo." Standing six-foot five-inches tall, Big Slim was a former Louisiana State football player and Texas oil-field roustabout. As a forerunner of Neal Cassady, he was a type that would infatuate Kerouac from then on, a charming derelict who never had to beg because some woman would always take care of him. In a later letter to Cassady, Kerouac described how he and and Big Slim hatched a plot to break out of the "nuthatch" but were apprehended and subsequently trans-ferred to Washington by train, accompanied by five guards carrying strait-jackets in case they misbehaved.

During the trip, Jack had a sexual experience which he later alluded to cryptically in *Duluoz*, but described more fully to me as I edited the book and asked for clarification. On the train, he and Big Slim were locked in two different compartments while the guards waited outside in the corridor. "I took the opportunity to fantasize, or that is, to relieve myself of the horror of masculinity," he wrote in *Duluoz*, and added, " 'Heart' and 'Kiss' is only something's sung by gals." When I asked him to amplify the passage, ex-pecting him to say he had masturbated on the train, he said, "Blow jobs were pretty common in the nuthatch." For a macho male, "the horror of mas-culinity" would be to have sex with another man, but merely receiving fel-latio, according to many men, in no way compromises their status as heterosexuals. In the *Duluoz* passage, Kerouac seemed to be suggesting that he "relieved himself" of any compunction with regard to giving fellatio and experienced a breakthrough with his feelings, but couldn't talk about " 'heart' and 'kiss' " since only "gals" do that. When I asked him if he would consider "decoding the passage for the benefit of the reader," he gave it some thought but decided to leave it intact in the final manuscript.

Arriving at Bethesda Naval Hospital in Maryland, he told his doctor that his name was Samuel Johnson and asked to be executed by a firing squad. He added that he couldn't endure navy discipline and asked to be discharged in order to return to the Battle of the Atlantic as a civilian in the merchant marine. His diagnosis was changed from dementia praecox to "schizoid per-sonality" with "angel tendencies." By angel tendencies, the doctors meant delusional self-aggrandizement, but Kerouac and Ginsberg would later give the word "angel" a new meaning for their generation. Wayward individualists like Cassady and Ginsberg became "desolation angels" in Kerouac's work and "angel-headed hipsters" in Ginsberg's "Howl." At Bethesda, Jack sat by "the nut ward window" and rued having squandered the opportunity to learn a "trade" and support himself, since writing now looked like a "stupid 'lit-erary' deadend." He thought of killing himself, but the mundane daily rou-tines of the hospital staff, such as the updating of his chart, somehow saved him. He finally realized he could redeem himself in the eyes of the world and escape the stigma of being called a draft dodger by signing up again in the merchant marine and shipping out to a war zone immediately upon discharge from the navy.

In May 1943, the authorities released him, promising an honorable discharge on grounds of "indifferent character." He left Bethesda with a government handout of fifteen dollars, but was stripped of his pension and most of his navy clothes, including his warm peacoat, peacap, and woolen bell-bottoms. It was a crisp spring day. He strolled down G Street in the capital, looking in on honky-tonks and penny arcades. He fell in with a marine, and they sat in a public park passing a bottle back and forth. They picked up a sailor and went to a hotel room, where the sailor, in his bathrobe, looked out the window and observed that it was "cock weather," Kerouac recalled in *Vanity of Duluoz*, adding, "I was sticking it up my ass with Mobilgas." Describing the same scene in *Visions of Cody*, he wrote that he'd been "hungup" until "cock weather" changed his life. In *Duluoz*, the scene has the same pivotal significance, marking a turning point. His life immediately "pivots," he wrote, and thereafter he embarks on an existence as a homeless wanderer, gathering the subject matter for his greatest work. When he read the "cock weather" scene in *Duluoz* aloud to me, I asked him to explain its baffling images and observed that he seemed to have undergone some form of sexual sea change in the hotel room. He indeed had, he admitted, though he used the word "education" and added that he "wasn't the only one getting it up the ass with Mobilgas. The Marine and I kept that sailor busy." I told him that my understanding of this part of the book was that a deep surrender had been required on his part—the crack-up, followed by the hotel-room epiphany—for him to lay claim to his true nature and artistic destiny. "I knew I could count on your empathy," he said. I didn't have the heart to continue pressing for more explicitness in his writing.[2]

Returning to New York on a steamy June morning in 1943, Kerouac found his parents living in an apartment over a drugstore at 133-01 Cross Bay Boulevard in Ozone Park, Queens. Leo was employed as a linotypist while Gabrielle was manufacturing army shoes. Their next-door neighbors were the parents of movie tough guy John Garfield, and Kerouac later wrote novelist Alan Harrington that he imagined himself as a combination of Garfield and Prince Myshkin, the saintly protagonist of Dostoyevsky's *The Idiot*. Kerouac and Garfield were in fact exact opposites: Garfield paid the rent but never showed up at home, whereas Kerouac showed up at home but never paid the rent. He saw Walt Disney's *Fantasia* fourteen times and wrote Sammy that the film was "magnificent," mentioning his favorite segments: Bach's *Toccata and Fugue in D Minor*, Mussorgsky's *Night on Bald Mountain*, and Schubert's *Ave Maria*. Sammy was caught up in one of the climactic struggles of World War II, the invasion of Italy, which General Eisenhower, the Allied commander-in-chief, called "the first page in the liberation of the European continent." Sammy still managed to get letters through to Jack, and in one he said he'd finally come to accept Jack's macho friends, such as G. J., who seemed like a pretty good egg after all. Jack shared Sammy's letter with G. J., and an old breach between his best friends was mended, if not the schism Jack felt in himself between the creative and masculine aspects of his character.

He hitchhiked from Queens to Asbury Park to see his old girlfriend Edie Parker, who was spending the summer with her grandmother. "Something like love throbbed" in him for Edie, he wrote in *The Town and the City*, in which he represented Edie as "his dear, wild, glad-eyed Judie of the college days." By writing "something like love," he implied that what he felt for her was less than the real thing, but she welcomed him back into her bed, despite his debaucheries with assorted men and women that had left his penis disfigured by venereal warts, though far from droopy. She could scarcely believe that he'd returned to her, but he said, "Yeah, yeah," and dashed out to a drugstore for rubbers. Later, at the beach, she flaunted him in front of a crowd of girls and toyed with him like a doll, even festooning him with earrings and necklaces. "Beautiful cunts passed by," he recalled in *Visions of Cody*, and the girls inquired, " 'What is this boy here, a gypsy?' . . . I had these . . . staples on my cock. . . . I had a hard-on, and I simply . . . fucked her." Edie confirmed years later that they had sex in Asbury Park and then read *Finnegans Wake* aloud to each other. Even her grandmother found him irresistible, and he moved in and lived with them for a couple of weeks.

Deciding to ship out again, he signed on the U.S.S. *George Weems* and kissed Edie goodbye. "You're a rat but I love you," she said. "Who cares?" he replied, but he cared far more than he was willing to admit, as a recently published letter demonstrates. He missed her, "strangely enough," he wrote, and promised her he would be true. Before he left the United States, he and his father went on a binge with Big Slim, who appeared unexpectedly in Ozone Park. Recounting the evening twenty years later, Kerouac called it an example of God's perfection: "Big Slim in his prime, Pop in his prime, me in my careless 1943 youth." It was the last time he'd see Big Slim, who ended up herding cattle in East Texas.[3]

Loaded with five-hundred-pound bombs earmarked for Nazi targets such as Dresden and Hamburg, the U.S.S. *George Weems* departed for Liverpool in late June with Kerouac standing the four-to-eight watch. Though the North Atlantic was still a battle zone, Germany's Admiral Karl Dönitz had withdrawn all U-boats from the area the previous month after relentless bombardment from Allied ships equipped with a lethal new weapon. The hedgehog, a multiple-barreled depth-charge mortar, hurled twenty-four bombs simultaneously in an oval pattern over a U-boat, virtually guaranteeing a hit. (Years later, Dönitz wrote in his autobiography that by May 1943 he knew he'd lost the Battle of the Atlantic.) On the *Weems*, Kerouac's job was to scan the horizon for mines, periscope wakes, or anything suspicious-looking. He complained to Edie that the voyage was tense and dismal, but his finest moment in World War II occurred on his bow watch when he spotted a German mine bobbing in the ocean. He immediately reported it to the bridge, the *Weems*'s navy convoy was alerted, and shortly he heard the mine being detonated by one of the *Weems*'s escorts. His scrupulous, sharp-eyed discharge of duty may have saved thousands of American lives, not to mention the *Weems*'s cargo of five-hundred-pound bombs, though as a German sympathizer, Kerouac felt sorry for "poor old sweet Dresden."

Off duty, he lay in bed and wrote Edie about the British authors he was reading as part of his homework for a forthcoming visit to London. John Galsworthy's three-generation family saga strengthened Jack's resolve to make his life's work one continuous succession of sequels. He also read—and urged Edie to read—Marguerite Radclyffe Hall's 1928 lesbian novel, *The Well of Loneliness*, which Radclyffe Hall said she wrote to prove that homosexuals were "born . . . not made." He and Edie seemed inclined to explore the parameters of their sexuality together when and if he returned from the North Atlantic. The *Weems* arrived finally in Liverpool, and he went ashore dressed in an impressive uniform he designed himself: black leather jacket and visored hat. Despite the fact that England was still a battlefront, in constant danger of Luftwaffe bombings, Kerouac set off across the midlands, determined to spend his two-day leave in London. Luckily, his visit came during a hiatus in the blitz, which had already killed fourteen hundred civilians, left twelve thousand homeless, and damaged thousands of buildings, including Buckingham Palace, which took several direct hits.

According to the Kerouac archive in Lowell, Jack had sex one night in London with a woman named Lillian, and they copulated twice. The following morning she said, "One more time, ducks, and then I gets ready for tonight's duty." That evening, he attended a concert at Royal Albert Hall, where John Barbirolli, former maestro of the New York Philharmonic, was conducting Tchaikovsky. Though an air raid was in progress, the audience chose to remain rather than flee to a shelter. Jack's train trip back to Liverpool, 175 miles northwest of London, was uneventful, though some of the cities en route, such as Coventry, had been leveled by Stuka bombers. During an air-raid blackout, he had to grope his way to the dock where the *Weems* was moored. On the way, a woman whom he described as "another bag like Lillian" propositioned him. He asked her where they could make love during a bombing raid, and she replied, "Up against a monument, dearie," referring to the monolithic statuary along Liverpool's waterfront. Ignoring the German bombs, he enjoyed a final sex act with a woman before going back to sea.

During a violent storm on the return voyage, the *Weems* was attacked by German submarines. Jack sat in the galley with the rest of the crew, playing checkers and drinking hot chocolate. As torpedoes whizzed by, they grimly realized they'd be lost if one of them connected, since lifeboats couldn't be lowered in a storm. Luckily, the ship survived both the storm and the Germans, and later, during lulls on board, Jack mapped out "The Duluoz Legend," which he would spend the rest of his life writing. He managed to stay sober until they made it back to Brooklyn, and then got drunk at the crew's farewell beer party. Afterward, he went into Manhattan to see Edie, who was still living with Joan Vollmer Adams in apartment No. 28 at 420 West 119th Street. In *Visions of Cody*, he described how Edie answered the door in shorts, exclaimed that she'd never expected him to return to her, and flew into his arms. Joan, who'd been teaching Edie how to give oral sex, kidded them and said that Edie was really "gonna get . . . screwed tonight." Jack replied, "Yeah, that's right," but later revealed that Edie "blew" him for the first time, adding that Joan "had told her '*Blow* Jack.'" He gave me substantially the same account when we discussed his World War II homecoming chapter in *Vanity of Duluoz*. "The girls had been playing around when I was away," he said. Joan had told Edie, "I'll show you how to please a man like Jack. Don't blow. *Suck*."

It is significant that Jack urged Edie to read *The Well of Loneliness*, which endorsed homosexuality as healthy and biologically determined rather than as an aberration. He suggested in *Visions of Cody* that both he and Edie were drawn to their own sex and had been fumbling and frustrated in their heterosexual efforts until the clever Joan showed them they could have all the orgasms they wanted with oral stimulation. In *Cody*, Kerouac's erotic memories of Edie were a jumble of "saddened biceptual, bisexual condomidance," as he put it in the most Joycean of his novels. At this point in his life, neither cunnilingus nor coitus appealed to him without extraordinary measures that went beyond the realm of foreplay. "I could complain about the honey in a woman's cunt," he wrote, "or sing a song about how you can suffocate on steam in a closed tunnel." Though he defined the ideal woman as one with "the inward desire to do nothing but get fucked," he was so enraged when this desire was directed at him that he wanted to "spit at [her] ruby lips." When Edie learned to disguise her "real cunt" by drawing lacy, gauzy scarves across it, he went wild with desire, and the squiggle of pubic hair on her inner thigh was so stimulating that he told her he'd gladly turn over his weekly paycheck if she'd "suck me off by the washing machine." With that kind of action he was willing to forego his desire for his own gender: "No more Rimbauds," he promised. Their lovemaking routine began with Jack grabbing her legs and spreading her thighs apart "forcibly," as he called her his "doe," his "rabbit," and his "fuck." Edie would "lie back and watch" as he made love to her, and he liked for her to cover her breasts with transparent dark lace. Reaching under the lace, he massaged her nipples until they hardened under his touch, which excited him tremendously because it meant he had pleased her in "the only way" he could. Finally, ready to penetrate her "juicy hole," he gave her what she said she wanted: "violent love." She liked it "hard," and after all their imaginative foreplay, he found that he could make love to her "your way . . . doll, run on ahead, f, f, f, f, f, f, f, f, f, f, fuck f f f fuck f f f fuck."

A Kerouac letter first published in 1995 reveals that he called Edie "Mommy" and she called him "Daddy." According to Edie, they'd conceived a child before he went to sea on the *Weems*, and she'd aborted it in his absence. The baby was a boy, and she insisted it was Jack's. In a 1981 article in *Moody Street Irregulars*, a Kerouac newsletter, she described the abortion as "forced labor at five months." Years later, in *Vanity of Duluoz*, Kerouac seemed eager to disclaim any possibility of fatherhood, writing that neither he nor Edie was capable of having children because she was anemic and he was sterile. Sterility ran in his family, he claimed, but he was being disingenuous. His father had three children, and his uncle Joseph had four. Jack was "very angry" that Edie aborted his son, she stated, but he would have been much angrier had she had the baby, as his subsequent paternity battles with another woman amply demonstrated.

Deeply in love, Edie was excited by the "new world" Kerouac opened up for her. She invited him to stay as long as he wanted in the apartment she was sharing with Joan Vollmer, though they only had a few pieces of furniture. He basically moved in and started living with her, but still paid regular visits to his parents in Ozone Park. It seemed like a perfect setup: Edie was happy because she had Jack, and Jack was happy because she had a bank account. And she was generous with it, often boasting that she had "spending money and then some" just a few blocks away at the Corn Exchange Bank at Broadway and 110th Street. That may well have been the main source of her appeal to the perpetually impoverished Kerouac, but they also had an active sex life together, according to Kerouac's sex list, which revealed that he and Edie made love a hundred times.[4]

The building where they lived, 420 West 119th Street between Amsterdam and Morningside near the Kingsley Arms, was "swanky" in Edie's estimation. There was a switchboard operator in the lobby as well as an open gilt-cage elevator. Situated on the fourth floor, the apartment had two bedrooms, a large kitchen, and a spacious living room overlooking the courtyard. Sunlight poured in through four large windows, and they could step out onto a long fire escape and use it for sunbathing. The apartment would shortly become the scene of the Beat Generation's first tribal home, the precursor of the Beat crash pad of the fifties and the hippie commune of the sixties.

Edie's roommate and sometime sexual mentor, Joan Vollmer Adams, was destined to become the tragic muse of Beat prehistory when William S. Burroughs shot and killed her in the following decade. A journalism student, she came from Albany, New York, where she'd been close to her father but distant from her mother, whom she'd alienated with her independence and frank contempt for anything that smacked of conformity and middle-class values. After Joan's husband went away to war and she started rooming with Edie, they became, in Edie's description, "two good-looking girls who always had men around." One of Joan's lovers was a Poughkeepsie man named Duncan Purcell, and the handsome John L. Fitzgerald was an occasional beau, though "Fitz" was so unaware of his desirability that he'd once picked up "West End Mary," a notorious Morningside Heights hag, and brought her home. Joan also dated a Columbia undergraduate named John Kingsland, an aficionado of Oscar Wilde, whom Ginsberg later described as "a prodigious 16-year-old overdeveloped and worldly wise sybarite."

Joan "was slow about everything," Edie recalled, "from reading to speaking and cooking." She was also one of the earliest prototypes of the Beat "chick" of the forties and the Jules Feiffer "strange wild creature" of the fifties—the unconventional and brave antecedents of the liberated woman of the sixties. A free spirit, Joan referred to almost everything outside her immediate circle as "bourgeois." She was also the "most intelligent woman I have ever known," Edie added. Kerouac liked Joan from the start and wrote in *Visions of Cody* that he "screwed her" at least once. He was impressed that her daily reading included *P.M.*, the *Daily Worker*, the *New York Times*, the *New York Herald Tribune*, the *New York Post*, and the *New York Daily News*. Her taste in literature was impeccable; her favorite writer was Proust, whom she could quote and discuss "with insight," Edie recalled. Joan had a pretty, heart-shaped face, an upturned nose, and large, warm, wide-set brown eyes. She stood approximately five-foot-seven and wore her shoulder-length brown hair in bangs, sometimes tying it back with a pastel bandanna. She had a "boy's figure," Edie noted, with "chunky legs like an athlete," and when she walked, "her calves wiggled." This was offset by "nice boobs," added Edie, who considered Joan to be "the "most feminine girl I ever knew." In black-and-white photos, which probably do not do her justice, Joan has the same rather mousy prettiness of Ethel Rosenberg, the alleged Communist spy who was electrocuted by the U.S. government during the hysterical Red witch-hunt of the early 1950s. If Edie was the Beat Generation's Zelda Fitzgerald, then its Madame de Staël, if not its Gertrude Stein, was Joan Vollmer Adams Burroughs. In two successive apartments in the early forties, Joan and Edie provided the Beats with a literary salon where many of the revolutionary artistic, political, and cultural ideas and styles of the mid–twentieth century were conceived.

In 1943, Kerouac hadn't yet coined the term "Beat Generation," but Edie recalled that she frequently used the word *beat*, because she was so often exhausted from her job as a longshoreman. The capable Edie worked as a forklift operator at the docks, loading GI mattresses onto liberty ships. " 'Beat' was a very old expression," she recalled. "It meant being tired. I said this a lot back then." After work, she and Jack often retired to the West End Cafe for dinner and beer, and to mingle with the students, seamen, and naval cadets who made up the dingy saloon's clientele. Both Edie and Joan believed in Jack and lavished their allowances on him, but he tried to contribute his share to the apartment, stealing food from restaurants and soda fountains where he occasionally found part-time work. At one point, he held a job as a switchboard operator in a hotel near the Columbia campus. Joan worked at home, addressing envelopes and typing student papers, and Jack often assisted her, since he was an expert typist and could also correct spelling and punctuation. He was trying, so far without success, to sell his stories and articles about life at sea, and sometimes he stayed up all night typing them.

With marriage in mind, Edie took him to Grosse Pointe in 1943 to meet her relatives. Though she liked to boast that she was "from wealth," Jack's executor, John Sampas, disclosed in 1995 that "Edie's mother went to a shoe factory every morning and shopped afternoons." And even Edie, in more lucid moments, admitted, "Mom owned and ran Ground Gripper Shoes in Detroit, working six days per week, eight hours per day." She was hardly the American princess sometimes depicted in other biographies.

Back in New York, Jack at last introduced Edie to his parents. Gabrielle and Leo took them to a tavern on Liberty Avenue and Cross Bay Boulevard for drinks, and the two couples later sauntered home together arm-in-arm. According to Edie, she and Jack's mother were congenial, but from Gabrielle's viewpoint, Jack and Edie were "living in sin." Marriage to Edie, whom Jack portrayed in *The Town and the City* as an antsy, thrill-seeking manic-depressive, was the last thing he wanted, though she certainly fit his description in *Mexico City Blues* of what he was looking for in a wife: a simple-minded girl who had nothing on her agenda but romance and marriage. Still, every time Edie mentioned marriage he begged off, though he kept her on the string. He was genuinely fond of her, and later referred to her in a letter to Neal Cassady as his "mad chick." Edie liked going to jazz clubs with him, and they heard Billie Holiday so often on Fifty-second Street that they adopted her song, "I Cover the Waterfront," as their special favorite. Lady Day, who liked to meet her fans, sometimes sat down at Jack and Edie's table. They met other musicians as well, and one night, while listening to Slam Stewart, Kerouac began his lifelong practice of plucking at a phantom bass.

As Edie became more loving, Jack began to draw away from her and to look for male friends to lay her off on, the way he'd passed Mary Carney on to one of his friends in Lowell. Eventually Jack and Edie evolved into what Edie described as "soul mates." In *The Town and the City*, the protagonist looked on the Edie character as "his sister," turning her over to another man with the observation, "The time has come for every single one American male to go out and be a pimp. Let all the young women be whores." Accordingly, he attempted to give Edie to a new friend, Lucien Carr, whom Edie introduced him to at the West End one night.[5]

Together with Joan and Edie, Lucien Carr was one of the Beat Generation's original scene-makers. A weirdly winsome and complicated teenager, Lucien had recently enrolled at Columbia and immediately attracted a coterie of followers. From a vaguely privileged background in St. Louis, where a prosperous grandparent had been a dealer in jute and hemp fibers, Lucien had been deserted by his father, who'd walked out on his family to become a shepherd in Wyoming and died while Lucien was still a child. Lucien hated both his parents, according to his son, the best-selling crime novelist Caleb Carr, who was interviewed by Daniel Pinchbeck in 1995 for the *New York Times Magazine*. As a schoolboy, Lucien had attracted his scoutmaster, a man fourteen years his senior. Like the serial killer stalking boy prostitutes in Caleb Carr's *The Alienist*, David Eames Kammerer doggedly followed Lucien from school to school, and Lucien apparently tolerated the six-foot-tall, red-haired Kammerer because he liked his sense of humor. Lucien had another unusual gay friend in St. Louis, the future novelist William Seward Burroughs II. Several years later, both Lucien and Burroughs found themselves in Chicago, Lucien attending the University of Chicago and Burroughs working as a bug exterminator. Inevitably, Kammerer showed up, and hijinks were sure to follow. "They always fooled around a lot together," wrote Burroughs's biographer Barry Miles, "and Bill was thrown out of Mrs. Murphy's rooming house because Kammerer and Carr tore up the Gideon Bible and pissed out the window."

When Lucien transferred to Columbia in New York, both Burroughs and Kammerer followed him to the city. Burroughs settled in Greenwich Village at 69 Bedford Street, just around the corner from Kammerer, who worked as the janitor in a building on Morton Street. Burroughs, the disenfranchised scion of the Burroughs Adding Machine Corporation, had been gay since childhood, according to Miles, and he "enjoyed the company of Kammerer and Carr." Like Kammerer, Burroughs, at thirty, was older than Lucien and had already graduated from Harvard, traveled abroad, suffered a nervous breakdown, and spent a month in Columbia-Presbyterian Hospital's Payne-Whitney psychiatric clinic, all while living on a two-hundred-dollar-a-month stipend from his family.

At Columbia, Lucien met Allen Ginsberg, a seventeen-year-old prelaw student from Paterson, New Jersey, and introduced him to Burroughs and Kammerer, drawing Ginsberg into his spooky circle of gay admirers. Ginsberg promptly fell in love with Lucien, whom he later described as "the most angelic-looking kid I ever saw, with blond hair." Although Lucien never achieved fame as a writer, he brought together the core group of the Beat Generation. Even before Kerouac was part of it, Lucien and Ginsberg gave the movement its first ideological moorings, which they called the "New Vision," a set of esthetic and ethical ideas derived from Rimbaud's *A Season in Hell* and William Butler Yeats's *A Vision*. While Ginsberg found Lucien to be "romantically glorious," he also noticed that Lucien was "completely repressed, frightening, and frustrating." Lucien later claimed that he didn't know any of them was gay, which he considered to be a "lonely, sorry life. . . . I had no idea that Allen was into homosexuality." He assumed that Ginsberg's overwhelming passion for him was nothing but hero worship.

Kerouac didn't care for Lucien at first, seeing him as a "mischievous little prick," but soon he too was seduced by Lucien's fancy line of blarney and "golden" good looks. When Kerouac and I discussed including Lucien's story in *Vanity of Duluoz*, Kerouac characterized his feelings for Lucien as a "fatal attraction," adding "We were like doomed lovers." Ann Charters, who interviewed Lucien for her Kerouac biography, felt that Lucien "exuded an indefinite but strong impression of homosexuality." Ginsberg stated in his *Journals Mid-Fifties*, published in 1995, that Lucien had "a prison in his soul." Not surprisingly, Lucien was fond of singing a song extolling rape, torture, and murder ("ruin me, ravage me"). Lucien would later tell Barry Miles that he was "trying to find values . . . that were valid," but his disdain for traditional values would lead to his downfall. The paradox of Lucien's life, as Kerouac wrote in a 1944 letter, was that he couldn't create art because he was paralyzed by self-hatred, which blossomed, like a poison flower, into a hatred of all mankind. Lucien later denied that he'd ever aspired to create literature. "I was never really interested in writing," he said, and added that Kerouac "had to write . . . like you gotta breathe or shit." Kerouac respected Lucien's "perfection of doubt," he later wrote Neal Cassady, and praised Lucien as a relentless "doubter" in the Emersonian tradition of constantly questioning society's ideas of virtue.

Having met Kerouac, Lucien now proceeded to involve him with Ginsberg and Burroughs. According to Ginsberg, Lucien described Kerouac to them in heroic, irresistible terms as a football star, poet, novelist, and sailor, and handed them Jack's address. At the time, Ginsberg was still a shy, virginal teenager, but he summoned the courage to call on Kerouac. No pair could have been more unlikely to found a literary movement, but the volcanic synergy produced by the meeting of Kerouac and Ginsberg would fuel American prose and poetry for decades to come. "Ginsberg met Jack in No. 62, 1944," Edie recalled, referring to the new apartment at 421 West 118th Street that she and Joan had recently leased. When Ginsberg arrived at noon, Jack had just gotten up, and he came to the door fresh from a bath. Ginsberg recalled that Jack was "very beautiful looking" in his white T-shirt, and Ginsberg's eyes fastened hungrily on his "sturdy peasant build." Kerouac hadn't yet had his breakfast, and as the two young men sat talking about the sea and poetry, Jack yelled for Edie to hurry up and bring his grub. To Ginsberg, Jack was highly desirable as a "big jock who was sensitive and intelligent about poetry."

Kerouac's own account of the visit was markedly different. He disliked Ginsberg on sight and "wanted to punch him in the mouth. He was a pushy little kike who had no business hanging around us older guys." He dismissed Ginsberg as someone who wanted to have sex with everyone he met, in a huge tub of dirty water. Edie too found Ginsberg to be sexually repugnant, but they were hospitable and offered him a beer. When Allen declined, Kerouac told him to shut up and called him a "little twitch."

After hearing both Lucien and Ginsberg effuse over Kerouac, Burroughs and Kammerer at last came to have a look for themselves. Burroughs wore his customary attire: a homburg, a Brooks Brothers suit, and a chesterfield. Again, Jack was just stepping out of the shower, to the delight of Burroughs, who would later write of a character in The Wild Boys, "Johnny has just taken a shower. Flesh steaming he walks across the room." Perching primly on a hassock, Burroughs quizzed Kerouac about going to sea on a merchant ship, but it was clear to Kerouac that Burroughs was interested in him as a piece of "rough trade," a term denoting a macho homosexual. To Edie, Burroughs looked like Sherlock Holmes, but Kerouac immediately liked him and relished his macabre sense of humor. One day, Jack felt, Burroughs would be "a shadow hovering over western literature." In recognition of what he regarded to be Burroughs's intellectual supremacy, he started calling him "Bull," despite the fact that Burroughs looked like Edith Sitwell.

Though surrounded by talented new friends, it was the handsome Lucien that Kerouac chose to spend his time with, drinking and talking until last call at the West End Cafe. "He was prettier than any woman I'd ever seen," Kerouac commented when he read one of the Lucien sections of *Vanity of Duluoz* to me on the phone. "I'm sure I ruined his grades at Columbia. When he wasn't around, I went chasing all over town after him, asking everybody where he was." Kammerer became so jealous of Jack that he tried to kill Jack's cat, Kitkat, and would have succeeded had Burroughs not freed the cat from the noose Kammerer had made from Burroughs's neckties. Kerouac would have killed Kammerer, he said, had he been present at the time. But in a dream Kerouac had, he saw himself and Kammerer in the same boat, driven by lust and to be pitied rather than scorned.

At the height of his popularity at Columbia, Lucien was like a magnet, striding across the campus followed by a retinue of "at least twelve eager students," Kerouac wrote, "among them Irwin Garden [Allen Ginsberg] . . . Joe Amsterdam [John Hollander], I think Arnie Jewel [Herbert Gold], all famous writers today, he's hurling back epigrammatical epithets at them and jumping over bushes to get away from them, and way back in the ivied corners of the quadrangle you might see poor Franz Mueller [David Kammerer] slowly taking up the rear in his long meditative strides." Lucien's girl was a patrician if somewhat abstracted Barnard coed named Celine Young, whom Edie thought resembled Marlene Dietrich. Jack was drawn to Celine and later described her in letters as a girl with a sweet smile, whom he'd love to travel with, and he also had erotic dreams about her "incorruptible hot soft and wet gash . . . ready to work, all lubricate." But he also saw her as "a menace," someone who couldn't decide if she wanted to spend her life with intellectuals or jocks. Meanwhile, she and Lucien often made love on the couch in Joan and Edie's apartment.

The publication of Kerouac's letters in 1995 revealed that part of Lucien's power over him was his ability to make Kerouac believe in himself as the inevitable literary hero of America's future. Kerouac could give the world "the new vision," Lucien said, but Kerouac realized he didn't yet command the style or subject matter to write a great life-changing work. For Kerouac, the new vision meant devoting his entire life to art. He felt so passionately in 1944 about the primacy of art that he cut his flesh and wrote a quotation from Nietzsche in blood: "Art is the highest task and the proper metaphysical activity of this life." Appropriating Lucien's term, Kerouac called the pursuit of excellence in art "Self-Ultimacy." It was a mistake, he felt, to write for money or recognition, and he was ashamed, he confided in his diary in 1944, that he had written half a million words since 1939 with the express purpose of gaining fame, not to mention "idolatry" and "sexual success."

It would remain for Ginsberg, years later, to give the most cogent expression of what these young men meant by the new vision: they wanted to be "seers," to have drug-induced visions, breakthroughs in consciousness, freedom to experiment sexually, and a total break from the past. Unfortunately, they did not always understand the ideas they acquired in their modern literature courses at Columbia, such as André Gide's *acte gratuit* and Nietzsche's *Übermensch* theory, which held that "supermen" were not accountable to society for their actions. They were impressed, too, by William Blake's opinion that "the path of excess leads to the palace of wisdom," but none of them seemed to realize that the path of excess also leads to liver disease, which eventually took out both Kerouac and Ginsberg.

Though Sammy was a medic on the Italian front, in a letter to Nin Kerouac repeated Burroughs's sick joke about becoming an ambulance driver in order to knock the gold fillings out of the mouths of fallen soldiers on the battlefield.[6] In January 1944, World War II entered its fierce, penultimate year, with the embattled Axis throwing everything it had at the increasingly victorious Allies. At Anzio, a beach town forty miles south of Nazi-held Rome, Sammy stormed ashore in January with thirty-six thousand Allied troops. Unfortunately, General Eisenhower had little interest in the Anzio operation, which had been promoted by Churchill; Ike was saving his guns for D-Day, the invasion of France, five months later. As a result, when the forces at Anzio were pinned down by German fire, they were left to perish on the beach. "The Italian campaign of 1944–45 was a serious strategic blunder," novelist James Jones later wrote in *WWII*. Jones praised the performance of WWII medical corpsmen for "the consummate tenderness" with which they handled and cared for the wounded and the dead. Sammy served at Anzio with "51 Station Hosp." and continued to write poetry, even in the thick of battle. In "Taste the Nightbane," published in *Stars and Stripes*, he described the "tortured hours" of the 125-day German bombardment, during which the beach was shelled every three hours, night and day, often by "Anzio Annie," a 280-millimeter, eleven-inch railway gun that could catapult 260-pound shells forty miles. Sammy's poem "Rhapsody in Red," also published in *Stars and Stripes*, caught the drama of a medic's life, describing how German Stukas destroyed his aid station, leaving the snow splattered "with scarlet glory." In a letter to Stella, Kerouac compared Sammy with WWI poet Rupert Brooke, describing Sammy's work as romantic in style but imbued with a sense of eternal truth.

Eleven years after Anzio, in a letter to Ginsberg, Kerouac recounted a vision he'd had of Sammy dashing through a hail of gunfire to save a fallen GI. "Sammy was wounded at Anzio beachhead," recalled Sammy's brother,

John, in a 1995 interview. "It was shrapnel from a bomb nearby." His injuries were critical, and he was evacuated by hospital ship. "Sammy was taken to Algeria," John added. In his hospital bed, Sammy requested a recording machine and made a record for Jack. "I weep for Adonais—he is dead," Sammy said, quoting Shelley's elegy to John Keats, who died in Rome in 1821. At the end of the message, Sammy's voice trailed off. "So long, Jack old boy," he said. "Take it easy." When Jack received the record from North Africa, he thought of Charles Boyer in the 1938 film *Algiers* and imagined Sammy as a martyr expiring in the Casbah. Sammy also sent a message to his family in Lowell, quoting a line from *Look Homeward, Angel*, "O lost, and by the wind grieved, ghost, come back again." The celebrated war correspondent Ernie Pyle left Anzio for London at this time, to cover D-Day. As Pyle flew over North Africa, above the hospital where Sammy lay, he looked out of his plane window and saw "the green peaks of the Atlas Mountains, lovely in the softening shroud of the dusk." Perhaps Sammy could see them too from his hospital bed below.

"Sammy died on March 2, 1944, from wounds at Anzio," John recalled. When Kerouac heard the news, he wrote an anguished elegy, which was first published in *Selected Letters* in 1995. Jack and Sammy had been *"Together!"* Kerouac wrote, and described the enduring love they'd shared. Then he mentioned their song, "I'll See You Again," and wondered where Sammy was now and whether he ever thought of Jack. Kerouac had once expressed the fear that he might not be able to survive without Sammy, and now he was certain he couldn't. There was nothing left to do but get drunk and dwell on the past, remembering *"d'amour,"* he wrote. Subsequently, in a letter to Ginsberg, Jack added that Sammy had died a Tathagata, referring to Siddhartha Gautama, the Buddha. In a way, the comparison made sense: As Kerouac wrote in a letter to Stella, both Siddhartha and Sammy, as young men, had renounced the security of home and family to help a suffering world, trudging the path of meekness and service. Kerouac had saved all of Sammy's "great compassionate" verses, and he was typing them up so that he could send Stella copies. He had seen Sammy's "sad eyes," he added, and now understood that Sammy had wept so often because he realized mankind had taken the wrong direction. The solution to all of man's problems was contained in three words, "Love Is All," the Buddhist belief that the practice of kindness leads to perfect wisdom.

Stella reciprocated by sending Jack Sammy's "old Goethean card" as a memento, and she apologized for being "morbid." Jack replied that death awaited them all sooner or later and assured her that he treasured the keepsake she'd sent. He also told her that she was an incorruptibly good person who commanded the respect of all who knew her. Then, in a lapse of sensitivity and tact, he told Stella that Sammy, Johnny Koumantzelis, and Billy Chandler had all been killed "for nothing." He still insisted that the United States never should have fought the Nazis and that World War II had been waged to improve the economy, completely ignoring that had the Germans won the war, he would have been executed as a dissident writer, Communist, sexual deviant, and hobo, and possibly even for racial "impurity," owing to Native American blood on his mother's side.

In 1967, when Kerouac read me the page in *Duluoz* dealing with Sammy's death, I remarked that I found his account "somewhat terse" and overshadowed by the abuse he'd heaped on Lieutenant General Mark Clark, commander of the U.S. Fifth Army. Kerouac explained that when Clark appointed Major-General John P. Lucas to command the Anglo-American forces at Anzio, he had warned Lucas, "Don't stick your neck out." Lucas's resultant caution and pessimism cost the lives of thousands of Allied soldiers. Kerouac added, "Mark Clark is personally responsible for every soldier that was killed at Salerno, too." I suggested to Kerouac that the passage would have more impact if he recounted his personal feelings on hearing that Sammy had fallen in battle. Quoting A. E. Housman, he said, "And round that early laurelled head will flock to gaze the strengthless dead and find unwithered on its curls the garland briefer than a girl's." Later, when the final manuscript arrived on my desk, I assumed it would include the Housman stanza, but it did not, and I felt it would be too painful to ask him why. Some thoughts, Wordsworth wrote, "lie too deep for tears."[7]

While the world struggled in the spring of 1944 with the forces of good and evil, Kerouac was fighting his own war on Morningside Heights, a personal battle between his opposing selves. He was torn by his love for Lucien Carr and the increasing pressure he felt to marry Edie and prove himself a man. He took Edie to Lowell on at least four occasions, introducing her as his future wife, but he seemed primarily interested in her money. Both she and Jack by now were staggering, blackout drunks. He scarcely remembered some of the trips he took, including one to the South, during which he stumbled around New Orleans and later met Thomas Wolfe's brother in Asheville. His funds ran out and he was reduced to begging from Edie, Gabrielle, and Leo, writing Edie on one occasion that he was dying of starvation. Finally, he realized his Southern trip was pointless and returned to an equally perplexing scene in New York.

Jack and Lucien's closeness continued to vex "Mother Kammerer," as Jack referred to Lucien's admirer, and the situation intensified when Kerouac and Ginsberg began to compete for Lucien's affections. Ginsberg tracked Lucien's "every move," Jack later wrote in a letter to Neal Cassady. Though already obsessed with Lucien, Ginsberg also fell in love with Jack but was too timid to confess his passion. Nevertheless, Jack sensed it and warned Ginsberg that "queerness" made him feel anxious. Ginsberg then reversed his strategy, dropped the sex issue, and attempted to snare Jack by spiritual means, contemplating a union of souls. But that didn't work either because Kerouac resented Ginsberg's self-appointed role as a "diabolic" despoiler of his spiritual life. Allen and Jack continued to vie for Lucien, and eventually Jack won. He began to call his beloved Lucien "Lou," and the insolent "Lou" called Jack a "has-been queen," Jack later recalled in a 1949 letter to Elbert

Lenrow. Kerouac was so spellbound by Lucien that he could not perceive what he later called Lucien's "shity [*sic*] little ego."

Even though World War II was still raging in the French countryside, Jack and Lucien decided to go to Paris and live together as artists. Discovering their plan, Kammerer tried to go abroad with them, and when this failed, he became insane with jealousy. Burroughs, who squandered his trust fund wining and dining Jack and Lucien at the Minetta Tavern and San Remo, later told Kerouac that he liked "brutal, bloody and degrading" exhibitions, but even the bloodthirsty Burroughs was shocked by the slaughter that disrupted the early Beat scene in the summer of 1944, when Lucien snapped one night and stabbed Kammerer to death. Lucien was nineteen at the time and in his sophomore year at Columbia. The entire university was rocked by the scandal, and all of the early Beats were swept up into the criminal investigation that followed, with the exception of Joan Vollmer Adams, who had temporarily moved out of the apartment, to have Paul Adams's baby at home in Albany.

On the night of the killing, Jack had left Lucien at the West End Cafe. A few minutes later, Jack encountered Kammerer on the Columbia campus, behind St. Paul's Chapel. Kammerer asked about Lucien's whereabouts, and after Kerouac told him, Kammerer proceeded to the bar, joining Lucien, Ginsberg, and other friends. According to Ginsberg's biographer, Barry Miles, "Lucien's attempt to escape to France brought matters to a head, and he and Kammerer got into a drunken argument." When the bar closed, they acquired a bottle of liquor, and though it was almost 3 A.M., they went into the darkness of Riverside Park, descending all the way to the lower levels by the Hudson River, one of the best-known trysting places of New York gays. As they were walking along the riverbank, according to a later newspaper account, Kammerer made "an indecent proposal" to Lucien, who took out his Boy Scout knife and jabbed it repeatedly into Kammerer's heart. "He died in my arms," Lucien said, according to *Vanity of Duluoz*. "He kept saying, 'so that's how it ends, so that's what happened to me.' "

After weighting Kammerer's body with rocks, Lucien dumped the corpse in the Hudson, but it wouldn't sink, and Lucien finally had to undress, wade in, and give Kammerer a shove. Face down, the body started floating downriver, its sandaled heels sticking ludicrously above the surface. For David Kammerer, there would indeed be "no moaning . . . when I put out to sea," as Tennyson wrote, but perhaps Blake offered a more fitting epitaph in *Auguries of Innocence*: "God appears, and God is light, to those poor souls who dwell in Night."

Dragging himself onto the riverbank, Lucien got dressed, climbed to Riverside Park, hailed a cab and, still stained with Kammerer's blood, rushed to Burroughs's apartment. Burroughs advised Lucien to get a lawyer, turn himself in, and plead self-defense. Instead, Lucien went uptown to visit Kerouac, who later helped Lucien dispose of the evidence, which included the weapon and Kammerer's eyeglasses. In 1995, at the Kerouac archive in Lowell, John Sampas said, "In Jack's journal, Lucien was laughing about a story of a guy who murdered twenty people."

Lucien surrendered to the police on August 16, 1944. He was booked for murder and sent to the Tombs, the dimly lit, decrepit lower Manhattan prison, where he was held without bail. Kerouac and Burroughs were arrested as material witnesses, having hindered the prosecution of a crime by failing to report it. This was soon upped to a more serious charge for Kerouac, who confessed that he had helped Lucien conceal evidence. Now he was an accessory after the fact, having aided a criminal after the commission of a crime, and subject to imprisonment. He was thrown in a cell in an Upper West Side precinct stationhouse. Burroughs was also jailed, but his father flew in from St. Louis and bailed him out for twenty-five hundred dollars. Kerouac knew that Leo didn't have that kind of money.

The following day, Kerouac was driven downtown to the district attorney's office. Under rigorous questioning about his sexual preferences, he apparently convinced the DA and a detective that he wasn't gay, and they immediately became more lenient, though later they would try to entrap him in homosexual acts. The DA lectured Jack on how Lucien had come very close to ruining his life, but the DA also realized that Jack was ignorant of the law and promised to go easy on him. Nevertheless, he put Jack in the Bronx jail for having failed to turn Lucien in. The DA was impressed that the *Daily News* was calling the homicide an "honor slaying," and if indeed Lucien was found to have been protecting himself against rape, he'd be charged with manslaughter instead of murder. The case hinged entirely, the DA added, on whether Lucien was homosexual. Jack insisted Lucien was straight, but both he and Lucien would be subject to further investigation. Jack was allowed to visit with Edie, who had also been brought in for questioning, and as soon as they were alone together, they both started crying from the strain.

Ginsberg and Celine Young were also brought in for interrogation. Jack was disgusted that Ginsberg proved to be of so little help, exploiting the crisis to promote his literary career and chattering to reporters about the "New Vision." Ginsberg had turned eighteen on June 3 and was awestruck to find himself suddenly thrust into the spotlight, but his biographer, Barry Miles, later argued that Ginsberg was helpful to Lucien, comforting his mother and settling his affairs at Columbia. Ginsberg also assumed full responsibility for Celine during Lucien's incarceration. Celine resembled Dante Gabriel Rossetti's Blessed Damozel, and her short stories were "very good," according to Ginsberg. Years later, in a letter to Alan Harrington, Kerouac expressed resentment that everyone in their circle escaped "unscathed" except for himself and Lucien, the "pale criminal."

Jack and Lucien were arraigned together in magistrate's court, where reporters noted that Lucien, carrying his copies of *A Season in Hell* and *A Vision*, looked wan and bookish. Yeats's weirdly amoral *Vision* appears, at least to some readers, to give one permission to violate traditionally ethical behavior in the process of self-reinvention. From certain angles, the Kammerer affair did indeed look like the effort of two very sick young men to reinvent themselves as macho males. In the courtroom, according to Kerouac's account in *Vanity of Duluoz*, Claude de Maubris, the character based on Lucien, whispers to Jack, "Heterosexuality all the way down the line."

Following the arraignment, the judge remanded Lucien to the Tombs, and Kerouac was locked up in the Bronx jail, commonly known as the "Bronx Opera House" because it was full of mobsters who'd "sung" on their bosses during a New York City racketeering crackdown. During liberty period each day, good-looking young Murder Inc. thugs—Mafia hit men—went to Jack's cell and attempted to seduce him. A friendly plainclothesman had already warned Jack that the "stoolies" had been promised fifty years off 199-year sentences if they could prove that Jack was gay. He resisted them, but the judge nonetheless set a hefty five-hundred-dollar bail. Jack was broke. Finally, the DA offered him his freedom in return for a one-hundred-dollar bond. Leo refused to put up the money and hung up on him. He then tried to get the money out of Edie, but she held out for marriage. He agreed, realizing that if he married her, the authorities would be convinced of his heterosexuality. Jack was released from jail long enough for the wedding ceremony, which was held at City Hall on August 22, 1944. His guard then hustled him back to his cell, and Edie promised to wangle the bond money out of her mother. In jail, Jack heard the inmates laughing at him, still unconvinced of his heterosexuality, and realized that he'd turned his life into an absurd, humiliating farce.

Lucien appeared in court on August 24 and "copp[ed] a manslaughter plea," Jack wrote. A hearing on his plea was held on October 6, 1944. Gabrielle told Jack, "There won't be no trial." Nevertheless, Lucien was sent to Elmira Reformatory in upstate New York for an indefinite term. With good behavior, he could be released within eighteen months, his family was assured. In 1997, after interviewing Caleb Carr, reporter Laura Reynolds Adler wrote that Lucien served two years for manslaughter. Problems had immediately developed in prison—Lucien's probation officer didn't like his attitude, which was characteristically arrogant and unrepentant; his values struck the officer as coldly intellectual. In letters to Kerouac, Celine wrote that the probation officer held no hope for Lucien's release unless he renounced his obvious pride in having killed Kammerer. Only occasionally, the officer said, did Lucien seem to regret the crime he'd committed. Lucien wrote Ginsberg complaining about prison discipline, but added that he was discovering heretofore unsuspected inner strengths. "Strong animal—man," Lucien said, according to Ginsberg. Lucien eventually repented of his "decadent philosophic nihilism" and began to feel guilty, finally accepting society's rules.

Kerouac's parents were relieved that their errant son, though a jailbird, was at last a respectable married man, and they paid him a visit in August, forgiving all. His marriage was a fraud, but Edie was nevertheless hoodwinked into coming up with the hundred-dollar bond, and Jack was released from prison. On September 1, 1944, he wrote Edie's mother that he and Edie were on their way to Detroit. He could hardly have sounded less enthusiastic, confiding to his mother-in-law that he would prefer to live apart from Edie, that their marriage had been ill-timed, and that he'd been forced into it less by desire than by "tragic events." A September 1944 notebook entry first released by Kerouac's estate in 1997 indicates that Jack and Edie settled in Grosse Pointe and that Jack repaid the bail money by taking a job in a war plant. In the same entry, he wrote that Gabrielle and Leo felt his marriage was doomed, but he was briefly hopeful of his and Edie's chances despite his inability to support a wife.

Predictably, it was all over in less than two months. Jack wrote Nin that he'd politely requested a divorce, and in early October 1944 he returned to New York. In a 1981 article, Edie wrote that she'd come home one day and caught Jack in bed with a Grosse Pointe girlfriend, Jane Beebe. "It started our split," she explained, adding that Jack would have been welcome to remain with her in Michigan, but he found it necessary, if he were to continue writing, to go elsewhere. To escape Edie's connubial expectations and her mother's "literary" patter about Pearl S. Buck, he'd spent most of his marriage locked in the bathroom reading Shakespeare and the Bible. Back home in Queens, he regretted that he'd not been clever enough to hold onto Edie because, as he cynically pointed out in *Book of Dreams*, she had "lots of money."

In the following months, he discovered the work of Arthur Koestler and gained some needed insights into the darker aspects of his character. In a letter to Nin, he wrote that all of his periods of creativity alternated with periods of self-destructiveness, as if his will to succeed and his will to fail were constantly at war. He was trapped in a vicious circle and could never finish important projects because of a "death-wish" that stemmed from his terror and guilt over Gerard. After he read Koestler, he realized that the problem went much deeper, to the heart of the human predicament itself. Koestler wrote:

> The creativity and the pathology of the human mind are, after all, two sides of the same medal coined in the evolutionary mint. The first is responsible for the splendor of our cathedrals, the second for the gargoyles that decorate them to remind us that the world is full of monsters, devils, and succubi. They reflect the streak of insanity which runs through the history of our species, and which indicates that somewhere along the line of its ascent to prominence something has gone wrong.

Due to this evolutionary glitch, part of the human brain remains reptilian, a leftover from prehistoric ancestors. In Koestler's view, the reptilian portion of the brain is responsible for the murderous, delusional streak in human nature. In the 1940s, the crazed messianism of the Third Reich and the genocidal behavior on both sides—saturation bombings, concentration camps, and atomic warfare—represented a triumph of the paranoid component in human nature and brought mankind to the brink of extinction.

Likewise, in Riverside Park that night in 1944, the same kind of ritual madness cost Kammerer his life, almost destroyed Carr and Kerouac, and covered everyone involved, including a homophobic judicial system, with dishonor.[8]

In the weeks following the killing, Kerouac imagined himself to be hounded by gay admirers, and despite his preference for their company, he sometimes resorted to extreme measures to discourage their advances. In his October 1944 notebook entry, he wrote that he boarded a merchant ship for Italy but got off in Norfolk, Virginia. The crew's gay bosun, an intimidating man who called Jack "Handsome," "Pretty Boy," "Baby Face," and "Sweetie Face," did not appeal to Jack. Jumping ship in wartime added to his general disgrace, and the merchant marine banned him for the duration.

He took a bus to New York and settled in Warren Hall, where Ginsberg was living. In an October notebook entry, Jack wrote that he began an affair with Lucien's girl, Celine. He later told Neal Cassady that he "was fuckin her regu-lar," but in the next breath, he revised that to "I only fucked her once." This was confirmed by his sex list, on which he noted only one instance of sex with Celine. *Visions of Cody* reveals that Jack enjoyed an explosive orgasm, "embedding my beautiful prick in the beautiful soft, wet between-legs slam . . . and coming with a bulging head." He worked just as feverishly on his writing and research, indicating in the October notebook entry that he returned to the Columbia campus and immersed himself in symbolism. In November he wrote that he was concealing his whereabouts from both Edie and his parents in order to devote himself to writing and to pursue a bohemian existence.

Using Ginsberg's Columbia library card, he checked out books by Arthur Koestler, Aldous Huxley, George Bernard Shaw, Thomas Hardy, and H. G. Wells. Determined to keep his writing efforts free of commercialism, he burned every page as he ripped it from the typewriter. "Jeez, Kerouac is neurotic," Allen observed in his journal. On the average, Jack and Allen got drunk together twice a week. They also shared meals in the dimly lit West End Cafe, hovering over Allen's bowl of potato soup like the peasants in van Gogh's *Potato Eaters*. Jack's notebook reveals that he came perilously close to starving that November. Without Ginsberg, he might not have survived. Still a virgin, Ginsberg felt awkward and unattractive, but dreamed of having a love affair with Jack. When Allen could conceal his lust no longer, he started building up his courage to tell Jack that he was gay, an admission that required considerable courage in the homophobic 1940s. Ginsberg's bold step came as he and Kerouac were talking one night in Allen's Warren Hall quarters, Jack in Allen's bed, and Allen lounging on a mattress on the floor. In 1972, Ginsberg recalled how certain he'd been that Kerouac would embrace his "throbbings and sweetness." He finally confessed to Jack that he was "really in love with Lucien. And I'm really in love with you. And I really want to sleep with you." "Oooooh no," Jack wailed. Allen wasn't his type, but he wanted to retain Allen's friendship. Jack was still fixated on Lucien, and he later told Neal Cassady, "I dig him, I always will." Yet Allen was striking in a lithe, dark-haired, lush-eyed way, and Jack proved to be a "passive lover," according to Ginsberg, when Ginsberg finally "made love" to him.

Their relationship shortly created yet another scandal at Columbia. It began when Allen wrote a *roman à clef* about the Kammerer killing and turned it in to his creative writing teacher, Professor Harrison Steeves, who was the chairman of the English department. Steeves objected to the subject matter and reported Allen to the assistant dean of Columbia, Nicholas McKnight. Such was the police-state atmosphere of American education in the 1940s that Dean McKnight, after perusing the manuscript, called Allen in and scolded him. Allen accused the dean of censorship. Flustered, the dean called Kerouac a "lout" and Allen's novel "smutty." Columbia was rabidly homophobic at the time, including even supposedly liberal teachers such as Lionel Trilling, who wrote in the *Partisan Review* that when he lectured on Gide at Columbia, he advised the young men in his class that Gide's scorn for "respectable life . . . doesn't of itself justify homosexuality."

Both Kerouac and Ginsberg preferred another Columbia teacher, Raymond Weaver, the discoverer of the manuscript of Melville's *Billy Budd*, who agreed to critique Jack's novel *The Sea Is My Brother*. Weaver was gay and "loved the football players," Ginsberg recalled. For years, Weaver and Trilling had been carrying on a running battle in the English department, and Trilling's wife, Diana, later wrote, "Weaver was anguished by his sexual deviance but handled it with courage and manliness." Through Weaver, who had spent time in Japan and studied Zen Buddhism, Kerouac learned more about Eastern thought and haiku poets. After declaring that Kerouac wrote "beautiful prose," Weaver handed him a bibliography that included the Egyptian *Book of the Dead*, the early Christian Gnostics, Plotinus, Melville's *Pierre*, and the American transcendentalists. This was Kerouac's and Ginsberg's first intensive exposure to Chinese and Japanese Zen Buddhism and Western Gnostic theology. The heretical Gnostic gospel encouraged humankind to break free from a corrupt world ruled by a perverse deity and to see the true world of emptiness and light. Such a revelation could only be achieved through a radical broadening of one's consciousness, Ginsberg later explained in the epigraph to *Kaddish and Other Poems*. Kerouac, who tended to see life as "a mean and heartless creation," welcomed the opportunity to view existence as a void or even as a dream of the gods that was already over.

Kerouac was largely responsible for Ginsberg's troubles at Columbia, which soon came to a head. Johnny, the bartender, reported Kerouac to the Columbia dean, blaming him for Ginsberg's drinking every night until last call. Columbia forced Ginsberg to move to on-campus quarters for closer supervision, and Ginsberg later scrawled obscenities on his dorm window, which came to the attention of the administration. Kerouac often stayed

overnight with Ginsberg in his suite in Livingston Hall, and one morning
Dean Ralph Furey walked in on them in bed together. Kerouac promptly
fled, leaving Ginsberg to face the music alone. Ginsberg was suspended from
the university.[9] Kerouac then moved in with Bill Burroughs on Riverside
Drive and became part of the hipster underworld of drugs and petty thievery.

Burroughs was nine years older than Jack, and his sexual tastes, later
described in his novel *Queer*, usually ran to "real uncut boy stuff. . . . Young
boys vibrating with life . . . maleness." Burroughs had only recently started
using hard drugs, largely due to his boredom with "living the kind of life
Harvard designs for you." Most of his acquaintances were thieves, and he'd
started buying stolen goods, including guns and morphine, in an effort to fit
in. Soon he was shooting up, dealing, and hanging out with thugs in a Times
Square hustler bar on Eighth Avenue near Forty-second Street, which soon
became one of Kerouac's favorite places. Through Burroughs, Kerouac met
the man who gave him the name for the Beat Generation. Herbert E.
Huncke, a small-time con man, thief, and gay hustler from Chicago, approached Kerouac in Times Square one night. "I'm beat," he said. Kerouac
later recalled that Huncke had a "radiant light shining out of his despairing
eyes." Huncke had picked up the word *beat* from "some midwest carnival
or junk cafeteria," Kerouac speculated. "It was a new language. . . . 'Beat'
originally meant poor, down and out, deadbeat, on the bum, sad, sleeping
in subways." In a letter to Ginsberg, Kerouac described Huncke as an embittered little man who could usually be found in Bickford's, nursing a cup
of coffee and plotting his next robbery. Huncke too recalled his first meeting
with Kerouac, who struck Huncke as a "typical, clean-cut college boy, as
green as the day is long." In Huncke's memory, Kerouac glanced about
eagerly and addressed casual remarks about the parade of hipsters to Burroughs. As Donald Kennison, Huncke's later editor, observed, Huncke was
the quintessential hipster, "gunning the streets, hungry for action and heart."
He was also a skillful storyteller, described by Kerouac in a letter to Neal
Cassady as "an actual genius."

Burroughs took Jack along to a gay orgy, and Jack felt guilty the next
day, canceling an appointment with Burroughs. His objection was one of
style rather than substance, he later told Ginsberg, explaining that he hadn't
liked the nelly queens or their "gossiping and snickering." Had more masculine partners been available, Kerouac would have come out; he told Ginsberg that he was prepared to accept every facet of his sexuality and to let all
his inhibitions "dissolve" in the heat of homoeroticism. He enjoyed an evening at the Everard Baths with Burroughs and Ginsberg and had sex with
French sailors, who performed fellatio on him. "He was very gay about it,"
Allen recalled.

Kerouac was enchanted by Burroughs's scintillating conversational raps,
bristling with lurid, campy vignettes, and finally one day Kerouac urged him
to write them down. "I don't want to hear anything literary," Burroughs
grumbled, but Jack laughed and told him, "You can't walk out on the Shake-

speare squad, Bill." Burroughs was eventually charmed into the writer's trade by Kerouac's beguiling smile, which Burroughs later described as "the sort of smile . . . you get from a priest who knows you will come to Jesus sooner or later." They began to collaborate on a 200-page murder mystery in 1945. Casting about for titles, they considered *And the Hippos Were Boiled in Their Tanks*, *The Philip Tourian Story*, *The Ryko Tourian Novel*, and *I Wish I Were You*, finally deciding on *And the Hippos Were Boiled in Their Tanks* for the working title. They attempted to imitate the fast-paced, sophisticated style of Dashiell Hammett, the founder of hard-boiled fiction and creator of both Sam Spade and Nick Charles. Burroughs was also an aficionado of Raymond Chandler and James M. Cain, whose tough but literate style and focus on the seamier side of life would later be reflected in Burroughs's novels. They got the *Hippos* title from a radio broadcast about a fire in the London Zoo, during which the hippos were literally cooked in their cages. Jack and Bill changed the setting from Columbia to Greenwich Village and worked a year on the story, each of them writing alternate chapters. Casting himself as "Will Dennison," Burroughs created scenes based on his experience as a bartender and filled them with lesbians, policemen, and soldiers. Kerouac portrayed himself as "Mike Royko," and focused on the killing itself, though he also wrote about the National Maritime Union hiring hall. One day, while reading a chapter of Bill's, Ginsberg had difficulty deciphering Bill's hurried handwriting and made a mistake, saying "naked lunch" instead of what Bill had written, "naked lust." Kerouac seized on "naked lunch" as a provocative title for a novel. Burroughs agreed, and when he used it on *Naked Lunch*, published in 1959, he acknowledged Kerouac's contribution on the first page. According to Kerouac, Lucien was angry when he heard that Jack and Bill were writing about him and ordered them to "bury it under a floorboard."

Under the pseudonym "Seward Lewis" (a compilation of Bill's and Jack's middle names), *Hippos* made the rounds of publishing houses, including Simon and Schuster, and was rejected by all. Burroughs lost interest in writing and concentrated on narcotics, but his passion for Jack remained undiminished, since it had been sexual rather than literary in the first place. For Burroughs, whom a friend described as "thirty-five going on ninety-five," the youthful Kerouac was a godsend. "Jack was gregarious," Burroughs recalled. "He liked to get out and drink and talk." Burroughs guided Jack through a year in the New York netherworld of drugs and shady characters. Burroughs's fascination with the criminal mind had begun at the age of thirteen when he'd read and reread *You Can't Win*, the autobiography of a petty thief named Jack Black, a drug addict, bindlestiff, and jailbird. Burroughs not only wanted to explore the depths of human evil to discover just how repulsive people could be, but also hoped to find out why the scum of the earth retained a vitality otherwise lacking in "dead" America.[10]

In January 1945, Jack and Edie tried a reconciliation and accepted Joan's invitation to rent a bedroom in her spacious new eighty-dollar-a-month, five-room apartment, No. 35 at 420 West 115th Street. Joan had given birth to a baby daughter, Julie, and was separated from her writer-serviceman husband, Paul Adams. In New York, she hoped to continue her education at Columbia's School of Journalism. To help her meet the rent on the apartment, Ginsberg and Burroughs also moved in. For a while, all three key figures of the Beat Generation, Kerouac, Ginsberg, and Burroughs, were living under one roof. The reconciliation between Jack and Edie foundered, according to Huncke, who said, "Apparently Kerouac wasn't too successful with her sexually." One night at 3 A.M., Jack walked in on Huncke and Edie having sex. "It was perfectly all right with Jack," Huncke recalled. "He made no fuss about it." Nevertheless, as Jack later wrote to Neal Cassady, he enjoyed sleeping with Edie and waking up to the cheery sound of her giggles "in the sheets."

Jack had sex with Ginsberg in the Village between some parked trucks on Christopher Street. "We were horny," Ginsberg recalled. They "jacked each other off," according to Barry Miles. The next time Jack and Allen passed "the trucks," the Village's well-known meat rack, they again stopped and masturbated each other. "Kerouac allowed Allen to blow him," wrote Miles, who added, "Allen fell completely in love." Kerouac and Ginsberg may well have had that moment in mind when they collaborated five years later on "Pull My Daisy," in which they wrote, "drink me when you're ready." That Kerouac's participation was not entirely passive when he and Allen had sex was indicated in *Mexico City Blues*'s "213th Chorus," which was dedicated to Allen and in which Kerouac invited Allen not only to "suck my lamppole," but to "pile my ane." He was impressed that Allen's penis was long enough to have a "hinge in the middle," he later told Timothy Leary. The most interesting order Kerouac issued to Allen in *Pull My Daisy*, however, was to destroy "the traitor" in his mind, which sounded like a desire for self-honesty. "Allen and Jack slept together occasionally," Huncke recalled. "Allen was in love with the whole bunch." According to Ginsberg, Kerouac at last began to be more reciprocal in their lovemaking, and thereafter their friendship deepened. "He was bending and stretching quite a bit to accommodate my emotions," Ginsberg recalled. "That's why I've always loved him, because I was able to completely unburden myself . . . and he was able to take it."

Yet it was as writers that Ginsberg and Kerouac had their deepest affinity, sharing their notebooks and works in progress and freely borrowing each other's ideas. Ginsberg always acknowledged that Kerouac was the master and he the student; he'd been studying prelaw at Columbia before he'd met Kerouac, and only later, under Kerouac's influence, had he begun to write poetry. "Kerouac was the first writer I ever met who heard his own writing, who listened to his own sentences as if they were musical, rhythmical constructions," said Ginsberg, who maintained that Kerouac created a sequence of sentences within a paragraph the same way saxophone gods Lester Young and Charlie Parker designed a jazz riff. In January and February 1945, according to Ginsberg's journal, he wrote his first good poems: "He Who Walks

Within the Womb," "I Have Been Unleashed," "This Stormy Foundation Bursts upon the Air," and "Now in This Park, by This Lakeside." Thanks to Kerouac, he was on his way to becoming America's best-known poet.[11]

In 1945, Kerouac began to expand his concept of Beat, which he defined as an attitude and a look, and his models were not literary figures but contemporary actors and musicians. Montgomery Clift's famous slouch was Beat, as were Dane Clark's tortured Dostoyevskian intensity and Brooklyn accent, Charlie Parker's black turtleneck sweater, John Garfield's portraits of battle-hardened, sardonic servicemen, and Marlon Brando's conga drums. As Brando wrote in his 1994 memoir, *Songs My Mother Taught Me*, "It was ecstasy sleeping on the sidewalk of Washington Square, realizing I had no commitments to anything or anyone." In Kerouac's gallery of Beat prototypes, hard-boiled private eyes like Humphrey Bogart had an honored place, as did Peter Lorre, on whose anguished visage the agony and ambivalence of mankind were definitively etched. To be Beat was to be yourself, at whatever cost. Brando would be the first Beat hero to create a sensation, in 1947, as the proud primal beast of *A Streetcar Named Desire*, and later as the leather-clad biker of *The Wild One*. To Kerouac, the original Beats shared a predominant characteristic: a "spirit of noninterference with the lives of others." Both Kerouac and Ginsberg saw them in a tragic light. Kerouac called them "ragged, beatific . . . down and out." To Ginsberg, they were mad geniuses, and in "Howl" he later alluded to Lucien and Kammerer's bloody date on the banks of the Hudson River; to Kerouac's brushes with insanity, warfare, and prisons; and to Burroughs and Huncke's pursuit of an "angry fix." Though Kerouac in *The Dharma Bums* would forecast the cultural revolution of the 1960s, at first his interest in the Beats was restricted to social notation. He focused on Beat manners—"a certain new gesture, or attitude, which I can only describe as a new *more* . . . a revolution in manners in America."

The most improbable members of the early Beat ménage were Drs. Alfred C. Kinsey and Wardell Pomeroy, who interviewed most of the Beats for their six-year study, *Sexual Behavior in the Human Male*. Years later, in *On the Road*, Kerouac recalled seeing Kinsey and an assistant in a Times Square gay bar in 1945. A fifty-one-year-old professor of zoology at Indiana University, Kinsey often came to New York on field trips and paid Huncke to line up interviewees. "All of us got into the habit of meeting at the Angle Bar," Huncke recalled, adding, "that would be Jack Kerouac . . . Allen Ginsberg . . . Bill [Burroughs] . . . Edie Parker." Eventually, according to Barry Miles, "Allen, Jack, Bill, and Joan all did interviews for the Kinsey Report." Interviewees were asked to describe their orgasms, and men were told to measure their sex organs, listing "length and circumference, normal and erect; angle, erect; curvature, erect; direction of carriage, erect." "I liked Kinsey," Huncke said, and referred to Kinsey's "marvelous sense of humor. . . . So he also became much of the scene. All during this period Jack would be there occasionally." In the most famous graph that appeared in *Sexual Behavior in the Human Male* on its publication in 1948, Kinsey defined male sexuality not in categories but as a continuum, with heterosexuality at one end and homosexuality at the other, with each individual man standing at some point on the scale, never one-hundred-percent straight or gay. He found no scientific justification for the categories *heterosexual, bisexual,* or *homosexual.* But the Kinsey revelation that shook American society to its roots was that one man in ten was gay and that from fifty to one hundred percent of the population had had homosexual experiences. In its denial of homoeroticism, Kinsey wrote, the whole society was sick. On publication, the 804-page "Kinsey Report," as it soon came to be known, sold 275,000 copies, an unprecedented amount for an academic, largely statistical tract. Over the years, the report and its methods have come under attack, but its social impact was enormous, eventually resulting in a shift in attitudes toward sex. Kinsey's interest in ridding America of sexual discrimination seemed more understandable after one of his biographers, James H. Jones, revealed in the *New York Times* in 1997 that Kinsey "was both homosexual and, from childhood on, a masochist who, as he grew older, pursued an interest in extreme sexuality with increasing compulsiveness."

Shortly after Bill Burroughs moved into her apartment, Burroughs and Joan Vollmer Adams became lovers. Ginsberg felt they were well-matched—wickedly witty, sharp-tongued, and sophisticated. Despite Burroughs's preference for men, Joan told him, "You're supposed to be a faggot [but] you're as good as a pimp in bed." Kerouac later told me that, in *Naked Lunch,* Burroughs was describing his own sex life with Joan, as well as the oral-sex tricks that Joan taught Edie, when he wrote, "She sucks rhythmically up and down, pausing on the up stroke and moving her head around in a circle. Her hand plays gently with his balls, slide down and middle finger up his ass. . . . She drinks his jissom which fills her mouth in great hot spurts. . . . [She] is strapping on a rubber penis: 'Steely Dan III from Yokohama,' she says, caressing the shaft."

Ginsberg regularly joined them in Joan's room, but only for conversation, and they talked into the early morning hours almost every night. Bill and Joan appeared to be a perfect couple, with Bill stretched out on the bed propped up on pillows and Joan lying next to him with her arms around him. To Allen, Joan was a beautiful woman, with an oval face, eyes that shone with intelligence, exquisite Cupid's bow lips, and a finely sculpted nose. Like Burroughs, she had a heroic brow and a high hairline.

The introduction of Burroughs into the apartment would prove to be a mixed blessing. Though he helped turn the parlor into the first creative cauldron of the Beat Generation, he brought in drugs, and this precipitated its downfall. Burroughs married Joan on January 17, 1945, and soon started bringing around morphine and marijuana, as well as undesirable characters. But the most insidious drug—Benzedrine, or "speed"—was introduced into their lives by Kerouac. He was first turned onto Benzedrine by Huncke's friend, a six-foot, redheaded gun moll named Priscilla Arminger who was known by her alias, Vicki Russell. She showed Jack how to break open Benzedrine inhalers, remove the soaked papers, roll them into pellets, and swallow them with coffee or Coke. The drug produced a feeling of excitement, confidence, and an urge to convey seemingly new insights, which made it irresistible to a compulsive writer like Kerouac. Jack and Vicki ended up "blasting benny" and rapping through the night, and they continued doing Benzedrine together for three days. "The next forty-eight hours I fucked her solid," he later told Neal. "That's a worldshaking cunt."

As a consequence of their association with Burroughs, both Jack and Joan became hopeless drug addicts. On speed, Kerouac lost a dangerous amount of weight very quickly. Ginsberg later described in "Howl" how they destroyed their health on Benzedrine, and how the drug dried up their ideas and writing ability. Kerouac's once-muscular body turned soft and mushy, and his hair began to fall out. In time, he came to fear and despise Benzedrine, but evidently he was still struggling to give it up as late as 1951, when he wrote Neal Cassady that he was suffering from phlebitis in his foot and trying to restrict himself to caffeine. According to *The Johns Hopkins Medical Handbook*, speed abuse can bring on strokes, but Kerouac's ailment, thrombophlebitis, is also one of the three most frequent complications of heroin addiction, so it seems likely that he was also dipping into Burroughs's morphine stash (heroin is derived from morphine). Kerouac's parents noticed his deterioration and begged him, to no avail, to dissociate himself from the "dope fiends and crooks" in the apartment. Though Joan had a new baby to care for, she took so much Benzedrine that she became a ghostly apparition, wandering around the city and getting lost. On one occasion, she was found in Whelan's Drug Store in Times Square, high on Benzedrine and carrying the baby in her arms. Then, just as everyone in the apartment was falling to pieces, the world outside at last began to pull itself together: World War II ended in August 1945.

It was a strange, uneasy peace, since the end of the war marked the beginning of the nuclear age. Poet W. H. Auden called it the age of anxiety, Kerouac called it the heyday of the Beat Generation, and politicians called it the cold war. In Ozone Park, between painful, malodorous stomach pumpings for the cancer that was killing him, Leo drew Jack to his side and muttered, "Beware of the niggers and the Jews." Intellectually and morally, Jack was a product of his father's isolationist Quebec background; anti-Semitism was a trait commonly found throughout French Canada. Unfortunately, Jack never rose above it. Nor was he alone. Though the Nazi genocide had killed fourteen million so-called racial inferiors, a postwar poll of U.S. occupation forces in Germany showed that twenty-two percent of American soldiers believed that the Germans had been right in exterminating the Jews, and fifty-one percent said Hitler had done Germany "a lot of good," according to journalist John Gunther.

Gunther blamed the soldiers' anti-Semitism on lack of education, but that could hardly explain the anti-Semitism that was rampant throughout the Anglo-American literary community. Ezra Pound was the most obvious example, broadcasting fascist propaganda before the U.S. government slapped him in an insane asylum. Thomas Wolfe wrote, in a September 1936 notebook entry, "In Germany you are free to speak and write that you do not like Jews and that you think Jews are bad, corrupt, and unpleasant people. In America you are not free to say this." Other major literary figures expressing anti-Semitic ideas included Theodore Dreiser, H. L. Mencken, T. S. Eliot, William Faulkner, Edgar Lee Masters, Eugene O'Neill, Vachel Lindsay, E. E. Cummings, Katherine Anne Porter, Tennessee Williams, and Graham Greene. Though Sigmund Freud long ago diagnosed racism as an illness, incredibly it has yet to be studied and treated as a disease. Certainly in the case of the anti-Semitic literary giants, their racism was accompanied by a host of mental aberrations. Kerouac and Graham Greene were homophobic and repressed homoerotics; Porter was antiblack and homophobic, despite her affair with a gay writer named William Goyen and sporadic lesbian relationships; Tennessee Williams was antiblack; and Faulkner suffered from sexual insecurity and alcoholism. Anti-Semitism was the dirty secret of American literature until it came to be dominated in the postwar years by estimable Jewish writers like Mailer, Saul Bellow, J. D. Salinger, Bernard Malamud, Isaac Bashevis Singer, and Philip Roth.

In 1945, while Kerouac nursed his anti-Semitic father in Queens, seventeen-year-old Eli Wiesel, the future Nobel laureate, was a world away in Buchenwald, holding his starved, dying father in his arms. Eli Wiesel realized, as Kerouac never would, that World War II had been worth fighting, that it had been, in Wiesel's words, "a struggle against received ideas and oppressive laws, a fight for freedom, for the right to say and write about whatever you pleased."[12]

Released by John Sampas in 1997, Jack's July 1945 notebook describes how the apartment began to break up that summer. Edie moved back to Asbury Park, and Jack jotted in his notebook that the marriage was discarded again at his instigation. Joan was lost to Benzedrine addiction, and when her ex-husband, Paul Adams, returned from the German front and came to New York to see their daughter Julie, he took one look at the speed freaks in the apartment and said, "This is what I fought for?" Joan glanced up from a drugged stupor and told him to "come off it." On speed, Kerouac had become homoerotically aggressive and was hitting on men in public, saying, "C'mon I'll fuck you," Ginsberg recalled. Drugs ripped through the inhibitions of everyone in the apartment, and Ginsberg wrote worshipful love letters to Kerouac, comparing himself with Aschenbach in *Death in Venice* and Kerouac with Tadzio. In November 1945, Kerouac reciprocated, telling Ginsberg that he loved him, but Benzedrine had reduced him to a state of "narcotic imbecility." Kerouac blamed his burnt-out condition on New York and on his former mentor, Burroughs. Having plundered each other for drugs and intellectual booty, neither Jack nor Bill was concerned for the other's welfare, and true friendship between them was impossible.[13]

Looking for a more wholesome hero, Kerouac focused on Hal Chase, whom he revered as a "cocksman" known for his varied and imaginative lovemaking techniques, including such exotic settings as a mirrored room. Haldon "Hal" Chase was Ginsberg's latest addition to the Beat menagerie, and it was Hal who expanded the parameters of the evolving Beat mystique to include the myth of the American West. From Denver, Colorado, Hal was a Columbia anthropology and archeology student who had served in the army in the ski troops. He moved into the apartment after the war. In Ginsberg's estimation, Hal was a "child of the rainbow" with "blond golden hair and good physique, an Indian hawk-nose and American boy State Fair fresh manners." Kerouac soon started monopolizing Hal, exactly as he'd done when he'd earlier taken Lucien Carr away from Ginsberg.

Jack admired Hal's ability to make out with any woman he approached in a bar or at a party, but Edie found Hal to be boringly narcissistic and full of himself. There could be no doubt, however, that Hal brought a new zest and energy to the apartment and helped to make it what it became at its best: the inaugural experiment in Beat communal living. Hal and the others dug into their psyches and had long analytical sessions in which they demanded complete honesty of each other. They were probably the only group in the world attempting this kind of psychological work in the forties; it would be another twenty years before the human potential movement and the first encounter groups.

One of the most famous early Beat rap sessions was the Wolfean vs. non-Wolfean debate referred to in Kerouac's November 13, 1945, letter to Ginsberg. One night, Jack, Allen, Bill, and Hal were all speeding when they decided to climb into bed and talk; Kerouac and Burroughs were in one bed, Ginsberg and Chase in the other. Hal viewed himself and Kerouac as Thomas Wolfe–type virile heterosexuals, while Burroughs and Ginsberg were "sinister . . . fairy Jew[s]" who liked Baudelaire and young boys. Ginsberg, who later confided in his journal that he'd only wanted to be kissed on the mouth and snuggle with "the fair boy's body," was understandably hurt by the anti-Semitic slur. In Kerouac's November 13, 1945, letter as it appears in the somewhat cryptic version edited by Ann Charters, Kerouac stated that Hal "operated his own self into an external sham calculated to hide his real fears." Hal's fears, Kerouac added, reflected his own fears. According to a passage in Visions of Cody, "Val [Hal] . . . was asleep and had his hand thrown over my cock and I was dreaming of cunts . . . and I woke up . . . with a hard-on." The Wolfean/non-Wolfean session became a reference point in Beat prehistory, supposedly separating the heterosexuals from the homosexuals. My reading of Kerouac's November 13, 1945, letter is that his confession of sham and fear reveal his repressed homoerotic side, and therefore the straight-gay distinction is less clear-cut than heretofore supposed. Kinsey's variable straight-gay scale had perhaps never been more to the point, but the Beats made the same mistake as the larger society and divided people into artificial sexual categories in order to discriminate against them.[14]

As their friendship deepened, Kerouac poured out all his literary dreams to Hal. His goal was to portray the entire social spectrum as Balzac had before him, and he intended to "conquer" America, the new literary locus of the world, as Balzac had encompassed all of France. Despite such grandiose notions, and although many other other writers of his generation were already emerging on the literary scene, nothing publishable emerged from the boozy, drugged, sexually stymied Kerouac in 1945. He was twenty-three, the exact age at which his contemporary Carson McCullers had made her debut in 1940 with *The Heart Is a Lonely Hunter*. Over the next five years, McCullers published *The Member of the Wedding* and *Reflections in a Golden Eye*, a record of quality that few if any of her peers would match in a comparable period. In a recently released letter to his future editor, Malcolm Cowley, Kerouac dismissed McCullers as one of modern fiction's affected "silly females," whose only gift was thinking up catchy titles.

Cowley was guilty of the same male chauvinism, having once told Scott Fitzgerald that women novelists "live spiritually in Beloit, Wisconsin," even those who masquerade as Left Bank bohemians. Despite such flippant and condescending dismissals, some of the best writing of mid–twentieth-century America was done by women, including Eudora Welty, Katherine Anne Porter, Flannery O'Connor, Jean Stafford, and Mary McCarthy, to name but a few. Other contemporaries being published by the mid-1940s included Gore Vidal, twenty, with *Williwaw*; Truman Capote, twenty-four, with *Other Voices, Other Rooms*; Saul Bellow, thirty, with *Dangling Man*; and Norman Mailer, twenty-four, with *The Naked and the Dead*, generally regarded as the best novel of World War II. But like Kerouac, many of his contemporaries would not be heard from until the 1950s, including Ginsberg, Burroughs, Flannery O'Connor, James Jones, William Styron, J. D. Salinger, Cynthia Ozick, James Baldwin, and Herman Wouk. Kerouac himself would not publish a book until 1950, and his March 1945 letter to Nin helped explain why: After *Hippos* failed to find a publisher, he developed writer's block. Though he and Burroughs were compatible as coauthors, they saw no reason to attempt a second novel together. Without a book contract to prove he was a publishable writer, Kerouac lost his confidence and gave up hope. Burroughs decided that *Hippos* was unpublishable, but almost half a century later the Kerouac estate revealed that the novel is part of its long-range posthumous publishing program.[15] Though neither Burroughs nor Kerouac realized it, another reason for their writing difficulties was the demoralization that accompanies alcoholism and drug addiction.

By mid-1945, Kerouac was so frantic to break into print that he resorted to hackwork, knocking out stories for true romance magazines, but even these were rejected. Since he was usually on speed, he may very well have been writing unpublishable nonsense. He was still working on a novel that had been in progress since his nineteenth year, and in a November letter to Ginsberg he revealed that he was perpetually loaded on Benzedrine because it enabled him to write huge quantities of prose. But, as Ginsberg had already discovered, Benzedrine made him turn out worthless "gibberish." The drug finally caught up with Kerouac, and in December 1945, he collapsed from thrombophlebitis and had to be hospitalized. He lay near death in a bed at Queens General with blood clots in his legs. In *Vanity of Duluoz*, he explicitly cited Benzedrine as the sole cause of his illness, and it also symbolized the dead end he'd reached with Lucien Carr, Burroughs, and Ginsberg, whom he now dismissed as ineffectual esthetes.[16] As usual, his friends made handy scapegoats. The strong person Kerouac sought was inside his own being but held hostage there by lies and drugs.

Soon after he went home from the hospital in 1946, Leo died in his arms, still only in his late fifties. "Take care of your mother whatever you do. Promise me," Leo said. "I promise," Jack said, and he meant it. Years later, in a letter to Joe Chaput, he wrote that he looked at his father's dead body slumped in the chair and noticed that his fingers were still stained from a lifetime of handling newsprint, lead, and printer's ink. Leo had been far from perfect, but he'd always kept pork chops on the table, as both Jack and Gabrielle were quick to point out. Jack noticed other blemishes on Leo's hands, but these were due to cirrhosis of the liver. Alcohol had so ravaged Leo's digestive tract that all the food he ate in his final year was instantly liquefied and robbed of its nutrients. His tortuous death goaded Jack into writing *The Town and the City*, which he envisaged as a book that would vindicate Leo, "a huge novel explaining everything to everybody." Gabrielle and Jack brought Leo's remains back to New England and buried him in an unmarked grave next to Gerard in Nashua, New Hampshire. Half a century later, Stella Sampas would donate an impressive granite monument bearing the names of Gerard, Leo, and Gabrielle, who died in 1973. Nin could not be present for her father's funeral because she was still away in the armed forces, where she met her second husband, a soldier named Paul Blake. As their family shrank, Jack and his mother clung to each other as never before.

A funeral service for Sammy Sampas was held in Lowell just after the war. "The army wrote and asked if we wanted Sammy's remains shipped home from Algeria," John Sampas recalled. "He was brought back to Lowell by train, and a military funeral was held at the Edson Cemetery. They gave you the flag. Sammy's medals are around somewhere, with Tony's and Nick's, from World War II." Sammy's memory invariably made Kerouac think of Verlaine, who once wrote: "You whose hope is past, here is peace at last." Though the patriarch of the large Sampas family was still in prison, Stella had fed and cared for several growing children as the older Sampas brothers had fought at the front. Stella was now twenty-seven, and although Jack was not yet divorced from Edie, he asked Stella to marry him. There could be no doubt that she adored him and wanted to say yes, but as she later explained, "I couldn't. I had a family to raise." One day, Jack and Stella took a long walk down Moody Street and paused on the banks of the Merrimack, reminiscing about how they'd once splashed around in the river, joyous and carefree. Again they discussed marriage, but the most Stella could promise was that she wouldn't marry anyone else.

Returning to his mother's apartment in Queens, Kerouac tore into *The Town and the City*, his sprawling epic of a family dispersing and fanning out over the country during World War II, which was essentially what his own family had just been through. Sunrise over Ozone Park often found him still at the typewriter, pounding out the novel's majestic, sonorous passages. Eventually the book totaled 1,183 pages. In the two years he worked on it, the manuscript was passed from hand to hand in the Beat underground until everyone he knew had read it, talked about it, and turned him into a legend years before the book was ever published. He always read his favorite passages aloud to Allen, who applauded Kerouac as a "poet-genius" and placed Jack's style in the grand novelistic tradition of Tolstoy and Balzac, but with an added dimension of Wolfean lyricism. It was not the experimental prose of Jack's later work in the 1950s, but straightforward narrative enriched by, in Allen's description, "long, symphonic-sentenced, heavily-voweled periods, a little with echo of Milton." *The Town and the City* was indeed traditional prose, but it heralded from its opening lines a brilliant new voice in contemporary fiction: "The town is Galloway. The Merrimac River, broad and placid, flows down to it from the New Hampshire hills, broken at the falls to make frothy havoc on the rocks." Today, those words are chiseled in stone on one of the mysterious dark monoliths by sculptor Ben Woitena that commemorate Kerouac in downtown Lowell. Even in 1946, Ginsberg knew that Kerouac was advancing the novel form to a historic milestone—a "great fusion of poetry and novel in America." Ginsberg was so exalted by Jack's poetic prose that he wrote his first publishable verse, which later appeared as *Gates of Wrath* (1947–1952).

Jack's only relief from his heavy work on the novel was occasional sex with Ginsberg. "It was interesting because Jack felt there was nothing homosexual about being the blowee, only the blower," Ron Lowe, Kerouac's Florida friend, recalled. "He said the young Ginsberg had been in love with him. Jack said, 'Gin used to blow me under the Brooklyn Bridge. I was young then and I came slow.' I was a little shocked. I came from a parochial background. To hear a man that freely admitting, despite his distinction of being the beneficiary instead of the benefactor, didn't cut with me. It was a distinction without a difference as far as I was concerned. I told Jack, 'A man asked me once if I was gay and I said no, but I do try to be cheerful.'" Yet the distinction was important to Kerouac, who somehow managed to convince himself that he could dip deeply and regularly into homoeroticism and still be a part of society's heterosexual tyranny. The cost of living so dishonestly was ever-increasing amounts of alcohol and drugs.

While Jack toiled on his novel in Ozone Park, Burroughs was getting into trouble with the law at the apartment, where he was arrested for forging

Dilaudid prescriptions, using a pad Huncke had stolen from a doctor in Brooklyn. Mortimer Burroughs again flew from St. Louis and bailed his thirty-two-year-old son out of jail. To pay for his heroin habit, Burroughs started robbing people in the subway—"working the hole," as he later put it in "Dead on Arrival"—and dealing heroin with a Times Square petty thief named Bill Garver. When Burroughs's case came to court, the judge was merciful since it was a first serious offense and gave him a four-month suspended sentence, but ordered him to go home to St. Louis where he could be supervised by Mortimer.

Joan was left alone in the apartment, fretting over how she was going to support Julie. Eventually, she rented rooms to Huncke and to cutthroats like Phil "The Sailor" White, with whom she had "a light affair," as she called it. When Kerouac arrived one day, she went completely berserk and took off all her clothes, revealing unsightly sores from Benzedrine abuse. So stoned she didn't recognize Jack, she demanded to know who he was, ordered him out of the apartment, and accused him of attempted rape. Ginsberg watched the entire scene while typing a ten-page introduction to his poem "Death in Violence."

The disintegration of the once creative Beat scene in the apartment was complete; the place was now little more than a warehouse for drugs and stolen goods. Eventually, Huncke was arrested and imprisoned for drug possession. Sailor also was arrested, and later hanged himself while awaiting trial in the Tombs. Marooned in the apartment with Ginsberg and unable to meet the rent, Joan overdosed on Benzedrine and was taken to Bellevue, where she became the first recorded case in New York City of a woman suffering from acute amphetamine psychosis. Julie was sent away to stay with relatives, and Joan remained in detox for ten days. With no one to pay the rent, the apartment passed into history. After closing it down and turning in the key, Ginsberg took a furnished room with an Irish family on West Ninety-second Street. Though the first Beat commune had ended in disaster, it had proven that an alternate lifestyle was indeed possible in America.

When Kerouac ventured into Manhattan from Queens during this time, he usually stayed with Hal Chase in Livingston Hall. War veterans were flocking to the campus, taking advantage of the GI Bill, and one of them, Ed White, a former navy man and a friend of Hal's from Denver, taught Kerouac the art of "sketching." Thereafter, like a painter with his sketchbook, Jack kept a notebook and wrote on-the-spot scenes, even when he was at a party or walking along the streets. Jack and Ed became so close they discussed going to Paris together and studying at the Sorbonne, but Ed was perhaps too "businesslike," Jack complained. Ginsberg felt that Ed ostracized him as a gay, and he was hurt when Jack invited Hal and Ed for Thanksgiving dinner in Ozone Park but excluded him. "Things going ill," Ginsberg confided in his journal in November, "loneliness, splenetic moods, boredom."

All that stopped in late 1946 when twenty-year-old Neal Cassady arrived in New York and radically changed both Kerouac's and Ginsberg's lives, meeting them first in the West End Cafe. Later, Hal and Ed, who knew Neal from Denver, took Jack up to Spanish Harlem on the subway, where Neal and his sixteen-year-old wife LuAnne Henderson were staying in a cold-water flat. In *Visions of Cody*, Neal, as "Cody Pomeray," answers the door nude, and Jack can see "Joanna Dawson [LuAnne]" on a couch in the shadows, hastily pulling herself together after sex. Jack notes that she is pimply but fresh and pretty, and that Cody's penis has a "big huge crown." Admiring Cody's "perfect build, large blue eyes," Jack thinks of a young Gene Autry, "hardjawed bigboned," and of the lion trainer Clyde Beatty. At first Jack doesn't view Cody as a possible friend. Cody brags of stealing cars, and strikes Jack as a potential murderer. But in Harlem they talk until dawn, and Jack finally falls asleep in a chair, still holding a cigarette butt retrieved from an ashtray. In the morning, Cody jumps up and begins to pace the apartment, finally ordering his wife to fix breakfast. She complies, as submissive as a sharecropper's drudge. As Cody dresses, Jack notices that his jeans and T-shirt cling to him "so gracefully . . . you couldn't buy a better fit from a custom tailor but only earn it from the Natural Tailor of Natural Joy." But there is nothing graceful about Cody's ideas or speech; in a spew of pseudointellectual babble, he says, "We'll never crystallize in our plans or come to any rockbottom pure realization, decision, whichever, or nothin without perfect action and knowledge not only philosophical and on an emotional plane but pragmatic and simple." As Cody's new mentor, Jack has his work cut out for him. "I thought of him as a heartbreaking new friend," Jack reflects.

Neal and LuAnne soon moved from Spanish Harlem to Tom Livornese's small apartment near Columbia at 103rd Street, but they were no longer welcome when it was discovered that everyone who came near them got crab lice. According to *Visions of Cody*, "Val [Hal] said . . . 'If you want to lay Joanna ask Cody.'" Not everyone was as charmed by Neal as Jack was. Edie, who was in and out of the Beat scene though she and Jack had annulled their marriage, called Neal "a clutz [sic]," and added that only naive young virgins fell for him. Hip women like Joan Burroughs and Celine Young were as unimpressed with Neal Cassady as Edie was. Burroughs actively disliked Neal and warned everyone that Neal would cut his own mother's throat "for gas money." Neal was just as critical of Burroughs and called him "as high-horse as a Governor in the Colonies, as nasty as an old Aunt, and as queer as the day is long." Though Kerouac sensed that Neal was a con man, he was dazzled and mystified by him. "I walked beside him on tiptoe," Jack recalled. "I didn't want to disturb the delicate balance that existed between this angel and me."

In *Visions of Cody*, the marriage of Cody and his child bride begins to fall apart amidst "horrible tearful scenes and . . . cocksucking in hotel rooms." Cody's wife pours out her "sob glob story" to Jack, who listens half-attentively, imagining "her legs spread revealing her cunt, and me there bending over her." Interviewed years later by Gifford and Lee, LuAnne Henderson revealed that her stepfather had been "interested in" her, and the situation had threatened to force her from her own home in Denver. Then Neal had come along, swept her into a hasty marriage, and cheated on her with every girl he met. In *Visions of Cody*, Joanna pushes Jack against the wall of a Harlem bar one night, pressing her body to his. Cody also wants Jack and suggests a ménage à trois. Later, the two men get in bed, with the girl "hot in the middle." She finds it flattering to have two sexy lovers in bed with her at the same time. She and Cody are both ripe for lovemaking, but Jack lies in a state of paralysis, "amazed, complicated, plotting." Realizing they've reached an impasse, Cody tells Jack and Joanna to relax, empty their minds of every fear and concern, and then "be straight in your soul and admit whatever feelings and act on them right away, don't let even a second rot." Jack lacks the courage, though not the desire, and later curses himself for missing the opportunity to learn "something about . . . ourselves we're dying by the hour to know and act upon immediately, that might very well be as Reich says *sexual*, some mystery in the bones themselves and not the shadows of the mind." Finally, the men each make love to Joanna, but separately and in private.

As revealed in *Cody*, the ultimate irony about Neal Cassady, a role model for a generation of heterosexual males as well as a sex object to women, was that his favorite fantasy was to be a clinging and submissive hausfrau. Cody wants to be "a sweet young cunt of sixteen so he could feel himself squishy and nice and squirm all over when some man had to look." As the loving bride of a rugged he-man, Cody wants to "spend all day over a hot stove and finger himself and feel the rub of his dress on his ass and wait for hubby who has one sixteen inches long."

Though in Kerouac's eyes Neal was a "bullnecked, rocknecked" athlete, cowboy, and tire-recapper, a seemingly invincible masculine juggernaut, Neal was basically a fragile child of an alcoholic who'd grown up in charitable, jail-like institutions such as the I. J. Mullen Home for Boys, a Denver facility for disadvantaged Catholic males. Literally and figuratively, Neal was still looking for his father or any strong male figure to latch onto. In Denver he'd been befriended by a high-school teacher named Justin Brierly, a Columbia alumnus who was also a lawyer and a committee member of the local Ivy League Scholarship Board. Brierly had steered Denver boys like Hal Chase into Columbia, but his interest in Neal was far from academic. In 1997, Steve Turner's *Angelheaded Hipster: A Life of Jack Kerouac* revealed that "Brierly had been sexually attracted to Neal, and managed to entice him into his first homosexual experience." Kerouac saw both sides of Neal from the start: the "young guy with a bony face that looks like it's been pressed against iron bars to get that dogged rocky look of suffering," and the coquettish bisexual who knew how to manipulate Kerouac by fluttering long lashes over "big blue flirtatious eyes."

One night, Neal appeared unexpectedly in Ozone Park just as Jack and Gabrielle were finishing supper and asked Jack to teach him how to write.

Kerouac tried to resist him, telling himself, "He's a guy, he's married, he works . . . go find your soul," but Neal proved irresistible, especially when he began to tell his life story, which Kerouac hastily jotted down and later recounted in *Cody*. Neal loved his father, and when his parents broke up, though he was only six, he chose to go on the road with his dad and live in Denver flophouses rather than stay with his mother and brothers. Court-mandated to return to his mother, he was beaten by his older brothers and ran away at fourteen to start a career of compulsive sex, car stealing, jail sentences, and self-education in public libraries. Wherever he was, he made sure that he had sex at least once a day. "To him," Jack wrote, "sex was the one and only holy and important thing in life." When Neal appeared in Kerouac's life in the late 1940s, he was exactly what Kerouac had been looking for, both personally and artistically: someone who combined the brotherly affection of Gerard, the spirituality of Sammy, the talent of Ginsberg, and the male beauty of Lucien Carr and Hal Chase. In Neal, Kerouac had found his mythic macho intellectual outlaw and would make him the paradigm of a new age as the rebellious hero of his most famous novel, *On the Road*. As Dean Moriarty, Cassady was destined to become one of the most famous characters in American fiction, one of the handful that readers know by name, like Ishmael, Huck Finn, Jay Gatsby, Jake Barnes, Robert E. Lee Prewitt, Captain Queeg, Holden Caulfield, and Yossarian.

Kerouac gave Neal a graphic demonstration of how to write that night, knocking out the account of the Lowell-Lawrence game in *The Town and the City*. Hovering over the typewriter with Jack, Neal said, "Write faster, so we can go out and get some cunt." Every time Jack paused to think or edit, Neal yelled, "Go! Grab that ball! Don't fumble it! Keep going!" Kerouac later told Ginsberg that it was "one of the best chapters in the book." It was as if Jack had been struck by "a kind of holy lightning," he later wrote in *On the Road*.[17] He had found another muse, the first since Sammy, and his life rattled onto a furious, fast track.

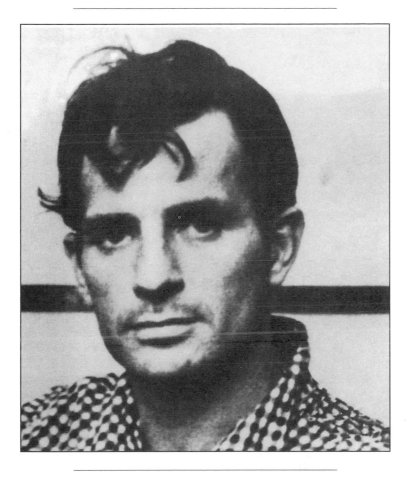

PART TWO

"THE ROAD IS BETTER THAN THE INN"
—Cervantes

FOUR

MUSCLES, MEAT, AND METAPHYSICS

At first, Kerouac seemed to lose Neal Cassady to Allen Ginsberg. Kerouac and Cassady had gone out looking for girls that night after the writing lesson, and they'd run into Ginsberg in Vicki Russell's West Eighty-ninth Street penthouse. In the past, Jack had often walked off with Allen's friends, like Lucien and Hal, but that night Allen walked off with Neal, who later proved to be the reciprocal lover of Allen's dreams and totally uninhibited in bed. In the most famous passage in *On the Road*, Kerouac described how he felt when Cassady and Ginsberg, as Dean Moriarty and Carlo Marx, left him in the middle of the street. "I shambled after as I've been doing all my life after people who interest me, because the only people for me are the mad ones, the ones who are mad to live, mad to talk, mad to be saved, desirous of everything at the same time, the ones who never yawn or say a commonplace thing, but burn, burn, burn like fabulous yellow roman candles exploding like spiders across the stars and in the middle you see the blue centerlight pop and everybody goes 'Awww!' "

Neal wasn't sure that Allen was gay, but he offered "to blow" Allen and "make" him have an orgasm, Allen revealed, in his poem, "Many Loves." In a journal entry, Allen added that he and Neal enjoyed "a wild weekend in sexual drama." Unlike Neal's second wife, Carolyn, who characterized Neal as a "sexual sadist," Allen compared Neal's lovemaking with "joyful yoga"—a sensual as well as a spiritual union of souls. According to a later lover of Neal's, Ann Murphy, an affair with Neal was a cornucopia of "muscles, meat, and metaphysics," and she described "his thick eight inches" with relish. Allen listed the acts they'd performed in bed, such as "his laying me" and "69," and prepared an agenda for future encounters, including "laying his mouth . . . a trip around the world . . . browning him . . . laying his anus . . . whipping."

But as enraptured as Allen was, he discovered that "Neal burned out compassion in his friends," as one of the Merry Pranksters put it in the 1960s, when Neal was a hero of the counterculture and driving Ken Kesey's famous hippie bus, *Further*. "I've almost used him up . . . and want no more of him," Allen wrote in his journal in early 1947. Neal's wife LuAnne left him in New York in March, fed up, she later told Gifford and Lee, with Neal's combination of irresponsibility and smothering possessiveness. "I never want to watch you lie around and masturbate and think of other girls and other things again," Dinah, the character based on LuAnne in John Clellon Holmes's novel *Go!*, says, and later explains to a woman friend, "You can't *care* for him . . . He's got to 'go' all the time, he's got to be leader, have lots of people around him . . . You just can't stick close to him if anything matters to you." Ginsberg would later be drawn to Neal again after seeing how passionately Kerouac cared for him, and how highly Kerouac esteemed Neal as a writer. In early 1947, most of Allen's friends at Columbia still regarded Neal as a jerk. "Lucien disliked Neal," Edie recalled.[1]

The snobberies of the Columbia crowd were not for Jack, who was glad to have Neal back in his life after all the others had amused themselves at Neal's expense and then discarded him. Several months before, Kerouac had begun the new year — 1947 — missing Neal and thinking about him, but he'd diverted himself by attending a round of glamorous parties thrown by his "Jewish millionaire friends" from Horace Mann. He took Lucien and Vicki along with him, and at one of the parties they saw socialite Gloria Vanderbilt. Vicki stole someone's purse and then crawled under a piano where Jack and Lucien had already retired to drink and talk. Jack ended up in bed with Vicki, but she threw up all over both of them, said, "Daddy, I'm no good," and told him to go to bed with Lucien. "*That's right man!*" Lucien said, letting out a fiendish shriek. Kerouac was grateful when Neal, who seemed more substantial than any of these friends, showed up again at his door in Ozone Park. Though Neal did not move in, they spent some time together, enough for Kerouac to realize that Neal had changed radically in the short time that had passed since their first meeting in Harlem.

The Neal Cassady who emerged from his affair with Ginsberg was not the Denver boy who'd mouthed clichés about "the world's great thinkers" only weeks earlier. Under Ginsberg's hip tutelage, Neal had become a cool customer with all the right moves and expressions. And after a few writing lessons with Jack in Ozone Park, Neal began to feel that he really might have a future as an author. They promised to meet again in Colorado later in the spring, but their plans were as tentative as their relationship; as Kerouac stated in *On the Road*, he and Neal did not become close friends in 1947. Nevertheless, by the time Neal announced he was returning to Denver in March, he had made enough of an impression on Jack to wind up in *The Town and the City* as "Paul Hathaway," a polygamist. And Jack was thinking of future times with Neal when he wrote the final passage, in which the protagonist leaves home after his father dies. "He was on the road again," Jack wrote, "traveling the continent westward . . . looking down along the shore in remembrance of the dearness of his father and of all life."

When Neal left for Denver on March 4, 1947, both Kerouac and Ginsberg went to the Greyhound Bus Terminal on Thirty-fourth Street to see him off. Ginsberg annoyed Kerouac by effusing over Neal's washboard abdominals, but what annoyed Kerouac even more was Neal's separate plan to meet Ginsberg in Denver. As Carolyn later wrote, "In an effort to keep everyone happy, Neal tried to juggle several relationships simultaneously." And he always kept them "secret from one another," she added. In the end, he invariably disappointed everyone, having taken on more commitments than he could handle. After Neal left, the old intimacy between Kerouac and Ginsberg was restored, and they "achieved a rapprochement," according to Barry Miles.[2] In Queens, Jack mapped out his trip to Colorado and decided to leave in July 1947. In the meantime, he accompanied his mother to Rocky Mount, North Carolina, for Nin's wedding to Paul Blake. Jack loved and admired Nin, whom he called "a smart 'kiddles,' " and thanked her for remembering his twenty-fifth birthday. She sent him a dollar, which could still buy ten glasses of beer, as he informed her in his March 20 thank-you note.

The Blakes' home would become Kerouac's headquarters for the next decade, and he would do some of his best writing in North Carolina, though he is rarely thought of in connection with the American South. In a letter to Burroughs, he described his two-week Southern jaunt in 1947 and commented on the snakes and alligators in Georgia's Okefenokee swamp, particularly a very old 'gator, said to be nine hundred years old, which meant, Kerouac calculated, that it had been around in the time of Alexander Nevsky, the medieval Russian conqueror. The 'gator had discovered the secret of life: the best thing to do, Kerouac wrote, was to give up all striving and loll around in a sunny swamp.

The early Beats were now scattered around the nation. Burroughs had gone to Texas with Joan, his stepdaughter Julie, and Herbert Huncke, and was cultivating a marijuana crop on what Joan described in a letter to Edie as a "broken-down 99-acre farm," approximately fifty miles north of Houston, in New Waverly. Burrough's scheme was to bring the harvested pot to New York in mason jars and get rich in the burgeoning Manhattan dope market.

Neal wrote Kerouac exuberant letters from the road, and they became Jack's main inspiration as he continued working on *The Town and the City*. On March 7, 1947, Neal gave a sizzling account of his bus ride to Denver, which made traveling with Cassady sound like the ultimate in instant gratification. The girl sitting next to him as the bus sped between Indianapolis and St. Louis wanted to "blow" him, Neal wrote, but he talked her into waiting until the next stop so they could get off and go to a hotel room.

Later in the trip, he seduced another passenger, a virginal schoolteacher, taking her to a park where, he later wrote, "I banged her." Thrilled to be deflowering a virgin, Neal "screwed as never before," he added. Awaiting his bus for Denver, he wrote Jack a letter while drunk and signed it, "To my Brother." Jack called it Neal's "great sex letter" when he shared it with Ginsberg, saying he wanted to write like Neal but couldn't. Actually, he wanted to live like Neal but couldn't; there is no evidence that Neal was ever an exceptional writer, but he represented to Kerouac the promise of dramatic breakthroughs in art and life. Jack was still struggling to squeeze out fifteen hundred words a day, producing the kind of formal prose he thought editors and critics would like. Neal urged him to try "dashing off" a completely spontaneous letter, warning that the danger of formal composition was just "say[ing] things rather than feel[ing] them." One should meditate before writing, and then "write rather than think what to write about," Neal advised. Kerouac read these words as if they were holy scripture, and indeed the effect they had on him was not unlike the Christian phenomenon of transfiguration—the sudden emanation of radiance from the person of Christ on the mountain. In the dynamics of Cassady's relationship with Kerouac, a reversal of roles had occurred. The student had become the master.[3]

With Neal away in Denver, Jack once again became the focus of Ginsberg's lust, and went along with Allen to a Passover seder at Louis Ginsberg's home in Paterson. Later, as they parted in the subway, Allen begged Jack to beat him, begging for "*any* kind of attention," Allen later explained. Kerouac refused, and Allen started "showing his cock to juvenile delinquents," he confessed. Equally importunate in his letters to Neal, Allen demanded sex and undying love, but Neal explained that he'd become involved with women again and was tired of "pricks & men." Ginsberg flew into a rage and called Neal a "double-crossing, faithless bitch." On April 10, Neal wrote that he was a bisexual who preferred women; he proposed that he and Ginsberg find a willing woman and make love to her until they became "truly straight," reflecting the popular psychiatric notion in the forties and fifties that gays could turn themselves into heterosexuals with sufficient practice. Neal's letters to Kerouac indicated that he'd lost all "peace of mind" because of juggling the two most important women in his life, LuAnne and the pretty and intelligent Carolyn, whom he'd just met. From a good Southern family, Carolyn represented Neal's new urge for respectability, and Neal represented Carolyn's desire for a walk on the wild side. They were both in for a bumpy ride.[4]

When Ginsberg finally read the manuscript of Kerouac's partially finished novel, he wrote Neal that *The Town and the City* was "very great" and that Kerouac's use of early 1940s autobiographical material justified all the Sturm und Drang of their lives at Columbia and around Times Square. Ginsberg felt that Kerouac had raced ahead of him artistically and created "a true and eternal world." In July, Ginsberg left for Denver on a Greyhound bus and, upon arrival, was immediately plunged into the chaos of Neal's tangled emotional life with two desirable and demanding women. In Queens, Kerouac wrapped up the first half of *The Town and the City*—six hundred pages—and put it aside, promising himself to finish it when he returned from his westward jaunt. He planned to see Neal and Allen in Denver on July 23 and then go on to the West Coast. On July 14, he wrote Burroughs that his prep-school friend Henri Cru had blown into town with two fat joints of Panama Red and was urging Jack to ship out with him from San Francisco. Jack was a "simpleton" for trusting the unreliable Cru, Ginsberg wrote in a letter to Mark Van Doren. Nonetheless, Jack finalized his plans to hitch to California, work together with Cru as electricians on Pacific ships, and save enough money to return to New York, where he hoped to finish his novel. On his way back from the coast, he would stop in Texas to visit Burroughs, Joan, and Huncke, and he also wanted to catch the Texas-Rice game, which for football fans was "always a killer," he wrote Burroughs.

Kerouac's first cross-country hitchhike began on July 17, 1947, aboard the 242nd Street Van Cortlandt Park train, which he took to the end of the line. As he set out in the wrong direction across the American continent, his experience bore out what Tom Snyder, founder of the Route 66 Association, said in Michael Wallis's *Route 66: The Mother Road*: "Open-road travelers are made more than born." In bitter tears, hitting his head with his fist, Kerouac realized too late what a mistake it had been to go forty miles north when he was California-bound. Swallowing his pride, he retreated to New York, where he caught a bus for Chicago. There he stayed in the Y, checked out the jazz scene in the Loop, and started hitchhiking west the next day. A dynamite truck took him through the green fields of Illinois, then across the intersection where Route 6 joins Route 66 "before they both shoot west for incredible distances." A few more rides and he'd traversed a thousand miles of midwestern plains. At last he entered Colorado and beheld the towering peaks of the Front Range. On July 28, from Denver, he wrote his mother that the weather was "cool and sunny," and tried to describe the majesty of the Rockies. One mile above sea level, Colorado is the most spectacular of the mountain states, with fifty-one peaks over fourteen thousand feet high. For a city boy from the cramped, industrial North, the West was both a revelation and a liberation. Denver seemed to float in its bowl-like setting on the eastern slope of the Rockies, and as soon as Kerouac arrived, he headed for Larimer Street, Neal's stomping ground. He looked in all the places Neal had told him about—pool halls, flophouses, diners, rail yards, and a gay bar—but there was no sign of Neal anywhere. He wondered why downtown Denver seemed so familiar to him, and then he realized it was exactly like Lowell—another endearing Grub Street, U.S.A.[5]

Denver's Columbia contingent, including Hal Chase and Ed White, welcomed Jack and provided accommodations. His friends disapproved of Ginsberg and Cassady's gay relationship and primly avoided them. Cassady's promiscuity struck them as gross, and his costume of T-shirt and jeans as too proletarian. Ginsberg had disgusted them by wearing swimming trunks in downtown Denver in broad daylight, sometimes with a dress shirt and bow tie. Finally, a new friend, Bob Burford, put Jack in touch with Ginsberg, and Ginsberg in turn took Jack to Neal. Once again, Neal answered the door naked. Behind him, Carolyn lay on the bed, blond and feline. Above her, on the wall, was her nude drawing of Neal, "enormous dangle and all," Kerouac noted in *On the Road*. Carolyn later attested that "the proportions of Neal's celebrated apparatus . . . are exaggerated" (indeed, Neal appears to have been perfectly average, as a photograph proved in Ginsberg's 1993 *Snapshot Poetics*). As obsessed with penis size as Kerouac was, Neal later said, in *Visions of Cody*, "I caught . . . an independent young guy . . . taking a piss behind the car . . . and he'd just woke up in the morning . . . and he had a big piss hard-on . . . and I was stupefied and knocked out by the size of his cock . . . what an enormous penis he had . . . I felt a great deal of envy."

Neal tried to divide his time three ways, splitting himself between Carolyn, Ginsberg, and Kerouac, and succeeded in satisfying no one. Carolyn immediately liked Kerouac and later wrote that his "brooding good looks and shy, gentle nature were comforting and attractive to me." He went to see her perform in the Maurice Maeterlinck play, *The Blue Bird*, at the University of Denver, and a few nights later, at a dance, Neal left Carolyn alone with Jack most of the evening, as if he wanted them to become romantically involved. "Dancing with Jack was the only time I felt the slightest doubt about my dedication to Neal," Carolyn recalled, "for here was the warm physical attraction Neal lacked." Jack was aware of her interest, and it made him nervous. Ginsberg later told her that Jack liked her but also feared her. In a 1991 interview, Carolyn said, "Women he admired he was afraid of. . . . I just can't think what else I could've done to make him afraid." On the dance floor, according to Carolyn, Jack said, "It's too bad, but that's how it is. Neal saw you first." (Interestingly, such compunctions had never prevented him from poaching Ginsberg's boyfriends.) Kerouac wrote his own version of that moment in his 1962 novel *Big Sur*, in which Carolyn appears as "Evelyn." Neal, as "Cody Pomeray," observes them "anxiously" as they dance, but he's too sensible to cut in because he knows they are only "a kind of romantic pair," rather than the real thing. Cassady knew that Kerouac was more interested in him than in Carolyn and therefore would never be a serious rival. Neal was aware, too, that Carolyn resented the way he thrust people on her sexually. She later confided to Jack that she became "so sick of all this sex business, that's all he talks about, his friends . . . all they think about is behinds." Jack, on the other hand, she found "refreshing," precisely because he put her under no sexual pressure and left the initiatives up to her. She liked Ginsberg for the same reason, writing, "Gays are always enjoyable because there's never any sexual threat." Despite Kerouac's fear of Carolyn, he also saw her as a kind of salvation. He could fall in love with her and still be free of commitment, knowing as he did that she could never be his because she belonged to Neal. But even this minimal emotional investment left him feeling uneasy.[6]

Though Ginsberg loved to wallow in Neal's messy life, Kerouac found it far too complicated and threatening, and switched over to the safer Hal Chase-Ed White nexus. According to Kerouac's sex list, he and Burford's sister, Bev, made love twenty-five times, but the high point of his Colorado visit came when everyone converged on Central City, thirty-five miles due west of Denver, for a historic weekend that helped define the Beat Generation. A ghost town tucked away in the Rockies, Central City held an annual six-week theater festival, hosting everyone from Mae West in *Diamond Lil* to the Metropolitan Opera. Central City had once been a prosperous mining town, but by 1947 the boardwalks were warped, raggedy curtains fluttered from broken hotel windows, stairways creaked, and in the mines rotting timbers barely contained tons of yellow mud. The Teller House boasted the original Face on the Barroom Floor, which had inspired a ballad. Neal told Ginsberg that everyone went to Central City to "drink, bang & fuck off." Carolyn was abandoned by Neal and left to sit alone in the bus after they arrived in Central City. Jack gravitated to Bob and Bev, Ed White, and other members of the Denver-Columbia set.

The Met's touring company was performing *Fidelio* at the opera house, and Kerouac was moved to tears at the afternoon performance. Beethoven's opera inspired the lines in *Road* that would become a rallying cry of the Beat Generation. Glancing around and failing to see Cassady and Ginsberg, Kerouac "realized they'd be out of place and unhappy. They were like the man with the dungeon stone and the gloom, rising from the underground, the sordid hipsters of America, a new beat generation that I was slowly joining." The character in the opera Kerouac referred to was Florestan, a political prisoner who was chained in a dark, subterranean cell and sang, "*Gott, welch Dunkel hier!*" ["God! This awful dark"], in one of the opera's better-known arias. Ultimately, justice triumphs over tyranny, and Florestan is led from his dungeon singing, "*O namen, namenlose Freude!*" ["Oh blissful hour, oh joy of heaven"]. Jack believed that Neal and Allen, in their honest if controversial declaration of passionate love, were leading their generation to a new freedom and happiness.

Both Kerouac and Ginsberg, in their mutual passion for Neal, were laying claim to their deepest instincts as artists and emerging into a new authenticity as human beings. Ginsberg turned twenty-one that summer, and his self-proclaimed role as a "Great Lover" impressed Jack and helped shape the evolving ethos of the Beat Generation, replacing pessimism with passion. Kerouac had previously criticized Ginsberg for sacrificing himself on the altar of romantic love, but in Denver he was touched by Ginsberg's courage. Ginsberg later wrote that Kerouac "redeemed himself" by at last endorsing homoeroticism, which set him apart from the chilly homophobia of the Denver-Columbia clique. Sensing power and passion in both camps, Jack felt loyalty both to Ginsberg and to the macho Denver contingent that had ostracized him. All that mattered was that everyone lay down their guns, come out of their trenches, get together, and live life at the pitch of passion;

that was the lesson brought home to Kerouac in the cleansing mountain air of Colorado.

After the opera matinee, Kerouac helped Bob Burford and others stage the first Beat party west of Manhattan, taking over an abandoned Victorian house and inviting everyone in from the street. In a sense, the party that started that night in the Rockies did not stop until Woodstock in 1969, for parties became the Beat Generation's breeding ground for ideas, art movements, and revolutions, eventually blossoming into poetry readings, happenings, demonstrations, and rock concerts. Without this coming together among the young, the culture of the isolated, dug-in middle class would have continued to dominate, and the social changes of the counterculture might never have come about. In Central City, as the East Coast Beats met their Western kinsmen for the first time, a new kind of "manifest destiny" was born. Sammy Sampas had predicted that "a new wind" would shake up the postwar world, and Kerouac felt the first tremors in the Rockies. He and his friends were an unstoppable subterranean force, "a wild yea-saying overburst of American joy; it was Western, the west wind, an ode from the Plains, something new, long prophesied, long a-coming." Without this vital infusion of Western energy, the Beat movement would probably have died out in the 1940s. For both Kerouac and Ginsberg, passion and partying laid the foundation for a burgeoning literary and social movement.[7] The essential characteristics of the new, post–East Coast Beat movement were unashamed sexuality, a growing sense of community and good fellowship, and a spirit of westering and renewal. As Kerouac wrote, he had truly crossed "the dividing line between the East of my youth and the West of my future."

Shortly after the festival, Kerouac left Denver and pressed on for California. As O. Henry once wrote, "East is East, and West is San Francisco." Kerouac was ineluctably drawn to the great capital on the Pacific, though California in the forties was still a national laughingstock: home of the movies, mind control, and high colonics. "There's no there out there," quipped Dorothy Parker, but westering has always run in the blood of Americans, whose ancestors broke away from the security of New England and the verdant piedmont of the Eastern states and crossed the Appalachians, the Rockies, and the High Sierras in three-mile-long caravans. "Bring me men to match my mountains . . . men with . . . new eras in their brains," wrote Sam Foss, whose words are inscribed on the state capital at Sacramento, and in 1947 Kerouac, an aimless drifter, yielded to some vague evolutionary imperative to lead a new Western migration. While the thrust of American life in 1947 was to organize and control the human spirit, Kerouac would attempt to unleash its anarchic energies. After the collapse of the New Vision–East Coast estheticism represented by Carr, Burroughs, and Ginsberg, Kerouac looked to the West for ideas and inspiration.

Many people believe that California's pioneering in the liberated manners and morals of the second half of the twentieth century commenced with Kerouac's arrival in San Francisco on August 10, 1947. Completing his

3,200-mile cross-country trip, he climbed off a bus at Market and Fourth, looking "like a haggard ghost," he wrote, but he perhaps better resembled Lenin at the Finland Station, as this moment represented the start of the Beat Generation's takeover of California. "There she was, Frisco," he wrote in *On the Road*, "long, bleak streets with trolley wires all shrouded in fog and whiteness." His relationship with the city that would eventually become the Beat mecca was not a matter of love at first sight. After two weeks, he dismissed San Francisco in a letter to Neal as "boring" and vastly inferior to Los Angeles and Denver. A few areas appealed because they reminded him of New York; Turk, Fillmore, Jones, Geary, and Howard were "very Greenwich Villagey," he wrote.

Kerouac's aggravation with San Francisco of course had nothing to do with the city and everything to do with his disappointment over Neal's failure to join him there. Though in Denver he'd learned to respect Ginsberg's honest expression of sexual passion, Kerouac grew bitter and jealous of Neal and Allen's intimacy. On August 26, after settling in Marin City, a suburb of San Francisco, he wrote Neal that, while he did not condemn Neal's "rapport" with Ginsberg, he felt excluded and bewildered by the affectionate language they used. Kerouac was still hoping against hope that the busy, emotionally overextended Neal would come to San Francisco, but as time passed it became clear that Neal was more interested in cultivating Carolyn and Allen. Kerouac's correspondence reveals the enormity of the role Neal was already playing in Kerouac's artistic development; he complained that without Neal at his side, he had no one to "feed" him new ideas or open him to new ways of thinking and perceiving.

Sausalito, a village just over the Golden Gate Bridge, was still a quaint backwater populated by a few fishermen when Kerouac settled there in 1947, and Mill Valley was little more than a cluster of quonset huts thrown up during the war for shipyard laborers. California's incomparable beauty and fascination would captivate Kerouac later on, but not on September 25, when he wrote Nin that "California stinks." On trips to the city, he scoffed at natives who attempted to emulate New York chic, like the Nob Hill women who wore fur coats in seventy-degree weather. They were nothing but pretentious, transplanted "Okies," he wrote. Superficial and devoid of Southern soul, the East's tragic sense, and the vitality of the Midwest, San Francisco had "nothing," he concluded, expressing a negativity about Baghdad by the Bay that would later give way to paeanistic perorations in *The Dharma Bums*, *The Subterraneans*, and *Big Sur*.[8]

In late August, Kerouac wrote Ginsberg and critiqued his poem, "Last Stanzas in Denver," which included the phrase, "Sad paradise." Jack misread it as "Sal Paradise," and later used it as his nom de plume in *On the Road*. Allen complained about the disrespect he'd been shown in Denver by Hal, Ed, and another Columbia student, Alan Temko, but Jack urged him to be Christlike and forgive all. In a letter to Neal, Jack observed that Hal, Ed, and Temko might possess the patina of intelligence conferred by college degrees, but only Neal had true wisdom, and he advised Neal to look to Burroughs for intellectual refinement though never for insight, which Neal possessed in greater measure than Burroughs could ever hope for.[9]

Predictably, Henri Cru hadn't lined up the promised merchant-seaman jobs, but he managed to get Jack hired as a security officer with Morrisson and Knudsen, Cru's employer in Marin City. Boasting that he was now a full-fledged member of the Sausalito Police Department, Jack wrote Neal that he was guarding a barracks housing construction workers being trained for jobs in the South Pacific. Although the pay was modest, he managed to send most of it to his mother, displaying a sense of decency for which the twenty-five-year-old Kerouac is rarely credited, though it required considerable sacrifice. He economized by bunking with Cru, sleeping in the same room with Cru and his attractive but shrewish girlfriend. In the circumstances, Jack was unable to work on *The Town and the City*, but he amused himself by adopting five cats, including three new kittens, and made them a cozy box, which he tucked in a hole in the floor. Animals never disappointed him the way people had, and in California he began to take out his spite on anyone unfortunate enough to cross his path. Because of his security job, he was armed with a .32 automatic, and he used it to scare girls along the Embarcadero, coming on like a Mafia hit man. Stumbling out of a bar into the fog one night, he drew his gun on a gay man and snarled that he was Nanny-Beater Kelly from Chicago. He confessed to Neal that he was acting like a lunatic.[10]

Trying his hand at movie scripting, he completed a forty-thousand-word scenario in six days, but the narrative muscle and snappy repartee required by films were not his strength, and his powers of description counted for little in Hollywood. His depression deepened when he learned that Neal was hitchhiking to Burroughs's farm in Texas with Ginsberg. Angry and envious, he denounced Neal and Allen's affair as "obnoxious" in a letter to Allen, but grew deferential when addressing Neal. One should strive to make life passionate and full, he wrote, but confessed that he could no longer make out with girls. On September 13, his luck changed; two girls were clamoring for him "to fuck them," but he couldn't be bothered. He was pursuing a ravishing girl named Odessa while simultaneously trying "to bang" her roommate. Then there was a petite girl from Seattle who would make a perfect wife, but he only wanted to "father" her. More stimulating was a rowing expedition in San Francisco Bay during which he was able to inspect the nude body of Cru's girl, Dianne. He'd been wondering whether she was a natural or bleached blonde, and now he knew: she was blond all over.[11]

He longed to be with Neal in Texas, but Neal told him there wouldn't be room in the jeep when he and Burroughs drove to New York in the fall with the marijuana harvest. Neal and Allen had arrived at Burroughs's ramshackle house on August 30, 1947, their relationship in ruins due to Neal's compulsive gender jumping. When Ginsberg finally nagged Cassady into giving him a "mercy fuck," the bed that Huncke rigged up for them collapsed, and they fell on the floor among scorpions. In "Hicksville," as Burroughs referred to New Waverly, Texas, Burroughs was doing three shots of heroin a day, and Joan was perpetually wired on Benzedrine. Huncke's legs were covered with boils, and his body was full of holes from repeated jabbing with heroin needles. Little Julie was now four years old and had a disturbing habit of gnawing her arm, which was covered with scars. No one bathed her, and Joan permitted the child to defecate in the Revere-Ware, the same pots she used for cooking. On July 21, Joan gave birth to William Seward Burroughs III in nearby Conroe, while still doing two inhalers of Benzedrine daily. She'd made no effort to kick during her pregnancy, and as a result the infant suffered from drug-withdrawal symptoms at birth and cried constantly.

The scene at the farm sounded repulsive to Carolyn, who had moved from Denver to San Francisco, where she was receiving ardent love letters from Neal. Brokenhearted, Ginsberg signed on a merchant ship at the port of Houston and shipped out for Africa. In Dakar, Senegal, he wrote "Dakar Doldrums," a sequel to his "Denver Doldrums." He was close to a nervous breakdown, and all that kept him going was Neal's vague promise that they'd reunite in New York later in the fall, but Kerouac was counting on similar assurances, as was Carolyn. At this point, Neal was calling the emotional shots in all their lives, which meant that they were at the mercy of "a psychopath" according to Holmes, who added that Neal "acted out everything that occurred to him" and never failed to seduce anyone he desired.[12]

Kerouac had a bad case of what he later called the San Francisco blues, and to be depressed in San Francisco was to be "bluer than eternity." On September 13, 1947, he wrote Neal that he was looking forward to their future life together, and he started his long trip home. On a bus to Los Angeles he fell in love with the girl across the aisle, a Mexican grape-picker named Bea Franco, whose eyes were "great big blue things with timidities inside." Slim-hipped, fragile, four-foot-ten Bea would later lend a rare grace to her scenes in On the Road. Though Kerouac required plenty of whiskey to do so, he seemed to be thoroughly comfortable with a woman for the first time, and drifted around the San Joachim Valley with Bea and her migrant-worker family for a couple of weeks. Supposedly they were job-hunting, but Jack agreed with Bea's brother, who said, "Today we drink, tomorrow we work." After picking cotton for $1.50 a day, Jack realized that he had not been in love after all and had only been playing at being a Chicano field hand in order to collect material for his writings.[13]

When his money ran out, he hitchhiked back to New York, and at last set foot on the familiar turf of Times Square, having racked up eight thousand miles since July. It was rush hour in Manhattan, and he saw New York as never before, through "innocent road eyes." The city no longer made sense to him; after the freedom he'd experienced and the adventures he'd had, he could only wonder why millions of people, trapped in artificial canyons, would battle each other for money, only to end up under a maze of tombstones, packed like sardines in outer-borough cemeteries. Later, at home in Queens, Gabrielle shook her head and told him how thin he looked. She had saved all the money he'd sent, and at last they were able to purchase an electric refrigerator, the first his family had ever owned. Neal had shown up on her doorstep, looking for Jack, and she'd put him up for a few nights, but he'd already left for California. Neal and Burroughs had sold a jeepful of marijuana, but it was green and uncured, and fetched only one hundred dollars.

Ginsberg returned from Africa and was as furious as Jack was that Neal had left New York for the West Coast. Though Carolyn appeared to have won Neal—he moved in with her in San Francisco in October—she later acknowledged that Neal was more interested in Allen and that "an accident of gender was all that put me where Allen wanted to be." She wouldn't be there for long. Neal wrote Allen that he'd decided to "break quickly" because Carolyn wanted to get married. He was still married to LuAnne, who had followed him to the coast, and they'd resumed their lovemaking. Feeling jilted, Ginsberg wrote Neal a poignant letter, threatening him and at the same time pleading for restoration of their sex life on any terms, even offering to perform "indecencies." With so many people making demands on him, Neal broke out in a painful case of hives. Hoping not to lose both of his literary friends, he was frantic to make amends with Kerouac and apologized on October 5, 1947, for his "desertion."[14]

Kerouac readily forgave him, largely because the letters Neal sent were full of juicy material. On the strength of Neal and Allen's moral support and Gabrielle's generosity—from her salary at a shoe factory, she kept Kerouac in paper, typewriter ribbons, cigarettes, and booze—Kerouac was able to tell Ginsberg on January 2, 1948, that *The Town and the City* would be finished in six weeks. In his journal, Kerouac added that the manuscript was a "Niagara of a novel," having grown to 280,000 words by the end of 1947, with a projected final length of 333,000 words. (The average published novel runs about 100,000 words.) After Jack typed a section for Neal's perusal, Neal sent back a "measly stupid page," Jack complained to Ginsberg. Neal tried to explain that he was preoccupied with a book of his own, which he was writing in diary form. It was the story of his life, and it did not sound promising. One of Neal's difficulties as a writer was his tendency to set impossible goals. A writer "must combine Wolfe and Flaubert—and Dickens," he wrote, and he might as well have thrown in God and Shakespeare. Though Neal's attempts at formal storytelling were undistinguished, his letters were packed with formulations that would become the bedrock of Kerouac's "spontaneous prose" esthetic. Prose should communicate itself as "a continuous chain of undisciplined thought," Neal wrote, and Kerouac took the theory and ran with it. More than anything else, it was Jack's determination to impress Neal that was responsible for his being able to finish *The Town and the City*.[15]

Jack spent Christmas 1947 in Queens with his mother. He would have a succession of girlfriends in 1948, including one referred to by Lucien's friend Tony Monacchio as "beautiful but dumb." In a letter to Ginsberg, Jack wrote that Lucien had been "dead drunk" at a party at Tony's, and though unable to walk without assistance, Lucien had still managed to look as dapper as Jay Gatsby, weaving around in his brown-and-white saddle shoes. Hal Chase and Jack remained close, and Hal brought his girl, Ginger, to dinner in Ozone Park. Jack later described Ginger, in a letter to Nin, as the kind of girl who'd slip into "ballet shorts" to perform parlor tricks, and he had a fling with her. He was also dallying with Ginsberg; high on Benzedrine, they enjoyed reciprocal sex in Ginsberg's West Twenty-seventh Street apartment. But Kerouac still disapproved of men trying to have a serious love relationship and was astonished, in retrospect, that everyone in their circle had lavished so much attention on Allen and Neal's romance.

Though Ginsberg had lost Neal, their open affair had stripped Ginsberg of his "masks and roles," and he achieved a personal and artistic freedom Jack and Neal would never know. Ironically, as Ginsberg grew stronger in New York, Neal fell apart in California and attempted to commit suicide. In September 1948, Neal was so anxious to get Ginsberg back, even though he and Carolyn now had a baby daughter, Cathleen Joanne, that he offered to support Ginsberg on Carolyn's wages. Begging Ginsberg to have sex with him, he promised to "splatter" Ginsberg with "come." In reply, Ginsberg jokingly asked Neal to send the "come" by return mail. Though no longer susceptible to Neal's wiles, Allen continued to love him and may have been the only one in their crowd to realize that Neal was the unhappiest of them all. Kerouac's conflicted feelings about homoeroticism prevented him from helping Ginsberg and Cassady through their 1947–1948 crisis, even though Ginsberg sent out many urgent cries for help. "Save me," he wrote Jack, but after it was all over, he reflected that no one had been sympathetic or understanding. In human terms, Ginsberg was perhaps the bravest and loneliest of the original Beats.

In April 1948, Jack was coming to the end of two-and-a-half years' work on The Town and the City, through "poverty, disease, and bereavement and madness," he told Ginsberg. From California, Neal requested an autographed copy of Jack's "great . . . tome." Ginsberg went out to Ozone Park to celebrate, and they stayed up two days talking, drinking beer, and reading their latest scenes and poems. Mostly, however, they "mooned" about Neal, according to Allen. Never suspecting what a devastating effect the news would have on Neal, Allen reported that Jack's novel was a masterpiece, one that exceeded his fondest dreams for any of them. Unfortunately, in the same letter, Allen scoffed at Neal's news that he had become a father. Furious, Neal replied that he and Allen were now hopelessly estranged and should cease communicating. Frustrated over his own writing efforts, which he described as "stupid trash," Neal gave up his literary ambitions and took a job as a brakeman on the Southern Pacific Railroad, working a potato local out of Pixley, California.[16]

With The Town and the City nearing completion, Jack began to think of possible editors and publishing houses, and in April 1948, he told Ginsberg that he longed for the same filial affection from his editor that had existed between Thomas Wolfe and his mentor at Charles Scribner's Sons, Maxwell Perkins. What he really wanted was a father, and he already saw Perkins in that role, apparently unaware that Perkins had died the previous year, on June 17, 1947. The enormity of Perkins's editorial contributions to *Look Homeward, Angel* was so well known that obituary writers described him as Wolfe's coauthor. In a May 18, 1948, letter to Ginsberg, Kerouac wrote that he'd submitted the manuscript to Scribner's two weeks earlier. *The Town and the City* received what people in the publishing business call "serious consideration," but the editor returned the manuscript with the observation that the ending was "messed up," and asked that it be revised and strengthened.[17] Kerouac did not yet know that such letters are meaningless unless accompanied by a contract.

In the summer of 1948, as Jack resumed work on the book, he started to meet other promising young writers in New York and to play a role in the city's variegated literary life, a rich mix of uptown intellectuals, midtown publishers, and downtown bohemians. On July 4, he attended a party at Ginsberg's apartment in East Harlem that brought several key figures of the Beat Generation together with some of the peripheral ones. While buying beer at a corner grocery, he ran into Alan Harrington, future author of *The Secret Swinger*, whom Jack referred to as "the faun." He was with an intense, personable young man with chiseled, aristocratic features.

This man was John Clellon Holmes, who would become an important friend in Kerouac's life and a powerful, articulate promoter of the Beat Generation. Only a mediocre novelist, Holmes's works, *Go!*, *The Horn*, and *Get Home Free*, would not be remembered. Holmes's first impression of Kerouac was as a "young John Garfield back in the neighborhood after college." In Holmes's 1952 novel *Go!*, Kerouac would appear as "Gene Pasternak," a young author who lived with his mother while writing a huge "clumsy valentine" of a novel that he already suspected the world was going to reject. Ginsberg appeared as "David Stofsky," a voluble, wild-eyed poet, and Holmes depicted himself as "Paul Hobbes," a tall, angular man with "a strangely unfinished air." Kerouac soon became Holmes's Neal Cassady, providing the more conservative, organized Holmes access to the wildness and inspired disorder of genius, which Holmes himself lacked. More perceptive than Ginsberg about Kerouac's innovative, post–*Town and the City* writings, Holmes replaced Ginsberg as Jack's closest literary ally, and Kerouac soon made Holmes's Lexington Avenue apartment his Manhattan headquarters.

At Ginsberg's soiree, Kerouac and a few friends captured the couch in the living room and became the stars of the party—described in *Go!* as figures of interest, mystery, and physical magnetism—while Ginsberg circulated merrily, like an Elsa Maxwell of the slums. At one point, an arrogant ex-lover of Tennessee Williams's, Bill Cannastra, started poking fun at one of the guests, but Ginsberg, a peacemaker even then, soothed everyone's feelings and called himself a wet-nurse to the Beat prima donnas. After the party, Kerouac went home with a girl who resembled the quintessential "beat chick" in Jules Feiffer's *Village Voice* cartoon strip or Gittel Mosca in William Gibson's *Two for the Seesaw*. As characterized later in *Go!*, Jack's date was slightly frantic and denounced "the corruption, depravity and general neuroticism of modern life." Though she stripped to her garter belt and performed an exotic dance for Jack, she announced that she was a virgin. Then she performed fellatio on him, but confessed she felt remarkably little, and Jack decided she must be a lesbian.[18]

At some point in the publishing saga of *The Town and the City*, Jack's former Columbia teacher Mark Van Doren became a key player. After Ginsberg touted the book as the Great American Novel, Van Doren urged Alfred Kazin, then a scout for Harcourt, Brace, to grant Kerouac an interview. It was scheduled, but at the last minute Jack had to cancel to escort his mother to Rocky Mount, where Nin had prematurely given birth to a son. Gabrielle remained with Nin to help care for the baby, and Jack returned to Ozone Park. An editor friend named Ed Stringham arranged for Jack to meet the editor-in-chief of Random House, but nothing came of this, and on June 27 he wrote Neal that Kazin had promised to read *The Town and the City* during the summer. If Kazin liked the manuscript and recommended it to a publisher, Jack could expect a two-thousand-dollar contract "on the spot," Ginsberg predicted.

Jack's hopes and projections began to soar, and he told a Lowell friend, Mike Fournier, that he was going to buy a ranch in the far West, stock it with three hundred head of cattle, and build two houses, one for himself and one for Mike. He was scouting for a partner and knew that Mike was a good outdoorsman and mechanic. Kerouac also sounded out Neal, explaining that he'd shortly be rich since his novel had "everything" from sex to suicide. After the success of *The Town and the City*, Hollywood would shower him with money to write starring vehicles for Lana Turner, and he'd be able to build a ranch house large enough for twenty people. To assuage Jack's horror of being alone, Neal and his family would come to live with Jack and his mother. If Jack and Neal grew bored with country life, they could roam the world and leave the womenfolk to run the ranch. After all, he added, he and Neal were the "two most important" authors in the United States.

When Neal and Carolyn read Jack's letter in San Francisco, they leapt at the ranch idea. Neal insisted that Ginsberg be included, since Ginsberg would do the "grubbing, scrubbing," and he proposed other communards, including Holmes, Huncke, and Burroughs. In the following weeks, Neal solicited government bureaus for pamphlets on ranching, water rights, and land permits. "I encouraged him for all I was worth," recalled Carolyn, who saw the commune as a chance for Neal to invest in property, rather than splurge on cars and drugs. Unlike the men, she was realistic enough to foresee conflict in Eden—wouldn't there be clashing egos among the communards? Completely misunderstanding, Jack blamed "female incompatibility" and condescendingly offered to help Carolyn transcend the "cattiness" endemic to womankind. He and Neal would permit the women to embrace one another "perversely," and presumably the men would do the same. Jack volunteered his mother's services as an all-around workhorse and earmarked one of the houses especially for his relatives. The other house would be for the hip contingent: the Cassadys plus Kerouac and his wife, who so far existed only in theory. Jack described his ideal spouse to Neal as an uninhibited party girl who would cheerfully clean the ranch house and cook for an endless stream of drop-ins and drifters.

Throughout the summer of 1948, Kerouac and the Cassadys continued to fantasize about a bucolic life in some sylvan refuge like Mendocino County or Muir Woods in Marin County, where Kerouac had seen cattle grazing not far from Stinson Beach. Though naive, chauvinistic, and impractical, Kerouac's dream ranch, as outlined in his letters to Neal and Carolyn, was an expression of the Beats' need for a new vision of human experience, one based on community, freedom, spontaneity, and love. In the same tradition of American idealism as Brook Farm and Sammy Sampas's Young Promethean paradise, Kerouac's utopian ranch also looked to the future, presaging the commune movement of the sixties. In 1970, twenty-two years after Kerouac conceived the first rural Beat commune, Yale law professor Charles A. Reich wrote in *The Greening of America*, "This is the revolution of the new generation. . . . Its ultimate creation will be a new and enduring wholeness and beauty—a renewed relationship of man to himself, to other men, to society, to nature, and to the land."

The Town and the City was still without a publishing contract, but on October 19, Jack wrote Hal that Kazin was at last reading the manuscript and would get it to editors at Random House, Knopf, Houghton Mifflin, and Little, Brown.[19] Kerouac's paranoia about publishers began during this period of struggle and disappointment over his first novel. He revealed in a letter to Neal that he feared the commercialism of the marketplace and the envy and resentment of literary professionals, whom he identified as critics and book editors. Like almost all writers, he loved editors and reviewers when they praised him, and hated them when they ignored him. When he finished revising the ending of *The Town and the City* for Scribner's, he resubmitted it, but the book was rejected in December 1948 despite Kazin's endorsement, and Kerouac was thrown into a depression for three days. "The bastards!" he said, according to Holmes. "After almost two months, they send it back with a rejection slip about paper costs and the risks of first novels! What do I care about all that!" On December 8, Kerouac wrote Neal that Little, Brown had declined *The Town and the City*, citing excessive length and prohibitive manufacturing costs. Little, Brown's rejection letter included high praise for his writing ability, but left him cursing editors and publishers as "cocksucking bastards" and accusing them of having "sheep's brains." One day, he predicted, they'd "come bleating" for him.[20]

Though Kerouac kept trying to sell *The Town and the City*, he realized it might take years, and his interests shifted elsewhere. During the fall he hitchhiked to Nin's house in Rocky Mount, where he hoped to earn two hundred dollars working at his brother-in-law's parking lot for the county fair, but heavy rains turned the lot into a huge mud puddle. Kerouac became infatuated with a nurse, referred to only as Ann B. in an October 3, 1948 letter to Neal. Though usually demure, Ann became "a shuddering cannon-ball" when Jack held her on the couch, and he wanted to seduce her but felt unworthy—she was a wholesome girl, and he was nothing but a lush and a freeloader. Besides, Ann was more attracted to a young doctor. Just as he'd once said he both loved Mary Carney and wanted to spit in her face, he told Neal that he wanted to marry Ann B., but then added, "I hate her." His letter at last took flight when he expressed his feelings for Neal, and he became so affectionate that he had to apologize for his "queerness" and for sounding so "sissy."

In a stunning confession, Kerouac told Neal that he was afraid his future biographers would one day come across the letter and use it as evidence that he was gay. For the benefit of posterity, he then went on to explain his position on homosexuality, defining it as hatred rather than love. His reasoning was that the penis had been created to fill the "void—(cunt)," and therefore no man could want another's penis "without envy." Suddenly recognizing the egregiousness of these remarks, he apologized to Neal, admitting that he'd made them so that students studying his novels in the future wouldn't be "disillusioned." The prospect of being pitied as a homosexual "goat" filled him with horror. The letter reveals Kerouac's constant fear of being thought gay, as well as his awareness that his passion for Neal was a dead giveaway. He was too intelligent not to recognize the baseness of his prejudices, and at such moments he resembled a Janus-like creature with a face looking two ways, spouting wrongheaded ideas and apologizing for them in the same breath.

In the end, Kerouac cannot be defined by his beliefs and prejudices any more than he can by his sexuality or even by his violent behavior. People are more than what they do and say. T. S. Eliot once wrote that Henry James had "a mind so fine that no idea could violate it." Kerouac did not have such a mind, but he did have such a heart, and its beauty and goodness are evident from the opening pages of *The Town and the City*, in which the Martin family, based on the Kerouacs and the Sampases, awaken to another day in the universe and create a kind of heaven on earth through love. Ken Kesey recognized this quality in Kerouac years later, defining it as "that rare warm glory that shines out of only the best efforts of the greatest artists . . . the light that uplifts and exhorts, that reveals us to each other as the glorious marvels we are."[21]

Returning to New York in October 1948, he enrolled at a popular adult-education college in Greenwich Village, the New School for Social Research, using his GI bill benefits. One night, he attended a folk dance at the school and wore his black leather jacket, plaid shirt, and blue jeans. Across the crowded dance floor, he spotted a dark and exotic girl — exactly his type. She was sitting alone at a corner table, drinking a Coke and apparently waiting for someone to ask her to dance.

"I just came in," he said, executing a courtly bow. "I saw you, and I wanted to get to you before anyone else did."

Nineteen-year-old Adele Morales, the future wife of Norman Mailer, regarded him with interest and decided he was precisely the kind of ex-GI she'd been looking for. "He could have been a movie star," she recalled in 1997, "solid with a strong body and good shoulders, even features, black hair and grey [sic] eyes and a beautifully shaped mouth." Jack swept her out of her chair, let out a rebel yell, and led her through a furious polka. He didn't introduce himself until after the dance, when he suggested they find a secluded spot.

"Adele's my name, and I feel the same," she said.

Clearly, she was a poet, he joked — her feet were long fellows. Charmed, she went with him to the San Remo on MacDougal Street, where he ordered a draft beer, bought her a Coke, and then embarrassed her by drumming on the tabletop with spoons and jumping up to improvise a jig. Finishing his beer, he ordered another, but ignored her empty Coke glass. "He's cheap," she thought, and she was even more vexed when he started scribbling in a notebook rather than paying attention to her.

"I'm a damn good writer," he explained.

When Adele told him she was half Spanish and half Peruvian Indian, he immediately became more attentive. Though she was ready for him to kiss her, all she received was a compliment: She looked like "an exotic tropical flower," he said. Flattered, she began to tell him about herself. She lived in Brooklyn and was studying painting, but she'd come to the New School primarily to meet men and dabble in esoteric "fun" courses such as Margaret Mead's anthropology class. Quickly switching the subject back to himself, Jack told her about his complicity in Lucien's crime, which made him seem glamorous to her. Then he began to talk about his mother, using terms that struck Adele as strangely romantic. Later, accompanying her home on the Sea Beach Express, he became excited when the train crossed over a bridge. "He jumped out of his seat," Adele recalled. "Jack never rose from a sitting position as much as he goosed himself into the air." Then, to the other passengers' consternation, he began to run up and down the aisle. Though she thought him odd, she later liked the way he kissed her good night, and she longed to see him again. "Adele was gorgeous," recalled novelist Barbara Probst Solomon. "She had a fire, a sexual kind of heat."

On one of their dates, Jack took Adele to a lecture at the New School. Afterward, he handed her the manuscript of *The Town and the City* and told her she was the first woman he'd asked to read it. Her mother perused it before Adele and announced, "He ain't no Dickens." Adele would have been well advised to tell her mother she wasn't a literary critic, but instead, on their next date, she informed Jack that his novel was boring. "Fuck you," he said, slamming down his beer so hard that he broke the handle off the mug. "You're a sore loser," she observed. "And you're a bitch," he said, grabbing his manuscript and walking out of the San Remo without paying the check. He didn't call her again for two years.[22]

Kerouac's studies at the New School included a course in the twentieth-century American novel with Elbert Lenrow as well as a creative writing class with Brom Weber. He also monitored Kazin's course in classic American writers. Kerouac had once denounced Kazin as a failed fiction writer, but now that he was counting on Kazin to get him published, he inundated the critic with fulsome compliments. In one letter, he wrote that Kazin was really more creative than critical, and he praised Kazin's lectures on Emerson and Thoreau, comparing them with sublime jazz riffs. In Weber's class, which was also attended by future *Godfather* author Mario Puzo, Jack began the first version of *On the Road*, but received little encouragement.[23] He probably would have given it up had Neal Cassady not suggested some vital field research.

In a December 8, 1948, letter to Neal, Jack demanded an instant response to his suggestion that he and Neal live and work together, regardless of Neal's obligations as a husband and father. Electrified by Jack's proposal, Neal decided to leave his wife and infant daughter, buy a new car, and drive east to be with Jack. According to Carolyn, Neal spent their life savings on a new 1949 Hudson Hornet sedan, and when she realized that he intended to leave her destitute, with no money even for baby food, she exploded. "I promised Jack," Neal sputtered, trying to explain his abrupt departure, but Carolyn said, "You mean to tell me it's more important to you to keep a promise to Jack than to your family? . . . Get out!" She suspected, rightly, that Neal was going through Denver to see LuAnne, to whom he was still sexually attracted. Just two weeks before Christmas, Neal abandoned Carolyn and Cathy and left to get Jack and LuAnne, explaining to Carolyn, "I'll be right back, just as quick as I can make it, baby." He was lying, as Kerouac's *Selected Letters* revealed in 1995. In a December 15, 1948, letter to Ginsberg, Kerouac wrote that Neal planned to spend a whole year with him in Arizona.[24]

Neal asked Jack for a ten-dollar loan to pacify someone to whom he owed two hundred dollars, as well as for funds for Carolyn and the baby to survive on. Jack agreed to send fifty dollars, but forwarded only ten, and Neal had to resort to desperate measures to raise gas money for the trip. He persuaded his friend Al Hinkle to marry a girl named Helen, whom they permitted to come along provided she'd pay everyone's expenses. "Helen is loaded," Neal told Carolyn. "It's a free ride, don't you see?" The fourth passenger in the Hornet was a hapless sailor who paid twenty-five dollars for a ride to Kansas, but who was summarily dumped in New Mexico.

In New York, while Jack waited for Neal to arrive, he spent time with a new girlfriend, Pauline. She had a "glorious body," Jack later told Neal, but her marriage to a truck driver had gone on the rocks because he was too staid to insert his fingers in her vagina. Eager to fix Neal up with a girl, Jack wrote Allen that he wanted Adele Morales for Neal. He was so excited about seeing Neal again that he completely lost interest in *The Town and the City*. John Clellon Holmes urged him to forget about Scribner's rejection and to keep the manuscript in circulation. "Just because a few editors can't seem to understand a really honest book, don't you lose faith in it," Holmes advised. Jack replied, "I really don't care about it any more," and added that he preferred Neal and the open road to elegant gays and Manhattan drawing rooms, but ideally he'd like to live in both worlds.[25]

Meanwhile, Neal was tearing across the continent at ninety miles per hour in what was left of the battered Hudson Hornet. Helen Hinkle was trying to enjoy her honeymoon with Al, but every time they made love, her diaphragm popped out—"a bad omen," she later confided to Carolyn. According to Neal's biographer William Plummer, after Helen spent all her money on gas, Al and Neal abandoned her in Tucson and headed north for Denver. By Helen's own account, however, she chose to bail out because Neal's daredevil driving left no time for pit stops despite nature's calls. They all arranged to meet later in New Orleans at Burroughs's home, and Helen proceeded to Louisiana on her own. Somewhere in New Mexico, Neal detoured to Denver, where he courted LuAnne, calling her "honeycunt," and then had sex with her for ten hours, concluding that he preferred her to Carolyn. He rang Jack long distance, but Gabrielle picked up the phone in Queens and cleverly extracted a promise from Neal to drive first to North Carolina. She and Jack planned to spend Christmas with Nin, and in order to save expensive train fares she wanted Neal to bring them back to New York before Jack and Neal went on the road. Neal agreed and said he'd be arriving around December 29.[26]

Laden with presents from New York, Jack and his mother shortly arrived at Nin's home for the 1948 holiday season. The little house at 1328 Tarboro Street, across a boulevard from a movie theater and a mall, later figured in both *On the Road* and *Visions of Cody*. It was going to be a perfect family Christmas, frosty and white, with snow steadily sifting through the Carolina evergreens. Nin's cozy parlor was warmed by an oil-burning stove, and her new furniture was upholstered in white cloth with red pinstripes. According to Nin's neighbor Helen Bone, the decor was "nice, real cute, just like her personality." Paul Blake Jr., Nin's baby son, started calling Gabrielle "Mémère," a diminutive of *grand-mère*, meaning "grandma" in her native Quebecois tongue. Soon everyone was calling her Mémère, and the name Gabrielle was virtually discarded.

Another neighbor, Sarah Langley, recalled that Mémère told everyone Jack was " 'going to be famous one day,' but we thought that was typical mother's love talking and didn't pay too much attention." Both Helen Bone and Sarah Langley admired Nin, calling her a cheery, happy-go-lucky woman, but Jack struck them as being different in every way. He seemed to be one of the few persons, even in the Carolina backwoods, to wear blue jeans in the 1940s; until Kerouac came along, Mrs. Bone had only seen field-workers in jeans. One day, Helen Bone asked Jack if he smoked. Smoked *what*, he asked. He wouldn't touch the kind of weed that the locals rolled, he said, referring to North Carolina's famous tobacco crop and implying he preferred pot. In fact, Kerouac smoked both tobacco and marijuana, and in one photograph, a pack of Pall Malls can be seen through his shirt pocket.

"Jack and Paul never got along and this really bothered Nin and Gabe," wrote John Dorfner, who interviewed Sarah Langley. "Kerouac would stay up all night writing and Paul would get very upset because the typewriter would keep him awake. It kind of vibrated through the walls of the house." But all differences were forgotten on Christmas Day, and Kerouac was delighted with Nin and Paul's present, a rolltop desk that he would use for some years. As he sat listening to his brother-in-law's Southern relatives exchange family gossip, Neal pulled up in the mud-spattered Hudson Hornet. Staggering from the car, Neal said he was "dog-tired" and ran for the bathroom. Jack went outside and peered through the car's slimy, opaque windshield at its withered occupants. LuAnne and Al Hinkle had been subsisting on rotting potatoes, and they had made it to Rocky Mount only because Neal knew how to run gas pumps back to zero. Though their appearance caused Nin's in-laws to raise their eyebrows, Neal quickly ingratiated himself with Mémère by offering to haul a load of old furniture that Nin had given her.[27]

In a matter of days, Jack and Neal made two trips of a thousand miles each from North Carolina to New York, braving winter storms while Neal drove seventy miles per hour and talked a blue streak. On the first trip, they deposited Hinkle and LuAnne in Mémère's apartment in Queens and returned to North Carolina for Mémère and the furniture. As they balled up and down the highways between Rocky Mount and Ozone Park, Neal gave Jack the answer he'd been seeking; he became the first person to tell Kerouac that the linear thinking of the West was a trap. "This is what *it's* about, man," Neal said, sticking his finger into his wadded fist, like a penis going into a vagina or an anus—the ultimate symbol of unity.

Though it was the dawn of the age of *The Man in the Gray Flannel Suit*, when financial success and social status were venerated above all else even if they meant "selling out," Neal suggested that salvation could be found only in *it*, by which he meant sex, jazz, drugs, and cars. Kerouac would later dismiss Neal's *it* philosophy as sheer vanity, but he embraced it at the time, having written Neal earlier that month that sexual gratification was "the basis of life." Mémère disagreed, and tartly observed that it was too bad Neal couldn't fit his wife and child into "*it*." As Carolyn Cassady revealed in her 1990 memoir, *Off the Road*, she had to apply for welfare when Neal deserted her and their four-month-old daughter. At one point, in a Medea-like moment of despair, Carolyn wished both herself and the baby dead. Unable to meet the rent, she packed up, moved to cheaper quarters near the Mission

Dolores, and borrowed money from her sister. "I was once again facing life alone," she resignedly wrote.[28]

On New Year's Eve, Mémêre stayed in Queens and listened to Guy Lombardo's broadcast from the Roosevelt Grill, while Jack and his friends went into Manhattan for a round of parties. Jack brought Pauline, but became more interested in LuAnne by the time they all attended a party in a basement apartment in the West Nineties. Watching Jack and LuAnne jealously, Neal and Pauline took revenge by going out to the Hudson and smooching. Jack's feelings were mixed: he was glad to be rid of Pauline, fearing she'd leave her husband and expect him to marry her, but his masculine vanity was affronted. He decided to get even with Neal by seducing LuAnne, but he was too drunk to maneuver her into the subbasement, where other couples were already making out in alcoves near the furnace. Presently, Neal came back from the car fired with energy, and darted from group to group, crouching like Groucho Marx. Lucien arrived and seemed resentful of Neal's hold on Jack, while Neal regarded Lucien as a square refugee from the Madison Avenue rat race, a throwback to the past. But Jack idolized both of them, Neal as his "blood brother" and Lucien as his "laird." According to Road, the laird had to be carried home after his girl decked him with "a roundhouse right."

Toward dawn, those who could still walk made their way to Holmes's apartment and continued to party through the first hours of January 1, 1949. When the West End Bar closed that morning, most of the customers drifted downtown and joined them. Dancing with LuAnne, Jack twirled her through a succession of daring gymnastic moves. Neal, who had stripped off his shirt, undershirt, shoes, and socks, got the next dance with LuAnne, which Holmes later described in Go!: "He gripped her hips with large hands and moved her to him and away as though he had tapped a world of grace and abandon inside her and could direct it at will. . . . The room's attention pivoted to them." Neal, who appeared as the character "Hart Kennedy" in Go!, inspired the title because he was always yelling, "Go! Go!" at jam sessions. He asked Holmes to lend him ten dollars, and Kerouac promised they'd repay it out of Mémêre's next paycheck.

In the first days of the new year, Neal remained broke and adrift in Manhattan. During an argument over his infidelities, he decked LuAnne, he told Ginsberg, with "a left thumb to the forehead." The blow fractured four bones at the base of his thumb, but did no damage, he later told Carolyn, to "that thick-skulled bitch." Later, Neal's injury was diagnosed as Bennets Fracture, and three settings were required over an agonizing period of twenty-one hours "on hard benches." Ultimately, Neal underwent an operation during which a doctor hammered a steel pin under his thumbnail to provide enough traction to prevent deformity. In a cast for a month, he developed osteomyelitis, and eventually his thumb had to be amputated at the first joint.

In January 1949, in their last days in New York, they were all at each other's throats in Ginsberg's apartment. As Ginsberg saw it, the main problem was Neal and LuAnne's "ill-starred obsession with one another . . . their secret lovelessness."[29]

One day Burroughs called from New Orleans, wondering when they were going to take Helen Hinkle off his hands and complaining that he wasn't running a hotel. On January 19, Jack, Neal, LuAnne, and Al Hinkle left New York in the Hudson, bound for New Orleans. They passed through Washington, D.C., just in time to see President Harry Truman's inauguration in front of the Capitol. In one of the first speeches of the cold war, Truman denounced Soviet aggression, and offered aid to foreign nations caught in the new struggle between totalitarianism and freedom.

The Beats pressed on to New Orleans, strangely happy in a nation gripped by terror. At Burroughs's house in Algiers, Helen Hinkle angrily confronted Al, who took her to the bedroom and made love to her. As Helen later recalled, one of the other women "comes in and asks if she can watch us screw," but Helen recoiled and thought, "Euuck." Outside in the yard, Burroughs and Kerouac were playing with Burroughs's guns, trying to outdraw each other. Burroughs was injecting morphine three times a day, while Joan, in a Benzedrine frenzy, performed pointless chores, like sweeping lizards off a tree. Neal later portrayed Joan's attitude as one of "blasé brittleness" but said nothing about about Bill's culpability in letting the children run around the weed-filled yard naked and defecate on the linoleum floor, which Joan had to scrub nightly with Lysol. Julie's hair was so filthy that it was "matted with dirt," Neal added in a letter to Ginsberg. Burroughs refused to lend money to Neal and warned Jack that he'd never make it to California alive, traveling with such a psychopath. But Jack set out for San Francisco with Neal and LuAnne, leaving the Hinkles behind in New Orleans where they'd decided to look for jobs.

In Texas, near Ozona, Neal shed his clothes and went romping in the dusk through sagebrush and tumbleweeds. "Neal did have a beautiful body," LuAnne recalled, adding, "we were all cavorting naked." Climbing back in the car, Neal insisted they remain unclothed and placed LuAnne between them in the front seat. LuAnne was "blushing, laughing," Kerouac recalled, "but just as composed as Queen Elizabeth, her pendant breasts full, round, soft and real in the light." As they drove across the Texas wilderness to Fort Stockton, LuAnne made love to both of them with her hands, caressing Jack's testicles. According to Kerouac, she used cold cream, but LuAnne later told interviewers, "I would have loved to have had . . . any kind of cream." She often guided the car while Neal fondled her with his one good hand, and motorists in the opposite lane gaped and swerved. In *Cody*, Kerouac celebrated LuAnne "with her yellow cunt in the sun, the first warm sun (approaching by the hour red old El Paso in the Sunset) since the blackened snows of New York winter, her squishy delicious cunt, wow, that Cody repeatedly penetrated and lubricated with his finger as he drove on." In El Paso, they went to the bus station, hoping to hustle gas money out of waiting passengers, but no one was around. Neal went off in the darkness with an ex-con, who said, "Let's mash somebody on the head and take his money." While they were gone, LuAnne continued to fondle Jack's testicles, while his palm inched up the inside of her thigh. Finally, Neal returned with enough money to get them to Tucson. There, broke and hungry, they stopped to visit the novelist Alan Harrington, who staked them to five dollars.[30]

Both Jack and LuAnne were completely in Neal's power, ready to devote the rest of their lives to him, but as soon as they reached San Francisco, Neal abruptly abandoned them in the middle of O'Farrell Street and went home to Carolyn. Watching him drive away, Jack called Neal a "bastard" and realized that Neal would always desert him any time it was expeditious for him to do so. Though broke, Jack and LuAnne checked into a fleabag hotel on O'Farrell and charmed the affable deskman into letting them pay at the end of the week. In their room, they went to bed and lay in each other's arms, remaining fully dressed. As a neon sign flashed outside the window, Jack told LuAnne the story of his novel-in-progress, *Dr. Sax*. For a few days, she kept them going on handouts from friends in tenderloin flophouses, but she didn't want to support Jack, despite finding him "extremely lovable and beautiful." In their crisis, he was as useless as a child crying for his mother. She decided to go back to a former fiancé and left Jack on the streets, starving and picking up cigarette butts. In one of the most beautiful and visionary passages in *On the Road*, Kerouac described a hallucination in which he saw an old woman who was his mother centuries ago. She scolded him for being so shiftless, and suddenly Kerouac felt himself at a strange, ecstatic threshold "where all the angels dove off and flew into the holy void of uncreated emptiness . . . innumerable lotus-lands falling open in the magic mothswarm of heaven." Somehow he knew that he and his mother had been struggling together through countless incarnations.[31]

Neal went crawling to Carolyn. "Surely Jack had some plan when he sent for you," she said. Neal promised that Jack would never come between them again, but as soon as Carolyn refused to lend him money, he left her and went looking for Jack, who had said he could get Mémère to wire emergency funds. Jack and Neal bought groceries, including baby food, and went home to Carolyn. She accepted the situation until she realized that Jack and Neal's intimacy excluded her. Aware of Carolyn's growing jealousy, Jack decided to return to New York and prepared a sackful of sandwiches to take along with him on the bus. Neal, whom Carolyn again kicked out when she discovered he was still seeing LuAnne, drove Jack to the station. Broke and hungry, Neal begged Jack for one of his sandwiches, but Jack refused, still angry that Neal had abandoned him on O'Farrell. In *On the Road*, Jack wrote that his ten sandwiches rotted before he got to the Dakotas, but he later told Ginsberg that there were fifteen sandwiches, only ten of which he ate before they spoiled. The gossipy Ginsberg then wrote Neal that Jack could easily have afforded to give him the five sandwiches that went bad. What Ginsberg didn't understand was how deeply

Neal had wounded Jack. As his bus pulled out of San Francisco, Jack didn't care if he ever saw Neal again.[32]

Despite ending in gloom and resentment, Jack and Neal's first trip together provided more than enough material for the first 178 pages of *On the Road*. Though Neal could not give him the love he wanted, he at least gave him a best-seller, and immortality.

FIVE

SUCKING ASSES TO GET PUBLISHED

His adventures with Neal released a flow of creative ideas in Kerouac, and as soon as he got back to New York in early 1949, he resumed work on *On the Road* as well as on other projects. *Dr. Sax*, which had been in the works for a while, was a novel of his youth in Lowell, with surrealistic interludes that he feared might be too "loony." One day, while working on *On the Road*, he got high on grass and began to write an account of Neal's youth, spinning out dazzling, gargantuan, free-associating sentences. Ultimately, these were dropped from *On the Road*, but were used in a later book, *Visions of Cody*, which is often referred to as the metaphysical, "vertical" version of *On the Road*, with less narrative and more depth.

Still trying to get *The Town and the City* published, on March 9 Kerouac sent several sample chapters to Mark Van Doren, along with the first two chapters of *Sax*. Though Van Doren was not impressed with *Sax*, he recommended *The Town and the City* to Robert Giroux at Harcourt, Brace, and a publishing breakthrough for Kerouac was at last at hand. Years later, in a June 29, 1955, letter to Ginsberg, Kerouac named several people whose efforts on his behalf led to the publication of his first novel, and Ginsberg headed the list. Ginsberg submitted the manuscript to Ed Stringham, an editor at the *New Yorker*. Stringham then passed it on to David Diamond, a composer who became infatuated with Kerouac. Diamond had influence with Kazin, who now held an advisory position at Harcourt, Brace.

Ann Charters, who later interviewed Kerouac, wrote that Kerouac personally took the manuscript in to Harcourt the day after Van Doren's call to Giroux in March 1949. Kerouac appeared in the editor's office in a jacket and necktie. "Giroux was immediately impressed," Charters wrote. In Giroux's 1981 R. R. Bowker Memorial Lecture he said, "One of the best means for an editor to acquire new authors is through other authors. Mark Van Doren sent Jack Kerouac to us with his first novel." Perhaps the deciding factor in the transaction, apart from the novel's merit, was that all three key players — Van Doren, Giroux, and Kerouac — were sons of Columbia. Giroux and Kerouac had something else in common: They were both of French descent, and both Catholics. Giroux was born April 8, 1914, and attended Regis High, a Jesuit institution in New York. He loved to lose himself in books and movies "so completely," he wrote, "that the world and time itself momentarily disappear." In the 1930s, he attended Columbia, where two of his favorite teachers were Van Doren and Raymond Weaver, and where he met a fellow student, Thomas Merton, who later gave Giroux "the biggest best-seller of my career." Merton's *The Seven Storey Mountain* was an autobiography written after the author entered the Trappist monastery near Gethsemane, Kentucky. Giroux published it in 1948, shortly before he met Kerouac, and the book shot to the top of the *New York Times* bestseller list, selling 600,000 hardcover copies. As a result, Giroux became editor-in-chief of Harcourt, Brace in 1948, and his new power in that position explains why Kerouac's difficult, unwieldy first novel, rejected everywhere else, got published at all.

Recalling his impression on first reading *The Town and the City*, Giroux said the manuscript was too long at eleven hundred pages but possessed "the lyricism and poetry of Thomas Wolfe's *Look Homeward, Angel*." He at once composed a letter to Kerouac offering a thousand-dollar advance against royalties, a substantial amount at the time, worth about $7,500 by 1990s' standards. Mailer's advance for *The Naked and the Dead*, published the previous year and, by 1949, the literary sensation of the decade, had only been $1250. Kerouac had just celebrated his twenty-seventh birthday, and on March 25, a few days before receiving Giroux's acceptance letter, he'd sat at his desk and made his first journal entry on yet another new version of *On the Road*. Though depressed by the storm of rejection slips that had greeted *The Town and the City*, he told Neal that he intended to continue writing fiction. Like Helen Hinkle, the Galatea Dunkel of *On the Road*, Jack was "a tenacious loser." A few days later, on March 29, he received Giroux's letter, read it, and fell to his knees, offering a "prayer of Thanksgiving." Then he opened his journal and wrote out the prayer, pressing hard on his pencil and going over the words a second time, as if to make sure God heard them. In a letter to Ed White, he wrote that it was a historic moment for "me and the family." When Mémère came home from the shoe factory and heard Jack's news, she was beside herself, especially when he told her that he was buying her a new Motorola TV set. Television was in its inaugural season, and the airwaves were jumping with the slapstick antics of forty-one-year-old Milton Berle, star of NBC's *Texaco Star Theater*. Mémère's Motorola was one of the first of

1,082,100 TV sets sold in America, of which 450,000 were purchased in New York City.[1]

Kerouac's friends reacted to his publishing coup with elation and envy. Neal wrote that he felt "so Glad," but quickly dropped the subject and suggested that his own dubious feat of stealing five hundred cars overshadowed Kerouac's entry into what he called "the big boys" league. To Neal, even Huncke was somehow superior to Jack by virtue of having spent more time in jails and asylums than Kerouac had. Lucien and Ginsberg discussed Jack's contract as they stood on Fifth Avenue watching the 1949 Easter parade. Lucien had started to write stories, and Ginsberg immediately assumed that Lucien was potentially a better artist than Kerouac and would eventually emerge as a significant figure in history. According to Barry Miles, Jack's triumph left Ginsberg feeling jealous and depressed.

The news of Kerouac's contract also met with mixed reactions at Columbia, where Lionel Trilling confided in his notebook, "I predicted that it would not be good & insisted. But later I saw with what bitterness I had made the prediction—not wanting Kerouac's book to be good because if the book of an accessory to a murder is good, how can one of mine be?—The continuing sense that wickedness—or is it my notion of courage—is essential for creation." Years later, Trilling's widow, Diana, explained that Trilling had hated himself for lacking the wildness he scorned in Kerouac, and he blamed his failure to write fiction successfully on the very qualities that he was esteemed for: his conscience, decency, quietness, moderation, and reasonableness. The critic would much rather have been a novelist like Hemingway, Mailer, or perhaps even Kerouac. On Morningside Heights, the only voice raised in praise of Kerouac was that of the benign Van Doren, who congratulated Jack and gave him a glowing blurb, writing, "John Kerouac is wiser than Thomas Wolfe, with whom he will be compared. In his first novel he is serious, warm, rich and mature. He is, in other words, a responsible writer, and much may be expected of him." Kazin also contributed a blurb, but Giroux did not use it on the jacket due to Kazin's connection with the company.[2]

Kerouac and Giroux began to revise and cut the manuscript at Harcourt, Brace's offices at 383 Madison Avenue. Giroux loved The Town and the City, according to John Clellon Holmes, and Kerouac idolized Giroux as an editor in the Max Perkins-Fitzgerald-Hemingway tradition. Giroux was only eight years older than Kerouac, but Holmes heard Jack refer him as "my father." Though the genteel Giroux was a regular at the Metropolitan Opera and the Century Club, he went out to Queens when Kerouac invited him to dinner, and trudged up the stairs to Mémère's spotlessly clean apartment over the drugstore. Looking for conversational common ground with the matronly skiving-machine operator, Giroux mentioned that his father had been French Canadian. She liked him at once, and Giroux found her "very funny, very salty," he recalled. Turning to Jack and talking about Giroux as if he weren't in the room, Mémère observed, "This man is like a banker.

Stick with him. Stay away from those other bums." Correcting her, Giroux said, "I'm an editor."

Like most people, Mémère had no idea what book editors actually do. As Giroux explained years later in his Bowker lecture, an editor is "a person who works closely with authors. . . . Editors developed from publishers' outside readers—literary consultants who were usually writers themselves and who recommended or advised against publication of the manuscripts the publisher sent them." By the final decade of the twentieth century, book publishing had produced only one famous editor, the fabled Max Perkins, yet Giroux's role model as an editor was not Perkins but the Englishman Edward Garnett, who launched Joseph Conrad, D. H. Lawrence, and John Galsworthy. Another editor Giroux admired was Edmund Malone, who helped James Boswell complete his biography of Dr. Johnson. Giroux, who started out as a market researcher and publicist for CBS, owed his own publishing career to British editor Frank Morley, who would later become Kerouac's U.K. editor for the Eyre & Spottiswoode edition of *The Town and the City* and who was the brother of Christopher Morley, the author of *Kitty Foyle* and editor of *Saturday Review* from 1924 to 1941. At CBS, Giroux had compiled two books based on European broadcasts, entitled *Crisis 1938*, and Frank Morley, then an editor at Faber & Faber, attempted to acquire them. CBS refused Morley's offer due to company policy. When Morley left Faber in 1939 and went to the United States to head the trade department of Harcourt, Brace, he hired Giroux as a junior editor beginning on January 2, 1940, for less than Giroux had earned at CBS.

Through Morley, Giroux met important authors such as Isaiah Berlin, Herbert Read, and T. S. Eliot, and began to build one of the strongest lists in publishing. Great editors are made by luck, but survive through pluck; their careers are founded on authors they inherit from their bosses or from other editors who are fired or quit, but after that, they're on their own. Giroux scored his first best-seller, *The Human Comedy* by William Saroyan, because Morley had assigned it to him. While still in his initial year as an editor, Giroux got another lucky break handling Edmund Wilson's *To the Finland Station: A Study in the Writing and Acting of History*, which became a modern classic. At a certain point, an editor must become self-sustaining and acquire authors from his own contacts, such as literary agents, friends, and scouts, or—as Giroux had just acquired Kerouac—through other authors. Giroux continued to compile a lustrous list, editing Carl Sandburg, Bernard Malamud, and Flannery O'Connor.

Kerouac and Giroux worked on *The Town and the City* for months, according to Holmes. They became quite close, as first-time authors and editors sometimes do, at least during the early period of their relationship when both are riding on a wave of hope. The honeymoon invariably ends as soon as the book is published. If the author becomes famous, he frequently moves to another firm for more money, not only out of greed, but to put any reminder of his obscure past behind him. If the book fails, he usually blames the editor and publisher for not advertising it enough. In 1949, Kerouac was grateful to be "taken up for a season," Holmes recalled, and added that Giroux introduced him around town as the literary world's bright new star. "Christ," Jack told Holmes, "I've got it made." He enthused in a letter to Ginsberg that Giroux was a powerful establishment figure who rubbed elbows with Eliot, Pound, Merton, and Robert Lowell. Moreover, Giroux was a shareholder at Harcourt and owned a subscription membership to the Metropolitan Opera, which meant to Kerouac that Giroux was on the same social footing as the Rockefellers. Then, in the most revealing passage, Kerouac told Ginsberg that Giroux liked him, that they were going to plays and the opera together, and that in Giroux he had discovered a "great" lifetime companion. Evidently, Giroux and Kerouac also considered traveling abroad together, for Kerouac wrote Neal that he wanted to learn Italian because Giroux was going to Rome the following spring. According to Temko, who visited Giroux's office with Kerouac, Giroux "doted on Jack and, of course, Jack was not above exploiting this kind of thing."[3]

On April 23, Kerouac wrote Harrington that he'd rented a tuxedo and ceased to regard himself as Beat. While at the Metropolitan Opera House one night, in the club circle, he found himself being admired by Gore Vidal, the literary wunderkind of the forties and the grandson of U.S. Senator T. P. Gore of Oklahoma. Only twenty-four, Vidal was already the author of two published novels, *Williwaw* and the notorious 1948 gay shocker, *The City and the Pillar*. Vidal later recalled:

> Jack was with a publisher, and I was with a friend of the publisher, a brilliant alcoholic writer . . . The writer had paid both Jack and Jack's beloved Nemesis, Neal Cassady, for sex . . . We are standing at the back of the opera box, which is so crowded that our faces are only a few inches apart. I feel the heat from his body. The eyes are bright and clear and blue; the body muscular . . . a drop of water slides alongside his left ear and down his pale cheek, not sweat, but water that he must have just used to comb his thick black Indian-like hair. We were also coming on to each other like two pieces of trade — yes, I was attracted.

Several years later, Kerouac and Vidal had an assignation in the Chelsea Hotel, and Vidal wrote, "I fucked him." If Kerouac was smitten, he failed to mention it in *Some of the Dharma*, written around the same time. As a homophobic homoerotic, he denied enjoying sex with men, but continued to have it. "Queers are not artists," he pontificated. "Truman Capote simpers . . . Gore Vidal stands legs akimbo in a Baroque garden in Italy." Proust, he conceded, was "the only fop who could write."[4]

In a 1949 letter to Ed White, Kerouac confided that he was bored with New York and intended to spend the rest of his thousand-dollar advance on moving his entire family to Denver, including Mémêre, Nin, Paul, and Paul

Jr. He leased a small clapboard house outside Denver on the road to Central City, and returned to New York in time to attend a June 15 cocktail party hosted by the Book-of-the-Month Club. He vainly hoped that *The Town and the City* would be made a full selection, earning him a quick fifty thousand dollars or more, but the book proved far too controversial for the conservative mail-order club. Back in Denver, with all his family around him, he got a construction job, rode bareback in a rodeo, and read François de Malherbe's poetry, Shakespeare in Racine's French translation, and Truman Capote.

Soon it became clear that moving to Denver had been a mistake; their home in suburban Westwood was remote and inconvenient with muddy, unpaved roads, and neither Jack nor Mémère could drive. Ed White later told the *Denver Post*, "It was doomed to failure, of course. Jack wasn't terribly practical." Soon both Jack and Mémère longed to return to the East, which only weeks before Kerouac had been damning as effete. Mémère missed Radio City Music Hall, preferring the Rockettes to the Rockies, and feared that the mountains were going to fall and crush her. She managed to get her skiving job back and returned to New York by bus on July 4, just seven weeks after having arrived in Denver. Paul Blake complained that the fishing in Colorado wasn't as good as at home and returned to North Carolina with Nin and Paul Jr. On June 24, 1949, Jack wrote Holmes that he'd wasted his entire advance on a harebrained misadventure, but he remained in Colorado because Giroux was coming out to stay with him on July 15. Jack was already planning to hit Giroux up for an advance for *On the Road*, his novel-in-progress.

Holmes later told Gifford and Lee that Giroux "liked Jack—maybe even more than liked Jack. . . . Giroux came out and they hitchhiked together." Interviewed by Charters in 1972, Giroux recalled going to Denver, but said he only hitchhiked for half an hour, and it wasn't his first time to do so. But in Kerouac's letter to Ginsberg, first published in 1995, Kerouac wrote that Giroux hitchhiked with him into the wilderness in order to gain a better understanding of the experiences related in *On the Road*, and in a letter to Ed White, he added that Giroux was "a fine young man," approximately thirty-five years old, with prematurely graying hair.

The kind of attention being lavished on Kerouac was typical of the postwar mania for discovering young novelists, a fad that gripped both the publishing industry and the popular imagination. The myth of the Great American Novel was still alive, and the media scrutinized budding novelists as if looking for signs of the Second Coming. Even before Capote's first book, *Other Voices, Other Rooms*, was published in 1948, *Life* Magazine splashed his photograph over a full page, and the accompanying article was headlined, "Young U.S. Writers: A Refreshing Group of Newcomers on the Literary Scene Is Ready to Tackle Almost Anything." Thomas Heggen, Jean Stafford, Calder Willingham, and Gore Vidal were among the writers featured in *Life*, and Vidal later observed, "After the war everybody was waiting for the next Hemingway-Fitzgerald generation to appear. . . . That's why a new novel by

one of us was considered an interesting event." The British critic Cyril Con-
nolly, who found nothing comparable in England, wrote, "The hunt for
young authors who, while maintaining a prestige value . . . may yet somehow
win the coveted jackpot is feverish and incessant."

Kerouac enjoyed the feeling of power that his friendship with Giroux
conferred, and in a July 28, 1949, letter to Neal, he overflowed with schemes
to cash in on this important connection. Jack naively believed that Giroux,
whom he described as publishing's hottest star, was going to make him rich
and famous. He was eager to share his imagined good fortune with Neal, but
only as a way of turning Neal into an emotional hostage. He pledged to
devote the remainder of his life to managing Neal's literary career and helping Neal financially. He was wildly off-target in prophesying that Neal would
emerge a better writer than either Ginsberg or Burroughs, and he was even
willing to bet everything he had on Neal. Then he proceeded to give Neal
some tips about the manipulation of New York editors, and in another letter
he coached poet Philip Whalen on the art of "sucking asses to get published,"
cruelly characterizing top-echelon editors such as Giroux, Malcolm Cowley,
Donald Allen, Louis Simpson, and Kenneth Rexroth as the "Farting-
Through-Silk set." These paragons of the literary establishment could be
charmed, fooled, manipulated, and used, and in his letters to Neal, Kerouac
portrayed himself as the Svengali who could teach Neal and other aspiring
Beat writers how to finagle contracts out of publishers. Flirting was part of
the game, but it took more than sex appeal to get published. If Neal would
only get a Brooks Brothers suit and stop coming on like a desperado, he
could take Madison Avenue by storm. All such Machiavellian strategies
availed Kerouac of nothing with Giroux, who published none of the other
Beats and dropped Kerouac after one book.

Although Giroux agreed to look at Ginsberg's poetry, Kerouac later told
Neal that Giroux did not consider Ginsberg's demented imagery to be a good
influence on Kerouac. In any event, Ginsberg was temporarily out of action,
having been arrested with Huncke and a gang of thieves, jailed in the Long
Island House of Detention, and later committed to a locked ward at the
Columbia Presbyterian Psychiatric Institute. Ginsberg would have been sent
to prison had it not been for the timely intervention of Lionel Trilling, who
persuaded a psychiatrist to vouch that Ginsberg was mad. Ginsberg wrote
Kerouac that he'd lost his mind, explaining that he had recently been breaking off in the middle of serious conversations and giggling hysterically. Van
Doren also tried to help Ginsberg, but Burroughs, who spoke from vast experience of arrests and grand juries, insisted that Ginsberg was mistaken to
listen to Columbia's "liberal fruit[s]," whose meddling could land him in the
madhouse for the rest of his life. Burroughs pointed out that Ginsberg had
done nothing worse than harbor stolen goods, and the prosecution could
never prove he'd known the gang was pulling robberies. But Ginsberg felt
that Burroughs's evil influence was the cause of all his problems, and he
chose to spend the next seven months in a psychiatric lockup behind Colum-

bia-Presbyterian's "gate of darkness." Kerouac tried to keep Ginsberg's spirits up, writing letters from Denver that were full of gossip and progress reports on *Dr. Sax*. Remembering his own days in a psychiatric ward, Kerouac pointed out that Ginsberg, while trying to persuade the doctors that he was not insane, should not persuade himself as well. According to Barry Miles, Kerouac's "valuable friendship helped Allen to bolster his shattered ego and take charge of his life again."

In Denver, after Kerouac and Giroux worked on *The Town and the City*, Kerouac saw his editor off at the airport and suddenly felt bereft. If Kerouac had attempted, as planned, to extract money out of Giroux for *On the Road*, he had not succeeded, for he was broke and had to take on backbreaking labor in the Denver fruit market. One evening, exhausted and lonely, he strolled through a black neighborhood, an experience that inspired one of the most resonant and controversial passages in *On the Road*. "At lilac evening I walked with every muscle aching among the lights of 27th and Welton in the Denver colored section, wishing I were a Negro, feeling that the best the white world had offered was not enough ecstasy for me, not enough life, joy, kicks, darkness, music, not enough night." The passage would later enrage James Baldwin, who found it condescending and typical of white stereotypes of black sexuality. Eldridge Cleaver disagreed, however, seeing it as a clarion call to the civil rights movement.[5]

In July 1949, Jack and Neal's love for one another crested, and Neal promised that he would keep Carolyn out of their way if Kerouac would only come to San Francisco and live with him. In her biography of Kerouac, Charters wrote, "By some definitions of the word Jack was in love with Neal, by his own definition he wasn't." Nevertheless, under the impression that he would have Neal completely to himself, Jack gave up his house in Denver and left for San Francisco. As he crossed the Colorado-Utah state line in an eleven-dollar travel-bureau car, he had an insight about his destiny. "I saw God in the sky," he later wrote, and added that God pointed a finger at him and said, "You're on the road to heaven."

At 2 A.M. one morning in the summer of 1949, he arrived at the Cassadys' rickety cottage at 29 Russell Street on Russian Hill, and once again Neal appeared in the doorway naked, as if offering a foretaste of the "slambanging big sodomies" that Kerouac would later describe in *Visions of Cody*. Carolyn, who'd been in bed with Neal and was three months pregnant, confirmed in her memoir that Neal "got up—as usual in the altogether." According to Carolyn, Jack said, "My God, man, what if it had been someone else?" Describing the same moment in *On the Road*, Kerouac focused on Neal's total self-acceptance and emancipation from American puritanism, writing, "It might have been the President knocking for all he cared. He received the world in the raw." Kerouac represented Neal, as Dean Moriarty, as saying, "You've finally come to *me*," signifying Neal's conquest of Jack, and Jack's decision to become emotionally enslaved by Neal again, despite having been abandoned by him on O'Farrell Street earlier the same year.

From her bedroom upstairs, Carolyn overheard them whispering and plotting adventures, and immediately foresaw the end of her marriage. In the following days, Jack and Neal's camaraderie left her feeling as if she'd once again been deserted. "Frisco jazz was at its rawest peak," Kerouac wrote, adding that he and Neal were at the clubs every night. On his first visit he'd hated San Francisco, but now with Neal at his side he loved it. Later, in his novels, he would turn the city into the Beat Pamplona, the geographical focus and cradle of a generation. "It was summer, August 1949, and Frisco was blowing mad," he wrote in *Visions of Cody*.

Fed up, Carolyn finally threw them out. "He's all you want," she told Neal. "Leave me alone. . . . Go." She didn't really want Neal to leave and was only trying to get his attention, but Neal and Jack packed and left together, as if they'd been waiting for an excuse. Carolyn, with only three dollars, once again faced desertion, but Kerouac was so happy that he blushed and wept for joy. He and Neal set out for New York in a travel-bureau car, referred to in *On the Road* as the fag Plymouth because Kerouac considered Chrysler products to be weak and girlish, without real acceleration or horsepower, a description that was as misogynous as it was homophobic. The car was driven by a gay man who managed to get Neal into bed in Sacramento, much to Kerouac's chagrin. In *Visions of Cody*, he wrote:

> That night the gangbelly broke loose between Cody and the skinny skeleton, sick. Cody thrashed him on rugs in the dark, monstrous huge fuck, Olympian perversities, slambanging big sodomies that made me sick, subsided with him for money; the money never came. He'd treated the boy like a girl! "You can't trust these people when you give them (exactly) what they want." I sat in the castrated toilet listening and peeking, at one point it appeared Cody had thrown over legs in the air like a dead hen . . . I was horrified . . .

Despite such prudish disapproval, Kerouac's peeking from "the castrated toilet" betrayed his painful awareness that he was the true loser: unmanned by nonparticipation, excluded from the bedroom of life, and consigned by fear to a commode, a receptacle of waste and dead matter. As Ginsberg wrote in his introduction to the 1972 unabridged version of *Visions of Cody*, the scene "alas was excised from *On the Road* thus removing one dimension of American Hero and misleading thousands of highschool boys for decades." Ginsberg noted that Kerouac "probably should have got into the act for his own happy good, not drunk himself to death with sinful visions. . . . I enjoyed both Cody [Neal] and Jack, many times in many ways jolly bodily and in soul love, and wish Jack had been physically tenderer to Cody or vice versa, done 'em both good, some love balm over that bleak manly power they had, displayed, were forced to endure and die with."

The day following the "monstrous huge fuck," Jack and Neal had a fight,

which Jack later recounted in *On the Road*, and it too occurred in a toilet—
this one in a roadside restaurant. Kerouac was relieving himself when he
stepped back from the urinal and said, "Dig this trick." He then stopped his
urine flow and moved to another urinal so Neal could get to the sink. Neal
warned him that he was going to ruin his kidneys. Jack flew into a rage and
revealed what was really on his mind. "I'm no old fag like that fag," he said,
but obviously he was jealous. Neal was completely crushed and bewildered.
He had nothing against making love to another man, but Kerouac had presented himself as unavailable, and Neal had always respected that, with the
exception of suggesting bisexual threesomes. Neal stalked from the restaurant
in tears. When Kerouac described the same trip in *Visions of Cody*, he wrote,
"Cody is full of shit: let him go . . . go sleeping on the other side of the
world."

Afterward, Neal drove the car in a blind rage, charging through Reno,
Battle Mountain, Elko, and Salt Lake City, finally pulling into Denver. They
gave up the car and parted company with Neal's gay sex partner. Neal then
started a fruitless search for his hobo father, finding only his half brother,
who wanted nothing to do with him. Everyone scorned Neal for deserting
Carolyn, and they called Jack a home wrecker. At last, Jack began to realize
that Neal was on a death trip and would never amount to anything. In Denver, Neal went on a car-stealing binge, committing grand larceny, and Kerouac was in danger of arrest and imprisonment as an accomplice. They made
it out of town in another drive-away vehicle, a 1947 Cadillac described by
Neal as a "big heavy hard-assed car . . . humps along like a bumblebee." Sick
and hungover, they fled Denver ahead of the cops with two stunned, speech-
less passengers, Jesuit college boys, and went "hurling into the dawn." As the
students cowered in the rear seat, they drove to New Raymer to visit a rancher
who'd once employed Neal as a cowboy. On the way, Neal wrecked the
Caddy, which had to be dragged from a ditch. The rancher was hospitable
but obviously disillusioned with Neal, like everyone else by now, and wary
of him as a con man. As the frazzled travelers headed for Chicago in the
damaged car, Neal reminded Jack of Captain Ahab in *Moby-Dick*. At the
wheel, Neal became a gaunt fanatic forcing the car beyond its limits. America
was not yet paved with freeways, and Neal was negotiating two-lane blacktop
roads at 110 miles per hour, booming through a succession of sleepy towns
like Pine Bluff, Kimball, Ogallala, North Platte, Grand Island, Carroll, and
Ames. Having hitched through these remote places in 1947, Jack reflected,
"I was beginning to cross and recross towns in America as though I were a
traveling salesman," but no one was buying his "bag of tricks." By the time
they reached Chicago, they'd covered twelve hundred miles in seventeen
hours, and the Cadillac was lurching spastically and dying at every stoplight.
After depositing their passengers at the YMCA, they quickly turned the car
in and, to escape the owner's wrath, dashed for a city bus. Then they took
another bus to Detroit, where Jack looked up Edie. She was mentally unstable, Jack wrote Nin, and he was "all through with it," he added. They ar-

ranged to ride to New York as paying passengers in a new Chrysler, finally completing what Jack referred to in *Visions of Cody* as "a wildgoose chase."[6]

The Town and the City had not sold to the movies, so Kerouac lacked the funds for the Italian trip he'd dreamed of treating Neal to. Instead, they faced the grim New York winter in Mémère's new apartment in Richmond Hill, Queens, at 94-21 134th Street, not far from the old place in Ozone Park. Mémère was furious at Neal for deserting his family, and told him to shove off in two days. Neal was ready to go—for him, the only point of life was "a fast car, a coast to reach, and a woman at the end of the road." For Kerouac, however, there was no such sense of purpose or destination, and at the conclusion of *On the Road*'s spectacular Part Three he could write only, "There was no more land." He was like the Clifford Odets character Mae Doyle in *Clash by Night*, who said, "Home is where you go when you run out of places."

A few days later at a party in Manhattan, Jack spotted a beautiful woman, Diana Hansen, the "Inez" of *On the Road* and "Diane" of *Visions of Cody*. Though Diana later told Carolyn that it was Ginsberg who introduced her to Neal, Jack wrote, "She was a raving fucking beauty the first moment we saw her walk in. . . . She said 'I always wanted to meet a real cowboy' and I called him over." Diana was sitting in a chair, and Neal seduced her in five minutes, kneeling at her feet, gazing up at her, then burying his face in her lap. She was a cultivated girl from Long Island, a Barnard graduate who worked at an advertising agency, and she may have done some modeling. "I saw him fuck her for the first time," Holmes recalled. "I saw him score. That's one of those two-minute things."

Jack found that he could no longer relate to Neal, that "everything blew out on that Cadillac trip East," and now there was nothing left for Jack to do but sit at home and fret over lost dreams and fallen heroes. Neal moved in with Diana, who was married to a poet but soon became pregnant by Neal. After work each day in a parking lot, Neal lounged around her home in the East Eighties in a hip-length silk Chinese kimono, "with his dork showing underneath it—just the tip," Holmes recalled. Much of the time, Neal sat in a dark room with a red light, smoked pot, and masturbated to pornography. "All she wanted was for him to love her and she was willing for anything," said Holmes. Neal told Jack that Carolyn and Diana talked to each other long distance, and discussed his "joint."[7]

According to Gifford and Lee, it was during this hiatus in Kerouac and Cassady's relationship that Kerouac "moved deeper into his friendship with Giroux" and his work on revising *The Town and the City*. On September 28, 1949, from Richmond Hill, Jack wrote his former New School teacher, Elbert Lenrow, that he was going to the Harcourt offices quite regularly in order to work on revisions, and he proposed bringing Giroux to Lenrow's home for an evening of "music and talk." Giroux still had him under pressure to cut *The Town and the City*. Editors customarily require cuts, not only to improve a book's pace and narrative quality but to keep the retail price down to whatever the trade will bear, which was about $3.50 in 1950. The greatest expense in manufacturing a book is not composition or printing, but paper and the cloth used in the binding. *The Town and the City* somehow had to be stuffed into a five-hundred-page, $3.50 package, or there would be no profit for the publisher and no royalties for the author. Finally, the book was set in type, and on November 1, Giroux wired Jack: "PROOFS BOOK ONE HERE COME IN COME IN WHEREVER YOU ARE." While still in proofs, the book sold to Eyre & Spottiswoode. Like most authors, Jack was delighted that his work would appear on both sides of the Atlantic, and when his British editor, Frank Morley, visited the U.S., he discovered a new drinking buddy.

As the book went through the publishing process, Kerouac, like most authors, was assailed by a multitude of doubts. He complained in a letter to Hal that the manuscript had been slashed to four hundred pages, which transformed it from a dark masterpiece into a marketable but conventional work of fiction. Hal urged Jack to withdraw the book and take it to another house, but common sense triumphed over authorial vanity, and Kerouac abided by his contract. If anything, Giroux could have cut the book even more, and the gaggle of Martin brothers should have been combined into a single protagonist; in the published version, many readers would find it impossible to tell the boys apart. According to *Some of the Dharma*, Giroux also toned down Kerouac's language, advising the author, "This is not a poetic age." More lenient than harsh, Giroux's editing saved a deeply flawed first novel from total obscurity.

Unlike Kerouac, Norman Mailer was grateful when his editor, a freelancer named Charlie Devlin, drastically cut *The Naked and the Dead*, another brilliant but diffuse first novel. "He edited it for about four weeks . . . fifty hours a week," Mailer recalled. "He was like a lawn mower . . . and . . . a very powerful thinker." Mailer's recognition of the editor's role in the novel's eventual success was almost unique in recorded publishing history. Thomas Wolfe's defection from Scribner's to Harper, after Max Perkins's heroic editing jobs on *Look Homeward, Angel* and *Of Time and the River* became public knowledge, was far more typical of author-editor relations.

Publication of *The Town and the City* was set for February 1950, and Giroux promised an aggressive publishing program. The sales representatives were expected to bring in twenty thousand advance subscriptions from the bookstores, and an advertising budget of seventy-five hundred dollars was set. Fifteen thousand copies were printed, and of these, 10,500 were bound. The remaining loose sheets were stored at the company's warehouse in the event of reorders.

The finished book was bound in red cloth, with the author's name and the title stamped in gold on the spine, and there was a monogram in gold on the front binding—all signs of special treatment for a valued author. Before the book went to press, Jack decided to use the name "John Kerouac." For the back ad (publishing parlance for the back of the dust jacket), Jack posed for the photographer, Arni, whose portrait of Jack was at once sensitive and moody, yet as rugged as Rudolph Valentino. Jack approved the photo, though he thought he looked like a "faggot." The front of the dustjacket, in blue, green, and brown, depicted Lowell, but Kerouac didn't like it, later writing Morley that the Eyre & Spottiswoode jacket design was far superior to Harcourt's. Hoping to stir up some local publicity, he wrote Charles Sampas at the *Sun* just after Christmas 1949, stating proudly that his novel would arrive in bookstores throughout the United States on February 23, 1950, and that the subject was Lowell.[8]

Allen Ginsberg emerged from the psychiatric hospital, and Jack and Neal got together with him to collaborate on a poem, "Pull My Daisy." A hip intellectual named Jay Landesman published it under the title "Song: Fie My Fum" in *Neurotica*, an underground magazine about "neurotic society from the inside." "Pull My Daisy" represented Kerouac and Ginsberg's first commercial publication, but hardly constituted a literary debut, since Landesman used only four verses, or about half the poem, and published it as part of a longer piece, "Report From the Asylum—Afterthoughts of a Shock Patient" by Carl Solomon, who used the pseudonym "Carl Goy." As fellow psychiatric patients at Columbia Presbyterian, Ginsberg and Solomon had become friends. According to Ginsberg, Jack contributed jazzy images to Ginsberg's rather staid verse. Ginsberg later confessed that he got down on his knees to induce Landesman to publish the poem. On doctor's orders, Ginsberg was trying to turn himself into a heterosexual and was now looking, without much success, for a hip but warm and loving woman. For the next five years, Ginsberg would enjoy, according to Miles, "a series of apparently satisfactory heterosexual relationships."[9]

Diana Hansen was one of the very few New York Beats to have an apartment, and Jack and Allen both made liberal use of it, Jack coming in from Queens, and Ginsberg visiting from New Jersey. On weekends they all went to the San Remo bar. W. H. Auden, who was forty-three in 1950, was often there with his lover, Chester Kallman, and his secretary, Alan Ansen. Auden found Kerouac attractive and listened patiently as the young novelist described *The Town and the City* and various works-in-progress, later offering to read Kerouac's manuscripts. At the time, the rumpled, hard-drinking Oxford bard was considered by most critics to be the greatest living poet after T. S. Eliot. Having renounced his British citizenship, Auden lived at 7 Cornelia Street, as well as in Cherry Grove, the gay Fire Island resort. Auden's "The Age of Anxiety," which won the 1948 Pulitzer Prize in poetry, had no direct connection with the cold war, but came to symbolize the mood of the fifties. It was set in a New York bar, where the habitués, including a young naval recruit, were wasting their lives while awaiting some signal or reason to begin living. Though T. S. Eliot, who was Auden's editor at Faber & Faber, called "The Age of Anxiety" Auden's "best work to date" and Leonard Bernstein set it to music, critics were befuddled, perhaps because a major influence on Auden's poem, as on much of Kerouac's writing, was Joyce's indecipherable *Finnegans Wake*. While Auden felt free to experiment in his own work, he did not extend the same privilege to Kerouac and warned him that *Dr. Sax* was too rough and unsalvageable, Kerouac revealed in a letter to Stella.[10]

One night in the Village, Jack ran into Adele Morales as she emerged from a class at the New School. She hardly recognized him in his tweedy Ivy League clothes, and though their last parting had been unpleasant, she was again drawn to his strong body and handsome face. She'd recently broken up with Ed Fancher—future founder, with Norman Mailer and Dan Wolf, of the *Village Voice*—and had attempted suicide. As she and Jack talked in front of the New School, he said his novel was being published by Harcourt. "That's wonderful, Jack," she told him. "I'm really happy for you." This time, she wisely reserved comment on his writing, despite her conviction that it was nothing but "overheated prose," and hugged him warmly. She volunteered the information that she'd moved from Brooklyn to Manhattan. Taking the bait, he asked for her telephone number and suggested a date. "I knew very few about-to-be-published writers," she thought. "Maybe this was a new chapter for me." Shortly thereafter, Jack showed her off at the West End, introducing her to Holmes and Ginsberg. In the following days, as they became lovers, he took her to Holmes's apartment and finally to Neal's, where Jack was spending most of his nights. The meager accommodations and nasty cockroaches left Adele as cold as did Kerouac's lovemaking. "Sex was not his major thrust in more ways than one," she complained in her memoir. "He rushed the act, the same way he hurried through everything else. It seemed to me he was only interested in the big event. What led up to it was of minor interest." With many of his other girls, however, foreplay was often the part of sex he enjoyed most. Jack's mother described Adele as a Bea Franco with brains, and although he liked working-class Hispanics, Adele was perhaps more of a hot-blooded Latin spitfire than he'd bargained for. Nevertheless, according to Kerouac's sex list, he and Adele made it through the sex act twenty-five times.

Kerouac was not the only man to find Adele sexually challenging. According to critic and gallery owner Nathan "Nat" Halper, Adele "had a reputation of being very, *very* good in bed . . . [with] pretensions to secret, primitive knowledge." She could also be rather frightening. Critic Seymour Krim, a friend of Kerouac's, called Adele "a pisser . . . an attractive, flirty girl. . . . She chased me around the room with scissors, trying to cut off [my] tie. . . . There was a perversity there."

One of Adele's problems in both her relationship with Kerouac and later with Mailer was the heady intellectual company she found herself in. "I was just out to have a good time," she recalled. "I loved sex, and I always wanted to be in love." She was not yet an alcoholic, so the Beat parties Jack took her to in Holmes's apartment, where everyone was sloshed on cheap wine and pot, held little interest for her. Though Adele thought Neal Cassady sexy, comparing him with matinee idols of later eras, Paul Newman and Sean Penn, she sensed at once that Neal was in serious competition with her for Kerouac. "He didn't like me," she wrote. "He was possessive of Jack and jealous because I was Jack's girl." Finally she tired of watching Jack and Neal "hugging, pummeling, and punching each other" and invited Jack to spend his nights at her place. After a few weeks, she suggested, "There are other things in a relationship besides fucking."

"Like what?" he asked.

They fought over her practice of using Orthocreme on her diaphragm to prevent pregnancy. "He hated getting it on his cock," Adele recalled. Eventually they drifted apart. "I was getting bored," she wrote, explaining, "most of the men I fell in love with always had a close friend." Kerouac had Cassady, Ed Fancher had Dan Wolf, and Mailer had actor Mickey Knox. Adele would later brand Mailer a "Mama's boy," an appellation often applied to Kerouac as well. Her need for drama was not shared by Kerouac; she liked to live "from crisis to crisis" and have "screaming fights" followed by "love duets," she wrote. Adele got all that and more when she met, and later married, Norman Mailer.[11]

Giroux notified Jack in early 1950 of a slight delay in the February publication date. According to Giroux, David O. Selznick, producer of *Gone With the Wind*, was reading the galleys at his Culver City studio, which had recently released the hit Orson Welles thriller *The Third Man*. Jack told Ed White that if the book sold to the movies, they'd go to Paris together and Jack would marry an inexperienced, *complaisante* French girl, one he could train. *The Town and the City* finally came out on March 2, 1950, and was dedicated to Robert Giroux, "Friend and Editor." On publication day the book was fairly well received by the critics, among them Charles Poore, the daily *New York Times* reviewer, who acknowledged "the depth and breadth of his vision" but harped on Jack's debt to Thomas Wolfe. The Sunday *Times Book Review* saluted Jack's novel as a "rough diamond of a book," but the reviewer, John Brooks, found the portrait of New York City "exaggerated," possibly because he'd never met anyone like Ginsberg, Huncke, and Kammerer, all of whom appeared in the book under fictional names. *Newsweek* praised the novel as "almost a major work" but found "the longwinded nonsense of its intellectuals . . . well-nigh unreadable." Kerouac's favorite review was that of Yvonne Le Maître in the Worcester, Massachusetts, *Travailleur*. In her notice, Le Maître gently chided the author for concealing his French-Canadian roots. Kerouac wrote her a gracious letter, promising he'd never make the same mistake again. He added that he might even write a French-Canadian novel in French.

The Town and the City also had its detractors, notably Howard Mumford Jones, who wrote in *Saturday Review* that it was "radically deficient in structure and style." The *New Yorker* dismissed Kerouac as "ponderous, shambling . . . tiresome." Predictably, the *Lowell Sun* was outraged by the author's inference that his hometown was "the stinkingest stinking town" and their reviewer also objected to Kerouac's "women of easy virtue" and "Greenwich Village queers." However, *Sun* columnist Charles Sampas plugged Jack in his January 4, 1950, column, alerting his readers to "The Great Lowell Novel," and the paper purchased serialization rights, running numerous excerpts along with photographs illustrating the people and places depicted in the narrative. Giroux sent Kerouac to Lowell for a book-signing at the Bon Marché department store on Merrimack Street, and Spike Morissette stood in line to get his signed copy. "Hi! I told you so," Spike said. "But . . . you should add more spice to your writing if you want to sell." Tears welled in Jack's eyes when he recognized his old sandlot pal Roland Salvas in line, and he stood to embrace him. After a radio interview, he returned to Queens and in the following weeks watched in horror and disbelief as his book sank without a trace, the fate of most first novels.

In a dyspeptic letter to Yvonne Le Maître in September 1950, Kerouac grumbled that *The Town and the City* was no longer selling and that no one had "discovered" him. He blamed the plethora of other publications, but the truth was that *The Town and the City* posed insuperable difficulties for the casual reader. Despite the lyricism of its descriptive passages and the poignance of isolated scenes, the novel was burdened with too many poorly drawn characters: identical young men and faceless young women. In December Jack wrote Neal an acrimonious letter calling the nation's review press "cocksuckers." Decades later, *The Town and the City* would be rediscovered, and a new generation of readers would validate Kerouac's own high estimate of the book, expressed in a 1950 letter to Neal as comparable to early Tolstoy. In 1997, almost half a century after publication, the novel is still in print.[12]

Realizing he wasn't going to make a living from writing, Jack entertained the thought of becoming a hustler, as he confessed in a letter to Holmes in the spring of 1950. That he already possessed a hustler's mentality was shown in his Farting-Through-Silk letter, but he lacked the style and finesse to be a successful courtesan, demonstrating no aptitude for cultivating the prominent gays, such as Broadway lyricist John Latouche, who threw themselves at him. The downtown scene, which was hopping in 1950 with Beat bashes regularly being thrown by Lucien Carr and Bill Cannastra, was more to his liking. Lucien lived on Twenty-first Street, and Cannastra's loft was only three doors down. According to Ginsberg, Lucien was going with Liz Lehrman, a painter. In a letter to Neal, Ginsberg wrote that he, Kerouac, and Lucien were kissing each other and singing the Yale alma mater song. At Cannastra's, Kerouac found that he could get drunk and be as homoerotic as he pleased. Auden, a regular at Cannastra's loft, wittily observed after reading Fitzgerald's *This Side of Paradise* that American men didn't seem to care for women at all. What they really wanted, Auden suggested, was "to be blown by a stranger" while perusing the daily paper, and "to be fucked" by their best friend after a few beers.

In Cannastra's flamboyantly decadent downtown salon, regulars included Tennessee Williams, Chester Kallman, Holmes, dance critic Edwin Denby,

New Yorker poetry editor Howard Moss, and Random House editor William Frankel. Cannastra was an influential Beat trendsetter and scene-maker from 1948 to 1950, and at his parties the Beat Generation coalesced as writers and painters exchanged ideas and mingled with editors and critics. Kerouac met painters Nell Blaine, Larry Rivers, and Alfred Leslie and, through them, Jackson Pollock and Willem de Kooning. Later on, Kerouac would collaborate with Rivers and Leslie on the film version of *Pull My Daisy*. Kerouac tried his hand at painting, scrawling primitive, stark, powerful crucifixes on bar napkins. Like Pollock's action painting, Kerouac's graphics as well as his fiction and poetry demonstrate that the process and the final product are one and the same.[13]

Though Cannastra preferred sex with men and had a male lover, he lived with an attractive woman from Albany named Joan Haverty. In a letter to Neal, Ginsberg described Joan as emotionally vulnerable and disturbed, adding that her self-abnegation and innocence made it easy for Cannastra to play Svengali to her Galatea. Joan sometimes dressed in drag as a sailor and joined Cannastra in kinky games, peeping through windows. Ginsberg found her to be impossibly smug, and he assumed she was a "fag hag" because she seemed curiously asexual in relation to straight men, with whom she wanted nothing but companionship. Both Kerouac and Ginsberg pursued her sexually and had affairs with her, but Kerouac got involved first with her lover, Cannastra, just as he'd first loved Sammy Sampas and, only subsequently, his sister Stella.

Cannastra was brash and daring enough to draw Kerouac out homoerotically more than any other man had ever succeeded in doing. At 3 A.M., in the middle of Sixteenth Street and Seventh Avenue, Cannastra told Kerouac, "Let's take all our clothes off," Kerouac recalled. Though Kerouac insisted on keeping his shorts on, Cannastra was completely nude as they ran around the block. On another occasion, Cannastra invited Jack to peer through a peephole into his bathroom. "We saw a lot of things," Kerouac later admitted in the *Paris Review*. Finally backing away from Cannastra's "glory hole," Jack said he wasn't "interested in that," and Cannastra observed, "You're not interested in anything." Kerouac told Al Aronowitz of the *New York Post* that he had group sex with Cannastra, and he admitted to *Paris Review* interviewers that he had sex "on a lot of couches with young men." When Jack tried to talk about *The Town and the City*, Cannastra kidded him, calling him "Queen of the May!" and "Your Highness!" In describing their sexual romps to the *Paris Review*, Kerouac added, "Auden would come the next day, the next afternoon, for cocktails. Maybe with Chester Kallman. Tennessee Williams." Unfortunately, the brilliant Cannastra was so self-destructive that no one expected him to survive for very long. Kerouac once saw him teetering on the edge of a rooftop, six stories high, and Ginsberg wrote in "Howl" that Cannastra cavorted on broken glass when he was drunk, and often vomited blood.[14]

During the same period, Kerouac was attracted to a colleague of Lucien's at UP. Jack referred to her as a "honey-brunette" and made love to her twenty-five times, according to his sex list. He was shopping for a woman to replace Mémère and take care of him and support him while he wrote *On the Road*, which he called, at this point, *Gone on the Road*. Though already romantically involved with Lucien, she let Jack stay in her apartment and drink her liquor, and he began to refer to her as his last girl friend and first grand passion. Lucien refused to give her up, and when Jack threatened to drop them both, Lucien shrugged, clearly indicating that he would regard the loss of Kerouac's friendship as no tragedy. Jack told Ginsberg he was hurt that Lucien could be so cold.[15]

Kerouac had expected a royalty payment on his first Harcourt statement, but to his surprise and dismay, he had not yet earned out his advance and received no further money on *The Town and the City*. Refusing to concede defeat, he finally persuaded Justin Brierly to intercede with Giroux, assuming that the publisher would not refuse a powerful Columbia alumnus who'd just appeared at a campus groundbreaking with Dwight D. Eisenhower, the new president of Columbia University. Brierly managed to convince Harcourt to foot the bill for a Denver book-signing party, and Giroux considerately approved $120 for Jack's plane fare. Jack later took a bus to Denver and pocketed the balance. In late May 1950, he was greeted by old friends in Denver, including the Hinkles and Beverly Burford, who found him a basement apartment and decorated it for him. Signing books at Daniels & Fisher Store Co., he looked like a dapper young barrister in his flannel suit and perfectly knotted dark tie. Ed White and all the old Denver gang showed up to support him, and Brierly's photograph of the occasion showed Kerouac enjoying the most delectable of authorial chores, greeting readers and signing books.

In June 1950, Neal arrived in Denver unexpectedly, driving a 1937 Ford jalopy and announced that he was taking Jack to Mexico. Carolyn had filed for divorce, though their daughter Jamie had been born on January 26. Neal had then married Diana Hansen, committing bigamy, since the divorce was not yet final. Abandoning the pregnant Diana in New York, he fled to Denver and picked up Kerouac, and in June they drove 1,767 miles to Mexico City to visit Burroughs. In *On the Road*, Kerouac described it as "the most pleasant and graceful billowy trip in the world," and Mexico struck him as "the magic land at the end of the road."[16]

He was entering the Third World for the first time, and the primitive "Fellaheen Indians," or peasants, were a revelation. The "civilized" world he'd left behind was gripped in cold war paranoia. The United States had started building the hydrogen bomb in January 1950, and the Korean War had begun on June 24. Kerouac wrote Jim Sampas, who served in the armed forces, that without divine intervention, the world was lost, and they'd might as well get ready to die. But high on grass, bouncing along the Mexican roads in Neal's old car, he experienced a happy hallucination: a microburst of gold shot from the sky, rushed at the car, and poured into his startled eyes. This was the moment, he later wrote, that at last made *On the Road* possible, the "great occasion" when he understood the meaning of Neal as an American icon. In his vision, Neal was God, and God had the face of President Franklin D. Roosevelt, the crippled hero who had saved the world from oppression and slavery. For all his faults, Neal was, like Jane Austen's Emma, faultless — an example of nature at it most triumphant. Though he drove like a psycho, passing eighteen-wheelers on narrow bridges and barely missing oncoming cars, he seemed to create the spaces he needed with his amazing coordination and confidence, and he always delivered his passengers safely to their destination. He was freedom personified, or so he appeared to those like Kerouac, who tended to idealize and deify him.

When Neal and Jack reached Mexico City in June 1950, Mexican hipsters had already preceded them, establishing a beachhead on Redondas Street, the scene of what Kerouac called "beat (poor) Mexican nightlife," where they peddled dope and crucifixes. The local hipsters looked cool in their wide-brimmed sombreros and zoot suit jackets, which were worn over bare chests. Jack and Neal found an apartment close to Bill and Joan Burroughs, who had fled the United States after Bill's last drug bust and were living at 37 Cerrada de Medellin with their children. Burroughs was writing *Junky*, one of the classic confessional romans à clef of Beat literature. Joan, on finding that Benzedrine was not available in Mexico City, had discovered tequila, which she drank from 8 A.M. until she passed out. Burroughs was free to have as much sex as he wanted with Mexican boys, who charged only forty cents. He and Joan were stalled sexually, locked in terminal conflict.

Kerouac soon discovered how mistaken he'd been to turn Neal into his personal god. As a result of drinking cheap wine and trailing after Neal through a succession of bordellos during a weeklong binge, Jack contracted amoebic dysentery, and Neal again deserted him. "Gotta get back to my life," he said, and vanished after stealing a few dollars from Jack, who was bedridden and barely conscious. Fortunately, Bill and Joan nursed him back to health.

Once he recovered, he found himself at loose ends in Mexico City, stayed stoned, smoking fifteen joints a day, and helped himself to Bill's morphine. When he finally went back to work, he attempted to combine *Dr. Sax* and *On the Road* into one long novel, giving Sal a childhood in Lowell, but it was a bad idea, and he soon dropped it. After another hallucination in which he saw himself canonized as the saintly hero and prophetic author of *On the Road*, he left Mexico City in July 1950 and began walking to New York, carrying two-and-a-half pounds of Mexican grass wrapped in silk and lashed to his waist. After he crossed the border at Laredo, he seemed to receive another sign that his life would always be that of a wandering mystic. In Dilley, Texas, an old man with long white hair approached him, said "Go moan for man," and disappeared into the darkness of the hot midsummer night. After that, Jack seemed to accept that it was his destiny to walk across America on foot, often in total darkness. He continued his homeward journey with a renewed sense of purpose, occasionally getting a ride. Despite the pain and heartbreak of his Mexican misadventure, *On the Road* was taking shape inside his soul.[17]

In New York, Kerouac struck John Clellon Holmes as having been "savaged" and "burned down." Together with Holmes and Lucien Carr, he went to Cape Cod to rest up and to contemplate the big question posed in his journals and letters in 1950: What was his true voice? He wrote Neal that he'd been attempting to find his own style ever since their Mexican trip. He knew that he was an effective mime, that *The Town and the City* was a fair impersonation of Wolfean thunder, and that he could imitate the voices of many other writers: the deafening silence of Fyodor Dostoyevsky; Louis-Ferdinand Celine's yelling; Mark Twain's riverboat banter; Henry James's aloofness; and Herman Melville's Shakespearean soliloquizing. On the beaches of Cape Cod in the summer of 1950, Kerouac began to have an inkling that his own voice would be that of a railroad man like Neal, but in order to claim it he would first have to break through the mannered literary elocutions he'd devised for publishers and critics. He turned again to Neal's letters, his Rosetta Stone for modern vernacular, and began to find his "middle style," the one he'd shortly use in *On the Road*.

Provincetown that summer seemed like an extension of Manhattan, and on Commercial Street or at the beach tourists rubbed elbows with Norman Mailer, Tennessee Williams, Mary McCarthy, Edmund Wilson, Dwight Macdonald, Franz Kline, Larry Rivers, Gerry Mulligan, Zoot Sims, and Stan Getz. Mailer and his wife Bea were in their final year together, and by the following summer Kerouac's old girlfriend Adele Morales would be living with Mailer in P-town. According to painter Fay Donoghue, a friend of Mailer's, "Given what was in the air, the whole Beat thing, [Adele's] cachet was that she had been involved with Kerouac. Norman was . . . great fun to be with but by no means the most famous writer in P-Town." In 1950, Kerouac was attracted to Helen Parker, John Dos Passos's ex-fiancee. He asked her to return to Mexico with him, but she explained that she was already romantically involved with Ginsberg. Eventually, she spurned both Jack and Allen in favor of folk singer Ramblin' Jack Elliott.[18]

Back in Manhattan, Kerouac crashed in Seymour Wyse's Chelsea apartment at Twenty-fourth Street and Ninth Avenue. In a single day, he wrote twenty thousand words of *On the Road*, mostly concerning Neal, and showed it to Holmes, asking if he should go on with the book. Neither Ginsberg nor Cassady were supportive of his recent efforts; Ginsberg called him a megalomaniac when Jack expressed satisfaction over his writing, and Neal suggested that marijuana was giving Jack delusions of grandeur. They were both wrong. Kerouac was beginning to hit his stride as a writer, but only Holmes was sharp enough to see it, and he alone encouraged Kerouac to stick with *On the Road*.[19]

One day in the autumn of 1950, Kerouac and Holmes went to Cannastra's loft together and found him sitting among empty beer bottles and broken records, talking to a woman who was wearing only a slip. Later, as they all walked down the street on their way to a party, Cannastra started snapping the aerials off parked cars. As he presented the aerials to Kerouac and remarked, "Wands, Your Highness, wands," Holmes was reminded of Jupiter clutching "bolts of lightning." Joan Haverty realized that Cannastra was depressed because he'd just received a Dear John letter from his fiancée. Somewhat later on, in early October, Ginsberg and Cannastra sat in the San Remo discussing death for five hours, and Ginsberg read Cannastra a recent poem containing a reference to a grave that would prove sadly prophetic. Cannastra said he liked a Howard Moss poem that portrayed love as such a miracle that it could make plants move and water speak.

Not long thereafter, Kerouac went to Cannastra's loft to borrow money and later ended up with Cannastra, Alan Harrington, Lucien, and Lucien's girl in a bar full of toughs, all spoiling for a fight. Cannastra yelled, "Up your ass with Mobilgas," and Lucien, looking exotic in his red shirt and with five o'clock shadow, started flirting dangerously with some hoodlums in the bar, Kerouac later wrote Neal. Sensing trouble, the owner's son, a soldier, told them to get out, but Lucien made one of his sassy remarks, and the soldier threw beer at him. Grabbing the glass, Lucien ground it in the soldier's face, and the soldier slugged him. Rushing to Lucien's aid, Jack seized him and headed for the door. One of the hoodlums flew at Jack, but Jack smashed him in the mouth. He felt confident that he could have taken on the whole bar, had Harrington, Cannastra, and Lucien only been capable of helping him, but they were useless, Jack later complained to Neal, and they permitted two of the toughs to pin Jack's arms behind him, kick him in his testicles, and begin to beat him to death. He later explained to Neal why his companions were such wimps: Lucien and Cannastra were "masochistic," and Harrington was no fighter. Murder was in the air, but Jack escaped with nothing worse than a battered face, thanks to a "quarterback sneak" recalled from his gridiron days. Drunk, they staggered out of the bar in the early morning hours, and Jack became separated from Cannastra on Bleecker Street.[20]

A woman named Ann Adams later gave Ginsberg an eyewitness account of what happened next, and Ginsberg relayed the gruesome details in a letter to Neal on October 31, 1950. Cannastra, Lucien, and a few others wandered around and ended up at Ann Adams's house, and then decided to move on to Lucien's apartment. Their intention was to take the subway to Lucien's, get some money, and then continue partying, though it was nearly dawn. By now, Cannastra and Lucien were quite drunk and affectionately grabbing one another, Ginsberg recalled. On the subway, waiting for the train to start, they began to talk about the Bleecker Tavern, where a Negro woman named Winnie hung out. Clowning around, Cannastra started climbing out the window of the train just as the doors slammed shut. When he tried to get back in, he discovered to his horror that he was stuck, having apparently misjudged the size of the opening in relation to his body. As the train began to move, he was completely helpless. With half his torso hanging out the window and half in the car, he was unable to gain any purchase or even maintain balance. His friends tried to pull him back without success. As the train sped out of the station and roared into the tunnel, they held onto him, and his coat started to rip. They tried to reach his shoulders, but he was too far out the window. When Cannastra realized that he was doomed, he let out blood-curdling screams, begging for help. A line of pillars rushed at him. He cringed and ducked his head, but it slammed against the first pillar with a hideous thud. Then, with pulverizing force, his body was yanked through the window and immediately vanished beneath the wheels of the train. Someone pulled the emergency cord, and the train ground to a halt. Ann Adams rushed to the last car and looked out. Cannastra was lying on the tracks, his skull cracked open, with his brain visible from one temple. According to Holmes, his body had been caught in the wheels and dragged fifty-five feet. He was pronounced dead on arrival at Columbus Hospital.

William Frankel said that Cannastra's death marked a turning point in the lives of everyone in the Beat circle, frightening them into making commitments they'd previously avoided. Kerouac immediately felt a panicky urge to marry and settle down, though he was serious about no one. He called Holmes at 5 P.M. on the day following the accident to report that no one had claimed Cannastra's body. He had a vague impression that Cannastra's parents lived "somewhere upstate, no one knew where," Holmes later wrote. "I didn't love him," Holmes reflected. "Did anyone love him?" Both Kerouac and Ginsberg had loved Cannastra, though only Ginsberg would write about him. Kerouac's relationship with Cannastra was too overtly homoerotic for him to feel comfortable dealing with it in his novels; it was "too hot to handle," as he put it to me, though he did mention Cannastra briefly in *Visions of Cody* as "Finistra." Ginsberg eulogized Cannastra in a poem, calling him a "great angel," and in another poem he wrote that Cannastra, who had practiced law, had been mercifully spared being ground up like "raw meat" in the legal profession. In "Howl," Cannastra was immortalized as the hipster who toppled from a subway car. Tennessee Williams, who had been carrying on a running affair with Cannastra since 1944, later reminisced about Cannastra's "warm sort of puppy-dog playfulness of nature. He was beat before there were 'beats' . . . Bill was way out of his closet and he was always drunk but a good drunk, I mean a wildly exuberant drunk, and he was a good lay."

Kerouac met Holmes and other friends of Cannastra's at a Village bar for a wake. With a shiver and a shrug, Holmes remembered Cannastra's famous parties, which had "blossomed in so many nights and afternoons like bright evil flowers," and the torrent of booze that had been "vomited and flushed away, and that had run out at last." Kerouac said it was "the end of an era," but Holmes's wife, Marian, scolded him for talking about Cannastra in such impersonal terms, and Kerouac said, "Oh, Christ, I didn't mean it that way." In 1950, there was still a Hoboken ferry at the bottom of Christopher Street, and they all wandered down to it in the chill October air and took it to Jersey for steamed clams. But once they were standing on River Street, they forgot about the clams and made a beeline for a pub with a red Rheingold neon sign. According to Ginsberg, the key question on everyone's mind was whether Cannastra had committed suicide or been the victim of a bizarre accident. Carl Solomon referred to Cannastra's death as "an invitation wrapped in a joke." Ginsberg concluded that Cannastra had had no idea that his dangerous games might one day end in death, or that his blind willfulness had always been working toward catastrophe. Life, Ginsberg believed, was like a machine, and the fuel was one's intuition. His long discussion of death with Cannastra a few nights before the accident had been a clear warning, though neither he nor Cannastra had recognized it. Through intuition one could escape the tyranny of chance, but what Ginsberg failed to take into account was alcohol's power to destroy intuition. None of them saw that Cannastra's drunken state that night had impaired his judgment.

Bob Burford recalled that people started calling them the Lost Generation, but Kerouac insisted, "This is a Beat Generation." After Cannastra's death, the Beats began to disperse, deserting the San Remo, and pursuing creative projects or new relationships. Kerouac disappeared into Queens, brooded on solitary marijuana highs, and on the rare occasions when he rejoined the crowd in Manhattan he looked like a Fitzgeraldean survivor of the twenties, wondering what to do now that the path of excess had once again led to tragedy.[21] Jack was busy writing On the Road, and Holmes was finishing Go!, in an as-yet-unwitting race to come out with the first Beat Generation novel. Ginsberg, who was still trying to become interested in women, pursued Cannastra's former girl, Joan Haverty, but only because he wanted to live in Cannastra's spacious, inexpensive loft. Ginsberg was still drawn to men. His passion for Larry Rivers was unreciprocated, but he allegedly seduced a twenty-year-old poet on the Village scene, Gregory Corso, a tousle-haired delinquent.[22]

Meanwhile, in early November 1950, Kerouac was on his way to a party at Lucien's when he saw a light in the window of Cannastra's loft and called up. Joan Haverty stuck her head out, and invited him in for hot chocolate. It took Kerouac only one night to edge Ginsberg out of the picture and move into the loft. In a letter to Neal he wrote that he felt alive and strong again after months of writing and rewriting On the Road. Joan was an attractive, dark-haired girl who was stunning enough to be a model, but Jack mistook her for a doormat, someone to cook and wash for him while he wrote. An accomplished dressmaker, Joan was on her own in New York at the age of twenty, alienated from her family in Albany. Until the age of fourteen she had lived in Hollywood, growing up in her parents' house off Sunset Boulevard at Fountain Avenue. She reminded Jack of Gloria Jean, the dewy-eyed charmer in W. C. Fields's Never Give a Sucker an Even Break. To Holmes, she was an irrepressible jeune fille—fair, fresh, and guileless. The only holdout was Neal, who thought it insane of Kerouac even to contemplate marriage. In whorehouses, Jack was unable to achieve an erection, Neal disclosed in a November 25 letter to Ginsberg, adding that Kerouac was a great lover only in fantasy. The same could not be said of Neal, who masturbated at least once a day and again at night, but seemed to get the job done with others as well. Though Kerouac sensed himself edging ever closer to the altar, he knew he was making a terrible mistake, later revealing in *Visions of Cody* that he didn't love Joan or even like her and knew it eight days before they wed. When Elbert Lenrow lent Jack five dollars for the license, Lenrow sensed that the union was doomed.

Jack and Joan's wedding ceremony took place at 6 P.M. on November 17, 1950, one month after Cannastra's death, in Judge Lupiano's apartment, with Ginsberg, Lucien, and Holmes as Jack's best men. At 7 P.M., a strangely subdued group of twenty invited guests filed into the loft to celebrate, but crashers soon swelled the party to a hundred. The final tally was even larger, according to Joan, who arrived at the loft to discover two hundred people, most of them complete strangers to her. Ginsberg and a friend climbed to the roof to smoke pot, so they wouldn't subject the other guests to the threat of arrest and imprisonment. Stoned, they went back down to the party where, to Ginsberg's bleary eyes, sober guests such as Bill Frankel and John Hollander seemed subdued and conservative. Lucien attended with Lizzie Lehrman, and also present were Holmes, Lenrow, Carl Solomon, Alan Harrington, Alan Ansen, and "Winnie," presumably the barmaid Cannastra had been thinking of before his accident. The guests struck Joan as a slouchy bunch of freeloaders and dipsomaniacs, and she was uncomfortably aware of being appraised with the avid interest of museum-goers inspecting a Renoir. The party ended, to her disappointment, without anyone having kissed her or wished her well. Nor was she delighted to discover that the beer keg had leaked, and someone had spilled a whole platter of hors d'oeuvers behind the refrigerator.[23]

Jack passed out and missed his own wedding night, but Joan helped him undress and put him to bed. He made up for his dereliction the following night, and wrote Neal on November 21 that he had gotten Joan pregnant on November 18. Neal replied that he hoped they'd conceived a son with large ears and an even larger penis. Joan soon discovered that she was expected to earn their keep, and she took a department store job at the beginning of the Christmas rush, while Jack wrote in the loft or lay in bed depressed. On December 3, he wrote Neal that he had been hired by Twentieth-Century Fox to read books at home and prepare synopses for the story department. By December 14, he was able to tell Neal that *On the Road* had been lassoed and wrestled to the ground.[24]

The marriage was probably the worst decision Kerouac ever made. Just two years later, he wrote Stella that Joan was "insane." He explained to Neal and Carolyn that Joan had been a lonely child reared in a fatherless family, and that her mother had passed her hatred of the male sex on to her daughter. Joan and her mother then dumped all their rage and frustration on Kerouac, or so Jack said; the perceptive Seymour Wyse defended Joan, finding her cheery and animated, and knew the real problem was Jack's insistence on leading a separate existence apart from any woman he got involved with — behavior guaranteed to induce insanity in any marriage partner.

According to Carolyn, Neal resented Jack's marriage because he'd been planning to travel alone with Jack in the coming months. Neal saw nothing but disaster ahead for Jack and Joan. In a letter to Ginsberg, he argued that Jack would never be able to satisfy Joan's sexual demands and that Joan was not clever enough to realize that the only way she could hold Jack was by giving him plenty of space. But Neal's own deficiencies as a husband and lover hardly qualified him as a marriage counselor. Carolyn later told *Rolling Stone*, "The only way he was not able to do it was when I was offering or willing. It had to be rape. Until finally I only submitted because I was afraid of him. At last, then, I said, 'I can't stand it anymore, kill me or whatever,' and much to my surprise he was very nice about it, he seemed to understand." Neal had his complaints about Carolyn too and wrote Ginsberg on May 15, 1951, that he was afraid he'd worn her out. As a result, he found other sex partners and also began to masturbate more. Attempting to resolve their sexual issues, Carolyn told Neal that she knew she disappointed him, but pointed out that if he were more faithful and dependable, she would become a more loving wife. But she lost hope when she saw a letter of Neal's to Jack, in which he wrote that he masturbated three times daily, however much reciprocal sex he was also having, and used to ejaculate a dozen times during all-day masturbatory sessions. After reading this, Carolyn told Neal his sex obsession was repulsive and potentially dangerous to both of them.[25]

Though Joan went to work to pay the rent while Jack wrote, eventually they were unable to afford the loft and so moved in with Mémère in Queens. It was an impossible arrangement from the start. Mémère lectured Joan about how to take care of Jack and then competed with her by indulging Jack's every whim. He tried to work on *On the Road*, but Joan distracted him by stacking rolls of cloth and other dressmaking supplies on his rolltop desk. Despite this aggravation, he was coming up with numerous alternate titles for *On the Road*, including "Love on the Road," "Look Out for Your Boy," "Hit the Road," and "Lost on the Road." While stoned one night, he wrote Neal that he was playing his Cuban bongo drums while Joan showered and Mémère sat in front of her Magnavox watching the Korean War news. Two million Chinese communists had charged Allied troops in Korea, and President Truman had written in his diary, "It looks like World War III is here." It had certainly arrived in Queens; Jack and Joan got into an argument about Truman, and Jack curtly informed her that a wife should never oppose her husband in any matter. Joan was so upset that she accidentally burned Seymour Wyse's trousers, which Jack had brought home for her to peg and iron.[26]

The major literary news during the winter of 1950 was the awarding of the Nobel Prize to William Faulkner, with whom Kerouac felt an affinity; they were both autodidacts and both drunks. Kerouac liked to read Faulkner's novel about hard-drinking pilots, *Pylon*, while high on marijuana. Of the two literary lions of the fifties, Hemingway and Faulkner, Kerouac preferred Faulkner and advised Neal in a 1950 letter to avoid the posturing and spareness of Hemingway. Yet the greatest literary influence on Kerouac was not any of the published writers of his time, but Neal Cassady's "Joan Anderson Letter," perhaps the most famous document in Beat history and the work that shaped all of Kerouac's future writings.[27] Jack found the letter on the front steps when he left the apartment in Richmond Hill on December 17 and perused it on the subway to Manhattan on his way to work. He spent another two hours studying the letter while sitting in a cafeteria. At 6 P.M., he returned to Queens and Joan started reading the letter, becoming so absorbed that dinner was an hour late. It was one of the finest pieces of prose any American writer had ever achieved, Jack wrote Neal. Unfortunately, only a fragment of the letter survives. In a 1995 interview, John Sampas said, "Allen Ginsberg and Gerd Stern lost the 'Joan Anderson Letter.'" After Jack read it, he acclaimed Neal as the literary lion of Denver, which made Ginsberg so eager to read it that he broke into Jack's quarters and stole it. Ginsberg was still in feverish competition with Jack over Neal's affections as well as the shaping of Neal's talent.

Set in Denver during Christmas 1946, the "Joan Anderson Letter" recounts Neal's escape from a bathroom window after being caught making love to Mary Ann "Cherry Mary" Fairland and his hospital visit to another girlfriend, Joan Anderson, following her suicide attempt. Apparently, Neal intended to use the letter in an autobiographical novel that Jack and Allen had been trying to get him to write. Published in *The Portable Beat Reader* in 1992, the surviving fragment contains lines like, "I ripped into her like a maniac and she loved it. . . . On ordinary occasions, however, I'd just pull it out and shove—to her bottom if we were secluded, to her mouth if not." In Kerouac biographies, the length of the letter is usually reported at thirteen thousand words, the figure given in Kerouac's December 27, 1950, letter to Neal. But some years later, in the *Paris Review*, Kerouac said the "Joan Anderson Letter" was forty thousand words long, and he repeated his original estimation of it as "the greatest piece of writing I ever saw." The surviving fragment fails to bear out such claims, but the original document was better, Kerouac indicated in the *Paris Review*. Besides Joan and Cherry Mary, the original dealt with a Christmas holiday weekend in seedy Denver settings such as pool rooms, flophouses, and jails cells, with incidents Kerouac called "hilarious and tragic." Neither of those words describes the 1997 movie based on Neal's letter, *The Last Time I Committed Suicide*, which seems pointless despite solid performances by Thomas Jane, Claire Forlani, and Keanu Reeves. Whatever the literary quality of the "Joan Anderson Letter," it galvanized the "middle" style of *On the Road*, Kerouac's best novel. He called Neal's prose "kickwriting"—first-person-singular arias composed in fits of soul-bearing frenzy—and henceforth Kerouac decided to write only when his material transported him into a state of ecstasy. In the *Paris Review*, he attributed *On the Road*'s uninhibited style entirely to the impact of Cassady's letters.

Neal was surprised at the electrifying effect the "Joan Anderson Letter" had on Kerouac and Ginsberg. Aware that both men idolized him, he modestly dismissed their encomiums as starry-eyed flattery and insisted that his life amounted to nothing but a mirage and a rainbow. The letter was the product of a three-day Benzedrine binge, he confessed. Ginsberg offered to edit the letter, promising that Van Doren and Trilling could use their influence to get it published as a novelette or an entry in the *Short Story* contest, but Neal cavalierly brushed off such suggestions. He didn't have the time or inclination to do additional work on it and was reserving his energy for *The First Third*, which seemed odd, since he hated his novel and called it an embarrassing flatulence. Like most people who attempt to learn to write, play a musical instrument, paint a picture, or master any of the arts, Neal came to the conclusion that writing was simply too much work. Kerouac, who seemed determined to turn everyone in his life into an author, was also encouraging Joan to write and called her, in a letter to Neal, a talented newcomer worth watching. Her talents were infinitesimal, and she squandered them on unpromising subjects such as how happy she felt upon arising in the morning, despite Jack's advice that she should write about a sex maniac who'd abused children in the Los Angeles of her youth.[28]

Almost immediately after receiving the "Joan Anderson Letter," Kerouac began a series of confessional letters to Neal in which he unintentionally outlined most of his novels for the next ten years, beginning with *On the Road* and including the Lowell novels. First published in 1995, the letters contain some of Kerouac's best writing, and they occupy sixty pages in *Selected Letters: 1940–1956*. He narrated the story of his life and revealed that his major preoccupations, which would shortly become the subjects of his novels, were Gerard's death, childhood homoeroticism and ghoulish fantasies, religious visions, teenage sexual experiences, his crack-up in the navy, his heartbreak when Neal abandoned him and LuAnne in San Francisco, fears of being homosexual, and his road trips with Neal. "Jack rehearsed his novels in his letters and note books," John Sampas said in 1995, but Jack's December 28, 1950–January 10, 1951, letters to Neal are also brilliant in their own right.

The competition between Kerouac's wife and mother became unbearable in early January 1951. Joan moved out, returned to Manhattan, and rented an apartment at 454 West Twentieth Street. Jack tagged after her, bringing his rolltop desk, and she let him move in. She found a job waiting tables at Stouffer's, and Jack was earning thirty-five dollars a week from his reader's job at Twentieth-Century Fox. After begging them to move to San Francisco, Neal arrived in New York in February 1951, ready to transport them across the continent, but they couldn't afford to relocate. "I'm sure it hurt Neal and bowled him over," Carolyn Cassady wrote. Neal feared that

Jack's yearning for family life had superseded his need for Neal. While still in New York, Neal attempted a reconciliation with Diana Hansen, but she kicked him out when he proposed moving her to Watsonville, where he'd make love to her on off-nights from Carolyn. The moment of Jack and Neal's parting provided both *On the Road* and *Visions of Cody* with their powerful final scenes. Jack was trying to get to a Duke Ellington concert with Joan and Henri Cru, who had leased a limo for the evening. Neal, shivering in his thin West Coast clothes, asked for a lift to Penn Station, but Cru refused, and Neal was left on the street. Jack and Joan told him they might come out to the coast in a month or so, and roared off in the limo. On Steve Allen's TV show years later, Kerouac said he and Neal both realized they had to go on to later stages of their lives. "Adios," he wrote in *Visions of Cody*, "Adios, King."[29]

Jack's marriage seemed to disintegrate shortly after he and Neal said goodbye. In a February 20, 1951, letter to Alfred Kazin, Kerouac volunteered a surprisingly intimate fact about his married life, which was all the more unusual since he and Kazin were not close friends, and the occasion for the letter was an impersonal request for help in obtaining a Guggenheim grant. He felt like a prisoner in the marriage and compared himself with the homicidal protagonist of *An American Tragedy*, a young man who, like Kerouac, dreamed of wealth, but was stuck with a working-class girl, whom he impregnated and ultimately murdered. Roberta Alden, the unfortunate factory girl in Theodore Dreiser's novel, lived in a rented room, and in Kerouac's letter to Kazin, he characterized his marriage to Joan as a tawdry, boarding-house affair, unbearable and depressing. Joan was miserable too and had started screaming at him. When he complained to Seymour Wyse, Seymour said, "The problem, Jack, is you're not bringing 'ome the bycon."[30]

Despite their difficulties, Kerouac loved Joan. In a 1951 letter to Neal, he confided that he kept a special place in his heart for her and always would. *On the Road*, he later told *Saturday Review*, was written expressly for Joan. Beginning April 2, 1951, while living with her, he conquered the last technical hurdles, and *On the Road* took its final form as an elegiac ode to Neal (as Dean Moriarty), narrated by his sidekick, Kerouac (as Sal Paradise). One of the last creative issues was whether to sketch in the characters' backgrounds or just skip "all such throat-clearing scenes," as he put it to me when we later discussed the same issue with regard to *Desolation Angels*. In the end, he kept his narrative as brisk and simple as Burroughs's no-frills reportage in *Junky*, which Kerouac read and admired when Burroughs sent him the manuscript. The universal rejection of Burroughs's book by New York editors when Ginsberg, acting as agent, first offered it to them glumly foreshadowed the mauling they'd soon give *On the Road*. In his decline letter — editors use the word decline rather than rejection — Jason Epstein, an editor at Doubleday, deemed Burroughs's prose inferior and said he wouldn't touch such a hot subject unless the author were a head of state. According to Ginsberg, Doubleday viewed drug addicts as shameful and beneath the dignity of a reputable imprint. Not many years later Mailer saluted Burroughs as "the only American novelist living today who may conceivably be possessed by genius."

The main catalyst for what came to be known as the definitive, "scroll" version of *On the Road*, written in April 1951, was Neal and his sinewy, onrushing "Joan Anderson Letter," which showed Jack how a hip, organic style could capture the essence of their travels and spiritual longings.[31] Rarely sleeping, Kerouac wrote the final draft in twenty days as Joan supplied him with bowls of steaming pea soup and mugs of hot coffee. He placed a screen around his rolltop so his light wouldn't keep her awake, and he asked her to sleep next to him as he worked. He typed furiously, a hundred words per minute, using what he described to Neal on May 22 as tracing paper that he'd found among Cannastra's possessions. Scotch-taping these sheets together, he created a 120-foot-long roll. Other biographies are full of contradictory claims about the scroll, mostly because of Kerouac's own conflicting reference to it on the "Steve Allen Show" as "Teletype paper." The scroll has survived and it is on deposit in the Berg Collection at the New York Public Library though it is still owned by the Kerouac estate. Interviewed in 1995, John Sampas stated, "It is *tracing paper*, the kind architects used." Kerouac created it because he did not want to interrupt the flow of his prose by stopping to change paper in the typewriter carriage. The scroll proved to be so effective that he completed twelve thousand words the first day, frequently shedding his sweat-drenched T-shirts. From April 2 to 22 he averaged six thousand words per day, energized by regular messages from Neal, such as the postcard dated April Fool's in which Neal stated with eloquent simplicity and brevity that he adored Jack.

According to Holmes, Jack and Joan's feuds became combative as he neared the end of the novel. Joan later maintained that she kicked Jack out on May 5. He then spent most of his time at Lucien's West Twenty-first Street loft, but one evening he returned to the apartment without warning and found Joan in bed with a co-worker from the restaurant where she was employed. He retreated to Richmond Hill and Mémère to lick his wounds, but after a few days, he moved his rolltop desk to Lucien's place in Chelsea and continued writing. Lucien could hear Jack typing when he left for the UP office in the morning, and the typewriter was still going when Lucien turned in at night. "I suppose he must have stopped sometimes to eat and sleep, but you couldn't prove it by me," Lucien recalled. Holmes arrived one day to lunch with Jack, Lucien, Temko, and Liz Lehrman, and Jack unrolled the scroll until it stretched thirty feet from the typewriter.

A week later, Kerouac finished *On the Road*, completing the final fifteen-thousand-word segment, largely an account of his Mexican expedition with Neal, on the last day. Lucien's cocker spaniel gnawed through the end of the roll and destroyed several feet of it. "It had perforce to be rewritten," Lucien recalled, "but I know for a fact that that was the *only* part of *On the Road* that was rewritten." In a single month, Jack had created a 125,000-

word novel, and it was a masterpiece, a revelatory knockout spiked with epiphanies and riotous innovation. It displayed Kerouac's wonderful "middle style," which fell between *The Town and the City* and the "spontaneous prose" he adopted in the autumn of 1951. Kerouac toted the entire three-inch-thick scroll to Holmes, who described it as a single paragraph, single-spaced, and using the real names of Ginsberg, Cassady, Burroughs, Hal Chase, and others, instead of the later invented ones.[32] The scroll was ridiculed at first by all who saw it, including Holmes, who compared it with a salami, but after Holmes read it, he told Jack he'd brought off something special. Perhaps the main reason for the pristine quality of the prose was that, despite legends to the contrary, Jack remained relatively drug-free while writing *On the Road*. In a letter to Neal, he stated emphatically that the only drug he used was coffee, and he added that caffeine was far better for a writer than Benzedrine, marijuana, or any other mood-altering drug, because coffee triggered additional reserves of brainpower.

The next person to read *On the Road* was Ginsberg, who somewhat reservedly called it well-written but at least acknowledged its newly minted quality. Ginsberg had been more astute in his assessment of *The Town and the City*, but he'd never properly evaluate *On the Road*, the jewel in the Kerouac canon, for which Kerouac would one day curse him. Immediately after reading the scroll, Ginsberg fired off a gossipy letter to Neal on May 7, telling him that Jack's novel was all about Neal, and noting that the ending was weak, because Jack had held back from showing that Neal was doomed. Jack was alarmed when he discovered Ginsberg's indiscretion and hastened to reassure Neal on May 22 that he was not forecasting Neal's death in *On the Road*, but he confirmed that it was indeed about Neal's life. He further characterized it as a radical change from anything he'd ever written, and indeed from any other book ever published. He foresaw that critics would hate it.

Neal wrote Ginsberg a witty letter suggesting alternate endings to *On the Road*, and in one, Neal died of prostate cancer induced by habitual masturbation. The other endings foreshadowed actual calamities in Neal's future; in one, he ended up in San Quentin, and in another, he suffered a serious injury while working on the railroad, dying without realizing his full potential. Neal's own writing had come to a standstill because, as he wrote Jack, marijuana had numbed his mind and warped his perception. In evaluating *On the Road*, Neal was as wrongheaded as Ginsberg, dismissing it as frivolous and insignificant. Kerouac would be well advised to put it aside, Neal added, unless he was willing to follow Neal's advice and blend it with *Dr. Sax*. Better still, it should be shelved for the present and later incorporated into a massive Proustian chronicle, a multivolume edition that would indeed be the Great American Novel. Neal had always been too hard on himself, "sweating over his inadequacies as a writer," as Carolyn put it, setting impossible goals, and feeling he had to be as good as Flaubert. For that reason, he imposed the same inappropriate standards on Jack and failed to recognize

On the Road as the novel that defined a generation. Lucien too missed the novel's essence—its jazz-like extemporaneousness and impudent pop-art freshness—and called it "shit," Jack wrote Neal on June 24, 1951. If Kerouac had followed the advice of well-meaning friends to tighten the narrative and sharpen the focus, he would have ruined *On the Road* and destroyed its form-shattering innovations.[33]

Despite faltering support from Ginsberg, who reread the novel and finally decided it was at least Beat, Kerouac was full of elation and confidence the day he rang Giroux from the loft and told him that *On the Road* had been completed. Later, in Giroux's office, Kerouac dramatically unfurled the scroll on the floor. "Here's your novel," he said. Instead of the expected exclamations of wonder and delight, Giroux said, "How the hell can the printer work from this?" Kerouac looked at him in shock. "But Jack, how can you make corrections on a manuscript like that?" Giroux asked. "After all, the idea of separate sheets of paper is to make it easier to rewrite."

"I don't make any corrections," Kerouac said, according to Giroux. "Everything's down there just the way I want it. That's the way it is. That's the way it will be." Kerouac then "stormed out in a rage," Giroux recalled, adding, "I never read a word of it." In a smoking 1952 letter to Ginsberg, Kerouac placed the primary blame for the agonies he experienced in connection with *On the Road* on Ginsberg and Giroux, and attributed to them the excremental odor of Manhattan.

He went to Joan's apartment battered but unbowed, Joan recalled, and denounced Giroux as a "crass idiot." Giroux later said, "That was my first experience as an editor with this my-words-are-sacred attitude in a writer. And I told him, 'Even Shakespeare, who, they say, didn't blot many words, blotted some, after all.' " Giroux subsequently claimed that the Shakespeare remark was a misquote. Kerouac wrote in *Playboy* in 1959 that Harcourt rejected *On the Road* because the company's sales manager, Ed Hodge, thought it a dud, and Kerouac noted that Giroux said, "Jack, this is just like Dostoyevsky, but what can I do at this time?" In a June 24, 1951 letter to Neal, Kerouac wrote that Giroux blamed the president of the company, advised Jack to stick to the traditional style of *The Town and the City*, and objected to *On the Road* as too experimental and possibly unlawful due to its cast of pot-smoking Beats and flagrant homosexuals. In 1966, Kerouac told Charters that after Giroux informed him of the sales manager's veto, "I said all right, I'll take it to Viking, and they sat on it for seven years." Failing to realize that the author-editor relationship is strictly business, Kerouac had naively assumed Giroux to be his friend for life, especially after their experiences together in the West, and he was not prepared for the abrupt termination of their relations. A year or so after the fiasco at Harcourt, he wrote a touching letter to Giroux, pondering whether their friendship had ever been real and concluding that in the end it had been purely professional.[34]

Even worse than the rejection of his second novel, from Kerouac's standpoint, was the news that Joan was pregnant. They met on Lucien's roof for a summit conference, and Jack explained that he wanted children but his book had been rejected and so he couldn't support a family in the foreseeable future. Joan locked him out of the apartment. The marriage was over. Sexually, at least, it had been more active than indicated in previous biographies. Kerouac's sex list reveals that he and his second wife made love one hundred and fifty times. They must have had sex almost daily during the seven months they were wed. Though Kerouac went into the relationship cynically, to get Cannastra's loft as well as a housekeeper, cook, and financial support, something changed in the course of their marriage. According to Neal, Kerouac experienced difficulty in achieving an erection prior to his marriage. Frequency is not a measure of whether a couple is intimate or has a successful relationship, but the blunt statistic in the archive indicates that Joan restored his potency. He considered the marriage a mistake, but he also wrote in *Visions of Cody* that in destroying it, he threw away his life.

Homeless again, Jack sought refuge in Lucien's loft, casting himself on the mercy of perhaps his most steadfast and reliable friend. Joan found herself in the frequent predicament of Beat wives: Like Carolyn, she was pregnant and abandoned, and she went home to Albany to have the baby. Janet "Jan" Michele, a daughter, was born on February 16, 1952. Later, when Joan took legal action, naming Jack as the father, he told Mémère that Joan had been unfaithful and that the baby wasn't his. Over four decades later, at the Kerouac archive, John Sampas released a notebook entry of Kerouac's dated March 21, 1962, in which he wrote: "Janet is NOT my daughter (because I remember Angelo 'Rosario' in my bed a month in 1951)." According to Carolyn Cassady, Kerouac told her and Neal in early 1952, "I caught her with this Puerto Rican a couple of times, see, and now she's pregnant and says it's my child—ha—it ain't *my* child." In 1995, John Sampas disclosed a separate notebook entry dated March 15, 1961, in which Kerouac denies paternity. In the 1960s, Joe Chaput asked Jack if he'd ever had a daughter, and Jack told him that he must be insane even to wonder.[35]

Mounting pressures combined with Jack's history of alcohol and drug abuse brought on a near-fatal attack of thrombophlebitis in the summer of 1951. Fortunately, Jack had gone to North Carolina and was cared for by Nin and Mémère. Apparently he spent some time recovering in Rocky Mount Sanitarium and was virtually immobile for a month, his legs propped on a chair. He edited the *On the Road* scroll; began *Pic*, his Huck Finn–type novella, which he would not complete for another eighteen years; read Melville, Lawrence, Blake, and Whitman; and listened to baseball games.

Returning to New York, Kerouac became embroiled in another competitive struggle with Ginsberg over Lucien. On August 31, he wrote Neal that he and Lucien were contemplating a trip to Mexico, and Ginsberg was so jealous that he was chasing after Lucien and devouring him with hungry, calculating eyes. Kerouac's phlebitis struck again on August 11, and he entered the Kingsbridge VA Hospital in the Bronx. Ginsberg leapt at the chance to replace him as Lucien's traveling companion. They left without visiting Kerouac, but later he was glad he hadn't gone with them, realizing that the antics of Lucien, Joan, and Ginsberg in Mexico would have finished him off.[36]

Burroughs had left Joan with the children at 210 Orizaba Street, a Mexican slum, and gone to Ecuador with a Florida GI named Lewis Marker. Later, he returned to Orizaba Street. On September 6, shortly after Ginsberg and Lucien Carr left Mexico, Burroughs drove himself into an anxiety attack over his predicament—that of a gay man trying to be a straight husband and father—and shot Joan through the head, killing her. It was an accident, he pleaded, but later added in *Queer*, "Murder is the national neurosis of Mexico." During a drunken "William Tell" parlor game, he'd ordered Joan to place a glass on her head so he could shoot it off with a Star .380 automatic. They'd consumed eight or ten drinks and had never performed the game before. Burroughs took aim at close range and fired. Joan slumped to the floor. Burroughs's friend, Lewis Marker, said, "Bill, your bullet has hit her forehead." Joan was pronounced dead on arrival at the Red Cross Hospital. Burroughs was arrested and charged with *imprudencia criminal*, but he wrote Ginsberg in January 1952 that he'd been sprung from jail and intended to "beat [the] rap." For two thousand dollars, a lawyer named Bernabe Jurado had arranged his release, and Mort Burroughs flew down from St. Louis with the $2,312 bail money. In San Francisco, when Carolyn heard of Joan's death, she mused, "Bill, the perfect marksman. How could it have happened?" Burroughs blamed a faulty gun, complaining that the sights were off. Joan was only twenty-seven, and Burroughs later confessed in *Queer*, "Hate and mischance blew the shot." He did not marry again, and when his affair with Marker was over, he undertook a passionate, slobbering pursuit of Ginsberg. Finally Burroughs moved to Tangier, where boys were plentiful. Kerouac reflected in *Visions of Cody*, "Mexico, drunk, June dying, I might have gone under."

Convinced that Joan's death was accidental and that Bill treasured her memory, Kerouac immortalized her as "June" in *Visions of Cody* and *Vanity of Duluoz*, as "Mary Dennison" in *The Town and the City*, and as "Jane" in *On the Road* and *The Subterraneans*. Perhaps her most characteristic line occurred in *Cody* when she advised Edie: "*Blow* Jack!" She would also grace several of Ginsberg's poems. In "The Names," she's the perennial hostess— generous, loving, and a bit melancholy. In "Dream Record: June 8, 1955," she lies forgotten in a seldom-visited grave in a Mexican garden, her epitaph obscured by the rain. In Carolyn's opinion, Joan committed suicide: When Bill's pointed revolver offered a quick and easy way out she raised her head in the final nanosecond and stopped the bullet. Ginsberg felt that Joan had long been trying to involve them all in a group suicide, including her children. After her death, Julie and Willie were raised by separate sets of grandparents. Though Joan Burroughs would never be regarded as such, she was the best example of the Beats' abuse of women, a sacrifice on the altar of bogus masculinity and dishonest sexuality.[37]

Shortly after Kerouac was released from the hospital, two patrol cars arrived at his mother's apartment in Richmond Hill and hauled him off in the middle of the night. He was booked for failing to support his pregnant wife, but in an October 1951 letter to Neal, he called Joan Haverty foolish for having him jailed, because he'd already assured her that he'd pay her prenatal doctor bill of five dollars per week privately and not through the court. He spent half an hour in jail with several Hispanic men who'd been nabbed for failure to pay child support, later referring to them as battered husbands. Upon Jack's release his mother told him she was moving south to live with Nin; from now on he'd have to fend for himself. He considered his dwindling options, and his correspondence with Stella indicates that he briefly considered returning to Lowell. Stella told him that her family was now running a bar in downtown Lowell. George Sampas had served his prison term, and the family had purchased the "Old 66" bar on Gorham Street for him to run. Jack asked Stella if he might hitch a ride to Lowell with Nick Sampas, a master sergeant in the Army, who was stationed in New York.

Meanwhile, Jack revised On the Road, typed it up as a regular manuscript, and gave it to an agent, Rae Everitt of MCA. An editor at Farrar, Straus suggested numerous revisions, but returned the manuscript without a contract. By June 24, 1951, Jack had broken off relations with MCA; in a letter to Neal he mentioned that his agent was now William Morris. To retrieve On the Road from MCA, Ginsberg invaded the offices of the entertainment colossus and snatched the dusty manuscript from the floor of a cluttered closet in the literary department.[38]

On October 9, Kerouac wrote Neal that he had completely reconceived On the Road. The new version was no longer a straightforward "horizontal" narrative of their road trips. It had become a "vertical, metaphysical" portrait of Neal. This was Visions of Cody, which Ginsberg described as an "in-depth" rendering of On the Road. Kerouac later told Joe Chaput that Cody was his favorite book. Drawing heavily on the "Joan Anderson Letter" and other Cassady material, it represented the full flowering of the writing method Kerouac called spontaneous prose. Some of his most familiar phrases occur in Cody, including, "The unspeakable visions of the individual" and "I struggle in the dark with the enormity of my soul, trying desperately to be a great rememberer redeeming life from darkness."[39] Despite the chaos of his personal life, he was in his prime as a writer, and the 1950s would be his best decade.

Burroughs too, now that Joan was out of the way, experienced a creative surge. He asked Kerouac to help him break into publishing by acting as his literary agent. Completing another draft of Junky, he decided to send it to Kerouac, but a friend lost it in a restaurant in Jacksonville, Florida. Fortunately Burroughs owned another draft, and asked Kerouac to handle it, since

Ginsberg had failed to find him a publisher. On July 30, 1951, Kerouac submitted *Junky* to James Laughlin at New Directions, the highly respected avant-garde publisher, promoting it as the most candid account of drug addiction to date. Kerouac was no more successful than Ginsberg had been, and seven months later he still hadn't heard from Laughlin. On February 24, 1952, he wrote a prodding letter, inquiring if anyone had even read the manuscript. Laughlin finally turned it down.

Resuming his role as Burroughs's agent, Ginsberg sold *Junky* the following year to Ace Books as a paperback original and also managed to stimulate Ace's interest in *On the Road*. Ace specialized in comic books, Westerns, whodunits, Gothic romances, and sci-fi — Frank Herbert and L. Ron Hubbard were Ace authors — and seemed an unlikely house for the Beats, but Ginsberg's old psychiatric-ward friend, Carl Solomon, was an editor there; he was also the nephew of the owner, A. A. Wyn. Evidently, Kerouac rehired Rae Everitt, for it was she who presented his terms to Ace for *On the Road*: a one-thousand-dollar advance, two-hundred-fifty payable on signing, with the balance to be paid at one hundred dollars per month. Solomon still had to persuade the conservative Wyn to take a chance on such a daring book, and as Kerouac awaited their decision, he decided to leave New York. Not the least of his motives was to escape the clutches of Joan and the Domestic Relations Court.[40]

Though homeless and jobless, Jack contemplated two prospects that old friends held out to him: Henri Cru suggested they hop a cargo ship and sail around the world together, and Neal invited him to San Francisco after Jack inquired whether Neal could get him a job as a brakeman on the Southern Pacific. In a passionate letter later quoted in Carolyn's memoir *Off the Road*, Neal declared his love for Jack, writing, "You love me, don't you? I love you, don't I?" Neal could hardly wait for Jack to arrive, and he painted an alluring picture of their future together as the van Gogh and Gauguin of literature, Jack writing masterpieces in the attic on Russell Street, while Neal benefited from Jack's editing and surged ahead with his own writing. Warning Jack that their life in San Francisco would not be restricted to "cunt and kicks," Neal then proceeded to offer all that and more if Jack would come back to him. He promised a car, a typewriter, free rent, use of his book and record collection and tape recorder, golf clubs, tennis racket, baseballs, pornography, Dexedrine, whores, and even, amazingly, his own wife, assuring Jack that Carolyn was also in love with him and would pamper him like his mother. He volunteered her services as washerwoman, portrait painter, and coffeemaker. And in case of a mental crack-up, never a remote possibility for any of them, an analyst at the nearby free clinic charged only fifty cents per visit. Since Carolyn had expelled Jack from 29 Russell Street less than two years previously, Neal promised, "Carolyn wants to try and make it up to you. We could try by way of a few group orgies." There would also be employment for Jack, since the railroad company Neal worked for was advertising for brakemen.

Henri Cru continued to woo Jack with visions of Oriental splendors they'd discover together on a world cruise, and guaranteed Jack a berth on a merchant freighter moored in Hoboken. While Cru managed to make it onto the ship, no job materialized for Jack, and Cru steamed out of Hoboken without him. However, he lent Jack sixty dollars for bus fare to California and promised he'd find a job for him on the ship, which would be docking on Christmas Eve, 1951 in San Pedro, California, just south of Los Angeles. Mémère contributed another thirty dollars toward bus fare, and Jack set out for San Francisco, planning to spend a few days with the Cassadys on Russian Hill before rendezvousing with Cru. On the bus from New York to California, high on Benzedrine and woozy on liquor supplied by friendly air force passengers, Jack noted in his journal that he'd crossed the Mississippi for the ninth time. He was road-weary, but as he later wrote in *Lonesome Traveler*, basically the same "old Ti Jean who'll go anywhere follow anyone for adventure."

In San Francisco, the freewheeling Cassady had painted himself into a corner with marital and family responsibilities. In desperation, he urged Jack to live with him and Carolyn indefinitely, hoping to have it both ways—an unconventional life and respectability at the same time. Neal and Carolyn now had three children: Cathy, four; Jamie, two; and a new baby, John Allen, who was named after both Kerouac and Ginsberg. Carolyn had convinced herself that the only way to hold Neal was to absorb Kerouac into the marriage, since neither man would give up the other. In December 1951, Kerouac settled in at 29 Russell Street after an abortive trip to San Pedro, where Cru had again failed to line up a merchant seaman's job for him. Kerouac made himself cozy in the Cassadys' roomy attic, but things soon began to go awry; he seemed determined to drive a wedge between Neal and Carolyn, even interrupting them while they were "fucking," he confessed in a February 8, 1952, letter to Holmes. As a result of Kerouac's intrusions, Carolyn developed a serious malady, Bell's palsy, which the doctor attributed to emotional strain. "They gave me a rubber band attached to a paper clip to wear over my ear and hook into my mouth," she wrote, "and an eye patch for my left eye which wouldn't close. I felt about as unattractive as anyone could."[41]

Neal tried to keep everyone happy by involving Carolyn and Jack in an affair, assuming that eventually they'd all end up in bed together. The next time Neal's railroad job called him away, he gave permission to "my best pal and my best gal" to make love, and Carolyn served Jack a romantic candlelight dinner. Later, sitting beside him on the bed, she fondly recalled how they'd danced so closely in Denver years ago when they'd first met. He turned to her, smiled, and said very quietly, "I wanted to take you away from Neal." They kept looking at each other, but he was no longer smiling. She wondered aloud whether Jack remembered the tune that had been playing that night in Denver. "Too Close for Comfort," he said, and moved closer. Gazing into each other's eyes, they both put their wine glasses down at the same time, in a moment that Carolyn later described as "perfect contact." Everything was perfect that night for Carolyn, who'd never liked Neal's rough, quick lovemaking; Jack seemed to fill her veins with "warm, carbonated water," she later wrote, describing him as "a tender and considerate lover, though somewhat inhibited, and I suspected he wished I was more aggressive, but that I could never be." The next morning, she dashed from the sofabed to her room upstairs before the children awoke. Jack followed her, kissed her on the forehead, and then continued upstairs to his attic. Carolyn drifted into sleep, luxuriating in "a flood of soothing warmth."

According to Kerouac's list, he and Carolyn made love thirty times in the course of their affair. He lived in her house from roughly the beginning of 1952 until the end of April. Their encounters seemed to Carolyn to be infrequent, but at least the affair succeeded in moving her from the far edges to the center of Jack and Neal's relationship, which had long ago eclipsed her marriage. "Now, I was part of all they did," she wrote. "I felt like the sun of their solar system, all revolved around me." Neal suddenly became a better lover, because Kerouac's desire for Carolyn made her sexier to Neal, and the threat to his marriage made him feel less ensnared by family ties. In the curious dynamics of their three-way relationship, Neal was using Jack to reignite his passion for his wife; Jack was using Carolyn to be close to Neal; and Carolyn was doing what she could to keep her home and family together.[42]

While living with the Cassadys, Kerouac continued to revise and tinker with *On the Road* until Carolyn feared that "the *Road* might become an interminable highway." Indeed, in its various forms the novel seemed to have taken over Jack's life. Carolyn discouraged Jack from revealing anything about *On the Road* to her, because the novel recounted so many of her husband's infidelities. The more she heard Neal laughing as he read the manuscript, reliving his peccadilloes, the more anxious she became that he'd be inspired to repeat them.

Despite Jack's obsessive involvement with *On the Road*, the transcendent artistic accomplishment of this period was his *Finnegans Wake*, the incredibly difficult and incomparably rewarding *Visions of Cody*. The final manuscript was five hundred and twelve pages, and he wrote it from October 1951 to May 1952, beginning it in Queens and finishing it in Neal's attic on Russian Hill. "That was the best place I ever wrote in," Jack recalled. "It rained every day, and I had wine, marijuana, and once in a while his wife would sneak in. I wrote it mostly by hand, some typed on Neal's typewriter." *Cody* includes a stupendous account of Joan Crawford filming *Sudden Fear* next door to the Cassadys, entitled "Joan Rawshanks in the Fog." The novel is both a recap of *On the Road* and a sequel to it; the narrative begins in the autumn of 1951, as Jack sits in the green-walled toilet of the El station at Third Avenue and Forty-seventh Street, masturbating and wondering how, since he's broke, he'll get to California to see Neal:

There's absolutely no sense whatever in lettin your pants down a la shittin and then, cause you're too lazy to get up, or make other shifts, simply milk the cow (with appropriate thoughts) and let the milk at its sweet keen pitch spurt downward, between thighs, when the urge at that moment is upward, onward, out, straining, to make everything come out as though gathering it from all corners of the loins to purse it out the shivering push bone.

Later, as he completed *Cody* in San Francisco, he used Neal's tape recorder, and together Jack and Neal took spontaneous prose "to the edges of language where the babble of the subconscious begins," as Jack later put in in *Escapade* magazine. Carolyn, who was working as a waitress to meet the higher grocery bill entailed by Jack's continued presence in their home, recalled, "During this time Neal and Jack experimented with their 'voices' and enticed stories from each other into the Ekotape. I would come home, kick off my wet shoes and head for the refrigerator." The text of *Cody* incorporated Jack and Neal's raw, unedited tape recordings, which give the reader the sensation of being caught up in a storm of language:

> Cody: Sit on my pole, or make a grab for it either way—Nay, I
>   know, nay, nay: a pole, a pole, I have a golden pole.
>
> Jack: A golden pole? With rings of frizzly slagrous iron from the
>   maw of dinosauric hillbottoms up-wheeled through a
>   rackshaft? . . .
>
> Cody: Ah me morning-star.
>
> Jack: It's a blue rose, the morning-star is like a blue rose in the
>   Hair of the Archangel.

For sheer linguistic boldness and exuberance, there is perhaps nothing quite like *Cody* in American literature, with the exception of Gertrude Stein's outrageous and delightful *Geographical History of the United States*. Though Kerouac had little interest in Stein's work, he "liked 'Melanctha' a little bit," he later told the *Paris Review*, referring to a story about an uneducated black girl in Stein's 1909 book, *Three Lives*. Like Stein, Kerouac often used words for their associational and aural values rather than strictly for meaning, and he employed repetition to enhance rhythmic verbal themes. And again like Stein, he blazed new trails in experimental writing, freeing language and literature from the chains of convention. In 1997, author and educator Douglas Brinkley called *Cody* "one of postwar America's authentic masterworks . . . a pioneering work of modernist fiction."[43]

In New York, Ginsberg grew envious of Jack and Neal and created an impossible situation at Ace Books, though his malice may have been unconscious. Appointing himself Neal's agent, Ginsberg pelted Carl Solomon with

several Cassady projects, even while various Kerouac manuscripts and proposals were still under consideration. With identical subject matter and similar styles, Kerouac and Cassady should never have been on simultaneous
submission to the same house, because it placed them in competition for
contracts. Evidently judging Cassady to be a more important writer than
Kerouac, Solomon warned Cassady to beware of Kerouac's influence. Ginsberg thus unintentionally undercut Kerouac's chances at Ace, but Kerouac
also had himself to blame, for he wrote Solomon at the end of 1951 that
Neal had created "A GREAT NOVEL." In the end, nothing came of Kerouac's association with Ace except for the $250 advance, which Jack gave to
Mémère. He then had to work as a baggage handler and yard clerk on the
Southern Pacific Railroad for pocket money. Giroux also declined the latest
version of On the Road, and Jack assumed it was because the editor thought
him stubborn and capricious.[44]

When Burroughs invited Jack to stay with him in Mexico City, Jack
seized the opportunity to free himself from the somewhat cloying scene at
the Cassadys. Though he appreciated the Cassadys' patronage, he was never
comfortable for very long in a sexual relationship with a woman, and he had
many other complaints, some of them churlish. Neal's liquor cabinet was
always empty, he carped in a letter to Ginsberg, though he did nothing to
replenish either the liquor or dope supplies he'd decimated. In Kerouac's
opinion, family responsibilities and financial woes were dragging Neal down
and destroying him as an artist, and it would take something catastrophic to
free him from what Jack saw as the bondage of domestic life. Unsurprisingly,
the Cassadys were not reluctant to see Kerouac go, having supported him for
the past four months, and they even gave him a ride out of town. They'd
decided to visit Carolyn's parents in Tennessee in May, and they drove Kerouac as far as the Mexican border at Nogales, south of Tucson, Arizona. Hurt
when Neal refused to stop for a roadside picnic, Jack subsequently told Ginsberg that Neal had seemed unduly eager to hustle him out of the United
States. Later that day, in the Mexican village of Guymas, Jack was ecstatic
again to be among the "Fellaheen," a term he used to denote the indigenous
folk of the Americas. After smoking opium with a hipster named Enrique,
they played with a huge dildo made from gesso, strapping it on and "prodding" each other, according to a letter Jack later wrote Allen. Enrique accompanied Jack by bus all the way to Mexico City, where they arrived at
dawn.[45]

Burroughs was alone in Apartment 5 at 210 Orizaba, and his blue eyes
looked innocent of any crime to Kerouac. Still shaken, Burroughs seemed
rootless and incomplete without Joan. After urging Jack to get rid of Enrique,
Burroughs began to court Jack, taking him to the Ballet Mexicano, to Te-
nencingo for hunting in the mountains, and to the turkish baths. At first,
Burroughs seemed willing to share his home, drugs, and food. He was shooting seven grams of morphine a month for only thirty dollars, and Jack helped

himself to Burroughs's supply. They also took peyote together, though Burroughs realized that drugs had ruined his life, robbing him of self-determination and hope. Burroughs showed Jack the manuscript of *Queer*, and Jack assured him that powerful litterateurs such as Giroux, Vidal, and Glenway Wescott would devour it. Each day, Kerouac smoked marijuana, shot morphine, and worked furiously on *Dr. Sax*, sealing himself in Burroughs's toilet and hoping his pot smoke wouldn't drift to the street and attract the police. On the title page he wrote "A Novella of Children and Evil, The Myth of the Rainy Night." Then he crossed it out, and wrote "Doctor Sax."

Soon tiring of supporting Kerouac, Burroughs complained that getting a penny out of his impecunious houseguest was more difficult than extracting an impacted wisdom tooth. Finally, almost bankrupt, Burroughs scorned Kerouac as insensitive, unthoughtful, and egocentric in an angry letter to Ginsberg. Why Burroughs continued to tolerate Kerouac was at last explained by Kerouac's friend Joe Chaput in 1978, who said that Kerouac told him Burroughs became so persistent in his amorousness that Jack at last permitted Burroughs to perform fellatio on him. The book Burroughs was working on as Kerouac stayed with him in Mexico City, *Queer*, was about Burroughs's penchant for repressed homoerotic types and drifters similar to Kerouac. In the opening scene, Burroughs possibly had Kerouac in mind when he observed that one of his friends was "as queer as I am. . . . If not queerer. But he won't accept it. . . . He is just in it for all he can get." When Jack spurned Burroughs's second pass, Burroughs cut off his food and drug supply, and Kerouac's weight plummeted from 170 to 158 pounds.[46] Appealing to Carolyn, whom he referred to as "kerouacass gal," Jack begged for enough money to get him out of Mexico by bus. He missed Neal and Carolyn so much, he wrote, that he wept when he thought of them, but Neal's interest had shifted to Ginsberg again. Neal wrote Ginsberg love letters urging him to come to San Francisco and make love to him and Carolyn. Allen replied in a letter to Carolyn that he was ready to have sex with one and all, unlike Kerouac, who'd been frightened of the ménage à trois Neal had proposed earlier in the year. Carolyn preferred a monogamous relationship with her husband but remained open-minded, feeling "if we all lived together, pressures could be siphoned off in small doses in a variety of ways."[47]

Kerouac wangled twenty dollars out of a financially strapped Burroughs and returned by bus to North Carolina, throwing himself on his mother's mercy. Mémère was in no position to help him; she had only one room in Nin's house and was working as Nin's maid in return for room and board. Both women nagged Jack to get a job so he could support himself and Mémère, and he briefly considered going to sea long enough to be able to buy Mémère a trailer home to place in Nin's backyard. The neighbors, Helen Bone and Sarah Langley, recalled that "Nin was always sure that Jack would be killed in Mexico . . . because of the kind of people that he associated with when he was down in Mexico City. . . . Nin and Gabe thought that when he left to go out on the road, that might be the end of him." Jack wasn't getting along with his brother-in-law any better than ever.

Finally completed in North Carolina, *Dr. Sax* was one of Kerouac's most daring novels. That he finished it at all was miraculous, considering that everyone from Van Doren to Giroux had advised him to drop it. In a letter to Neal, Jack wrote that Giroux disdained Sax-like fantasy figures and urged Jack to concentrate instead on real people. And in a letter to Stella, he revealed that Van Doren found *Dr. Sax* too special, advising Jack to shelve it. Ace rejected the novel, but despite these votes of no confidence from both commercial publishing and academia, *Dr. Sax* in the years to come would be ranked near the top of the Kerouac oeuvre by both critics and biographers. Tom Clark calls it "arguably Jack's finest novel," and Dennis McNally considers it "his masterpiece . . . a wonderful prose study of the magic space between shadow and light." Kerouac described it to Hal as a novel about the American Dream as experienced in childhood. Exploring virgin territory, Kerouac was again testing the parameters of the novel form, pushing it toward surrealism. According to Lucien, Kerouac said, "It's the greatest book I ever wrote, or that I will write."

In my estimation, both *On the Road* and *The Dharma Bums* are better novels, but *Dr. Sax* is a gem, flashing with some of Kerouac's most evocative images ("the wrinkly tar corner . . . Rainy funerals for little boys"). The story concerns Jack's attempts to survive the ghostly traumas of childhood, but it also takes the reader on a fantastic mystical and spiritual trip. Its two dominant symbols are a huge bird, representing the Lord's resurrection on Easter morning, and the Giant Serpent of evil, which explodes from the bowels of the earth to consume Lowell during the flood of 1936, coiling "out of a hundred miles of hugeness and slime—the mighty green coil turned in the sun slithering with under-world masses and vapors." Suddenly, a darkness falls over the town, and at first everyone thinks it's a thunderhead, but slowly they realize it's God descending from the heavens. "There in the blinding white sky of churchbells and wild disaster hung this huge black bird that must have been two or three miles long, two or three miles wide, and with a wing spread of ten or fifteen miles across the air." With a motion "as slow as Eternity," the bird plucks the Giant Serpent from the ground and ascends with it "into the bedazzling blue hole of heaven." At last, the little boy who narrates the novel, along with the entire town of Lowell, is delivered from terror, and "our Spring is free to fallow and grow wild in its own green juices." Dr. Sax, who was based partly on Burroughs, concludes with another of Kerouac's memorable lines, "The universe disposes of its own evil . . . By God."[48]

Ace rejected *Dr. Sax* along with *Visions of Cody* and *On the Road*, and Ginsberg made a terrible mistake as Kerouac's literary agent, repeating the publisher's wrongheaded and sometimes malicious criticism of these ground-breaking books. Kerouac's editor, Carl Solomon, continued to suffer from mental illness. He wrote a peculiar letter to Jack, stating that authors were nothing but "trade" and editors were their "aunties." As Solomon's behavior grew increasingly aberrant, he stabbed a book, threw his shoes and briefcase at oncoming cars, left his wife, hurled paint on his walls, and flooded his apartment. Eventually he was locked up in Bellevue.

Such derangement helped explain his rejection of *On the Road*, but there could be little excuse for Ginsberg's June 11, 1952, letter in which he savaged Kerouac's writing as unpublishable and called it a "goddam junk-yard." Ginsberg was referring to the rewritten version of *On the Road*, which reflected Kerouac's advanced technique of spontaneous prose, and which, twenty years later, would be published as part of *Visions of Cody*. Ginsberg complained that it had too much sex and was eccentric and incoherent— insane in the worst possible way. After ripping it apart to Jack, Allen wrote to Neal on July 3 and gossiped that Jack had deliberately ruined his novel in a misguided effort to show publishers how far he could go in challenging their rules of composition. The taped conversations with Neal were pure gibberish, and only readers who'd had sex with Jack would understand them. Allen himself was still writing commonplace, academic verse, though within two years, with *Howl*, he would be writing exactly like Jack.

When *Cody* was posthumously published in 1972, Ginsberg wrote the introduction and executed a complete about-face, hailing it as "a work of primitive genius" comparable to the work of Rousseau, Wolfe, and Tolstoy, and calling Jack's free-flowing prose "a consistent panegyric to heroism of mind." After Kerouac became famous, the tapes seemed to Ginsberg to be "the sacramentalization of everyday reality . . . a model to study." The acrimonious language of Ginsberg's 1952 letter to Jack suggests that he was using the occasion to settle a number of old scores. Ginsberg always hated it when Kerouac portrayed him in his novels as a nebbish among hunks, and in an indignant aside about *Dr. Sax*, he wrote that Kerouac should not have stepped outside the framework of the book to comment on Neal's large penis, Lucien's no-longer-blond hair, or Ginsberg's insanity.[49]

Kerouac's belief in *On the Road* and *Visions of Cody* remained un-shaken, and he wrote to Stella that *On the Road* was a visionary American work, but so offbeat that no publisher would touch it. Nonetheless, he told her he was confident it would one day be discovered. He added that he regarded himself as the Ezra Pound of his generation, and explained that Pound had influenced Stein, Hemingway, and Eliot, but had ended up in a psychiatric hospital. On October 8, Kerouac finally fired off an understand-ably intemperate reply to Ginsberg's June 11 letter, stating that both Ginsberg and Holmes had betrayed him. Holmes's portrait of the early Beats, *Go!*, was published in 1952, by Scribner's, and Kerouac felt he'd been scooped and exploited. Even worse, Holmes was now proposing to write a jazz novel using the title, *Horn*, which Jack had planned to call his own projected, but never written, jazz epic. Kerouac threatened to come to New York and punch out the bespectacled Ginsberg and Holmes, but he didn't want to waste his time taking off so many glasses. He called them both queers, swore never to speak to Ginsberg again, and suggested that Ginsberg henceforth save his blow jobs for Gregory Corso. He hoped Corso, who had served time in Clinton Prison in Dannemora, New York, would stab Ginsberg. The one positive note in Jack's otherwise vitriolic letter was his faith in *On the Road*, which he defended as a classic. He understood that Ginsberg hated it out of envy and jealousy. In conclusion, he vowed to have nothing more to do with the petty and egotistical New York literary scene.

At Ace, Solomon and Wyn caught the edge of Kerouac's wrath in a coruscating letter dated August 5, 1952. Responding to Ace's charge that *On the Road* was an unintelligible hodgepodge, Kerouac reminded them of the fate of masterpieces such as *Sister Carrie*, which Doubleday suppressed, and Joyce's *Ulysses*, which went unpublished in the United States for many years. He also cited Hemingway's short stories, which editors at the *Saturday Evening Post*, *Popular Magazine*, the *Dial*, and *Red Book* rejected as too flimsy and fragmentary. He predicted that *On the Road* would one day be hailed for transcending old European fiction models as one of the first truly modern books. He refused to carry out Ace's revisions, likening himself to Michelangelo being asked to cut his David down to reasonable size, and asked if he should send them an IOU for their $250 advance. His ego at such times would seem odious were his foresight not so absolutely on target. By the 1990s, all the things he predicted for *On the Road* and *Visions of Cody* had come true many times over. But in the fifties, he was near despair, and wrote Carolyn that he'd been screwed by the book business and that it looked now as if his destiny was to be ripped off by third-rate pulp publishers.[50]

For the rest of the summer, he moved around restlessly between North Carolina and New York, feeling welcome in neither place. He started speaking to Holmes again, realizing how barren his life was without his few precious friends. He wrote Holmes that he was thirty years old, insolvent, loathed by his wife, who wanted him thrown in jail, and had a daughter he never wanted to lay eyes on. His mood improved, however, when Neal tracked him down in Rocky Mount and insisted that Jack come to live with him and Carolyn in their new home in San Jose, a nine-room house they'd rented for only seventy-five dollars a month. Moreover, Neal had lined up a job for him at Southern Pacific. Carolyn, whose palsy had subsided after six months of physical therapy, also implored him to come back and save their marriage, since she and Neal were "still not making it" without Jack. On funds borrowed from Justin Brierly, Jack started hitchhiking to California and got as far as Denver. After visiting with Ed White and the Burfords, and making love to a Swedish woman named Edeltrude, he hitched the rest of the way to San Francisco, subsisting on twenty-five dollars Neal wired on September 2.

Completing the last leg of the journey, he jumped on the "Zipper" — railroad parlance for Zephyr, a fast freight — and rode it to San Jose, where Neal and Carolyn met him in their Model-A Ford. Neal left to catch a freight to Watsonville, and Jack and Carolyn immediately fell into each other's arms and started kissing. "The fog wrapped a blanket around us," she recalled. In his checkered shirt, Jack looked big and virile to her, and they were so excited they spilled his bottle of wine as they grappled in the jalopy. "His ardor returned undampened," she wrote. Once inside the house, Jack took a bath, Carolyn fixed him a snack, and then they went to bed, where Carolyn once again found Kerouac to be a lover of "tenderness and appreciation." She was tempted to spend the night with him, but finally returned to her own room lest the children discover them. At breakfast, after a moment of awkwardness, the children swarmed all over him, and when they went outside, they still held onto his hands. He seemed more himself with the kids, perhaps because they expected nothing from him but fun. The Cassadys' home was roomy and comfortable, with walnut trees and blackberries in the backyard, roses and a towering palm in front, and a marijuana crop in the vacant lot next door.[51]

Jack began his training as a railroad brakeman. As he later recalled in "October in the Railroad Earth," he worked the "Saturday afternoon local to Hollister out of San Jose miles away across verdurous fields of prune and juice joy." Earning six hundred dollars a month, he saved it in order to return to Mexico and write. He was a good railroad man, though not a great one like Neal, who thought nothing of jumping on and off trains traveling at twenty miles per hour. Kerouac had once been fast enough on the gridiron but, as Carolyn noted, he lacked "the swift and agile moves necessary for freight-car switching." Al Hinkle agreed, explaining that Kerouac was a "poor brakeman" because he was "afraid of the wheels. He was afraid of getting off and getting on." Work this dangerous could not be done while stoned, and Neal, a self-described pothead, received ten demerits for derailing a locomotive. Having loved trains since childhood, Kerouac valued his job too much to jeopardize it by getting high while kicking boxcars. His job on the Southern Pacific turned him into the best poet of American railroads since Wolfe. "Bam the main line of the old SP and the train flashing by, all gone howling around the bend to Burlingame to Mountain View to the sweet San Joses of the night," he wrote in "October in the Railroad Earth."[52]

One evening when Carolyn and Jack were dining alone, he said, "God . . . I love you." Later, they danced to mambo records and held each other close. The months they spent together in San Jose were "golden," she wrote, and his words of love warmed her for the rest of her life. Sometimes she would sit on the edge of his bed, holding the baby, Johnny, as Jack read letters from Mémère and Nin. He took long walks with the Cassadys' daughters, Cathy and Jamie, and taught them to write poetry. Though Jack and Neal were rarely at home at the same time due to overlapping shifts, there were times, Carolyn recalled, when all three of them sat around the big circular oak dining table, talking while the children romped in the kitchen.

As Carolyn listened, Jack and Neal made tape recordings. In one of them, Jack read from the just-completed *Dr. Sax*. "Tragedies of darkness hid in the shadows!" he boomed, using a mock-serious, W. C. Fields voice. Years later, as I worked on this book, Carolyn made a copy of the recording for me, and at last I realized that Kerouac intended his more Shakespearean passages to be read in a histrionic, almost comic way. His recitation has all the eye-popping melodrama of John Barrymore doing *Hamlet*. It added a whole new dimension of camp to *Dr. Sax*.

In an October 4, 1952, letter to Ginsberg, Neal wrote that he wanted to have sex with Jack and Carolyn, but Jack was making it difficult. He called Jack the solitary lover of Carolyn and added that Carolyn gave Jack oral sex. At one point, Jack seemed almost ready to participate in a ménage à trois but backed down, and Neal told Ginsberg that he was close to giving up all hope of maneuvering Jack into a threesome. Uncomfortable under such pressure, Kerouac wrote Holmes on October 12 that he could no longer endure his predicament in Neal's home. According to Carolyn, as Jack drew closer to her and the children, Neal became jealous and wanted Kerouac back again as his adoring sidekick. "The wanderlust was tugging at Neal again," she wrote, "and the Mexican sun at Jack." As was so often the case in Kerouac's life, money issues were the deciding factor. When Neal finally tired of Jack's freeloading in the fall of 1952 and told him to pay for his own food, Jack stormed out of the house and out of San Jose, checking into a four-dollar-a-week hotel room on Third and Howard in San Francisco.[53]

After the complexities of open marriage, Jack treasured the privacy of his skid row hideaway. He acquired a Zenlike reverence for his few possessions: a hot plate, the wire he rigged over it to make raisin toast, a covered campfire skillet for fluffy fried eggs, and a few groceries tightly wrapped in a brown carton. He discovered that if you treat even the humblest chore with reverence — washing dishes as if you were bathing the baby Jesus — then every task becomes a joy. Each morning, he would lift his brakeman's lantern from a peg on the door and run for the Zipper. Roaring down to Watsonville on the freight train, he would lean from the side of a boxcar and give signals. According to Hinkle, Kerouac sought out hobos and spent time with them in boxcars, underpasses, and rail yards, and on remote embankments. He discovered that some of the dispossessed felt free of all responsibility and expectation and had more fun than "normal" people ever suspected. He often quoted a passage from Dwight Goddard's *Buddhist Bible*: "Oh for this one rare occurrence gladly would I give ten thousand pieces of gold! A hat is on my head, a bundle on my back, and my staff, the refreshing breeze and the full moon." At night, back in San Francisco, he made his way through the bums and winos to his flophouse and was recognized and accepted as a genuine Third Street "bo." He wrote Ginsberg that he was happy for the first time since his sandlot days. The jazz joints of Little Harlem were just around the corner from his hotel. After hearing Billie Holiday sing, he talked with her and later looked after her dog, cradling it in his arms.[54]

Waiting for a freight one night at the depot, he fell asleep on a lumpy couch and suddenly was awakened by Neal, who hovered over him and began crooning to him and urging him to return to San Jose. According to Carolyn, Jack was back with them in less than a month. Again, he and Carolyn became lovers, but it was a mistake, and Jack wrote Stella that he was in a black depression, contemplating suicide. Carolyn remembered that Jack made love "with an air of apology. I felt that he never gave of himself completely; he preferred the woman to manage the event (so he could say, 'It wasn't *my* idea — or *my* fault'?)." Any pleasure they derived from each other, she felt, was "due to my efforts to be alert to his moods and desires without imposing my own." He was more vulnerable than any other male she had ever known, and he had the tenderest heart, she recalled. Jack responded to her maternal nature by developing a serious codependency, begging her, though she was a mother with small children to care for, to leave her family for a while and come to Mexico with him. Carolyn decided she could regard it as a long-needed vacation, and agreed to go. But Neal grew jealous and insisted on going to Mexico with Kerouac himself, promising Carolyn that he would leave Kerouac in Mexico City with Burroughs, score some dope, return to California, and take care of the children, while Carolyn joined Jack in Mexico. In December, Jack and Neal left, driving Neal's old Nash. In the end, Carolyn never made the trip at all and bitterly wrote, "What good was it to be loved by two men if I couldn't have either?"

When Kerouac and Cassady arrived in Mexico City in late 1952, Burroughs's life was still in turmoil. His lawsuit had been compromised when his lawyer, Jurado, shot a seventeen-year-old for sideswiping his Cadillac and damaging a prized tailfin. Jurado fired a bullet into the boy's leg and then fled to Rio. Burroughs jumped bail, left Mexico City, and headed for Panama via Florida. Kerouac too was fleeing the law, since Joan Haverty was still pursuing him for child support, and in Mexico City he went under the name "Señor Jean Levesque." Neal and Burroughs despised each other as heartily as ever, and Neal soon returned to his family.

For twelve dollars a month, Kerouac rented a small adobe hut on Burroughs's roof at 210 Orizaba, which could only be reached with difficulty by climbing a flight of rickety metal stairs insecurely attached to the building's crumbly stucco walls. Kerouac enjoyed sitting in the sunshine on the roof of the old apartment building and watching Indian women wash their clothes. Though the two cell-like rooms in his hut had no electricity and were damp and malodorous, he was at peace there, free of emotional entanglements, and he felt like he was suspended in the sky over Mexico City.

William Maynard Garver, the junkie coat thief from Times Square who lived downstairs, became Jack's closest friend. Garver lured young people into his room by offering dope. He derived a special kick from converting drug virgins into addicts. Slipping back into Benzedrine addiction, Kerouac loved to sit up all day and night rapping with Garver, who was an expert on Minoan civilization. Kerouac also became fascinated with Garver's pusher friend Dave and started recording Dave's life story for a novel about a drug dealer. Nothing came of the project, or of a novel he wrote in French in five days about himself and Neal.

More promising was a new fiction project dealing with Mary Carney and high-school love, which became *Maggie Cassidy*. Kerouac was in his most prolific period, and stories and ideas were overflowing. He wrote Carolyn that he was working on a major novel that would be his last chance for success, and in a letter to Holmes, he described it as his ultimate opus. Dealing with a generation of hipsters who were impoverished and doomed, the novel would be a hyped-up, thousand-page, Dostoyevskian version of *The Town and the City*, and he intended to change the title of *On the Road* to *Visions of Neal Pomeray* in order to call his new epic *On the Road*. The novel would recapitulate his growing up in Lowell and then go on to portray Jack, Holmes, and all the others on the Beat scene, but it never jelled. During this period he preferred the shorter novella form and turned each of his experiences into autonomous, gemlike works such as *Dr. Sax*, *Maggie Cassidy*, and *Visions of Gerard* or the tour de force bop monologue, *The Subterraneans*. He already sensed before he'd even written these books that they were somehow beyond fiction and even beyond the ancient tradition of storytelling; as he told Holmes, they belonged to the realm of vision. In Mexico City in December 1952, Kerouac completely abandoned the conventional epic narrative form of *The Town and the City* and entered the creative period that would produce his revelatory shorter novels of the early 1950s.[55]

In his loneliness, he pleaded for Holmes and Ginsberg to visit him, promising a lot of good talk and cheap sex and promoting Mexico City as a Beat Sodom and Gomorrah. He also tried to lure Carolyn to his tenement penthouse, where they would drink wine, smoke marijuana, dance the mambo, and eat oysters before making love. In California, Carolyn read his letter and dreamed of joining him, but Neal wouldn't permit it. "Serves him right for stealing other men's wives," Neal said. Carolyn and Neal argued, and she reminded him that he had pushed her into having an affair with Jack in the first place. Neal told her to advise Jack to find his own women for a change. She was naturally happy that Neal wanted her again, and reflected that Jack "had been the cement to bind our little family closer together." She started to compose a Dear John letter to Jack, but he spared her the trouble, writing that he'd decided to leave Mexico City and spend Christmas with his mother in Queens. "Poor Jack," she reflected. "He just couldn't be alone for long. Everything had worked out for the best, and his mother would be happier, too." Thanks to the various games the Cassadys had played with Kerouac, Carolyn's sex life with Neal had never been so good, "almost like a honeymoon," she recalled.[56]

While still in Mexico City, Kerouac received an unexpected gift from Holmes, who sent him fifty dollars out of the eight thousand he'd received as the first installment of *Go!*'s twenty-thousand-dollar paperback sale to Bantam Books. However, *Go!* would never appear as a Bantam paperback due to the publisher's fear of lawsuits; most censorship cases in the fifties were over paperback books. Holmes had also come into eighty thousand dollars from his parents' estate. For the hard-strapped Kerouac, the fifty-dollar windfall, on which he could survive for months, effectively patched up a major breach. Kerouac had been outraged when Holmes appropriated the term "Beat Generation" in a November 16, 1952, article, "This Is the Beat Generation," in the *New York Times Magazine,* even though Holmes credited Kerouac as the originator of the term. Gilbert Millstein, who had written a favorable review of *Go!* in the *Times,* called Holmes up and said, "What in hell is this whole 'Beat Generation' thing? . . . Come in and let's talk about it." Subsequently, Millstein arranged with Louis Bergman of the *Times Magazine* for Holmes to do the article, and it created a sensation. It was also rather shallow: Holmes wrote that the Beats drank "to 'come down' or to 'get high,' not to illustrate anything. Their excursions into drugs or promiscuity come out of curiosity, not disillusionment."

In Lowell, the sharp-eyed Stella saw the article, sent it to Jack, and told him she was glad the *Times* had recognized him. Stella felt his writings were of great inspiration to ordinary people. Making a pun, she added that book publishers' neglect of him "beat" her. Jack replied to her, gratefully calling her his "lucky leadingstar." Then he promised her they'd one day be together, and mentioned his and Sammy's song, "I'll See You Again." He intended eventually to return to Lowell, settle down, and marry. Stella confided to Aida Panagiotakos that Jack wanted to make her his bride. Jack's absence from the best-seller lists did nothing to lessen his appeal to Stella, she assured him, and he wrote back promising to bring her an exotic present from the Orient (at the time, he was again nursing vain hopes of traveling in China).

In the same warm mood, he wrote Holmes that he wanted them to remain friends for life. Only weeks before, he had written Ginsberg that *Go!* was a putrid abomination and had dismissed Holmes as a leech and a dunce, but the fifty dollars suddenly made *Go!*—and Holmes—look much better. Though he could never bring himself to praise *Go!* to Holmes, he wrote Ginsberg in November 1952 that it wasn't so bad once he saw Scribner's finished copies, and he told Holmes to put pressure on the publisher to keep the stores well stocked, as there seemed to be a run on it (the Scribner edition sold only twenty-five hundred copies). Holmes invited Kerouac to live and write in his country house in Connecticut, and Jack was already delirious over the prospect. Holmes had bought a fourteen-room colonial house in Old Saybrook, and he began to write his jazz novel, *The Horn.* Kerouac was working on the same subject and had already planned a chapter on Billie Holiday, to be called "The Heroine of the Hip Generation." Holmes would publish *The Horn* a few years later, in 1958, and dedicate it, "For Shirley, who listened and for Jack Kerouac, who talked." And talked too much, evidently, for his own good. Kerouac warned Holmes that he had already announced his plans for *Hold Your Horn High*, a novel of Lester Young, Billie Holiday, Zoot Sims, Gerald "Wig" Wiggins, Stan Getz, and Miles Davis — the entire jazz scene since 1935, as seen through the eyes of his friend Seymour Wyse. Apparently, Jack never finished his jazz novel, for no such manuscript exists in his archive in Lowell, according to John Sampas.

If Holmes was sometimes a friend Kerouac could ill afford, Ginsberg was also dangerous, especially in his role as Kerouac's literary agent, because he was frequently dead wrong about the artistic direction Kerouac should take. Ginsberg disapproved of Kerouac's latest project, *Maggie Cassidy*, and believed Kerouac should concentrate on the supposedly mature world of Lucien and Cessa Carr and on the themes of matrimony and social life. This might have been good advice for John O'Hara or John Updike, but if Kerouac had followed it, he would not have written *Maggie Cassidy*, *Visions of Gerard*, or *Dr. Sax*, some of his finest creations. He chided Allen for selling out to commercial publishing interests and pointed out that as an artist, he would continue to delve into his own soul for material. He fired the twenty-six-year-old Ginsberg, and told him on November 8, 1952, that he was going to name Holmes his literary agent for *Dr. Sax*.[57]

Shortly before Christmas 1952, Kerouac began hitchhiking from Mexico City to Queens, stopping in New Orleans long enough to visit a brothel called The House of the Rising Sun. "The madam met me and . . . said, 'Young man, I'm gonna teach you the meaning of lust,' " Kerouac later told Joe Chaput. "She unzipped my fly and pulled down my pants." Back on the road, exposed to the winter elements, he pushed his health to the limit, drinking and taking Benzedrine. His legs became inflamed, signaling another attack of thrombophlebitis. He arrived in New York in time to spend Christmas with Mémêre, who had returned from Rocky Mount and rented another apartment in Richmond Hill. Mémêre was again working in a shoe factory, and her refrigerator was full of beer, steak, and eggs. Under her care, Jack's health soon began to improve. Joan was still trying to chase him down for child support, and for a while he virtually exiled himself in Queens.

Lucien and Cessa threw a hectic holiday soiree. Kerouac later wrote the Cassadys that Lucien looked like an stodgy old wire-service rewrite man in his bushy mustache and horn-rimmed glasses. Ginsberg was bloated and unsightly, and Helen Parker seemed matronly and antiquated. After far too much to drink, Kerouac went home with Ginsberg, who had an apartment on the Lower East Side. Kerouac fell asleep in a blackout and when he came to the next day, he walked off with Ginsberg's *Complete Oeuvres Genet*, though he promised in a note to return it. Jack decided to deliver a finished copy of *Dr. Sax* to Van Doren, but the professor wasn't at home. His son, Charles, answered the door and was hospitable and chatty. Charles's girlfriend became excited and gushy when Jack described his latest enthusiasm, Buddhism, and he gave her some tips on how to practice Buddhist meditations. Then Charles told Jack that Giroux was going to publish his first novel, and Jack later relayed this news to Ginsberg in campy, risqué language. (Charles Van Doren later achieved notoriety as a contestant on a TV quiz show and was hailed as a new breed of intellectual pop hero on the cover of *Time*. Subsequently exposed for having cheated on the show, Charles Van Doren fell into disgrace.) After Kerouac's visit, Mark Van Doren sent him a note about *Dr. Sax*, rejecting the completed manuscript as tedious and senseless. In response to Kerouac's continuous pleas for help in finding a publisher, Van Doren admitted that *Dr. Sax* was unique, but he couldn't imagine any publisher taking it on. After that, Kerouac testily wrote off his old Columbia teacher, criticizing him in a letter to Ginsberg as a hollow man. Had Van Doren proved more useful, no doubt he'd have retained the saintly status Kerouac had accorded him in *Visions of Cody*.[58]

Kerouac's interest in Buddhism in the early fifties when very little literature was available on the subject in the Western world placed him again at the cutting edge of cultural developments. The Zen authority in America was D. T. Suzuki, an octogenarian professor at Columbia. Ginsberg was reading Suzuki's *Introduction to Zen Buddhism*, and in a May 14, 1953, letter to Neal, Ginsberg discoursed at length on satori, a state of spiritual enlightenment and an aspect of Zen Buddhism that Kerouac found especially absorbing. Satori is a flash of insight capable of changing one's life; Kerouac had been exploring such visionary experiences for years. Unfortunately, his alcoholism was rapidly advancing to the stage that satori would no longer be possible for him, since alcoholics exist in a state of confusion that precludes spiritual experience. On New Year's Eve, Kerouac and Ginsberg shared a cab home after a party, and Kerouac drunkenly burst into sobs, bemoaning that he was in his thirties but no smarter than ever.[59]

Kerouac had not entirely forgiven Ginsberg for trashing *On the Road*, and in January 1953, Ginsberg wrote Neal that Jack had begun to shun him. At home, Kerouac occupied himself with a new, but never completed, novel about his experiences on the coast division of the Southern Pacific. He told Carolyn that he was shying away from relationships because he'd found women too possessive, and he was giving up any hope of leading a fulfilling personal life. He occasionally dated Ginsberg's old girlfriend, Dusty, who posed no threat since she liked girls. Free from sexual pressures and anxieties, he wrote like a streak in early 1953, finishing *Maggie Cassidy* in approximately six weeks.[60] Though it covered some of the same ground as *The Town and the City*, *Maggie* succeeded where the earlier novel had faltered, largely because Kerouac now focused on a single protagonist, "Jack Duluoz," rather than dividing himself into a half-dozen autobiographical clones. One of his best-paced stories, *Maggie* reads like the crack of a bullwhip. Because of his multiple-book option at Ace, the manuscript had to be shown there first, but they turned it down.

Ace published Burroughs's *Junky* in 1953 as a lurid paperback original subtitled "Confessions of an Unredeemed Drug Addict." Kerouac was annoyed to read in David Dempsey's column in the *New York Times* that the gifted young literary author of *The Town and the City* supported Burroughs's novel. Since Burroughs himself disowned authorship of *Junky*, publishing it under the pseudonym William Lee, Kerouac grew even angrier when he discovered that Ginsberg had planted the item. In a stern letter of reprimand and warning, he informed Ginsberg that, in any further transactions, he must go through Jack's new agent, Phyllis Jackson. More than Kerouac's pride was involved; he was hiding from Joan, and he could ill afford to have his name appear in newspapers. All of his friends were aware that his mail had to be addressed to an alias, and always to a decoy address, never to his home, lest he be traced by the Brooklyn DA's Uniform Support of Dependents Bureau. Out of loyalty to Burroughs, Kerouac eventually contributed a blurb, calling *Junky* the only authoritative contemporary work on drug addiction and referring to the author as a venomous Nazi-like savant.[61]

Kerouac had acquired his new agent, the clever and powerful Phyllis Jackson of MCA, through Holmes, and Kerouac gave her *Maggie Cassidy*, *On the Road*, and *Dr. Sax* to represent. In perhaps the most important move of Kerouac's publishing career, Jackson submitted Kerouac to Viking Press's distinguished literary consultant, Malcolm Cowley, who was also a critic and author of *Exile's Return*, a highly regarded study of the Lost Generation. Phyllis suggested that it would be a good idea for Cowley to take her young author to lunch. At the restaurant, Kerouac was uneasy with the tweedy, professorial editor. Though Cowley was not interested in reading *Dr. Sax*, a decision he would live to regret, Kerouac described the story to him. Cowley predicted that if Kerouac would delete the novel's brilliant imagery and turn it into a simple tale of a New England boyhood, it would be worth fifty thousand dollars. But Kerouac protected *Dr. Sax*'s phantasmagorical magic and refused to disfigure his novel. Half joking, Kerouac said that if he were William Faulkner, Viking would publish *Dr. Sax* exactly as written. In the Mephistophelian way that editors sometimes have, Cowley replied that Viking would agree to take a loss on *Dr. Sax* if Kerouac would also give them a blockbuster. Cowley later read *On the Road* "with great interest and enthusiasm," he recalled, but asked for revisions that Kerouac found unacceptable. Kerouac wrote Carolyn that henceforth the only contract he'd sign would be one drawn up by God, and he'd accept no revisions except those wrought by time. The only slant or angle he'd tolerate in his writing would be the sunshine on his face, and he had no hope of royalties beyond whatever reward came to him in the afterlife. Though his life appeared chaotic and unprincipled in many ways, he had the courage and integrity to defend his work against desecration, however well-intentioned. Sometimes, in retrospect, he rued his sense of honor, and when he still remained a publishing outcast in 1955, two years after meeting Cowley, he acknowledged in a letter to Cowley that he'd been mistaken in spurning the editor's offer to put *On the Road* under contract in 1953.

Neither Phyllis Jackson nor Cowley gave up on Kerouac. Referring to *On the Road*, Cowley recalled, "The manuscript stayed on my desk." Soon,

Cowley was calling Phyllis fairly regularly, asking, "How's your fellow, John Kerouac? What's he up to now?" Phyllis told Kerouac that he should feel free to drop in and consult with Cowley at Viking from time to time, and Cowley later recalled that Kerouac occasionally appeared in his office, often accompanied by Ginsberg. One day, Cowley asked Jack to show him the Beat scene in Greenwich Village, and Jack took him to all the hipster hangouts. While they were barhopping, Kerouac remarked that one day there would be only two religions in the world. "Which two?" Cowley asked, feeling certain that Kerouac would include the Catholic Church. "Mohammedanism and Buddhism," Jack replied.

Despite the congeniality of his relationship with Cowly, Kerouac's writing career was stymied, and in the spring of 1953 he resumed traveling, going first to Montreal in one of his periodic searches for his roots. He had a fleeting déjà vu sensation of being among his own kind at last, but passed out in a Ste. Catherine Street whorehouse. When he came to, he left Montreal, peremptorily dismissing the elegant city as "Northern Gloomtown," and Canada as "shit."[62]

He returned briefly to New York, and then in April 1953 he rode by bus to California in search of work. Neal had been seriously injured while operating the brakes atop a boxcar, which had rammed into the bumper and knocked him to the ground. "The force of his fall tore the foot backwards, nearly severing it completely," Carolyn recalled. According to Ginsberg's 1993 book *Snapshot Poetics*, Neal had heroically "averted a train crash." The break was in his right ankle, which for years had to be wired into place, leaving it stiff. Jack, who was suffering from a terrible nose infection and migraine headaches, visited Neal in the hospital and took advantage of the occasion to stock up on one million units of penicillin as well as barbiturates for his migraines.

Eventually Neal returned to San Jose and began the long legal process of trying to collect thousands of dollars in accident benefits. Jack found railroad work in San Luis Obispo, a quiet mountain town about 250 miles south of San Francisco that reminded him of Nashua. The Southern Pacific Railroad hired him as a brakeman on freight runs in the mountains around Santa Margarita. He lived in a six-dollar-a-week room in the Colonial Hotel on Santa Barbara Avenue and wrote his mother on April 25, urging her to move to California and live with him. Houses were too expensive, but he was saving his money and he promised to buy them a trailer.

In June, Kerouac got drunk in San Francisco with his North Beach friend Al Sublette and decided to go back to sea. Hanging around the maritime union hall, he eventually took a job as a bedroom steward aboard the S.S. *William Carruth*, bound for Panama. The night before sailing, he went on a binge with Sublette, downing thirty beers and ten whiskeys. The next morning, he barely managed to stagger aboard, later describing in "Slobs of the Kitchen Sea" what alcohol had done to him: "the slow paralysis of fingers, hands—the spectre and horror of a man once rosy babe now a shivering ghost." He added that "all true drinkers" were "kings of pain." On board, he was given a new assignment as a "goddam scullion," and he found himself waiting tables and washing pots and pans again just as he'd done in 1942. But once in Panama, he loved the tropical huts and the muddy earthiness of the place. He could sense the South American continent looming just beyond the swamp, beginning with Colombia. The voyage home passed in a haze of liquor and Benzedrine. Approaching New Orleans, he stared drunkenly at the Mississippi River, "where all America pours . . . her mud and hopes . . . into the doom of the Gulf." In July 1953, he jumped ship with three hundred dollars' pay and three hundred from his railroad job in uncashed checks and headed for New York.[63]

In his absence, Ginsberg had once again taken over his agenting as well as his power of attorney. Kerouac's manuscripts were gathering dust in Mémêre's apartment, and Ginsberg later wrote Neal, somewhat wearily, that he had retrieved them and was beginning to "peddle" them once again. Though Phyllis Jackson had already established the vital connection with Cowley, Ginsberg called at Viking in July 1953 and started trying to turn Cowley into the "elderly grandfather for the Beats," according to Cowley. The editor had no interest in the other Beats, but he still wanted to publish Kerouac, whom he referred to as the best unpublished writer in the world. However, Cowley continued to reject *Dr. Sax* and *Visions of Cody* as too innovative for a mainstream trade house. He recommended *On the Road* at Viking's weekly editorial meeting, "but no, they wouldn't publish it," he recalled. Cowley also began to promote Kerouac to editors of literary quarterlies, including Arabel Porter, who launched *New World Writing*, an important paperback series.[64] Cowley's plan was to build up Kerouac's reputation with excerpts from his works in distinguished quarterlies, hoping this exposure would make him more attractive to hardcover publishers. It was sound strategy.

For all Kerouac's publishing woes, he was in some respects the most fortunate of authors. In Malcolm Cowley, he had the support of an awesome editor who not only got books published but controlled their critical reception and sales.

SIX

ORGASM, BUDDHISM, AND THE ART OF WRITING

Like many people in the fifties, Kerouac read Wilhelm Reich's *The Function of the Orgasm* and was impressed with Reich's thesis that having a lot of sex would dispel psychosomatic ills. Reich's emphasis on the primacy of vigorous heterosexual genital contact convinced Kerouac, who was thirty-one, that he had to have a grand passion, and soon. In August 1953, he wrote to the Cassadys that the key to life, he'd discovered in Reich, was heterosexuality — "man cock, woman cunt" — and that a man had to do more than stimulate a woman's clitoris; he had to bring her to vaginal climax. He began to spend more time that summer cruising Manhattan bars and visiting Ginsberg's East Seventh Street apartment between Avenues B and C, half a block from Tompkins Square Park. More than ever before, he was on the prowl for a good woman to have sex with.

Ginsberg's apartment was now the gathering place of the new "subterraneans," as Jack and Allen called Gregory Corso and other youthful newcomers to the hip scene. The name embraced the original Beat crowd as well, including Bill Burroughs, Alan Ansen, and Ed Stringham. Another popular salon was Adele Morales and Norman Mailer's loft on Monroe Street in the shadows of the Manhattan Bridge, "which was 'subterranean' in the same way we were using the word, Kerouac and I, and the way Kerouac used it later for the title of his novel *The Subterraneans*," Ginsberg recalled. "The loft had the same atmosphere as [*Barbary Shore*], that kind of Dostoyevskian man-of-the-underground quality, which I thought was great." As Mailer's mistress, Adele Morales loved Mailer's "beautiful cock," she wrote in her memoir, because it could sustain an erection for as long as Mailer kept his mind

on a "country landscape, green meadows, trees, and a blue sky," and sometimes that was for considerable periods. The downside of their relationship
was his whiskey-fueled temper. " 'Stupid bitch,' he would say," Adele recalled, " 'you're a piece of meat.' " He spent a lifetime suppressing his feelings of tenderness and spirituality, disdaining them as unmasculine, and like
Kerouac, he cultivated macho drinking buddies—in Mailer's case, prizefighter Roger Donahue. At one of Adele and Norman's parties, Marlon
Brando sat quietly with a girl on his lap, never budging or speaking, even
when punks invaded the loft and hit Mailer on the head with a hammer,
drawing blood. Montgomery Clift rushed to Mailer's aid, and another guest,
Emma Clara "Ecey" Gwaltney, speculated, "Maybe Montgomery Clift had
a crush on him at that point."

Though Mailer's scene was downtown geographically, in every other way
it was light years removed from the Beat milieu of Kerouac and Ginsberg.
Kevin McCarthy recalled seeing "the Plimpton types" pulling up at Mailer's
Lower East Side loft and climbing his fire escape in black tie. George Plimpton was a charming socialite who ran the *Paris Review*, a powerful literary
quarterly that would shortly figure in Kerouac's career, but Plimpton's crowd
did not frequent Ginsberg's salon, where everyone smoked cigarette butts,
panhandled for drugs, or—like Kerouac, who'd become known as a
"mooch"—cadged drinks. Moreover, the people in Ginsberg's apartment
were largely homoerotic, though by no means exclusively so. Corso was now
Ginsberg's roommate, but when Burroughs returned to the city that summer,
he stayed in the apartment during August, and became Ginsberg's lover. "He
liked to come while being screwed," Ginsberg recalled, adding that Burroughs giggled like a British nanny in bed. Hoping to intimidate Corso
and drive him from the apartment, Burroughs brought out his machete and
started chopping up a pile of Peruvian yage. Soon, Corso cleared out, and
Burroughs tried to "schlupp" Ginsberg—a Burroughs term for a telepathic
union of souls.[1]

In August, at a party given by Ginsberg, Kerouac met Alene Lee, a beautiful black girl who was helping Ginsberg type Burroughs's manuscripts,
Queer and *The Yage Letters*. Kerouac later portrayed her as "Mardou Fox"
in *The Subterraneans*. They made love forty times, according to his sex list.
Since their affair lasted only thirty days, the figure demonstrates Kerouac's
passionate attraction to Alene; she was his feminine ideal, a dark-skinned
throwback to Bea Franco, but also a dazzlingly contemporary Manhattan
type, a classic Beat "chick": bright, exotic, and sufficiently neurotic to require
psychoanalysis on a daily basis. Jack spotted her across Ginsberg's living room,
which was cluttered with manuscripts and record albums and swarming with
people. He admired her petite, slightly tomboyish figure, mocha skin, and
exquisite features. Ginsberg had been attracted to her briefly and then had
dropped her except as a friend who was always welcome among the junkies,
musicians, and poets who hung out at 206 East Seventh Street. Kerouac
immediately began to fantasize about having Alene "between my legs while

kneeling on the floor of the toilet, I on the seat, with her special cool lips and Indian-like hard high soft cheekbones," he wrote. Though he was supposedly seeking standard Reichian missionary-position intercourse, the closer he got to scoring with Alene, the more he reverted to exclusively oral fantasies. At Ginsberg's party, she was standing not far from him, talking to one of the several subterranean men who felt rather possessive about her. Alene had noticed Jack, too, and admired his Hawaiian shirt, she later told interviewers Gifford and Lee, as well as his "incredibly good-looking, really handsome . . . big blue eyes and black, Indian-type hair."

Kerouac portrayed himself in *The Subterraneans* as "Leo Percepied," a young novelist at the peak of his physical attractiveness, "so beautiful" that one of the girls in his crowd found it impossible to look at him. Leo Percepied could scarcely have been more autobiographical, bearing the given name of Jack's father. His surname may have derived from *percipient*, "one who perceives," or from the French words *percé* and *pied* (pinched foot). Like Jack, Percepied was an alcoholic and a self-described Canuck who did not speak English until he was five or six years old. *The Subterraneans* marked the first time that Kerouac honestly presented himself as an alcoholic and egomaniac. All of Percepied's virtues had "long been drowned under years of drugtaking and desiring to die," Kerouac wrote, "a drunk really, always staying late, freeloading, shouting, foolish." Some of the new-style "cool" subterraneans found Jack to be unfashionably "hot," projecting more heat than light in his tense, animated raps. But to Alene, his somewhat passé enthusiasm and energy seemed endearing. Though she was just as insecure as Kerouac, she appeared to be graceful and confident, and she seemed to have a special status among the subterranean males as a kind of hipster high priestess. He portrayed her in *The Subterraneans* as the communal girlfriend of the whole clique, including William Gaddis, future author of *The Recognitions*; saxophone player Alan Eager; and Mason Hoffenberg, later coauthor, with Terry Southern, of *Candy*. When Kerouac failed at first to come on to Alene forcefully, she concluded that he was a square from Brooklyn or New Jersey, and left Allen's party alone. Crestfallen, he assumed that he wasn't her type and that she preferred less rugged-looking hipsters.

Playing cupid, Ginsberg subsequently arranged for Jack and Alene to meet again in his apartment, and this time they connected. Jack went home with her to her apartment in Paradise Alley, a courtyard on East Eleventh Street near Avenue A, and he fell in love with her. Alene had a way of curling into his body, whether they were dancing or she was just sitting on his lap and telling him the story of her life. As he got to know her better, he realized she was intense to the point of "hospital type insanity," a black counterpart to Peyton Loftis, Styron's suicidal heroine in *Lie Down in Darkness*, who hallucinated pink flamingos prancing on Harlem rooftops. Kerouac represented Alene Lee, as Mardou Fox, as flipping out while crouching naked on a wooden back-alley fence. But she managed to hold down a regular job, working at a health book company run by an editor of the left-wing newspaper *P.M.*, and handling books such as *Blackstrap Molasses, Sauer-kraut, Urine: Water of Life*.

Though Kerouac felt like an outsider among the subterraneans, Alene recalled, "If you saw him with his friends, even if he were stone-drunk, he was accepted and loved." Kerouac wrote of her in almost rapturous terms in *The Subterraneans*, recalling his "shuddering" orgasm and her remark, " 'I was lost suddenly' and she was lost with me tho not coming herself but frantic in my franticness (Reich's beclouding of the senses) and how she loved it." Her senses were not so clouded that she failed to notice she wasn't getting off, and years later she stated flatly that their relationship was strictly nonsexual. She looked on Kerouac not as a lover but as "a brother, someone I knew very well." Somewhere along the line, Kerouac's man cock–woman cunt formula had stopped working.

Sexually, Leo Percepied reflects Kerouac's divided nature. In the novel, he goes in for gay bashing but lets Mardou go home alone so he can spend the evening with gay friends, drooling over "pornographic (homo male sexual) pictures and listening to Marlene Dietrich records." Accompanied by a sadomasochistic sidekick who's also a husband and father, Leo goes cruising for sailors. Later, a queenly male friend observes, "You and that there Sam Vedder go around the Beach picking up sailors and giving them dope and he makes them only so he can bite, I've heard about you." Leo's motives for making Mardou his mistress are suspect from the start. Overly concerned that the other men in the group not think him gay, he uses Mardou as a way of convincing them he's straight. When one of the subterraneans accuses him outright of being a homosexual, he begins to imagine himself as the white gay man in the Turkish bath in Tennessee Williams's story, "Desire and the Black Masseur," and Mardou as the "big buck nigger" who cannibalizes him.

When Leo fails to bring women to orgasm, he blames them for his ineptitude and accuses them of being frigid. Mardou "did not gain orgasm from normal copulation and only after awhile from stimulation as applied by myself," he wrote. But the following passage indicates that they progressed to coitus: "The insides itself I should say the best, the richest, most fecund moist warm and full of hidden soft slidy mountains, also the pull and force of the muscles being so powerful she unknowing often vice-like closes over and makes a dam-up and hurt." He fears that her vagina will injure him, due to her "contraction and greatstrength of womb" and that he'll have to go to the hospital and have his penis bandaged. On such fears, Jack's hope of discovering the ultimate act of self-realization in Reichian orgasm finally ran aground. Norman Mailer at this time was undergoing a similar trial with the sensually free Adele Morales, but salvation through sex would prove equally elusive for them. In Mailer's sexually graphic *The Time of Her Time*, after Sergius O'Shaugnessy brings his Greenwich Village girlfriend to orgasm she walks out on him, sneering, "Your whole life is a lie, and you do nothing but run away from the homosexual that is you." Evidently lust, even the Reichian variety so esteemed by both Kerouac and Mailer, does nothing to heal a shattered spirit or a dishonest heart. Kerouac's man cock–woman cunt equation lacked love, the essential ingredient for the kind of redemption he was seeking.

Recalling her affair with Kerouac, Alene stated that she had never taken him seriously as a lover, finding him to be "helpless. We were both really play-acting at serious life." In the novel, the affair begins to unravel when she tells him he's too old to be living with his mother, essentially delivering the same message as the girl in *The Time of Her Time*. There were other issues, and they were just as damaging to true intimacy as Kerouac's one-sided orgasms. As a racist, he was ashamed of Alene for being a Negro. One day, he took her to meet Lucien and Cessa, who'd just had their baby. "And what part of India are you from?" Lucien asked. Alene could never again respect Jack, knowing that he had lied to Lucien and tried to pass her off as Indian. But worse was to come. Soon, Jack started behaving in ways that seemed deliberately calculated to drive her away and end their affair.

One night Kerouac and Burroughs saw Gore Vidal in the San Remo, and Kerouac decided to ditch Alene and go home with Vidal. "I've got to see Gore Vidal!" Jack said, according to Alene. "It's a historic literary occasion!" She dragged Jack away from Vidal and into the street, but he stood on his head to convince her he was sober and could make his way home without her.

"It's him or me goddamit," she said, according to Kerouac. He chose Vidal.

"We're through," she said, stomping off.[2]

In *The Subterraneans*, Kerouac wrote only sketchily of his tryst with Vidal, whom he portrayed as "Arial Lavalina." Selling himself rather cheaply, Percepied asks Lavalina for fifty cents and then goes to Lavalina's hotel room to spend the night. In the morning, he wakes up from an alcoholic blackout, remembering nothing, but Lavalina gives him a dollar. Later, he returns the dollar to Lavalina with a note apologizing for having misled him into expecting sex. In tossing the dollar back and forth, the men were vying for the label "rough trade." Kerouac liked the designation because male prostitutes, often known as rough trade, can have sex with men and still think of themselves as straight. Vidal's delusions were of another order: He thought he was "butch" enough to qualify as rough trade. Both, of course, were kidding themselves. At first, they were two monstrous egos clashing in the night.

Forty-two years after their sexual encounter, Vidal finally filled in the missing pieces, writing in his memoir, "August 23, 1953, Jack brought Burroughs and me together at the San Remo bar . . . Hot night. Jack was manic. Sea captain's hat. T-shirt. Like Marlon Brando in *Streetcar*. Drinking beer . . . Jack was loud . . . drunk." The three writers left the San Remo together and went to a lesbian bar, Tony Pastor's. In the cab, Jack kissed Vidal's hand and called him "dear." Afterward, on the street, Jack started cutting up, swinging on a lamppost like Tarzan. When Burroughs abruptly left them, Vidal assumed he was disgusted with Jack's behavior, but in reality Burroughs also had a crush on Vidal and departed in a fit of jealousy. Vidal then told Jack he was going uptown, but Jack suggested, "Let's get a room around here." Vidal, who was twenty-eight to Jack's thirty-one, usually never went to bed with anyone older than he, but suddenly he remembered the drop of water on Jack's neck years ago at the Metropolitan Opera. Now the sweat was real, and he felt an overpowering desire for Jack. At the desk in the shabby Chelsea Hotel, they each signed their real names on the register, hoping that biographers would one day celebrate their decision "to couple," Vidal confessed.

Upstairs, Jack suggested they take a shower together. "To my surprise, he was circumcised," Vidal noticed, and later wrote, "Jack and I were an ... unlikely pairing, classic trade meets classic trade, and who will *do* what?" But Jack immediately began to perform fellatio on Vidal, who recalled, "the blow job—a pro forma affair ... I put a quick stop to. ... We rubbed bellies. ... I finally flipped him over on his stomach, not an easy job as he was as much heavier than I. ... Jack raised his head from the pillow to look at me over his left shoulder. ... He stared at me a moment ... forehead half covered with sweaty dark curls—then he sighed as his head dropped back onto the pillow." The following morning, Vidal savored the way Kerouac "smelled ... What was irresistible in Jack at his sanest was the sweetness of his character ... animal charm." Kerouac came away from their liaison feeling both proud to have conquered a literary lion and resentful, calling Vidal a pompous "little fag" in a letter to Cowley the following November.

But Kerouac was as drawn to homoeroticism as he was repelled by it, and one night at the San Remo he bragged about having had sex with Vidal, compromising his already shaky heterosexual status among the subterraneans. "Jack was rather proud of the fact that he blew you," Ginsberg later told Vidal. Vidal was writing for network television and was annoyed to hear "that Jack had announced this momentous feat to the entire clientele of the San Remo bar," he recalled. One of the men who overheard Kerouac's boast was a Westinghouse advertising executive who was involved with Vidal on the television program, *Studio One.* "I don't think," said the adman, "that this is such a good advertisement for you, not to mention Westinghouse."[3]

In an even more blatant attempt to drive Alene out of his life, Kerouac practically shoved her into bed with Corso. As a result, Jack and Alene's affair was over by October, and Kerouac's remarkable haste in writing about it suggests that he undertook it primarily to get material. He dashed from Alene's bed to his mother's apartment in Queens, loaded up on Benzedrine, and wrote *The Subterraneans* in three nights, he later told Joe Chaput, according to Joe's son Phil—and the novel's final lines indicate that he wasn't exaggerating: "And I go home having lost her love. And write this book."

Afraid Alene would sue him, he changed the setting of the story from Greenwich Village to San Francisco's North Beach.

The change doesn't entirely work. *The Subterraneans* is such an obsessive, claustrophobic Manhattan story that it never really makes sense in the open, breezy air of San Francisco, nor does the novel's famous pushcart scene. Based on a prank involving Corso and Kerouac, who stole a pushcart and rolled it all the way to Ginsberg's apartment, the episode is not as plausible on San Francisco's hills as it would be on the pancake flatness of Manhattan. But *The Subterraneans* belongs to New York in an even deeper sense as a classic Greenwich Village love story in which two neurotics tear each other to pieces. After Kerouac completed the novel, Alene called him and said she was working as a waitress at Rikers restaurant near the Columbia campus at Broadway and 115th Street. He had promised to show her the manuscript, and he kept his word, taking it to her home. She later remembered him depositing it like a small boy bringing in a dead animal from the backyard. When she read it, she felt sick, because their affair "was still raw," she recalled. "If you want me to," Jack said, "I'll throw it in the fire." They were sitting in front of a fireplace, and she would have let him burn it had she not been so certain that he had stashed another copy of the manuscript somewhere.[4]

Technically a tour de force, *The Subterraneans* seems to have been expelled in one long breath, like a heroic if overbearingly manic jazz riff. Ginsberg recognized it as a prose innovation, calling it "the long jazz line" and later employing it to historic effect in "Howl." Thematically, the novel is a sexual tragicomedy of errors in which all the lovers are mismatched, a conundrum that often occurs in Kerouac's fiction. In a bar scene, Kerouac, as Percepied, says, " 'Frank's leching after Adam, Adam's leching after Yuri,' and Yuri'd thrown in 'And I'm leching after you.' " (The character key for the passage is as follows: Frank = Burroughs, Adam = Ginsberg, and Yuri = Corso.) Percepied is torn between Mardou and his mother, and between homoeroticism and heterosexuality. After being with his girl, he always goes home feeling guilty, "finding my mother glum and all-weekend-alone in a chair with her shawl." Whatever one thinks of the story, *The Subterraneans* is a stunning stream-of-consciousness feat that gives the impression of a single sentence blurted by a tortured, wild-eyed fanatic.

Kerouac was on a creative roll, and no other novelist was producing comparable fiction at the rate he established in the late forties and early fifties, with *On the Road*, *Visions of Cody*, *Dr. Sax*, *Maggie Cassidy*, and *The Subterraneans* completed in a five-year period. Only Tennessee Williams, in the theater, could match such a record, with *A Streetcar Named Desire*, *Summer and Smoke*, *The Rose Tattoo*, and *Camino Real* produced in the same time frame. With a little encouragement, Kerouac no doubt would have completed even more of the projects he started at this time but dropped in the face of publisher indifference, such as the *Gone With the Wind*–type historical novel that he referred to in a letter to Cowley, not to mention his dope-dealer novel, his railroad novel, and his jazz novel. His sole champion besides Cowley was a mild-mannered, bespectacled, soft-spoken paperback editor named Arabel Porter, who advised him that she was trying to excerpt a section from *On the Road* for *New World Writing*. Kerouac immediately wrote to Cowley and thanked him for staging an effective campaign to get him published. Unfortunately he also included a number of gratuitous, crack-pot, slanderous slurs at Vidal, even threatening to write an exposé of homosexual authors such as Vidal and Paul Bowles. This was a verbal form of gay-bashing, and since Kerouac had recently had sex with Vidal, it also represented a new low in hypocrisy, guilt, and self-hatred.

He sank into a depression that laid him low for the fall of 1953. After his affair with Alene, he retired to Richmond Hill feeling like an imbecile for lavishing so much time on *Doctor Sax*, *On the Road*, and other "reject-able wild prose madhouse enormities." He thought seriously of becoming a farmer and wrote Neal that if he grew his own food he could survive an H-bomb apocalypse. Replying on December 4, 1953, Neal discouraged Jack's agricultural fantasy and urged him to come to San Jose and work as a parking-lot attendant. With his last thirty dollars, Kerouac immediately started making plans to leave for the coast. Mémère decided she wanted to go too and settle among the palm trees, far from the bitter Northeastern winter. She told Jack to go ahead first and find a home for them. His departure in the winter of 1953–1954 was part of the general exodus of Beats from New York, marking the end of their first creative period. Kerouac hitchhiked to San Jose, Bur-roughs settled in Tangier, Ginsberg went to the Yucatan, and Corso moved to Cambridge, Massachusetts, and each in his way would spread the Beat philosophy and style.[5]

That philosophy was given a new dimension by Kerouac's adoption of Buddhism in late 1953. In December he started compiling his vast Buddhist bible, *Some of the Dharma*, a compendium of prayers, meditations, notes, poems, and diaries in which he set forth his view of life and further developed his esthetic theories regarding automatic writing. In Kerouac's universe, nothing is real but the mind, and everyone is part of this Universal Mind Essence that he defined as God. Individuals as well as the planets and stars are nothing but temporal accumulations of atoms that only appear to be real, but the great oversoul of which we all partake is not only real but goes on forever. In *Some of the Dharma*, Kerouac wrote that if he received the Nobel Prize he would tell the world, "All things are different forms of the same thing . . . Universal Mind," and he firmly believed that his own mind, ego, and personality were not his but "manifestation[s] of universal essence."

Both in terms of theme and style, the impact of Buddhism on Kerouac's writing was more significant than anyone could have assessed before the publication of *Some of the Dharma* in 1997. In early 1954, as he launched himself into the book, he redefined his mission as an artist, writing that he would create a "lifework teaching-book" to "enlighten the world and wake it from its sad mistaken dream of rue and rage." He wanted to relieve people of their stresses and tensions by showing them how to "return to mind" through meditation and prayer. The implications for his spontaneous-prose esthetic were enormous. In artistic terms, truth could be elicited through a style that tapped the true nature of Universal Mind Essence, or God as manifested in the human mind. Again, Kerouac stressed the sacredness of the first, unedited utterance because it mirrors "pure, universal intuition. . . . the original and perfect nature of man, which comes, goes, and never returns, like a cloud in the blue sky. . . . I preach . . . man's infinite Mind seeking perfect restoration." Technique in writing, for Kerouac, was not "changing words and halting and erasing and rearranging," but finding "deep form, as ored up from the bottom of the Mind unplanned . . . *the secret of writing is in the rhythm of urgency.*" Years later, describing the mature Kerouac style, Ken Kesey praised "the fluid grace of the prose and the integrity achieved by that famous fastashandscantype method of writing." Kerouac's stylistic discovery, spontaneous prose, was still considered controversial even within the Beat movement in the mid-1950s. Buddhism in a sense assured its future, lending a holy sanction to spontaneity and galvanizing his themes. His task as the author of the Duluoz Legend, he announced in *Some of the Dharma*, was "discovering the Dharma and trying to teach it, 1953–1955." He had arrived at a moment of artistic synthesis in which form and content became one; some of his best writing was before him.

Buddhism was the subject of lively debate when Kerouac arrived at Neal and Carolyn Cassady's home in San Jose on February 5, 1954, Neal's twenty-eighth birthday. As Jack later wrote to Carolyn and Neal, it was a "brilliant, radiant sympathetic, sinless" night of communication among friends. Jack got loaded and eagerly launched into a theological discussion, explaining that *dharma* is a Sanskrit word meaning "that which binds, supports, sustains"; it is the ultimate law of all creation in both Hinduism and Buddhism, and it also denotes individual right conduct. As a Buddhist, Kerouac believed in the self-regulating power of the universe; one gets exactly what one gives out, like a man bouncing a rubber ball against a wall. At this Neal bristled, preferring the Biblical version of the same doctrine; raising his finger like Billy Graham, he intoned, "Whatsoever you sow, that shall ye also reap."

Neal introduced Kerouac to the teachings of a Christian proponent of Buddhist philosophy named Edgar Cayce, expatiating on Cayce so persuasively that Jack wrote in *Some of the Dharma*, "How stupid I was to doubt any of the miracles of Jesus, Buddha, Edgar Cayce, Ste. Theresa or myself." A great diagnostician and miraculous healer, Cayce was born in Hopkinsville, Kentucky in 1877, and died in Virginia Beach, Virginia, in 1945. Like Kerouac, Cayce had visionary experiences from the time he was six or seven years old; upon his death he left a legacy of fourteen thousand telepathic clairvoyant statements on subjects ranging from reincarnation to medicine, business, health, and exercise. Though uneducated, Cayce was able to tap incredible masses of knowledge by hypnotizing himself and going into trances. Like Thoreau, Emerson, Whitman, and Kerouac, Cayce embraced the Buddhist concepts of karma (earned fate) and reincarnation and, also like them, he believed that man originated as a spirit rather than as a physical body. In Cayce's cosmology, particles of the universal spirit manifested themselves in matter, possibly out of a drive for adventure and fun, but this disrupted an orderly pattern of evolution that was then in process on the earth.

Man, utilizing his brilliant Faustian creativity and technological expertise for self-centered ends, succeeded in ensnaring himself in materialistic pursuits and lost sight of his essential nature as a projection of God. The resulting turmoil and strife, according to Cayce, has been going on for ten million years, with man reincarnating himself over and over, trying to get it right, but often slipping back into his obsession with material pleasures.

To a degree, Cayce and Kerouac shared the same tragic view of the human condition, but they parted company radically on the issues of reincarnation and karma. Kerouac saw both as a curse on mankind, a grim cycle of birth, rebirth, and endless suffering. "A mistake has been discovered at the heart of the universe, and its name is existence," he wrote in *Some of the Dharma*; "all sentient life is tortured." Men are blinded to the reality of the spirit by their obsession with material objects and by desire and ambition. For most people, "life is a curse, not worth living," Kerouac believed. "The universe is a dream already ended." Kerouac's own hopelessness was traceable to his drinking and drugging, which robbed him of the stillness and clarity required for meditation and prayer. In rare intervals of sobriety he was able to meditate long enough to receive a glimpse of the ecstasy he was denying himself while drunk or drugged. *Some of the Dharma* is in part a disturbing log of an alcoholic's doomed spiritual quest and a dirge over his expulsion, through intoxicants, from "the golden central hall of knowing . . . Nirvana . . . a strange chamber of great inward glory . . . from out of [which] you emerge with loving-kindness, compassion, gladness and equanimity." By the end of the book, Kerouac, unchanged by Buddhism, continues to blame the world's ills on women, homosexuals, and book publishers. Time and again he promises to abandon alcohol and drugs and to give up the friends who place these temptations before him, but invariably he reverts to his old patterns.

Far more optimistic than Kerouac was able to be, Edgar Cayce held that reincarnation is man's way of progressing spiritually through eons of time, and that karma is good, for it brings us the experiences that we need to grow. Our spiritual progress requires more than one lifetime; as Christ explained, "Unless a man be born again he cannot see the kingdom of heaven." According to Cayce, karma is balanced by grace—God's unlimited and unmerited love. Cayce's son, Hugh Lynn, once explained, "We move under the law of Grace the moment that we begin to forgive ourselves and others. . . . To forgive our self is to rid our self of guilt. To forgive others is to rid our self of the resentments and hate which twist our souls and make us sick. Anger is a thought pattern, and we build karma from thought patterns as surely as from deeds. . . . Grace is the love of God pouring out continuously on man. . . . We come under the law of Grace whenever we choose it instead of the law of Karma." As creatures of free will, we may choose the path of our soul, including the family and circumstances into which we are born. Then, through meditation, we can connect with God, and rid ourselves of obsessions, prejudices, and biases, rather than carry them over into another lifetime. Unfortunately, Kerouac was unwilling to surrender any of his defects, including anti-Semitism, misogyny, resentment of publishers, substance abuse, and homophobia; no wonder he feared and hated the ideas of karma and reincarnation and, in true alcoholic fashion, insisted on instant Nirvana.

During Kerouac's visit with the Cassadys in San Jose, he and Neal agreed on the merits of Edgar Cayce's philosophy but clashed over Neal's other religious enthusiasm, Oral Roberts. Kerouac raised violent objections when Neal "fell for" Oral Roberts's fanatical fundamentalist preachings. "Okie Horseshit," Kerouac wrote in *Some of the Dharma*, scorning the revivalist's "Phallic Dynamism—there was an Asexual Angel in Jesus and Buddha, no ignorant screaming and self-infatuated blabbering." Though Carolyn perceived a new chasm opening between Jack and Neal, the latter's religious awakening had the effect of projecting Kerouac deeper into his own spirituality. At the San Jose library, Kerouac conducted research for *Buddha Tells Us*, his biography of Siddhartha Gautama, the founder of Buddhism, who lived in the foothills of the Himalayas in the 6th century B.C. Later described by the Kerouac estate as "a handbook for Western understanding of Buddhist teachings," *Buddha Tells Us* is sometimes referred to as *Wake Up*, and in it Kerouac wrote:

> Buddha means the awakened one. Until recently most people thought of the Buddha as a big fat rococo sitting figure. . . . The actual Buddha was a handsome young prince who . . . cut off his long golden hair with his sword and sat down with the holy men of the India of his day and died at the age of eighty a lean venerable wanderer of ancient roads and elephant woods.

Kerouac's interest in Eastern philosophy anticipated that of general Western culture by a decade or more, and Neal's discovery of Cayce came a dozen years before author Jess Stearn brought Cayce to the attention of the public in his best-seller, *The Sleeping Prophet*. In an even more profound sense, the transformations Kerouac and Cassady were undergoing in 1954 would not be felt by the populace at large until the end of the century, when more and more people seemed to be forsaking drugs and drama for lives based on spiritual values, meditation, and sobriety. Kerouac typed up a hundred pages of notes on Buddhism in February 1954; they were eventually incorporated into *Some of the Dharma*, which was completed two years later on March 15, 1956. By the time Viking at last published the book in 1997, 1.5 million Americans were Buddhists, and *Time* magazine was featuring Buddhism on its cover. As the *Los Angeles Times* observed, Kerouac was a "hero and prophet to everyone but himself," and as Tom Clark wrote in the *San Francisco Chronicle*, "The book was an idea forty years ahead of its time." *Publisher's Weekly* found *Some of the Dharma* "extraordinary . . . an important early record of one Westerner's—and, by extension, Western culture's—encounter with the East."[6]

Alcohol and drugs were not the only reasons Kerouac's Buddhism failed to bring him the peace he sought. In *Some of the Dharma*, he attributed his loneliness to his having no Buddhist friends to share his ideas with, but the real issue was his own self-centered isolation. World-weary, loveless, and a fugitive from the law, he was bored at thirty-two. He missed the point of the Buddhist principles he espoused — that salvation comes through altruistic motives. But at least he was beginning to acknowledge that alcoholism lay at the root of all his problems. "Drinking heavily, you abandon people," he wrote, "and they abandon you — and you abandon yourself — It's a form of partial self murder."

At the Cassady home in San Jose, Jack and Neal smoked so much pot that they became paranoid and suspicious of each other. Despite Kerouac's intellectual grasp of the Buddhist precept that all conflict arises over matters of possession, he fought so bitterly with Neal over how to divide twenty dollars worth of grass that he packed his duffel bag and moved to San Francisco. Carolyn zeroed in on their ridiculous contretemps when she observed that Jack and Neal's quarrels were "like lover's fights — petty, heartrending and caused by other factors under the surface." Kerouac later wrote Carolyn that he disapproved of Neal's sadomasochistic sex play, calling it an indulgence for which Neal would accrue bad karma. He also noted Neal's treatment of his children, citing the time Neal slapped his daughter Cathy across the room. Neal was equally disenchanted with Jack and accused him of being a parasite. The Cassadys' hopes for a liberated, open marriage with Jack were finally dashed by jealousy and competitiveness. "It's not good to have this three-way play against each other, because we want each other and each resents the third," Carolyn wrote. Ginsberg soon replaced Kerouac in the Cassady household, but Carolyn kicked him out when she walked in on Allen and Neal having sex. Kerouac heard of the fracas and called Carolyn "Miss Virago," reminding her in a letter that Allen and Neal had been friends long before she'd entered the picture. Getting on his gay-chauvinist high horse, Burroughs observed that in disposing of Ginsberg, Carolyn at last had her man to herself, "what every U.S. bitch of them wants," he snarled.[7]

In San Francisco, Jack took up residence again in the Cameo Hotel in a three-dollar-a-week room and wrote his first book of poetry, *San Francisco Blues*. One of the few major novelists since Thomas Hardy to write important poems, Kerouac had loved poetry ever since he'd written his first verse in childhood to a parochial-school classmate, a love that continued under the influence of Sammy Sampas. Fresh and vivid, Kerouac's poetry was a flight taken at the height of his powers as a writer, and he later described *San Francisco Blues* as "my first book of poems, written back in 1954 & hinting the approach of the final blues poetry form I developed for the *Mexico City Blues*." The first explicit examples of Buddhism in his imaginative work occur in these verses, which he wrote in a pocket notebook while sitting in a chair beside his hotel window, drinking out of a jug of California Tokay and watching the teeming street life below. In portraying the cops, sailors, whores, and winos of skid row, he was striving for the same effect as a jazz blues chorus. The San Francisco poems were among the many that were discovered after Kerouac's death in his meticulously organized files, according to the estate. Though Kerouac would never be recognized as an important poet in his lifetime, Ginsberg called him a "major . . . seminal" poet of the second half of the twentieth century. With Kerouac, Ginsberg added, "a human voice" entered modern poetry, introducing a rush of American idiom. But when Kerouac showed his poems to Mark Van Doren in 1954, the English professor wouldn't even acknowledge that they were poetry.[8]

In the spring, Kerouac returned to New York by bus, writing Carolyn on April 23, 1954, that he'd barely made it to Queens without starving but felt stronger than ever because hunger induced anger, and anger led to self-knowledge. Neal wasn't impressed and jibed in a letter to Ginsberg that Jack had run home to "mama." In the tranquility of Mémère's apartment, Jack achieved the kind of work that Neal could only dream of, surging ahead on *Book of Dreams*, a remarkable example of the Beat principle of total self-disclosure. "I love my home," he wrote in *Some of the Dharma*, "because here is my chow & my retreat." Then, in a May letter to Ginsberg, he talked frankly about his desperation as an alcoholic. Although he was occasionally able to stop drinking, he fell off the wagon as soon as he became bored, and he still didn't realize that his boredom was the result of living only for himself, offering so little service to others, and being a burden on so many. His vulnerability was a magnet for impossibly dysfunctional girls, the latest being a junkie friend of Iris Brody's. Iris, who in the following decade would die of a drug overdose, was a Greenwich Village painter known as one of the "Three Graces of the San Remo." In 1953–1954, the Three Graces introduced fashions that would dominate the hip scene for the next fifteen years, including wire-framed glasses, granny dresses, beads, and long ironed hair.

On August 24, 1954, Kerouac felt he'd reached "the lowest point" since embracing Buddhism the preceding December. The issue was still his alcoholism; he knew he should stay sober in his search for the truth, but life for him without alcohol was "too dreary," he confessed in *Some of the Dharma*. He missed his principal codependents of this period, the Cassady family, and wrote Carolyn a touching, affectionate letter. One of her daughters, Cathy, had told Kerouac, "Don't you know that I am Pooh Bear," he reported in *Some of the Dharma*, referring to one of the lovable creatures in A. A. Milne's classic children's story, *Winnie the Pooh*. He revised the final passage of *On the Road* to read, in part, "the children must be crying . . . don't you know that god is Pooh Bear."

Fortunately, he was not as strapped for money as usual. Thanks to his railroad jobs, he was receiving unemployment checks and could help his mother meet expenses. He waited in vain for good news from publishers. *On the Road* was on offer to Little, Brown, whose editor, the stuttering, somewhat pompous but gifted and likable Seymour (Sam) Lawrence, had once turned down Kerouac's gripping chapter on Leo's death in *The Town and the City* with a knuckle-rapping lecture on craftsmanship. In a letter to Ginsberg, Kerouac objected to the impertinence of "that little queen." When Lawrence subsequently rejected *On the Road*, Kerouac complained to Ginsberg that the editor sat on the manuscript for six months in 1954 and kept buying time by assuring Kerouac's agent that he loved the book. According to Lawrence, his conservative colleagues were to blame, but he managed to round up twelve recommendations for publication from associates at Little, Brown's more liberal and literary subsidiary, the Atlantic Monthly Press. Unfortunately, one of the Little, Brown editors was powerful enough to blackball it. Despite Lawrence's aggressive and persistent advocacy of *On the Road*, he infuriated Kerouac in his rejection letter by offering yet another of his vacuous pontifications on the art of writing, and Kerouac dubbed him "Little shit S."

Though Kerouac would later be portrayed as an artist who loved writing books but hated the writing game, in reality he relished the politics of publishing and had proudly brandished the clout he'd briefly possessed as Harcourt's fair-haired boy. What he hated was rejection and powerlessness, and he reacted by vilifying both editors and publishers. "Fuck these . . . Lawrences," he wrote Ginsberg, and he damned all editors as "pissyass . . . minimizers." Kerouac and Ginsberg considered setting up an independent press to publish their own works as well as those of Burroughs and Cassady, but they lacked the necessary capital of a thousand dollars. Their first list would have been one of the most formidable in publishing history, including *On the Road, Howl and Other Poems, Naked Lunch*, and the *Joan Anderson Letter*.

Malcolm Cowley was exempted from Kerouac's contempt for publishers, at least for the present, because he plugged Kerouac in the August 21, 1954, issue of *Saturday Review*, writing, "It was John Kerouac who invented the phrase [Beat Generation], and his unpublished narrative 'On the Road' is the best record of their lives." In a letter to Ginsberg on August 23, Kerouac wrote that Cowley was still promoting him in New York literary and publishing circles, and Cowley's efforts finally paid off. Arabel Porter purchased excerpts from *On the Road* and *Visions of Cody* for *New World Writing*, paying Kerouac $120. The selections dealt with Jack and Neal discovering the San Francisco jazz scene and included a passage in which they heard Anita O'Day in her Chicago nightclub. With Kerouac's customary flair for titles, he called the selection "Jazz of the Beat Generation." Acceptance by an editor was always a tonic, and he celebrated by swearing off liquor, explaining to Ginsberg that, at thirty-three, he was too old to drink, and he'd also given up smoking and all-night parties. In *Some of the Dharma* he confidently wrote, "The reason not to drink any alcohol at all is to attain permanently to the shivering bliss of pure blood. To keep the mind from confusion." But a short while later he confessed that he'd "been drinking like a fiend," passing out two times in August and numerous times in July 1954, "like a man hit over the head. . . . I drink to destroy myself." In his letter to Ginsberg, he displayed his usual split personality with regard to homoeroticism, advising Ginsberg in one breath to marry a rich girl and join the yachting set, and in the next assuring him that plenty of gay sex partners could be found in San Francisco at the Black Cat on Columbus at Montgomery.[9]

Kerouac had acquired a new agent in May 1954, one who would remain with him for the rest of his life. Recommended by Giroux, Sterling Lord was a dark-haired, fair-skinned, well-built collegiate tennis champ from the Midwest, a man of quiet charm and grave good manners. In August, Kerouac advised him that he intended to use the name "Jean-Louis" as a pseudonym due to the autobiographical nature of his novels. The anonymity of a nom de plume, Jack explained, would shield him from litigation. He feared not only libel suits from the people he wrote about, but child-support suits from the irate and indefatigably litigious Joan Haverty. Sterling began circulating *On the Road* under its new title, *Beat Generation*, and pitched it to Bill Rainey, an editor at E. P. Dutton. Optimistic about getting a contract, Rainey held onto the manuscript for weeks. A typically conservative New York publishing house, Dutton had surprised the trade by issuing Françoise Sagan's controversial French novel, *Bonjour Tristesse*, which dealt with a then-taboo subject, a love affair between a young woman and an older man. Despite Sterling's skills as a subtle and persuasive salesman, Dutton declined *On the Road*. Nonetheless, Kerouac was convinced that his career was at last being directed by a master and told Mémère to "Trust in the Lord."[10] Not even Sterling Lord, however, could stem the tide of decline letters in which top editors racked their brains to come up with logical reasons for turning down a modern classic.

Again, Buddhism helped Kerouac accept rejection and privation. In *Some of the Dharma* he renounced society's "system of lures," including publishing, which was nothing but a "self-caress." After reading the *Diamond Sutra*, he wrote Ginsberg that he'd glimpsed heaven, which he defined as the here and now. He wrote Burroughs that he'd given up sex, except for masturbation, but Burroughs told him he was going too far and that only cowards renounced pleasure and its attendant suffering. When Kerouac heard that Ginsberg had also taken up masturbation, he warned him against it, advising that "mast'ion" was not the same thing as Buddhist abstinence for it constituted a method of evading the problem while falling short of the solution. Kerouac had completely soured on women and wrote that their "slit" was a gaping wound that reminded him of homicide; women made him "sick." In *Some of the Dharma*, one of Kerouac's most misogynistic books, he used Buddhist asceticism as an excuse to berate womankind, calling them "semen nurses," castrators, grave-makers, and crocodiles. "The True man eschews women, has no children, and seeks No-Return to the dreary wheel of life & death. He is constantly on his guard against lust & concupiscence & cupidity." But he told Ginsberg that after a drink, he was still game for anything.[11]

In this dark mood, he wrote his nightmarish sci-fi tale, "cityCityCITY," a visionary portrait of an overpopulated dystopia governed by computers capable of wiping out whole neighborhoods at will. In a letter the following year to Ginsberg, he revealed that he'd written the story at the height of the hysterical Communist witch-hunt—the army-McCarthy hearings—and intended it as a preview of the world's future as a police state straight out of Kafka. He asked Burroughs to collaborate with him on an expanded, novel-length version of the same idea, but the collaboration failed to take off. He continued to develop the story on his own; in a letter to Carolyn on August 26, 1954, he wrote that "cityCityCITY" was shaping up as a spectacular sci-fi novel. However, several years later in *Evergreen Review*, he dismissed the entire sci-fi genre as one of the "modern bizarre structures . . . [that] arise from language being dead," which no doubt explains why he dropped the form.[12]

On October 27, Kerouac confided in a letter to Alfred Kazin that Malcolm Cowley had now decided he liked both *Dr. Sax* and *The Subterraneans* but couldn't convince Viking to make an offer. Jack viewed *The Subterraneans* as a love story, but he made it sound like a very odd one indeed, comparing the protagonist with Dostoyevsky's ax-murderer, Raskolnikov. He characterized his newly invented prose style as a jazz-tossed ocean of language. Though he felt his writing was as smooth as butter, he told Kazin that Robert Giroux refused outright to subject himself to unpolished prose and insisted on more formal composition. Rather pathetically, Kerouac begged Kazin to read his various unpublished novels since no one else would, and he couldn't continue writing without some feedback.[13]

At this point, virtually the entire commercial publishing industry—known by insiders as "the trade"—had turned its back on Kerouac. There was a remarkable irony in this. In his celebrated 1951 critical study, *After the Lost Generation*, John V. Aldridge complained that Norman Mailer and other post-WWII novelists—Vance Bourjaily, Irwin Shaw, Merle Miller, Paul Bowles, John Horne Burns, Gore Vidal, and Truman Capote—had failed to come up with a new literary movement because they lacked the spirit of protest and innovation that had animated Hemingway, Fitzgerald, Dos Passos, and other writers of the 1920s. The Lost Generation authors had radically transformed the language of fiction, and now there was nothing left for the younger writers to do but endlessly repeat old, outdated styles. While Aldridge was applauded for this observation, Kerouac continued to wave a radical new literary movement under the noses of the literary establishment, who ignored him. Aldridge lived in comfortable Roxbury, Connecticut, near William and Rose Styron and, somewhat later, Arthur Miller and Marilyn Monroe, and Norman Mailer and Adele Morales—perhaps too far from the barricades to hear the sound of the very revolution he was calling for.

————

Kerouac's return trip to Lowell in the autumn of 1954 occasioned another historic advance in his formulation of the Beat philosophy, to which he now added his powerful and far-reaching advocacy of nonviolence. Feeling homesick, he'd gone to Lowell to research his nonfiction portrait of the city, *A Book of Memory*. One day, he passed by Stella's house but was too shy to call on her, later writing her that he'd visit the Sampas home the next time he came to Lowell. Stella was now working as the forewoman of a shoe factory above the Giant Store on the corner of Broadway and Dutton Street. No one recognized Kerouac as he strolled around town, stopping at one point in front of Leo's old Spotlite print shop on the canal, now an abandoned hovel teeming with ghostly memories. In Ste. Jeanne d'Arc Church, Kerouac was meditating when an insight about the true meaning of the Beat Generation overwhelmed him. The word *Beat* meant "beatific," he realized, and suddenly the movement acquired significant new moral and philosophical underpinnings, ones that would deeply influence the counterculture of the sixties and strip aggression and war of much of their glamour.

"Woe unto those who think that the Beat Generation means crime, delinquency, immortality, amorality," Kerouac wrote, showing how far he'd come from his own criminal behavior of the 1940s. Now he defined Beat in terms of what Gerard had told him in childhood: "Ti Jean never hurt any living being . . . all are going to heaven straight into God's snowy arms so never hurt anything and if you see anybody hurt anything stop them as best you can." Kerouac was not exactly telling the truth when he wrote, "I have never had anything to do with violence, hatred, cruelty," but at least now he embraced better values than the nihilistic ones he and Lucien had gleaned from Gide, Nietzsche, Yeats, and Rimbaud. His new goal, he wrote, was "to be in a state of beatitude, like St. Francis . . . practicing endurance, kindness, cultivating joy of heart"—and all these could be achieved through sobriety and meditation. Though he foresaw that "the dope thing will die out," unfortunately it didn't for Kerouac, whose life continued to be littered with benny tubes and roaches.

He genuinely tried to incorporate the Beat principle of nonviolence in all his affairs, vowing in *Some of the Dharma* to forswear even arguing and fighting. In the future, if someone insulted him, he would "give it back and say 'What do I want with your insult. You'll have more use for it than I have.'" Carried into the streets by Ginsberg and others, Kerouac's nonviolent type of social dissent would help reshape the world in the sixties.

In 1954, as he continued walking through Lowell, he came to Moody Street and, as he later wrote in *Some of the Dharma*, he longed to share his new Buddhist insights with G. J. Apostolos—particularly his realization that all our thinking, worries, and anxieties are "powerless . . . to influence . . . the Ultimate Enlightening Nature of Mind-Essence." He searched all the clubs and bars hoping to find a drinking buddy, but none of his old cronies were around and he went away dejected. He abandoned his latest project, *A Book of Memory*, after discovering that he could no longer write the carefully crafted sentences that publishers wanted. On October 6, 1954, he wrote, "I shall now give up Modern Prose, which I invented." As revealed in *Some of the Dharma*, he decided to become a hermit, patterning himself after Thoreau in his hut at Walden Pond. But Kerouac had more in common with his fellow Columbia alumnus Thomas Merton, who was described by Carol Zaleski, author of *The Life of the World to Come*, as a "champion of eremitism . . . torn by desires of solitude and sociability, silence and self-expression, monastic obedience and beatnik spontaneity." Kerouac saw himself as a Buddhist monk roaming the deserts and mountains in search of *samapatti* (transcendental spiritual powers). But even as he made these plans, he acknowledged the pointlessness of geographics and stated that salvation requires not an outward odyssey but an inward voyage to "the hole in your mind." Only there could one find "the true Morphine . . . Samapatti intelligence apprehending knowledge directly by intuition." In *Some of the Dharma*, he added that he'd experienced a "superb happiness" during his October 1954 Lowell visit, realizing that if he'd "stop guzzling . . . a new life would begin." Before long, he "got a GAY idea" and resumed his drinking, "ending again in despair and blind nerves."[14]

Returning from Lowell, Kerouac's bus pulled into Manhattan at 10 P.M., and while walking in midtown, sipping from a pint of inexpensive port, he saw Adele Morales with Norman Mailer, whom he later portrayed in *Desolation Angels* as "Harvey Marker," author of *Naked and the Doomed*. Though Kerouac and Mailer had much more in common than Adele — they shared a penchant for criminal types, homophobia, and a love of offbeat places like Mexico City — Kerouac's newly assumed beatific posture was in stark contrast to the moral position Mailer was forming in the 1950s. Just as Kerouac was renouncing violence, Mailer began to espouse it, arguing that rage is detrimental to creativity when turned inward upon oneself, and should instead be unleashed upon the public. Externalizing violence is both healing and cathartic, or so Mailer thought at the time.

Though Kerouac and Mailer diverged ideologically, they respected each other. Mailer was trying to thrash his way out of the failure of his second novel, *Barbary Shore*, but he was still regarded as the creator of a heroic WWII combat novel that could never be matched. Kerouac, though spurned by publishers, was considered the only authentic hipster on the literary scene, and had a mushrooming underground reputation. They had both been ostracized by the book trade for writing experimental books that were morally suspect. Bennett Cerf of Random House not only declined the iconoclastic Mailer novel *The Deer Park*, but tried to scare other publishers out of taking it, warning Walter Minton of Putnam's that it was "bad for the industry." Minton published it anyway, in 1955. Writing in the *New York Herald Tribune*, Cowley called it "serious and reckless . . . an advance over *The Naked and the Dead*. . . . Mailer, though not a finished novelist, is one of the two or three most talented writers of his generation."

When Kerouac ran into Adele and Norman on Third Avenue he avoided them, later writing in *Desolation Angels*, "I just dont even look, but down-street I turn just as they turn, curious lookings." While sponsoring *Desolation Angels* at Coward-McCann a decade later, I asked Kerouac why he avoided Mailer that day since they were both literary outcasts and might have lent each other moral support. "Ha," he said, "Mailer would have wanted a sparring match, and I gave up fighting for art, just like I gave up football for art."

After snubbing Norman and Adele, Jack proceeded to the Village and ducked into a familiar neighborhood bar. A Negro hipster in a beret asked him what he did for a living, and Kerouac replied that he was the best writer in the United States. The black hepcat shook his hand and identified himself as the best jazz pianist in America. He was Cecil Taylor, and when he later played a set, he seemed to aim it directly at Jack. Afterward, Kerouac went down to the waterfront, taking nips from his bottle and occasionally stopping to warm his hands over flaming barrels left by stevedores. October always made him feel that everything was exactly as it should be — "old melancholy October, tender and loving and sad."[15]

He managed to remain sober for eight days, writing on October 12, 1954, that he had conquered his compulsion to drink by eating well, staying away from slippery people and slippery places, and taking long walks. But a notebook entry in *Some of the Dharma* reveals that he slipped again on October 13. "Got drunk," he wrote, adding, "replunged . . . in insensitive ignorance of the past 14 years." On December 19, he noted that he'd hit the worst bottom of his life — his wife had put out a warrant for his arrest, he was hounded by the police, plagiarized by his friends, devastated by pot, Benzedrine, tobacco, and goofballs, and he was mutilating himself by burning his hands. "Also full of alcoholic sorrow," he added.

As Christmas 1954 approached, he sobered up again and even succeeded in hypnotizing himself and practicing *dhyana*, a trance-like state of contemplation and ecstasy, three times daily. On December 23 he thought of writing a Buddhist novel but discarded the notion lest it rekindle his cast-off ambitions and "re-attach" him to "self-attainment." Following his third dhyana of the day he started drinking wine, later lamenting that alcohol had doomed him to another reincarnation. "The reason I'm suffering now," he wrote in *Some of the Dharma*, "is not because I'm JK but because I'm a bearer of self. . . . 'I' won't be reborn, *self* will be." He would have to keep reincarnating until he was willing to walk through his problems sober instead of drinking over them. He became convinced that if he could remain sober long enough to achieve the perfect meditation, he would annihilate selfhood and escape the suffering of further rebirths. On December 25, he at last caught a glimpse of his soul, "a glorious feeling of Mind Essence . . . I am a Tathagata [the fully enlightened one] truly tho not even yet an Arhat [monk] free from the intoxicants." He emerged from his meditation knowing that it no longer mattered whether he wrote or not; his true calling was to be a "Tao Hobo." In Taoism, which was used to adapt early Buddhism to Chinese patterns of thought, the Tao, or Way, is characterized by humility, passivity, and rejection of materialistic values, and it espouses a primitive preliterate form of society. As a Tao Hobo, Kerouac intended to meditate until he succeeded in "fumigating the universe with mind-essence."

He would have been better off leaving the universe to its own devices and focusing on the character flaws that were killing him. The new year, 1955, began inauspiciously for Kerouac, who permitted mercurial and fickle editors to drive him into fits of blind rage. Alfred A. Knopf Inc., the same house that turned down *The Deer Park*, teased Kerouac cruelly, promising to give *On the Road* careful consideration if he'd retype the dog-eared, coffee-stained manuscript, which had taken considerable punishment in its humiliating trek through New York and Boston publishing houses. He stayed up late many nights preparing a fresh copy only to have it returned later in January with a letter from editor Joe Fox that Kerouac described in *Some of the Dharma* as "ridiculous." He later explained to Ginsberg that Fox was arch and disdainful, calling *On the Road* bad fiction and complaining about lack of structure. According to *Some of the Dharma*, Fox found *On the Road's* "mystique" of the U.S.A. "touching" but not especially convincing, a judgment that struck Kerouac as "unfounded" since the America depicted by Carl Sandburg, Walt Whitman, and Thomas Wolfe was "made of the same stuff as my sublimities." On January 11, 1955, he angrily jotted, "KNOPF-SHMOPF-KAPOP," and swore that he'd never again write "systematic books of literature."

The Subterraneans was faring no better than *On the Road*, though Sam Lawrence at least declined *Subterraneans* with a reluctant, eloquent, and tearful letter. Lawrence loved Kerouac's style, but he shortsightedly discounted the Beats and urged the author to find more socially acceptable subject matter. That made about as much sense as asking Eudora Welty to cover the Indianapolis 500. Despairingly, Kerouac felt an urge to douse "the fire of writing and clear away the smoke and ashes of publishing." Later in January, he contested Joan Haverty's suit against him in court, producing a note from a doctor at the VA hospital verifying his phlebitis. He brought along a stack of Buddhist books to read in jail in case the decision went against him. Joan was trying to force him to admit he was Jan's father and win child support. Jack had tried to work and earn money, taking a job the previous year as a brakeman on the New York dock railway, but he'd suffered an attack of phlebitis in his arm. His once-powerful legs were sore, swollen, and wrapped like an old woman's. Joan seemed to take pity on him, explaining she hadn't been aware of his illness. "The dotter," as Jack referred to Jan, was four years old, and he looked at photographs of the blue-eyed child, murmuring, "Not my kid." But he later wrote Ginsberg that Jan in fact resembled him and could indeed be his offspring. Ginsberg had arranged for his brother, Eugene Brooks, to represent Jack in court. The tired-looking judge, who readily agreed that Kerouac was desperately sick, set the case aside. When Jack returned to his mother's apartment, he sat retaping his legs but continued to gamble with his life by drinking wine, taking Benzedrine, and smoking cigarettes. He had discovered a powerful spiritual tool in Buddhist meditation but unfortunately couldn't stay sober long enough to use it.

Exasperated with publishers by the end of January 1955, Kerouac ordered his agent to return all his unpublished work. He was sick of well-meaning editors who championed his books but returned them with lame notes blaming lack of house support. Then he would see the same editors at the San Remo, and they would fawn on him, thrilled to be in the presence of a bona fide subterranean and pumping him for tips on how to be hip, slick, and cool. One editor, he later told me, even asked him to write a nonfiction guide on how to be "groovy." "You asshole," Kerouac replied, "don't you know that's what *On the Road* is?" In a fit of pique, he instructed Sterling henceforth to charge all editors one hundred dollars per reading of *On the Road* since he saw no reason to continue entertaining them for free. The novel had been sitting around publishers' offices so long that it was hopelessly out-of-date, containing nothing about Kerouac's conversion to Buddhism. In *Some of the Dharma*, he reflected that the only way the novel could conceivably be issued now would be if a publisher were willing to designate it a "pre-enlightenment" work. But when he received the galleys of "Jazz of the Beat Generation" from Arabel Porter, he changed his mind and told Sterling to continue sending around his manuscripts, including *On the Road*.

His future editor Donald Allen recalled, "I had had some editorial experience of Jack Kerouac's *On the Road* as early as '54 and '55 when I had copy edited the 'Jazz of the Beat Generation' episode for *New World Writing* and had read the whole manuscript for a publisher." According to a later friend, John Montgomery, Kerouac was not entirely pleased with the editing of "Jazz of the Beat Generation" and thought *New World Writing* "did him a great disservice in splitting an approximately five hundred-word sentence in two." He didn't dare publish under his own name; Joan might slap him with another lawsuit. His decision to use the nom de plume Jean-Louis in *New World Writing* No. 7 was a horrendous career mistake, undermining Cowley's efforts to establish his name. Cowley was understandably upset, having just referred to him in print as "John Kerouac." In San Francisco, Ginsberg, who'd been showing *Visions of Cody* to Bay Area poets and critics including Robert Duncan and Kenneth Rexroth, proudly told everyone that Jean-Louis was his friend Kerouac and persuaded them to read "Jazz of the Beat Generation." Rexroth featured Kerouac's story on a radio broadcast about *New World Writing* and compared him with Celine and Genet. After reading *Visions of Cody*, Robert Duncan said, "Any man who can write fifty pages of description of reflections within a polished car bumper is a great genius in the tradition of Gertrude Stein consciousness prose."[16]

Meanwhile, in February 1955, Kerouac strolled around a sharecropper's farm in North Carolina accompanied by his nephew "Little Paul," pondering the nature of the universe. On February 18 he began *Buddha Tells Us*, and found that writing about Siddhartha grounded and centered him. "The haunting sensation of the world's unreality, momentariness, and pitiful sorrow has been somewhat dissipated," he noted, "and again the world seems solid and real." He celebrated his thirty-third birthday on March 12, the same day Charlie Parker, his idol, died in New York, having drunk and drugged himself to death. Parker was just a year and a half older than Jack, and the major poem Jack would compose the following summer, *Mexico City Blues*, was an elegy for Parker. "The inspiration of his saxophone work suffuses the poem," wrote critic James T. Jones in his excellent book-length study, *A Map of Mexico City Blues: Jack Kerouac as Poet*. On March 28, Kerouac seemed to be following Parker to the gates of insanity and death, admitting that he was "battered all over" from a three-day binge in New York, which left him "a sorrowing mess." He had to recant his claim that Buddhism had cured him of alcoholism, and he told Neal Cassady that the only way he could deal with his boredom was to drink himself into oblivion. He thought of committing suicide by dissolving forty sleeping pills in a glass of water and gulping them down but knew he would vomit his "horror back on out." His mother, tired of supporting him with her meager earnings as a sweatshop cobbler, packed him off to North Carolina to sponge off Nin and Paul for a while. From Rocky Mount, he sent jittery letters to his agent, impatiently inquiring about the status of various manuscripts. When James Laughlin of the avant-garde New Directions declined *Dr. Sax*, Kerouac told Sterling Lord that he was slowly going insane in the back country of North Carolina. There was ample evidence of this in some of Jack's instructions to Sterling. Though Kerouac was well aware that Giroux hated his wildcat style and had no intention of publishing him, he told Sterling to dump a pile of manuscripts, including *Maggie Cassidy*, *Dr. Sax*, and *The Subterraneans*, on Giroux's desk for the editor's personal delectation. The cost of writing one major novel after another only to see them disappear into a vacuum was obviously beginning to tell.

In North Carolina, Jack's sister and brother-in-law were opening a television business, into which Mémêre sank her few savings. Determined that Jack should earn his keep, Nin put him to work in Blake's Television Shop, which opened at 1311 Raleigh Road. Color television had just been introduced, with a 12.5-inch Westinghouse set retailing at $1295. When only thirty sets were sold nationally, however, the company immediately lowered the price to $1110. A typical item carried in Paul and Nin's store was a transparency that could be placed over black-and-white television screens to give the illusion of color. Jack called it "Colyalcolor," a word that shows up in both *The Dharma Bums* and *Some of the Dharma*, signifying the blissful emptiness Kerouac sometimes found in Buddhism. His job, which paid seventy-five cents an hour, was to move television sets whenever the regular helper called in sick, but Jack couldn't stay sober long enough to be trusted.

Again he contemplated committing suicide with his barbiturate cocktail, writing in *Some of the Dharma* that he intended to drink "poison death . . . soon." Fortunately, a new literary form he devised—called "flashes," brief, two-line "daydreams" of enlightenment—kept him sufficiently occupied to dispel thoughts of suicide. In *Some of the Dharma* he confided that "instead of drinkin sleepin pills," he decided to sleep around the clock, going into a mystic meditation called *samadhi* and composing his *Book of Flashes*, which would transport readers "to Nirvana with 'me.'"

Jack tried to share his interest in Nirvana with his mother and sister, but they were busy working to cover his expenses and derided his obsession with Buddhism. When Mémère complained of a back ache, he prescribed a long walk, but what she probably needed was respite from supporting a grown son. Her kindness and generosity to him were bottomless, and when he asked her for material for *Visions of Gerard*, she gladly shared her memories. On April 5, 1955, he had a "great talk with Ma" during which she gave him one of the novel's radiant images, that of Gerard ascending to heaven in a white chariot. Jack also wrote a short poem, "The Wine Prayer," beseeching Avalokitesvara, the Hearer and Answerer of Prayer, to free him from bondage to alcohol and drugs. Then, invoking all his saints—Gerard, Buddha, Sakyamuni, Leo Kerouac, Jesus, St. Francis, and Avalokitesvara—he cried out, "HELP ME . . . not to drink," for he sensed his life was going to be cut short, and he needed his strength to complete the Duluoz Legend. Concocting a curse on alcohol, he resolved to say, "a bottle of death," the next time he was was offered beer, wine, whiskey, or mescal. His chances for remaining sober were nil and he knew it, writing, "It's going to take years to destroy the formed habit." But it would take more than years—what was required was nothing less than a change of consciousness, and Kerouac was too isolated and self-absorbed for any meaningful change to take place in his life.

Inevitably, he slipped, and as usual the effects of his drinking were worse than ever, for alcoholism is a progressive disease. On April 15, 1955, he wrote Neal that he now had to drink during hangovers in order to control his violent shaking. Despite his knowledge of Neal's capriciousness, he deluded himself into seeing Neal as his salvation, heaping flattery on him, calling him America's best author, and trying to set Neal against Carolyn, promising plenty of thrills if Neal would come to North Carolina. Afraid he'd gone too far, Jack denied that he was "queer," as if that would win him points with Neal, who was highly rated as a lover by San Francisco painter Robert LaVigne. Neal didn't bother to acknowledge Jack's letter, but when Carolyn found it, she discovered that Jack had betrayed her by trying to lure Neal back to North Carolina. She had already lost Neal to the suicidal Natalie Jackson, whom Helen Hinkle described as "weird . . . staring into space—catatonic." When Al Hinkle revealed that Natalie was known around the North Beach for her expertise in performing oral sex, Carolyn immediately thought, that "made more sense." Kerouac realized that Neal was ignoring him and quickly switched his attentions to Carolyn. She sensed Jack's loneliness and longed to resume their affair but later wrote, "I knew it could never be the same as before." After receiving Jack's morose letters, Ginsberg noted in his journal on June 8, 1955, that Jack was "sunk in woe & loneliness from Rocky Mount."[17]

Kerouac had hoped that publishers would respond more favorably to his nonfiction religious books than they had to his novels, but *Buddha Tells Us* was "received coldly" even by his own agent, he wrote Ginsberg. Nothing, however, could shake his certainty that *Buddha Tells Us* was "a lake of light," he wrote in *Some of the Dharma*. If he could only get the book through the "Money changers," he knew people would love it, for it held the key to peace of mind. Unexpectedly, Giroux requested a copy, asking to see Jack as well, though *not* any of his impromptu novels. Jack set to work typing *Buddha*, and meanwhile told Giroux he'd expect a publishing decision on the book in thirty days. He still had not learned that it is editors, not authors, who set the deadlines (an expression frequently heard in overworked, understaffed editorial departments is, "If they want a quick answer, the answer is no").

When Kerouac heard from neither Giroux nor Lord, he seriously considered firing Sterling as his agent. On May 20, in an anguished letter to Ginsberg, he wrote that no one in New York was answering his letters or calls. Finally, at the end of his patience, he ordered Sterling to return all his manuscripts at once, effectively terminating him. When this too was ignored, Jack consulted Burroughs, who called Lord's behavior "a deliberate affront."

According to Montgomery, Kerouac decided that magazines and publishing houses were operated by persons "with a gang mentality." Kerouac's view exaggerated the case, but editors and agents logically give priority to their successful authors. When Kerouac had first told Lord that he'd finished *Buddha*, he'd expected enthusiasm but instead Sterling had only inquired if it was "any good." As his agent's silent treatment continued, Kerouac complained to Ginsberg about the "rats" on Madison Avenue. Giroux finally told Lord, but not Jack, that he'd thought better of it and didn't want to see Jack's Buddhist tracts after all. Jack was puzzled; Giroux had other religious writers on his list, notably Merton, but what Jack didn't realize was that while a substantial market existed for Catholic books, Western publishers were understandably reluctant to gamble on Eastern philosophy (even when *Some of the Dharma* was finally published in 1997, sales were moderate despite good reviews). *Buddha Tells Us* was shown to Viking, but Cowley declined it, urging Jack to stick to fiction since he was a natural-born storyteller. Sterling ventured the opinion that Kerouac had exaggerated the importance of Cowley's role in his career, and Jack angrily retorted that Cowley was the only person who'd ever done anything for him. Kerouac then made the mistake of complaining about Sterling to his sister Nin, who immediately seized the opportunity to become Jack's agent, though she knew nothing about literature and even less about contracts.[18]

Fortunately, good news at last began to trickle in from the publishing world, and Jack sidestepped Nin's offer. His story "cityCityCITY" sold to his poet friend David Burnett at *New American Reader* for fifty dollars. More significantly, "The Mexican Girl," a selection from *On the Road*, sold to the *Paris Review*, an important showcase for new talent. According to Cowley, *Paris Review* fiction editor Peter Matthiessen, future author of *At Play in the*

Certificate of Baptism

Go in Peace
and the Lord
be with You

CHURCH OF

St. Louis de France

Lowell, Massachusetts

⌒ This is to Certify ⌒

That *Jean Louis Kerouac*

Child of *Léo Kirouac*

and *Gabrielle Levesque*

born in *Lowell, Mass.*

on the *12* day of *Mars* 19*22*

⌒ Was Baptized ⌒

on the *19* day of *mars* 19*22*

According to the Rite of the Roman Catholic Church

by the Rev. *D. W. Boisvert*

the Sponsors being *Jean-Baptiste Kirouac*

and *Rosanna Kirouac* as appears

from the Baptismal Register of this Church.

Dated *23 June 1984*

Rev Roger N Jacques Pastor.
Associate

FOR NOTATIONS SEE REVERSE SIDE.   COTTER CHURCH SUPPLIES • LOS ANGELES • BC 101

Jack's baptismal certificate from the Parish of St. Louis de France in Centralville, a French-Canadian section of Lowell, where French spellings were still used (*mars* instead of March). To Kerouac, birth represented the beginning of the tragedy of consciousness—the dance of life that ends in death.

RIGHT: Lowell High School, where Kerouac learned to love Edwin Arlington Robinson, Robert Frost, and Emily Dickinson, and where he achieved his first successes on the gridiron and with the girls. "I hung out at the empty halls, classrooms—sometimes met Pauline Cole under the clock," he wrote in *Maggie Cassidy*.

(Ellis Amburn)

LEFT: City Hall, built in 1893, in downtown Lowell. The statue, *Winged Victory*, commemorates the first two Lowell soldiers killed in the Civil War; Kerouac wanted to replace it with a nude statue of himself.

RIGHT: St. Jean Baptiste, described in *Maggie Cassidy* as the "Ponderous Chartres Cathedral of the slums," the church where Kerouac was an altar boy and the site of his funeral.

35 Burnaby Street in Lowell's Centralville, where Kerouac lived in 1925–1926. Explaining how he acquired his idealism from his "holy brother" Gerard, Kerouac wrote, "Gerard showed up at the cottage on Burnaby street (when I was three) with the little boy... 'Ya faim, he's hungry.'"

The model for the "Castle" in *Doctor Sax*. "My ghost, personal angel... secret lover... came to Lowell as part of a great general movement of evil—to the secret Castle," Kerouac wrote.

Perpetually in flight from landlords and bill collectors, Jack's family moved in 1927 to 320 Hildreth Street.

Climax Runner: According to sports writer Glenn Stout, Kerouac became the star of the Lowell High varsity football team during his senior year. He scored the only touchdown in the big Thanksgiving game with Lawrence.

Kerouac once told me that Sammy Sampas (pictured here in uniform, 1942) was his muse and remained so, even after his death, through his sister Stella (center), whom Kerouac married. One of the last things Jack wrote was an October 4, 1969, card to Charles G. Sampas (left), reminiscing about football days at Lowell High.

"The family that drinks together," Kerouac said, giving me this picture (taken in Times Square in 1943) to run on the end sheets of *Vanity of Duluoz*. Jack was delighted when I compared his mother (center right) with Fay Bainter and his sister (center left) with Gail Russell, both wartime movie stars. His dad, Leo (far right), joined them for a night on the town.

Kenneth Rexroth, whose attacks against Kerouac in the major review press of the fifties and sixties almost destroyed Kerouac's career. The feud started when Rexroth denigrated *Dr. Sax* in manuscript; it accelerated during a dinner-party quarrel, and raged out of control when Kerouac roomed with Robert Creeley, who'd cuckolded Rexroth.

Lucien Carr (shown in 1960), whose killing of David Kammerer landed Kerouac in jail (for abetting a homicide) in 1944. Lucien later worked at UPI News, having cleaned up his act after being released from jail. Carr is the father of the best-selling novelist Caleb Carr, author of *The Alienist* and *Angel of Darkness*.

RIGHT: Gary Snyder, the "Japhy Ryder" of *The Dharma Bums*. Kerouac told me that Snyder called him a "bodhisattva…a wise angel." Kerouac admired Snyder's rugged passion for the wilderness and knowledge of Zen.

BELOW: Adele Morales, Kerouac's former girlfriend, snuggling up to her husband, Norman Mailer, outside New York's Felony Court in 1960. Mailer had recently stabbed her.

OPPOSITE PAGE: Allen Ginsberg at a protest in 1964. As Kerouac's alcoholism led him into a steady decline, Ginsberg came to replace Kerouac as the voice of the Beats and many other groups. When I suggested to Kerouac that he should take his rightful place as leader of the sixties counterculture, he refused and said, "Ginsberg's messianic robes don't suit him."

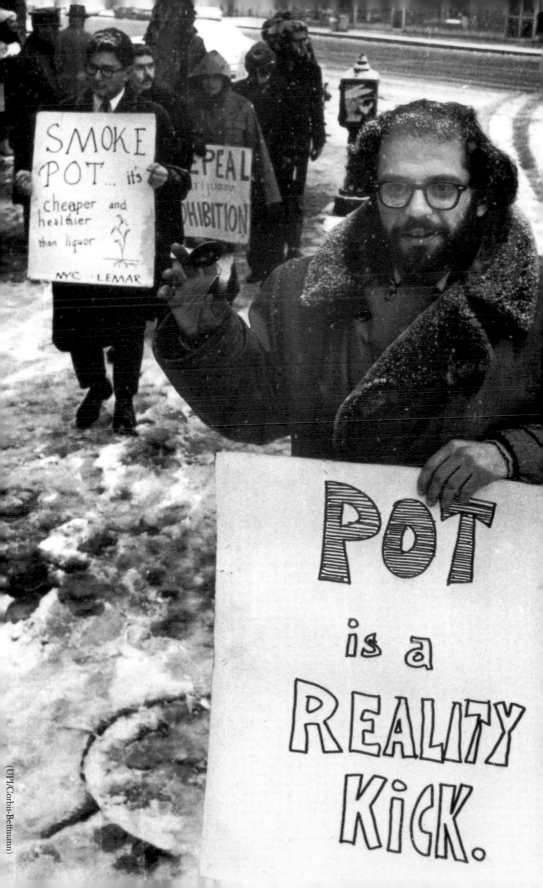

SMOKE POT... it's
cheaper and
healthier
than liquor

NYC · LEMAR

EPEAL
PHIBITION

POT
is a
REALITY
KICK.

(Billy Koumantzelis collection)

ABOVE: "Jack was in limbo and he didn't make it out," said Billy Koumantzelis (left), seen drinking with Kerouac in Nick Sampas's bar in Lowell in the late 1960s. The woman's identity is not known.

OPPOSITE PAGE: William Burroughs, an early mentor of Jack's, in Paris in 1960. They collaborated on an unpublished novel and had sex on one occasion in Mexico.

COWARD-McCANN, INC. *Publishers*

200 MADISON AVENUE, NEW YORK, N. Y. 10016

November 19, 1964

Mr. Jack Kerouac
5155 10th Avenue North
St. Petersburg, Fla.

Dear Jack,

Many thanks for your quick and good letter answering all questions about
setting up DESOLATION ANGELS. I'm awfully glad to have you and it and the
whole thing's a big pleasure to do because I've read you since ROAD and
liked you all along. A lot of your strongest qualities come out in this
work, and a hell of a lot of charm -- I always remember especially the wild
wonderful talk between Duluoz and the poets, a rare case of conversation
coming out as spontaneous poetry.

Well, with your letter now, I'm ready to go to the printer as soon as the
script arrives back from you. Not a minute to lose, really, since we publish in April, and I want to have the finished book in hand plenty of time
before actual publication -- to get it around in the right hands and get
talk started.

Sterling I believe is checking with you about Seymour Krim for the introduction and I'd like to make a strong pitch for him here. Dwight Macdonald,
though willing to read the ms, on speculation, seemed pretty uninformed
about your work and not really able to supply the literary and historical
framework I'd like in the introduction. This would be no problem for Seymour Krim, who does already know your work very well and agrees with me
about the importance it has, its effects not only on literature but on life
as well. Things in general have not been the same since ON THE ROAD, and
it's time this was spelled out in no uncertain terms.

You've got me excited about the new novel, VANITY OF DULUOZ, so
I'll keep your hideaway top secret. I envy you St. Petersburg.
weather all fall, New York the last few days has begun to act u
and it's drippy and foggy and funky.

I saw friends of yours at a party the other night at Richard H
Allen and Peter were there, but it was a busy-busy N.Y. party
get a chance to talk. It was a publication party for Sandy Fr
brother's book, YARBOROUGH, and the confusing mixture of gues
off-putting -- society folk from Philadelphia, editors, write
but none of this bothered ████████ who opened his fly at one po
other asked Lee Pollack why she and Jackson couldn't have any

-2-

Nov

Mr. Jack Kerouac

Hope you'll say to go ahead with Seymour Krim, who'll giv
I like the way you sign off and I'll do the same . . .

Your friend,

Ellis Amburn
Editor

EA:as

COWARD-McCANN, INC. *Publishers*

200 MADISON AVENUE, NEW YORK, N. Y. 10016

May 7, 1965

Mr. Jack Kerouac
5155 10th Avenue North
St. Petersburg, Fla.

Dear Jack:

An advance check will be going along to Sterling on Monday.

I'm enclosing some reviews, which run from good to bad. Time magazine, interestingly, is the best. Some of the reviewers seem to
me just hopeless, crotch-bound reactionaries, still unable to let
themselves go, still unable to scale that wall they've erected between literature and life, as Frank O'Hara once put it. What puz-
zles me is how some people can resist the utterly irresistible, in-
toxicating flights of language in Desolation Angels, some of the
best you've written.

Our advertising campaign will be starting shortly. The book will
be featured in our full-page ad May 16 in The Sunday Times Book
Review. You will have an ad June 3 in the New York Review of Books;
June 6 in the San Francisco Chronicle; June 8 in the daily New York
Times; and in the Evergreen Review in August. This is ambitious,
and I know you will find it heartening.

Yours,

Ellis Amburn
Editor

EA:as
Encs.

COWARD-McCANN, INC. *Publishers*

200 MADISON AVENUE, NEW YORK, N. Y. 100

July 17, 1967

Mr. Jack Kerouac
c/o The Sterling Lord Agency
75 East 55th Street
New York, N. Y. 10022

Dear Jack:

You really did get it in, and it really is good.
We're going ahead for the winter list.

I'd love to have some pictures of you as a kid, as
a football star, as a college student, as a sailor.
Particularly eager to have something circa 1946 or
somewhat earlier, like the picture you refer to (hope
you have it) of you and Claude on the steps of Low
Memorial.

In many ways Vanity of Duluoz is the most direct,
personal and generous of your books. It is exactly
what you said it would be, the story of an adventurous education, and the style is perfect for it.

Yours,

Ellis Amburn
Senior Editor

EA:as
cc: Sterling Lord

Kerouac scrupulously filed most of the letters I sent him as we worked together on
his two final novels. The personal nature
of my role as a confidant allowed us to
abandon traditional business mannerisms
and correspond as friends.

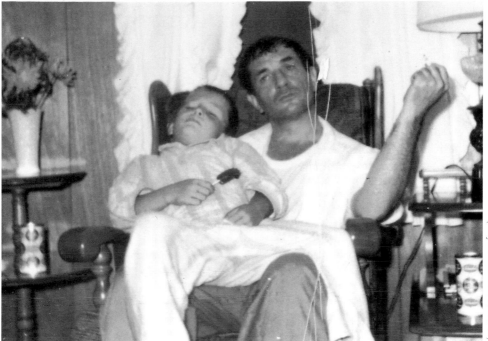

Kerouac, towards the end of his life, with Billy Koumantzelis's son. The children loved Jack, who engaged them in exciting games and often provided hilarious antics for their enjoyment, such as his Jekyll-and-Hyde transformation act.

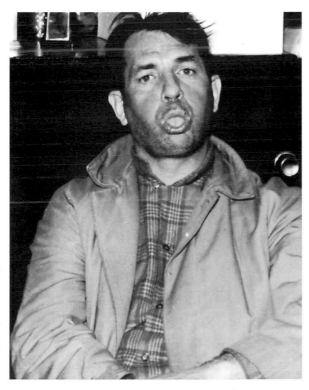

According to friends, Kerouac, shown here in the late 1960s in Lowell, was demonstrating how to give head.

The corner lot in St. Petersburg, Florida, where Kerouac was living at the time of his death. After hemorrhaging in the bathroom of this house, Kerouac was taken to the hospital, where "he kind of burst," recalled neighbor Betty Watley.

Ron Lowe, Kerouac's St. Petersburg, Florida, friend, was with Kerouac at the end, and stood in a puddle of Kerouac's blood as he tried to help him at the hospital.

Jan Kerouac claimed to be Jack's daughter. She died in June 1996, at the age of forty-four, after a bitter dispute over control of the Kerouac archive, though she had met Jack Kerouac only twice.

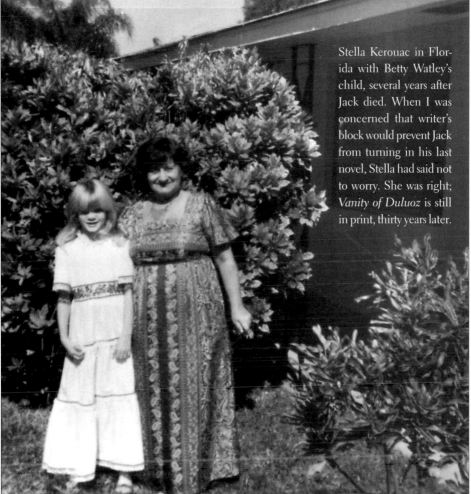

Stella Kerouac in Florida with Betty Watley's child, several years after Jack died. When I was concerned that writer's block would prevent Jack from turning in his last novel, Stella had said not to worry. She was right; *Vanity of Duluoz* is still in print, thirty years later.

(Betty Watley)

DEDICATED TO

Σταυροῦλα

Means "From the Cross" in Greek, and is also my wife's first name—STAVROULA.

Extra, special thanks to Ellis Amburn for his empathetic brilliance and expertise.

From *Vanity of Duluoz*, which Kerouac dedicated to his wife Stella and me.

RIGHT: The pallbearers carrying Jack's casket out of Archambault Funeral Parlor.

BELOW: I went to the Edson Cemetery and watched young people make pilgrimages to Kerouac's grave in Lowell, leaving notes, prayers, joints, and empty beer cans and bottles. It seemed an ironic celebration of what ultimately killed Jack.

LEFT: Kerouac's death certificate, which shows the cause of death: gastrointestinal hemorrhage from cirrhosis of the liver.

BELOW: Tony Sampas, Allen Ginsberg, and Billy Koumantzelis (left to right), at the Rainbow Bar in Lowell, 1988. These three of Kerouac's pallbearers got together at the Kerouac symposium in Lowell to celebrate Jack's life and writing.

(Billy Koumantzelis collection)

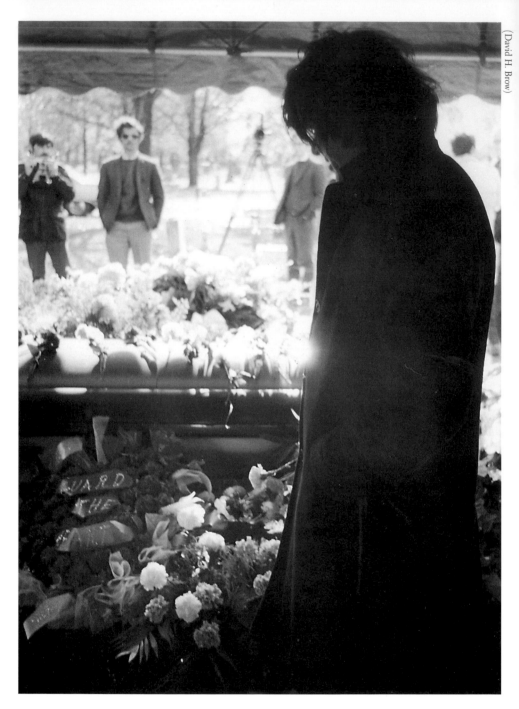

Gregory Corso at Jack's casket, 1969. At the funeral, Stella Kerouac accused him of neglecting Kerouac before his death. Corso considered dragging the corpse from the coffin and heaving it across the room; it was hypocritical, he felt, to mourn a body that no longer contained Kerouac's spirit.

Fields of the Lord, apparently wanted Kerouac "to revise and chasten the style." Cowley too urged Kerouac to tone down his language. Using a baseball analogy, Cowley pointed out that curveballs were great, but it was good to get them over home plate "and communicate." Kerouac knew that he wrote better than those who presumed to advise him, and confirmation was shortly forthcoming from Martha Foley, who selected "The Mexican Girl" for inclusion in *The Best American Short Stories 1956*. At last he decided to use his real name; he wrote Cowley to inform Peter Matthiessen that he was coming out of the closet as Jack Kerouac. Having found a market for Jack's stories, Cowley wrote him on June 7, 1955, requesting another brief, autonomous section of *On the Road* for submission to Plimpton at the *Paris Review*. Jack sent in "Ghost of the Susquehanna," a splendid and eerie hitchhiking episode. At last, everything was falling into place for his emergence as an important author.[19]

Cowley's position as a consultant rather than a full-time editor at Viking limited his ability to force through contracts. When Viking acquired a powerful new editor, Keith Jennison, Cowley shrewdly enlisted his support for *On the Road*. Other editors at the house fell into line, including Ellen Levine, who memoed that Kerouac was "fresh, new (and fascinating)," and though she felt the novel needed "a lot of work," it was so important that it "must be published even if it is a literary and financial failure." When it appeared that Dodd, Mead's Allen Klots also wanted to make an offer, Kerouac came to New York and tried to get Viking to issue small monthly payments while he prepared the new updated version of *On the Road* featuring Ray Smith as a wandering bhikku. In *Some of the Dharma* he referred to his "Begging Bowl Contract—$25 a month." Jennison observed, "You certainly aren't holding us up, boy," but Cowley demurred, blithely suggesting that Jack support himself with part-time employment. Due to swollen veins in his foot, Kerouac was unable to hold down a job, and he told Ginsberg that he was hurt by Cowley's heartlessness. Though Jennison patted Kerouac on the back reassuringly and both editors said they wanted to reconsider *On the Road*, Jack went away from the meeting disappointed, later writing in *Some of the Dharma*, "When I asked for $25 a month they smiled and their eyes twinkled." But he knew he'd acquired a useful ally in Jennison, whom he also liked personally (Jennison took the photograph of Kerouac that appeared the following decade on the paperback of *Tristessa*).

On July 12, 1955, Cowley wrote Lord to say that he wanted another look at *On the Road*, and later that summer he agreed to write a foreword to the manuscript, hoping to impress the top executives at Viking who had the final say. Kerouac, who knew the value of the eminent critic's imprimatur, told Sterling that Cowley was a saint for resuscitating his career. Cowley's endorsement in the form of a blurb or foreword could jump-start *On the Road* and might even land it on the best-seller list. Meanwhile, Kerouac generously shared his contacts at Viking with other Beat writers, extracting a promise from Cowley to read *Naked Lunch*. He also pushed Corso's work, collecting some of Corso's poems to show David Burnett. Such energy, persistence, and unity, spearheaded by Kerouac and Ginsberg, fomented the beginning of the Beat Generation's emergence as a literary movement in 1955.[20]

Before leaving New York, Jack lunched with Giroux and gave him *Dr. Sax* and *Buddha Tells Us*, but Giroux chose not to publish these works. Later, in *Some of the Dharma*, Jack consigned the editor to his personal limbo of "Lost Angels" and "Devils," with Robert Lax, Latouche, and Ginsberg, though he added that God loved them and would forgive them. *Buddha Tells Us* went off to Philosophical Library, and Kerouac looked forward to hearing the opinion of the learned editors. Instead, they asked him to underwrite six hundred copies at $3.50 each, adding that his book was "very well written." Since he didn't have $2100, he rejected their quasi-vanity proposal and changed the title of the book to the jazzier and religiously nonspecific *Wake Up*. In another disheartening development, Arabel Porter declined "Joan Rawshanks in the Fog" from *Visions of Cody*, as well as the final chapter of *The Subterraneans*. Jack told Sterling to show the latter to Criterion and *Dr. Sax* to Arthur Cohen at Noonday Press. Since Allen Klots had been such a good if ultimately ineffective promoter of *On the Road* at Dodd, Mead, Jack wanted him to see *Maggie Cassidy* and *The Subterraneans*. Sterling probably never had a client who kept him so busy or made him less money. His belief in Kerouac and his unwavering loyalty through long, lean years were unusual in a business in which shifting allegiances are commonplace. In *Some of the Dharma*, Kerouac admitted that he'd needlessly antagonized "older genera- tion helpers" such as Giroux, Van Doren, and Kazin by hawking "hipsterism and beatness." The "generation-instinct" that had motivated Kerouac to de- fine his era seemed irrelevant and misguided in a world that he now viewed as timeless and "intrinsically empty."[21]

In July 1955, Jack returned to Rocky Mount by bus, later complaining in a letter to Cowley that a blood clot on his left ankle was "biggern a baseball." Unable to afford the penicillin prescribed by doctors, he longed to go to Mexico City where the drug was administered in pharmacies, on the spot, at a dollar a shot and where the high altitude would have a healing effect on his circulatory system. In a July 4 letter begging Cowley for money, he wrote that he was praying that Cowley's and Jennison's efforts would eventuate in a contract for *On the Road*. Elsewhere, Kerouac denied that he ever prayed, but desperation had turned him into a foxhole Christian and made him see that Buddhist meditation perhaps wasn't enough. "Save me," he implored Cowley, threatening to forsake literature and kill himself if Vi- king declined *On the Road*. The worst thing about poverty, he told Cowley, was not being able to buy a beer.[22]

Later, with a few hundred dollars from his stories and a two-hundred- dollar grant Cowley wangled from the National Institute of Arts and Letters, Kerouac set out on another transcontinental hitchhike. In the July heat of the Southland, he headed for Tulsa, where he could connect with Route 66 and take America's "Main Street" all the way to L.A. But the few cars and trucks he managed to hail down were all going in another direction, and he ended up in Victoria, Texas, after enduring "a horrible trip through hell," he wrote in *Some of the Dharma*. Later, standing on Main Street in Houston, he decided to go to Mexico, to escape the "organized viciousness" of the United States. But on Monterrey's skid row, he missed the States and old friends such as "queer Bill [Burroughs] digging boys in mid-night bars of Mexico." He decided to live in Mexico City for the same reason that he'd embraced Buddhism's Universal Mind Essence and advocated spontaneous prose — Mexicans struck him as primitive, natural, and closer to God than over-civilized Europeans. "Fellaheen," he wrote, "is Antifaust, Unanglosaxon . . . Unsquare, Ungothic." The last thing he wanted to be was "literary," he added. Putting all hope of publishing and recognition behind him, he vowed to live like a holy man and disappear into monastic solitude.

He did nothing of the sort. One of the most exciting, momentous years for Kerouac — and the Beat Generation — lay ahead: 1955 would be symbolized by the dark, brooding, sensuous Mexican landscape, the setting of both *Mexico City Blues* and *Tristessa*, and by the sparkling air of northern California, where Kerouac would ring in the San Francisco Poetry Renaissance. His novel of Mexico, *Tristessa*, is a hymn to his twenty-eight year-old Indian peasant lover, Esperanza Villanueva, whom he met shortly after arriving in Mexico City. Settling again in Orizaba Street, he crashed the first few nights with his pusher friend, Bill Garver, and later rented his old "mud block" hut atop the building. Esperanza was the widow of Burroughs's morphine dealer, Dave; a junkie, pusher, and prostitute, she was known on the streets as "Saragossa." Kerouac fell in love with her one afternoon while buying "Miss Green" from her, he related in an August 7, 1955, letter to Ginsberg. Miss Green was a euphemism for marijuana, indicating that he began as one of Esperanza's dope customers before becoming her lover.

Recent evidence uncovered at the Kerouac archive in Lowell in 1995–1997 shows that Kerouac's relationship with Esperanza was one of the most passionate and intense of his life. According to Kerouac's sex list, he and Esperanza had sex fifty-six times. Since they were together only forty-two days, obviously their relationship was overwhelmingly sensual. The fact that she was addicted, starving, and dying said volumes about what turned Kerouac on: He liked dark ghetto denizens, vulnerable, helpless, and weak. In a way it was pathetic, but there was also something triumphant in the new, more accurate picture of Kerouac. He was capable, after all, of giving and receiving more joy than indicated in the memoirs of some of his girlfriends.

New archival evidence also sheds a different light on Kerouac's experience as a Buddhist, which was not as celibate as heretofore thought, and on his writings during this period. Other biographies give a perhaps incomplete impression of his state of mind in the summer of 1955, as he wrote an important work, *Mexico City Blues*, as well as *Tristessa*, a brief but glowing novel quite unlike anything else in his *oeuvre*. Clark writes that Kerouac was "desperate," McNally maintains he was "lost in a never-never land," Gifford and Lee portray him as abstinent and "innocent," Charters claims that he was incapable of a close relationship with Esperanza because she was not white, and Nicosia even goes so far as to deny the existence of their romance. In none of these accounts do we get a true sense of what Kerouac's six weeks in Mexico City were really like, why it was a time of such high productivity, and why his fiction and poetry that summer were of such exceptional quality.

In fact, he was not nearly as unhappy as other biographers believe, as indicated by the fact that he and Esperanza had sex, by his own count, an average of 1.3 times a day, a veritable festival of the senses. When I researched this book at the archive, Kerouac's sex list seemed absurd and bizarre to me at first, a bit of sexual braggadocio, like notches on a belt. But when John Sampas told me that Kerouac had saved many of the letters I had written him and produced them from the archive, I realized that the sex list sprang from the same meticulous archival passion, as well as from the compulsive reportorial regimen that makes Kerouac's work such a solid document of mid-twentieth-century experience.

There is little consensus regarding Esperanza's physical appearance. Kerouac described her elegant high cheekbones, her delicate, fine-boned body, the "peachy coffee" color of her complexion, and her deep-set Garbo eyelids. He doted on "the lean hocks of her rear." He loved the gutsy way she stood her ground, "legs spread . . . like a junkey [sic] on a corner in Harlem." But when Ginsberg met her the following year, he found her to be "thin and weak from morphine addiction," according to Miles. Kerouac's view of her seemed "hopelessly sentimental" to Ginsberg. Corso, who also met her, later said, "She was out of it." They missed the point that it was her drugged condition — she was going through ten grams of morphine a month — that in large part made her such a uniquely effective lover for Kerouac. Morphine sex is a driven wallow in totally self-absorbed sensuality, involving few expectations of definitive results and consequently no performance anxiety. In view of Kerouac's sexual hang-ups and his fear of wholesome white women like Carolyn, Esperanza was a perfect partner. She contributed substantially to the emotional equanimity and sense of well-being that enabled him to turn out some of his best work in the six weeks they were together.

Ironically, Kerouac's racism also played into the success of their mating. Like many racists, he was prejudiced everywhere except in bed, where his partner's perceived subhuman status neutralized his feelings of inadequacy and enhanced his virility. Despite *Esquire*'s claim at the time that "Latins are lousy lovers," Kerouac was not the only fifties macho role model to go for Hispanics. Both Brando and John Wayne preferred dark-skinned women. Kerouac first realized he loved Esperanza when it dawned on him that she was like the brave women played by Katy Jurado and Jean Peters in Brando's movie of the Mexican revolution, *Viva Zapata!* Esperanza always seemed to know exactly what to do and say to make Jack feel strong and virile. She had also delighted her late husband, Dave, whom Burroughs gave the fictional name "Old Ike," and occasionally she still talked about how much she adored Dave. Much older than Esperanza, he had died at fifty-five of high blood pressure the previous November. Esperanza had been involved with him since the age of sixteen, when he'd taken her off the street and used his profits from rich junkie clients to keep her in style. Jack still thought of Dave as his "old buddy" from his previous stay at Orizaba Street when he'd taken notes for *Dave*, his projected story of a drug dealer.

Esperanza cleverly found the way to Jack's heart by telling him that he'd one day be rich from his writings. He began to sense that he was on the verge of a breakthrough and that fame as well as money were within his grasp. Why then, Esperanza asked, was he "*muy dolorosa* [full of pain]?" He replied that he was "sad because all *la vida es dolorosa*." She agreed but reminded him that "life is love too." Assuming her junkie stance, she threw a bump and grind in the direction of the bed and observed, "A million pesos does not move — but when you got the friend, the friend give it to you in the bed." He knew that Esperanza could feel his pain, and it made him love her more.[23] The impression he gave in *Tristessa* and to friends that this was a period of rigorous celibacy was due to his ardent conversion to Buddhism and his determination to present himself as a pure "dharma bum." The humiliation of being a failed novelist had become so unbearable that he could no longer face his friends as a writer. He assumed the mantle of a holy man, a Buddhist free of all desire, including the desire to be published.

Surprisingly, he succeeded in this role perhaps as profoundly as he did as an artist. A great teacher is known by his pupils, and Kerouac's accomplishment as Ginsberg's guru was impressive; Ginsberg spread "the True Meaning, or Dharma" throughout the western world in the sixties. Some of Kerouac's best 1955 letters were Buddhist tracts addressed to Ginsberg, who later said, "The first Buddhism I learned was from Jack, and maybe some of the deepest." Ginsberg proved to be such a good pupil that Kerouac eventually relinquished his "Einstein" role, assuring Ginsberg that they were "fellow disciples" of the Buddha.

Many have viewed the mid-fifties as barren wilderness years for Kerouac; his major novels were behind him, though still unpublished, and he was exiled from trade publishing and ignored by critics. But these were nonetheless important and fruitful years, especially in terms of the influence he would later have on millions. At roughly the same age as Siddhartha and Christ, he began in this period what can only be called his ministry.

In popularizing Buddhism and redefining morality for a generation, Kerouac's spiritual impact on America was one of the strongest since that of Cotton Mather, the seventeenth-century Puritan clergyman whose hysterical endorsement of the Salem witchcraft persecution contributed to the intolerance and fanaticism of American religion well into the modern era. As an antidote to Mather's emphasis on guilt and sin, Kerouac in some small but significant degree may have altered the course of American destiny. The seepage of Eastern thought into Western philosophy and religion via Kerouac and his disciples helped liberate a generation from centuries of enslavement to the Puritan work ethic and, like a lifting of Maule's curse, freed them from shame and repression. When Kerouac first told the story of Buddha in the mid-fifties, few even knew who Buddha was, but they quickly learned as Kerouac's unpublished religious treatises and letters circulated among the subterraneans of the fifties. In his biography of the Buddha, Kerouac wrote, "Having eaten the humbling, the dreary meal, downcast yet joyful, he who had worn garments of silk and whose attendants had held a white umbrella over him, walked on in rags in the burning sunshine of the jungle solitude." In 1955, Kerouac, a homeless wanderer, would shortly popularize Beat Generation concepts in San Francisco and begin to disseminate a message of mystical-religious awareness.[24]

The first one hundred and fifty poems or "choruses" of *Mexico City Blues* were completed just two weeks after Jack arrived at Orizaba Street. He assured Sterling that the book would give modern poetry what *On the Road* and *Cody* had given modern prose: a return to unpremeditated, authentic language. In two more weeks, he completed the remaining ninety-four choruses and told Sterling that his "Jazz Session" was bound to shake up the poetry establishment. Whatever its effect on literature, the book succeeded to an astonishing degree in approximating the "talking horns" of the jazz musicians Kerouac been listening to and studying for years.

Much of *Mexico City Blues* was written in Bill Garver's room. Garver came from Pittsburgh, where his father had run a large plumbing factory and had bequeathed him a yearly income. Kerouac felt safe and comfortable with Garver because, as he told Ginsberg, Garver was straight and therefore put him under no pressure for sexual favors, as so many of Kerouac's benefactors had done and would continue to do. At the end of a day's writing, he would show his poems to Garver, who'd always say, "Oh boy, that's good." The entirety of *Mexico City Blues* was handwritten.

Aware that he could never support himself by writing poetry, Kerouac tried to convince Cowley to advance money for a commercial historical novel on the Zapotec Indians. He envisaged it as another *Forever Amber*, promising Cowley to lard the narrative with passionate Latino sex revels. Unlikely as it sounded, the proposed novel was essentially no different from subsequent Mailer potboilers such as *Ancient Evenings*, but Kerouac found no takers at Viking. Cowley was appalled by the prospect of handling a novel with sex orgies and advised Jack to find some other way to make money.[25]

Garver kept Kerouac in drugs that summer, and Kerouac reciprocated by emptying Garver's urine bucket for him and going on occasional dope runs. Kerouac's affair with Esperanza ended when he deferred to Garver's love for her, merging into Esperanza and Garver's affair as he had with Neal and Carolyn. "I'm always the King sucker who was made out to be the positional son in woman and man relationships," he wrote at the conclusion of *Tristessa*. There wasn't much left of Esperanza to love; by the end of the summer, one of her legs was paralyzed for a month, and her arms had developed cysts from goofballs and morphine. Kerouac found it easy to give her up, realizing "what would I do with her once I'd won her?" But while the affair had lasted, she'd been a superb Mimi to his Rodolfo, two bohemian lovers in a Mexican garret drinking wine and shooting up by candlelight as he crafted immortal poems. When Ginsberg read *Mexico City Blues* he recognized it as a poetic breakthrough and over the next few years would try without success to get it published. Even fellow poets who ran small presses turned it down, including Lawrence Ferlinghetti and LeRoi Jones. The seemingly effortless grace of Kerouac's rhythmic line and his speed of composition stirred resentment in fellow poets, most of whom refused to dignify Kerouac's verse by calling it poetry.

In *Mexico City Blues* Kerouac wrote the Beat Generation's *Four Quartets*, a hip meditation on life, death, and the cosmos. Though new preoccupations like Buddhism, goofballs, and morphine crop up in the poem, none of them is permitted to overwhelm a text that is vintage Kerouac, replete with Gerard riding through in his snow-white wagon, Mémêre as the earth mother Jack keeps falling in love with, and Leo dying for the umpteenth time. Charlie Parker, Glenn Miller, Gore Vidal, Westbrook Pegler, FDR, Garver, Ginsberg, Corso, and Burroughs the cast of the poet's life—stroll in and out of the choruses, setting the distinctive style of the New American Poetry also found in the gossipy fifties poems of Frank O'Hara. Felicitous images abound, and the poet's awe, terror, and wonder at the mystery of existence are definitively captured in the mega-image of a cosmic meat grinder spewing life into the void in a never-ending stream of creation that includes everything from Michelangelo to maggots. Baffled by the squirming spectacle of seemingly senseless reproduction, the poet sighs that he'd prefer to remain comfortable and secure in God's bosom, eternally unreincarnated. Buddhism offers the comforting thought that, however frantic the rat race of life, everyone wins in the end since materiality is illusory. Although there is no way to escape the suffering inherent in human life, the poem resonates like Beethoven's "Ode to Joy" with its affirmation that mankind ultimately luxuriates in the milk and honey of God's grace. Charlie Parker appears as Buddha, transporting everyone to the doors of infinity. Parker's message is simply that the universe is unfolding in everyone's best interest. In the coda, Kerouac asks Parker to pray for him.[26]

There was something different and nearly perfect about Kerouac's work that summer. The frenzied experiences of *On the Road* and *The Subterraneans* were far behind him. The big party with Neal was over, and the time had come for a summing up. Death seems to hover over *Mexico City Blues* just as it hovered over Jack and Esperanza as they injected potentially lethal drugs. Both of them fell ill, and Kerouac wrote Ginsberg in August that his leg pained him constantly; it was one of the most dangerous, thrilling, and productive times of Kerouac's life.

Ginsberg was also writing a major poem that summer, still called "Howl for Carl Solomon," and he sent it to Jack in Mexico City. Though Kerouac was sick from drug abuse, preoccupied with two important works of his own, and so broke that he was reduced to asking friends to take up a collection to get him out of Mexico, he was kinder to "Howl" than Ginsberg had been to *On the Road*, praising it as a mighty poem in his August 19 letter to Ginsberg. Eschewing the analytical nitpicking to which Ginsberg had subjected *On the Road*, Kerouac cautioned Ginsberg not to change a word of "Howl." A work of art, he said, should never be compromised by second thoughts, and a writer must always resist the temptation to indulge in Monday-morning quarterbacking. The first draft is the only valid draft; revisions, rewritings, and editor's intrusions produce nothing but weary rehashes. In Kerouac's response to "Howl," he thoughtfully cited specific examples of his favorite lines, including the one about a compulsive writer like Kerouac who went around flashing both his penis and his prose. On the dedication page of the published book, Ginsberg acknowledged that part of the text as well as the title came from Kerouac, the "new Buddha of American prose." (Ginsberg corrected himself in 1980, stating that he'd thought of the title himself.) Kerouac's only lapse of judgment was to say in his letter that "Howl" included too many homosexual references. One only need imagine the poem without Ginsberg's cauterizing honesty to see how wrong Kerouac was. Nonetheless, Ginsberg replied that everything good in "Howl" was but recycled Kerouac, graciously adding that it would take him many years to approximate Kerouac's mastery of the spontaneous form.[27]

Deciding to resume his trip to California, Kerouac boarded a bus in Mexico City on September 9 and took it as far as El Paso. From there he started hitchhiking, but drivers roared past him and sped on toward Las Cruces and Deming, New Mexico, leaving him in a cloud of dust. Rides eventually materialized, and he made it across the deserts and mountains to the west. In L.A. he caught the Zipper to Santa Barbara, and then started looking for rides again on U.S. 101. A blond bombshell in a new persimmon-colored, simonized 1955 Mercury Montclair stopped and gave him a lift all the way to San Francisco, a ride he subsequently described in "Good Blonde" as his ultimate hitchhiking experience. The blonde was wearing a white strapless bathing suit and a gold ankle bracelet, and was driving barefoot. As he admired her creamy armpits, she complained that she'd driven from Fort Worth, Texas, without a night's sleep. Jack promptly dug through the dirty underwear and cheap Mexican trinkets in his backpack and produced an ample supply of Benzedrine. "Crazy!" she said, and as the speed took effect, they both started gabbing, sweating, and laughing, jazz blaring from the dashboard radio. Floorboarding the Mercury, she balled into San Luis Obispo at 110 miles per hour and then, just north of town, shot straight up an almost vertical mountain until they were brushing the clouds. All the while, her mad rap continued. Everyone in Texas was getting stoned, she said, including her small brothers and sisters, and even tobacco-chewing farmers were beginning to cultivate "loco weed" in their yards. Later, describing the "good blonde" ride to Holmes, Jack wrote that the peace and happiness the Beats had forecast in 1948 was coming true; President Eisenhower was dismantling the military-industrial complex, and war would soon be a thing of the past. In San Francisco, the blonde let Kerouac off at the South San Francisco rail yards, and they talked about meeting again some day but probably never did. After making his way to the downtown area, Jack bought a bottle of wine and checked into a skid row hotel for the night.[28]

The next day he found Ginsberg washing dishes in Berkeley and working on his M.A. in English literature at the University of California. Allen lived in a thirty-five-dollar-a-month, ramshackle, rose-covered cottage at 1624 Milvia Street, and he had surrounded himself with some of the most exciting poets on the San Francisco scene. Though Ginsberg had been in the city since 1954, and veteran poet Kenneth Rexroth had been there even longer, the critical mass needed to ignite the San Francisco Poetry Renaissance did not occur until Kerouac's appearance in 1955. His fame preceded him in the Bay Area where he was already regarded as an important poet by many of Allen's friends, including Gary Snyder and Philip Whalen. They'd devoured Allen's copy of *Mexico City Blues* and reacted to it with the same shock of recognition that an earlier generation had felt on discovering Pound and Eliot. Kerouac made them realize that they could be themselves, that it was no longer necessary to echo the then-official poetic sound of Eliot or Frost.

In late September, Kerouac and Cowley discussed possible libel problems, one of the last obstacles to the publication of *On the Road*. Kerouac told the editor not to worry about Justin Brierly, since mutual friends had already assured him that Justin would be delighted to appear in *On the Road* as "Denver D. Doll." He changed Bea Franco's hometown from Selma to Sabinal, California, and told Cowley that Carolyn Cassady wouldn't sue, since he was now her sometime lover. Most of the place names in the book underwent radical alteration, such as Rocky Mount, which became Testament, Virginia. As for editorial changes, Kerouac offered full cooperation; hungry authors without publishing contracts usually do. He told Cowley to make all the changes he wanted. The editor even secured Kerouac's permission to implement a controversial revision first suggested in 1953 — and angrily rejected by the author at that time — to combine the first and second trips in *On the Road*. Five years without a book contract had reduced Kerouac to a meek supplicant. But *On the Road* hit a legal snag at Viking, and the manuscript remained with the company's attorney until November. On October 12, Cowley warned that altering the characters' names and appearances was just the tip of the legal iceberg. Anyone could sue him who felt they'd been held up to ridicule or shame. The novel posed horrendous legal issues because it was not a work of fiction, in Cowley's estimation, but a documentary journal.

On November 8, Cowley dropped another bombshell. Before *On the Road* could be accepted for publication, Viking's attorney required signed releases from both Neal and Allen. At this crucial point, Neal and Allen could have held Kerouac up for a cut of the book, but they proved to be true friends. Both signed releases on November 14 during a jam session. But the threat of litigation continued to haunt Jack, who suddenly wanted to get releases from every Beat character he'd written about. They were scattered all over the world, many of them without addresses. He tried to drown his fears in liquor, and Gary Snyder pointed out that he was drinking excessively. He snapped at Gary like a willful child, telling him he'd do anything he wanted to do.

Legal complications held up the publication of On the Road for another eighteen months. On December 26, 1956, Kerouac wrote Jennison that he was still fussing with the manuscript, scrupulously excising any references that could even remotely be construed by living prototypes as unflattering. But in the fall of 1955, with publication at last virtually assured, Kerouac settled down in Ginsberg's cottage, where he spent three of the best months of his life. High on inexpensive California wines from the nearby Napa Valley, he held court in Berkeley, met the bright young writers in Ginsberg's set, and dreamed of a film version of On the Road, which, he informed Sterling, should star Brando in the leading role as Dean Moriarty, with Montgomery Clift playing Sal Paradise. He expected the sale of film rights to fetch $150,000. He was not as optimistic about Sterling's ability to sell his latest manuscripts, Tristessa and Mexico City Blues, and he was right: they were destined for the bottom drawer, at least for the present.

One day, Neal came by Allen's cottage to see Jack, accompanied by his inamorata, Natalie Jackson, whom Jack would describe in The Dharma Bums as "Rosie Buchanan," a "real gone chick," lanky and attractive, known to "everybody of any consequence" in North Beach as a would-be author and artist's model who was beside herself with joy to be Neal's current girlfriend. Natalie made a tape-recording of Jack's "Jazz of the Beat Generation," and Jack wrote Sterling that they were discussing a possible record album; it was the first sign of what would later become a substantial career for Kerouac as a recording artist. John Montgomery, who appeared as "Henry Morley" in The Dharma Bums, recalled Natalie as an unkempt but kind woman who thoughtfully offered to share her marijuana joints. When Kerouac, Cassady, and Ginsberg got together to read their works and talk all night, Peter Orlovsky, Ginsberg's new boyfriend, was impressed with the verbal fireworks. Kerouac was jealous and resentful that Ginsberg had a lover who looked straight and was younger, better built, and more "manly" than either Kerouac or Cassady. In anger, Jack stuck his fist through the bathroom door and accused Ginsberg of being a lecher. Orlovsky immediately liked Jack, finding him a "rugged-looking . . . athlete."[29]

In late September 1955, Ginsberg introduced Kerouac to the reigning doyen of the local literary scene, the fifty-year-old Rexroth, who later appeared as "Rheinhold Cacoethes" in The Dharma Bums. Kerouac's other new friends, Snyder and Whalen, both shared Kerouac's interest in Buddhism, and both had read "Jazz of the Beat Generation" in New World

Writing. Then a twenty-five-year-old graduate student of Chinese and Japanese at Berkeley, the green-eyed, sun-tanned Snyder had published poems in the *Berkeley Bussei*, issued annually by the Berkeley Young Buddhist Association. Both Snyder and Whalen had worked as fire lookouts in the Cascades, and Jack immediately admired these atypically outdoorsy poets, wondering if he could be a forest ranger too. Eight years Kerouac's junior, Snyder looked to Kerouac for guidance as a poet, while Kerouac looked to Snyder for wisdom. "As a poet I hold the most archaic values," Snyder said, "the fertility of the soil, the magic of animals, the power-vision of solitude, initiation and rebirth, love and ecstasy, the common work of the tribe." The phrase "dharma [truth] bum" was given to Kerouac by Snyder, whom Kerouac called "the number one Dharma Bum of them all." This period represents the high point of Kerouac's ministry: he viewed himself as a "religious wanderer" trudging "the immense triangular arc of New York to Mexico City to San Francisco" for the purpose of enlightening people and thereby gaining a foothold in heaven. As predicted in *The Town and the City*, he consciously assumed the role of cultural avatar at this time, and his influence began to be felt even though his fame as the author of *On the Road* was still two years in the future. Gary Snyder was a significant conduit of that influence.

In *The Dharma Bums*, Snyder appears as "Japhy Ryder . . . five foot seven, but strong and wiry and fast and muscular." A Buddhist orgy seems a contradiction in terms, but that was what Snyder, Kerouac, Ginsberg, and a beautiful girl named "Princess" had, though Snyder called it "yabyum." Kerouac represented Snyder, as Japhy, arriving in the Berkeley cottage with Princess and immediately taking off his clothes. Ginsberg and Princess did likewise, and then they all made love as Kerouac looked on timorously. Ginsberg's biographer, Miles, later explained, "It was an Oriental form of sex based on the mystical formula: 'Om, the thunderbolt in the void.' " In practice, the men provided the thunderbolt, and Princess supplied the void. At last, Jack asked Snyder if it would be all right for him to kiss Princess's arm. Snyder told him to go for it, and Kerouac made love to Princess as they luxuriated in warm bathwater. The yabyum experience sealed a uniquely deep and spiritual bonding between Kerouac and Snyder.

Years later, Snyder called Kerouac an "American mythographer" and said his novels would always stand as the classic expression of the "myth of the twentieth century. . . . Jack saw me . . . as [an] archetypal . . . American of the West . . . anarchist, libertarian . . . hobo, railroad bum, working man." In short, Snyder was a Neal Cassady with brains and talent. For Kerouac, Snyder would have been the perfect friend except for one drawback: try as he might, he could never drag Snyder down to the level of his own low-bottom alcoholism.

In a letter to Whalen, Kerouac unreservedly stated that Whalen and Snyder were the most nearly perfect human beings he'd ever encountered. Whalen was a big, smiling, thirty-two-year-old Oregonian who eventually moved to Japan and lived there until 1971. Returning to the U.S., Whalen was ordained as a Buddhist monk in 1972, becoming head monk at the Zen Mountain Center in Tassajara Springs, California, in 1975, and subsequently abbot of the Hartford Street Zen Center in San Francisco. In *The Dharma Bums*, Kerouac portrayed Whalen as Warren Coughlin, "a hundred and eighty pounds of poet meat." Kerouac prompted Whalen to write "Big Baby Buddha Golden 65 Feet High," according to Ginsberg, who added that Snyder, Michael McClure, and the other young San Francisco poets were "curious . . . sometimes inspired" by Jack. What Kerouac had to offer these young men, most of whom had been trained in formal poetry at institutions like Berkeley or Reed College, was, according to Snyder, the bravery to make their poems "be right there with the moment totally." Snyder once referred to Kerouac as a bodhisattva. As Kerouac later told me, "A bodhisattva is like an angel, a wise angel. Snyder believed my sincerity could light up the dark corners of the world." Philip Whalen ascribed his career as a poet to the combined influence of Kerouac and Ginsberg. Seeing them in operation in San Francisco in October 1955 made Whalen feel that being a writer was a great calling. They were the first truly literary people Whalen had ever met, "living . . . writing . . . picking it up out of the air, out of books, out of . . . people," Whalen explained.[30]

The epochal poetry reading that launched the Beat Generation on the West Coast occurred on October 7, 1955, at the Six Gallery, a cooperative art gallery located in a converted auto-repair garage at Union and Fillmore. A minuscule but potent forerunner of 1969's Woodstock, the Six Gallery reading was a cultural watershed, the first significant gathering of like-minded dropouts from American materialism. Originally, it was to have been organized by Michael McClure, but Joanna McClure was expecting a baby, and as Michael explained to Ginsberg at a party for W. H. Auden, he was too busy to round up six good poets in the Bay Area. The shrewd Ginsberg immediately saw a chance to establish his reputation in San Francisco and volunteered to chair the reading. As a guest in Ginsberg's Milvia Street cottage, Kerouac gleefully observed the Byzantine workings of Bay Area literary politics as Ginsberg and Snyder shaped the historic event. The six poets selected to read were Snyder, Whalen, Rexroth, McClure, Ginsberg, and Philip Lamantia. As Robert Duncan later observed, they were all street poets, and they were about to take San Francisco by storm. "Save the invitation," Gary said, according to his friend Will Petersen, "some day it will be worth something."

Describing the fervency of the San Francisco poets in 1955, McClure said the competitiveness of the group forced "whole new areas into being." Looking back on the event forty years later, critic Rebecca Solnit wrote in the catalog of the Whitney Museum's 1995 Beat retrospective show that "the central moment in . . . Beat culture . . . the moment Jack Kerouac mythologized in *The Dharma Bums*," was Ginsberg's premier reading of "Howl" at the Six Gallery. Kerouac described the occasion as "a historic night." Ginsberg urged Kerouac to participate as one of the readers, but Kerouac refused, explaining in a September 20, 1955, letter to Cowley that he was too shy to go on stage. He suspected that poetry readings were silly, and told Cowley that it was beneath a poet's dignity to masquerade as a clown.

On October 7, Lawrence Ferlinghetti, driving an old Austin, carried Kerouac, Ginsberg, and Corso to the Six Gallery. A thirty-six-year-old former New Yorker, Ferlinghetti had earned his doctoral degree at the Sorbonne before settling in San Francisco and starting the magazine *City Lights*, named after the Charlie Chaplin movie. The magazine operated out of the second floor of a building at Broadway and Columbus in North Beach. Ferlinghetti later opened the City Lights Bookstore on the floor below and kept it open until midnight and 2 A.M. on weekends. He also established a book publishing company called City Lights, which published Ferlinghetti's *Pictures of the Gone World* in 1955 in the Pocket Poet Series. "The 'Howl' reading . . . immediately dissolved the rust of a couple of decades of American poetry [which was] really in the doldrums at the time," Ferlinghetti recalled. "It was a whole new ball game."

Before the reading, Neal took the poets to Vesuvio's, a bar on the corner of Columbus and what is today Jack Kerouac Alley. As the poets ordered drinks, Jack sized them up and decided that Snyder, who resembled a lumberjack in his Italian mountain-climbing boots, was the only he-man among them. In *The Dharma Bums*, Ginsberg was "Alvah Goldbook," a "hornrimmed intellectual hepcat with black hair"; McClure was "Ike O'Shay," "delicate" and "handsome"; and Lamantia was "Francis DaPavia," an ethereal, aristocratic "Renaissance Italian." Leaving the bar, they went on to the gallery, where approximately one hundred and fifty people had gathered, including Ferlinghetti's wife, Kirby; Robert Duncan, who'd previously read at the Six; writer Jack Goodwin; Berkeley librarian John Montgomery; Orlovsky; Neal, in his brakeman's uniform, complete with watch and vest; Natalie; and what appeared to be the entire Bay Area bohemian poetry intelligentsia. They were packed into the the large twenty-five-by-twenty-five-foot room, which had a dirt floor, white walls, and a restroom with a door that wouldn't lock. McClure later described the audience as made up of "poets . . . Anarchists . . . Stalinists . . . professors . . . painters . . . bohemians . . . visionaries . . . idealists and grinning cynics." In front was a small, hastily improvised dais with six thronelike chairs in a semicircle, and behind the dais was an exhibition of sculptures by Fred Martin: muslin-wrapped orange crates that had been dredged through plaster of paris and had come out looking like battered surrealistic living-room chairs and sofas. "I was the one who got things jumping," Kerouac wrote in *The Dharma Bums*, and he admitted in a letter to Holmes that he was quite drunk. He succeeded in relaxing the somewhat stiff, self-conscious audience by plowing through the crowd and brashly demanding dimes and quarters for wine, but McClure later recalled that other people were taking up collections and going out for wine as well.

The program began with some introductory remarks by Rexroth, and then each poet rose to do his reading, coming to the front of the dais and nodding or waving to friends in the audience. Lamantia went first, reciting posthumous poems by his late friend John Hoffman, whom Ginsberg and Carl Solomon had known, and who'd expired of a peyote overdose in Mexico City. McClure later described Hoffman's lovely verses "that left orange stripes and colored visions in the air." Kerouac, at his most sexist, nearly burst out laughing when he saw Lamantia's long white fingers shuffling the pink onion-skin pages and heard his dainty British inflections. Neal stood in the crowd behind Natalie, with his arms encircling her. Jack went up to them and gave Natalie a drink from his bottle. She flashed a grateful smile, and he moved on, wandering among the clusters of people, facing the audience rather than the dais, and offering everyone a drink. Finally, he went to the stage and sat down at stage right, uttering audible exclamations of wonder and delight. Lamantia and McClure appreciated Jack's infectious energy, but Rexroth resented him. According to Ferlinghetti, Kerouac eventually lay on the floor near the stage, and everyone assumed he'd passed out, but Ferlinghetti realized he was simply relaxing and registering everything—the Boswell of the Beats. Rexroth got up to introduce McClure, speaking in a facetious, faintly amusing voice. McClure then read "Point Lobos: Animism," a lyric poem inspired by a ruggedly beautiful point of land between Carmel-by-the-Sea and Big Sur in north central California. McClure wanted to express how "everything (breath . . . ripple in the tidepool, cloud, and stone) was alive and spirited . . . a frightening and joyous awareness of my undersoul." Next, McClure read "For the Death of 100 Whales," a poem that pioneered a new theme in American life in 1955—the diversity and freedom of the environment—and prefigured the ecology movement. Whalen came on next, reading "Plus Ça Change," a metaphoric poem that charmed the audience with what McClure called its "naked joy of portraying metamorphosis and of exemplifying and aiding change in the universe."

During the 10:30 P.M. intermission, Kerouac and a drinking buddy named Bob Donlin took up another collection for booze, then hit the streets in a wobbly, raunchy condition, Kerouac later wrote Holmes. A blue-eyed, black-haired Boston Irishman who later appeared in *Desolation Angels* as Rob Donnelly, Donlin told Kerouac, when he realized they were from the same part of New England, that there were more Bostonians at the gallery than there were in Massachusetts. Jack later indicated to Holmes that he and Donlin got into trouble when they stumbled down to the waterfront looking for liquor. As they staggered back with the wine bottles, they tripped and fell in the street and started vomiting. By the time they reappeared at the Six Gallery, Jack had "scabs" on his face, he later told Holmes.

Mingling in the crowd, Neal approached Ginsberg's lover, Orlovsky, and said, "Come over here, Peter, come stand next to me," Orlovsky recalled. When he asked Neal why, Neal said, "I don't know anybody here." Neal's biographer, Plummer, later wrote that Neal "felt somewhat peripheral to the event." As the Beat Generation's muse since 1946, Neal logically should have

been on the stage reading the "Joan Anderson Letter." According to Steve
Turner, author of *Angelheaded Hipster*, Neal lacked "the confidence to appear in public."

Rexroth introduced Ginsberg, who was tipsy but managed to read in a
"small and intensely lucid" voice, McClure recalled. In the poem's opening
verses Ginsberg described how most of his friends had been ruined by heroin,
marijuana, turpentine, alcohol, peyote, wine, Benzedrine, and beer, and he
used four-letter words that had rarely, if ever, been heard in public. As Mc-
Clure later revealed in a *Lowell Sun* interview, the audience listened in
shocked silence except for Kerouac, who bravely started shouting "GO" in
cadence with Ginsberg's recitation. In Kerouac's and Cassady's use of the
word *go*, the embryonic counterculture heard its rallying cry for the first time.
Two years later, Mailer wrote in *The White Negro* that *go* projected a "sense
that after . . . years of monotony, boredom, and depression . . . one has
amassed enough energy to meet an exciting opportunity . . . one is ready to
go, ready to gamble."

As Kerouac rooted for Ginsberg that night, Ginsberg's voice began to
soar, and the audience joined Kerouac in his contrapuntal interjections. By
then, Kerouac was standing in front of the crowd, passing his bottle. Suddenly
he saw an old girlfriend, Jinny Baker, an attractive twenty-three-year-old Japanese woman. As they chatted, she seemed to be apologizing for a fight they'd
had in the past, babbling that she'd been responsible and was now sorry, and
adding that she'd broken her back. Jack proclaimed his love for her, but
privately told Snyder that she was insane. One of the members of the audience, Jack Goodwin, later recalled that "Carrowac" drank Burgundy and scat-
sang lines from "Howl" whenever Ginsberg paused for breath. Kerouac's
unique contribution, Goodwin added, was that he turned an uptight poetry
reading into an audience-participation event not unlike a holy-roller revival-
tent meeting, with everyone chanting in rhythm. Ruth Witt-Diamant, who'd
sponsored readings at the Six and the Poetry Center, motioned frantically for
Ginsberg to tone down his sexually explicit language, fearing scandal and
arrest, but she finally gave up. Neal beamed with pride as he heard Allen
celebrate him as Colorado's gift to beauty and virility. As soon as Allen finished, Neal rushed to the stage and shook his hand, and Jack assured Allen
that he was going to be famous. Everyone else was "standing in wonder,"
McClure recalled, "knowing . . . that a barrier had been broken . . . a human
voice and body had been hurled against the harsh wall of America and its
supporting armies . . . academies and institutions."

"Howl" was a tough act to follow, but according to Snyder's friend Will Petersen, Snyder projected heroic confidence "in an impoverished Taoist unpublished poet sort of way." Ginsberg was still wearing standard establishment
garb—a charcoal gray suit, white shirt, and tie—but Snyder wore Levis. He
quickly took command of the audience, reading his erudite and effervescent
nature poem, "A Berry Feast." With its crisp evocation of sparkling creeks and

stealthy trout, the poem sounded a strong new voice in American letters and also helped awaken the world's ecological consciousness. In *The Dharma Bums* Kerouac would be one of the first to salute Snyder for his "anarchistic" criticism of a society that destroys its forests to create ugly and dehumanizing suburban housing developments. McClure later observed that Snyder's poem created a space in which people could see the damage that had been done to nature and humankind. Snyder was Kerouac's personal favorite that night, for Snyder had something hopeful to offer, whereas Ginsberg struck him, in retrospect, as overwrought and bitter, and Whalen seemed obscure.

The gallery emptied slowly, as if no one wanted to leave. Ten minutes later, as John Montgomery stood outside, he overheard a girl say that her shivers and goosebumps were at last subsiding. "Everybody was milling around wondering what had happened and what would come next in American poetry," Kerouac recalled in *The Dharma Bums*. The poets all went together to Sam Wo, Snyder's favorite Chinese restaurant, for a post-performance celebration, then on to a popular Beat hangout on Grant Avenue, the Place, and finally, according to Barry Miles, to an orgy.

Not until 1995, with the publication of Kerouac's letters, was it known that the evening had a dreadful ending for Jack. He described it to Holmes as the most depressing night of his life, adding that not even Dylan Thomas or Faulkner could have drunk himself into such a colossal stupor. At times Kerouac was so craven in his alcoholism that he'd shamelessly guzzle the flat, tepid dregs from abandoned glasses and bottles.[31]

The day following the reading, Ferlinghetti offered Ginsberg a publishing contract for *Howl and Other Poems*, and Van Doren and William Carlos Williams were the first to send congratulatory letters. A local though not yet a national celebrity, Ginsberg was happy to share the limelight with Kerouac, and took him along when he was invited to McClure's home. They brought a small stash of marijuana in a matchbox, and everyone got off. McClure was impressed with Jack's spirituality and intense self-consciousness. As they discussed *Mexico City Blues* and McClure's poetry collection, *Dark Brown*, they drank muscatel, and McClure recalled that Jack made "half drunk, beautiful slurry sounds"; he would recite a poem and then offer a preposterous, fantastical commentary. Kerouac and McClure later became close, and McClure observed that there were two Kerouacs: the brazen, inebriated extrovert, and the quiet, meditative visionary author. In neither guise did Kerouac strike McClure as a forceful male and certainly not as a natural-born leader, but McClure always sensed his potential power as an agent of social and cultural change. "The long-term bio-politics . . . our effect on everything . . . in that sense Jack is, was, and will be a leader." McClure told Ginsberg that "Howl" reminded him of *Queen Mab*, Shelley's first lengthy poem, and later wrote that "Howl" turned Allen from a repressed, studious outsider into an "epic vocal bard."

In the following days, the Berkeley Buddhist Church study group asked

Kerouac to give a reading of *Mexico City Blues*, still unpublished but rapidly becoming an underground classic. Kerouac's performance did not rival the sensation of Ginsberg's at the Six, but the Buddhists admired his poems enough to print a few choruses in *The Bussei*.[32]

Neal and Carolyn invited Jack to their new home at 18231 Bancroft Avenue in Los Gatos, fifty miles south of San Francisco, and they sampled some of the grass Jack had brought from Mexico. The scene at the Cassadys was more bizarre than ever. Though Neal was now spending most of his time in San Francisco with Natalie, he didn't want to lose Carolyn. He assigned a handsome stranger to keep Carolyn company, and she later referred to the man as "Pat," describing him in her memoir as "a tall, muscular Adonis, bronzed and blond." Neal soon regretted his decision, scorning Pat as egotistical and ridiculous, but Neal's children loved Pat and began to refer to him as "Daddy."

One evening, Kerouac attended an unorthodox, liberal Catholic church service with Neal and Carolyn, an experience that later became the basis for Kerouac's film, *Pull My Daisy*. Carolyn invited the priest, whom she described as "a slight, handsome young Swiss," to Los Gatos to meet Kerouac, Ginsberg, Neal, and Pat. At one point, after drinking a great deal of wine, Kerouac sat down at the priest's feet, leaned affectionately against his knee, and started quoting the Diamond Sutra. "I love you," Jack said, gazing up at the cleric, who smiled in quiet acceptance of Jack's feelings. Everyone else seemed embarrassed and pretended to ignore Jack's declaration, though it marked one of the defining moments of the Beat Generation as a paradoxical compound of beatific reverence, open lust, and bold heresy.

Two matronly church women had accompanied the priest to Los Gatos, and Ginsberg impishly sat down between them. Since his success at the Six Gallery, he had been suggesting at every social situation he found himself in that everyone strip naked. On this occasion, he said, "Now then, what about sex?" Kerouac giggled, but the ethereal young priest remained undaunted and pointed out that the sex drive can be used for pleasure and reproduction or to create imaginative works and philosophies for the good of mankind and one's own spiritual progress. "I love you," Jack repeated.

Beverly Burford, whose young niece was being coached in ballet by Carolyn, later told Kerouac biographers Gifford and Lee that Carolyn "was very involved with a progressive priest that she was going to marry and dump Neal." But that night Carolyn's passion was focused exclusively on Kerouac. They had the house to themselves, since Neal had gone back to San Francisco to be with Natalie. After the children went to bed, Jack and Carolyn "outdid" themselves, she recalled, and neither slept that night, hungrily making love, "grasping and clutching . . . pouring into each other our pent-up affection and sorrow." Finally, at dawn, Jack took his sleeping bag outside, since the children would soon be stirring. At breakfast, he appeared to be hungover, but he opened a beer and started maneuvering his way out of another emotional attachment. He told Carolyn that Neal still loved her, even though Neal was living with Natalie. Carolyn must "surrender" herself to Neal, he insisted. Carolyn knew she could never possess Jack the way she wanted to, any more than she could control Neal. "Both of you do very well in loving me 'indifferently,'" she observed.

It was a fair, gusty morning, and Jack and Carolyn stood close to each other on the patio, watching the clouds tumble and toss overhead. Neal's fatal flaw, Carolyn observed, was that he mistook marijuana for a shortcut to spirituality, and no such thing exists. If Neal would only meditate instead of getting stoned, he would find the peace that eluded him. Jack needed no convincing of marijuana's dangers, having already stated in *Some of the Dharma* that the poisons in pot induce temporary panic, the very opposite of the serenity he sought. Perhaps the cure for his addictions, he decided, was to go to the mountains and meditate, like Larry Darrell, the worldly protagonist of W. Somerset Maugham's *The Razor's Edge*, who found enlightenment in the Himalayas and converted to Hinduism. Meanwhile, he advised Carolyn to stick with Neal at any cost. The Cassady family provided a domestic anchor that Jack didn't want to lose, or he'd be totally adrift. "Just you do what he wants and know he's great," Jack said, epitomizing the Beat attitude toward women, which was no different from that of the larger society in the 1950s.[33] It served none of them well, neither the men who tyrannized the women, nor the women who enabled them to do so.

Neal suddenly burst in and swept them off to a racetrack for a day of betting on the horses. He had worked out a peculiar system that he swore was foolproof—always bet on the third-choice horse, since the first and second are overrated—but he usually lost, and finally he went broke. One day, in desperation, he took Natalie to the bank and talked her into forging Carolyn's signature in order to withdraw ten thousand dollars, all that remained of his court settlement for his ankle injury, as he later confessed to a Catholic priest, Rev. Harley. Neal then proceeded to gamble away the entire amount in six weeks. Natalie, already mentally unstable, suffered a nervous breakdown brought on by her despair over Neal, and by her guilt over having wasted Carolyn's and the children's life savings. Neal tried to dump Natalie on Kerouac, but he didn't want her either, especially after he discovered that he couldn't restore her sanity by mouthing Buddhist nostrums about emptiness. She was convinced that the police were about to destroy all nonconformists. Abandoned by both Cassady and Kerouac, Natalie committed suicide by slashing herself with broken glass and then leaping from the roof of Neal's tenement in San Francisco, according to Neal's correspondence with Harley.

Like Joan Burroughs, the tragic Natalie would find her niche in Beat history. As Maria Damon writes in "Victors of Catastrophe: Beat Occlusions,"

Elise Cowen, Natalie Jackson, V. R. ("Bunny") Lang, and Joan Burroughs remain . . . significant icons of inspiration, pathos, and creative intelligence. . . . While the. . . . Beat men may have slighted the creative powers of the women in their immediate circles, Sappho, Emily Dickinson, Gertrude Stein, and Hilda Doolittle ("H. D.") were . . . acknowledged as ma(s)ters . . . Their poetics and their homoerotic lives served as models for experimental writing and transgressive sexual exploration.[34]

Carolyn Cassady appears to have survived through a combination of moral strength and emotional detachment. Looking back on her life with Jack and Neal from the vantage point of 1995, she said, "I was not romantically 'in love' with either of them. I was a sexual cripple and so never cared about that part."

After Natalie's death, Jack again escaped the complexities of the Cassadys' ménage and returned to Ginsberg's cottage in Berkeley. On November 9, 1955, he wrote Stella, who'd been sounding lonely and forlorn in recent letters, about a walk he'd taken with Ginsberg and Whalen along the docks. At one point, Jack commented on a dusty sunflower withering in litter and industrial grime, calling it a victim of civilization. The incident inspired a major Ginsberg poem, "Sunflower Sutra." In Jack's letter to Stella, he assured her that she too was a sunflower and that her soul would never be sullied by the world. Referring to her as Estella of Stars, he expressed his love and promised to visit her in Lowell in the spring of 1956. He seemed close to proposing, telling her that she was adored by numerous suitors, but he pulled back, writing instead that he was a Japanese-style Buddhist pilgrim who required solitude in the mountains or desert.

Jack had just returned from an expedition in the High Sierras, where he had found both bliss and a sense of purpose while mountain climbing with Snyder and Montgomery. They had scaled the twelve-thousand-foot Matterhorn, a peak on the northern side of Yosemite, and Snyder, as uninhibited as ever, had gone naked part of the way. As a mountain climber, Kerouac was more of a sprinter than a two-miler, according to Montgomery. Kerouac's account of the climb in *The Dharma Bums* is a spectacular foray into nature writing and bull's-eye prophecy. A vision comes to him on the mountaintop, revealing that his mission is to lead humanity and incite a generation of young people to drop out of the rat race and hit the road. "I see a vision of a great rucksack revolution," he wrote, "millions of young Americans wandering around . . . giving visions of eternal freedom to everybody. . . . How truly great and wise America will be, with all this energy and exuberance . . . focused on the Dharma." The role he saw for himself as a dharma bum was derived from the *Diamond Sutra*, which held that "Great Beings of Enlightenment, in teaching the Verity (Dharma) to others, should first free themselves from all exquisite or disgusting tastes." Alcohol and sex would prove to be difficult tastes to shed. Back in the city, Kerouac's breathless account of his vision was met with gentle cynicism by North Beach coffeehouse wits. According to Montgomery, a phrase often overheard at the

Place, Vesuvio's, and the Triéste was: "I'll take them to twelve thousand feet and fuck."[35]

Natalie Jackson's violent death in 1955 had the same effect on North Beach hipsters as Cannastra's had had five years previously on their Greenwich Village counterparts. Suddenly they recognized the dangers of the Beat life, and some of them, including Kerouac and Cassady, even fled San Francisco. Kerouac represented Gary Snyder, as Japhy Ryder in *The Dharma Bums*, as saying that Natalie "was a flower we let wither." Neal returned to his family, but he appeared to Carolyn to be gazing into a chasm, viewing his own irreversible descent into hell. Kerouac was also depressed. Now that he'd resumed drinking, he became surly and testy, alienating many San Francisco friends. He was frustrated and angry that some of them still refused to heed his Buddhist message of acceptance and renunciation. While visiting a young woman's home in Berkeley with Ginsberg and Snyder, he began to discourse on the illusory nature of the self. "Well, I don't care," Ginsberg said, Kerouac reported in *Some of the Dharma*, "I'm gonna go right along and just be Allen G[insberg]." Enraged, Jack started yelling and threatening to leave. Refusing to be intimidated, Ginsberg told him to go ahead and leave, and Jack stalked out in a huff.

As news of the Kerouac-Ginsberg altercation swept the Bay Area poetry scene, Kerouac became convinced that "G[insberg] envies me and hates me," he wrote in *Some of the Dharma*. Kenneth Rexroth, who was one of the most powerful book reviewers in America, was offended by reports of Kerouac's temper tantrum but nevertheless included him among the guests when he invited leading Beat figures such as Cassady, Ginsberg, Whalen, and Orlovsky to his home for dinner one evening. At one point Kerouac demanded more wine, though he'd already had too much. "Just because you're a genius you think you can act RUDE and UNMANNERLY!" Rexroth screamed, according to *Some of the Dharma*. With a sweeping gesture that included the other Beat guests, Rexroth said, "Get out of my house, all of you!"

"Aw you're frightening me to death!" Kerouac quipped, making an enemy for life. Not until the publication in 1995 of Kerouac's January 16, 1956, letter to Snyder did the real issue between Kerouac and Rexroth emerge at last. Kerouac was irked because Rexroth had attacked *Dr. Sax* after having read it in manuscript, and his remarks struck Kerouac as spiteful, jealous, and blind to the fact that Jack had taken huge risks, eschewing conventional narrative in favor of allegory, myth, and magic. Kerouac aired numerous other complaints about Rexroth in his letter to Snyder, casting aspersions on Rexroth's masculinity and calling him an old hag. It was well known that Rexroth promoted the careers of young writers in order to insure their subservience to him as the West Coast's literary panjandrum, and that he boasted of having slept with every woman in California. Kerouac poked fun at such egotistical posturings and told Snyder that he'd like to urinate on Rexroth and his retinue of groveling disciples. In *The Dharma Bums*, Kerouac would further alienate Rexroth by spoofing him at the Six Gallery reading as an "old anarchist fud." He would pay dearly for these slights, since Rexroth was at the height of his popularity as a critic and was often called on by the *New York Times Book Review* to evaluate new authors.

After Kerouac's clashes with Ginsberg and Rexroth, he moved out of Ginsberg's cottage and into the Cameo Hotel. Due to a "broken footbone," Jack limped as he made his way each day through the derelicts on skid row. At night he listened to the tugboats in the bay and to the wheezing of a dying old man next door. Finally, he decided to go back on the road, cursing San Francisco as a city of infidels. In late November 1955, Philip Whalen gave him a farewell dinner at a Chinese restaurant. Jack denounced Ginsberg and Rexroth for turning against him, pointing out that Ginsberg had been a covert detractor for years; at last his influence over Jack was at an end. Whatever the real or imagined issues between them, Kerouac was probably just smarting because Ginsberg had momentarily upstaged him.[36]

Still suffering from his injured toe, Kerouac dragged his weighty belongings "down Hobo Street," he wrote in *Some of the Dharma*, but his spirits lifted as soon as he arrived at the Cassadys' home, where he "ended up in the sunny grass with . . . Sweet Carolyn." During the next few days, Carolyn noticed that he was more concerned than ever about his homelessness. Jamie, Cathy, and Johnny, the Cassadys' children, fascinated him, and he wrote down everything they said, later turning their childish observations into "*pops*," short verses defined in *Some of the Dharma* as " 'little Samadhis' . . . aimed towards enlightenment." He finally left Los Gatos on a gray afternoon, hoisting his fifty-pound rucksack and walking off in the fog, bound for North Carolina to celebrate Christmas 1955 with his family. It was another hard, three-thousand-mile journey in boxcars and on flatbed trucks, sleeping in fields and cringing when policemen stuck their flashlights in his face and routed him. In a letter to Snyder, he expressed astonishment that it was against the law in the United States to sleep in the countryside, adding that the police had made him a fugitive in his own land.

He learned how to survive on the road from the hoboes he met in rail yards. They showed him how to bathe in the water that dripped from "reefers"—refrigerated boxcars—and one kindly bindlestiff gave him a cure for his swollen legs: headstands performed daily for three to five minutes. After three months of following the hobo's advice, Jack no longer complained of phlebitis, and he decided the 'bo must have been a Buddha.

En route from California to North Carolina, Kerouac almost killed himself on a fourteen-car Diesel, the Arizona Zipper, when he jumped from the top of a moving boxcar, but luckily he landed uninjured in a ditch. In a bums' cafeteria on South Main in L.A., he breakfasted for seventeen cents and wrote "Little Main Street Blues." Then he bought a bottle of wine and sat drinking it in a sun-splashed parking lot behind a Chinese restaurant. It was December 14, 1955.

Contemplating his alcoholism, he realized the tragic price he was paying for medicating his boredom with booze. Hangovers were making him suicidal and turning him into a zombie—the "notself" he chillingly described in *Some of the Dharma*. He felt completely empty, and in a perverse negation of everything Buddhism stands for, he wrote to Snyder that nothing really matters in life. In his alcoholic confusion he had twisted Buddhism into a justification for hopelessness. But Buddhism is not about devaluing life; it's about treasuring life and treating everyone with infinite kindness, tolerance, and understanding. Plunged into three-day depressions, Kerouac considered attending Alcoholics Anonymous meetings, but revealed in *Some of the Dharma* that AA made him feel "sad and hangovery." It was not AA, of course, but alcohol that gave him hangovers. Kerouac wrote that by switching from heavy drinking to "lil bit this and lil bit that," and by limiting himself to one drink a day at cocktail time, he could conquer his disease, but his drinking only got worse when he tried to control it. He reached the nadir of alcoholic denial when he claimed in *Some of the Dharma* that he'd experienced his "highest visions of Buddhist Emptiness when drunk," but added four pages later that, having overdosed on codeine and alcohol, his mind was so ravaged that he couldn't even think.

On December 15, 1955, outside Riverside, California, fifty-five miles from central L.A., he hacked his way through bramble and bamboo to a dry riverbed bottom. In the privacy of the bushes, he took off his clothes and walked around naked, fantasizing about the firm behinds of California girls until he became "hard and juicy," he wrote in *Some of the Dharma*. After building a campfire, he prepared a hot, satisfying supper of tea, beans, and macaroni. Then, the light from the fire dancing in his eyes, he wrote a poem, "Little Pure Land Blues," describing his riverbottom hideaway and his fear of the police. It was almost Christmas, 1955, and though he was fighting a head cold and exposed to the raw night air, he prayed in the poem for the welfare of others, asking his angels to hover over every rooftop. Writing about the same evening in *Some of the Dharma*, he wondered why he was still being denied enlightenment despite his rigorous Buddhist studies; then, deciding that alcohol was to blame, he resolved to do "no more systematic drinking." Dreaming of hot-fudge sundaes and Broadway shows, he ticked off six new novels he'd write after *Visions of Gerard*: *Visions of Mike*, *Visions of Nin*, *Visions of G. J.*, *Visions of Sebastian*, *Visions of Bill*, and *Visions of Gary* (only *Visions of Gerard* would ever be completed). At last he went to sleep, shivering but grateful to be a free person in a cold sleeping bag rather than an emotional hostage in a warm bed.

In the U.S.–Mexico border towns of Mexicali and Calexico, he couldn't resist stocking up on inexpensive drugs, purchasing sixty codeinattas and fifty Benzedrines for $3.50. Later, as border guards searched his bag, he reflected that his karma was about to land him in jail. But the guards tired of sifting through the mess in his backpack — French fries, raisins, peanuts, carrots, and whole wheat bread — and waved him through customs. He had exactly $62.10 to make it across the continent to Rocky Mount. Fortunately, he fell in with a friendly truck driver, Charley Burchette, and after they drank tequila and sampled Mexicali's "sultry whores," Kerouac rode with him all the way to Springfield, Ohio — a glorious, twenty-four-hundred-mile transcontinental jaunt, accomplished in ninety hours. In Springfield, the bitter cold finally drove him off the road, and he bought a twelve-dollar bus ticket to North Carolina.[37]

On December 21, he stepped from the bus onto Route 64, still three miles from Nin's house in Big Easonburg Woods. As he walked home over icy country roads, he was freezing, but he was glad to be in the southeast for a white Christmas. In *Some of the Dharma*, he recalled approaching the house and standing "in the frosty yard watching Ma at her dishes in the kitchen, piteous-faced. . . . Poor Gabe in this harsh life." Going inside, he embraced his mother and promised he'd never injure her again. Mémêre surprised him by saying she was leaving shortly for Brooklyn, where her stepmother was dying. Too late, Jack realized that he should have remained in Los Gatos for a family Christmas with the Cassadys. Feeling a desire to drink, he tried to fight it but finally fell off the wagon on Christmas Eve. As a contented cat purred in his lap, he drank wine in front of the TV set, watching Mass from St. Patrick's Cathedral in New York. Before he passed out, he wrote a "drinking pome" and later mailed a copy to Gary Snyder. Published in 1995 in *Selected Letters* and again in 1997 in *Some of the Dharma*, it was a sprightly Yuletide ditty full of pixilated musicians and purehearted priests.

On the morning of December 27, 1955, he began writing a major work, *Visions of Gerard*, the story of the first few years of his life. "Took Benny for kickoff," he confessed in *Some of the Dharma*, but the drug didn't help. Later, puzzling over why he'd been blocked on the novel's "big opening day," he admitted that Benzedrine numbed his brain and made him worthless for normal life. Doggedly adhering to Buddhist tradition, he meditated and prayed every night in a clearing deep in the piney woods. Emulating Siddhartha, who'd meditated beneath the bodhi tree, Kerouac sat under a gnarled twin tree near a brook he called Buddha Creek.

Pleasantly aware that the Beats were changing modern life and thought, he was convinced that a small group of Buddhist thinkers — including himself, Whalen, and Snyder — had already had a calming effect on the American temperament, and that by 1958 the transformation would be complete. Surprisingly, some of the earliest symptoms of cultural change occurred in the mainstream of society rather than on its Beat fringes. In January 1956, a surprise best-seller called *The Search for Bridey Murphy* suddenly had millions of people talking about reincarnation. The book had come about as a result of Thomas Sugrue's 1942 biography of Edgar Cayce, *There Is A River*, which inspired Morey Bernstein to hypnotize a Colorado housewife and regress her to a previous life in Ireland. Nin voraciously consumed *Bridey*

Murphy and asked Jack to tell her everything he knew on the subject of reincarnation. He immediately wrote the Cassadys to send him the address of the Cayce Association for Research and Enlightenment so he could request pamphlets. In Los Gatos, Neal excitedly reminded Carolyn that Cayce had predicted a spiritual revival throughout the world between 1958 and 1998. He sent Jack the address—Seventh and Atlantic Avenue, Virginia Beach, Virginia, considered by many to be the world's mecca for psychic phenomena. In Rocky Mount, Kerouac noted in *Some of the Dharma* that his present life was nothing but an "echo" of a previous incarnation as a bloodthirsty tyrant and perpetrator of genocide. That would certainly explain his anti-Semitic streak; other Kerouac incarnations sounded more benign, including ones as Avalokitesvara, a bhikku; Asvhaghosha, a desert monk; a Chinese Buddhist; an Aztec; Shakespeare; a British highwayman; and Balzac.[38]

He began 1956 afire with ambitious plans. Suddenly recalling a youthful aptitude for sports reporting, he considered forsaking fiction to write for a Manhattan daily. On New Year's Eve, he had a drink and toasted the comic-strip character Major Hoople, acknowledging the absurdity of his resolution to stay sober and feeling "worse than King Job." He wanted to work part-time as a forest ranger and earn enough money to spend the rest of the year writing fiction in Mexico City, where he'd establish a Mexican Buddhist monastery just outside the city limits, with no rules or regulations. A second monastery would be opened on Neal's property in Los Gatos, and students could major in "Emptiness-hood," he told Whalen. (After Jack's death, Ginsberg and poet Anne Waldman established the Kerouac School of Disembodied Poetics at the Naropa Institute in Boulder, Colorado.) Despite Nin's faddish intoxication with *Bridey Murphy*, she poked fun at Jack's Buddhism, and he drowned her out by warbling Frank Sinatra's "You're Learning the Blues." Living rent-free on her glassed-in back porch, he threw open all six windows when he slept, snug in his duck-down bag. His requirements were few: a cot, a typewriter, a desk, and a screen for privacy. All his books, including Proust and William Blake, were in the living-room bookcase. He was proud of his complete, unabridged editions, and wrote Carolyn that his copies of the classics lent an air of distinction and affluence to Nin's home. Mémère gave him enough money to subsist, though he needed little, helping himself to the Blakes' larder. In return for Mémère's having poured her life savings into Paul's television business, she and Jack were theoretically welcome as permanent nonpaying guests in perpetuity. In addition, Mémère was still working as Nin's maid. The arrangement satisfied no one.[39]

In the first weeks of 1956, Jack was phenomenally productive, completing his short novel *Visions of Gerard* and bringing *Some of the Dharma* up to three hundred pages. Like many authors, including John O'Hara, Kerouac preferred to write at night, often working by candlelight. Though *Visions of Gerard* gives an impression of serenity, even of sacredness, it shot out of him in ten days of unrelenting Benzedrine abuse. On January 5, he wrote Whalen that he was working at an unprecedented pace, and on the seventh he completed the six-thousand-word schoolyard and confessional scenes between 1 and 3 A.M. Chronologically *Gerard* was the first installment of "The Duluoz Legend," and Kerouac offered in the Whalen letter yet another explanation of the derivation of "Duluoz," claiming it was a Breton name that he'd decided to use in place of his own in what he now envisaged as a never-ending saga of his life. By the time he reached the last chapter of *Gerard*, he was throwing up from Benzedrine abuse. Everything he wrote in that condition, he confided in *Some of the Dharma*, was, predictably, "a crock." After catching up on his sleep, he went back to the last chapter, working through the night at the kitchen table. On January 10, he completed the novel's Christmas Eve chapter and the account of Gerard's endless night of unbearable pain. On the eleventh, the author had his own night of pain, writing twelve pages and immediately consigning them to the wastebasket. Seven straight nights on Benzedrine left him wired, brain-dead, and *"bored,"* he wrote in *Some of the Dharma*, adding that speed rendered him incapable of meditation, devoid of purpose, and sick of writing. But he drew strength from what Burroughs said at Fugazzy's in 1953—that Kerouac was the best author in the United States—and at 1 A.M. on January 16, he finished *Visions of Gerard*, pushing the manuscript aside with the anxious thought that it might be too soppy. Perhaps his most vulnerable work, the novel was open to the charge of sentimentality for its candid love of family life and in its wrenching grief over mortality. Yet those qualities also defined the novel's greatness, which lay in its reverence for existence and its mystical sense of eternal life.

Quickly recovering his cockiness, Kerouac announced in *Some of the Dharma* that he'd now attained total control of his art and could be mentioned in the same breath with Mozart and Rembrandt. In a January 16 letter to Whalen, he crowed that he could write better than any other author alive. On the same day he wrote Snyder and said he would call the novel *St. Gerard the Child* but feared people would ridicule him. Snyder had decided to go to Japan to study Zen Buddhism, and Kerouac promised to join him there if the book earned money; he wanted to spend an afternoon in a teahouse, pay homage to Buddha, and then disappear into an opium den. Teetering between terror and grandiosity, Kerouac recorded in *Some of the Dharma* that he was praying to Gerard to save him from alcohol. Soon, however, he moaned that his head was splitting from the combined effects of codeine and liquor.

Tightly focused on the final year of Gerard's life, 1925, and drawn from nothing but dim, dewy memories of Jack's fourth year, Mémère's stories, and a few old letters of Leo's, *Visions of Gerard* would probably never have been written had Mémère not gone to New York to attend a funeral. In North Carolina she usually kept Jack up all night, gabbing and nipping from a bottle. Her absence was thus fortuitous. With its jewel-like clarity and sure, unimpeded narrative line, *Visions of Gerard* is as pure and distilled as Hemingway's *The Old Man and the Sea*. Fortunately, Kerouac's announced intention to attack Jews produced only one anonymous reference to them in *Gerard* as "blood-louts." Despite drugs, alcohol, and a mind beclouded with racism and sexism, he achieved in *Gerard* a kind of requiem mass in novel form, and often called it his favorite work.[40]

At the end of January, he took the train to Brooklyn for his step-grandmother's funeral, staying at 293 State Street with an aunt who upset him by continually shifting the sleeping arrangements. His real purpose in coming to New York was business: He wanted to discuss his backlog of unpublished manuscripts with Sterling and to see Cowley about getting *On the Road* in acceptable shape for a contract. Upon his return to North Carolina on February 7, Kerouac wrote Whalen that the trip had been disappointing, and at first he blamed New York. As an alcoholic in denial, he automatically attributed his misery to people, places, and things, seldom admitting that the real cause was his drinking, which made him rude and reckless. After one too many in a Greenwich Village bar, he ran into Alene, but she humiliated him, kissing every other man in the saloon. His smug subterranean drinking buddies rubbed it in, making him feel like a failure.

Jack's only champion, he told Holmes, was Lucien's wife, Cessa, who graciously invited him to the Carrs' Sheridan Square apartment. Cessa was pregnant with a son, whom they later named Caleb (and whose future novel, *The Angel of Darkness*, would be a 1997 main selection of the Book-of-the-Month Club). Lucien liked Kerouac's concept of a completely empty universe so much that he said he was going to write a sutra that would contain nothing but blank pages. When Jack said goodbye to Lucien on his final night in New York, Lucien gave him a bottle of sherry—the last thing Kerouac needed—and he polished it off while walking home across the Brooklyn Bridge, his scarf wrapped up to his ears.

Later, in his poem "The Brooklyn Bridge Blues," Jack related a strange story about his mother's behavior in New York. He told his aunt that he'd given Mémère fifty dollars from his American Academy grant, but Mémère denied it to his face. Having portrayed herself as Jack's sole means of support for years, she was disinclined to relinquish the role over a mere fifty dollars. Lucien shamed Jack for squabbling with his mother over money. The episode shocked him into recognizing, at last, the true source of his problems. "It's *not* New York that is rude, forgetful, cold," Kerouac wrote in *Some of the Dharma*, "it's ME."

Back in Rocky Mount, he considered withdrawing all his manuscripts unless they were put under contract in 1956. He also steamed over what to do about Ginsberg, whom he loved but envied. On February 24, he wrote Lucien that Ginsberg was reciting his "dirty" poem up and down the West Coast. The solitary reason Ginsberg was becoming famous, claimed a resentful Kerouac, was his willingness to say *prick* and *pussy* in public, the only writer to do so since Henry Miller. Stung by Kerouac's barbs, Ginsberg stopped speaking to him. Kerouac admitted that he fulminated about Rexroth and Ginsberg so much simply because he was broke and out of liquor, bored, and had nothing better to occupy his mind. Soon, he attempted to make amends by sending Ginsberg Buddhist material and a Sanskrit prayer, referring to them in a letter to Whalen as "holy assholies." He was no longer angry, and could not imagine life without Ginsberg. But he warned Whalen that no male was safe with Allen, who could insert his "Hebrew National" stealthily and without warning. A falling-out occurred when Ginsberg made unwanted sexual advances to Snyder during their Seattle–San Francisco tour in 1956, a trip described in Snyder's poem, "Night Highway Ninety-Nine." Jack discussed the Snyder-Ginsberg contretemps in a letter to Snyder that winter; the problem, in Jack's view, was that Ginsberg couldn't control his lust, and Jack blamed Allen's father, gossiping to Snyder that Louis Ginsberg had called Allen his "loverboy." Jack feared Allen was detouring from the path of dharma and heading in the direction of Tangier, Burroughs, and Arab boys. He was right, but it was no detour; Ginsberg was simply being true to himself. The enormous difference between Kerouac and Ginsberg, which emerged powerfully at this time, was Ginsberg's active engagement with life, represented by his willingness to go onstage at the Six Gallery, while Kerouac served the wine. The difference would become critical in the following decade, when Ginsberg took to the trenches as a new generation's moral leader, and Kerouac completely disappeared from view.[41]

On the Road hit yet another in a seemingly endless succession of obstructions. While in New York, Jack had attempted to see Cowley at Viking, but Cowley was away, teaching at Stanford University. Evidently, Kerouac had forgotten that Cowley had advised him in an October 12, 1955, letter that he'd be in Palo Alto after January 2, 1956. Kerouac had just been in that part of California, and it was maddening for him to learn, too late, that one of the purposes of Cowley's California trip had been to oversee the final polishing of On the Road. The confusion resulted in a six-month delay in publication.[42]

Thanks to a forceful recommendation from Whalen, Kerouac was offered a U.S. Forest Service job on February 7, 1956, and he immediately wrote Carolyn that it was the opportunity of a lifetime. Over the summer, he would be paid $230 a month to be a fire lookout on Desolation Peak in the Mount Baker National Forest near Marblemount, Washington. He was less excited about his publishing situation, which was at a standstill, and he complained to Sterling on February 24 that he was not satisfied with the management of his affairs. On the same day, he complained to Lucien that Sterling had received the manuscript of Visions of Gerard but had neglected to comment on it. He was beginning to despair of ever finding a business representative or editor who understood him. Like many authors, he did not comprehend that it is unrealistic to expect compliments and love in a business relationship.[43]

By March, he felt so unwelcome in Nin's house that he wrote Carolyn he'd soon be homeless. According to Kerouac, his brother-in-law had gone back on his promise to Mémêre that she and Jack could live with them indefinitely. Now Mémêre was talking of moving to California with Jack, but she suddenly fell ill and started sneezing and coughing. On March 10, two days before his thirty-fourth birthday, Jack decided to use his new spiritual tools to treat her. He hypnotized himself, and the cure for Mémêre's ailment (linament and brandy) was revealed to him in a trance. When she recovered, he noted in *Some of the Dharma* that he'd now become a "healer." Perhaps he was, but sometimes he used Buddhism to justify and rationalize his drinking. People fall ill, he wrote, as self-punishment for wrongs previously committed; his phlebitis, for example, was a karmic rebuke for his brutality on the gridiron. The obvious cause, of course, was drug and alcohol abuse.[44]

In mid-March 1956 he wrote Carolyn that he was returning to San Francisco, and that his mother would shortly join him there. Mémêre wanted to spend the rest of her life on the West Coast and was already dreaming of lavish dinners in Chinatown, but Jack's letter to Carolyn made it clear that Mémêre would have little time for relaxation; he was already scouting out shoe-factory jobs for her in the Bay Area. Though he wanted to purchase a quaint little bungalow in Berkeley, he was so far from being able to mortgage a house that he had to borrow fifty dollars from Mémêre for travel expenses.

On his last night of meditating at Buddha Creek that spring, he realized everyone was a "starbody," and the purpose of life was to awake to this eternal self. Finishing *Some of the Dharma* on March 15, he wrote that the Beat Generation was nothing but an insane illusion. Nevertheless, he asked himself if his just-completed, four-hundred-and-twenty-page Buddhist screed wasn't perhaps the dry run for a heroic work of fiction that could be called *The Tathagata*. He answered himself resoundingly in the negative, admitting how little he'd gained from Buddhism; "rich wine," he wrote, had prevented him from achieving *samapatti* in his present lifetime. But he didn't despair, because he assumed that he would be granted "a billion lifetimes as Writing Buddhas" to express "what Samadhis and Samapattis show." In the grip of alcoholism he'd cunningly found a way to pervert the philosophy of reincarnation. "Drink yr. Port & Shut Orp," he blearily reasoned at the end of *Some of the Dharma*, giving himself permission to continue drinking in his present incarnation but promising to stay sober in the next.

Unfortunately for Kerouac, reincarnation doesn't work that way, at least according to Ruth Montgomery, the Cayce expert I published with Kerouac on the same Coward-McCann list in the 1960s. On a visit with Ruth and her husband Bob in their home near Cayce's A.R.E. headquarters in Virginia Beach, Ruth and I discussed the possibility of her writing a book on reincarnation. "It's a good idea to discipline yourself to become the kind of person now that you'd like to be the next time around," Ruth told me, and I was so intrigued that I commissioned her to write *Here and Hereafter*. In that book, which became a 1968 best-seller as well as a pioneering New Age work, Ruth wrote, "An entity who is unable to curb his overindulgence in liquor or sex can carry that obsession with him beyond the grave, where the longing for it proves so irresistible that he returns, almost immediately, without the philosophical preparation that could permit him to select his next incarnation with wisdom." When I shared this passage with Kerouac, he was quite upset, commenting, "Sounds like you could get caught in a hideous vortex, just like I said in 'the wheel of the quivering meat conception.' Reincarnation stinks. I was pretty much over it by '59."

In April 1956, Kerouac set out again for California. A neighbor drove him to Highway 64, where he got a ride from a high-school student as far as the country town of Nashville, North Carolina. Then he sweated while walking in the afternoon sun for thirty minutes before a sailor stopped and drove him to Greenville, South Carolina. Later, during a storm in Georgia, Kerouac drank a half pint of wine and decided to catch a Greyhound to El Paso. From Texas, he hitchhiked across New Mexico, Arizona, and California. Finally arriving at the L.A. rail yards, he jumped on a local and rode it up to Santa Barbara. After a swim at the beach, he caught the Midnight Ghost to San Francisco and fell asleep under a truck that was lashed to a flatbed. By the time he reached San Francisco, he was tired and had one dollar in his pocket. Gary Snyder, who was staying in a cabin in Marin County, invited Jack to bunk with him throughout the spring. Though Snyder was a man of action and Kerouac was passive and usually hung over, they accepted each other totally, forming the most uniquely trouble-free partnership of Kerouac's life.

Set in an evergreen grove in Mill Valley, Snyder's shack, "Marin-An," was so rudimentary that it had no glass in the windows. Each morning Snyder and Kerouac would watch the sun appear over a nearby stand of fragrant eucalyptus trees, and then Snyder would jump up and get a good fire going in the stove as he whistled merrily. "Well don't just lay there in your sleeping bag pullin your puddin," he'd tell Kerouac, "get up and fetch some water. Yodelayee hoo!" Whenever Michael McClure came to visit, he always sensed an "uncanny stillness" within Marin-An, as if the cabin were a chapel. Down the slope at 348 Montford Avenue stood the home of Locke McCorkle, who was characterized by Jack in *Desolation Angels* as "Kevin McLoch," a "serious, beautiful man, 23, with blue eyes, perfect teeth, handsome Irish charm, and a lovely melodious way of speaking." In Snyder's cabin and in McCorkle's house, Kerouac spent some of the happiest days he would ever know. Snyder's common sense, integrity, and eloquence would win him the Pulitzer Prize for *Turtle Island* in 1975, and these same qualities animated everything he said and did with Kerouac in 1956. They cooked meals for each other, went on long hikes, and prayed for all living creatures.

Snyder was on the brink of his departure for Japan, where he would undergo formal training in Zen Buddhism for the next twelve years. In 1956 he was already pioneering "the emergent Pacific culture," he later wrote in *No Nature*. Kerouac listed Snyder's various causes as "soil conservation, the Tennessee Valley Authority, astronomy, geology, Hsuan Tsung's travels, Chinese painting theory, reforestation, Oceanic ecology and food chains." Having previously worked in the Skagit mountain region where Jack would shortly take up his post on Desolation Peak, Snyder was able to teach Jack how to survive in the wilderness, and Jack eagerly soaked up every lesson, from camping to composing koans. Sometimes Snyder would coach Kerouac and McClure in a Zen running meditation as they jogged single file along the tracks at night. Parties usually started in Locke McCorkle's house and ended up in Snyder's cabin, and the girls often danced naked. Some of the men would also take off their clothes. One day, Jack saw a nude Ginsberg and Orlovsky standing by a bonfire, casually conversing with two men in business suits. Though Kerouac customarily sat quietly in meditation, with his eyes closed, at one gathering he went up to Alan Watts, portrayed as "Arthur Whane" in *The Dharma Bums*, and asked him to define Buddhism. Replying that Buddhism was getting to know as many people as possible, Watts then walked off to shake hands with everyone present. When Watts wrote in *The Realist* magazine that Kerouac had "Zen flesh but no Zen bones," Kerouac called Watts an authentic if somewhat foppish Buddhist. According to Whalen, everyone adored Kerouac, but Whalen added that Jack made it difficult, turning away every compliment and insisting that he was a huge failure. He could also be quite nasty, and eventually he turned on everyone, calling them hopeless fuckups. Catholicism was to blame, Whalen felt, because it had given Kerouac a "dirty me" complex.

Just before Snyder left for Japan, he took Jack on a long hike up Mount Tamalpais to Muir Woods, and then down a steep path to Stinson Beach for a swim in the Pacific. In Snyder's poem, "On Vulture Peak," he wrote that he and Jack got drunk, took off their clothes, and squatted on the beach as they enjoyed a mess of steamed mussels. In *The Dharma Bums*, Kerouac recalled beach picnics with Snyder when they spread out their meals of salami, Ry-Krisp, cheese, and wine on a piece of paper in the sand. Snyder's message, as interpreted by Kerouac in *The Dharma Bums*, was that spirituality lay in getting close to the basic elements, "rock air fire and wood." The only issue separating the two friends was Jack's drinking. Gary warned Jack that he was missing out on his own life; Jack angrily insisted on his right to self-destruct. According to Gary, "Jack wanted to get out of the world," and he seemed to be surrounded by "a palpable aura of fame and death." In an essay on the religiosity of the Beat Generation, Snyder maintained that drugs could be used to seek personal insight but only with "intelligent" caution and prudence. Staying stoned all the time is a dead end, a life without "intellect, will, and compassion; and a personal drug kick is of no use to anyone else in the world." He sadly foresaw that Kerouac would end up blowing bubbles in the gutter. One day, he asked Jack how he could possibly expect to connect with his spirit when his mind was "muddled" and his body was falling apart.

"I'm not sick," Jack replied "I'm fine." But of course he wasn't; his refusal to let Snyder help him was perhaps Kerouac's last chance to save his own life, for no one else would ever command as much respect from him as Snyder did. In *Some of the Dharma* Kerouac wrote that he would continue to search for "some expedient means" to give up alcohol. He wanted a "DRY STRONG HAPPINESS," knowing that "WET WEAK UNIIAPPINESS (hangover)" was ruining his body, draining his enthusiasm and joy, and affecting his brain. But every time he tried to reduce his intake of alcohol, he found that controlled drinking inevitably led to further binges. Nothing less than total abstinence would cure him of his obsession, but he was unwilling to pursue a "new life of holy purpose," he wrote, if it meant sacrificing alcohol.

On the Road was still stalled at the editing stage. Usually a book is put under contract before it's edited, but Viking reversed the process, holding off Kerouac's contract as a way forcing him to accept editorial changes. The problem was that Kerouac and Cowley couldn't seem to get together geographically in order to work on the manuscript. Cowley went to Palo Alto to teach a creative writing course at Stanford, but the trimester ended by the time Kerouac returned to California, and Cowley was now back in New York. As a result, Cowley edited On the Road alone and unilaterally, for which Kerouac, as he later told me, would never forgive him. Despite repeated pleas from Jack, Viking did not pay the thousand-dollar advance requested by Lord for another nine months. At one point in the spring of 1956, Kerouac wrote Cowley that such treatment was both humiliating and unjust. After Kerouac supplied the releases the publisher requested, he assumed he was past the legal hurdles, but then he discovered that the publisher was still fretting about Justin Brierly, the prominent Denver citizen who'd first seduced Neal Cassady. Kerouac applied additional camouflage to his portrait of Brierly as "Denver D. Doll," according to Locke McCorkle, but Brierly's interest in young men was still evident.

News from home was equally distressing. On April 1, Mémère wrote Jack a desperate letter describing her situation in Nin's home as intolerable. Mémère was running out of money, and Jack had better become a successful author, she wrote, or they'd never survive. Despite these distractions, Kerouac produced two important new works that spring that further defined Beat spirituality. Up until then, his Buddhist writings had been mostly biographical or translations. Gary Snyder encouraged him to write an original sutra — an aphoristic doctrinal narrative traditionally regarded as a discourse of the Buddha — and the result was The Scripture of the Golden Eternity. Kerouac wrote it in Locke McCorkle's shack in Mill Valley, and for once he went back over his prose carefully, making many emendations and burnishing the writing to a fine sheen. "It was a scripture," he explained. "I had no right to be spontaneous." In the tradition of Pascal's Pensees, one of his favorite books, Golden Eternity was a collection of Buddhist-cum-Beat epigrams, such as, "Cats yawn because they realize that there's nothing to do," and "We're waiting for the realization that this is the golden eternity." In Kerouac's world, all is emptiness, but emptiness is the pure thought of God. "God is not outside us but is just us," he wrote, echoing the Biblical insight, "The kingdom of God is within." With lines like, "The world is nothing but a dream and is just thought of and the everlasting eternity pays no attention to it," Kerouac's sutra shimmers with intimations of cosmic peace and well-being.

When Gary Snyder departed for Japan, Kerouac, Robert Creeley, and a few other friends gave him a farewell party on May 15, 1956, at Stinson Beach, and everyone dashed into the surf.[45] With Snyder's departure, Kerouac lost a brilliant friend but gained another in Creeley, who moved into Marin-An as his roommate. In a letter to Holmes, Kerouac described Creeley as a darkly handsome man with a black eyepatch. According to Ginsberg, Creeley's 1952 volume of verse, Le Fou, and numerous subsequent collections made him "the leading representative of postmodernist poetry in the U.S.A." Creeley had been a teacher at Black Mountain College in North Carolina and editor of the Black Mountain Review. When the college closed from lack of funds, he drifted to San Francisco, where Ginsberg introduced him to Kerouac. Creeley appointed Ginsberg contributing editor for the spring 1957 issue of Black Mountain Review, and Ginsberg selected Kerouac's "October in the Railroad Earth," excerpts from Burroughs's Naked Lunch, and his own poem, "America."

Creeley later recalled that Kerouac's voice was "soft, bemusing, in no way self-assertive. Gentle . . . without any intent to be so." The day Snyder left, Kerouac and Creeley went to a bar called the Cellar, and after they'd had a few drinks it became disturbingly obvious to Jack that Creeley was cracking up. They were sitting in front of the bandstand, where Tommy Flannigan was playing with a trio, when suddenly Creeley started banging on the table with his beer bottle. They assumed they were "classically with it," Creeley recalled, but the bouncer, a man named Trent, Dylan Thomas's former bodyguard, thought otherwise. After Trent ordered them to leave, Kerouac tried to maneuver the fractious Creeley past the bouncer, but Trent landed a blow that sent an eye tooth through Creeley's lip, and blood streamed out.

Kerouac later told Holmes that he'd twice had to wrestle Creeley to the floor and shield his body to keep him from being beaten to death. After their expulsion from the Cellar, Kerouac took Creeley to the pension of some French Canadian friends who gave them ice, towels, and brandy for Creeley's pain. Finally, Kerouac deposited Creeley with a friend, Ann Hirshon, who lived in South San Francisco on the other side of the city from Marin County. Then Jack trudged back over the Golden Gate Bridge to Locke McCorkle's house, where he collapsed from exhaustion. Whatever Kerouac's faults, he did not abandon friends in trouble, and Creeley gratefully acknowledged his kindness and patience in the preface to the posthumously published Good Blonde.

Kerouac and Creeley were among the most attractive and available males on the Bay Area Beat scene, and they brought both glamour and chaos to the parties they attended in the week they lived together. They would stand at a corner of the dance floor, pounding on frying pans and double broilers while downing their drinks. As if Kerouac's relations with Rexroth were not already sour enough, Creeley started having an affair with Rexroth's wife, Marthe, and Jack allowed the lovers to use his cottage. After Kerouac's complicity in his cuckolding, Rexroth's hatred for Jack turned into a blazing obsession. Creeley's troubles continued to mount: He insulted a policeman and spent the weekend in the Bryant Street Jail. With Neal's help, Kerouac finally hustled Creeley out of San Francisco for his own good. While careening through North Beach, Neal kept telling Creeley that he was concerned for his welfare, and Creeley marveled that Neal could steer the car with so few glances at the road. Years later, what Creeley recalled was "how particular such friendships were."

When Marthe left Rexroth to live with Creeley, Rexroth had a nervous breakdown, and he somehow convinced himself that Kerouac and Cassady were the cause of his woes. When he recovered, he swore to destroy them both. Kerouac, who was much more of a literary politician than anyone had ever supposed prior to the publication of his letters in 1995, immediately appealed to Gary Snyder to intercede with Rexroth. Foreseeing that Rexroth would one day demolish him in the review press, Kerouac begged Snyder to explain to Rexroth that he'd only become involved with Creeley because Creeley was "flipping" and in need of protection. But Snyder had his own reputation to think of, and his agenda did not include cleaning up Kerouac's messes. More typical of Snyder's generous nature was the meditation bell he sent to Mémêre from Japan.[46]

Kerouac's *I Ching* advised him to feed people, so he threw his doors open to hoboes and drifters. As a result, a motley crew was often assembled in the hut, passionately arguing poetry and philosophy as Kerouac bent over the stove, frying tasty johnnycakes (yellow corn meal, chopped onions, salt, and water) or a meatless but hearty slumgullion (eggs and potatoes scrambled together), and brewing aromatic tea. Bob Donlin crashed in the cabin while recovering from a spree; looking rather like actor Robert Mitchum, Donlin appears in Peter Orlovsky's famous photo of Neal, Allen, Robert LaVigne, and Ferlinghetti standing in front of City Lights on a sunny day. At the cabin, when no one was around, Kerouac relaxed naked in the backyard and took sponge baths. Sometimes he cooked his supper naked while camping on Mount Tam. Another guest at Marin-An was poet Lew Welch, a future collaborator of Kerouac's who'd once been a roommate of Snyder's and Whalen's at Reed College. Creeley recalled that Lew Welch would often collect mussels for a quick lunch.

Kerouac's *Old Angel Midnight*, later famous for its mysterious and resonant opening phrase, "Friday afternoon in the universe," came about when Jack started doodling in the cabin one day; the doodle turned into a long exercise in automatic writing. One of his most inaccessible pieces, it makes large demands on the reader: Kerouac's purpose was nothing less than to capture the sound of the cosmos. Arthur C. Clarke, Carl Sagan, and Stanley Kubrick would later turn to Vangelis and Strauss when trying to simulate the elusive music of the spheres, but to Kerouac (as to Emily Dickinson, who wrote, "I heard a fly buzz—when I died") the cosmos sounded pretty much the same as one's backyard: "cats wailing in the wail-bar wildbar wartfence moonlight midnight Angel Dolophine immensity." McClure later defined *Old Angel Midnight* as Kerouac's rhapsody on the dynamics of memory, dreams, and consciousness. Comparing the text with a buccaneer's treasure trove, McClure wrote that he could sit for hours "running the fingers of my mind through the shining doubloons and emeralds and pull out a crusty necklace of pearls and precious stones draped with sea moss." According to John Sampas, Kerouac started *Old Angel Midnight* on May 28, 1956, and originally considered the title *Sebastian Midnight*, then changed it to *Lucien Midnight*, and finally decided on *Old Angel Midnight*. "It represents Gerard, Sebastian, Neal," Sampas explained. "Jack was closer to Lucien than to Ginsberg or Burroughs. Jack was about the love between two guys." According to Dennis McNally, Jack changed the title from *Old Lucien Midnight* due to Lucien's objections. Lucien wrote Ginsberg that he found it disconcerting when friends mentioned him in their works and that included the dedication page, a reference to the fact that Ginsberg had listed Lucien among the dedicatees in *Howl and Other Poems*. Lucien's name was deleted from subsequent printings.[47]

Kerouac's rivalry with Ginsberg at last subsided to the point that he was calling Ginsberg a living saint. Kerouac took his new girl, a brunette from Berkeley, to visit Ginsberg, and she was outraged when Peter started massaging Allen while both men were naked. Jack's girl was a Marilyn Monroe–type who affected Marilyn's pucker and "ululululululululululating" wiggle, he wrote Holmes. He took her back to Mill Valley and tried to seduce her on the kitchen floor, but she interrupted him, asking what kind of car he owned. Under the impression that all published novelists were rich, she was disillusioned when she discovered he couldn't even drive, and she lost all interest in him. In May 1956, Jack again attended a reading of "Howl," this one at a small Berkeley theater where nude line drawings of Ginsberg and Orlovsky making love were tacked to the walls. Ann Charters, an English major at the University of California at the time, attended the reading with Orlovsky and later described Kerouac as looking "darkly intense." Situating himself near the stage, Kerouac noisily instructed Rexroth how to conduct the program, and no sooner had the crowd settled down than Kerouac passed the hat as usual and went out for wine. Later, he handed mash notes to Ginsberg as he recited his poem in a low, confident voice. The poet Richard Eberhart was present and later wrote up the event for the *New York Times Book Review*. Published the following September, the article singled out Ginsberg as the leader of a revolutionary literary movement. When West Coast poets such as Rexroth, Duncan, and McClure saw the piece, they felt neglected, and a new rivalry began to fractionalize the budding San Francisco Poetry Renaissance.

In June 1956, it was time for Kerouac to begin his firewatcher job in the northwestern wilderness, but he still hadn't received Cowley's editing suggestions for *On the Road*. He fired off an angry postcard threatening to withdraw the novel if he hadn't received a contract by October 1.[48] With their corporate armor and legal resources, publishers are notoriously indifferent to threats from indigent authors, and Viking ignored the postcard. Without a regular full-time editor, Kerouac was constantly falling between the cracks at Viking. Neither Keith Jennison, an acquisitions editor, nor Cowley, a consultant, fulfilled the role of a "working" or "line" editor, and Kerouac became an orphan at Viking. But there were compensations, as time would prove. In Cowley, one of America's best known men of letters, Kerouac had an advocate who wielded more power in the literary world than more professional editors could ever hope for.

PART THREE

SUCCESS, LOVE, MARRIAGE, MADNESS

SEVEN

STARVATION RIDGE

On June 18, 1956, Kerouac hitchhiked up the coast to Desolation Peak, passing through some of America's most spectacular scenery: the Redwood Forest and the beginning of the Cascade range in Oregon. Arriving at the port of Seattle, he beheld the capital of the great American Northwest, which he later praised in *The Dharma Bums*, thus adding another town to the Beat map. Seattle was all that Gary Snyder had promised it would be: "wet, immense, timbered, mountainous, cold, exhilarating, challenging."

After shopping for warm clothes in Goodwill stores, Kerouac went out to Highway 99, a few miles from Seattle, and caught a series of short rides. Highways 1-G and 17-A took him into the vast mountain country, finally dead-ending at Diablo Dam. From then on, it was dirt roads, and his rides came from loggers, uranium prospectors, and farmers. Even out here, there was an occasional grocery store or bar, though the bartender in one old tavern was so feeble he could hardly draw Jack's beer. "I'd rather die in a glacial cave," Jack thought, "than in an eternity afternoon room of dust like this." Finally, he reached the last town in the Skagit valley, Sedro-Woolley, and followed narrow roads along rivers and cliffs. His last ride came from a drunken wrangler with sideburns, who skidded to a stop at the Marblemount Ranger Station.

For the next week, at fire school, Kerouac wore a tin hat and learned fire-watching with a group of young men, digging fire lines and dousing flames. With forty-five dollars' worth of groceries purchased on credit in Marblemount, he headed for his fire station, traveling first by truck, then on a giant Pittsburgh-type lift that hoisted him up to the level of Diablo Lake, and then by boat. A mule skinner brought Jack's pack mules along a gorge trail that had been blazed during a gold rush in the nineteenth century. At Ross Dam, Kerouac took a forest service float further into the wilds, and finally an assistant forest ranger joined him and the mule skinner for the horseback ride amidst a downpour to Desolation Peak. All the while, the mule skinner offered advice on how to endure the coming months of solitude. Evidently it was all right to talk to yourself, as long as you didn't answer back. At five thousand feet, they left the steep rocky trails and entered a mountain meadow. They rode on through fog and swirling mists, and at sixty-six hundred feet, in a hailstorm, Kerouac got off his horse and led it the rest of the way. Finally, he saw his cabin nestled among firs, flowers, and patches of snow on a ledge called Starvation Ridge.[1]

Inside the ten-by-ten-foot cabin, the floor was covered with dirt and rat excrement, and the windows were completely blackened by grime. Nevertheless, Kerouac was relieved to discover that the cabin was secure and solidly built, with steel rods rooted deep in concrete. The mule skinner and the ranger helped him set up his station and get his radio going, and the next morning they said goodbye and vanished into fog and snow. Alone on the side of the mountain, Kerouac could see nothing but blowing fog, and he set about cleaning the hut. That night, he went outside to meditate and saw the evening star over Canada. In the middle of the night, he suddenly woke up and thought he saw a monster like the Abominable Snowman at the window, but it was Mount Hozomeen, far away in Canada. The foggy clouds had parted at last, and it looked like van Gogh's *Starry Night* outside, with the aurora borealis sending streamers of light into the night sky.

The next morning, Jack walked out into an alpine paradise of blue sky and endless vistas of lake and timber. Down below, the boats in Lake Ross were too small to see, but he could make out their trails in the water. Suddenly, it felt good to be alone, with nothing to do but rest and eat, and no one to please but himself. His drinking water came from a snowfield in back of the hut, and he only required a bucketful of snow per day. He danced and sang in the open air and had rarely felt so happy. As in Snyder's cabin or Jack's fleabag hotel room, housekeeping chores were performed as if they were holy rituals, which had the effect of transforming drudgery into joy. He baked muffins and made a stew, and his pea-and-bacon soup was scrumptious. He made raspberry Jell-O and kept it in a jar in the snowfield. He brought in a bouquet of wildflowers. He rolled his own cigarettes, often while looking down at clouds a thousand feet below.

Midday was often hot and airless, with plagues of insects, but he welcomed them as his only living companions. Nights were cool, and the lake below was "moon-laned." Sometimes, meditating in the woods, it was so still that when Jack made a slight motion in the grass, he could hear the hooves of deers running away in the distance. During one meditation, he thought he heard Avalokitesvara the Hearer and Answerer of Prayer say to him that he would shortly be given the means to show his generation how completely free they were. When he opened his eyes, he saw a shooting star and said, "Okay, world, I'll love ya." The books inspired by his mountain solitude, *The Dharma Bums* and *Desolation Angels*, were the products of that love.

The sole requirements of his job were to scan the horizon for smoke, operate a two-way radio, clean the hut, and occasionally go outside with his earmuff hat on to chop wood. (Years later, when John Montgomery made the climb to Starvation Ridge, an old ranger who still remembered Kerouac complained that he turned off his radio so he could write without interruption.) August rolled in like thunder, and in *The Dharma Bums*, Kerouac's style rose majestically to the occasion: "Mad raging sunsets poured in seafoams of cloud through unimaginable crags." Snowstorms battered the cabin, but it stood firm. Thunder in the mountains reminded him somehow of Mémère's all-encompassing love. On the mountain, he recovered his health and looked young and vital again; his hair grew long, his eyes seemed a purer blue, and his skin had a healthy, ruddy tan. He had brought along no alcohol, and he may have suffered withdrawal symptoms, but it is impossible to know for sure, as he wrote no letters during this time. No mention is made of D.T.'s in the fire-watching sections of *The Dharma Bums* and *Desolation Angels*, but certainly something prevented the fundamental life change he sought in the mountain. In his wilderness isolation, he learned nothing, except that in sixty-three days a grown man leaves a pile of excrement approximately the height and size of an infant. Alan Watts, it seemed, was right: the point of life was to meet as many people as possible. Spiritual awakenings probably occur more often through selfless service on the streets of Calcutta than in self-centered solitude on Desolation Peak. On Kerouac's sixty-third day on the mountain, he contemplated his column of feces for the last time. With the autumn rains, the season abruptly ended, and a voice on the radio ordered all the lookouts to come down from their perches.

At least he'd detoxed. In his mountain meditations, he'd reconnected with his spirit and realized, "I am God," not in an egotistical sense, but in the same spirit as the biblical injunction, "Be still and know that I am God." But faith without service, he soon discovered, was no defense against alcoholism. In early September, he resumed a life that was as self-absorbed as before, making a beeline for the first bar he came to. Some observers thought he'd become unhinged by too much isolation. An old-timer told John Montgomery in 1991 that Kerouac "babbled to himself after he returned to Marblemount briefly after the fire season."[2] From Seattle, Kerouac took a bus to San Francisco and arrived on a Sunday via the Oakland-Bay Bridge, feeling a renewed love for the city and for civilization generally.

After checking into the Bell Hotel, he went in search of drinking buddies at the Place and the Cellar, at last running into poet Bob Kaufman, whom he'd later portray as "Chuck Berman" in *Desolation Angels*. Kaufman was a black man who'd once barged into a party, grabbed Jack away from Neal, and started dancing with him to a Chet Baker record. Jack later wrote of the "perfect grace of his dancing . . . like Joe Louis." Kaufman struck Kerouac as the perfect prototype of the new Beat hero: weary, defeated, resigned, and gloriously cool. Kaufman wrote jazz poems like "Round About Midnight," inspired by Thelonious Monk, that dealt with funky, tender lovers with melancholy voices and tentative smiles. Born in New Orleans in 1925, Kaufman was one of thirteen children born to a German Jewish father and a black Roman Catholic mother from Martinique. In 1954 Kaufman went to San Francisco, where he lived openly with a white woman. Poet Mona Lisa Saloy later wrote in *Beat Culture*, "Bob Kaufman used jazz music as a creative vehicle, reading to standing-room-only crowds in San Francisco's North Beach clubs as early as 1953. . . . Charlie Parker and Billie Holiday . . . often visited his apartment after gigs . . . Kaufman coined the word 'beatnik' — not Herb Caen of the *San Francisco Chronicle*." It seems unlikely, however, that *beatnik* could have been coined before October 4, 1957, when the Soviet Union announced that it had successfully launched *Sputnik*, the first artificial satellite to orbit the earth. Beat detractors seized on the suffix *nik*, which had not been previously used in English, to give the Beat Generation a pejorative, un-American connotation.[3]

The North Beach scene to which Kerouac returned from Desolation Peak showed the effects of the sensational Six Gallery reading. San Francisco was celebrating poets and poetry in a way the world hadn't seen since the heyday of Lord Byron. Ginsberg was the man of the hour, having returned from the Arctic Circle where he'd worked aboard the USNS *Sgt. Jack J. Pendleton* delivering material to refurbish the distant-early-warning-line radar system. When *Howl* was published in 1956, hip young people walked down the street holding the stark black-and-white City Lights paperback edition in front of their faces, unable to tear their eyes away from it. "The poem has created a furor of praise or abuse whenever read or heard," Richard Eberhart wrote in the *New York Times Magazine*.

Poetry readings became the fashionable place to be seen in San Francisco. "I saw Kerouac read at the Bagel Shop, up the hill from City Lights," Ed Crusoe, a merchant seaman, recalled. "That was the origin of the bohemian coffeehouse movement. Somebody was beating on bongo drums that day — maybe Kerouac. North Beach at the time was full of burnt-out Korean War veterans, and some World War II vets, drunk on wine, making do on pensions." Kerouac stayed with Ginsberg and Orlovsky in a Potrero Hill housing project, and Corso was living with a Frenchwoman in North Beach and planning a poetry reading for later in the fall. Kerouac was no longer angry at Corso for making love to Alene because he now realized that he'd wanted to get rid of her anyway.

With Ginsberg, Kerouac, and Corso now all on the West Coast, their combined energy soon attracted the attention of sharp-eyed Manhattan trend-spotters and fashion-setters. Though impoverished poets represented the polar opposite of the then-current American model of success, *Mademoiselle* magazine, anxious to keep its audience of educated young women abreast of the latest cultural developments, dispatched a photographer to the coast to pose

Kerouac and his friends for a spread on "Flaming Cool Youth of San Francisco Poetry." Kerouac wore a large silver crucifix that Corso lent him, but *Mademoiselle* airbrushed the crucifix out of the picture, finding it blasphemous. Published the following February, the article presented an alluring picture of San Francisco's North Beach as the subterranean mecca, with nightclubs like the hungry i and the Purple Onion, coffeehouses, and low rents. But Kerouac soon observed dissension and rivalry among the "desolation angels," as he called the San Francisco poets. Two of them, McClure and Duncan, had refused to be photographed with the others, deciding they'd pursue their artistic destinies independent of the movement. Ginsberg tried to form a united front now that a coalition had been forged between East Coast and West Coast Beats, but Kerouac too opted out, writing in *Desolation Angels* that he wanted to go his "own way." Ginsberg would have to wait until the sixties to stage his revolution with the help of the even more disaffected baby boomers.[4]

After a week among the disputatious San Francisco poets, Kerouac left the city and visited briefly with the Cassadys in Los Gatos. Carolyn found him to be lost and morose, and she no longer wanted to make love with him. He confided that living alone on Desolation Peak had been a mistake; he'd almost lost his mind from isolation and ennui, and he'd never again go into seclusion. Discovering this fact about himself laid waste to his dream of achieving Buddhist self-containment, and he threw himself into partying in San Francisco. On his next visit to Los Gatos, he appeared "worn out" to Carolyn. Jack brought Corso along, but Neal and Corso didn't like each other, and Corso poked fun at Neal's veneration of TV revivalist Oral Roberts.

None of the Beats seemed to grasp that spirituality is a matter of action, not something gleaned from books or preachers or visions but rather found in the thick of life where needy people are crying for help. That is why truly spiritual people like Albert Schweitzer and Mother Teresa claimed to have been helped by the lepers and dying people they worked among. They knew that only to those who give is happiness given. Though Kerouac's art was a transcendent creation and an enduring gift to the world, it did not afford him an opportunity to connect with people on the direct level where love and mutual help are transmitted. He was locked in selfhood, and it became his prison.

In the fall of 1956, Kerouac mapped out his future in a letter to John Montgomery; his immediate plan was to go to Mexico City, where he seemed to do his best writing. He intended to use the journal he had kept on the mountain as the basis for a major novel, *Desolation Angels*, which would portray the core Beat group—Ginsberg, Cassady, Corso, and the Orlovsky brothers, Peter and Lafcadio—and trace their recent travels and adventures. Afterward, he would spend Christmas in Orlando, Florida, where Nin and her family had moved, and then he would travel abroad with Ginsberg to Paris and probably Africa, since Burroughs had told him that Tangier was *"the place."* Then, his wanderlust presumably sated, he'd make northern

California his permanent home, settling in a hut in Marin County for the remainder of his days.[5]

In September or October, Kerouac set out again for Mexico City. By now a seasoned bindlestiff, he jumped on the Zipper and rode it as far as Los Angeles. Later, while trying to sleep near a highway in Arizona, he was hassled by the police. He would write in "The Vanishing American Hobo," "I myself was a hobo but I had to give it up around 1956 because . . . I was surrounded by three squad cars in Tucson at 2 AM." At last arriving in Mexico City, he once again rented the rooftop adobe on Orizaba Street, where he wrote *Desolation Angels*, a meditative account of mountain solitude followed by a gossipy narrative of the San Francisco Poetry Renaissance. To relax after writing, he would stroll down bawdy Panama Street where beautiful Mexican prostitutes were available for forty-eight cents. When he had sex with them, he made them purchase and use something he called Sanitubes in a letter to Montgomery. He went back on all kinds of dope, usually morphine and whatever else Garver had in his room, and briefly saw Esperanza again, but she had drugged herself to the limit and was "completely gone," he wrote Sterling.

After finishing *Tristessa*, Kerouac found that he had pretty much used up all of his material as a writer, and in *Desolation Angels* he was writing about what had happened to him only a month before. On his Mexico City rooftop, he turned again to painting, using housepaint mixed with glue. He finished a portrait of Gerard and one of God, and announced that he would be a first-rate painter within a few years. In 1995, his paintings were hung in the Whitney Museum as part of a Beat retrospective, no doubt primarily because of his literary fame, but they were substantial enough to rate full-length book treatment, with color reproductions. New York University art professor Ed Adler's study of Kerouac as an abstract expressionist has been scheduled for publication by Viking.

Kerouac made some radical decisions regarding publishers in 1956, instructing Sterling on October 7 to withdraw *On the Road* from Viking. Cowley had failed to meet the deadline Kerouac had set for a contract, and Jack told Sterling to sell the book as a paperback original since he no longer cared about getting reviewed by what he referred to as the "fags" at the *New York Times*. Paradoxically, his homophobia was increasing in direct proportion to his homoerotic activity. Though Kerouac was having sex with boys in Mexico City, he lied about it in *Desolation Angels*, writing that he was "a non-queer" but that "60% or 70% of our best writers (if not 90%) are queers." Despite having made important artistic breakthroughs, he was no closer than ever to a personal one, and in denying his true nature, he was denying the most basic aspect of life. Mailer's "The White Negro" expressed the same deep-seated homophobia and misogyny, even to the extent of disdaining femininity as a weakness. The most uncool thing any hipster could do, Mailer wrote, was to "lose your control, reveal the buried weaker more feminine part of your nature." Such assumptions were completely typical of the fifties, when sexism and racism were rampant and often bore the stamp of social and political sanction.[6]

In October, the new *Evergreen Review* offered to publish *The Subterraneans*, paying a penny a word. Kerouac accepted, instructing Sterling to advise the editor, Donald Allen, that if they'd pay him one cent a word for every word he'd ever written, he'd be a multimillionaire. In a postscript, he decided to leave *On the Road* with Viking after all; he didn't want to be rude to Malcolm Cowley, who had proved to be a professional genie and a cozy friend. As the architect of Kerouac's career, Cowley was building Jack's reputation as a serious writer brick by brick, using his literary contacts to place Kerouac's writing in the nation's most prestigious quarterlies. Kerouac realized that such exposure could net him book offers from all over the world.[7]

Ginsberg, Orlovsky, Corso, and Orlovsky's teenage brother, Lafcadio, all came to visit Kerouac in Mexico City in November, taking an apartment downstairs at Orizaba Street. Lafcadio, who rarely spoke, reminded Jack of Gerard. Though Peter was said to be straight, he had fallen in love with Ginsberg's brilliant mind and was willing to do anything Ginsberg asked. Ironically, Peter had been shy and virginal as a heterosexual and afraid to approach the opposite sex, but now he enjoyed frequent intercourse with women, thanks to Ginsberg's skill as a sexual catalyst. In a letter to Robert LaVigne, Ginsberg described how he and the twenty-three-year-old Peter sometimes had three-way sex: Allen would "screw dog" a girl as she knelt and performed fellatio on Orlovsky; then they would switch positions and eventually just play around, obsessing on each other's "cocks and cunts."

In 1989, after interviewing Ginsberg, Barry Miles revealed that Kerouac, Ginsberg, and Peter Orlovsky went home with some Mexican boys, played spin the bottle, got undressed, and all had sex together. They also made it with some of the more shapely girls on Panama Street, Kerouac told Montgomery. Jack introduced Ginsberg and Corso to Esperanza, but she struck them as just another hopeless, emaciated junkie. Corso was appalled by the poverty of Mexico and wanted to escape as quickly as possible.

At one point, the three Beat leaders sat down for what amounted to a summit conference. Having brought their ideas to a degree of public notice in San Francisco, they considered their next move, and everyone agreed that it was time to become expatriates and carry the Beat movement abroad. Burroughs continued to promote Tangier, inviting both Kerouac and Ginsberg to stay with him at the Villa Mouneria. They all agreed to rendezvous in North Africa in early 1957, but Ginsberg convinced Kerouac to return to New York first, because Ginsberg felt certain that Kerouac was about to "get published, meet everybody, make money, become a big international traveling author, sign autographs for old ladies in Ozone Park." And in Orlando, Florida, he might have added, for Mémère was now living with Nin and her family at 1219 Yates Avenue in Orlando, future home of Disney World.[8]

Kerouac and his friends packed themselves into an expense-share car with two other people, strapped their rucksacks and a bicycle to the top, and drove to New York. Near San Antonio, Texas, the exhausted travelers stopped to rest. Kerouac climbed out and spread his sleeping bag on a dry river bottom. A simpatico buddy slithered in with him and they spooned the night away, oblivious to the subfreezing weather. Later, in West Virginia, Jack took over the wheel and at last taught himself how to handle a car. In Manhattan, the driver stopped and let them out in Greenwich Village, where the Beat scene was at its still-authentic, 1956–1957 prefame peak. Kerouac soon accumulated various girlfriends, but his life also took another distinctly homoerotic turn, and again the two sides of his nature were at war with each other. Intriguingly gaunt, almost haggard at 155 pounds, and hollow-eyed from the privations of poverty and homelessness, he noticed that both women and men in New York looked at him the way men gawk at strippers: mesmerized, hungry, spellbound.

Helen Weaver became his mistress. Dark-haired and attractive, she was the roommate of Lucien's former girlfriend, Helen Elliott, and the two Helens lived across the street from the White Horse Tavern on Hudson Street in a quaint old brick building that Jack though of as Dickensian. Kerouac and Weaver could not have been more simpatico; she had majored in English literature at Oberlin and wanted to be a writer herself. Fluent in French, she would later become a professional translator. In *Desolation Angels*, Jack wrote that they made love the first time on the floor of her bedroom, as Jack, recreating the Marlon Brando/Eva-Marie Saint scene in *On the Waterfront*, kissed her "down to the floor, like a foe. . . . We ate each other and plowed each other hungrily." In an interview forty years later, Weaver still spoke of Kerouac in a warm, affectionate voice and defined their lovemaking as classic heterosexual, male-dominant coupling, adding, "Oh, yes," for emphasis. In 1995, John Sampas revealed that Jack was seeing Helen Weaver, Joyce Johnson, and Dody Muller around the same time. Kerouac's sex list showed that he had sex with Weaver twenty-five times. Johnson later wrote in a memoir that both Weaver and Helen Elliott were "tall and boyish," and portrayed them as heavily psychoanalyzed party girls, who kept their apartment full of beer and men and liked to show off their long legs and to dance to Frank Sinatra and Elvis Presley. According to Kerouac, he gave Weaver her "first *extase*," and she let him move in. She had a job, so in some respects it was a perfect setup; he typed up *Tristessa* and *Desolation Angels*, flirted with Elliott while Weaver was away, and enjoyed candlelight dinners with both girls every evening.[9]

Elsewhere in the Village, Richard Howard, who would later win the Pulitzer Prize for poetry, put up Ginsberg, Corso, and the Orlovsky brothers. "They had the place to themselves because I was spending my nights with Sandy Friedman over on Bleecker Street," Howard explained in a 1995 interview. "Allen was putting together *Naked Lunch* on the floor—a loose typescript that he was composing, trying to make some kind of book out of it. They all hung around the apartment about a week. I was writing dictionaries for a living over on Twenty-third Street at Funk & Wagnalls. I had to come home to get something one day. When I walked in, they were all just getting up, in various stages of disrepair. Gregory was rising from one of the little foam-rubber beds. He was not ever in my estimation a very attractive person, but he stretched his bare-chested, chicken-breasted nudity and asked, 'You like Gregory's body?' "[10]

A tireless promoter of Beat writers, Ginsberg paid visits to magazine, newspaper, and book editors, using his expertise as a former San Francisco advertising executive to pitch the Beat Generation as a revolutionary lifestyle and literary movement. On little but chutzpah, hype, and *cojones*, he succeeded in convincing the *Village Voice* that the Beats were news, and the editors scheduled interviews with Kerouac, Ginsberg, and Corso.

While living in Helen Weaver's apartment, Kerouac wrote five hours daily, from midafternoon until dinner, content at last to be in a situation free from financial worries. But, never adept at tolerating sexual pressure, he frequently disappeared to go on long binges with Lucien. Kerouac had never gotten over his fixation with Lucien. In *Desolation Angels*, in which Lucien appears as "Julien," he wrote, "I had once seen a photo of Julien when he was 14, in his mother's house, and was amazed that any person could be so beautiful. Blond, with an actual halo of light around his hair, strong hard features, those Oriental eyes—I'd thought 'Shit would *I* have liked Julien when he was 14 looking like that?' but no sooner I tell his sister what a great picture it was she hid it . . . The little boy too beautiful for the world but finally saved by a wife." Just as Kerouac had been the third member of the Cassady marriage in California, he now became a regular in Lucien's household; however, in *Desolation Angels* he represented Lucien, as Julien, as saying, "If I catch you making any pass at Nessa I'll kill you."[11]

Meanwhile, Cowley continued to edit *On the Road*, and he asked Jack to consolidate some of the trips described in the book and to eliminate others in order to provide "more of a continuous narrative." He also said that the book should have less swinging "back and forth between East Coast and West Coast like a huge pendulum." On one occasion, Jack was two hours late for an appointment, finally showing up at Viking high on a pint of liquor. Helen Weaver recalled that he was typing *Desolation Angels* and *Tristessa* while also carrying out *On the Road* revisions. According to Cowley, "he revised, and revised well." Yet Kerouac complained to me in the following decade that Cowley "tried to ruin" *On the Road*, although he did not say that Cowley ever succeeded in actually doing so or in damaging the book in any way. I gathered that Kerouac agreed to many of Cowley's suggestions, but never incorporated them into the manuscript. Many authors do this on the assumption that editors won't have the time to read through the manuscript again.

The publication of Kerouac's letters offered fresh evidence that there was not as much difference between the original scroll and the published version of *On the Road* as previously thought, and that Kerouac succeeded in tricking Cowley into thinking that he had made extensive structural revisions when actually he had not. In Kerouac's June 23, 1957, letter to John Clellon

Holmes, he wrote that the bound book of On the Road was identical to the scroll. Then he confided his "secret," revealing that Viking was under the false impression that he had spent the past five years extensively rewriting the manuscript. On the contrary, he told Holmes, the bound book was the "shining original." In 1986, Kerouac scholar Dave Moore compared the first few pages of the Viking bound book with the scroll, and found only name changes and some minor textual adjustments that were made not as a result of Cowley's editing, but during Jack's retyping of the manuscript. According to Holmes, much of the material on terminal destinations such as New York and San Francisco was deleted by Kerouac, before Cowley's editing, because Kerouac felt the city adventures detracted from the more fascinating road experiences. Kerouac discussed Viking's handling of On the Road in Desolation Angels, writing, "They advanced me $1000 payable at $100 a month installments and the editors (without my knowledge) bent their wrenny heads over my faultless prose and prepared the book for publication with a million faux pas of human ogreishness." My own feeling, from all Kerouac said to me about the handling of On the Road, was that he effectively resisted Cowley's editing, only to be ambushed later by Viking's copy department. Unless given instructions to the contrary, copy editors routinely standardize all punctuation, grammar, and syntax, following house style, which is exactly what most writers need. But again, Dave Moore's investigative work is revealing: he discovered no substantial differences in style and punctuation between the scroll and the Viking bound book, and concluded, "The book as we have it today preserves the freshness and vitality of Kerouac's original high-speed outpouring of 35 years ago."[12]

On the Road was at last accepted by Viking the week before Christmas 1956, and announced for fall 1957 publication. Kerouac mentioned in a letter to Holmes that the publisher was sending him all over Manhattan to secure even more libel releases. Cowley's crucial "acceptance report" stated that On the Road was "a narrative based on fact, but with names and events sufficiently disguised to call it a novel." Kerouac was the spokesman for "a new age," and On the Road would "stand for a long time" as the classic of postwar bohemian life, Cowley predicted. He had attempted in editing the manuscript to correct "the two problems of libel and obscenity." Not until March 1, 1957, would a Viking interoffice memo headed "Kerouac's On the Road—The Libel Reading" advise that the novel was "clean now."[13]

As Christmas 1956 approached, Kerouac and Ginsberg jointly wrote Carolyn. They boasted that Kerouac was living in spacious, sunny splendor amid Chinese mattings, Picasso prints, a hi-fi, and large cats, but complained that Jack's sexy mistress and benefactor was altogether too clinging and possessive. As his affair with Helen fell apart, he retreated to Lucien's apartment; he also participated in an orgy with Diane DiPrima, a petite, bosomy, red-haired, twenty-two-year-old poet, and the two gay men with whom she was staying. A second-generation Italian from Brooklyn, DiPrima published her first book of poems, This Kind of Bird Flies Backwards, the following year. In "Three Laments," she described herself as a cool Beat chick whose philosophy was to go with the flow of experience and swing with whatever was swinging. In another poem, the powerful "Brass Furnace Going Out: Song, After an Abortion," she chastised her lover for walking out on her at the first sign of trouble. When DiPrima met Kerouac, she had recently dropped out of Swarthmore College, and had discovered "Howl," reading it to all her friends. When she learned that Ginsberg and Kerouac were back in town, she sent Ginsberg a sheaf of poems and invited him to visit her in Soho. Ginsberg was amused by her verses, and took Kerouac and Orlovsky along when he called on DiPrima at a barnlike third-floor loft on Prince Street, bringing jugs of wine and killer grass and hashish. Leslie, one of DiPrima's male friends, was a ballet dancer, "beautiful and sad and fragile and gay," in DiPrima's description. After passing around a joint, Jack treated them to a lengthy, silver-tongued disquisition on poetry and art. Then he grabbed DiPrima's manuscripts "and proceeded to uncorrect the poems," she recalled, "rolling the original bumpy lines off his tongue, making the stops and awkwardness beautiful."

DiPrima noticed that Ginsberg, her idol, was attracted to Leslie, and she suggested they spend the night. Ginsberg and Orlovsky immediately shoved the couch all the way to the back room, placed it next to the bed, arranged the potted plants in a circle, and lighted some Indian incense, creating a sensuous space, like a clearing in a rain forest. Leslie placed candles next to the bed and turned off the overhead light. Although DiPrima enjoyed fondling "the cocks with which I found myself surrounded," she was having her period and felt embarrassed by the "Tampax sticking out of my cunt." Leading with his head, the way he'd once played football, Jack massaged her breasts with his face and the top of his head, while Ginsberg delivered an erudite discourse on menstruation, pointing out that animals in estrus always bleed a bit, providing surplus lubrication and heightened kicks due to an alteration of hormones. It sounded wonderful, and to the cheers of all, DiPrima dislodged her Tampax and heaved it across the loft. "Jack began by gallantly going down on me to prove that he didn't mind a little blood," she remembered, and then he made love to her forcefully as she "squirmed down on his cock, getting it all inside of me, feeling good and full." In her estimation, unlike Adele Mailer's, Kerouac was "a long, slow, easy fuck." Ginsberg later remembered it as "a big all-night orgy." After Jack and Diane's simultaneous orgasm, Jack took a break and rolled a joint, sucking on it deeply and holding the smoke in his lungs as he passed it to Diane. As she toked, she took stock of the others, noting that Ginsberg was sprawled across the bed, and "Leslie was fucking him in the ass."

DiPrima's and Ginsberg's separate accounts of what happened that night offer striking contrasts. Claiming that Kerouac was hetereosexual, DiPrima wrote "Finding himself in a bed with three faggots and me, he wanted some pussy and decided he was going to get it." In Ginsberg's account, however, Kerouac's behavior was decidedly gay. "Jack Kerouac and Peter and I all got into bed with her and a couple of dancer friends she had," Ginsberg recalled, "she and Jack and me sucking the cock of this really pretty looking dancer boy." Their accounts also differed with regard to Orlovsky; Ginsberg included him in the action, but DiPrima wrote that after Orlovsky gave them all lingering kisses, he cut out.[14]

Despite these unrestrained forays into bisexuality and homoeroticism, Kerouac continued to go in for verbal gay bashing. In a letter to Cassady, he boasted that he had regained his clout in publishing circles, and urged Neal to send him a manuscript to submit to New York's "fairy editors." Though he disparaged them, he was counting on the same editors to pay him enough for a new Mercedes-Benz. He was not above accepting a stolen overcoat from his old friend Henri Cru. It was made of vicuna, like the one that rocked the Eisenhower administration the following year when Ike's assistant, Sherman Adams, accepted gifts from New England industrialist Bernard Goldfine. Though Jack's vicuna coat came to his ankles, he wore it to brunch at the St. Regis with Salvador Dali, who'd told Ginsberg at a gallery opening that he'd like to meet some of the current crop of younger poets. Dali's wife, Gala, thought Kerouac, Ginsberg, Orlovsky, and Corso too shabbily dressed to be entertained at the St. Regis, and invited them all to Sunday brunch later on at the Russian Tea Room. Dali sat studying Kerouac and finally said, "He is more beautiful than M. Brando." Kerouac later told me that he and Dali "frisked each other in the men's room" and that he also enjoyed a flirtation with Dali's wife.[15]

At Christmas, Jack went to Orlando to spend the 1956 holiday season with his family. He stopped en route in Washington, D.C., where Corso was houseguesting with poet Randall Jarrell, whom they'd earlier met at a dinner party given by Ruth Witt-Diamant in San Francisco. A forty-three-year-old air force veteran who had served in World War II, Jarrell emerged as a major poet in the postwar years, and his 1954 novel, *Pictures From an Institution*, satirized life in a women's college. After a trip to San Francisco, he became convinced that the Beats were reviving poetry as a relevant art form, and he invited Corso to the capital. Jack "had a ball," he wrote Ginsberg, and described Jarrell as large, courteous, and "sweet." He gave Jarrell his vicuna coat in exchange for Jarrell's more practical air force fur-collared leather jacket, and the generous Jarrell threw in a snazzy red sweater and a "sharp hep cap." Jack wrote *Washington DC Blues* in Jarrell's living room, while the distinguished poet and Corso went to visit a psychiatrist friend. Jarrell predicted that Kerouac would one day be wealthy, but in the meantime he generously offered to help Kerouac financially by recommending him for fellowships and writing grants. A decade later, in 1965, the kindly, fifty-one-year-old Jarrell committed suicide. Like Sylvia Plath, Theodore Roethke, and John Berryman, all of whom killed themselves, Jarrell was a victim of mental illness.[16]

Leaving Washington during the 1956 Christmas season, Kerouac took a bus to Florida. Drunk on half a bottle of Jack Daniels, he lost his manuscripts, including *Desolation Angels*, *Washington DC Blues*, and the second half of

Tristessa, as well as numerous paintings. As his whole life flashed before his eyes, he at last saw the connection between his drinking and the horrible things that were always happening to him, and he began to cry. Alcohol had now divested him of his manuscripts, the only "little tricks to make life livable" that he had left. He saw the faces of those who'd often been his only source of hope—Mémère, Lucien, Ginsberg, and Helen Weaver—but nothing could relieve his despair. Fortunately, he learned in Raleigh, North Carolina, that his rucksack had been found, with all his writings, and it was being shipped ahead to Orlando.

His good luck continued when he reached Nin's home. He received an uncharacteristically warm welcome from the Blakes, who had prepared a special room and arranged all his unpublished papers on his rolltop desk. Mémère was grateful to have been reprieved once again from the skiving machine, and was drawing on her social security and once more earning her keep as her daughter's housemaid, taking out the garbage, cooking meals, washing dishes, ironing, and running the vacuum cleaner. Though aging and weary, she was being used as a vassal, slaving "her ass off," as Kerouac had once described Mémère in her shoe-factory days.

Sterling had advanced forty dollars against the thousand-dollar advance for *On the Road*, and Jack bought presents for everyone at home. Christmas Eve found the Kerouacs and Blakes sprawled in front of the television, loaded on martinis. Mémère passed out during midnight mass from St. Patrick's. By New Year's Day 1957, she finally got around to preparing the traditional Yuletide turkey dinner. When Jack left Orlando shortly thereafter, he told Mémère that he would buy her a house if *On the Road* made money. "*Oui Jean*, I *do* want a lil home of my own," she said, but warned him that "bums" like Ginsberg, Carr, and Burroughs were out to destroy him. He took the train to New York and stayed again with Weaver, extolling her exquisitely smooth skin in a letter to Neal. He added that Allen was still in love with Neal and wanted to take the male dominant ("husband") position while making love to him. Kerouac felt the same way about Neal, he confessed.[17]

At last on January 11, 1957, Kerouac signed the contract for *On the Road*. Later, Ginsberg took him along with Corso and Orlovsky to meet William Carlos Williams in Rutherford, New Jersey, and Kerouac thought the seventy-two-year-old bard seemed bored. Williams later stated that Kerouac and his friends acted like "bums," smoking marijuana and drinking so much that his wife Flossie had to go to the wine cellar to restock the liquor cabinet. They all read their poems, and Williams preferred Orlovsky's. In 1957, Williams wrote to Theodore Roethke about "Karuak and Corso" and commented that Western civilization, with the advent of the Beats, had advanced to the stage of "anything goes," and he was all in favor of it. Even if they were bums, he respected the Beats' defiance of conventions.[18]

During the winter of 1956–1957, Kerouac alienated one girlfriend too many with his drinking and found himself on the street, shivering in a snowstorm. He went to Lucien's apartment in Sheridan Square, but they got into a drunken fight, and Jack later checked into the Marlton Hotel on Eighth Street, where he continued typing *Desolation Angels*. Ginsberg knew he was broke, and fixed him up with Joyce Johnson, who worked as an assistant at MCA. This was before her two marriages, and she was still Joyce Glassman. Her policy was "nothing-to-lose, try anything." After staking Kerouac to a meal, she let him move in. Conveniently, her Upper West Side apartment was not far from Jack's old watering hole, the West End Cafe.

"He lived like a homeless person for much of his life," Johnson recalled in 1995 at the annual Kerouac conference in Lowell. "He was a fragile, exhausted man who came up to New York for the experience of fame." They had sex the first night, and she later wrote that "he wasn't fierce but oddly brotherly." Her favorite memory of their affair was "lying with my head on his chest, his heart pulsing against my ear. His smooth hard powerful arms are around me, and I'm burying my face into them because I like them so much." But all too soon, she added, "Jack leaves me. He goes into the small back bedroom . . . pulls the window all the way up, closes the door, and lies down on the floor in his sleeping bag alone. . . . I didn't really mind, that was the strange part." She accepted the arrangement, but later wrote, "I hate Jack's woman-hatred."

One night he left her alone and went downtown to the White Horse Tavern in the West Village. Mailer was holding forth at the bar, "talking anarchy with a beer mug in his hand," Kerouac recalled. Though Mailer was top dog in rural Connecticut's well-heeled literary pack, he was promoting himself as a rebel, hoping to jump on the Beat bandwagon. "Kerouac thought that Norman was being an intellectual fool," Ginsberg said. "The whole point of *On the Road* . . . had to do with American tenderheartedness. . . . Kerouac's take on 'The White Negro' was that it was well-intentioned but poisonous, in the sense that it encouraged an image of violence." Adele Morales, who'd lived with Mailer since 1951 and had married him in April 1955, was pregnant that winter, but friends were alarmed at the couple's combativeness.

The women in Kerouac's life could be very assertive when his inconstancy pitted them against each other. According to Kerouac, Helen Weaver and Joyce Johnson fought over him in the White Horse. However, in Johnson's account, Jack was in Weaver's apartment, and Johnson gave him an ultimatum to meet her at the bar in fifteen minutes or their affair would be over. He chose to go with Johnson, at least for the present. She gave him plenty of lebensraum, not to mention hearty English-style breakfasts.

Joyce Johnson later described Kerouac in his thirty-fourth year as "beautiful. You're not supposed to say a man is beautiful, but he is." Deeply in love with him, she asked if she could accompany him to Tangier, but he refused. His plan was to go to North Africa early in 1957 and meet Burroughs and Ginsberg; then he would go on to Spain to write, and finally he would travel to Paris in the spring, where he hoped to meet Louis-Ferdinand Celine. Jack's ship, the Yugoslavian freighter *Slovenia*, docked at the Brooklyn Busch

Terminal in February 1957. Lucien and Cessa Carr, with their children Caleb and Simon, drove Jack and Joyce to the pier. He was to be one of only two passengers aboard the freighter and he would have a comfortable double stateroom, which he later described in a travel piece, "Big Trip to Europe." They partied in Jack's cabin, drinking the champagne Lucien had brought. The tweedy, horn-rimmed Lucien seemed to Joyce to be much older than his thirty-one years, and despite his punkish, uneven haircut, he struck her as a quaint anachronism, adrift in memories of the West End Cafe, the early forties, and Edie and Joan's apartment.

Lucien and his family left around dusk, but Jack asked Joyce to stay with him, as the ship wasn't sailing until the following day. It was a strange night. He woke up at 11 P.M. and insisted on going out for a drink. They ended up taking a subway into Manhattan, and he got drunk on bourbon at the West End. He kept talking about death, and he later represented Joyce, as Alyce Newman in *Desolation Angels*, as saying, "That's because you're sick from drinking too much." She advised him to "sleep it off man." The bartender was looking at him as if he were dead, Jack complained, and Joyce said, according to Jack, "Maybe you are." They spent the night in her apartment, and he had a nightmare in which all his friends were aboard an endless train to the graveyard. When he left her the next day, he promised they'd meet again.[19]

Kerouac's winter passage to Africa was rough and stormy. In Tangier, he settled in with Burroughs, who at forty-four looked amazingly hale and hearty considering his drug habit. They lived at No. 1 Calle Magallanes in the Spanish quarter, and Jack helped Bill type *Naked Lunch*. By 1957, Burroughs was trying his hand at Kerouac-style automatic writing, typing at high speeds for six hours at a stretch. But Kerouac was an even faster typist, and Burroughs kept feeding him chapters. Jack experienced a bad reaction to Burroughs's visceral imagery and had nightmares in which he pulled mile-long salamis out of his mouth. The whole point of writing *Naked Lunch*, Burroughs said, was "shitting out my educated Middlewest background for once and for all. It's a matter of catharsis where I say the most horrible thing I can think of."

After spending some time among Burroughs's Tangier friends, Kerouac dismissed them, in a letter to Joyce, as an "international hive of queens." Burroughs had been in Tangier since the early fifties, first at Anthony Reitshorst's famous male whorehouse at No. 1 Calle de los Arcos, not far from the Socco Chico, and then, since 1955, at the Villa Mouneria, where many of the tenants were female prostitutes. For a while, Burroughs had had sporadic sex with Kiki, a Spanish boy, but Kiki had run off with a Cuban bandleader, who'd later stabbed him to death for sleeping with members of his all-girl orchestra. When Burroughs wrote, he was always drugged on homemade *majoun*, a hashish candy that he cooked on a small spirit stove. A heady combination of chopped kif, honey, cinnamon, caraway seeds, and ground nutmeg, *majoun* helped him stay off hard drugs, which was probably the only reason that *Naked Lunch* was ever completed. Paul Bowles came to visit, later recalling, "There were hundreds of pages of yellow foolscap all over the floor . . . with heel prints on them, rat droppings, bits of old sandwiches, sardines. . . . As he finished a page, he'd just throw it on the floor." Burroughs, who was again taking an interest in women, confided to Ginsberg that he liked to look at "tits" and still became aroused every time he inspected "a cunt." Nevertheless, Burroughs kept a twenty-year-old male lover, whom he introduced to Kerouac in a gay bar. The young man had the same "sweet sad smile," Jack noted, that Burroughs's lovers always had.

As in Mexico City, Jack rented a rooftop room for twenty dollars a month, with a tile patio facing the vivid green waters of the bay. He had a view of tall, slender minarets rising gracefully from a clutter of mosques and flat Moroccan tenement roofs. It was chilly in Jack's room, and Burroughs bought him a kerosene stove in the medina as payment for his excellent typing. Burroughs lived on the main floor in a small, whitewashed, damp room that opened onto a garden. Paul Lund, a gangster from Birmingham, England, was a neighbor, and he often dropped in at 4 P.M. for cocktails. He regaled Burroughs and Kerouac with stories of holdups and jail sentences, which later appeared in both *Naked Lunch* and *Desolation Angels* (Jack changed Lund's name to "John Banks"). A firm believer that serious writers should cultivate eccentrics, Burroughs listened carefully, hoping to pick up colorful gangster slang, and he relished expressions such as, "There she is jugglin me sweetbreads with her tongue!"

Sometimes, Lund and Kerouac brought veiled, dark-eyed, three-dollar whores to Kerouac's room, where the girls shed their floor-length *jalabas* but stayed in their high heels. Kerouac and Lund "took turns with the trick-turners," Kerouac recalled, and in a letter to Neal he added that the whores did a lot of heavy breathing, either enjoying themselves or putting on a very good show. As a pothead, Kerouac was in paradise, writing to Neal that North Africa was ruled by "t-smokers."

At night, Burroughs brought his binoculars to Kerouac's rooftop apartment, and they enjoyed the harbor view, alight with brightly illuminated boats arriving from Casablanca. A beacon from the harbor strafed Kerouac's room at regular intervals. Burroughs told Jack he was looking forward to Ginsberg's arrival. Still in love with Ginsberg, Burroughs rested his head against Jack's shoulder and sobbed. "Grownup men," Kerouac huffed, had no business fooling around with "Vaseline and KY." Burroughs ridiculed Kerouac, calling him a "great bore," but at least "secondbest to *nothing*."

Jack roamed the medina in a cloud of self-administered toxins, all available at the local drugstore, including Sympatina for ups, Diosan for downs, and Soneryl for a complete knockout blow. In the medina, he dined in a Spanish restaurant on shrimp soup with noodles, pork in tomato sauce, bread, a fried egg, an orange, espresso, and wine — all for thirty-five cents. But Burroughs's drugs made him feel paranoid, and a big wad of Burroughs's home-brewed black opium plunged him into a thirty-six-hour funk. As he lay vomiting in his room and overhearing "the creaks of pederast love" from the apartment next door, he longed for the seclusion he'd known on Starvation Ridge. It wasn't the pederasty he objected to, but the fact that "the sweet smiling sad Latin boy went into my bathroom and laid a huge dung in the bidet." The opium that made Kerouac so ill had been cut with arsenic.[20]

Grove editor Don Allen sent him the galley proofs for *The Subterraneans*, which *Evergreen Review* was running in its entirety, as the first inside account of a Beat Generation love story. *Evergreen* was on the verge of becoming the No. 1 periodical of hip young Americans—a 1950s equivalent of *Rolling Stone*—and a one-shot serialization was a considerable coup. But Jack stopped it dead in its tracks. Don Allen had "pulled a Giroux," Jack fulminated in a letter to Holmes, charging that the editor had transformed his shaggy marathon sentences into "faggish" drivel. Don Allen's editing amounted to emasculation, he charged, and he ordered Sterling Lord to kill it unless *Evergreen* restored the text to its original form. *Evergreen* dropped *The Subterraneans* and substituted Jack's excellent "October in the Railroad Earth." Grove Press, owner of *Evergreen*, later recouped its losses by publishing *The Subterraneans* in book form in 1958, exactly as Jack had written it. Viking announced that *On the Road* would be published in the fall, and Jack started worrying about libel suits.

In late March 1957, Ginsberg and Orlovsky arrived in Tangier. Ginsberg photographed Jack on the beach; at thirty-five, Kerouac was again in top physical shape, with formidable biceps, flat washerboard abdominals, and powerful legs that showed no sign of boils, scars, or swelling from phlebitis. Predictably, Burroughs was jealous of Ginsberg's lover, Peter Orlovsky, and made condescending remarks, alienating Peter. Ginsberg considered Burroughs a great writer and priceless teacher, but the trip fell far short of Ginsberg's announced intention: he and Peter had come to Tangier, as Allen put it, "to fuck [Burroughs]—to exhaust his desires." Instead, Ginsberg collaborated with Burroughs on *Naked Lunch*, incorporating excerpts from Burroughs's letters to him from 1953–1956.

Ginsberg attracted a parade of hipsters to Villa Mouneria, but Kerouac didn't like the supercilious late fifties Beat style and ruefully reflected, "To think that I had so much to do with it, too, in fact at that very moment the manuscript of *Road* was being linotyped for imminent publication and I was already sick of the whole subject." Without Kerouac, the united front that Ginsberg had dreamed of fell to pieces, and by April, Kerouac was gone, on a boat to Marseilles. He loved Ginsberg and Burroughs too much to tell them the truth: "They bored me," he wrote in *Desolation Angels*, but so did "everything else." Boredom, a typical alcoholic complaint, is the sign of a totally selfish, self-centered existence. For years, Jack's life had been dominated by drugs, alcohol, sex, obsessive work, and physical and emotional violence, and he was completely burned out. The dreaded "notself" had come back to haunt him.

Leaving Burroughs's jaded African scene behind, Kerouac sought peace and quiet in the south of France. In Marseilles, early on a Sunday morning, he sat in a bar drinking hot coffee and felt as if he were back in Lowell's Little Canada, where the shops had the same names, such as *épicerie* and *boucherie*. He rode on a comfortable local bus to Aix-en-Provence, where he drank vermouth at a sidewalk café and gazed at the smoky blue hills in the distance, realizing how exact Cézanne's colors were. Then, in the Cathedral of St. Sauveur, he sat on his eighty-pound rucksack and wept, listening to the choirboys and wondering about all the babies that had been baptized in the sixth-century Romanesque stone baptistry, "all with eyes of lucid liquid diamond understanding." He trudged five miles looking for a ride, but as he later observed in *Lonesome Traveler*, hitchhiking was all but nonexistent in France because motorists had no room in their tiny compacts for extra passengers. He finally gave up at Eguilles and took a bus through the Arles region, where he looked out on "the restless afternoon trees of van Gogh." At Avignon, which seemed to rise from the dust of centuries, he felt the suffocating boredom of French provincialism and understood why Madame Bovary committed suicide. But he had no complaints about the cuisine or the prices; a five-course meal of vegetable soup, omelet, broiled hare, mashed potatoes, red wine, bread, and flan cost only $1.75.

He took the Paris Express, arriving at the Gare de Lyon at dawn. On first glimpsing the endless boulevards spoking out in all directions and bordered by majestic beaux-arts apartments, he thought, "Yes, they made themselves a *city!*" He hiked twenty miles each day and slept in dismal hotels run by Turkish pimps, rarely able to get a room for more than one night. But he feasted on onion soup, *pâté de maison*, and bread for twenty-five cents in Les Halles. On the Left Bank, he ran into Corso, who was writing erotica for the Olympia Press. Though Jack attracted plenty of young women in the sidewalk cafés in Place St. Germain, they called him a "jerk" the minute they discovered he "just wanted them to spread their legs," he recalled. He spent the night sleeping on the floor, listening to Corso make love to his French girlfriend. The following day, he left for London by train, forgetting to look up Louis-Ferdinand Celine, who lived in Meudon, a southwest suburb of Paris, and was still spouting anti-Semitic diatribes.

Seymour Wyse put Kerouac up in his flat in St. John's Wood in northwest London, though Kerouac also stayed at a hotel in Leicester Square. He wrote to Holmes that Seymour was disillusioned with him for becoming a heavy drinker. In an article entitled "The Day I Met Jack Kerouac," Jim Burns remembered seeing Jack drunk and boisterous in a public toilet in Leicester Square. Returning to the United States in May 1957 aboard the *Nieuw Amsterdam*, Kerouac realized that he'd come to Europe too late in life, "just when I became disgusted with any new experience of any kind." Throughout France, England, and now aboard the ship, people stared at him for wearing the same clothes he'd worn hitchhiking across the country or living on Desolation Peak—jeans, a lumberjack shirt, and a zippered windbreaker—a style that would shortly sweep the world. Young girls tried to lure him into shipboard romances, but he was more interested in the fabulous food, including cold roast beef and Dutch powdered-sugar raisin bread.[21]

Joyce sheltered him again when he returned to New York. She had quit her sixty-dollar-a-week job at MCA to become a secretary at Farrar, Straus. Robert Giroux had moved to the same house, as editor-in-chief, and Joyce later disclosed that Jack's quarrel with Giroux had been smoothed over by the passage of time and was now regarded as "a mock-heroic encounter between the artist/savage and the gentleman." Joyce was disappointed when she discovered that Jack was only in town long enough to pick up one of his hundred-dollar installments from Viking, and then he was off to Florida to collect Mémère, move them both to San Francisco, and fulfill his promise to his father to take care of his mother. Joyce went to the bathroom and cried, realizing that Jack had not come back to America for her, but for Mémère. She begged him to stay at least a week, but he told her to "get yourself a little husband."

Mémère was already packing for the move west when Jack joined her in Orlando. The most touching items in the heap of possessions she'd accumulated over the years were some curtains she'd never hung, because she'd never been in one place long enough to do so. As Jack stated in *Desolation Angels*, she was the best person in his life; he was amazed that many writers seemed to hate and neglect their mothers. In Mémère, he could sense infinite maternal love—perhaps the closest thing on earth to God's love—when he stood watching her "mending the rips in a bloody shirt with quiet eternal bowed head over needle." They shipped their belongings to Philip Whalen in Berkeley, and on May 6, 1957, set out for California on a Greyhound bus. It was an excruciating, four-day ordeal, but they managed to turn it into a joyride, staying drunk most of the way on Juarez bourbon. Arriving in Los Angeles at dawn, they wandered among derelicts and prostitutes, looking in vain for a coffee shop. After riding a bus up north through the San Joaquin Valley in the dead of night, they finally arrived in Berkeley and walked up Milvia Street to Whalen's cottage. The gracious, thirty-four-year-old Whalen looked at Mémère and told Jack, "I like her." Whalen later described her as a devout woman who pinned religious medals on her underwear.

The next day, Jack rented an apartment at 1943 Berkeley Way just off University Avenue, with a view of the Golden Gate Bridge some ten miles in the distance. Like many Easterners who migrate to northern California, Mémère was expecting sunshine and instead got fog and chill. She went around clutching her shawl to her shoulders and rattling her rosary beads. An inveterate night worker, Jack slept in the daytime, and Mémère fell into a funk, isolating herself in the apartment. At night, Jack lit candles and worked on *Old Angel Midnight*, or went to the Place in North Beach. On Wednesdays, the Place featured "Blabbermouth Night," and anyone could get up on the little balcony over the room and perform. "The literati of North Beach flocked to the Place," recalled Linda Gravenites, who met her first husband, Patrick Cassidy, there. "They had a poetry night, and a jazz band played behind the bar." Jack often stumbled home drunk, frightening his mother, who'd begun to see that he was killing himself. By the time their furniture arrived, she had already soured on California and was longing for the companionship of her daughter and grandson. When Whalen came over and shared a bottle of wine with Mémêre, he realized it would be pointless for her to unpack.

Trying somehow to redeem his ill-advised move, Kerouac wrote to Joyce on June 11, 1957, urging her to join him in California and bring along her lesbian friends, Elise and Sheila. She gave up her apartment, moved in with a friend, and started saving for the move west. But she heard no more from him and blamed Mémêre, calling her "my overwhelming adversary." Her real adversary, of course, was Jack himself, specifically his preference for what she called his "boy gang." She moved to the grim Yorkshire Hotel, home of perpetual postgraduates who couldn't cut the umbilical cord with Columbia, and continued to await word from Jack.[22]

In Oakland, Neal finally reappeared in Jack's life, asking for ten dollars to buy some weed. He quickly disappeared again, and Jack had to chase him down one night at the Place to dun him for the money.

Three days later, in August 1957, Jack tore open a parcel from Viking and took out his complimentary copies of *On the Road*. Suddenly and unexpectedly, Neal, the hero of the book, appeared in Jack's Berkeley Way apartment, accompanied by virtually the entire cast of the novel, including LuAnne, Helen and Al Hinkle, and a friend of Neal's named Doug Ferguson. The advance copies had a promotional wrapper over the dustjacket, which publishers sometimes use when they have very high hopes for a title. The message on the wrapper stated that the novel was destined to provoke "violently conflicting reactions" in the public and the review press. The blurb, which sounded as if Malcolm Cowley had composed it, stated that a group of rebellious Americans had risen after World War I and called themselves the Lost Generation. Hemingway was their spokesperson. And now another group had emerged from World War II, and was "roaming America in a wild, desperate search for identity and purpose"; this was the Beat Generation. "Jack Kerouac is the voice of this group and this is his novel." After a few apologies for the salacious nature of story, the jacket copy saluted *On the Road* as a genuine "publishing event." That kind of endorsement from a respected house like Viking still carried enormous weight with the review press in the fifties, and the omens for a best-seller were good.

Jack hastily shoved the copies underneath the bed. "You're all going to be mad at me," he said, according to Helen Hinkle. Al told him not to worry, since none of them really cared what was in the book; they were more interested in going out for a drink. Understandably, Kerouac was crestfallen, but his feelings on this occasion were far more complex than Al and the others could have imagined. Kerouac felt guilty, as if he'd betrayed Neal by writing about him and had now been caught red-handed with the "poor crazy sad book." Neal accepted the copy Jack handed him. He went outside in back of the apartment and started reading it while chinning himself on some metal bars. He then began to swing from the rafters like a monkey, Al recalled. Kerouac stood around anxiously explaining why he'd written certain scenes, and apologizing for others, but "none of us cared," LuAnne said. Kerouac's set was hardly a literary one; sadly, he could not share his excitement with the very people he'd written about.

They went to a North Beach bar, and Jack noticed that Neal had been behaving strangely ever since he'd opened *On the Road*. When they said goodbye that day, Neal nervously averted his gaze and seemed distant and shifty. The others wandered off, and Jack was left alone, feeling deserted.

When Neal later showed the book to Carolyn, she asked what he thought of it, and Neal replied that he liked Jack's account of their adventures, but the celebration of his drinking, screwing, and carjacking embarrassed him. "He wasn't proud of this side of his nature," Carolyn said. "He had tried very hard to overcome it." But according to Kerouac, Neal hadn't changed at all; he shortly asked Jack if there were any girls available around Berkeley. In *Desolation Angels*, Jack acknowledged that Neal loved Carolyn and the children and valued his job, but after sunset he was "hot for old lovers," and for weed, lively conversation, and music.

Thinking better of his plan to live with Joyce, Kerouac rang her from a bar in Berkeley and started disparaging San Francisco, attempting to dissuade her from joining him. Though he promised nothing, he indicated that they might continue their affair in Mexico later on. She didn't hear from him again for nearly a month, and when she tried to find him, ringing the Place long-distance, he wasn't around. The bartender was hardly reassuring, telling her, "Kerouac? Everyone wants to speak to *him*."

When friends dragged Jack home drunk one night, Mémère looked at him in horror and asked if he was deliberately trying to destroy himself. McClure remembered that she treated Jack like royalty, and regularly pulled him back from the brink of suicide. When Jack inscribed Mémère's copy of *On the Road*, he wrote that the royalties would buy her a dream house, along with the rest and contentment she deserved after long years of toiling for "Ti Jean your son the author." Mémère tried reading the novel, but only got as far as page thirty-four before giving up. "He told me I'd get mad at him," she later explained to *New York Post* reporter Alfred G. Aronowitz. "But I'll read it some day."

Jack and Mémère's California misadventure ended abruptly only six weeks after it had begun. Leaving their furniture behind, they boarded a Greyhound in mid-July and returned to Florida. Jack settled Mémère in a small forty-five-dollar-a-month porch apartment a couple of blocks from Nin's place in Orlando, just around the corner from where she'd lived only six weeks before. Mémère was pleased with her new home, largely because it had a bar in the kitchen, which she christened "Gabe's Place." But Jack was uncomfortable in the small apartment, and his room lacked an air conditioner in the middle of an oppressive tropical summer. He wanted to finish *Desolation Angels* and work on other projects, and he thought again of all the good writing he'd accomplished in Mexico City. Despite the dope they took, he was always productive and contented when he hung out with Bill Garver. After blowing up at his nephew for eating all of his Pecan Sandies cookies, he impulsively left Orlando on July 23 and returned to Mexico City by bus, feeling like "the 20th Century Scrivener of Soul Stories going down again to Gloom Mexico for no particular good reason."

At Orizaba Street, Kerouac was greeted with the shocking news that his friend Garver was "*murio.*" At the end, the old overcoat thief had run out of morphine—every junkie's nightmare—and had chosen suicide over the agonies of narcotic withdrawal, swallowing forty sodium amytal tablets. Jack fled Orizaba Street, never to return, and wrote Joyce passionate letters from the Marble Hotel in downtown Mexico City, urging her to join him, and hinting at the saturnalia they'd enjoy while watching their reflection in the "sex-orgy" mirrors surrounding his double bed.

Joyce would have run to him "without any inducements at all," she recalled. Giroux had just promoted her from secretary to editorial assistant, but she walked into his office and announced that she was leaving for Mexico to write a novel and live with Kerouac. Giroux seemed mildly surprised, but raised no objection, and she bought her plane ticket. In Mexico City, Jack was caught in an earthquake, and though he survived it uninjured, everyone in the huge apartment building across from his hotel was killed. He decided to leave the city as soon as possible. In a letter to Alan Ansen, who was in Tangier finishing the typing of *Naked Lunch* for Burroughs, Kerouac wrote that his fellaheen, ethnic kick was over. Ironically, just as Kerouac was about to make the Beat Generation famous, he lost interest in it. For him, the Beat epoch that had begun at Columbia in the early forties had ended in the early fifties at the height of his road adventures with Neal. Now, at thirty-five, he was a little too old for that kind of life, and his interests, such as they were, lay elsewhere. When he saw his short story "The Mexican Girl" in the fashionable *Paris Review*, he thought, "Just as I'm about to really skid into decay'd middle age my books'll start selling." All he really wanted to do was follow Gary Snyder to Japan, but he couldn't afford it.

Kerouac wrote at once to prevent Joyce from coming to Mexico City, suggesting that she keep her job and lay aside funds for her own personal "writing-time," and perhaps move to Paris. He believed she could become "the first great woman writer of the world," and he assured her she could "write a big book." Meanwhile, he hoped she'd look for an apartment for them in New York, and he would join her there shortly.

In Orlando in late August, he tried to work on *Visions of Gary*, his book about Snyder, and *Secret Mullings About Bill*, a memoir of Burroughs. The local papers, alerted by Viking that *On the Road* was shaping up as an important publishing event, took note of Kerouac's presence in Orlando. Shortly thereafter Jack was aware of neighbors spying on him as he attempted to sunbathe or read in the yard.

Kerouac was broke and unable to go to New York to promote his novel, which had a September 5 publication date. He appealed to Joyce, who dug into her "writing-time" savings and sent him thirty dollars to get a bus ticket to New York. On the last day of August, he wrote her that he was eager to embrace her again. On September 2, she moved out of the Yorkshire and into a new apartment in the West Sixties, between Columbus Avenue and Central Park West. In his final letter to her from Orlando, he was already referring to her place as *their* apartment. By September 4, Joyce was expecting him momentarily and fielding urgent calls from Viking's publicist, who said *Time* wanted to interview Jack on publication day. *Time*'s coverage, which included a simultaneous interview with Ginsberg in Paris, was a gauge of the tremendous advance interest in *On the Road*. The second issue of *Evergreen Review*, in which Kerouac and Ginsberg appeared with "October in the Railroad Earth" and "Howl," respectively, was the most popular in the history of little magazines, and it sold out several printings in rapid succession.[23]

At long last, the climax runner was back in the game.

EIGHT

TOUCHDOWN

Still dressed for sunny Florida in a flashy blue Hawaiian shirt, Kerouac arrived in Manhattan on a Greyhound bus late on the afternoon of September 4, 1957. He was about to go public for the first time in seven years, and the prospect of publishing his second novel filled him with both joy and apprehension. As long ago as 1954, he'd told Alfred Kazin that he'd created a new way of writing, and at last, in *On the Road*, his innovative jazzlike style was to have its long-delayed debut. Naturally, he was leery of what the critics and the public would make of a novel that broke all the rules, but it was reassuring, when he reached West Sixty-eighth Street, to see Joyce running down the street to meet him, and to learn that the *New York Times* was reviewing his novel. A good notice in the daily edition — a distinction accorded only a fraction of the forty thousand titles published annually in the United States at the time — could send a book straight onto the best-seller list.

That night, Jack and Joyce had sex and later fell into "the blacked-out sleep that comes after making love," she recalled. According to Kerouac's own records, he made love with Joyce seventy-five times during the course of their relationship. By Joyce's reckoning, they knew each other for nearly two years, during which time Kerouac flitted in and out of her life for brief periods. She and Jack discussed marriage, but she didn't count on it, and she reflected, "Well, I'm having this experience now, and it will probably end, but I will have had these two years."

Later on the night of September 4, they suddenly woke up from a heavy sleep, got dressed, and rushed down to the newsstand at Broadway and Sixty-sixth Street, where the next morning's *Times* always arrived around midnight.

Jack told Joyce that he was not expecting a rave. The news vendor stood at the entrance to the subway, opening up a bundle of September 5 papers that had just been delivered by truck. They purchased a copy, and rushed past the dramatic page-one photograph of Negro students being jeered and turned away by rifle-toting national guard militiamen at Central High School in Little Rock, Arkansas. Well inside the paper, in a regular column called "Books of the Times," Gilbert Millstein echoed Viking's dust-jacket claims for *On the Road* in one of the most graphic displays on record of an editor's power to engineer an author's critical reception. In language that was almost identical to Viking's promotional copy, Millstein hailed the book's publication as "a historic occasion," which was only a slight variation of Cowley's hype of the novel as "a publishing event." Cowley's blurb had invoked the Lost Generation and Ernest Hemingway, and set Kerouac up as the leader of the new Beat Generation. Point by point, Millstein virtually paraphrased Cowley, writing that *The Sun Also Rises* was the great novel of the twenties, and *On the Road* caught the spirit of the postwar generation as no other novel had. That one claim, backed by the power of the *Times*, could make *On the Road* a best seller. Millstein went on to give a sensitive analysis of Kerouac's strengths, comparing the road trips with Wolfe's great train accounts in *Of Time and the River*, and noting that Kerouac's jazz writing had never been matched in American literature, "either for insight, style or technical virtuosity."

"It's good, isn't it?" Jack said, after reading the review in silence.

"Yes," Joyce replied. "It's very good."

They went to Donnelly's Bar for a beer, opened the paper, and read the review again, studying each line. Jack shook his head and seemed to be oddly perplexed. In Joyce's opinion, he was stunned by the implied responsibilities of being named the leader of his generation by the *Times*. In the past, he had dreamed of being a spokesperson for the entire world, but in the intervening years, his alcoholism and publishing failures had filled him with fear and dread; down deep, he knew that he was bored and no longer had anything of value to say. Though he still felt an obligation to share his Buddhist enlightenment with other people — to free them from the bondage of worry, desire, and ambition — he wrote in *Some of the Dharma* that he wanted no part of what he called "a new disease *messiana*." Nevertheless, Jack woke up a celebrity the next morning.

In keeping with the irony that invariably accompanied Kerouac's fortunes, the *Times* rave was a fluke. The all-powerful daily *Times* review was usually written by the paper's regular book critic, Orville Prescott, who was derisively known as "Prissy" because of his prudish taste. Prescott would certainly have panned *On the Road*, but he was on vacation in early September. By this odd, fortuitous twist of fate, Kerouac's novel fell into the hands of the same man who five years previously had reviewed Holmes's *Go!* and then assigned Holmes to write "This Is the Beat Generation" for the *New York Times Magazine*. In 1985, Millstein remembered looking at Viking's review copy of *On the Road* while summering on Cape Cod: "I read the book and

I was simply stunned, simply stunned." The review he wrote would become one of the most famous and influential in the history of literary criticism.

Ginsberg had predicted that the greats of literature would ponder Kerouac's name, and Pulitzer Prize-winning poet and dramatist Archibald MacLeish was one of the first. As Librarian of Congress, MacLeish had served as the nation's putative poet laureate in the years before that office was officially established. MacLeish praised *On the Road* to his Harvard class, Nelson Algren sent a wire full of warm praise, and Charles Olson, whose 1950 essay "Projective Verse" had anticipated the Beats by calling for a poetry based on the vernacular, called Kerouac "the greatest writer in America." The phrase "on the road" entered the language and would crop up in the years to come in everything from a song by Willie Nelson to a letter by Flannery O'Connor to her editor, Robert Giroux. Kerouac realized he was famous when he went to a club in the Village and a youth at a nearby table said to his buddies, "Look, there's Jack Kerouac, right *there!*" The *Village Voice* noted that *On the Road* had taken New York's bohemian quarter by storm. People were seen carrying the book on the Village's broad avenues and quaint back streets, flipping through its pages in the Eighth Street Bookstore and Marlboro's, and perusing it on their way to work in subway stations at Sheridan Square, Fourteenth Street, Astor Place, and Bleecker Street.[1]

Future authors and celebrities later recalled reading *On the Road*, and some of them said it changed their lives. Among the novel's aficionados were Jacqueline Kennedy, Ken Kesey, Larry Rivers, Tom Hayden, LeRoi Jones (Imamu Amiri Baraka), Ed Sanders, and Robert Stone. "We all tried to imitate it," said Kesey, a twenty-two-year-old University of Oregon student and future author of *One Flew Over the Cuckoo's Nest*. Hunter Thompson, then an eighteen-year-old sports editor in Jersey Shore, Pennsylvania, recalled, "Kerouac turned me on to the idea that writing was fun, that you wrote about what you did." Future "Merry Prankster" Ron "Hassler" Bevirt recalled that for conservative, middle-class teenagers, *On the Road* was a "tremendous trip . . . the first word that we got . . . about this gassy, groovy stuff going on." Gordon Lish, later a Knopf editor, "swallowed" the novel, "hook, line, and sinker," he remembered, "and went looking for Dean Moriarty." Lish left his home in Arizona and headed for San Francisco, as thousands, perhaps millions, after him would do.

In a chain reaction, Kerouac's influence leapt from segment to segment of the culture, seizing the imagination of musicians such as Bob Dylan, André Previn, Janis Joplin, Van Morrison, Ramblin' Jack Elliott, King Crimson, Art Pepper, Mark Murphy, Jethro Tull, Tom Waits, Ricky Lee Jones, David Amram, and David Bowie, and actors such as Jack Nicholson, Kim Novak, Nick Nolte, and David Carradine. Future rock idol Jim Morrison, who in 1957 was still shocking his high-school classmates with skits about "butt-picking and masturbation," devoured *On the Road* while alone in his room in Alameda, a city in the San Francisco Bay area. The novel held him spellbound for four hours, according to Morrison's biographers, Jerry Hopkins and Danny Sugarman. The following day he resumed reading the book, and this time he made notes, often copying entire passages. Morrison was drawn to both the Ginsberg and Cassady characters, and he started imitating Moriarty, especially his "hee-hee-hee-hee" giggle. Morrison went to North Beach and searched out Kerouac's haunts, and even went to City Lights and met Ferlinghetti.

Though Kerouac later announced in *Playboy* that the Beat Generation was "a swinging group of new American men intent on joy," both men and women immediately asserted their right to be a part of it. In New York, Hettie Cohen, LeRoi Jones's girlfriend, who later described herself as "a small dark twenty-two-year-old Jew from Laurelton, Queens," called *On the Road* "the new, hot book . . . I love Jack Kerouac's footloose heroes, who've upset complacent America simply by driving through it." Kerouac's first impact on readers, whether male or female, was to make them break away from whatever had been holding them back, like Janis Joplin, who crammed *On the Road* into her knapsack in Port Arthur, Texas, and headed for North Beach. But Kerouac's impact went deeper than that, as one reader, Jim Christy, later recalled. "He infused that rush of words with some vague and indescribable longing which really unites everybody," Christy wrote. "And it is this that made him an outsider of modern Western culture much more than the portrayal of a drug-booze subterranean footloose lifestyle . . . that hushed awe in the face of the mystery of the world." The *Village Voice* reviewer, Arthur Ossterreicher, presciently recognized on September 18, 1957, that Kerouac was not just another writer, and *On the Road* not simply a novel, but "a rallying point for the elusive spirit of rebellion of these times, that silent scornful sit-down strike of the disaffiliated. The ugliness of American life appears on every page of *On the Road* but does not fill it. . . . Beneath the beatness on the surface of everything, Kerouac finds beatitude."

On the day after Millstein's review, Keith Jennison visited Kerouac and gave him half a case of champagne, which Joyce served with orange juice. Every few minutes, the phone rang—a reporter requesting an interview, a publicist inviting Jack to an important book party, or an old friend blurting effusive congratulations. Jennison probably thought so much champagne would last awhile, but three bottles were polished off in a compulsive frenzy that disturbed the editor, who took Joyce aside before leaving and said, "Take care of this man." All too soon, she fell into the role of enabler, bailing Jack out of his difficulties rather than letting him hit bottom and perhaps change.

In the first week after publication, Holmes received thirty-five requests for introductions to Kerouac, which was more typical of the emergence of a rock star or sports hero than an author. Kerouac's fans mistook him for the Dean Moriarty character, and didn't realize he was the timorous Sal Paradise. "The way they talked to me made me feel like an impostor," Kerouac later told me. At one party, he added, a woman said, "I'll fuck you in the john."

People who hadn't thought of him in years, such as his ex-wife Edie Parker, suddenly resurfaced, eager to share the limelight. Edie had been through a marriage to a businessman, and now suggested a round-the-world tour with Jack. He wasn't interested, and his curt dismissal of his former wife made Joyce wonder if she wouldn't soon be in for the same treatment. At Viking's publication party in his honor, he was mobbed by well-wishers, all vying to take credit for the novel's success, and he later complained to Neal about shrieking reporters, as well as publishers who got loaded and unfurled the *Road* scroll on the carpet.

Ironically, Jack had already turned against *On the Road*, and he wrote Elbert Lenrow, on January 13, 1958, that he no longer liked the novel. Few but his closest intimates knew that the book was over six years old and was already regarded as obsolete by its author.[2]

Other biographies have perpetuated the myth that fame and success destroyed Kerouac, when in reality his drinking had long before established the suicidal direction of his life. In fact, his long-delayed breakthrough was probably the only reason he survived another eleven years, for it was unlikely by 1957 that he could have endured another year of failure and obscurity. Following the debut of *Road*, fame didn't change his behavior; it just made him feel guilty about his actions because of their increased visibility. "Drunk alatime," he wrote Neal. He was in no condition to confront interviewers, most of whom wanted him to talk about sex and drugs and to confirm popular clichés about the Beats.

Explaining Buddhism and Christianity to CBS's grand inquisitor, Mike Wallace, as Kerouac attempted to do during an appearance on the televised evening news, was like trying to communicate the beatitudes to Attila the Hun. Kerouac needed all his wits about him to impart the spiritual message he had spent years working on, most recently in his Buddhist studies, teachings, and writings, but his alcohol and drug abuse robbed him of the ability to discuss substantive issues. "Jesus said to see the Kingdom of Heaven you must lose yourself," he told Wallace, who shot back, "Then the Beat Generation loves death? . . . The Beat people want to lose themselves." Wallace seemed determined to put the Beat Generation in a negative light. During this interview, years before the advent of Timothy Leary, Kerouac introduced the subject of drugs as a path to enlightenment, but Wallace said drugs were "a self-destructive way to seek God." He was right, but he was also obtuse to ignore Kerouac's interest in consciousness expansion, a subject that had rarely been broached since Huxley's *The Doors of Perception* in 1954.

Though Kerouac felt he disgraced himself again on John Wingate's pioneering *Nightbeat* talk show televised on WOR-TV, Hunter S. Thompson later revealed in *The Proud Highway* that at the West End Cafe, hundreds gathered to watch Kerouac's first network television interview. As soon as Kerouac appeared on camera, the West End erupted in cheers, and Kerouac was greeted like the "Bob Dylan of his day," Thompson recalled. At WOR, Kerouac feared he'd made a fool of himself in front of forty million viewers by invoking the name of God and stressing the importance of faith, but at the West End, Hunter Thompson was electrified when he heard Kerouac say, "I'm waiting for God to show me his face." In Thompson's opinion,

Kerouac was saying he wanted "to believe in something" and that made him the "spokesman" for everyone in the fifties. Kerouac, who had brought a bottle to WOR, did not suspect that he was changing people's lives as he spoke. The entire interview was a struggle, because Wingate, like other interviewers, wanted a facile characterization of the Beats, something succinct and quotable, but Kerouac insisted on being true to his beliefs and spoke from his heart. The Beats were "basically a religious generation," he said. "We love everything, Billy Graham, the Big Ten, rock and roll, Zen, apple pie, Eisenhower—we dig it all. We're in the vanguard of the new religion."

He later wrote Neal that he had crammed God down Wingate's throat, and in retaliation Wingate had introduced the subject of narcotics, hoping for a more controversial interview. Reluctant to discuss drugs lest he get himself busted, Kerouac completely clammed up. After the show, he went out and got drunk with Wingate. Jack feared he'd ruined the show. But Holmes received calls from many people he knew, saying they had to meet Kerouac because "he knows everything." One woman admitted to Holmes that she would do anything to make love to Kerouac. Joyce, who had accompanied Jack to WOR, was convinced it had been a mistake for him to bare his soul, but as Hunter Thompson's 1997 book made clear, the *Nightbeat* appearance helped many nonbelieving members of the Beat Generation who'd been spiritually starved before Kerouac told them it was hip to believe in God again.[3]

On the Road became the most publicized literary event of the year, though James Gould Cozzens's *By Love Possessed*, a well-made novel about a respectable citizen toying with criminality, dominated the best-seller lists. Kerouac's fame continued to spread, and Mémère was delighted to be inundated by letters from distant relatives, who'd previously snubbed her but now begged her to come for long visits. According to the *Boston Sunday Globe*, Kerouac made forty thousand dollars from *On the Road*, but there was a hefty tax bite. In the weeks immediately following publication, the novel sold out its first printing, a second printing was ordered on September 20, and a third shortly thereafter—unmistakable signs of a best-seller in the making. "Everything exploded," Kerouac wrote Neal. Warner Brothers was willing to pay $110,000 for movie rights, with Jack playing Sal Paradise, but Jack claimed his agent turned down the offer. Promising to make Neal a star, Jack told Neal he could play himself in the movie. In a 1995 interview, John Sampas said, "Jack did a two-page scenario of how it should be done." *Billboard* reported in June 1958 that Brando was set to play Dean Moriarty, and folksinger Theodore Bikel, later Mary Martin's co-star in the Broadway musical *The Sound of Music*, was to play either Kerouac or Ginsberg. The Earl ("Fatha") Hines Orchestra would be prominently featured in the film, which was to be shot in San Francisco. Nothing came of the project, and the film rights lay dormant for decades.

Lillian Hellman, the Broadway playwright and sometime producer, urged Kerouac to write a play entitled *The Beat Generation*. Kerouac assembled the script from unpublished manuscripts such as *Visions of Cody* and *Desolation Angels*, but the mercurial Hellman soon lost interest. Magazines were eager for Beat articles, and Sterling closed deals with *Esquire* ($500), *Playboy* ($500), and *Pageant* ($300). The British rights to *On the Road* were acquired by André Deutsch, and translation rights were sold to French, Italian, and German publishers. Viking's subsidiary rights department arranged a minor book-club sale to the Book Find Club. No doubt influenced by its most discerning editor, Arabel Porter, the New American Library bought the paperback rights and published the book in a fifty-cent edition a year later, with the blurb, "The riotous odyssey of two American drop-outs, by the drop-out who started it all."

In September, Kerouac quickly tired of performing the sociological routine required by reporters, who invariably asked him to identify the word *beat*. Repeatedly, he related how he'd first heard Herbert Huncke utter it in Times Square, and how subsequently he'd expanded it to include the Christian concept, "beatific," but no one wanted to hear about the spiritual thrust of the Beat Generation. As Ginsberg later pointed out, Kerouac attempted in his interviews to explain "the necessary beatness or darkness that precedes opening up to light, egolessness, giving room for religious illumination." The true meaning of the term was expressed in *On the Road's* famous affirmation: "Everything belongs to me because I am poor."

Exhausted and drained after the Wingate show, Kerouac hid out in Joyce's apartment for two days, hardly speaking to her. Though she was only twenty-one and admitted she was no expert on fame, she advised him to refuse requests for press and TV interviews when he didn't feel well. He followed her counsel for a few days, but it was unnatural behavior for an author with a new book in the stores, and he soon resumed his promotional efforts. Joyce later wrote that fame's fleeting thrills were responsible for corrupting Kerouac and destroying his dreams, but there are numerous examples of integrated, sober persons who seem to handle their celebrity with no difficulty. Furthermore, even when drunk, Kerouac managed to drive home some of his ideas in the media. "People hitherto out of step with the Beat Generation are catching up by reading 'On the Road' by Jack Kerouac," wrote one reporter. "The beatniks . . . don't like middle-class obsession with objects and conformity; they expand their minds with drugs or religion (many check out Zen Buddhism)."

Millstein gave a party for Kerouac, but the guest of honor refused to show. "Hours went by," Holmes recalled, "and people kept piling in, and no Jack." Kerouac's drinking destroyed this unique opportunity to buttress his position in New York literary and publishing circles. Suffering from alcoholic shakes, he stayed in bed, and Joyce finally rang Millstein with his regrets. "I can't come down," Kerouac told Holmes. "I've got the D.T.'s, but I know you've come into town. Can you get out, and come up and see me?" Holmes slipped out of the party, leaving Millstein to explain Kerouac's nonappearance to thirty to forty guests who'd come to meet the self-proclaimed "Marlon

Brando of literature." Uptown, Holmes found Jack in bed, clutching his head in terror and babbling that he no longer knew who he was.

Gracious and forgiving, Millstein subsequently met Kerouac and liked him so much as "an appealing combination of visionary and wordling" that he later arranged a nightclub appearance for Jack as a stand-up performer. Millstein described Kerouac's voice as having "a childlike timbre ... oddly at variance with ... [his] physical strength; ... it was also ... nervous and compelling." It seemed to Millstein that Kerouac would be the perfect person to introduce to New Yorkers the San Francisco phenomenon of jazz-poetry readings. Max Gordon, the owner of the Village Vanguard, loved the idea, and negotiations were set in motion for Kerouac to become a cabaret performer, marking a first for a serious novelist.[4] Meanwhile, he began to reel from a vicious critical backlash.

In Millstein, Kerouac had made a powerful friend, but the rest of the review press resented *On the Road* for rejecting the conformist values of Eisenhower America, and launched an anti-Kerouac campaign that would hound him for the rest of his life. The first attack came three days after the daily *Times* review, in the then rather stodgy Sunday *New York Times Book Review*. David Dempsey, immortalized in a contributor's note as "a freelance writer and critic of fiction," was weirdly schizoid, applauding Kerouac's novel as "enormously readable and entertaining," but dismissing the characters as sideshow "freaks ... fascinating although ... hardly part of our lives." John Updike parodied Kerouac in the *New Yorker*, presenting Jack and Neal as children named Lee and Gogi, and confining their transcontinental crossings to a "sad backyard" in the "American noon." Hemingway's future biographer, Carlos Baker, was no more perceptive in *Saturday Review*, shrugging off *On the Road* as a "dizzy travelogue" full of "verbal goofballs." Benjamin DeMott sneeringly wrote in *Hudson Review* that Kerouac was "a slob running a temperature." In a review entitled "Restless Rebels" in the *Herald Tribune Book Review*, Gene Baro called the novel "infantile, perversely negative." *Encounter's* R. W. Grandsden got nothing out of Kerouac but a "series of Neanderthal grunts." Phoebe Adams of *Atlantic Monthly* found Jack "more convincing as an eccentric than as a representative of any segment of humanity." *Time* at least saw Kerouac in a generational context, as "a kind of literary James Dean ... Wolfelike ... Whitmanesque," but failed to spot Dean Moriarty as the cultural paradigm he would shortly become, writing him off as "uncooperative." According to the *San Francisco Chronicle*, the novel was about "something everybody talks about and nobody does anything about, the delinquent younger generation." Jack's Columbia classmate Herbert Gold lashed out in *Playboy*, shrilling, "Kerouac sees himself as the Prophet and Charlie Parker as God." Subsequently, in the *Nation*, Gold suggested that *On the Road* was "proof of illness," that Ginsberg, the "Carlo Marx" of the novel, was "perverse," and that Kerouac was a mouthpiece for "male hustlers."

In a hysterical and paranoid *Partisan Review* broadside called "The

Know-Nothing Bohemians," another Columbia alumnus, Norman Podhoretz, accused the Beats of wanting to "kill the intellectuals," of being "hostile to civilization," and of worshiping "primitivism, instinct, energy, [and] 'blood.' " He denounced Kerouac for espousing "mystical doctrines, irrationalist philosophies," and "left-wing Reichianism." Continuing his campaign in *Esquire*, Podhoretz wrote that Kerouac wanted to "replace civilization by the street gang." Podhoretz later boasted that his *Partisan* attack was "damaging to Kerouac's standing as a novelist." Kerouac met him at a party and accused him of critical overkill. "I could not get that conversation out of my head," Podhoretz later wrote. "I was thrown into a serious funk." Podhoretz knew that as a critic he should be championing the innovative writers of his time, just as Edmund Wilson had supported the authors of the Lost Generation, but instead Podhoretz "was for some reason choosing to act as an enemy of the writers of mine," he admitted. History subsequently showed, according to Dennis King's perceptive article, "Norman Podhoretz's War on Kerouac," that "Podhoretz's, and the liberal literary establishment's, original attacks on the Beats in the 1950s constituted an appalling error of critical judgment—comparable in its irrationality to the French Academy's hounding of impressionist painters in the later nineteenth century."

Yet the critical barb that hurt Kerouac's reputation the most came not from the critics but from Truman Capote, who got into a fight with Norman Mailer about Kerouac on David Susskind's TV talk show, *Open End*. Mailer defended Kerouac's "rapid" writing, but Capote interrupted him, and said, "Writing! That's not writing, it's just . . . typing!"

Some time after the Russians launched Sputnik, the press started referring to Kerouac as a *beatnik*. Herb Caen in his *San Francisco Chronicle* column was the most frequent offender. Kerouac scolded Caen when he encountered him in a North Beach bar in the late fifties, but Caen insisted he hadn't intended the word to be a put-down. "I'm King of the Beats, but I'm not a Beatnik," Kerouac said to a painter friend, Hugo Weber, but he frequently used the word in his writings after 1957.

Despite the flurry of attention following publication of *On the Road*, Kerouac tried to relax with old friends like the Carrs and spent a weekend at their country home in Cherry Valley. Though the Carrs' small children were in the house, the adults would talk and drink all night. Sometimes when the children awoke in the morning, everyone had passed out, and there was no one to fix breakfast. Simon Carr, one of Lucien's sons, chose to be a painter when he grew up because "it's the opposite of talking," he said. "The bottom line of a great painting is silence. I associate the beats with the more difficult times we had as a family."⁵

Jack's celebrity began to bring him brilliant new friends like the thirty-three-year-old Zurich-born photographer Robert Frank, who wanted to film *On the*

Road, but the asking price of over one hundred thousand dollars was out of his range. In 1955 Frank had been awarded a Guggenheim grant to write about the United States and had spent a year driving around the country with his family. He asked Kerouac to contribute the preface for his forthcoming book of photographs, *The Americans*, and Kerouac quickly turned out a resonant evocation of Frank's work, writing that Frank's pictures explored "that crazy feeling in America when the sun is hot on the streets and music comes out of the jukebox or from a nearby funeral." In his association with Frank, Kerouac was again on the cutting edge of artistic innovation. In 1995, Whitney Museum curator John G. Hanhardt wrote, "Like the improvisatory line of jazz, Frank's shooting technique picked out of gesture and incident a powerful visual emblem of American vernacular culture." On publication *The Americans* was misinterpreted as anti-American and attacked by critics, but it would influence generations of artists in divergent fields, including rock star Bruce Springsteen, who found Frank's pictures and Kerouac's text an inspiration for his bleak *Nebraska* album. Cameramen came to treasure Frank's spontaneous photographic style and to regard *The Americans* as a textbook on street journalism.[6]

One night shortly after publication of *On the Road*, Bob Donlin came across Kerouac in the Five Spot with two reporters from the *New York Times*. After greeting Donlin, who told Jack he'd seen a rave review in the Miami airport on his way to New York, Jack got lost in a long drunken ramble, and the reporters walked out. He then left the Five Spot with Donlin and went to a bar in the Bowery. "This guy is famous," Donlin recalled, "and we're in this crummy bar . . . and they won't serve Jack because he was too out of control." In Jack's hotel room the next morning, they shared a six-pack for breakfast. Though scheduled for a *Playboy* photo shoot later in the day, Jack continued to drink, "ranting and raving" about *On the Road*, Bob recalled. By the time the photographers arrived, Jack was "pretty stiff," Bob added. The cameramen snapped some pictures, but when the photos were viewed at *Playboy*, according to Bob, the editors "took one look at Jack and scrapped the whole project."

After seven weeks in the city, Kerouac caught a train for Orlando, and Donlin and some friends accompanied him to Penn Station. On the way, Jack stopped at a White Castle to buy some hamburgers and sodas for the trip. "Jack," Bob said, "you're successful now. . . . Why are you buying hamburgers when they have a nice dining car in the train?" Jack told them he was too embarrassed to use the diner and preferred to remain in his compartment. According to Carolyn, he was wiped out by the critical drubbing accorded *On the Road*. "They cast him into a new hell," she wrote. "Neal and I, too, were surprised. . . . The reviewers . . . were like angry dogs." *On the Road* triumphed over its would-be executioners and hit the *New York Times* best-seller list. Kerouac heard the news in Florida in October, and predicted his book would be number one by Christmas. *On the Road* remained among the top-ten best-selling books for the next five weeks, and though it never made number one, the novel went on to launch an industry as the Beat Generation caught on commercially. The Beat image was exploited to promote and disseminate books, magazines, movies, TV shows, bongo drums, records, black turtleneck sweaters, jeans, fruit boots, leotards, black skirts, Fred Braun sandals, berets, and a whole lifestyle epitomized by coffeehouses, poetry readings, and sexual freedom. Poet Ted Jones and photographer Fred McDarrah even set up a Rent-a-Beatnik service, charging fees to liven up parties with beatniks carrying bongo drums and reading poetry. Kerouac later told me that a condom manufacturer asked him to endorse a "Beat rubber," but he refused. "I told them a more sensible idea would be a Beat Your Meat masturbation kit, with a joint, a hanky, and dirty pictures," he said.

Viking had an option for Jack's next book, and he emptied a rucksack full of masterpieces for Cowley and Jennison to choose from: *Dr. Sax, Maggie Cassidy, Visions of Gerard, Tristessa, Visions of Cody, Desolation Angels, Mexico City Blues, Old Angel Midnight*, and *Some of the Dharma*. Amazingly, Viking took none of them. Years later, with no apparent change of heart, Cowley said he hadn't cared for *Maggie Cassidy* or *Visions of Cody*. "*Dr. Sax* I think I was completely wrong about," he admitted. "I should have forced *Dr. Sax* down Viking's throat."

There is an eerie parallel between Cowley's conviction that nothing was quite good enough to follow *On the Road* and Max Perkins's reluctance to publish much of what Wolfe showed him after the 1929 success of *Look Homeward, Angel*. Editors and critics both have a tendency to expect authors to top themselves with each new book, as if the creation of art were some sort of championship contest. Though Wolfe's touchy ego was a strong factor in his decision to leave Scribner's, Wolfe himself blamed Perkins for their split, citing the deadly six-year hiatus between the publication of his first and second novels, during which time Perkins passed on *K-19*, Wolfe's railroad novel, as well as on *The October Fair*. In a bitter letter to Perkins, Wolfe complained that they'd "stalled around" on *The October Fair* until he'd "gone stale on it." Wolfe told Perkins that "your counsel and your caution" were the cause of the collapse of his career and finances in the early 1930s. Even after the worldwide success of *Of Time and the River* in 1935, Perkins again was tepid in his response to Wolfe's follow-up project, *The Vision of Spangler's Paul*, which later became *The Web and the Rock* and *You Can't Go Home Again*, published by Harper. In Kerouac's case, as Ginsberg pointed out, *Dr. Sax* was his "logical next book," but when Viking passed on it and also let all his other unpublished manuscripts go, Sterling was left with no choice but to hold a literary rummage sale. All of Kerouac's orphans would find homes, but Viking's defection meant that he would never have a responsible and consistent publishing program for his impressive backlog of manuscripts. One book a year from the same author is all the book trade and review press can handle without becoming impossibly jaded, yet this basic publishing truth was ignored as a decade's worth of Kerouac titles suddenly flooded the market over the next few years. They should have been spread out over a decade instead of being indiscriminately flung at the public and the press. As a result, the author's reputation sustained damage that would not be repaired until long after his death.

Both *Maggie Cassidy* and *Tristessa* ended up as Avon paperback originals, which meant that they'd never be properly reviewed. However, Avon's advance for the two titles, fifteen thousand dollars, was more money than Kerouac had ever seen, and he was glad to have it. *Mexico City Blues*, *The Subterraneans*, and *Dr. Sax* went to Grove. No one wanted *Visions of Cody*, though New Directions brought out 750 numbered copies of a fragmentary excerpt. Kerouac's 1956 sutra, *The Scripture of the Golden Eternity*, was issued by Totem Press, a minor imprint. Gray Williams, an editor at McGraw-Hill, put together "a lot of magazine stuff," as Kerouac called it, and published the pieces as *Lonesome Traveler* in 1960. Though a landmark travel book, *Lonesome Traveler* was lost, like the others, in a disorganized welter of Kerouac titles that were "privished" — book-trade parlance for inept publishing — between 1958 and 1960. "It killed him that his books were just being ignored and being tossed off as inconsequential," recalled David Amram, with whom Kerouac would shortly produce a historic series of jazz-in-poetry readings [7]

Though Viking had no interest in Kerouac as an author, it valued him as a property and sought to capitalize on him while interest in the Beats remained high. Cowley urged him to write a novel of childhood, but to avoid the surrealistic and expressionistic trappings of *Dr. Sax*. In Orlando, Kerouac sat at his desk at 1418½ Clouser Street, but found he couldn't write to order, and he went through ten fifths of Schenley's whiskey in eighteen days. Nin's family, which had previously withdrawn its welcome mat, now clamored for his attention and appeared at Mémère's far too frequently for dinner. Viking finally tired of waiting for the hard-to-please Cowley to get a new Kerouac title onto the list, and one of Cowley's colleagues at the house suggested a sequel to *On the Road*. The publisher approached Kerouac and held out the promise of a contract if he would give them a quickie surefire follow-up to his best-seller. "Jack . . . did his *Dharma Bums*," Cowley recalled. "I had nothing at all to do with that." Without Cowley's sponsorship, Kerouac's affairs at Viking would shortly fall into chaos, but he knocked out *The Dharma Bums* in ten sessions in November 1957, fifteen thousand words at a time, and sent it in. Again, Kerouac's relationship with his publisher resembled that of his idol, Thomas Wolfe, with Charles Scribner's Sons. Wolfe complained that Max Perkins rushed him into delivering *Of Time and the River*, the sequel to *Look Homeward, Angel*, six months before it was ready. Viking was equally anxious for another *On the Road*, and Kerouac gave it to them in *The Dharma Bums*, which was immediately accepted for publication. Kerouac ran into editorial problems when Viking attempted to standardize his prose. "He had a terrible fight with Viking about the changes that this editor and the copyediting department had made in the style," Cowley recalled. "Later on he got mixed up and thought I was responsible for them. I never saw the manuscript for *The Dharma Bums*." The experience was so onerous that Jack came to regard the novel as a potboiler, but it was in fact one of his best and most influential books, with its memorable portrait of Snyder as pioneer nature lover and environmentalist, and its lively account of the woodsy bohemia of the late 1950s.[8]

In Orlando, as Jack recovered from the nerve-racking excesses of his last trip to New York and the subsequent writing blitz that produced *The Dharma Bums*, he was in no mood to hear that Joyce Johnson was planning to join him in Florida. His affairs and marriages had always coincided with a desperate need for shelter, but after the success of *On the Road*, he would be less dependent on girlfriends for a place to stay. "Joyce Johnson was coming to Florida on a surprise visit," John Sampas revealed in 1995. Kerouac's executor cited a document in which Henri Cru warned Jack, "The trap is set. Please don't fall in it." According to Joyce, she wrote and asked permission to visit, but was refused. "I'd evidently gone much too far," she related, "daring to suggest Mémère and I and Jack could be under the same roof." But Mémère was hardly the issue, for when Jack returned to New York, it was not for the purpose of resuming his relationship with Joyce. He stated in a letter to Joyce that he did not want to marry and settle down until he was sixty-nine years old, citing the figure that denotes the primary position for mutual oral sex. (The same number appears four times in the assemblage Kerouac created for the bound typescript of *Book of Dreams*, displayed at the Whitney in 1995; for Kerouac, sixty-nine promised pleasure without the possible consequences of parenthood or emotional entanglements). He was content, as he wrote Charles Sampas, to remain in Florida in the autumn of 1957, and he described his life with Mémère as idyllic, with daily highballs of rye and Coca-Cola. Though the rent was only forty-five dollars a month, Mémère had a spacious yard, spread out over an acre, with orange, tangerine, and grapefruit trees.[9]

When Kerouac returned to New York at the end of 1957, he galvanized the East Coast poetry reading movement, and helped open "a million coffee bars," Burroughs recalled. In her essay "Beat Culture: America Revisioned," Lisa Phillips, a curator at the Whitney Museum of American Art, notes, "The first jazz poetry readings in New York [were] organized by David Amram and Jack Kerouac." Amram was a serious young jazz musician and composer who later scored Kerouac's film *Pull My Daisy*, Arthur Miller's play *After the Fall*, and the William Inge–Elia Kazan movie *Splendor in the Grass*. Kerouac met him at the Five Spot, a Village club where Amram often played with his group. One night, Amram noticed that Jack was listening very intently as Amram played his French horn. The instrument fascinated Jack because of its "ancient sound from preconscious past." Amram played the rest of the set straight at Jack, and later they went to Amram's Christopher Street apartment, where Kerouac gave an impromptu poetry reading. Hearing in Jack's voice the kinds of sounds that only a very good tenor saxophone player or singer can create, Amram sensed that Kerouac instinctively understood the language of jazz "in all its complexities and subtleties of rhythm and nuance."

Amram and a group of poets staged a reading at the Brata Art Gallery on East Tenth Street, which Amram later described as the first example of jazz-poetry fusion in New York City; Kerouac acted as master of ceremonies and also read his poetry. Though the Brata performance was largely improvised, Amram's description of the prior planning that went into it sheds light on how fifties jazz-poetry fusion came about. Amram read over the poems first and marked places for musical interpolation; then he'd perform the kind of music that suited the material—pop, blues, jazz, neo-classical, Renaissance, or even "modal music" to give a feeling of rainfall, the ocean, Route 66, or Iowa cornfields. The Brata reading was not advertised, but word spread throughout the Village, and on the night of the performance the gallery was packed despite a drenching rainfall. Kerouac, Lamantia, Howard Hart, and Jack Micheline read their poems to Amram's mellow French horn accompaniment. Kerouac's performance was boldly and ingeniously improvisational, like nothing any of them had heard before. He would suddenly break into song in the middle of a poem—"not just scatting," Amram recalled, "but humming and singing." Amram would join in, and they'd perform duets. "It really went over great," Amram said. After the Brata reading, Kerouac and the other participants attended a large party, and Kerouac told Amram that he and Lamantia wanted to do more readings. Several days later, they all met in Amram's apartment, and performances were scheduled for early the following year at the Circle in the Square, the leading theater of the fifties off-Broadway renaissance.[10]

At Christmas 1957, Kerouac was booked into the Village Vanguard as a nightclub act. "One of the most revolutionary achievements of the Beat era," wrote Lisa Phillips, "was a change of venue for art: out of the academies, museums, and concert halls and into the streets, coffeehouses, and nightclubs." Gilbert Millstein and impresario Max Gordon scheduled Kerouac's gig during the Christmas holidays, when the city would be crowded with students from Ivy League colleges, many of whom were already avid fans of Kerouac's writing. The Vanguard, a narrow subterranean space located a few blocks from Sheridan Square on Seventh Avenue, was one of Manhattan's most famous bistros, noted for blues and modern jazz. Kerouac told *Newsday* that he was paid two hundred dollars per performance at the club. Unfortunately, it did not occur to him to have musicians back him up, according to Millstein, who went to the Vanguard opening night. Jack was staying in Henri Cru's apartment, although at some point during his engagement at the Vanguard they quarreled, and Jack moved to the Marlton Hotel. Cru, who had blown up to three hundred pounds after becoming a chef, was present opening night, as was Lucien, who noticed that Jack was petrified with stage fright. Trying to calm him, Lucien said, "Let's see what's happening tonight, Jack." Completely disoriented, probably already drunk, Jack said, "I haven't got my shoes on, I can't do my fingers, read this sunumbitch." Cru snapped a picture of Jack showing him in a button-down Brooks Brothers shirt open at the collar, with his unruly black hair spilling over his brow, looking reproachfully at the camera, mouth and chin set in a kind of sullen pucker. He seemed to be on the verge of tears.

The Vanguard was not an easy room to play. Its audiences were accustomed to blues greats such as Muddy Waters, Huddie Ledbetter, Joe Williams, Helen Humes, Josh White, and Dinah Washington, who had no trouble filling the noisy room with their big voices. As Kerouac went on that night, Steve Allen, the popular comic, writer, and pianist, arrived and took his table up front. With his horn-rimmed glasses and shiny pompadour, Allen was one of the most recognizable celebrities of the fifties, having originated NBC's legendary *Tonight Show* and played the title role in the movie *The Benny Goodman Story*. After reading Kerouac's article about his experience as a fire lookout, Allen had written him a fan letter, telling him it was "one of the most beautiful examples of nature-writing" he'd ever seen. Allen was less impressed with Kerouac as a nightclub performer. Jack sauntered onstage, looked around, and read a few paragraphs from *On the Road* and some poems. That was it. "The first show was a disaster," Allen said, according to music writer David Perry, who contributed the liner notes for a 1990 reissue of Kerouac's recordings.

During the break, Allen tactfully observed to Millstein that Jack's reading could use some "unobtrusive musical accompaniment." Millstein immediately asked if Allen would go on with Kerouac for the second show, though Millstein felt "the collaboration of two personalities more dissimilar, for whatever purpose, could not readily be imagined." Jack Kerouac was the epitome of nonconformity while Steve Allen represented the ultimate in mass-audience appeal and establishment superstardom. But at the beginning of the second show, Kerouac proudly introduced his new partner, and the team of Kerouac and Allen proved to be a sensational act. Allen modestly recalled, "I don't know if Jack needed accompaniment or a line of dancing girls, but the second show turned out much better. . . . He was like a musician [with] a gentle sense of humor and a nonpushy personality. . . . He was cool."

After the show, Millstein suggested that Kerouac and Allen cut a record together, one that would combine jazz and poetry. The LP *Poetry for the Beat Generation* was conceived that night. Lucien, who attended all of Jack's Vanguard performances, was, as usual, unimpressed, and he dismissed Jack's collaboration with Steve Allen, noting that the house was down to ten customers by the time Jack overcame his stage fright. "Come on, Jack!" Steve said, according to Lucien, who added that Jack loved being teamed with "this millionaire number one."

The episode made Jack keenly aware of the advantages of backup instrumentalists; for the rest of the gig he performed to musical accompaniment. One night his reading was particularly impassioned and effective; as recounted in Kerouac's posthumously published *Heaven and Other Poems*, Lee Konitz, a jazz musician Kerouac idolized, told him he was not just reading, he was "singing." John Montgomery, a California mountain-climbing part-ner, showed up one night carrying his rucksack and watched the show from the bar. Kerouac performed "extremely well," he recalled, adding that Bev-erly Kenny, a young singer whose specialty was "emotionless flatted notes," accompanied Jack's reading, and that after the show a dozen adoring fans surrounded Jack and swept him off to a party.

The night Amram caught his act, Kerouac "flipped out," Amram re-called, but even in that condition he was the best poetry performer Amram had seen since Dylan Thomas. Joyce, who attended late in the run, reported that Kerouac made his entrance to a drumroll; then, inexplicably, he sat with his back to the audience, swigging from a bottle of Thunderbird wine and grooving to Zoot Sims. Finally, the largely collegiate audience began to clap and heckle, and one of the musicians told him, "Hey man, time to do your gig." He started reading, but long before he finished, the house had emptied out, except for Joyce, who at last emerged from the shadows at the back of the room and kissed him on the mouth. Though a hip looking girl was waiting to go home with him, he took Joyce to the Marlton, and later moved in with her again.

Just when his cabaret act began to come together, he destroyed it. "Jack got written up in *Time* magazine because of his thing at the Vanguard, which actually didn't come off that well because he was too nervous and got drunk," Amram said, explaining that Jack would miss shows while hanging out on Seventh Avenue with fans and fellow poets who plied him with wine. The Vanguard engagement was canceled after one week. Jack told Montgomery that the management complained he was attracting too many drifters in san-dals and dungarees. Montgomery noticed that Jack was drinking more alco-hol than his body could tolerate. In denial as usual, Kerouac told the *Village Voice*, "I'm no Jackie Gleason. I'm a poet." But despite the consensus of other biographers that Kerouac bombed at the Vanguard, he was good enough to attract a major recording contract, and he later turned out three superb LPs.[11]

In January 1958, Kerouac returned to Florida where he busied himself with *The Dharma Bums* and dickered, not very effectively, with Hollywood over the movie sale of *On the Road*. Director Donn Pennebaker, who was involved in one of the attempts to film the book, said, "I knew there had to be some way to translate Kerouac's particular angst, his fidgety enthusiasm and love of things around him, people around him, into film terms.... Kerouac and Neal Cassady lived at a hundred-mile-an-hour clip . . . their es-sences were intertwined." Though Francis Ford Coppola would later acquire the rights and hire Michael Herr to write the screenplay, *On the Road* still had not been filmed as of 1998. The picaresque narrative no doubt presented plot problems, but both *Easy Rider* and *The Big Chill* proved that Hollywood was capable of turning out hip movies. Carolyn Cassady's book *Heart Beat*, recounting the Kerouac-Cassady ménage à trois, was filmed in 1979, starring Sissy Spacek as Carolyn, Nick Nolte as Neal, and John Heard as Jack, but it was depressingly downbeat and muted, like a middle-aged *Jules and Jim*. Coppola's version of *On the Road* sounded equally unpromising after it was announced that the film would be shot in black and white, which could not possibly capture the spectacular spirit and scenery of *On the Road*.

At one point in 1957, during the novel's run on the best-seller charts, Kerouac asked Neal if being the book's protagonist had changed his life and whether people were "chasing" him. Though Neal did not answer, he later told his confessor, Rev. Harley, that he was "puffed with pride" as he flaunted his fame among the subterraneans on Grant Avenue and as the conductor on the busy San Jose–San Francisco commuter train. He became addicted to any kind of attention, even the "backhanded plaudits" sarcastically tendered by detractors. Neal's eventual downfall was precipitated by his dealing grass during layovers in North Beach. The bust was entirely Kerouac's fault, or so Burroughs claimed; having published nothing since 1953's *Junky*, Burroughs resented Kerouac's best-selling status and his growing international fame. Burroughs suggested in a 1958 letter to Ginsberg that *On the Road* had come to the attention of the police in northern California, and they'd quickly gone looking for the real Dean Moriarty, car thief and drug addict. But Neal's biographer, Plummer, laid the blame on Neal's own indiscretions and the pride he took in being Johnny Potseed — "marijuana central for the city of San Francisco." According to Ginsberg, Neal had always been "heroic, but uncool."[12] Ginsberg too was under legal pressure. A San Francisco court tried Ferlinghetti for distributing *Howl*, calling the poem obscene, but the publisher was acquitted in 1957.

When Neal was finally arrested and jailed for possession of marijuana in 1958, he blamed his own recklessness and poor choice of friends. He was "Quentin-bound," he warned Carolyn, unless she used their house as security for his twelve-thousand-dollar bond. She refused, knowing that he would jump bail and leave her and their children (six, eight, and nine years old) homeless. A Superior Court judge sentenced him to San Quentin for five years to life, and he was locked in a 4.5-by-7.5-by-9.5-foot cell. Sadly, the man who epitomized freedom and inspired a revolution in American writing now found himself behind bars without even "stationery, or toothpaste, or soap," as Neal complained in a letter to Carolyn. Kerouac told Ginsberg that he couldn't help Neal because the bad publicity would embarrass Mémêre, and he added, rather lamely, that he'd warned Neal about the dangers of dealing. Neal's hobo father showed more compassion and sent a five-dollar money order from Denver. Eventually, Kerouac bought Neal a typewriter — a payback, he told Carolyn, for all the meals they'd staked him to, though he said nothing about his indebtedness to Neal's "Joan Anderson Letter." In his categorical denial that *On the Road* was in any way responsible for Neal's imprisonment, Kerouac seemed to be protesting too much, and there was evidence of a guilty conscience in his correspondence with Carolyn. She was quick to write Jack and absolve him of all blame, but Neal was bitter about the novel. When fellow inmates complained that it was always checked out of the prison library, he wrote Carolyn he'd be happy if the book had no readers at all. He admitted to Rev. Harley that *On the Road* was scrupulously correct as a factual account, but he objected to Kerouac's so-called holy visions on marijuana, which struck him as sacrilegious. Like Jack, Neal was a foxhole Christian, and he became a religious fanatic in prison, compiling a list of all 262 popes from St. Peter in A.D. 64 to John XXIII in 1958.[13]

In February 1958, Kerouac was riding high as the brightest star of the new poetry-reading craze. He performed two midnight shows at the Circle in the Square, where the readings were now more theatrically staged, with searchlights, fog lights, and highway high beams raking audiences and performers. Kerouac kept the audience in a state of wary anticipation; they never knew when he'd suddenly grab his head, look around like a scared animal, and retreat into the wings. Amram called it "fantastic go-go theater." In Kerouac, the largely collegiate audiences began to embrace a new concept of literature and theater: a glory in roughness, a raw, living texture, bold and unfinished as a Pollock or a de Kooning. It was radically different from the staid classrooms and polite literary cocktail parties of the time. This was the generation that would lead the freedom marches of the 1960s, but no one had yet ignited their spirit of rebellion. Kerouac confronted them face-to-face, as poets had done since the time of Homer, going directly to the people to give them a sense of themselves, their nation, their potential, and their gods. "Heroic poetry is a phantom finger swept over all the strings, arousing from man's whole nature a song of answering harmony," wrote Yeats. "It is the poetry of action, for such alone can arouse the whole nature of man."

One night, Kerouac stirred his listeners to such a pitch they could no longer contain themselves, and they started yelling questions and comments at him. Instead of being offended, he encouraged their outbursts; "he'd answer in a real, super down-home party style," Amram told interviewers Gifford and Lee. "It was audience-attack, but always with a cosmic sense of humor." Now that he'd dispensed with stiff oratorical and theatrical conventions, Kerouac relaxed and made up poems on the spot to Amram's French-horn riffs. "He used his voice just like another horn," Amram related in his memoir *Vibrations*. "Spontaneous bop prosody"—Ginsberg's definition of Kerouac's art—perhaps reached its peak during these jazz-poetry-fusion concerts. At intermission, ambitious young writers flocked to Kerouac, and Amram noticed that he always greeted them with warmth, gave them his full attention, and lovingly shared his experience and hope. A new sense of community swept through the subterraneans of bohemia, and they would shortly fill the coffeehouses of the world, setting the style of the sixties.[14]

The Subterraneans was published by Grove on March 5, 1958, and it found the media waiting with a raised hatchet. The no-longer-Silent Generation may have found its bard, but the establishment felt threatened and horrified. Henry Luce's conservative *Time* magazine called Kerouac the "latrine laureate of Hobohemia . . . ambisextrous and hipsterical." In the *New York Times Book Review*, Dempsey defended America's morals against an author who "celebrates the self as something irresponsible, without ever identifying it with a world of objective, relevant values." Rexroth wrote in the *San Francisco Chronicle*, "Kerouac portrays, in really heartbreaking fashion, the terror and exaltation of a world he never made." Then, in a gratuitous aside, he added, "Herbert Gold is right: Jack is a square, a Columbia boy who went slumming on Minetta alley ten years ago and got hooked." Rexroth renewed his attack in the *Nation*, making one of the most unlikely charges ever leveled against Kerouac, calling him a puppet of the Eastern publishing establishment. In May, Rexroth lashed out again, writing in the *New Yorker*, "I've *lived* in the kind of world that Jack Kerouac *imagines* he has lived in." Jack sent Rexroth a letter objecting to his jibes, but Rexroth ignored it.

The Subterraneans also had its champions. Henry Miller wrote, "Believe me, there's nothing clean, nothing healthy, nothing promising about this age of wonders—except the telling. And the Kerouacs will probably have the last word." The *San Francisco Examiner* called it "a book of raw power and awesome beauty," and the *New York Herald Tribune* praised Jack as a jazz poet and his sentences as "tempestuous sweeps and whorls" that had the same "rich music of Gerard Manley Hopkins or Dylan Thomas." But Amram later recalled how the barrage of negative criticism affected Kerouac. "It broke his heart. . . . All the people who really should have been proud to know him and be on his side and help him . . . were just jealous [and] missed a wonderful chance to learn from a master." According to Montgomery, Jack said he and Ginsberg "had sat at the feet of all American critics they could find and had learned from none." But despite critical opprobrium, *The Subterraneans* quickly sold twelve thousand paperback copies upon publication in simultaneous hardcover and trade paperback.[15]

Jack began a new career as a recording artist in March, when he cut his first LP with Steve Allen in New York. Arriving from Florida for the session, which had been arranged by mail, he went into the studio to meet Allen just after lunch, carrying a suitcase stuffed with handwritten fiction and poetry manuscripts. Allen later described the suitcase as the sort available in dime stores for four dollars and often seen in backwater bus stations at two in the morning. Kerouac took out a bottle of seventy-nine-cent rotgut wine and then placed his bag on the piano to use as a music stand. "There was no rehearsal," Allen recalled. "We had no idea what would happen." In Jack's account, Allen seated himself at the piano and lightly stroked the keys, producing lovely chords; Jack stuck his hand into the suitcase "as if blindfolded" and pulled out a few pages. After a cursory perusal of the material, Allen said, "Okay," and signaled the engineer to roll the tape. After every cut, Jack passed his pint of Thunderbird to Allen, who accepted it, Jack recalled, with "charitable gaiety." Allen later explained that he'd shared Jack's "cheap wine" only to keep his co-star happy. Many a tippler has copped the same plea, but Allen was not an alcoholic. Later in their relationship, he would witness the terrible seriousness of Jack's drinking problem and recoil from it.

They recorded the entire LP in one hour. "I was the performer, he wasn't," Allen remembered. "He simply read. No dramatics, no histrionics." The strength of the record, apart from the brilliance of Kerouac's prose, lay in the delightful subtlety of their interaction. According to Bob Thiele, Dot's A&R man, the two artists "were on the same wavelength." Describing the first cut, "October in the Railroad Earth," David Perry wrote that Kerouac's "voice dances excitedly around everything from a San Francisco alley to puffs of clouds. . . . Allen's somewhat staid jazzy riffs lend a smoky Sinatra bar-belting air to the project."

When they completed the fourteenth track, an engineer said, "Great, that's a great first take," but Kerouac said, "It's the only take." Just before the album went on sale, Dot president Randy Wood suppressed it and halted pressing of the record. "This is obscene," he told Thiele. "I wouldn't even let my son listen to it." Millstein, who contributed the liner notes, said the recording industry should be ashamed of itself, adding that he would not have given his endorsement to a pornographic LP. Thiele resigned from Dot, and later he and Allen reissued the album on the Hanover/Signature label. Millstein predicted that the censorship controversy would boost sales, and he was right. The LP enjoyed a period of popularity according to Beat memorabilia dealer Stephen Ronan, who said, "Jazz and poetry became a vogue." Ferlinghetti and Rexroth subsequently released LPs with jazz accompaniment, but Ronan called them both undistinguished; the poets simply raised "their usual reading voices to accommodate the music being played behind them. Kerouac, on the other hand, was one of the musicians."[16]

On March 12, Jack observed his thirty-sixth birthday, and he continued to do poetry readings. "My wife was a waitress in an espresso coffeehouse," recalled novelist Robert Stone, who saw Kerouac "around giving readings. . . . We were certainly in awe of him." Joyce Johnson attended a reading at midnight in a small Bleecker Street theater, and LeRoi and Hettie Jones also saw Kerouac read. "The poetry-reading circuit came into its own," LeRoi recalled. "There was a sense of community growing among some of the young writers, and I was one of them as well as the editor of one of their magazines [Yugen]." After poetry readings degenerated into commercial, coffeehouse clichés, Kerouac and Amram went underground and staged forty to fifty readings in the homes of Lucien Carr, Alfred Leslie, and Robert Frank. In their memoirs, Amram and Joyce Johnson gave contradictory characterizations of Kerouac at this time. Joyce claimed that Jack's greatest ambition was to go to Hollywood and become one of Frank Sinatra's drinking buddies. But Amram had a very different impression, writing that Kerouac did not aspire to be another "Milton Berle," but was "amazingly honest and uncorrupted."[17]

For once in his life, Jack had enough money to make a down payment on a house, and in late March 1958, he purchased a roomy old place in Northport, a town on the North Shore of Long Island that reminded him of New England. Since the house was not available for immediate occupancy, he drifted around Manhattan, and while drinking in the Village, he got into a bar brawl that left him staggering and bleeding from head wounds. Once again he vowed to mend his ways. On April 10, he returned to Florida to help Mémêre pack for the move to Northport. Robert Frank accompanied him for a *Life* spread "on the road to Florida," as Frank put it. Later, Frank recalled how Kerouac was "suffering through" his splendid fame, and how he adored Mémêre, music, children, and the United States. *Life* eventually scrapped the story, and *Esquire* considered picking it up, but dropped the idea when Kerouac passed out in the magazine's New York office.

After Jack and Mémêre moved to Northport in April, he wrote, "A peaceful sorrow at home is the best I'll ever be able to offer the world, and so I told my Desolation Angels goodbye. A new life for me." He was through with the Beat life, he wrote Ginsberg, adding that he might see old friends for an occasional beer, but only rarely. Joyce Johnson came out to Northport for a visit, but Jack explained that Mémêre didn't allow extramarital sex in the house. "I told Joyce Glassman [Johnson's maiden name] to never come here and bother me again," Kerouac wrote in a letter to Henri Cru, first released by Jack's estate in 1995, "but she keeps coming anyway and says she loves me. . . . ' "18

Both Joyce and Ginsberg later painted bleak pictures of Jack's life in Northport, colored perhaps by their disappointment over being banished from the house. A more objective observer, reporter Mike McGrady, who profiled Jack for *Newsday*, presented a different view. "For the first time since his boyhood in Lowell [Kerouac was] dug in, rooted, off the road." Kerouac enjoyed meeting his neighbors, playing softball, drinking beer with local fishermen, and joking with teenagers. "The resulting portrait is less tragic than that presented in Ann Charters's *Kerouac* or Dennis McNally's *Desolate Angel*," wrote William Gargan, who reviewed the McGrady piece when it was published in an anthology, *The Kerouac We Knew*. The house adjoined the high-school football field, and in the fall, Jack watched practice scrimmages from his upstairs study window, recalling his touchdown runs on the Lowell varsity.

Jack and Mémêre both blamed his past troubles on his Beat associates, but neither of them realized their own drinking posed a greater danger. Mémêre even started opening and censoring Jack's mail, thinking she could shield him from the influence of Ginsberg and Burroughs. "I was his benefactor all my life," she said in a *New York Post* interview. "He always lives with me, outside of when he travels." When she intercepted a letter from Ginsberg that mentioned cocaine, she wrote to him and threatened to have him thrown in jail. She bombarded Burroughs with hate mail, and he retaliated by calling her "a stupid, small-minded vindictive peasant." Jack completely backed up his mother, and an infuriated Burroughs snapped that she had Jack "sewn up like an incision." To Kerouac, she seemed his only bulwark against the hailstorm of abusive criticism aimed at him at the height of the Beat craze. Even his Lowell relatives turned against him, griping that he had disgraced the family name. "They write an awful lot of things about him that's not so," Mémère told the *Post*. "I know. I'm his mother." For instance, in her syndicated daily column "Broadway," Dorothy Kilgallen wrote, "The purchase of a not-exactly-Bohemian $30,000 house is one of the out-of-character things Jack Kerouac has been able to accomplish since the publication of his various beatnik efforts." But Kilgallen was wrong about the price; Jack had paid fourteen thousand dollars for the house. Like most celebrities, he complained about the loss of privacy, but he loved being famous, and he threw his doors open to fans, who came bearing liquor and grass. They vomited in his study and slobbered over Mémère's dinners. Despite her protestations of vigilance, she was usually loaded herself.[19]

Kerouac's first album was so successful that Thiele asked him to cut another LP with Steve Allen. Kerouac agreed to record again on the condition that, instead of Allen, he could work with his favorite tenor sax players, Al Cohn and Zoot Sims. Thiele agreed, and for this session, Kerouac chose to read his unpublished haikus and blues poems. American haiku differs somewhat from Japanese haiku, which is restricted to exactly seventeen syllables. Due to the difference in language structure, Kerouac allowed some latitude as to length, though not much. To be successful, a haiku must pack universal meaning into three lines. "A sentence that's short and sweet with a sudden jump of thought is a kind of haiku," he wrote.

The session began in a mood of high elation as Kerouac read his short, aphoristic verses, pausing between each one to give the musicians a chance to play five-second interpretive solos. The saxophonists took turns, Sims playing after the first haiku, Cohn after the next, and so on. When one of Kerouac's haikus described a cat gingerly stepping through the morning frost, Zoot Sims suggested the balletic lightness of feline movement. Al Cohn responded to Kerouac's description of a lonely businessman coming home from work, walking through an abandoned football field, with a forlorn blues improvisation. When Kerouac zoomed in on the "self-shat" strand of silk from a busy worm, Zoot Sims supplied an appropriately rococo commentary. Poet and musicians seemed to be tossing a ball back and forth, and the game became more competitive and exciting as the cut progressed. The musicians' witty comebacks sometimes reduced Kerouac to giggles of delight. At the end of the cut, everyone yelled for joy.

Trouble began at the start of side two, when Kerouac told the musicians to play "behind" him as he read, and he cautioned an engineer to make sure that he could be heard over the music. Apparently, the musicians felt they'd been demoted, and all the zest and creativity suddenly went out of the LP like air escaping from a balloon. Kerouac's jazz-poetry experiment worked best when he allowed his musicians full partnership, but it withered into Muzak when he dominated the session. He couldn't understand why the musicians were so cold and distant when they finished the take. He'd wanted to go out and have a few drinks together, but after the session, Sims and Cohn packed their instruments and left without a word. Thiele called out for Jack to come and listen to the playbacks, but there was no response, and he finally found Jack squatting in a corner and weeping as he leaned his head against the wall. "My favorite saxophone players left me," he said. "They don't even want to listen to these playbacks." Thiele went to an Eighth Avenue bar with Jack and congratulated him on cutting "a great LP," but Jack started acting crazy, periodically going out to the curb and throwing empties at passing cabs. He kept asking why his musicians had deserted him before the playback. "Frankly," Thiele recalled, "I was frightened. He was out of control." Hailing two cabs, Thiele put Kerouac in one and then jumped in the other. "That was the last time I saw Jack, a true genius," he said.

First as an LP and later as a cassette, *Kerouac: Blues and Haikus* was destined for a long life. In 1990, over thirty years after its initial release, Ginsberg contributed a piece for the booklet accompanying the Rhino re-issue, writing, "*Blues and Haikus* remain for me the classic of all Beat era jazz poetry recordings." Some of the material appeared in Jack's *Heaven and Other Poems*, which critic Michael Powell called "the single most readable of Kerouac's 'poetry' titles." Kerouac's haiku about a dead fly he found in his medicine cabinet—a magical evocation of all mortality—was a favorite of both Snyder and Ginsberg. According to critic Barbara Ungar, the "housefly" haiku is a perfect example of the genre because Kerouac enters completely into "the essence of an object or a moment," stirring in the reader a subtle reminder of the ephemeral nature of existence. "His haikus describe the rare moments when Kerouac found inner peace, when he stopped running long enough to look and feel deeply the nature of this tragic, fleeting world," Ungar observed. In 1966, in Ginsberg's *Paris Review* interview, he called Kerouac "still the best poet in America," and pointed out that other poets often struggle for weeks to write haikus, but Kerouac "thinks in haikus, every time he writes anything. . . . He's the only one in the U.S. who knows how to write haikus. . . . Snyder has to labor for years in a Zen monastery to produce one haiku about shitting off a log." Snyder once explained that the most expert haiku poets are often shown up by newcomers due to the high premium haiku places on spontaneity and speed of composition. That was why Kerouac's "first thought–best thought" esthetic worked so well in this exacting poetic form; "he did beautiful little haiku," Snyder said.[20]

Ginsberg returned from world travels in 1958 a famous man, and a subtle transference of power took place in the Beat movement with the leadership passing from the recessive Kerouac to the visible and voluble Ginsberg. Now a homeowner and an established author, Kerouac announced to old friends that he was a Republican, traditionally the party of the status quo. He was having sweet dreams in which "Eisenhower is president of heroic America thru gray decades up to 1980's and we're all amazed to see him champion childlike cause after childlike cause, arms folded, a Saint, & I like him," he wrote in *Book of Dreams*.

The world-leadership role Kerouac had once forecast for himself, described in both *The Town and the City* and *The Dharma Bums*, he now unwittingly abrogated, and Ginsberg immediately stepped into the void as quickly and effectively as he'd previously taken over the San Francisco Poetry Renaissance when McClure stepped down from chairing the Six Gallery reading. Even before the 1960s, Ginsberg set in motion a proactive revolutionary program, starting with his protest against cold-war politics. He also took up Neal's cause, proclaiming in a demonstration in California that Neal was being unduly punished for holding three marijuana joints, and agitating for his release from San Quentin. Kerouac wanted no part of Ginsberg's militancy, and wrote Snyder on July 14 that he disliked Ginsberg's political grandstanding. Then, making a clean sweep of former associates, he added in a letter to Ed White that he would travel no more "silly roads" with Neal. Kerouac even avoided friends such as Snyder and Whalen, fearing that he'd lose his hard-won celebrity if the police ever caught him with pot heads.

In Northport, he donned a pair of overalls, the same kind he'd worn in boyhood; he tended his garden, watched his American Beauty roses grow, and drank iced white port. Ginsberg sought him out, but Kerouac refused to receive him, saying, "What good would it do?" His loneliness drove him into some odd alliances. A group of Long Island teenage boys adopted him; for Kerouac it was almost like a return to the sandlots and "adolescent homosexual ball[s]" of Lowell. According to Peter Orlovsky, Kerouac consorted with gangs of kids who would storm into restaurants naked to shock the customers. Soon, Kerouac's phlebitis returned, along with alcoholic rashes. He shut himself up in the house and continued to drink. The Dexamils he took to trigger his writing did nothing to dissolve his writer's block, leaving him only constipated and infected with boils.

Kerouac thought that perhaps the famous Zen interpreter, Dr. D. T. Suzuki, could help him, and he visited the venerable sage on October 15, 1958, in Manhattan. A small man, Suzuki lived in book-lined rooms with wood paneling on West Ninety-fourth Street. Having carefully arranged three chairs for Jack and his companions, Suzuki sat behind a table, quietly studying them. Jack noticed that Suzuki's eyelashes were very long, which somehow made him think of a saying about the Dharma—that it took root very gradually but could never be dislodged. Suzuki asked his guests to speak distinctly, explaining that he was partially deaf. Almost shouting, Jack asked Dr. Suzuki why Bodhidharma came from the west. Dr. Suzuki at once realized that Kerouac's problem was alcohol, and told him to switch to green tea. Then he advised Jack and his friends to "sit here quietly," Jack recalled in *Berkeley Bussei*, and in a few minutes Dr. Suzuki came back and served "thick and soupy" green tea in fragile, battered and chipped bowls. Shortly, Suzuki showed them to the door, admonishing Jack to stick to green tea. On the sidewalk, Jack looked back and saw Suzuki standing in the doorway. Speaking from his heart, Jack said he wanted to move in with Suzuki and spend the rest of his days with him. "Sometime," Suzuki said, raising a finger and giggling.

Kerouac and Ginsberg shared a cab downtown to Viking's publication party for *The Dharma Bums*. In Ginsberg's subsequent review of the novel in the *Village Voice*, he hailed it as an "extraordinary mystic testament," and in a letter to Jack, he called it "a great piece of religion." On their way downtown that day, Ginsberg correctly predicted that Kerouac would "get attacked for being enlightened." With the exception of the *New York Times Book Review*, whose critic, Nancy Wilson Ross, treated *The Dharma Bums* with respect, the other prestige publications bore out Ginsberg's prophecy. *Time* headlined its review "The Yabyum Kid: How the Campfire Boys Discovered Buddhism." The daily *Times* reviewer, Charles Poore, mistook the novel for a "machine-age parody on the great American migrations of the nineteenth century." In yet another *Times* piece, J. Donald Adams attacked the novel's keen prevision of the sixties, referring to "[such] absurdities as its vision of millions of young Americans strapping on knapsacks."

But at last Kerouac had written a book that was clean enough for his mother to read. In her copy, he scrawled that *The Dharma Bums* would pay the mortgage and keep them in cat food and brandy, and added that references to her could be found on pages 132, 133, and 148. Mémère still hadn't read the novel by the following spring, and Jack finally ordered her to do so, in front of the *New York Post*'s Al Aronowitz. "He's a good boy," Mémère told the reporter.

Unfortunately, Ginsberg labeled *The Dharma Bums* a travelogue, which would later lead critics to underestimate the novel and rate it below such bravura feats as *Visions of Cody* and *The Subterraneans*. Though Kerouac himself viewed *The Dharma Bums* as hackwork, it represented, at least in some respects, an important advance over his previous work. Without reverting to traditional fictional techniques, he succeeded in molding and shaping his material into a dramatic and coherent narrative that conveyed his themes with power and precision, yet retained his trademark stream of consciousness and jazzy, hopped-up rhythm. Ginsberg's real reasons for underrating the novel became clear with the publication of his correspondence, in which he stated that he resented Kerouac's portrayal of him as "Alvah Goldbook," finding the character to be "too inconsistent mentally." Ginsberg's advice on technique was the worst he'd given Jack since his infamous *On the Road* letter, demonstrating once again that going to a competitor for career guidance is like going to a butcher for brain surgery. Assuming that Kerouac's cleaner prose was the result of exhaustion, Ginsberg lectured him to return to "Wildbooks" like *Dr. Sax*. But Kerouac's new, leaner style represented a technical advance that not even the author yet appreciated, and to revert to the surrealism of *Dr. Sax* or the long jazz line of *The Subterraneans* would have represented a stylistic setback. Henry Miller did not share Ginsberg's reservations about *The Dharma Bums*, and wrote a letter full of unqualified praise.

Ginsberg's *Village Voice* review also did Kerouac personal harm. Typically indiscreet, Ginsberg revealed that Kerouac was on the verge of a crackup. Though basically a decent man, Ginsberg was increasingly competitive, itching to become as famous and glamorous as Jack, something he would never quite achieve. Though he knew how sensitive both Jack and his mother were, he wrote, "I begin to see why Pound went paranoiac." Unduly impatient to replace Jack as king of the Beats, Ginsberg lacked Kerouac's charisma, formidable physical assets, and clout as a best-selling novelist. Ironically, Jack was so eager to shed the title that he issued a public announcement over UPI, dissociating himself from the movement. Lucien, who still worked at the wire service, sent out the interview, but the media continued to regard Kerouac as the spokesperson for his generation. TV talk-show host Ben Hecht tried to provoke him into criticizing Eisenhower, the Pope, and Secretary of State John Foster Dulles, goading him with cracks like, "Why are you afraid to speak out your mind?" Kerouac wouldn't budge, and he suggested they discuss the things he loved, like Christ and (in a rare departure from his customary anti-Semitism) the Star of David. At a subsequent panel discussion at Hunter College on November 6, he regaled the audience with an imitation of Hecht, whining, "What's wrong with this country." Suddenly becoming serious, he announced that the cosmos was "one vast sea of compassion . . . beneath . . . this show of personality and cruelty."[21]

Gregory Corso, whose cold-war classic, "Bomb," was published as a broadside by City Lights, accompanied Jack on jaunts around the Village. Kerouac was invariably greeted as a conquering hero or challenged by drunken tourists spoiling to test their mettle against the new Hemingway. Adele came back into Kerouac's life and invited him to Perry Street, where she and Norman Mailer were living. "I went along," Ginsberg recalled. "Jack was . . . withdrawn and shy, while Norman was friendly. . . . But [Kerouac] was very proud of being the greatest writer in America. Norman loved Kerouac . . . saw him as a . . . great innocent. . . . He felt more hard and sophisticated and worldly . . . whereas Kerouac . . . was thinking in Buddhist terms." Like Kerouac, Mailer was temporarily burnt out as a novelist following widespread critical attacks on *The Deer Park*. Mailer wrote no more fiction for ten years, staying drugged on pot, Seconal, Miltown, Benzedrine, and alcohol. Adele had also become an alcoholic, and was so overbearingly aggressive that friends of Mailer such as novelist Chandler Brossard found her impossible to deal with. At one party Adele approached Brossard and told him she liked "juicy, fuckable men," but that he was "dry and unfuckable." Brossard told Norman, "You've gotta get this woman away from me." But Mailer liked to see her fight and often goaded her on.

Adele responded in kind. Though Kerouac was an ex-lover, she invited him, along with Steve Allen, to one of their parties. "I liked the idea of my famous ex-lover and my famous husband being in the same room with me," Adele wrote, "especially since the duplex was a far cry from my cold-water flat in the days when Jack and I had been lovers." According to Adele, Kerouac got drunk and hid under the dining room table, explaining that he could hear better than he could see. Years later, when we were working on the Mailer passage in *Desolation Angels*, Jack recalled the party. The guests pumped him about how to become famous, but they did not care for his answer. "You work like a dog," he said. "You live like a hobo." At thirty-five, Mailer noted the intense media attention being focused on the Beats in 1958, and began to seek confirmation that he was the greatest novelist of his time. When no such accolade was forthcoming, he at last realized he was "on the wrong train," recalled Barbara Probst Solomon. "It wasn't easy to get caught short being a leftover Dreiser or Dos Passos . . . so when he looked over his shoulder and there was the Beat Generation, he knew he had to do something to compete."

In *Advertisements for Myself*, Mailer brazenly claimed that no other living writer was in his class. With the exception of Kerouac, almost every serious novelist in the world was outraged, and wrote "Fuck you" and "Up Yours" when invited by James Jones to inscribe his copy of *Advertisements for Myself*. "I didn't hold it against Mailer," Kerouac told me a few years later. "It's natural to be your own favorite writer. But what Mailer really wanted to be was the most psychotic, and we'd already been through that." Following a decade of Beat violence that included manslaughter, jails, mental institutions, and suicide, Kerouac had turned to the beatitudes, Christ's promise on a mountain in Galilee that the meek will inherit the earth. "Mailer was trying to stir up competition and rivalry in 'Talent in the Room,'" Kerouac told me, "and he tried to lay a violent trip on us in 'White Negro,' bomb us back to the stone age, or the nut house. No thanks." Nevertheless "The White Negro" would be carried by the baby boomers into the sixties, along with *On the Road* and *The Dharma Bums*, as a guidebook to revolution.

Meanwhile, the big cocktail party of the fifties went on. During a visit to New York from Tangier, Paul Bowles recalled seeing Kerouac at a bash given by Chandler Cowles. Bowles's companion was Gore Vidal. Kerouac chatted with W. H. Auden and then left the party with Vidal and Bowles. "Gore and I went with him to an apartment in the Village," Bowles wrote. "During the evening Jack grew expansive on beer." When Bowles and Vidal left Kerouac that evening, Jack handed Paul a paperback copy of *The Subterraneans* in which he'd written, "To Paul—a man completely devoid of bullshit." The inscription was disingenuous at best: In *Some of the Dharma* Kerouac included Bowles in a group of writers he stigmatized as "raving social climbers," a description that also fit Kerouac. When Bowles's wife, Jane, author of the 1954 Broadway play *In the Summer House*, read *The Subterraneans*, she said, "But are they all going through a Celine period, or what?" Paul reflected, "The Beat writers, in particular . . . Ginsberg, Corso, and Kerouac, were receiving enormous publicity at that moment."[22]

Jack fell in love again in late October 1958. Dody Muller was a painter, and one of her collaborations with Willem de Kooning would be included in the Whitney's *Beat Culture* retrospective. Jack and Dody met through Robert Frank and his sculptor wife Mary. Thirty-two years old and the widow of a painter named Jan Muller, Dody had a studio in the Village, which Kerouac soon turned into a crash pad, inviting in numerous drinking buddies, most of them disreputable. Dody was dark, attractive, and vibrant, the way Jack liked his women. They made love fifty times, according to Kerouac's sex list. Jack asked her to marry him and move to Paris. She liked him well enough, later describing him in somewhat familial terms as "sweet and kind," but when she met Mémêre, she shuddered at the prospect of being caught between them. "[My mother] doesn't like my girlfriend," Kerouac confided to Aronowitz, "because she has long, long hair and doesn't tie it up. . . . My mother calls her *la sauvage* — the savage." In Northport, Dody was appalled by the sight of Mémêre guzzling cheap whiskey and crossing herself while watching Bishop Fulton J. Sheen on television. Like Joyce, Dody tried to help out in the kitchen, but she didn't meet Mémêre's strict sanitation requirements, and Mémêre rewashed every dish that Dody touched. Jack and his mother quarreled like lovers, Dody noticed, and she even suspected them of incest.

At the Cedar Tavern, Jack became involved with all of Dody's friends, including de Kooning. Jack started painting again, inspired by Dody's generous coaching and a studio full of supplies. He was eighty-sixed from most of the bars in the Village, including the Cedar, where he annoyed the owners by urinating in the sink and pouring beer into poet Kenneth Koch's hat. Afterward, Jack stood in the street, and painter Stan Twardowicz, a Cedar regular, brought a beer out to him.

Uptown friends like Steve Allen were also concerned about Kerouac's alcoholism. Allen compared Jack's "strong self-destructive streak" to Lenny Bruce's, calling it "a pity." He was charmed by Kerouac's naturalness and lack of pretension and said Kerouac had "no airs at all of I'm a Great Writer." They began to see each other socially. Allen and his wife, TV star Jayne Meadows, invited Kerouac to dinner, and he arrived at 1009 Park Avenue at 5:30 P.M. His hosts asked if he wanted a cocktail before dinner, and he asked for brandy. A full bottle was placed on the coffee table, and Kerouac polished it off, according to Allen, "with little visible effect on his behavior." In his normal speaking voice, which Steve characterized as "soft, loose," Jack held forth brilliantly on two of his favorite novels, Louis-Ferdinand Celine's *Journey to the End of the Night* and *Death on the Installment Plan*, savoring the author's misanthropic verbiage and his portrait of existence as rotten and mad. Dinner was served at 7:30 P.M., and afterward Kerouac asked for another drink. Having depleted his host's supply of brandy, he now started in on his scotch, and went through two bottles. "His mind raced on at a great pace, as did mine, as the two of us talked endlessly, for hours," Steve recalled. Around midnight, Jayne decided she'd had enough. Though, according to Steve, she found Jack "amusing," she had a professional engagement the next day, and she started yawning and making pointed references to the lateness of the hour, trying as tactfully as she could to let their guest know that the party was over. Despite his admiration for what he called Jack's "boyish charm," Steve too was eager for Jack to leave so they could retire. Impervious to their hints, Jack continued to drink and ramble.

"Jack, it's been the kick of all time, but I'm really wiped out," Steve finally said at 2:30 A.M.

"I'm not goin' home," Jack replied. "Oh, don't worry, I'll split . . . I'll find somebody else who's up. Can I use your phone?"

"Sure," Steve said, and Jack frantically dialed everyone he knew, until someone finally invited him over. In the following days, Steve read some of Celine's work, and he and Jack had lively discussions about France's evil genius, whose latest novel, *Castle to Castle*, concerned the grotesque Nazi world he'd experienced while fleeing across Europe in World War II. Kerouac and Allen remained friends, and Kerouac's sex list reveals that Jack once made love to a girl who worked in the studio with Steve Allen.[23]

When Mémère left Northport to visit Nin in Florida during the 1958 Christmas holidays, Jack relaxed at home with Dody, and they enjoyed long walks on the beach, but mostly they drank. He was still seeing Helen Weaver and Joyce Johnson. One night, in front of Joyce, he started making out with Helen. Joyce pulled him out to the street and called him "a big bag of wind!" He retorted, "Unrequited love's a bore." She stormed off, hoping he would follow, but he didn't. He spent Christmas in Northport with Robert Lax, the editor of *Jubilee: A Magazine of the Church and Her People*, who had published some of Kerouac's poems. Lax was a friend and Columbia classmate of Thomas Merton and Robert Giroux, and Kerouac had once written Giroux that he found Bob Lax to be "sweet." Lax offered to get Kerouac admitted to the L'Eau Vive monastery at Soissy-sur-Seine to meet with Merton, and Kerouac considered it for a while, but finally gave up the idea, deciding it would conflict with his Buddhism. Thereafter, Lax humorously referred to Kerouac as "J-Louis Chinaboy." On Christmas Eve, they drank wine and read selections from *Finnegans Wake* and from Jack's unpublished manuscripts. The following year, Kerouac's Catholic poems were published by Jubilee in a volume entitled *Hymn—God Pray for Me*. In *Cerrada Medellin Blues*, Kerouac wrote that he loved Bob Lax, but not the purgative that bears the same name. Kerouac gave *Jubilee* his 1955 story "Statue of Christ" but worried that it might be too Buddhist for them. In 1959 Kerouac's interest in Buddhism would radically diminish. "I am a Catholic," he wrote in one of the concluding chapters of *Some of the Dharma*.[24]

After the holidays, Mémère returned to Northport. She staged a harrowing scene when Robert Frank and Alfred Leslie, who had entered a filmmaking partnership, drove out with Dody to discuss producing underground films with Jack. "Jewboy," Mémère hissed at Leslie, and she locked her liquor cabinet, having promised Leo that she would never entertain a Jew in her home. Dody found her behavior to be vile and depraved, but there was a poignant and tragic reason behind it. Mémère struck out at Jack's friends because she'd convinced herself that they—rather than alcoholism—were the cause of his drinking. If she ever admitted that alcohol was his problem, she'd have to admit that it was hers as well, and give up drinking. That, as a determined alcoholic, she would never do.

Once Jack quieted his mother down, he listened to the filmmakers' plans to produce a Kerouac movie. It was a historic moment in the Beat movement, the meeting of three gifted men of similar sensibilities: the leading practictioner of spontaneous writing, the master of the grab shot, and a second-generation abstract-expressionist action painter. The point of Alfred Leslie's paintings, wrote critic and filmmaker Robert C. Morgan, "was to convey raw emotion—social angst . . . through the trace or sign of rapid-fire gesture. . . . His . . . works . . . were built-up surfaces on which layer after layer of gestural nuance was applied . . . until the final resolution was determined in a sudden flash of intuitive know-how." Kerouac, Frank, and Leslie were about to create one of the Beat Generation's signature works, *Pull My Daisy*, later acknowledged as the first underground film.

Robert Frank began by reminding Jack that he wanted to film *On the Road*. Leslie pointed out that going on location would be too expensive. They then proposed an anthology-type movie that would be made up of three thirty-minute segments: Isaac Babel's *The Sin of Jesus*; a Zero Mostel starring vehicle called *Mr. Z*, a story based on Frank's memory of a man in Paris who'd lived with scores of mannequins; and a Kerouac story. Jack played them a tape he'd made of himself reading the play he'd written for Lillian Hellman, *The Beat Generation*. In retrospect, he rather agreed with Hellman that it had no merit, but Leslie liked Jack's performance so much that he thought of using the tape in a film and having the actors lipsynch Jack's reading. In the end, Leslie and Frank would film only the play's third act, an account of the Beats' visit with the liberal Catholic priest at the Cassadys' home. The Isaac Babel and Zero Mostel segments of the planned ninety-minute film would never be shot, and as a result Kerouac's lone segment, at thirty-minutes' running time, would have a difficult time finding a distributor. Kerouac agreed to write and perform the narration, as a voice-over. When they discovered that MGM had already copyrighted the title *The Beat Generation* for an exploitation film with Mamie Van Doren, they changed the title to *Pull My Daisy*, borrowing it from the old poem by Jack, Neal, and Allen. Principal photography was set to begin early in 1959.[25]

On New Year's Eve, Jack and Mémère toasted each other with martinis in Northport, and she said, "Happy New Year, dear boy, and I hope you'll be happy." Quoting her in a regular column he'd begun to write for *Escapade* magazine, Kerouac commented, "It no longer matters to me about 'happiness' . . . There's nothing to yearn after. . . . I raise a private toast to my mother and all beings (silently) wishing them the Sweet Dharma Truth . . . which blots out . . . ogroid earth." Jack saw 1959 in with Lucien Carr in Manhattan and then partied with the recently assembled cast and crew of *Pull My Daisy*. The film would pioneer what came to be known the following year as the New American Cinema. Kerouac, Frank, and Leslie were among a very small group of artists, including John Cassavetes, Shirley Clark, and Kenneth Anger, who envisaged a new world of film free from the clichés of formula-ridden Hollywood. Apart from *Pull My Daisy*, this movement would produce

Shadows, The Connection, and *Scorpio Rising,* which would introduce a freshness and immediacy not seen before in commercial movies.

Pull My Daisy started shooting in Leslie's loft at 108 Fourth Avenue on January 2, with a budget of fifteen thousand dollars. Kerouac was under the impression that the actors received five dollars a day, but Ginsberg later revealed that he, Orlovsky, and Corso were paid eighteen dollars daily to clown around. Amram, who wrote the musical score, contributed his services gratis. Codirector Leslie insisted that the set was as orderly as a Hitchcock shoot, but Amram recalled total anarchy: boisterous, stoned, drunken days of improvisation. One day, Kerouac and Dody monitored the filming from Leslie's elevated loft bed. Jack advised Corso, who was playing him in the film, to stop trying to imitate him and simply be himself. The only professional actor in the cast was the breathtaking French beauty, Delphine Seyrig, who later became a star of the "New Wave" French cinema as the leading lady in Alain Renais's *Last Year in Marienbad.* She was briefly a part of the Beat scene as the wife of American painter Jack Youngerman. On January 10, Orlovsky wrote Carolyn that Seyrig, a "good looking actriss [sic]," was playing Carolyn in the film. According to Amram, Seyrig wanted to analyze the script, but this was met with ridicule and laughter. Ginsberg walked around the loft naked. Larry Rivers, who was playing Neal, complained that anyone could steal a scene by taking off his clothes. Refusing to be upstaged, Rivers grabbed his saxophone and played it throughout the scene. "I never understood this goofy little masterpiece as it was being filmed," Rivers recalled in his memoir *What Did I Do?,* "but it was pleasurable playing the part of a stoned train conductor carrying a kerosene lamp in the company of such beat luminaries."

Leslie found Kerouac's presence to be distracting. He had never approved of Kerouac's use of black slang, which struck him as a form of discrimination, and he was angered when Kerouac dragged a Bowery derelict into the loft before the production began. "I was going to disrupt everything so I wasn't allowed at the filming," Kerouac recalled. "I was around the corner in an artist's studio." But according to film historian Blaine Allan, who interviewed Leslie and Dody Muller, Kerouac was not barred from the set. After six weeks, the shooting was completed, and Leslie and Frank drove out to Northport with Dody to screen the footage for Jack. Unaccustomed to viewing film without sound, Jack disliked *Pull My Daisy* on first viewing, but he agreed to lay down the soundtrack in the studio of his old friend Jerry Newman. Arriving drunk, Kerouac had more liquor and reefer at the studio, and turned the session into a party that went on for a day and a half. He threw away his notes and improvised a new script as he recorded. The result was a magnificent verbal and poetic tapestry that pulled the film together, and transformed *Pull My Daisy* into a classic example of spontaneous bop prosody.

At the wrap party, fellow artists showered Kerouac with the respect that had largely been denied him in the book world, but that now came to him from actors, filmmakers, and musicians. An invitational screening was held at 11:30 A.M. on May 12, 1959, at the Museum of Modern Art. Holmes recalled that Kerouac was "somewhat shy" about his role in the proceedings and mentioned that the film bore little relation to his play but "did its own thing well." As Kerouac introduced Holmes to Frank, it was clear to Holmes that Kerouac admired the filmmaker and "liked" *Pull My Daisy*. "He thought that Allen & Gregory & Peter were great . . . he liked Dave Amram and Larry Rivers," Holmes added.

Kerouac went pub-crawling with de Kooning, and was kicked out of Birdland, along with jazz drummer Elvin Jones. De Kooning was kind and infinitely patient with Kerouac, though the painter was very unlike Kerouac, Jackson Pollock, and many other sexually fragile men of their generation who chose to armor themselves with machismo and overt homophobia. De Kooning moved freely and comfortably through the largely gay world of New York art galleries, and even looked on the famous gay curator and poet Frank O'Hara as a "good omen," O'Hara's biographer, Brad Gooch, wrote. "Evidently free of Pollock's homophobia, de Kooning often greeted O'Hara at the Cedar with a big juicy kiss." Blond, smooth-skinned, and always smiling, de Kooning had been a housepainter in Rotterdam when he'd decided to become the best painter since Picasso and Miro. In the opinion of many, he succeeded.

Pull My Daisy was a metaphor not only for the Beat Generation, but for the mystery of human life in the cosmos. As the movie begins, Kerouac's voice announces that it is "early morning in the universe." Carolyn is shown in a cramped tenement room with her children, while Neal is away working on the railroad. Then the poets arrive, followed by the preacher and two uptight matrons. When Neal joins them, havoc sets in, and Carolyn throws them all out. "The film conveys an anti-establishment boys club atmosphere that shields a homoerotic subtext of relationships and pairing within the Beat movement," wrote John G. Hanhardt, film curator of the Whitney Museum and author of "A Movement Toward the Real: *Pull My Daisy* and the American Independent Film, 1950–65." In a larger sense, the film explores the conflict between the Beats and American rationalism, as represented by the church, and resolves it by showing that everyone is crazy on both sides. Through image and poetic narration, the film achieves a small miracle: By the end, the crowded tenement room seems as vast and unfathomable as the universe, and Kerouac's little Los Gatos anecdote becomes what one reviewer called "a poetic mystery as elusive as reality itself."

Once again, Kerouac was at the forefront of an art movement that would have wide-ranging social and political implications. According to Hanhardt, "*Pull My Daisy* heralded a new American cinema much as the Beat poets articulated a new American poetics in literature . . . [and] laid the foundation for the counterculture of the 1960s." Kerouac's radically destabilized narrative swept away the rigid cause-and-effect rules that had governed scenarists since *The Great Train Robbery*. Leslie's seemingly improvisatory style and Frank's fluid photography brought to filmmaking all the spontaneity of Kerouac's revolutionary free-form esthetic, and influenced future underground as well as mainstream films. Amram's haunting score and singer Anita Ellis's powerful rendition of "The Crazy Daisy" drenched the entire enterprise in a jazzy ambience. On November 11, 1959, Manhattan's most prestigious film society, Cinema Sixteen, screened *Pull My Daisy* on a bill with John Cassavetes's *Shadows* as a program entitled "The Cinema of Improvisation."

The new experimental-film press immediately recognized the movie's innovative quality. "*Pull My Daisy* clearly point[s] . . . toward a new thematic, a new sensitivity," Jonas Mekas wrote, and Hanhardt later categorically singled out *Pull My Daisy* as "the key Beat film of its generation." *Film Culture* awarded *Pull My Daisy* its second annual Independent Film Award: "In its camera work, it effectively breaks with the official rules of slick polished . . . cinematographic schmaltz. It breathes an immediacy that the cinema of today vitally needs if it is to be a living and contemporary art."[26]

Kerouac's second triumph in 1959 came on May 13, when he cut *Readings by Jack Kerouac on the Beat Generation*, completing the three-record deal that jazz impresario Norman Grantz had signed him to. Producer Bill Randle spent hundreds of hours helping Jack select material from his published and unpublished works. The final selections were drawn from *Old Angel Midnight*, *The Subterraneans*, *Visions of Cody*, *Mexico City Blues*, and *Book of Blues*. No musicians accompanied him this time, but it was perhaps the most musical of his albums, thanks to the suppleness of his voice and jazzlike vocal riffs. Steve Allen looked in on the session, and Ginsberg and Corso dropped by the studio, bringing numerous girl groupies. Randle objected that Jack sometimes departed from his texts, and huffed that he should have done his editing before the session, but it was Kerouac's variations on the text that gave the LP its feeling of excitement.

Some of Kerouac's best books—*Dr. Sax*, *Maggie Cassidy*, and *Mexico City Blues*—were unimaginatively and routinely issued in 1959, and they were uniformly savaged by book reviewers. The usually perceptive Ralph J. Gleason panned *Dr. Sax* in the *San Francisco Chronicle*, writing that Kerouac had gone "all Joycean on us . . . and failed." "Juvenile scrimshaw," sniffed the *Atlantic*'s Phoebe Adams, and Dempsey, his old nemesis at the *New York Times Book Review*, dismissed *Dr. Sax* as "not only bad Kerouac, but a bad book . . . largely psychopathic . . . pretentious and unreadable farrago of childhood fantasy-play." When the *Times* reviewed *Mexico City Blues*, published October 20, Rexroth wrote, "The naive effrontery of this book is more pitiful than ridiculous." But in 1982, McClure called the same book Kerouac's "masterpiece . . . a religious poem startling in its majesty and comedy and gentleness and vision." In *A Map of Mexico City Blues*, James T. Jones wrote, "Whether Rexroth was really castigating Kerouac for his bad manners at Rexroth's San Francisco salon or trying to get at Kerouac's friend . . . Creeley, who had had an affair with Rexroth's wife, or merely venting some private frustration in literary terms, the *Times* piece is a model of unethical behavior in print." Though Creeley defended *Mexico City Blues* in *Po-*

etry and Anthony Hecht praised it in *Hudson Review*, the *Times* effectively killed the only volume of Kerouac's poetry published during his lifetime. *Visions of Cody* was virtually ignored when issued in abridged form, and when *Maggie Cassidy* appeared, *Saturday Review* critic John Ciardi called Kerouac "a high school athlete who went from Lowell, Massachusetts, to Skid Row, losing his eraser en route." Kerouac had once joked that Ciardi didn't know how to put on a condom. According to Ciardi biographer Edward M. Cifelli, Ciardi drank a bottle of J. W. Dant, a 100-proof Kentucky sour mash, every day, and his alcoholism and diabetes reduced him to impotency.[27]

Financially, Kerouac was faring better than he was with book reviewers. In early 1959, he told Aronowitz that he had netted twenty thousand dollars in the year since becoming famous (over a hundred thousand dollars by late 1990s standards). *Maggie Cassidy* sold 125,000 copies, a respectable if not sensational mass-market performance. *On the Road* racked up paperback sales of half a million copies for Signet and hardcover sales of twenty thousand for Viking. *The Dharma Bums* had a hardcover first printing of thirteen thousand at Viking, and the British edition sold a healthy (for England) four thousand copies. Jack had three thousand dollars in the bank, the Northport house was paid for, he was expecting eight thousand dollars from his first royalty payment in 1959, and the final twelve-thousand-dollar installment on the sale of *The Subterraneans* to MGM was payable in mid-1959. Had he owned a piece of the merchandising that stemmed from *On the Road*, he'd have been a multimillionaire.

Though the TV situation comedy *Dobie Gillis* was based on Max Shulman short stories, the Beat character, Maynard G. Krebs, was created expressly for the TV show following the success of *On the Road*. Running from 1960 to 1964, *Route 66*, a sanitized retread of *On the Road*, was a hit series for 116 episodes and worth millions of dollars. "The idea was for everybody to rediscover the United States through our characters' eyes," recalled Martin Milner, who played Tod Stiles. George Maharis, a dead ringer for Kerouac, played Tod's sidekick, Buz Murdock. Enraged, Kerouac charged plagiarism, and he attempted unsuccessfully to sue on two different occasions.[28]

Though Kerouac was satisfied with his home in Northport, by mid-1959 Mémère could no longer stand being separated from her daughter and grandchild. Jack offered to move back to Florida and build a duplex so that he and Mémère, as well as Nin and her family, could all live together. The idea was quickly quashed by Paul Blake, and Jack then offered to build adjoining houses, paying all construction costs. Paul found this proposal acceptable, and in June, Kerouac sold 34 Gilbert Street while Mémère went down to Florida to look for a temporary rental. Dody Muller had left Kerouac after a stream of filthy street people, the only companions left who'd tolerate Kerouac's self-centered monologues, had befouled her apartment. Dody began an affair with de Kooning, and Jack became involved with Lois Sorrells, a twenty-four-year-old Northport woman. But his primary alliance was with his mother, and since she was as alcoholic as he, they drifted into a whirlpool of dizzying moves around Northport and up and down the Eastern seaboard. Mémère wrote from Florida that everything had "blown up"; the Blakes' marriage was in trouble, and Mémère no longer thought it a good idea for Jack and her to move to Florida. Instead, as Jack told his Grove editor, Don Allen, Mémère decided she wanted to return to Northport. Once again, Jack went house-hunting and purchased a small new cottage with a basement office at 49 Earl Avenue. Settling in, he placed a crucifix over his bed and a picture of the Virgin Mary on the wall, along with prints of El Greco, Picasso, van Gogh, Rouault, Rousseau, and Gauguin paintings.

When Whalen went to visit, he found Jack and Mémère passed out; he was unable to rouse them. Jack was putting away a quart of whiskey a day, and Mémère wasn't far behind. Don Allen also visited, arriving in Northport with Grove owner Barney Rosset and Jack's French editors, Claude Galli-mard and Michel Mohrt. Seated at a round captain's table in the kitchen, Jack and his guests discussed his unpublished manuscripts, and "Mémère served a delicious and hearty supper," Allen recalled. "Jack and I made a short foray to a nearby liquor store and bar." Jack gave Don a sheaf of poems, but the editor didn't succeed in getting *Heaven and Other Poems* published until long after Kerouac's death.[29]

In mid-November 1959, Kerouac flew to Los Angeles to appear on *The Steve Allen Plymouth Show*. According to John Montgomery, Kerouac bolstered his courage in a waterfront bar in Venice, L.A.'s seedy beatnik enclave. Rehearsals, which Kerouac found stressful, were held across town at a Burbank studio. "One hundred technicians waiting for me to start reading, Steve Allen watching me expectant as he plunks the piano, I sit there on the dunce's stool and refuse to read a word or open my mouth," Kerouac recalled. Steve begged him to cooperate, but Kerouac refused and rushed to a bar across the street where he got drunk, he later confessed in *Big Sur*. But he certainly didn't look drunk in the extraordinary color film clip of the show that has survived. At the beginning of the segment, Steve sits at a white grand piano, and his hands move gracefully across the keyboard, picking out a jazz pattern. Turning slightly toward the audience, he says, "In the early 1950s the nation recognized in its midst a social revolution called the Beat Generation." Describing *On the Road* as a "powerful and successful" novel, he recounts how it became a bestseller and turned its author into "the embodiment of this new generation. So here he is, Jack Kerouac."

Kerouac enters, looking healthy and photogenic in his tweed jacket and open-necked polo shirt. Indulging in a bit of behind-the-scenes gossip, Steve tells the audience that the author had been very nervous at rehearsal. Then he asks Jack if he's still uncomfortable.

"Oh, no," Jack replies, leaning on the closed piano cover, using it as a lectern, but in the next few moments, as he attempts to field queries from the urbane, affable Steve, he almost chokes on embarrassment and seems close to tears. Allen asks him how long it took him to complete *On the Road*.

"Three weeks," Jack replies, barely audible.

Next, Steve wants to know how long Jack drifted around the country collecting material for the book.

"Seven years," Jack replies. Chuckling, Steve observes that with *him* it was "just the other way around"—he hitchhiked for three weeks and needed seven years to write it up. Then Steve apologizes for posing the "tired" question that Jack must have heard from a hundred interviewers and fans: What, exactly, does *beat* mean?

"Well, sympathetic," Jack says, smiling but emphatically indicating it's his last word on the subject. A shrewd interviewer, Allen realizes that he at last has Jack primed to give a good reading. The audience is expecting to hear Jack read from *On the Road* as agreed, but Jack cagily finds a way to include a passage from *Visions of Cody*, a book he prefers to *On the Road*. Before reading it, he explains that people often ask him why he wrote *On the Road*. Everything he writes is "true" because he believes in what he sees and reports it as it is. Then he reads a passage from *Visions of Cody*, the annunciation scene at the Colorado state line, where Kerouac had a vision of God telling him to "go moan for man," and to write truly of the world. "My heart opened up to God," Jack says, and then he segues into *On the Road*, describing how in the final passages he told of his buddy Dean Moriarty coming "all the way from the West coast" to visit him for just a couple of days. "We'd just been back and forth across the country several times in cars," Jack says, "but now our travels were over. We were still great friends, but we had to go into later phases of our lives." All nervousness gone now, he begins to read the coda with such authority and feeling that many in the audience are moved to tears: "Old Dean's gone. . . . So in America when the sun goes down and I sit on the old broken-down river pier watching the long, long skies over New Jersey and sense all that raw land that rolls in one unbelievable huge bulge over to the West Coast . . . I think of Dean Moriarty." From the instant Jack said "*gone!*" the meaning of the coda became poignantly clear; it was about the temporality of life, and how the comings and goings of loved ones, and ultimately of life itself, must be accepted as part of living.

Steve Allen remembered Jack reciting "great rolling period-shy paragraphs." The show was seen by thirty million viewers, and Kerouac received two thousand dollars for his appearance. In *Big Sur*, he recalled "surprising everybody the night of the show by doing my job of reading just fine." Later, the producers took him out in a group that included Mamie Van Doren, the wife of bandleader Ray Anthony. Kerouac evidently made a pass, was rebuffed, and spitefully lashed out, calling her "a big bore trying to read me her poetry and won't talk love because in Hollywood man love is for sale."

In his book *More Funny People*, Steve Allen recalled seeing a "slightly intoxicated" Kerouac two nights later. "We had just left a recording studio on Sunset Boulevard near CBS and our farewells, for no particular reason, had turned to horseplay." As Steve started walking down a quiet residential side street to his parked car, Jack couldn't stand to see the evening end. He started "shouting mildly obscene pleasantries." Steve turned and waved, calling out "somewhat less raucously—not because I had any better sense than he but because I was sober. . . . Jack was not speaking to me in his own voice, he was imitating Dayton Allen. 'Steve Allen,' he was shouting, at half past midnight, 'how's your sister? And why . . . not.' " In *Moody Street Irregulars*, Steve explained that Dayton Allen, one of the comics on his show, was a Groucho Marx type known for his trademark expression *Whyyyy not?*, delivered in a goofy fashion. After Jack had yelled at Allen that night, Allen paused on the sidewalk and laughed long enough for Jack to realize he'd got the joke. "And then he was gone," Allen recalled.[30]

Before leaving for the San Francisco International Film Festival, where he was to be honored for *Pull My Daisy*, Jack looked in on the filming of *The Subterraneans* at the mammoth MGM studio in Culver City, which in 1959 was still a bustling production center. MGM's major picture that year, *Ben-Hur*, brought the studio a record-shattering eleven Academy Awards, including the best-actor Oscar for Charlton Heston. *The Subterraneans* had begun with high hopes on Kerouac's part, when he'd met with producer Arthur Freed, the man responsible for many of the vintage MGM musicals, including *Singin' in the Rain* and *An American in Paris*. But on seeing some of the footage at the studio, Kerouac realized that *The Subterraneans* was a "travesty" of his novel, he later told John Clellon Holmes.

MGM ads promised to lay bare "love among the new bohemians," but the film cringed from reality and watered the interracial love story down to suit middle-class prejudices. The black heroine was turned into a white girl played by Leslie Caron, the lovable gamine of *Lili* and *Gigi*. As Leo Percepied, wholesome George Peppard embraces Mardou before the final fadeout and tells her, "You cook, I'll write." The *Hollywood Reporter* rather liked Peppard, writing that he "talks and acts like a legitimate Beat." Kerouac disagreed, complaining that Peppard had portrayed him as a rowdy; Jack himself would never have settled his differences with Corso, played by Roddy McDowall, by threatening to break his arm. Other cast members included Jim Hutton, the father of future star Timothy Hutton, as Ginsberg, and future *Rowan and Martin's Laugh-in* star Arte Johnson as Gore Vidal. Even *Time*, one of Kerouac's worst enemies, was offended, grumbling that the movie "bears about as much relationship to Jack Kerouac's novel as Hollywood does to Endsville." In *Saturday Review*, Hollis Alpert noted that the film was exactly like producer Freed's musicals, except "the score and lyrics are missing."

Jack's trip from L.A. to San Francisco that week took him from the ridiculous to the sublime: *Pull My Daisy* was receiving top honors at the film festival. Kerouac arrived on the verge of a nervous collapse, blaming his condition, in a letter to Neal, on the Steve Allen show and other movieland "folderol." He went to an Italian club on Grant Street and sang along with a jazz combo, later spending the night with Jacky Westrope, a woman whose husband, a jockey, had recently been killed. Though Neal was cooped up in a miserable cell in San Quentin, Jack gloatingly described the "widow's mansion" and other luxuries in his rather insensitive letter to Neal. Westrope predicted that Kerouac was overdue for some sort of calamity, but he boasted to Neal that he was as invincible as Balzac. Jack later stayed with Whalen at one of the pioneering communes, Hyphen-House, at 1713 Buchanan, near Post, which Kerouac later described as a multiracial hostel for hip couples and singles. In *Big Sur*, he represented Lenore Kandel—author of the later counterculture poem, "To Fuck With Love"—as "Romana Schwartz," who walked around the house in "purple panties . . . nothing else on . . . she's . . . a nudist . . . also intelligent, well read, writes poetry, is a Zen student, knows everything, is in fact just simply a big healthy Rumanian Jewess who wants to marry a good hardy man." Others at Hyphen-House included John Montgomery and two future collaborators of Kerouac's, Lew Welch and a Japanese poet named Albert Saijo. Jack ran into his old friend Helen Elliott, and her name later appeared on Kerouac's sex list with no number, but with the notation, "Calif."

Though Jack didn't get in touch with Carolyn, she heard in Los Gatos that he was cheered at the film festival when *Pull My Daisy* was screened. Called to the stage, he was so intoxicated that he fell down twice as members of the audience gasped. *Pull My Daisy* was awarded the first prize for Best American Experimental Film for 1959, and Kerouac's narration was praised as "the most beautiful since that of *The River*," Pare Lorenz's 1938 documentary about the Tennessee Valley Authority. Jack antagonized many people at the festival, showing up drunk and acting ridiculous during group interviews with Robert Frank and Alfred Leslie. Wearing a workshirt to a formal party in his honor at the Matador, he was refused entrance by the doorman, but Leslie interceded and Jack was finally admitted. Once inside, he was shunned by the other guests until debonair David Niven, winner of the 1958 best-actor Oscar for *Separate Tables*, lifted his glass to Kerouac, invited him to sit at his table, and said, "Strike another blow for freedom, Mr. Kerouac!"[31]

Jack promised Neal that he'd go to San Quentin on November 21 at 9 A.M. to address the inmates in a prison class on comparative religion. But he not only failed to show, he even refused to visit Neal, lest ever-present journalists report that he approved of drugs and lawbreaking. For weeks thereafter, in letters to Carolyn, Neal bitterly attacked Kerouac, while Kerouac, in his correspondence with Neal, made excuses about how occupied he'd been with the rich and famous in San Francisco. Neal lumped Kerouac together with *Chronicle* columnist Herb Caen as "pure puke," and he wrote that neither Kerouac, Ginsberg, nor any of his other "sicknik" friends had sent him a penny. Neal failed to see that there was a certain justice in Jack's snubs, after the way Neal had ditched him in San Francisco and Mexico City.

To compensate for what Neal referred to as Kerouac's "defection," Alan Watts agreed to address the convicts at San Quentin. In the coming months,

Neal would adjust to prison life, despite some physical ailments, such as rectal polyps that were so large they provoked a prison doctor to exclaim, "What beauties." Recovering from alcohol and drug addiction, Neal began a program of self-improvement: he quit smoking, stopped masturbating, prayed hourly, lifted weights, and ran two hundred and fifty yards in fifty-three seconds. Prison, he wrote Carolyn, was exactly what he needed, and eventually he enjoyed everything about San Quentin except for missing his children. Certain that God was enlightening him, he embraced his confinement as a divinely ordained penance. Finally released the following year, on June 3, 1960, he immediately fell back into his old ways, however, and resumed drinking and drugging harder than ever.[32]

Before leaving San Francisco, Kerouac inveigled Whalen's roommates, Welch and Saijo, into driving him back home on Route 66 in "Willy," Lew's Jeep station wagon, which had a mattress in back. At one point along the twenty-four-hundred-mile highway, which spanned the continent from L.A. to Chicago, they stopped to steal a roadside cross commemorating a fatal highway crash. The act symbolized Kerouac's troubled return to Christianity after his long romance with Buddhism ended in 1959. In a letter to Whalen he wrote that the "sudden buddhism boom" he'd expected *The Dharma Bums* to bring about in the United States had not materialized, and he had nothing more to say about the dharma, which was "slipping away." He needed the comforts of Christianity; "life without heaven" was insupportable, he told Whalen. In Kerouac's understanding of Buddhism, the creation of the world had been a stupid mistake. He could no longer believe that theory, since he felt "the presence of angels." But Buddhism had not failed Kerouac so much as Kerouac had failed Buddhism; he'd willfully refused to follow the path of sobriety which, as he well knew, was required for enlightenment. He had foreseen the end of his Buddhist period in *Some of the Dharma*, writing that he preferred "the wine, the weed," and the rewards of fame.

In Las Vegas, Lew Welch gambled in a casino while Jack and Saijo visited a replica of Mount Vernon, George Washington's Virginia plantation home. Back in the jeep, Lew drove while Jack rode shotgun and Saijo meditated in the rear. Though Saijo remembered that Kerouac sometimes spelled them at the wheel, Kerouac was still too nervous to be a good driver. As a nisei—a person born in America to Japanese immigrants—Saijo had been confined in the California camp for Japanese American citizens during World War II until he was drafted, and then he fought alongside GIs in Italy. Kerouac's other companion, Lew Welch, resembled Neal Cassady in many ways. A superb driver and pyrotechnical monologist, Lew was later described by Carolyn Cassady as "a great delight . . . with thick, straight red hair . . . piercing blue eyes, slight of frame but wiry . . . intelligent . . . erudite . . . satirical." Lew drank as heavily as Kerouac and suffered from periodic liver breakdowns.

During the trip, Kerouac, Welch, and Saijo collaborated on haikus about Oklahoma windmills spinning in the wind and staid-looking grain elevators standing at attention on the Midwestern plains. These were posthumously published in 1973 in *Trip Trap: Haiku Along the Road From San Francisco to New York, 1959*. In East St. Louis, the queen city of Route 66, they stopped to catch a striptease show, perhaps following the advice given in Bobby Troup's 1941 song, "Get Your Kicks on Route 66." As Kerouac traversed the old highway for the last time in 1959, Route 66 was crumbling and would shortly be replaced by superhighways. Impressed by the German autobahn, President Eisenhower envisaged a 42,500-mile U.S. interstate system, and the Federal Aid Highway Act had been passed in 1956.

Back in Northport, Mémêre served Thanksgiving dinner, which Saijo later described as "wonderfully abundant." She liked Welch and Saijo, but both men soon left New York. Welch wanted to go hiking and camping on the Rogue River in Oregon (in 1971, he would disappear while hunting in the mountains near Nevada City, California, and never be found). Jack too wanted to go into the wilderness, and he wrote Neal on December 13 that the only desire he had left was for a house in the wilds of Oregon.[33] But he remained in New York, where *Pull My Daisy* had its commercial premiere at the newly opened New Yorker Theater the first week of April 1960, marking the first time that a short film was the main feature on a bill. It ran with Orson Welles's *The Magnificent Ambersons* the first week and Morris Engel's *The Little Fugitive* the next.

The film was the only unqualified critical success of Kerouac's career. *Esquire* film critic Dwight Macdonald called it "as refreshing as anything I've yet seen. . . . The narrative by Jack Kerouac . . . kept things rolling along on a tide of laughter and poetry, like a parody of the stage manager in *Our Town*, substituting a raucous city streets accent for the latter's folksy twang. . . . Kerouac shows an unexpected virtuosity at the Great American Art of kidding." In both *Film Culture* and the *Village Voice*, Mekas hailed Kerouac's narration as a work of "immediacy, poetry and magic that is without precedent in American Cinema . . . a portrait of the inner condition of an entire generation . . . the only true 'beat' film . . . in the sense that beat is an expression of the new generation's unconscious and spontaneous rejection of the middle class way . . . the most truthful American film." Peter Bogdanovich, future director of *Paper Moon* and *The Last Picture Show*, called it "brilliant."

Such accolades were out of proportion to the film's popular acceptance, which was nil. After two weeks at the nine-hundred-seat New Yorker, it virtually disappeared from screens. At just under thirty minutes, it was neither a short subject (not that any venue exists for those) nor a feature film, and no one knew how to distribute or show it. If Frank and Leslie had produced the other two shorts that were intended to make up a ninety-minute feature with *Pull My Daisy*, the film might have reached a wider audience. Ironically, *Pull My Daisy*, the brightest star in Kerouac's critical crown, was consigned to oblivion.[34]

Turning again to the novel form, Kerouac started terrorizing Lucien and

Cessa in early 1960 with threats to tell all about the Kammerer killing in his new project, *Vanity of Duluoz*. Ginsberg begged him to put the book aside, pointing out that Lucien was dead set against it. Reluctantly, Kerouac complied, but would offer it to me at Coward-McCann a few years later, and I would pay him to write it. The Kammerer killing was the high point of the novel, and a good example of Kerouac's honed-down, bare-bones late style.

Ferlinghetti called on Kerouac in Northport in April 1960 to review Kerouac's backlog of manuscripts for possible publication by City Lights. Subsequently, Ferlinghetti issued Jack's poem *Rimbaud*. *Book of Dreams*, described by the author as an eight-year record of his dreams, from 1952–1960, came from City Lights in 1961, and *Scattered Poems* was posthumously issued by Ferlinghetti in 1971. Ferlinghetti graciously invited Kerouac to come to the West Coast and use his cabin at Bixby Canyon in the Big Sur region, and Kerouac accepted, boarding a train for California on July 17, 1960. He felt he had to escape New York or perish.[35] He was 38, and about to collapse.

NINE

CRACK-UP

In 1960, the two key novelists of the postwar years—Jack Kerouac and Norman Mailer—both suffered nervous breakdowns. In the very process of trying to pull himself together in Big Sur, Kerouac "went mad," he wrote Carolyn. Mailer too was trying to reinvent himself, running for mayor of New York City, when he stabbed his wife, Adele. If the Beat parties were miniversions of Woodstock, the Mailers' parties were the precursors of Altamont. On the night of the stabbing, two hundred people, including scuzzy-looking deadbeats, bag women, pimps, and runaways, as well as Shel Silverstein, Leonard Lyons, C. Wright Mills, George Plimpton, Peter Duchin, Barney Rosset, Allen Ginsberg, Norman Podhoretz, Barbara Probst Solomon, Tony Franciosa, and Frank Corsaro, attended the Mailers' bash in their twelfth-floor sublet at Ninety-fourth Street. Adele was resentful that Mailer seemed more devoted to his mistresses and male friends than to her. At the fateful party, which was a birthday celebration for Mailer's prizefighter friend Roger Donahue, Adele disappeared into the bathroom with a girl, according to Bill Ward, editor of the *Provincetown Review*. "They were very cozy," he recalled. "That's possibly what might have triggered Norman." But Adele would later cite Gore Vidal's comment, "My dear, Norman has always been married to Mickey [Knox]. There's never been anyone else for him." At the end of the party, loaded on martinis, Adele called Mailer a "little faggot." Drunk and drugged, Mailer seized a kitchen knife and plunged it into her chest near her heart. Adele was taken to the hospital; Mailer was packed off to Bellevue, where he was diagnosed as having "an acute paranoid breakdown." Mailer's friend, H. L. "Doc" Humes, cofounder of the *Paris Review*, observed, "The precipitating factor was alcohol." Adele survived her ordeal, but her marriage to Mailer, which she later characterized as "our little dance of death," was over. Mailer escaped without a prison sentence.

Alcohol was also the precipitating factor of Kerouac's psychotic episode. Though Ferlinghetti provided a cabin for him to begin a new novel in, and a chance for peace and calm in Bixby Canyon near Big Sur, Kerouac got drunk as soon as he stepped off the California Zephyr in San Francisco. He was a wreck by the time he finally left the city by bus and rode one hundred and thirty miles down the coast to Monterey. He arrived after dark, the worst possible time to go to into the Big Sur region, a rugged wilderness of mountains, redwoods, and jagged coastline. No public transportation was available, so he took a cab from Monterey and began a half-hour ride. Highway 1 clings to mountainsides that are almost perpendicular to the roaring sea hundreds of feet below, with no guardrails but with many hairpin turns. Finally the driver deposited him in Bixby Canyon, and Kerouac groped his way in pitch-black darkness to Ferlinghetti's cabin, where he collapsed with a severe case of delirium tremens. After three weeks of lonely terror, he started walking back up to Monterey, a harrowing trek that left him exhausted, and limping on bleeding feet.[1]

He took a bus to San Francisco, rounded up an entourage, and descended on Neal and Carolyn in Los Gatos, again becoming enmeshed in their sticky emotional life. Jack noted that Neal was as magnetically appealing as ever, and he wrote in *Big Sur*, "women were always having transcontinental telephone talks about his dong." As usual, Neal had more women than he could handle and tried to fob off his new mistress, Jacqueline Gibson, on Kerouac, but according to Carolyn, Kerouac said, "She bores me." All Kerouac wanted was to resume his old, close relationship with Neal, but for a variety of reasons, this was no longer feasible. Both Jack and Neal were approaching forty, and both were now hanging out with younger men. Neal was obsessed with a convicted thief, fresh out of Soledad State Prison, who was physically a younger version of Kerouac—black-haired and muscular—while Kerouac was rather haplessly involved with a blond sixteen-year-old boy he'd admired at the nude baths. Kerouac's rage and frustration over his thwarted desires broke out in another attempt to sabotage Neal and Carolyn's marriage. He cruelly set up a confrontation between Neal's wife and mistress, bringing Jackie Gibson to Los Gatos and thrusting her on Carolyn. "I guess it was bound to happen sometime she'd come here," Carolyn told Jack. "I guess it was destined to be you who'd bring her." In the end, Neal remained with Carolyn, and Jack went off alone, "but not to any life of my own on the other end either, just a traveling stranger," he wrote in *Big Sur*. He spent his final night in San Francisco in bed with poet Bob Kaufman, who'd recently been roughed up by the police and thrown in jail for posting a notice about a poetry reading. The next morning, Kerouac left a note telling Kaufman he didn't even know his name, and added, "I have . . . slept with you and loved you." Linda Gravenites, who was later Janis Joplin's roommate, recalled, "Bob Kaufman was wonderful. I proofread his autobiographical book of poems, *Second April*, because I was hanging out with Bob and Bill Margolis, another North Beach poet. One day I was in Vesuvio's, and someone I was sitting with said, 'Oh, there's Jack Kerouac.' I looked over, and Jack was really drunk. He was slipping and sliding out of his chair and under the table."[2]

When Kerouac returned to Long Island, Mémère was shocked by his deterioration, and she wrote Holmes a pitiful letter, begging him to save her "boy," who was "going to pieces." But Holmes was as alcoholic as Jack, and he later confessed that he and Jack would get drunk together and happily reminisce about the past. "He drank a quart of brandy every single day," Holmes recalled. Sterling confirmed that "something just about like what he tells about in *Big Sur* actually took place. You'd call it a breakdown, I guess." In mid-October 1960, Kerouac spent three days in the East Village with Ginsberg, "finally ending in bed w/me & Peter like Silenus nekkid—his big thighs and belly," Ginsberg recalled, comparing Kerouac with a figure from Greek mythology, Silenus, who was a sly, cowardly old drunk. Ginsberg's East Second Street apartment had become the focus of the new sixties drug culture after Ginsberg's return from South America, where Peter Matthiessen had arranged for Ginsberg to acquire the hallucinogenic drug yage. The drug made Ginsberg feel that he was God, and, despite numerous bad trips, he became convinced that drugs could implement the old Beat goals of sexual and spiritual liberation. He wrote his long poem *Kaddish* on the Beats' drug of choice, Benzedrine.[3]

In November 1960, a splendid new era began in the United States with the election of the youthful president, John F. Kennedy. Increasingly conservative from 1960 on and convinced that nothing mattered, Kerouac didn't vote in the presidential election, but he favored Richard Nixon. To vote, he felt, would "encourage Caesarism." Ginsberg found both Nixon and Kennedy "obnoxious," he wrote Jack, adding that Nixon "take[s] the cake." His statement to Kerouac, "I HATE AMERICA!", was symptomatic of how out-of-step the Beats were with the country at the dawn of the New Frontier, as was Ginsberg's sentimental journey up to Harlem to shake Fidel Castro's hand. Kerouac was thrilled when First Lady Jacqueline Kennedy told *Reader's Digest* that she read everything from "Colette to Kerouac," but unfortunately her endorsement did not have the same effect on his sales that JFK's had on Ian Fleming's, when the new president revealed he was a James Bond addict.[4]

A significant factor in Kerouac's failure after his split from Viking was the total absence of a coherent publishing program. In pell-mell fashion, publishers continued to throw his books at the reviewers and the public, inundating them with no fewer than five new Kerouac titles in 1960, all of which were ignored. *The Scripture of the Golden Eternity* was issued by LeRoi Jones's Totem Press in the spring, followed by the Avon paperback original, *Tristessa*; the McGraw-Hill hardcover, *Lonesome Traveler*; and the City Lights broadside, *Rimbaud*. *Book of Dreams*, also issued by City Lights, received no reviews in New York, and only two in the rest of the nation. Kerouac wrote

318 SUCCESS, LOVE, MARRIAGE, MADNESS

Carolyn and Neal that he was so angry at critics that he was tempted to stop publishing altogether. And in a letter to Ginsberg he blamed the destruction of his reputation on the "Marxist" reviewers of New York. Ginsberg wrote Neal and Carolyn that Kerouac was threatening to kill himself.[5]

Jack's mood did not improve in early 1961 when his second wife, Joan, took him to court, still claiming he was Jan's father. Although the case would drag on to the end of the twentieth century, long after all the principals were dead, a document uncovered in the archive in Lowell in 1995 sheds an interesting light on Joan's allegations. On March 15, 1961, Kerouac wrote that a good friend of his "was laying" Joan, as was the nephew of his friend. Kerouac added that Joan had deserted her husband and children and wanted to use Kerouac as "the husband sucker." In a letter to the Cassadys, Jack added that Joan's husband "laid her up to 2 twins," but she "couldn't stand" him and returned to New York with her twins and Jan. Jack's lawyer, Ginsberg's brother Eugene Brooks, managed to get the paternity case postponed, but the legal pressures, combined with Jack's drinking in Manhattan, inevitably brought on a relapse of phlebitis. Jack was also afraid that Jacqueline Gibson, his Big Sur sex partner, would sue him for mentioning marriage and then walking out. He wrote the Cassadys that if he ever thought of having sex again, he would have his penis amputated.[6]

When he tried to write in Northport, he discovered that he had nothing to say, and even worse, he had no further interest in language or style. To combat boredom, he started bringing Northport riffraff into his and Mémêre's home, and Mémêre became frightened as the house filled up with sinister-looking creeps. Though he observed his thirty-ninth birthday on March 12, 1961, he carried on with teenagers until dawn, and Mémêre lay in bed wondering if she was going to be raped and murdered in her own home. She decided to flee once more to Nin in Florida, and Jack put his second Northport house up for sale.

In a newly released note in the Lowell archive, Kerouac outlined his next move. Part of the note was typewritten, the rest hastily handprinted, chronicling his April 1961 move with Mémêre to the Kingswood Manor in Orlando. They settled at 1309 Alfred Drive, just two houses from Nin. He wrote Don Allen in early June 1961 that his new quarters were "real fawncy" and described the terrazzo flooring, wall oven, shower stall, and heating and air-conditioning, as well as the handy supermarket down the street. The subdivision was surrounded by sturdy fences, but soon he was complaining in a letter to Carolyn that he couldn't abide the neighborhood any longer. Die-hard beatniks had succeeded in tracking him down, and he was under siege by "interrupting maniacs," including a Swedish tourist.[7]

His alcoholic geographics—frequent moves undertaken on the fallacious assumption that misery can be left behind—began to come even faster now, and suddenly he decided to leave Orlando and return to Mexico City. On another handprinted note in the Lowell archive, he wrote that in June 1961 he arrived in Mexico City and stayed at 13-A Cerrada de Medellin. In Mexico

City, his dark, uncomfortable apartment was below the duplex once inhabited by Bill and Joan Burroughs, and he seemed to be surrounded by ghosts of the past. He was due soon in New York for a court date, but thought it best to remain in Mexico for solitary meditation. In July 1961, he wrote the twenty-two choruses of *Cerrada Medellin Blues*, which were full of allusions to loneliness, drinking, guardian angels, and homoeroticism. If all the Beats got together, they would create one long penis, he wrote, in a homoerotic variation on Dorothy Parker's statement that if all the girls at Vassar were laid end to end, she wouldn't be surprised. Holmes was not only a friend, but an "almost lover," he wrote in the "8th Chorus" of the "Second Solo" of *Cerrada Medellin Blues*.

Usually too intoxicated to write, he rationalized that he was consuming Jesus' blood when he drank Benedictine, for surely the cross and "D.O.M." on the label sanctified it as a divine cocktail. When he heard of Hemingway's suicide in 1961, he wrote "Hemingway Blues," followed immediately by "Me Too Blues," mocking the final macho gesture of "Hoomingway," who blew his brains out in Idaho by triggering a shotgun with his big toe. In the same poem, there was a chilling image of the human brain as a creamy dessert specked with currants—or perhaps riddled with buckshot. Like Kerouac, Hemingway had found that writing interfered with his drinking, and he had produced little of significance after collecting the Nobel Prize for Literature in 1954.

Though Kerouac's major creative period was now behind him, he overcame his writer's block and managed to complete fifty-thousand words of fiction while in Mexico City, his first sustained attempt at narrative writing in four years. The new novel, which he at first called *An American Passed Here* and later used as Book Two, "Passing Through," in *Desolation Angels*, dealt with his experiences in Mexico City in the late fifties, his affairs with Weaver and Johnson, and his African and European travels, ending with his decision to renounce the Beat life and settle down with his mother on Long Island. He wrote Don Allen that he was in no rush to publish *Desolation Angels*; Barney Rosset at Grove had offered a thousand dollars, which Jack thought "measly," and so the novel went into the bottom drawer. Besides, critics were complaining that Kerouac books were a glut on the market. He was also holding back *Visions of Gerard*, waiting for a good offer and the proper timing. Kerouac was at last developing some professional publishing savvy.

He was thrown into a fit of loathing, he wrote Carolyn, when his packed suitcase was stolen from his room in Mexico City. His young Mexican Indian boyfriend had been buying Jack drinks and even professed to love him, but Jack suspected that his trick was implicated in the theft. As Kerouac later said to me after I purchased *An American Passed Here* for Coward-McCann, "A good lay ain't always worth the price you pay, even in Mexico, where you can get a blow job for a few pesos, and get fucked for free." In Mexico, he imagined a guardian angel hovering over him, inquiring why he'd forsaken

so many friends, and he thought longingly of Corso, Ginsberg, Diane Di-
Prima, LeRoi Jones, Snyder, Burroughs, Ray Bremser, Neal, Sammy, Esperanza, and Lucien. He cursed the world and immediately regretted it, mindful
of Thomas Merton's unshakable benevolence. After a final drinking binge,
he left his once-beloved Mexico City, never to come back again.[8]

Upon his return to Orlando, Kerouac learned that he was being exposed
in *Confidential* magazine, a scandal sheet that was the *National Enquirer* of
its day. As Kerouac consumed his daily fifth of Johnny Walker Red, he perused Joan Haverty's article, "My Ex-Husband, Jack Kerouac, Is an Ingrate."
Joan was under the impression that he had an annual income of fifty-
thousand dollars, based on inflated newspaper reports. Kerouac rarely had as
much as ten thousand in savings.

Unsurprisingly, his horrendous intake of Johnny Walker Red soon
brought on an abdominal hemorrhage. When he recovered, he went to New
York to face his paternity case. The *New York Daily News* headlined its
account, BEAT BARD DENIES HE'S THE DADDY-O. He met his alleged nine-
year-old daughter, Jan, in June 1961, when she was living with her mother
and twin half-sisters in a tenement on the Lower East Side. The court ordered
blood tests to determine paternity, and both Jack and Jan were tested, but
other biographical literature is inconclusive with regard to the results. Nicosia
did not specifically footnote his claim that "blood tests . . . showed that she
was possibly his daughter (at that time it was impossible to obtain conclusive
physical proof)." Nor, in an article written with Richard Gehr and published
in the *Village Voice*, did Joyce Johnson's son, Daniel Pinchbeck, document
his statement, "After the blood test he admitted Jan was his daughter." Nicosia claimed the exact opposite: "In his final appearance before Judge Benjamin Fine, Jack still denied the girl was his." In her memoir, Joyce wrote
that Kerouac told her Jan was not his daughter, though he carried a picture
of her in his wallet; Pinchbeck confirmed this in the *Voice*, writing that
Kerouac explicitly told Joyce, "This is not my daughter." McNally, author of
Desolate Angel, interviewed Eugene Brooks but did not document his allegation that "Jack 'lost' on the blood test and was forced to acknowledge
paternity."

In a statement to Joyce, later repeated by Pinchbeck in the *New York
Times Magazine*, Kerouac attempted to explain what appeared to some observers to be a family resemblance between Jack and Jan: "Jan's mother had
schemed to have an affair with a man who looked like [Jack]," Pinchbeck
wrote. The meeting between Kerouac and his alleged daughter was warm
and friendly, according to Jan's account. "It was a day for which I had been
waiting all my young life," she stated in a 1994 press conference. "Finally . . .
I was face to face with this handsome blue-eyed man I'd heard so much
about . . . who looked just like me and who was afraid to meet my gaze. . . .
I didn't see him again for six years."[9]

On October 24, 1961, from Orlando, Kerouac wrote his Italian editor,
Nanda Pivano, that he'd finished *Big Sur* in ten days. It was a fictional

account of his alcoholic crack-up the previous year. On megadoses of Benzedrine, he'd managed to cut through his hangovers long enough to turn out one of the most honest and shocking novels of his career, comparable in its unflinching depiction of alcoholism and insanity to Fitzgerald's *The Crack-Up*. In style, it was a "plain tale in a smooth buttery literate run," he told the *Paris Review*, explaining that it combined the mystical aura of *Tristessa*, the speedwriting of "The Railroad Earth," and the Dostoyevskian confessional hysteria of *The Subterraneans*. He typed the novel on a Teletype roll, single-spaced, at such a fast clip that it probably contained less fiction, he told Carolyn, than anything he'd ever written, and would immediately be recognized as an autobiographical document with easily recognizable characters. As a result, he developed a guilt complex over having exposed his California friends, and he felt so "shitty," he added, that he put the scroll away and, for a while, suppressed his own novel. "Notoriety and public confession is a frazzler of the heart," he told the *Paris Review*. But he celebrated the novel's completion by going through a case of cognac in a week, and he ended up in the hospital in a blackout.[10]

Back in New York, supposedly for a house-hunting trip to Vermont, he went on an excruciating month-long binge, which he described to Carolyn in January 1962. He and Lucien got into violent fights with each other and sometimes came home bloody. The White Horse Tavern banned him. After one blackout, he woke up missing hundreds of dollars.

He returned to Orlando on the train, retyped the *Big Sur* scroll on standard double-spaced pages, and dispatched the manuscript to Sterling, with carbon copies, so that it could be submitted simultaneously to more than one house. Kerouac was still considered to be a "hot property," and both Barney Rosset and Don Allen of Grove were panting to publish any new novel by him. Both Giroux and Cowley had declined *Wake Up* when it was still entitled *Your Essential Mind: Story of the Buddha*, and had treated it "coldly," Kerouac said, according to John Sampas. But *Big Sur* was offered to both Giroux and Cowley, and Giroux's offer of ten thousand dollars was eventually accepted. Jack was pleased by Sterling's news that Giroux also wanted *Visions of Gerard*. As Sterling had some leverage in the deal, Giroux agreed to make no editorial changes. "Jack had a clause in his contracts — no editing," Sterling said in a 1996 telephone conversation with me.

When *Big Sur* was published, many critics punished Kerouac for being an alcoholic, as if he'd willingly chosen the disease. In the sixties, years before First Lady Betty Ford and Elizabeth Taylor made the disease of alcoholism as respectable as cancer or tuberculosis, virtually no one admitted to being an alcoholic, and the subject was shrouded in shame and secrecy. Even Hunter Thompson refused to understand why someone as hip as Kerouac couldn't have a good time in Big Sur, and he wrote a friend that he would give one of his testicles to trade places with Jack so he could drink and drug with the beatniks. Having expected *Big Sur* to be a sexy California romp, Thompson resented Kerouac's searing documentary of a ruined life, and he summarily dismissed *Big Sur* as a "stupid, shitty book." *Time* scoffed at the novel's honest account of alcoholism and mental collapse, scorning the author as "ridiculous and . . . pathetic." Kerouac fired back at the magazine in an item in Mary Sampas's column in the *Sun*, dismissing *Time*'s anonymous reviewer as a "pantywaist." Herbert Gold wrote in *Saturday Review* that all of Kerouac's thirteen previously published books were "a flood of trivia," but at least Gold acknowledged that Jack was "on the right road at last . . . in focus, troubling and touching." William Wiegand, writing in the *New York Times Book Review*, seemed unaccountably pleased that Kerouac had suffered a nervous breakdown, but praised *Big Sur*'s "sense of structure and pacing . . . the scenes click and signify." Attempting to explain the continuing critical backlash against Kerouac, Ralph J. Gleason wrote in the *San Francisco Chronicle* that Kerouac had "committed the worst crime of those who go against the traditional in literature, he has been read." Kerouac assumed that he was a victim of reverse anti-Semitism, he wrote Carolyn in October 1962, but it was far likelier that the critics disdained him because he had achieved a celebrity status far beyond that usually accorded serious authors.[11]

As he turned forty in 1962, Kerouac had a premonition of death. Not even sure that he would live until he was fifty-two, the age at which his friend Franz Kline had died, he began to set his affairs in order and willed everything to his mother. He established highly organized files for his letters and manuscripts, leaving a substantial archive for future researchers. He bemoaned the emptiness of his life in Florida, telling Carolyn that he had neither male nor female friends, nor intellectual peers. But his main problem, he added, was alcohol. He joked that he still had his good looks because booze had pickled him, but acknowledged that beneath the surface, he was "cropping a corpse."

Longing to live again in New England, he left Florida and went looking for real estate on the Maine coast in the summer of 1962, but he stumbled into another bender and somehow ended up on Cape Cod. In a jazz club one night, he was brutally beaten by the black bouncer. He later regained consciousness in a muddy pasture, sobbing. Jack's penchant for making racist cracks left him increasingly susceptible to retribution in the 1960s as blacks made steady strides toward correcting America's centuries-old segregationist inequities and were less inclined to indulge bigoted clowns with big mouths.

Returning to Florida, Jack attempted to shed forty excess pounds by working out with weights and mowing the lawn, despite the humidity of the tropical summer. In early September, by plane and train, he traveled to the Holmeses' place in Old Saybrook, Connecticut. He consumed a quart of cognac daily for a week, and also drank wine, but refused to eat, shave, bathe, or get dressed in the morning, slouching through the days in pajama bottoms and T-shirt. Once, Holmes accompanied him on a real estate tour of Deep River, but Jack sat in the car, bravely trying to endure what Holmes called "drunk sweats." Finally, Jack gave up and darted into a bar. "Way down deep . . . he wants to die," Holmes confided in a journal entry, noting that

Kerouac could no longer bear his feelings of loss and estrangement. Though Jack's esthetic perceptions remained "dead certain," Holmes noted that in other areas he made no sense at all, blithering on about being Jesus one minute and the devil the next.[12]

Kerouac took a taxi from Old Saybrook to Lowell, though it was a 150-mile trip. His survival instinct was drawing him back to his hometown, perhaps the last place on earth that still retained an illusion of safety for him. Jack and his cabdriver, an Italian from New London named Bartalucci, arrived in Lowell at 3 A.M. He immediately went to Cuckoo O'Connell's bar and drank until he passed out. At closing time, his inert body wasn't noticed, and he spent the night in the bar. The following morning, he helped himself to the liquor stock and was shouting "Whoopee!" when the owner arrived and threatened to call the police. Jack started mumbling Stella's name, and at last the owner rang the Sampas home, informing Stella that a deranged bum was asking for her. She persuaded her brother, Tony, to look after Kerouac that night, and when Tony later left for a dice game, he turned Jack over to a bartender named Manuel "Chiefy" Nobriga, who worked at the Sampas-owned bar, Nicky's. Billy Koumantzelis joined them, and they went on to the SAC—the Sportsmen's Athletic Club—an after-hours lounge in the Acre. The SAC was, and remains today, a large, loud, friendly tavern with a rectangular bar in the middle of a large open space, surrounded by high tables, tall stools, and a dance floor. In 1995, Billy recalled, "Jack's popularity was nil at that time. I hadn't read his books, and haven't read a one of them to this day. He was just a guy I liked very much. He was gentle, kind. But Jack was in limbo, and he didn't make it out. He spent his last sixty dollars on the cab from Connecticut. He looked at me and said, 'You're an ugly bastard. There's no family resemblance between you and Johnny. What happened to you? Your brother was a Greek god.'"

After the bar closed, they left with Tony Sampas and went across the street to a housing project, where two girls they knew lived. "It was Tony Sampas's girl who happened to be over there," Billy recalled. "Jack made a move on her, he made a bad impression. He called her a lesbian. . . . I pulled him outside and said, 'What the fuck, you dope—you're in Lowell. We don't go for that. All night long you've been pullin' this fuckin' shit—pissin' on the lawn and swearin.' You don't act like that in Lowell—you don't go after anybody else's girlfriend.' It was toward the end of the night, and after two bottles of scotch, that I calmed him down. After that, he always said, 'What I like about Billy Koumantzelis is he says it like it is.'"

At some point during Kerouac's ten-day stay in Lowell, he asked Stella to marry him. "I don't know if he was serious," Tony recalled, "but he sure shook up Stella." Now in her early forties, Stella was still single, and still—according to her sister, Helen Surprenant—a virgin, despite being a bosomy, earthy woman, not unlike Anna Magnani. "George Soulis wanted to marry Stella," Betty Sampas, Stella's sister-in-law, said in a 1995 interview. But Stella had waited for Jack, according to both Aida Panagiotakos and John

Sampas. "She would see herself in anything he wrote, or on TV, when he appeared," Aida said. "She told me, 'He's going to marry me.' I thought it was a big joke. I ridiculed her, I really did." Stella recalled that whenever a new Kerouac title was published, "I'd say, 'Look at Jack Kerouac's new book,' and they'd look at the cover, flip through it and say, 'Very nice.' " Kerouac was always conscious of her love, and he told Holmes, "She wants to marry me. She's gonna wait for me."

During Jack's September 1962 visit, Stella accompanied him to a local radio show, "Dialogues in Great Books," at station WCAP to promote *Big Sur*. The interviewers, Charles Jarvis and Jim Curtis, noticed that Jack was swigging from a pint of booze. When Jarvis asked him what he thought of Ginsberg, Jack said, "He stinks." Launching into a discussion of *Big Sur*, Jack pointed out that the bound book contained many typographical errors and suggested the publisher should pay for them. Whenever Mémère had made mistakes in her job as a cobbler, she'd had to pay for the shoes, so why should publishers be any different?

One night he left a bar called Chuck's with Huck Finneral, a reedy, behatted eccentric who carried a business card that read: "Professional killer . . . virgins fixed . . . orgies organized, dinosaurs neutered, contracts & leases broken." Huck's philosophy of life was: "Better a wise madness than a foolish sanity." They drove to a friend's house in Merrimack, New Hampshire, and on the way, Jack sang "Moon River," calling it his favorite song. Composed by Henry Mancini and Johnny Mercer, "Moon River" was the theme song of the popular Audrey Hepburn movie *Breakfast at Tiffany's*. Sobbed by a harmonica, later swelling with strings and chorus, the plaintive tune's gentle but epic-like lyrics describe a dreamer and roamer not unlike Kerouac.

Huck Finneral became one of Jack's "huckleberry friends" in Lowell, and another was a thirty-four-year-old Canuck named Paul Bourgeois, who had spent seven years in a state prison. In an October 4 letter to Ginsberg, Jack stated that Bourgeois had an appointment in Washington with Secretary of State Dean Rusk to discuss the fate of three thousand half–French Canuck Iroquois Indians. Bourgeois was such a charmer that he convinced Kerouac that both Jack and Mémère were honorary members of this tribe. Jack decided to move to the Arctic and live among the Iroquois, taking Mémère along; he looked forward to participating in savage sacraments such as drinking deer blood. In Bourgeois, he had found a seemingly strong male to fill the void left when Neal stopped acknowledging his letters; Jack was "washed up" with Neal, he wrote Ed White. When Jack left Lowell and departed for New York by automobile, Bourgeois was at the wheel, and later on the plane to Florida, Bourgeois was in the seat next to him. Jack had paid his fare.[13]

At home in Orlando, at 1309 Alfred, both Nin and Mémère looked at Bourgeois and immediately smelled a hoax. He was nothing but a typical mill-town punk in Mémère's estimation, and in a letter to Lucien on October 22, Jack wrote that his family had debunked Bourgeois's claim of being a

Kerouac cousin and chief of the Moon Cloud Canucks. But Bourgeois remained an asset of sorts: in bars, he drew desirable people into Jack's orbit, so Jack kept him around, giving him the guest room. But they were both alpha males, prone to fighting, and one night Bourgeois shoved Jack through a window. Fearlessly stepping into the fray, Mémêre parted the combatants, and then kicked Bourgeois out, paying for his train transportation back to Lowell. Not until June 1963 did Jack finally state, in a letter to Ginsberg, that Bourgeois "was shit."

Jack and Mémêre's hope of forming a close family unit with Paul and Nin in Florida turned into a farce, as Kerouac's *Notebook No. 38*, shown me by the estate in 1995, indicates. Jack complained that he had to walk eight miles to collect his mail. He swore that even if he became a millionaire he'd leave no money to the Blakes. What particularly infuriated him was that he'd purchased a seven-dollar fifth of Scotch and given it to Paul, who took it off to a friend without offering Jack a drop. Mémêre, he added, wanted to return to Northport; she was distressed that her in-laws were snubbing her. Jack felt that he and his mother had been betrayed by Nin as well as Paul, and that the Kerouac family unity had been destroyed. He begged his mother to take his side in all issues, but she kept harping that he was letting people like Ginsberg, Burroughs, and Bourgeois kill him, and Jack found himself defending them. He felt helpless since he was always either drunk or hungover, and he swore off hard liquor, thinking, mistakenly, that it would be possible to sober up on beer. Nin's marriage was hanging by a thread; her husband took the five thousand dollars Jack lent him to build an annex to his house and spent it elsewhere. Jack complained in his notebook that he had to write off four thousand dollars.[14]

In their chronic alcoholic geographics, Jack and his mother continued to whiz up and down the East Coast like yo-yos on a string. As long as they could blame their unhappiness on externals, such as houses, relatives, and places, they could avoid facing their alcoholism. On November 1, 1962, Jack returned to Northport. Shortly before Christmas he bought a new ranch-style house with a fireplace, a wood-paneled rumpus room in the basement, and two baths, for twenty-four thousand dollars, arranging for his Florida mortgage to be transferred. It was snowing when he and Mémêre moved into 7 Judyann Court on Christmas Eve. The house was pleasantly situated, high above town, and only half a block from the high-school field. In spring 1963, he played baseball there with Stan Twardowicz and *Newsday* reporter Mike McGrady. Though he hardly looked like an athlete in his ragged red slippers, his sure swing and powerful arms still guaranteed a homer.

Mémêre surveyed her fine ranch house, her twenty-sixth home since Jack's birth, and reflected on how far she'd risen from the ghetto. To show her appreciation, she went to Woolworth's and bought Jack a lamp that was engraved, "Genius at Work." In Jack's bedroom, a rosary dangled from a lamp over his bed. He kissed his crucifix before retiring at night. In Mémêre's room, a bottle of Southern Comfort was stashed under the bed, and she kept the level carefully marked so she could see if Jack was stealing from it. In a *Newsday* interview, she was described as a "dimple-faced little old lady." Studying Jack through her glasses with anguished concern, she said, "It's your one fault, Jack. Too much you drink." The reporter added, "She sighs but hands him another can of beer." Kerouac resumed work on an old project, *Vanity of Duluoz*, but stopped after an attack of the D.T.'s. It would be a miracle if he ever wrote anything again.

"Stella came with Jack to Long Island," Betty Sampas revealed in 1995, explaining that Stella stayed with her Uncle Mike in nearby Huntington. Jack asked her to marry him, and Stella was willing, "but Mémêre put up a fuss," Betty said. "Stella then returned to Lowell." Carolyn Cassady became available to Jack in February 1963 when she decided to divorce Neal, who was still running around with other women. Though Jack had often professed to love Carolyn, he wrote her that he wasn't even sure he'd make it through the "next 24 hours." He advised her to raise her children by the principles of the Sermon on the Mount but said nothing about resuming their love affair.

Corso visited Jack in Northport to work together on a Beat philosophy article for *Playboy*. They got into a heated argument about civil rights, and Corso pointed out the discrepancy between Jack's pro-Negro stance in *On the Road* and the racist epithets he uttered on a daily basis. Jack stubbornly insisted that "poetic statements" in artistic works did not commit him to them in his personal life. The quarrel intensified as they drank, and eventually they dropped their *Playboy* collaboration. Jack's reactionary beliefs and prejudices also came between Snyder and him, after Snyder forwarded a paper by a Japanese girl who had subjected *The Subterraneans* to a psychological analysis. In a May 23, 1963, letter to Snyder, Jack called women "demons" and said they used their wiles to rob men of their freedom. That same year, women's lib was launched with the publication of Betty Friedan's *The Feminine Mystique* and male chauvinism became unfashionable, but Kerouac's misogyny remained unchanged.[15]

Though Kerouac proved too brittle to change with the times, both Snyder and Ginsberg were in the vanguard; in 1963, the two poets were both in India, discussing meditation with the Dalai Lama. Gurus throughout the subcontinent advised Ginsberg that he'd never attain higher consciousness unless he gave up drugs, and Ginsberg wrote Kerouac that he was finished with cosmic musings and had located his true feelings in his "belly." While in Saigon, he learned about the war in Vietnam, where President Kennedy had sent sixteen thousand military advisers in open defiance of the Geneva accords. The U.S. government was still concealing American involvement, but Ginsberg would soon be instrumental in exposing it. Upon his return to the States in 1963, he participated in a fourteen-hour protest, one of the first sixties antiwar rallies.

Kerouac was furious. In a letter to Holmes, he criticized Ginsberg's "messiah" complex, but Ginsberg was only assuming the spiritual role that Kerouac had once proposed for himself in the messianic passages of *The Town and the City*, *Visions of Cody*, and *The Dharma Bums*. On August 26, 1964, after the U.S. sent more soldiers to Vietnam, Kerouac said America ought to "get out" of Vietnam, adding, "the Viet Cong are getting money from Americans." According to Burroughs, whose *Naked Lunch* had at last been published to enormous acclaim, Kerouac had always been a political paradox: a peace-loving Buddhist in an Eisenhower jacket, with a prayer bell in one hand and a flamethrower in the other. Burroughs called it "double-think." Though Bob Dylan, the most influential singer-poet of the sixties, acknowledged Kerouac as his inspiration, Kerouac at first dismissed Dylan as "another fucking folksinger," but eventually he conceded, "Well, he's okay."[16]

Newly divorced from Carolyn, Neal popped back into Jack's life in July 1963, paying a visit to Northport. Jack found him to be as bright and lovable as ever, but objected vociferously to his tacky cronies, whom Jack characterized in a letter to Carolyn as flunkies. They raided Mémère's refrigerator and polished off "expensive delicacies," Jack complained. Since Neal's parole from San Quentin, he'd been in and out of jail, and his driver's license had been revoked. According to Carolyn, he went through eighteen cars in his first two years out of prison. At one point five wrecks were lined up in their driveway. Neal's car thefts had once seemed glamorous to Kerouac, but they terrified him in 1963. He came down with a case of D.T.'s, and his shakes got worse as he imagined police pulling up and hauling him and Mémère to jail with Neal's gang. Finally, Kerouac kicked them out, which effectively ended his relationship with Neal, though they would meet one more time. Jack then went on the wagon for a brief time.

In the late summer of 1963, Kerouac resumed his drinking. Biographer Tom Clark later saw a connection between this slip and a remark made by Joyce Johnson in *Esquire* that Kerouac had "settled down on Long Island with his mother." According to Clark, "The innuendo bothered Jack. He couldn't understand why anybody should make jokes about something as innocent as his love for Gabrielle." In a conversation with Ginsberg, Kerouac vowed he would never cast his mother "to the dogs of eternity." On a Farrar, Straus, and Giroux press release, he gratefully acknowledged that she had underwritten his novels "by working in shoe factories. . . . She's my friend as well as my mother." When he fell off the wagon, he found the effects of alcohol more devastating than ever; a classic symptom of the disease is that it continues to progress, even during periods of abstinence (as recovering alcoholics often say, "While I was sober, my disease was doing push-ups in the parking lot"). As a result, Kerouac's tolerance of alcohol was near its end, and he began to have physical symptoms that were increasingly frightening. In November 1963, shortly after the assassination of President Kennedy, he and Alene were walking through Greenwich Village on their way to the Ninth Circle, a bar and steak house, when he suddenly stopped.

"I can't walk that far without getting a drink," he said.

"Why not?" she asked.

"Because I break out into a sweat, and I have to have another drink."[17]

Robert Giroux published Jack's gentle, radiant fictional meditation, *Visions of Gerard*, in the fall of 1963, to notices that were more like character assassinations than reviews. It would take years for the novel to be recognized as a minor masterpiece — a great prayer in novel form, a fictional equivalent to Schubert's "Ave Maria." After accusing Kerouac of "cast[ing] his deficiencies about him like confetti," *Newsweek* wrote that "childhood is intrinsically a bore, and heartsy-flowery re-creations of it are intrinsically a fraud." In a piece entitled "A Yawping at the Grave," Saul Maloff complained in the *New York Times Book Review* on September 8 that Gerard could not be seen or heard because of Jack's "garrulous hipster yawping." Robert Phelps discounted the novel in the *New York Herald Tribune* as "grossly sentimental." Kerouac told Holmes on October 5 that his *Gerard* notices were like cobwebs stretched across his eyes. He was acutely aware that lesser talents like Edwin O'Connor and Allen Drury were picking up Pulitzer Prizes while he had yet to receive a single award.[18]

He felt as unloved personally as he felt unappreciated critically. One day, he appeared at Ginsberg's Lower East Side apartment and begged for sex. "I'm old," he said, "come on and give me a blow job." Though Ginsberg would once have happily obliged, he now found it an unappetizing prospect. Peter Orlovsky remembered having mercy sex with Kerouac, explaining, "Me and Allen . . . both blew him." Kerouac was so mired in sexual dishonesty that he kept insisting, even in the midst of fellatio, that he wasn't gay. Northport librarian Miklos Zsedely caught Kerouac in a more honest moment; in his taped interview for the Northport Public Library, Kerouac asserted there was nothing inherently wrong with homoeroticism, because "everything is the Holy Ghost." He added that "all the girls that Proust is writing about were boys."[19]

In May 1964, Boston College, which had once offered Kerouac a football scholarship, invited him to visit the campus as a noted author. In a letter to Rev. Sweeney, S. J., who'd extended the invitation, Kerouac offered to deliver an address on Jesus Christ. Two weeks later, he called Sweeney, and they talked at length, according to the priest, who said Kerouac was gentlemanly and sober. They began to correspond, and Sweeney revealed that he was an aficionado of *Visions of Gerard*, calling the novel "one of the most touching elegies I have read." He promised to pray for Jack, and he asked that Jack pray for him as well. Due to scheduling difficulties, occasioned by ceaseless moves from the Northeast to Florida, Jack never made it to Boston College. However, he invited the Jesuit to Northport for a visit, and they remained in touch for the rest of Kerouac's life. In the spring of 1964, Kerouac accepted a speaking engagement at Harvard College, but was so drunk and disorderly that the *Crimson* called him a "clown."

He appeared much sounder in both mind and body the following July, when *Newsday* reporter Val Duncan went to 7 Judyann Court for an interview. At forty-two, Kerouac still had stunning blue eyes and a face that was open and smiling. The reporter noted that Jack had been drinking all day and yet his eyes were not only bright but had "purity" in them, and when they shook hands, Kerouac's "great fist" was strong and dry and friendly. Jack executed one of his headstands for the reporter; the maneuver was accomplished with the style of a "champion gymnast," Duncan wrote. Due to rigorous workouts, Jack had brought his weight down to 190 pounds, and the reporter noticed his "rippling stomach muscles . . . bulging biceps . . . belly hard as a butcher block." Before posing for *Newsday*'s photographer, Jack went to the bathroom and shaved off a four-day growth of beard. He told Duncan he no longer visited Greenwich Village, blaming the politicization of the Beats, whose agenda, he felt, should have remained strictly esthetic. As racist as ever, he deplored activists who militated for civil rights. He was writing an article on Shakespeare for millionaire Huntington Hartford's short-lived slick magazine *Show*, and he described his current novel as a memoir of travel in Europe and North Africa. This was *An American Passed Here*, the novel I would shortly edit as "Passing Through" or "Book Two" in *Desolation Angels*. At the end of the interview, Kerouac asked the reporter to give him a lift to the nearest bar. "I'm out of Scotch and I need a shot," he explained. A little later, he shuffled into a tavern, still wearing his bedroom slippers.[20]

Nin fell desperately ill that summer, and Jack wrote Rev. Sweeney that he and Mémère were moving back to Florida to be near her. Nin was only forty-five years old, but already suffering from arteriosclerosis, and her weight dropped to ninety pounds. Kerouac sold the Northport house, and he and Mémère boarded the train for Florida. In St. Petersburg, he purchased a new house still under construction at 5515 Tenth Avenue North in a pleasant, upper-middle-class residential section. Interviewed in 1995, Betty Watley explained that Jack and Mémère stayed with Nin in Orlando, eighty-five miles to the northeast of St. Petersburg, during many of her last days. In a notebook entry first released by Kerouac's executor in 1995, Kerouac described the deplorable state of Nin's marriage. Paul Blake Sr. deserted Nin and their son after seventeen years.[21]

In St. Petersburg, Betty Watley lived only a block away from the Kerouacs. Jack hired Betty's husband to take care of the yard. "Jack was a nice guy when he was sober and most of the time when he was plastered and not upset," Betty recalled. "Mémère was very happy-go-lucky, and they got along real well. I never saw her as difficult; she was a typical Frenchwoman, and did a lot of cooking for Jack, and got heavy as she got older. There was a Publix grocery store within walking distance of them — they didn't have a car and neither did I. There was a lot of banter, and Mémère could take anything he'd dish out." When asked if she'd known Kerouac was a famous author, Betty replied, "I didn't care for the rough language in his books, or the type of people he wrote about. He would change gears when he talked about his writing, and that's when he seemed to be the happiest. Or when he was banging on his piano. I don't know if he ever really knew how to play it—he said he was trying to play jazz. He was a very lonely man. He liked my kids, and said he was going to teach my oldest, the nine-year-old, how to play the piano, but I don't know if they ever got around to that. He liked kids as long as they weren't his, and were no responsibility. He was a will o' the wisp, always looking for something and never really found it."

Kerouac's world now narrowed down to the bars and pool halls of St. Petersburg and Tampa, where he soon attracted a coterie of admirers and drinking companions. "St. Petersburg in the sixties wasn't ready for Kerouac in performance art," said Ron Lowe, a rock-and-roll singer who became one of Kerouac's closest friends. "He loved being the center of attention. Someone asked him what he was doing in St. Petersburg, and Jack said, 'Well, everybody's gotta be somewhere.'" They met in a bar where Ron was playing with his band. At first Ron thought Jack was "too old, too fat, too drunk to be the man that had held me and a whole generation in the palm of his hand, but you could tell it was Kerouac from the way he used the language." Ron sang a slow blues tune that night, and Kerouac paid him a compliment. "You make me cry," Jack said. Then he arrogantly demanded that Ron give him a ride home. The band finished at 2 A.M., and Jack wanted to cruise the beach. "You've got miles and miles of connected islands here," Ron explained in 1995. "They're called the Holiday Isles, a whole chain of them that runs from the tip of the peninsula at St. Petersburg. Jack and I drove around at probably twenty-five miles an hour, late at night, while all the lights were on blinker, no traffic, listening to some distant radio station that would have something besides Top Forty on it. Just for background music. Drove around and just talked and talked. He just wasn't wild about being here period because this is the slow lane. But when he would get a couple of drinks in him, his energy would perk up. The unrelieved dreariness that [his biographers] wrote of—it wasn't *unrelieved* dreariness. Before the high rises went up, the beach was quaint in those days—little one-story motels, little bars, little peeling white wooden shacks with weatherworn tables and chairs on a small porch."

When they pulled up at Jack's house, he tried to give Ron a couple of dollars for gas. "No, man," Ron said, "that's all right, you're welcome to the ride." Jack bent down and peered at him curiously. "Aw, come on in," he said. "We'll listen to some good music." Jack played Zoot Sims and Gerry Mulligan on his bulky reel-to-reel tape machine. "Unfortunately it was a dual track tape," Ron recalled. "On the other side was the Mozart high mass in C-sharp minor. We would be listening to the jazz for a while, and he would suddenly leap up across the room and punch this button and go from Zoot Sims to Mozart, which was a little bit of a shock. Then he'd push the button again, and you were back with Zoot and Gerry."

Ron had played football at Largo High and was a sporadic weight lifter.

At six-foot-one, he weighed three hundred pounds, but his doctor said he was solid muscle. "Mémère considered me a blessing because Jack had brought home a pretty bizarre collection of people over the years. I was sober and polite . . . Mémère used to cook for us. Good but uninspired fare, usually warmed-up leftovers. Jack once told me, 'Here I am, trapped by a promise, like the old Greek god in the River Styxx, you have to keep your promise regardless of how disastrous the consequences may be, if you made the promise.' He meant his promise to Leo that he would never allow his mother to be alone. Of course, his sister Caroline [Nin] had done a wonderful job of upholding the covenant. Then she died."

The end came for Nin at 1:45 P.M. on September 19, 1964, in the Florida Sanitarium and Hospital in Orlando. According to Nin's death certificate, she died of "coronary occlusion due to arteriosclerotic cardiovascular disease." In October, Kerouac wrote Rev. Sweeney to pray for Nin, and noted that she had died of a heart attack. Mémère was "disconsolate," he added. He described his present life as getting "drunk WAITING" for friends and then getting even drunker when they arrived. He told the priest that he had put a St. Benedict medal on his door.

The following week, Sweeney sent Jack a long letter of sympathy, but also addressed Jack's drinking problem. While alcohol was the "nearest refuge," he warned that it would destroy Jack's mind and ultimately kill him, and he begged Jack to strike a "Truce of God." If Jack turned his alcoholism over to a higher power, the priest advised, the "grace" of that higher power would remove his desire to drink. It was sound advice and very similar to the teachings of AA's Bill Wilson. In conclusion, the priest told Jack that his talent now required a dramatic technical advance, and suggested more discipline and structure. Following Sweeney's advice, Jack drank less for a few weeks, but then subsided again into chronic alcoholism.[22]

Jack's writing came to a standstill. He had some unpublished manuscripts, but *Big Sur* and *Gerard* had not sold well, and publishers were no longer clamoring for his novels. Jack needed money, and decided at last to release a couple of old fiction manuscripts, *Desolation Angels* and *An American Passed Here*. It was at this point that I came into Kerouac's life.

TEN

A PERSONAL REMINISCENCE

One day in 1964, Sterling Lord sent two Kerouac novels to my office at Coward-McCann. That night, I took home *Desolation Angels* and a somewhat shorter novel, then called *An American Passed Here*. I remember sitting on the couch in my railroad flat at 196 West Tenth Street, just around the corner from Sheridan Square, and lifting the yellowed pages of *Desolation Angels*. The author's typing, I noticed, was perfect, but the paper seemed like inexpensive "copy paper," as it's called in newspaper offices. I started reading, and then put the manuscript aside, distracted by Kerouac's raw, unpolished style. My first thought was that the novel would require too much interlinear editing—changes in virtually every line. For some reason, I decided to try reading it on marijuana, and I rolled a joint of Manhattan "wacky weed." I'd been smoking pot ever since the late 1950s when Warren Picower, a fellow editorial assistant at *Newsweek*, turned me on, but I rarely attempted to work while stoned. After I took a few tokes, Kerouac's prose almost knocked me off my Salvation Army couch: "Hundreds of miles of snowcovered rock all around, looming Mount Hozomeen on my north, vast snowy Jack to the south, the encharmed picture of the lake below to the west and the snowy hump of Mt. Baker beyond, and to the east the rilled and ridged monstrosities humping to the Cascade Ridge."

This was Kerouac's mature style, something I had never read before. It was written in 1956, after *On the Road*, which had sounded like Thomas Wolfe to me. Just as significantly, *Desolation Angels* was written before *The Dharma Bums*, which Jack had composed in a simpler style to please Viking. *Desolation Angels*, I realized, was his lost masterpiece, the final flowering of his great creative period in the fifties: the true voice of Kerouac. I stayed up most of the night finishing it, and then plowed into the second novel, *An American Passed Here*, which was fascinating, but not nearly as good. It had been written, Jack later explained, "in the summer of 1961 . . . in two different pads in Mexico City." By then, Kerouac had suffered a nervous breakdown and was no longer a juicy writer. But I found *An American Passed Here* to be of great historical interest; as a sequel to *Desolation Angels*, it continued the story of the original Beats as they moved on to Mexico, New York, Tangier, France, and London. I knew that I wanted to publish both books, and I already had a publishing theme in mind for them: "They did for the Beat Generation what Hemingway's *A Moveable Feast* had done for the Lost Generation; they showed us how literary and cultural movements are born." For the first time, I could see the connection between the Beats and the sixties counterculture, and I also realized that Kerouac's *oeuvre* was one long epic, like William Faulkner's Yoknapatawpha County novels. These qualities needed to be pointed out to a public that had forgotten an important writer.

Short books have a hard time succeeding in the competitive fiction market, which is dominated by bulky blockbusters. Our way around this with Kerouac would be to combine the two novels Sterling had submitted, and publish them as one, under the title *Desolation Angels*. Further, an introduction by a powerful and respected critic might get Kerouac good reviews and restore his career. I made a joint offer for both *Desolation Angels* and *An American Passed Here*, contingent upon the author's acceptance of my publishing program. Though the advance was modest, Sterling was pleased that I wanted to publish Kerouac with energy and imagination. He said he would ask the author to call me so I could describe the unusual publishing strategy I had in mind. A day or so later, my secretary Ann Sheldon appeared in my doorway and said, "Jack Kerouac on line one." Thrilled, and very curious to know what he'd sound like, I picked up the receiver. He was excited that I thought *Desolation Angels* an important book, and a warmth and intimacy came into his voice that were very beguiling. In *Jack Kerouac: A Biography*, Tom Clark accurately reported, "When Ellis Amburn suggested that Jack Kerouac conjoin *Desolation Angels* in one book with the 50,000 words written in 1961 in Mexico City (*An American Passed Here*), Kerouac agreed." That makes it sound so easy. But in fact, at first, Kerouac insisted on publishing the books separately.

"Won't I get more money with two advances?" he asked.

"This is my best offer," I replied, telling the truth.

He also objected to my idea of commissioning an influential critic to write an introduction. "Why should I give another writer a free ride?" he asked, according to the deal notes I scribbled on a desk calendar–address book. I told him that we were up against a critical backlash, that reviewers had never taken him seriously, and that the grand scheme in his novels— the Duluoz Legend—needed to be explicated, the way Malcolm Cowley had first mapped Yoknapatawpha County in the Viking Portable Faulkner. "*Cowley?*" he said. "That's the bastard that fucked over my prose at Viking."

I knew nothing of his publishing history at the time, but clearly I'd wandered into a minefield. Thanks to Sterling's persuasive powers, Kerouac finally accepted my publishing strategy, and we proceeded to contract.[1]

For the introduction, Kerouac suggested critic Dwight Macdonald, who had liked *Pull My Daisy* and who was hip enough, according to Adele Mailer, to throw nude beach parties on Cape Cod. I contacted Macdonald at the *New Yorker*, and while I found him to be very personable, he was not enthusiastic about Kerouac. I next tried Seymour Krim, a *Village Voice* writer and author of *Notes of a Near-Sighted Cannoneer*. I wrote Kerouac on November 19, 1964, "Sterling I believe is checking with you about Seymour Krim for the introduction and I'd like to make a strong pitch for him here. Dwight Macdonald, though willing to read the manuscript on speculation, seemed pretty uninformed about your work and not really able to supply the literary and historical framework I'd like in the introduction. This would be no problem for Seymour Krim, who does already know your work very well and agrees with me about the importance it has, its effects not only on literature but on life as well. Things in general have not been the same since *On the Road*, and it's time this was spelled out in no uncertain terms."

As soon as he received my letter, Kerouac called from Florida and said to go after Krim. Kerouac and I chatted a while that day, long enough to discover that we knew many of the same people. He expressed mild curiosity about some of them, including Larry Rivers, Patsy Southgate, and Helen Weaver. He was of two minds about the post-Beat scene that he'd supposedly left behind, the same one I was now part of. On the one hand, he told me to give out his address to no one, and I wrote him on November 19, "Rest assured I'll keep your hideaway top secret." On the other hand, he wanted to know what was going on. I was in a position to tell him, as I was running with the people Jack had known in Greenwich Village, Fire Island, and the Hamptons. Poetry readings and coffeehouses were largely a thing of the past, but the bars were as full as ever, and another generation was now eating the tasteless but inexpensive food at the Cedar. I remember going there with Joe LeSueur and Frank O'Hara; the air crackled with a sense of high camp and high purpose around those two, and it was never more electric than on the evening that Jerry Leiber and his wife Gaby treated the three of us, along with LeRoi and Hettie Jones, to a sumptuous dinner at Luchow's. The Five Spot and the Half Note were still going strong, and Charlie Mingus was the new jazz god. Everyone flocked to Washington Square to hear the folk singers, but overall the scene was relatively quiet, just before the storm of late sixties revolution. My friend Harriet Anderson, a Peyton Loftis-type deb from Nashville who'd worked in Putnam's subsidiary-rights department, introduced me to the same White Horse and Corner Bistro crowds that had drunk with Kerouac, including Bill Manville, who had written the *Village Voice*'s popular weekly column, "Saloon Society." Kerouac asked me to send him Manville's new book of the same title.

At one of Harriet's parties, she introduced me to David Amram and his roommate Lenny Gross, the editor of *Sexology* magazine. Amram produced his ubiquitous French horn and started playing a jazz solo. A little later, the curly-haired, cherubic Gross burst out laughing when Harriet told him I was Kerouac's editor. He explained he'd been in the audience the night Kerouac spoke at Brooklyn College in 1958. "I knew Kerouac still lived with his mother," Gross said, "so I asked him if she ever got nervous when he left home to make all those great trips in *On the Road*."

In Easthampton, where Kerouac had once been kicked out of a party by Lee Krasner Pollock, Truman Capote dropped by Joe LeSueur's while I was houseguesting one weekend. "Kerouac writes fiction nonfiction," Truman announced. "*I* write nonfiction fiction." Though disappointed that so few of Kerouac's contemporaries shared my enthusiasm for his writing, I continued to send accounts of "the scene" to him in Florida. "I saw friends of yours at a party the other night at Richard Howard's," I wrote. "Allen [Ginsberg] and Peter [Orlovsky] were there. . . . It was a publication party for Sandy Friedman's brother's book, *Yarborough* . . . society folk from Philadelphia, editors, writers, just-friends, but none of this bothered [one of the guests], who opened his fly at one point and at another asked Lee Pollock why she and Jackson couldn't have any children."

Kerouac was romantically drawn to Patsy Southgate, who lived with painter Mike Goldberg in a large townhouse behind the White Horse and was raising two small children, Luke and Carrie, from her marriage to Peter Matthiessen. In a 1996 interview, Patsy remembered Kerouac as "a disturbed cat. My heart sort of went out to him, but I realized that he counted on that. He ended up living with his mother."

The next time Kerouac called me, he asked again about what he called "the season in New York." I told him I'd dined with Frank O'Hara in art dealer Donald Droll's loft at 791 Broadway with Joe LeSueur, painter Roy Leaf, curator Kynaston McShine, and McGraw-Hill editor Peter Kemeny, and that Frank had told me, "I'm glad you're looking after Jack's books. Take care of him." Time had healed an old altercation between Kerouac and O'Hara. As Joe LeSueur recalled in 1997, "Kerouac was yelling at Frank, being awful to him, during the [1959] poetry reading at the Living Theater, and then later ran into him at the Cedar bar, and Frank would hardly speak to him. Kerouac started coming on to him, saying, 'What's the matter, don't you like me?' Frank said, 'It's your writing I like — it's not you.' Kerouac couldn't have been more pleased. It meant much more to him to be liked for his writing than for his character or personality, which is kind of touching, and very serious of Kerouac. He really cared about what he did."

At the office, I soon grew accustomed to the sight of Ann Sheldon in my door saying, "It's Jack again." Some days, he called more than once. He was eager to know the status of the proposed Seymour Krim introduction to *Desolation Angels*, and I told him that Sy Krim and I had arranged to meet at Mary Elizabeth's, a garment-district tearoom, to discuss it. Sy was a big, elegant guy, approximately thirty-five years old, bright, hip to every nuance of the cultural scene and particularly to what he called "the bitch of Manhattan," with its "hallucinated, pounding, chase-novel tension." At lunch, over Mary Elizabeth's strong straight-up martinis and home-cooked pot roast, Sy said that Kerouac was the one writer who had captured "that curious combination of agitation and rapture" that defined the Beat Generation. I liked the way he described Kerouac's style as "brave and unbelligerently up-yours." Kerouac's novels, he felt, were the best prose record of "our screwy neoadolescent era." However, by the time our butterscotch meringue pies arrived, I found myself expressing serious concern over several reservations Krim had voiced about Kerouac. In Sy's opinion, Kerouac had gone overboard when he'd compared himself with Proust, and Sy also felt that Kerouac was in danger of repeating himself unless he stopped writing autobiographical novels. "You can't criticize an author in his own book," I said very firmly. Krim did not argue, and he accepted the job. I explained that I was on a strict budget and could only afford a small honorarium. "Actually, I'd do it for nothing," Krim said. But after I returned to work, I ordered a check, and I sent it to him shortly after he signed a letter of agreement.[2]

Meanwhile, I passed on to Sterling Lord some editorial recommendations, and he promised to consult Kerouac about them. A few days later, Sterling told me that Kerouac didn't want to make any changes. I transmitted the manuscript to the copyediting department with instructions to the copy editor, Catherine Wilson, to leave the writing intact, but to flag misspellings and queries, which I'd then forward to the author. The extent of my contribution as Kerouac's editor on this book was small but crucial; by combining two minor novels, I'd created a major one. As I structured it, the original *Desolation Angels* became Book One, and *An American Passed Here* became Book Two, under the umbrella title *Desolation Angels*. Against my wishes, Kerouac changed the half-title of Book Two to the less effective "Passing Through." When I objected, he explained that *An American Passed Here* was "too good a title to throw away," and he said that he would use it "as the title of a whole book, some day, maybe." Years later, I learned from Tony Sampas that *Passing Through* was the title of one of Kerouac's favorite LPs.[3]

After looking over several artists' portfolios, I chose Sam Salant to design the dust jacket. According to my notes, "Told artist to show a novelist in the grand tradition, encompassing an entire generation." Taking me literally, Salant came up with a heroic image of Jack, his arms embracing a mass of humanity, including recognizable faces such as those of Ginsberg and Corso. I wrote a selling line, "The famous underground novel," and ran it under Salant's line drawing. Altogether, it was a provocative package, one that had "major novel" written all over it.

Kerouac told me that he was thrilled with the way we were treating his book, and I replied, "Your letter delighted me. I fussed over the physical details of the book a lot, and wanted it to be the best, so I'm all the more grateful for your thoughtfulness. Not many authors are that appreciative. I look forward to doing other books by Jack Kerouac." Later, in a scholarly article on *Desolation Angels* published in *Moody Street Irregulars*, Mike McCoy wrote, "Ellis Amburn was Jack Kerouac's last editor. . . . This was two jobs: working with Kerouac on the manuscript and trying to generate interest on the part of the readers and critics. . . . As Amburn himself says, 'Jack did not need editing—just encouragement and an appreciative reading.' " There was also an element of affection. Very early in our relationship, he signed a letter to me, "Your friend." In my next letter, I wrote back, "I like the way you sign off and I'll do the same. . . . Your friend, Ellis Amburn, Editor." Kerouac rang shortly thereafter, asking if Krim's introduction was ready yet. It wasn't, but it was during this call that he mentioned the late Harpo Marx, whose recent death Kerouac called "the greatest loss to slapstick since Molière."

On November 27, I wrote Jack again to thank him for going over the copyedited manuscript and for arranging the numbering of chapters and parts exactly as he wanted. "Also," I wrote, "thanks for the valuable information about the biographical aspect of the novel, and for telling me about Hicks-Jones and Tallman, all of which will be of interest to Seymour Krim for his introduction. I've also asked Krim to pay special attention to your italic preface to *Big Sur*, which is a good statement about your total work." Kerouac had directed my attention to various critical assessments of his work, including an essay by Warren Tallman published in 1959 entitled "Kerouac's Sound." Tallman compared *The Subterraneans* to bop music, in which each statement is followed by inventive digressions. While the plot traces Leo and Mardou's love-affair, the novel is awash in what Tallman called "improvised details," and these reach "down into the clutter of their lives among the guilts and shames . . . to steal their love from them. The truth is in the improvisations."

In my November 27 letter, I told Kerouac that his galleys would be ready in approximately one month. We were tentatively planning to publish in April 1965, and we had "not a minute to lose," I added, "since I want to have the finished book in hand in plenty of time before actual publication—to get it around in the right hands and get talk started."[4]

Early in 1965, Seymour Krim delivered his introductory essay, which was a lively, comprehensive revaluation of Kerouac's entire career, as requested. It had taken him weeks to write, and I had been patient, despite prodding memos from the production department. We had to postpone publication for a month. "It pulls no punches," Krim said. "I assess Kerouac's weaknesses as well as his strengths." I told him that Kerouac would never stand for being attacked in his own book, but Krim said, "Why don't you show it to Kerouac and see what he says?" I forwarded the intro to Sterling, urging him to tell Kerouac to accept it. Then, on February 8, I wrote Kerouac:

> . . . the introduction . . . is not only a highly significant essay on your work, but an invaluable publishing supplement that should help bring

new attention to all your past work as well as to *Desolation Angels*. Here is stated, in what I think are moving and genuine terms, your seminal importance. But what gives it force is Krim's honesty and candor; this is no publisher's puff, but a fully fleshed piece of criticism that accomplishes several things in addition to providing an appreciation of your work. For the whole new generation of readers that has come of age since *On the Road*, it supplies the necessary background. For reactionary reviewers who come up with the same old reservations, it disarms them by beating them to the punch. And for everyone, it beams a new and vital light on you and your work. We are scheduled to go to press this week, so please call me, person-to-person, collect, as soon as you can. We want to stick to our announced publication date of May 3, and will be able to if we can wrap up this last detail this week. All good wishes to you.

He called me all right, and he was fuming. "How dare that son-of-a-bitch knock me in my own book," he said, according to my notes. Subsequently, I tried to intercede with Krim, but he was as touchy as Kerouac and would brook no changes. I had no more time or energy to expend on Krim's introduction. In exasperation, I decided to let Kerouac and Krim slug it out. On February 13, Kerouac wrote Krim that he objected to the allegation that he was familiar with the homosexual subculture of New York, and he asked Krim to make it clear that he was a "non-participant . . . [in] homosexuality." Soon, Krim was burning up the line to me, railing about Kerouac's "hypocrisy." Why, he demanded, should we be dragged into Kerouac's "big lie"? I told him to cool down, and I'd talk to him later.

Joe LeSueur shared my office and had overheard part of the conversation. He was surprised that Kerouac would make such a fuss over being thought gay, and mentioned a well-known painter, John Button, who'd been to bed with Kerouac. I knew Button, who, at thirty-six, looked like musical star (and later director) Gower Champion and who was one of the best-known and most-loved persons in the downtown art scene. According to the *New York Times* art critic John Russell, Button's canvases were unexcelled in their ability to portray Manhattan with an "unemphatic but penetrating poetry." One evening, when I was visiting Button in his Lower East Side apartment, I mentioned that I was Jack Kerouac's editor. Button immediately told me about having had sex with Kerouac, and remarked, "He's hung like a cigarette butt."

Krim finally altered the gay reference in his introduction, writing that Kerouac's "French-Canadian-Catholic-Yankee arc was widened to compassionately include non-participating acceptance of the homosexuality of his literary pals." On February 18, I wrote Kerouac, "All those changes have now been made in the Krim intro."[5]

My efforts on behalf of *Desolation Angels* soon paid off in ways I had not dared to dream of. I had expected critical dividends, not monetary ones, but when the intro was seen by Bantam Books, we received an offer of twenty thousand dollars for paperback rights. Bantam's editors told me they didn't care much for Kerouac — it was the Krim introduction that sold them. At that point in the sixties, twenty thousand dollars was like a hundred thousand today, and on April 21, I wrote Kerouac:

> Congratulations! . . . It's a great sign of success for *Desolation Angels*, and I know you'll be heartened by this sale too. It's a damn good one, and we're all very proud of it and you. The monies will be forthcoming in three installments — a third on your next royalty statement, unless you need it earlier; a third on publication of the Bantam edition; and the final third six months after publication of the Bantam edition. You get 60% of the reprint sale. That means that on the first payment of $6,666, your share will be $3,999.60.

Shortly after the Bantam windfall, difficulties arose with Krim, who felt he deserved a share of the paperback sale. I pointed out that I couldn't rewrite the letter of agreement he'd signed, so he went to Kerouac. "I didn't want the damn introduction in first place," Kerouac said, Krim later told me. According to my April 21 letter to Kerouac, the Krim affair ended fairly amicably, though Krim received nothing from Bantam. "It's nice of you to write Seymour Krim," I wrote Kerouac, referring to a warm letter Kerouac had sent Krim, expressing his gratitude. "I would have written more," I added, "but got caught up in all the day-to-day doings here, especially preparations for the new sales conference."[6] At the conference, which was held at the Sheraton on Park Avenue, I delivered a passionate pitch, but later, at a company luncheon, some of the salesmen told me that bookstore owners were not looking forward to another Kerouac novel after the successive failures of *Big Sur* and *Visions of Gerard*. I still held out hope that positive press reviews would create renewed interest in Kerouac.

As publication day approached in the spring of 1965, no groundswell developed for the book. Almost twenty years later, in *Moody Street Irregulars*, Mike McCoy wrote, "Why there was such a lack of interest is hard to say. It certainly was not through lack of effort or imagination on the part of Ellis Amburn. But his frustration is evident." I had told McCoy, "Kerouac fans must have been out to lunch in the 1960s."

On publication day, May 3, 1965, I sent Kerouac a congratulatory telegram, but unfortunately there was no good news to report. To my surprise and delight, he called and thanked me for all the effort I'd made, and said, "I'll dedicate a novel to you some day." On the same day, Kerouac wrote to a Dutch fan, J. G. Biorkens, acknowledging receipt of Biorkens's book-length study of his work, which Kerouac said was "sensitive and 'hip.'" He praised Biorkens for realizing that jazz is not primarily sound, but phrasing, and added that he was going abroad in June. He wanted to go to Holland and meet Biorkens, though generally he planned to avoid literary folk and all American tourists. A recent girlfriend, Kerouac confided, was from Brussels; her name was Yseult Snepvangers, and she was a formidable woman. During a visit to her home, he had met the director of the Antwerp Symphony. Kerouac expressed heartfelt gratitude to Biorkens for championing his novels.[7]

Saul Maloff attacked *Desolation Angels* in the *Times Book Review*, calling it a "disaster" and an "inconsequential epic [about] exhibitionistic cults of coterie iconoclasts. . . . The characters are as fatuous in life as in art." On May 4, in the daily *Times*, Charles Poore dismissed Kerouac as "obsolete," but he could not disguise the fact that he enjoyed the novel; he compared it with the works of Saroyan and Wolfe. Kerouac caught "the color and sweep of human destiny," Poore wrote, but lest he appear to be endorsing the book, he accused the Beats of encouraging "narcotic experimentation" and wrote the novel off as "a nonclassic of a vanishing era." Nelson Algren wrote in *Book Week*, "Kerouac's prose is not prose: it is a form of self-indulgence." Hunter Thompson again turned on Kerouac, and in a letter to a friend, Thompson wrote that unless Kerouac were assassinated, all hipsters were in danger of being called the "Third Sex" generation.

Other notices, almost uniformly condescending, continued to trickle in, and on May 7, I wrote Kerouac:

> I'm enclosing some reviews, which run from good to bad. *Time* magazine, interestingly, is the best. . . . What puzzles me is how some people can resist the . . . intoxicating flights of language in *Desolation Angels*, some of the best you've written. Our advertising campaign will be starting shortly. The book will be featured in our full-page ad May 16 in the *Sunday Times Book Review*. You will have an ad June 3 in *The New York Review of Books*; June 6 in the *San Francisco Chronicle*; June 8 in the daily *New York Times*; and in the *Evergreen Review* in August. This is ambitious, and I know you will find it heartening.

Kerouac replied in early May, venting his anger over the reviews, especially one that appeared in the *New York Herald Tribune*. I replied on May 17, "Thanks for your spunky letter—the way I like to hear an author talk! The *Trib* is getting generally irresponsible—with the unwarranted attack on Norman Mailer comparing him with James M. Cain—and Tom Wolf's [sic] dirty-pool attack on William Shawn and the *New Yorker*. I think people are losing respect for the *Trib*, which has gone Merrick-showbiz. Enclosed is a copy of our ad from yesterday's *Times*—hope you like."

By the time *Desolation Angels* got its big critical break—from Dan Wakefield's unexpected rave in the *Atlantic* in July 1965—it was too late to do us any good. The ad campaign was over, so we couldn't publicize Wakefield's endorsement, and the bookstores had long ago written off Jack's novel. But Wakefield confirmed my claims, writing, "Probably no other American writer—no, not even Norman Mailer—has been subjected to such a barrage of ridicule, venom, and cute social acumen as Kerouac. If the Pulitzer Prize in fiction were given for the book that is most representative of American life, I would nominate *Desolation Angels*. . . . We seldom recognize a real American dream when we see one." Wakefield was Kerouac's lone champion in 1965, and bookstores soon began to return overstock to us for credit. In trade parlance, we had to "eat" most of the copies. But, according to many, the Krim intro planted the seeds of the Kerouac revival.[8]

Jack did some world traveling in 1965, going to Europe to research his short Grove Press book, *Satori in Paris*. Kerouac and I discussed the possibility of meeting in Europe in 1965, as indicated in my April 21 letter in which I wrote, "I might see you in London. I'm going there too, in September." But he preceded me overseas, visiting France that summer. When he returned to St. Petersburg in July, he wrote *Satori in Paris* in seven nights, printing it by hand, and he later read most of it to me on the phone. In the narrative, Kerouac searches for his family's genealogy in Paris and Brittany, but spends most of his time drinking, getting lost, and missing trains and planes. I thought it "disarming and lovable," and told him, "Your book is true to the mess that travel actually is, but no one else has ever admitted it."

Satori in Paris was indeed a classic travel piece, proving that, when one travels, everything that can go wrong usually does. I was so charmed by it that I missed the frightening signs, which occur throughout the book. All of his calls to me so far had been perfectly sober ones, and it had not yet dawned on me that he had a drinking problem. In retrospect, my remarks to him about *Satori in Paris* strike me as naive, especially when I commented that he was at his most appealing in this book, because he was utterly honest about himself, "even when you've had a few too many." He laughed and replied, "If you're big and fat, *be* big and fat." When I asked him about the French literary scene, he indicated that Michel Mohrt of Gallimard had somehow hurt his feelings, either hanging up on him or refusing to see him at the office. Nor had he called on Celine or Genet, as planned. "Not even," he added, "the Gallic Tristessa, Françoise Sagan. Didn't see the expatriates, either—why turn *la Rive gauche* into MacDougal Street? One's enough." He was uncomfortable with most literary people, and he found the "atmosphere of *litterature* sinister." Only much later, when I finally learned that he was an alcoholic, did I realize that he'd called on no one in Paris, but had isolated himself in churches, museums, and obscure *bistros* because he was ashamed of his drunkenness.[9]

"I remember you were on the phone a lot with Kerouac," my colleague Betty Prashker said in 1997. Before she went on to become a leading editor at Doubleday and subsequently at Crown, Betty occupied the office next to mine at Coward, building a list that included Alison Lurie and Muriel Rukeyser. "I was very excited that you had Kerouac," Betty recalled. "I would be trying to come in and talk with you, and Ann Sheldon would say, 'Oh, he said he's on the phone with Jack.' " It wasn't always business, either. One day Kerouac began talking about rock and roll, which had become the most popular music in the world since its controversial debut in the 1950s. "It's the sign of a new spirituality in the twilight of Western civilization," he said, and then quoted the "Trio of the Rhinemaidens" from *Götterdämmerung*: "*Frau Sonne, sende uns den Helden, der das Gold uns wie der gabe* [Fair sun god, send to us the hero, who again our gold will give us]!"

According to Kerouac, Elvis Presley, James Dean, and Marlon Brando represented a new American paradigm, replacing the old masculine model of aggression, violence, and misogyny. "Love is sweeping the country," he wrote in "America's New Trinity of Love: Dean, Brando, Presley." "All gone are the . . . barriers of ancient anti-womanism that go deep into primitive religion." As an example of the new "all-embracing, non-assertive" masculinity, he cited the famous abandoned-mansion scene in *Rebel Without a Cause*, in which Dean encourages Natalie Wood to include Sal Mineo in their love. As early as 1957 Kerouac predicted that the "Revolution of Love" would be sparked not by a novelist or philosopher but by a rock-and-roll star. In an earlier era, novelists had been the culture heroes in America, with Sinclair Lewis, Theodore Dreiser, and Ernest Hemingway looked up to as sages. In the sixties, guitar gods replaced novelists as generational spokespersons, but it was increasingly obvious with each new release from Bob Dylan that Kerouac and Burroughs were the source of some of rock's basic ideas and familiar lyrics. "It was Ginsberg and Jack Kerouac who inspired me at first," Dylan told *Playboy*. In a cover story, *Time* hailed rock as "the international anthem of a new and restless generation," but oddly neglected to identify its origins in Beat rebellion.

Kerouac told me that Ginsberg had recently been with Bob Dylan in London for Dylan's Royal Albert Hall concert, and that Ginsberg and Dylan were "thickern thieves." At a party after Dylan's concert, Ginsberg met the Beatles and lectured them about the Beat Generation. John Lennon subsequently contacted Kerouac, revealing that the band's name was derived from "Beat." "He was sorry he hadn't come to see me when they played Queens," Kerouac said, referring to the Beatles Shea Stadium concert in 1965. "I told him it's just as well, since my mother wouldn't let them in without a haircut. He wanted to know how to reach Jayne Mansfield, said he wanted to fuck her." The actress had starred in *The Girl Can't Help It*, one of the few "A" rock movies ever made.

Bob Dylan used one of Kerouac's trademark words in "Desolation Row" and another in "Subterranean Homesick Blues," but it was in "Like a Rolling Stone" and "Highway 61 Revisited" that Dylan's garrulous, rambling lyrics echoed Kerouac's style and upfront attitude. Kerouac was convinced that pop and rock could enrich each other by merging, but added, "The way rock is going, that'll never happen. I'm sticking to 'Moon River.'" Had Kerouac been more visible in New York, California, and London, and had he spent time with some of the rock musicians who swore by him, such as Jerry Garcia, he might well have influenced the future of rock and brought about the rock-pop fusion he desired. But he was no longer a part of the cultural scene, and increasingly his alcoholism would isolate him from a world he'd helped create.[10]

At some point following the publication of *Desolation Angels*, I signed up my second Kerouac novel. A reference to *Vanity of Duluoz* occurs in my November 19, 1964, letter to Kerouac, demonstrating that we had been discussing this novel from the outset of our association. He told me he had been struggling with *Duluoz* and that it was not going well. "I've already written up everything that ever happened to me," he said. I told him that he'd never written about being a football star at Columbia or about serving in World War II. At the time, I had not read *The Town and the City*, or I would have known that he'd already touched on these subjects. He did not correct me, fortunately, because if he had, I probably would have dropped my interest in *Vanity of Duluoz* and lost one of his most intriguing novels.

"I want to make a lot of money . . . ," he said, adding that perhaps he should try his hand at espionage fiction.

"That's very in vogue—what do you want to tell?"

"How about murder?"

"Now you're talking."

He further whetted my interest by saying he'd actually been involved in the David Kammerer killing. I immediately put *Vanity of Duluoz* under contract and began to pay him regular installments on his advance. Years later, in "Ellis Amburn: Editing the Final Words," Mike McCoy reported that the novel was in "outline form" and "Jack had apparently been trying to finish [it] . . . but was unable. . . . Amburn . . . gave Jack the needed push." When Mike McCoy contacted me for *Moody Street Irregulars*, I wrote him, "Jack had been hearing of the big bucks writers were beginning to get in the sixties and wanted a lot of money for *Vanity*, but the most I could get him, based on *Desolation Angels*'s hardcover sales . . . was something in the neighborhood of $7,500."[11]

Kerouac began writing again and often called to read me his favorite paragraphs. I remember his nostalgic conjuration of small-town Americans heading for sandlot football games on Saturday mornings, the men charging along "hands-a-pockets," carrying homemade stakes and chains for yard markers. I commented on how suddenly his prose could veer from Norman Rockwell Americana to black cynicism, and he said, "Yeah, you're seeing a writer's midlife crisis in action."

Kerouac always spoke clearly, never slurring his words, and I still had no inkling of his alcoholism, but every evening in Tampa, as I subsequently learned, his drinking turned him into another person altogether. He was a regular at a new hangout, the Wild Boar tavern, which opened in Tampa on Nebraska Avenue in August 1965. A customer named Lawrence R. Broer watched Kerouac and the owner, Gerry Wagner, who weighed 230 pounds, "bust bellies" one night, and then saw Kerouac lurch to a table in the corner, struggling for his breath. Broer went over and talked to Kerouac, and later recalled that he was "strong and muscular" but looked disheveled in his greasy lumberjack shirt and a pair of ragged overalls two sizes too large. Jack's burly physique had incongruously sprouted an old man's potbelly, though he was only forty-three. The belly was probably due to an enlarged liver. He claimed that someone had just tried to abduct him, but he and his sidekick, an ex-con named Cherokee Chief, had escaped into a cemetery. Kerouac reminded Broer of Zorba the Greek, swilling wine, pontificating, and quoting love poems. But underneath the ribaldry, Broer caught a glint of insanity in Kerouac's bulging, stricken eyes.

Suddenly, Kerouac stood up and began to dart from table to table. Plopping down beside a perfect stranger, he announced, "My father next to my brother lies." Moving on to another table, he said to a startled woman, "Ah, excuse me, Loretta Young." Then, suddenly making sense, he turned and told Broer, "There's nothing to life but just the living of it. . . . Get to know as many people as you can. . . . Just flow. . . . This is the Great Knowing. . . . Shut up, live, travel, adventure, bless, and don't be sorry." Later, Broer ran into him in the men's room, where he was admiring himself in the mirror, combing and preening and calling himself Rudolph Valentino. Broer asked him about Hemingway, and Kerouac said he disapproved of the wanton destruction of innocent wild animals, adding that he didn't need blood lust to prove his virility. "Look, I'll show you," he said, exposing himself.

In November 1965, Kerouac paid a visit to the Holmeses in Old Saybrook. Holmes was shocked by both his insatiable need for alcohol and his virulent anti-Semitism. Kerouac insisted that his Jew-baiting was benevolent — simply a way of stunning people into being their true selves. It seemed a spurious distinction at best. Sensibly, Tony Sampas took Jack to see a psychiatrist, who tried to warn Jack that his frequent use of the word "Jewboys" was dangerous; he also observed that Kerouac's main problems were his fear of his own "homosexual tendencies" and his fear of women. Kerouac grew combative and insulted the shrink. Back in Nicky's Bar, he mooched drinks until he passed out. "Jack's head was on the bar," Billy Koumantzelis recalled.

After his return to St. Petersburg, he bellied up to a bar, eyed a rangy John Wayne look-alike, and hit on him. The problem in Florida was never a lack of willing males, but a place to make out with them. There was little opportunity for any kind of passional life under the same roof with the hawk-eyed Mémère. "I doan like dem dere fags runnin' around de house naked," she said.

On the phone one day, Jack told me that he and his mother had suddenly decided to return to the Northeast. Having spent their lives moving from place to place, they couldn't break the habit though they were no longer running from bill collectors as in Leo's day. "We're pulling out of the subtropics or going crazy, one," Jack said, blaming "too many bloody sunsets, too many flatulent hurricanes, too many silly waterspouts. Florida lightning bolts are fat and jagged, like the ones in cartoons." In order to finish *Vanity of Duluoz*, he said he must return to New England, which he'd called, in *Visions of Cody*, "the tangled viney place where ... the dream began." "Maybe it will help me bring this novel off," he said. "Anywhere in New England will do. Sterling will give you my new address. Adios for now."[12]

In March, Kerouac sold the St. Petersburg house, and in May, he went to Hyannis, Massachusetts, ninety miles southeast of Lowell, and purchased a one-story Cape Cod house at 20 Bristol Avenue. He returned to Florida to collect Mémère, and Betty Watley drove them north in a tan Chrysler New Yorker driveaway. "The car was packed, you can imagine, with two or three cats," Betty recalled. "Mémère was drinking, and they were both pretty well looped. I drove the whole way, no one to spell me. Jack sat in the front with me, Mémère in the back, with the cats in their cat carriers." They drove 945 miles before at last stopping to rest in Washington, D.C. "We made it that far in one day, driving clear into the night," Betty said. "The next day, Sunday, Jack said, 'I know how to get around here,' but we kept driving around and around, sometimes on the sidewalk. We got lost. . . . Needless to say, he had probably been drinking, but we finally made it out of Washington. Actually it was a fun trip. Jack and Mémère were hilarious. She sang French songs."

A real estate agent met them in Hyannis, and Betty "turned around and came right back," she recalled. "I returned the car to the man who owned it and took a bus and came into Boston and got a plane from there. The next I heard from them was a letter from Mémère, who was waiting for a washer and a dryer to be delivered." Eventually, Mémère's maple furniture arrived, and she put up chintz curtains, trying to simulate Colonial decor.

Though Kerouac's alcoholic antics were witnessed by Kurt Vonnegut Jr. and others on Cape Cod, this was not the Kerouac I knew from our telephone conversations. Jack continued to ring me only when sober, for his drinking had not yet advanced to the point that he was willing to trash his relations with his publishing house, especially one that made money for him.

The first hint I had that Kerouac was in trouble came, unwittingly, from photographer Jerry Bauer, a personal friend of mine, who had photographed Kerouac at home in Northport. Both Bauer and I were in Rome that fall, and one evening, as we sat eating *gelato di pompelo* in the Piazza Navonna, I casually asked him to tell me what it had been like to meet Kerouac, and photograph him. Bauer shook his head, and said, as he recalled in a 1997 interview, "He drank beer after beer as the afternoon wore on. I'd taken the Long Island Railroad out there, and I don't think he was seeing many people then. His mother was quite nice. He was happy to see me. I really liked the guy; he was great fun, and very funny. There were crosses on the wall in his bedroom. He cooked me a hamburger for lunch. He still looked good; he had a handsome face, but he knew he was getting a pot belly. I gathered he was bisexual."

What I took away from my meeting with Jerry in Rome was a feeling that Kerouac drank too much, not that Jerry had harped on it, but perhaps because I'd always sensed something fragile in Kerouac during our telephone conversations, though I'd never been able to put a label on it. But the extent to which Kerouac's life was falling apart in 1966 never occurred to me until decades later when Tony Sampas told me, "I went up there on July 4, 1966, and Mémêre and Jack were shooting off fireworks. I was sure they were going to be arrested. The streets were crawling with police, going up and down the street arresting everybody who was making noise. That night, Jack yells, 'Where are all the beautiful girls coming from?' When we were put in jail, Jack looked at me and said, 'I'm sorry, man.'" After four hours, they were released.

In August 1966, for a bibliography Ann Charters was compiling of Kerouac's works, Charters drove up to Hyannis from New York. Jack helped her with the research, but then tried to have sex with her. Mémêre hustled Charters out of the house, warning that Jack had recently tried to kill her with a knife. Amazingly, in September, Kerouac still sounded sober in his talks with me. In one of them, he said his mother had suffered a stroke. "Her rear end still works, that's about all," he said, "except for her tongue. That's still flapping twenty-four hours a day. 'Get me this, get me that, wipe my snatch.' She needs care from a woman. I don't know what to do. The book's off for a while."

"Of course," I said. "Don't worry about it. I'll pray for your mother."

"Pray for yourself," he said, but with no malice, and added, "Thanks for not nudging me about the book."

Mémêre's left side was paralyzed, and though she eventually regained some feeling, she could not rise from bed without assistance. As always, Kerouac stuck by her, performing perhaps the most selfless and honorable service of his life. With medical bills, he needed money now more than ever, and fortuitously his Italian publisher, Mondadori, paid him a thousand dollars to go to Milan to promote its edition of *Big Sur*. He needed someone to look after Mémêre. "Jack called Stella and asked her to come to Hyannis," recalled John Sampas, who was living on Stevens Street with Stella and their mother, Maria. John urged Stella to go to Jack, assuring her that he would care for Maria. Stella shortly arrived in Hyannis, and Jack left for Milan.[13]

"The wops fucked me over," he told me upon his return, "absolutely threw me to the lions. But I got in a few punches. Oh, and I saw your buddy Jerry Bauer in Rome." The Italian promotional tour had been arranged by the agent, Fernanda ("Nanda") Pivano, who had originally recommended *Sulla Strada [On the Road]* to Arnoldo Mondadori Editore. After drinking two bottles of champagne, Kerouac made a shambles of his publication party in Milan's Cavour Bookshop. With good reason, the Italians found him to be "insolent and proud," John Montgomery wrote in "Kerouac and Italy." Jack called the long-suffering and compassionate Nanda a "Communist Jew spy" and passed out at a dinner party hosted by Arnoldo Mondadori. In Naples, he made an appearance at the Villa Pignatelli bookshop, and he caused a near-riot at the University of Napoli by vigorously defending U.S.

policy in Vietnam in front of an audience of radical students. Baffled by Kerouac's unexpected position on the war, the young Italians broke up the meeting in protest. "I snuck out like a football player," Kerouac said, "and ran to our sports car. Zoom! Sang in a nightclub, pounded the piano, had a real Mafia bodyguard."

Going on to Rome, he rang Jerry Bauer, who came to see him at his hotel. "The Albergo Barberini in Piazza Barberini is an okay hotel, not grand," Jerry recalled in 1997. "Jack had a nice room, and said he was happy to see a friend in Rome. He looked like he'd been drinking a bit, mainly beer. He acted perfectly correct. He didn't want to go out, and had been staying in the hotel.

" 'Jack,' I said, 'you've got to go see the Sistine Chapel, you've got to go to the Vatican.'

" 'The only thing I'm going to do is go out shopping and buy a cross for my mother,' he said. I gathered he'd been drinking in his room."

While in Rome, Kerouac dined at Restaurant Il Bolognese in Piazza del Popolo, accompanied by his escorts, Domenico Porzio and Giulia Niccolai, who recalled that Jack disapproved of the fashionable Cinecittá clientele, though this was the heyday of the Italian cinema, with auteurs such as Federico Fellini and Michelangelo Antonioni dominating the world's art theaters. He drank whiskey during a live TV interview in Rome, and imitated Mussolini on camera, asking, "Where's the Last Supper at?" The pious Italian press was understandably hostile, and used Kerouac's tour as an opportunity to assert the moral superiority of established values over the new radicalism of Italian youth. When he left Italy, Kerouac asked Porzio, "Where have I been during these days? Is Italy beautiful?"[14]

In early 1967, Kerouac telephoned my office, sounding perfectly normal as usual, and said he had moved to Lowell.

"Lowell," I said. "Why on earth?"

"Lowell, Massachusetts, is my hometown. Sweet Lowell by the river. I grew up here, and I've married a local girl, Stella Sampatacacus." He explained that his bride was Sammy's sister, and he identified Sammy as "the guy who encouraged me to write, killed in World War II." Stella had been in Hyannis, taking care of Mémêre, when Jack proposed to her in November 1966. She immediately called John.

"Should I marry Jack?" she asked.

"Yes," John said, he recalled in 1995.

"Who's going to take care of Mom?"

"I will. It will give you an opportunity to get out on your own. Marry your sweetheart."

John Clellon Holmes later revealed that Kerouac rang him in the middle of the wedding party, bombed but deliriously happy. The service took place in the Kerouac home in Hyannis, with the justice of the peace officiating. "I made her wedding dress—which was plain white with a veil," Stella's sister, Helen Surprenant said. After the ceremony, Jack relaxed in his study, enjoying a glass of Johnny Walker. Stella called Aida Panagiotakos in Lowell.

"Well, Jack and I are married," she said.

"*What?*" Aida exclaimed, "I never believed it was going to happen." In other biographies, the marriage is usually dismissed as rather pitiful, undertaken by Jack in order to provide Mémêre a full-time nurse, but intimates in Lowell, who observed the marriage at close range, disagree. "Stella was a lady, right from the heart," said Billy Koumantzelis. "That's one of the things Jack liked about her. She was sweet, genuine, and honest, and she always made you feel comfortable." Though Kerouac frankly told me that he needed someone to take care of his mother, he also spoke of his marriage to Stella as a consummation of his and Sammy's love. Some sort of displacement, a melding of brother and sister, had taken place in his mind. "Sammy looks out from her eyes," he said, "and speaks from her lips." In our first conversation, Stella told me, "Sammy passed the torch to me. Don't worry, your book will get done."

Fortunately, I was spared any knowledge of Kerouac's behavior in Hyannis until many years later. Soon after the wedding, in January 1967, police slapped him with two arrests for public drunkenness, and he accelerated his plans to get out of town. Later the same month, he put the Hyannis house up for sale, and left with Stella and Mémêre for Lowell, where he knew he would be protected by Stella's brothers, and by unofficial bodyguards like Billy Koumantzelis and Joe Chaput. He rented out the Hyannis house, as a source of additional income, and completed the move to Lowell in mid-January. In a letter to Rev. Sweeney, Kerouac wrote that his bride was Greek Orthodox and remarked that they would soon remarry in the Holy Trinity Church in Lowell. They were also contemplating a Catholic ceremony in Saint Louis-de-France. Messily scrawled, Jack's letter to Sweeney evidently was written while he was intoxicated: he signed himself as the "Secret Pope of America." Nevertheless, Sweeney replied that he would gladly perform the ceremony, and spelled out the permissions that would be required from the Lowell parish in order for a nonresident to celebrate an official Catholic service. In his reply, Kerouac thanked the priest and added that Frank Leahy had recently returned to the Boston-Lowell area. Leahy was supposed to have a comeback in 1967, and "so am I," he wrote.

Kerouac purchased a house in a fashionable section of Lowell known as the Highlands, where the elegant streets and gracious homes were a far cry from the wrinkly tar corners of Pawtucketville and Centralville, across the Merrimack River, where he'd grown up. Nevertheless, Centralville had been his first choice, and he'd tried to buy the white-frame house on Beaulieu Street where Gerard had died. The place had been well kept up over the years, but it was not for sale. Stella's brother, Nick, introduced him to the realtor who showed him the Highlands house—a handsome split-level, ranch-style structure at 271 Sanders Avenue.

Interviewed in 1995, the present owner, Dennis Scannell, Lowell High's current head football coach, said, "The Cohens had the house directly after Kerouac, and said Kerouac had stuff sitting on original John F. Kennedy [presidential campaign] posters. The floors were stained from his cats." Scannell and his wife Ann have lived at 271 Sanders for fourteen years, but they still hear screwball stories from Kerouac's old neighbors, who often saw him wandering around in his pajamas and slippers. Trying to keep him out of bars, Stella hid his clothes and shoes, but he went out anyway. "He was nuts, a complete night owl," said Scannell. "Neighbors directly behind Sanders Avenue said, 'He slept all day and partied all night. Drove us crazy playing a guitar.'"

Another resident, George Chigas, was nine years old when Kerouac moved to the neighborhood in 1967. One day, Chigas was playing football in the street with some friends when Kerouac came out of his house, wearing a dirty T-shirt and rubbing his stomach. Kerouac said George's parents had invited him to a party in their home earlier in the week, and he wanted to know if he could have some of their liquor, since he had exhausted his own supply. Another neighbor, Phil Coppola, recalled, "Kerouac came by one night in pajamas with a manuscript, offering to sell it for a hundred dollars, but would take twenty." Kerouac told Joe Chaput that he was going stir-crazy, because he was cooped up in the house day and night.

In taking over Mémère's care, Stella had lifted an enormous burden, and Jack began to read me exciting new passages from *Vanity of Duluoz*. The book was produced at great cost to Stella, though she never complained to me. According to Aida, Stella was swamped with work, taking care of both Mémère and Jack. "She had no free time to drive around and visit or have lunch like we used to do. She was tied up with Mémère and Jack and even her own mother. Mémère was both a severe diabetic and an invalid. Jack was almost as helpless. Stella did everything, she had to clean them, she had to dress them, do their laundry and feed them and take care of the house. It was a full-time twenty-four-hour job." "Stella gave up her whole life for our mother, Jack, and Gabe," said John Sampas.

For once, Mémère respected and liked one of Jack's women. Stella told her Lowell neighbor, Mary Rouses Karafelis, "Mary, she treats me like her daughter. I am so happy." Long accustomed to the self-sacrifice entailed by unconditional love and service, Stella raised no objection when she learned that her peculiar marriage to Kerouac would involve no sexual contact. They occupied separate bedrooms. During the day, Jack often repaired to a small upstairs study that reflected the fastidious order he brought to bear on his work, but never on his life. The room was so clean it was literally "shining," the *Paris Review* later reported.

Stella often answered the phone when I called, and I always enjoyed speaking with her, because her voice was so warm, soft, and gentle. She did not sound like a disappointed person, but like a contented wife, and she was the opposite of many of the authors' spouses or lovers I dealt with, often on a daily basis. Some of them were far more demanding and imperious than the authors themselves. One of them even insisted on designing a Pulitzer Prize–winning spouse's dust jacket, and the author later shoved the childish crayola drawing across my desk and expected me to use it. Stella Kerouac was a refreshing departure, invariably tactful, intelligent, noninterfering, and devoted to Jack and Mémêre. "This book is for you and me," she said to me one day, referring to *Vanity of Duluoz*. "He says you're holding things together in New York, and I'm holding things together at home." Tony Sampas was also invaluable, patiently listening every time Kerouac wanted to read a passage.

Though still paralyzed, Mémêre dominated 271 Sanders from her sick-bed, commandeering the dining room, which was located at the center of the house. She rang her bell when she needed attention, jangling it almost constantly. Wrote a *Boston Globe* reporter:

> A few feet away, just the other side of a thin plastic folding-accordian door . . . sits Jack Kerouac in a rocking chair. . . . "Completely surrounded by booze," in his own words, averaging 12 to 15 shots of whiskey and gulps of beer an hour, seven feet from his own television set, staring at the midday pap, his mind as sensitive as a frog's opened heart.

Stella finally gave up trying to keep Kerouac dry, but made sure he did his drinking at the family establishment, Nicky's, where her brothers could keep an eye on him. In 1995, Guy Lefebvre, who runs a framing shop in downtown Lowell, described what the bar was like in the sixties. "The strippers were so bad that I sat at the bar at Nicky's and watched the news, and nobody likes looking at naked women more than me. They took off everything and showed their sagging tits and sagging bellies. The median age was mid-thirties but they all looked about forty-eight. In most bars, all the women get good-looking at closing time, but it never got that late at Nicky's."

Kerouac strayed from Nicky's at his peril, always getting into trouble when his in-laws weren't around to control him. One evening, he stumbled into Omer's, a tough café and pool hall around the corner from Nicky's. His arrogance and self-proclaimed expertise on rising from the ghetto outraged the blacks. "We had to go and rescue him," Billy Koumantzelis recalled. "He got busted one time on Andover Street for peeing when loaded. Sergeant Flaherty arrested him. Flaherty was a great reader of Kerouac's books. He took Jack to the station, and for eight hours they enjoyed a literary discussion." According to Lowell's current chief of police, Ed Davis, Kerouac was also arrested at Nicky's by officer John Sheehan.

In March 1967, Kerouac read fresh passages of *Vanity of Duluoz* to me over the telephone, still sounding completely normal. As an ex-student of Columbia's graduate faculty of philosophy, I particularly enjoyed his evocation of the Quad: "Lights of the campus, lovers arm in arm, hurrying eager students in the flying leaves of late October, the library going with glow, all the books and pleasure and the big city of the world right at my broken feet." Any time he rang and started reading to me, I told Ann Sheldon, "Hold all calls." When Kerouac informed me his writer's block had come back, I read passages to him from his published work, such as, "We zoomed through small crossroads towns smack out of the darkness, and passed long lines of lounging harvest hands and cowboys in the night." Then I'd say, "You did that, Jack. You can do it again."

"Oh, yeah," he said, "what makes you so sure?"

I told him that I'd enjoyed his recent letter to me, and suggested he could write *Vanity of Duluoz* as if he were composing a letter to me or Stella.

"How about Neal?" he said.

"Anybody," I said. "It doesn't matter, so long as it's someone you trust. It could even be God."

"I know," he said, "I'll write it to Sammy." Then he reconsidered and said, "No, I'll write it to Stella. I'll start it, 'All right, wifey . . .' "[15]

I still had no knowledge of the private hell he was going through, but that began to change gradually in the spring of 1967. During one of his calls, I told him about the first East Coast Be-In, which was held in the Sheep Meadow in Central Park and attended by 250,000, including the poet Robert Lowell. The Sheep Meadow demonstration stemmed from the original San Francisco Be-In, which had been organized by Allen Ginsberg, Gary Snyder, Michael McClure, and Lenore Kandel. The Be-Ins forged a powerful new coalition of Beats, hippies, flower children, war protesters, rockers, drug advocates, and disenfranchised groups such as blacks, women, and gays. This became known as "the movement," which ultimately mushroomed until it was powerful enough to undermine two U.S. presidencies and help end the war in Vietnam. As the movement began to accelerate in the late 1960s, I said to Kerouac, "All of this comes straight out of you." I urged him to assume his rightful place as the founder of the postwar counterculture. "People want to see you," I said. "You should be up there on those flatbed trucks, addressing thousands."

"The hippies came out to Northport and tried to see me once," Kerouac said. "Ginsberg's messianic robes don't suit him." He explained that Ginsberg had dragged him into Timothy Leary's experiments with psychedelics at the beginning of the sixties. Ginsberg felt that the world's most influential people—beginning with Kerouac, Robert Lowell, Barney Rosset, LeRoi Jones, Willem de Kooning, Franz Kline, Thelonious Monk, and other hip VIPs—should be converted to psychedelics. Leary, who regarded *On the Road* as the "Upanishads of the Uprising," agreed to a kickoff psilocybin trip with Kerouac and Ginsberg in Ginsberg's Lower East Side apartment and to subsequent sessions with Lowell and Rosset. Kerouac and Leary got along well at first, contemplating Ginsberg's penis, playing Kerouac's baseball-solitaire game, and then going outside and using snowballs to toss football passes at each other. But the trip soon turned into a nightmare.

I later knew Leary and found him to be the egomaniac of all time. "My mind's never been the same since that bummer with Leary," Kerouac told me, adding, "Walking on water wasn't built in a day." By that he meant that psychedelics were incapable of changing society overnight, or perhaps at all.

Years later, Leary told me the session hadn't been a picnic for him either. Leary's agent, Ron Bernstein, had suggested I publish Leary at William Morrow, where I was an editor in the late 1970s, and one evening I accompanied Leary to Princeton, where he was to give a speech. At some point during the automobile ride from Manhattan, the subject of Kerouac came up. "Jack gave me my first bad trip," Leary said. "I rolled up in a ball and Ginsberg had to talk me out of it. *On the Road* looked to the future but its author was stuck in the past." Leary and Ginsberg had only themselves to blame for the fiasco; they'd dropped psilocybin pills with Kerouac even though they knew he was drunk and in no condition for a psychedelic trip.

On the phone, Kerouac described another bummer, this one with Ken Kesey. Neal Cassady had driven out to Northport in 1964 and urged Jack to return with him to Manhattan for a party at Kesey's. "I didn't care if Neal had been sucked in by the hippies—I didn't want be trotted out for the Merry Pranksters to inspect like some dinosaur," Jack said. In November 1964, Kesey and his Merry Pranksters had pulled into the city on a 1939 school bus, *Further*, which was painted in psychedelic Day-Glo colors. Neal was at the steering wheel. The lightning rod of the Beat movement in the forties and fifties, Neal was now a catalyst of hippie revolt, beginning with his momentous 1960 meeting with Leary in Cambridge, Massachusetts. Neal had converted the then forty-year-old Leary from a Harvard don into a swinger by having sex with girls under Leary's nose.

Neal's subsequent arrival on the hippie scene in the Haight-Ashbury was recalled by Linda Gravenites in a 1997 interview. "I was housesitting for the Grateful Dead at 710 Ashbury Street, and one day Jerry Garcia said Neal was a guru. Neal hung out at the Dead's house a lot, throwing a sledge hammer, eight or ten pounds, to develop his forearm muscles. He was an old speed freak, extremely intelligent, had a low tolerance for boredom, a maniac driver, really liked his ladies to be pretty strange so he wouldn't get bored. He liked dippy chicks because he couldn't figure out what they were going to do next. One day Neal and I were sitting in the kitchen. He wasn't talking for once, and I was thinking of what Jerry said. 'Hey, Neal, what's man's purpose,' I asked. He said, 'To dream.' I thought that was a marvelous answer. Artists have to pull it out of a dream and put it into form; living is like that too."

By 1964, Neal was regarded as a hero by Kesey, Jerry Garcia, and other leaders of the West Coast psychedelic movement. As Garcia put it, Neal was their authority on "subjects that haven't been identified yet." Kerouac, according to Ginsberg, was viewed by Kesey as "an elder master and a great American." Like many of the younger writers of the sixties, Kesey had been inspired by Kerouac's revival of the Thoreauvian tradition of gentle resistance to authority. Born on a Colorado farm, Kesey by 1959 was volunteering as a paid subject for hallucinogenic experiments at Veterans Hospital in Menlo Park. Later, he remained at the hospital to work as a ward attendant. As a fledgling writer, he sought out Kerouac's editor, Malcolm Cowley, Kerouac's agent, Sterling Lord, and Kerouac's publisher, Viking. *One Flew Over the Cuckoo's Nest*, Kesey's stream-of-consciousness novel, was published in 1962. An anarchic, lethally satirical work, it concerns the revolt of a group of inmates in an insane asylum against dehumanizing regimentation; their story symbolizes all attempts to extinguish human individuality. When the twenty-nine-year-old Kesey arrived in New York in 1964 shortly after the publication of his second novel, *Sometimes a Great Notion*, a saga of an Oregon logging family, a party was held for the Beats to endorse the hippie revolt. Everyone wanted to meet Kerouac and receive his blessing, evidently unaware of the author's conservative Republican bias.

"I didn't even want to go into town with Neal," Kerouac later told me. "Too many temptations, and I really wasn't very well at the time." As always, he succumbed to Neal's charm, and his first drink soon led to a dam-burst of booze. Photographs of Kerouac at Kesey's party that night reveal a waxy, white-faced wraith who looks more like a corpse than a living person. Neal, "upped to death and driving like he wanted to kill us both," had whisked Jack into Manhattan, Jack recalled, "and he hit me up for a wad of cash en route." Jack gave him ten dollars, which later caused Carolyn to reflect that Neal had sunk "from conman to beggar."

Jack and Neal arrived on the Upper East Side around 10 P.M., and for a while sat on the bus, *Further*, reminiscing with Ginsberg and Orlovsky. It was difficult for Kerouac to get excited about going to a party of acid–heads five years after he'd dropped psilocybin and fourteen years after tripping on peyote, but they finally went upstairs, and Neal excitedly showed Jack around. "Dig this, Jack, the tape recorders and the cameras, just like we used to do, only this time professionally," Neal said, enthusing over the equipment with which the Pranksters were chronicling their cross-country trip. Sensing Kerouac's discomfort, Kesey commented to Ginsberg, "We should have gone out to Northport quietly in the night." Robert Stone, who was among the guests, observed that Kerouac "couldn't find solace in people like . . . us. . . . He was drinking whiskey from a paper bag, and he was very pissed-off and at his most embittered. . . . Kerouac was eloquent on what jerkabouts we were." Stone shrewdly observed that Kerouac "was jealous that Ken Kesey had grabbed Neal as a bus driver."

Stone was right, but Jack's feelings about Kesey were even more complex. Ron Lowe told me in 1995, "Jack said Ken Kesey and that bunch killed Cassady, basically that they used him up. But if anything Neal was a volunteer." When Kerouac reminisced about the Pranksters party to me in 1967, he said he liked Kesey as a novelist, but he deplored "the chaos, the ugly lights, the loud tapes (no good jazz or nuthin'). The American flag was desecrated in my honor of all things." In fact, photographs of Kerouac at the party show him smiling and wearing the flag wrapped around his neck like a scarf. On one occasion, I tried to explain to Kerouac that he'd misperceived the hippies, who were in the process of reinventing America as a better place and who looked on Kerouac as their spiritual forebear. As journalist Lauren Kessler wrote, the Pranksters "served as a trans-generational bridge between the Beats and hippies. It was about staging a grand goof, about being yourself. . . . In the context of the times it was . . . liberating." I told Kerouac that we should be doing everything we could to enlist hippie support for his books, since the Beats had ignored *Desolation Angels*. When he said nothing, I became a little exasperated, and added, "Don't you realize that to get your books accepted anymore, we have to remind people that today's civil rights and antiwar revolts come straight out of the Beats?"

His reply shocked me into silence. In a strange, unfamiliar tone—cold and weak, almost trembling with fear and paranoia—he called the hippies "a bunch of communists," and added, "Whatever you do, don't give my address to Ginsberg, or any other communist. I don't take any credit for the hippies, don't want my name associated with them in any way." I couldn't believe what I was hearing, since I still thought of Kerouac as a radical. I remember hanging up the phone, feeling like I was on a sinking ship. My author was a political reactionary—the kiss of death in the sixties, the age of "radical chic," when editors were running after Eldridge Cleaver, Abbie Hoffman, Angela Y. Davis, and Malcolm X. My own list would soon include *Soledad Brothers*, a prison diary by black-power leader George Jackson. For the first time, I seriously wondered if I could continue publishing Kerouac; he wasn't selling, and I didn't like his politics. Several things kept me going. I had money invested in him, enormous respect for his body of work, and loyalty not only to Jack but to Stella, Mémère, and even to Sammy, the "Sabby Savakis" of *Vanity of Duluoz*.[16]

According to Kerouac's notebook entries for June 1967, Mémère was undergoing therapy for her paralysis. He brought her home from the hospital around the first of the month and tried to cheer her up by giving her two new cats named Timmy and Tuffy. The cats may have been a mistake; once Mémère was settled comfortably in bed with them, she saw no reason to do her exercises. Jack confessed in his notebook that he was drunk around the clock, and that he and Mémère had turned Stella into a slave. On Monday, June 12, he noted that another cat, Pitou, had expired at dawn as Mémère cuddled it on her breast. The skin on the cat's tail had turned black with gangrene. Remarking that his notebook had become unrelievedly depressing, Jack decided to give it up; all it displayed was spiritual bankruptcy, though he acknowledged that he was fortunate to have a good wife in Stella. One day, he found the therapists pulling Mémère's limp body through the house and told them to stop. One of the therapists explained that they were helping Mémère to learn to walk again, but it was clear to Jack that his mother had passed out. He ordered them to put her on the bed and later confirmed that she'd lapsed into unconsciousness during the exercise, but her therapists had continued to drag her slumped figure, thinking her merely difficult or lazy.

Ginsberg finally managed to track Kerouac down in Lowell, but he was not welcomed, and Kerouac accused him of plagiarism, charging that Allen had swiped his best ideas. At forty-one, Ginsberg had become the most famous poet in the United States, as well as an international symbol of the antiwar movement. His bearded visage peered from a best-selling poster that showed him dressed up as Uncle Sam.

Other old friends of Kerouac were not faring as well. "Bob Kaufman's brain turned to mush," Linda Gravenites recalled. Wavy Gravy, a counterculture celebrity, said, "All along the roadside, you see the smattered and charred and twisted remains of people who . . . read *On the Road* and . . . wanted nothing more than to be Neal Cassady. They'd take a lot of pills and they'd fry their brains and that would be it." Only in the historical context of a bland, oppressed culture could Neal Cassady, a carjacker from Denver, have become an icon in populist mythology. His message to the hippies was the same as it had been to the Beats: take it to the limit, and discover the illimitable spirit within. As Thelonious Monk once put it, "Every man is a genius just being his own self." Unfortunately, Cassady never heeded the famous warning that was circulated in the underground press in 1965: "Speed kills . . . can and will . . . freeze your mind and kill your body." Within five years of their first injection, most speed freaks were dead.

The most notorious guru of the decade, the Maharishi Mahesh Yogi, advised Ginsberg, "LSD has done its thing. Now forget it. Just let it drop." When Ginsberg pointed out that the Maharishi's audiences were made up almost entirely of acidheads, the guru remained unshaken and replied, "Meditation, meditation, meditation."

Kerouac made an effort to stop drinking and "tried a couple of AA meetings, but gave up," recalled a Lowell acquaintance, Gary Cheney. Jack soon hit the bars again, announcing, "I'm Jack Kerouac. I'm a famous writer from Lowell," according to Jay Pendergast, who drank with Jack at the SAC. Pendergast often watched Kerouac sidle up to "dingy unfocusing drones," and when he tried to blow his monologues at them, they would turn "hostile, frightened, uncomprehending" glares on him, mumbling "asshole." Nothing seemed to faze Jack any more, now that his "notself" was in charge. "This anonymity is what he wanted to experience," Pendergast said. Often, Jack would play his phantom bass in the SAC, plucking at the carpeted pole in the middle of the room, lost in an blackout. At Nicky's one night, he told the barmaid, Maureen Murphy Coimbra, "I have twenty-five-hundred mounted police coming in from Canada. They're gonna take care of you."

"Okay, Jack," she replied, "I'll handle it, don't worry about it."

Encouraged by her response, he rounded up Maureen, Tony Sampas, and Maureen's brother Danny and took them all home with him to Sanders Avenue. "We were in the study," Maureen recalled, "and Stella came downstairs and said, 'You'll have to leave now.' Jack told Stella, 'I took you out of the goddamn mills, and I put you in the study, and you're not throwing my friends out of my house.' I said, 'No, no, Jack, we'll go. She has to get up in the morning.' " On his better days, Kerouac would sit peacefully in Nicky's, reading the *Sun* at 4 P.M. and dreaming of starting a small community newspaper in Lowell.[17]

Vanity of Duluoz was largely written in ten bursts between mid-March and mid-May 1967. Kerouac and I were in touch regularly, and he told me that my "empathy" was his "companion and source of strength." He said my suggestion to write the book as a letter to someone he trusted had proved helpful, motivating him to conceive of the novel as an explanation to Stella of the obstacles he'd overcome to achieve fame. One day, he called to say the book was finally finished. John Sampas, who was working for a Boston investment firm, took the manuscript to his office, and asked a young woman to make photocopies. Soon it was on my desk in one of Sterling's familiar brown manuscript boxes.

I had so wanted to love the book, but the final manuscript was full of gratuitous racial and sexist slurs, and Kerouac's contract protected him from editorial changes. Over the years, he had read much of the text to me, but during these telephone calls, he had concentrated on what Ginsberg called "condensed cadenzas," or lyrical effusions, and the novel's pervasive negativity didn't hit me until I saw the completed manuscript. Though *Vanity of Duluoz* would fail on publication in 1968, the novel eventually was recognized as a classic of bitter, misanthropic honesty, and became a money-maker for the corporation. In 1998, it was still in print, and could be found in almost every large bookstore in the nation.

On July 17, I wrote Jack:

> You really did get it in, and it really is good. We're going ahead for the winter list. I'd love to have some pictures of you as a kid, as a football star, as a college student, as a sailor. Particularly eager to have something circa 1946 or somewhat earlier, like the picture you refer to (hope you have it) of you and Claude [Lucien] on the steps of Low Memorial. In many ways *Vanity of Duluoz* is the most direct, personal, and generous of your books. It is exactly what you said it would be, the story of an adventurous education, and the style is perfect for it.

I was moved by the dedication page, which read: "Dedicated to Stavroula. Means 'From the Cross' in Greek, and is also my wife's first name — Stavroula. Extra, special thanks to Ellis Amburn for his empathetic brilliance and expertise."

Ginsberg told Ken Kesey that *Vanity of Duluoz* was "Jack's best retrospective on America's Golden Disillusionment" and that it contained "some of the best football stuff ever written." In a letter to Dennis McNally, Ginsberg compared the barebones style of *Vanity of Duluoz* with a "mature painter's swift exact unerring brushwork," and praised the author's occasional "sleight-of-hand rhapsodies." Touchingly, Ginsberg asked what more could anyone expect of a "dying Kerouac," pointing out that even in the final two-year death grip of his alcoholism, Kerouac "outwrote all his peers excepting maybe Burroughs." Ginsberg was almost alone in appreciating Kerouac's output in the 1960s, calling it as substantial in amount and quality as that of any novelist of that decade. On the basis of *Visions of Gerard* and *Desolation Angels* alone, he was right.

Sensing that *Vanity of Duluoz* would be Kerouac's last major novel, I decided to turn the physical package into a kind of commemorative edition. I ordered an unusual dust jacket, including photographs of the author on both the front and the back. I asked Jack to dig into his family albums and send me photos of himself, Nin, Leo, and Mémère in Lowell and in New York.

On August 3, 1967, I wrote Kerouac, "Thanks for the great pictures. I think the one from high school, with you in tie and pullover, is one we'll use for the sales conference late this month." For the front cover, I chose a picture of Jack in his "35" football jersey, dashing for a touchdown. I presented the novel at our next sales conference, and later wrote Kerouac on September 12, "I'd like to have decorative endpapers for *Vanity of Duluoz*, and I've had the designers, Addelson & Eichinger, prepare them. A Xerox copy is enclosed, and I hope you like it as much as I do. As you can see, I've used the pictures you were nice enough to give me. I showed them to the salesmen at the sales conference, and everyone liked them so much they said please use them in the book. Tell me if it's okay by you, and I'll go ahead. All the best."[18]

As we prepared to issue the novel in 1968, there was a slight flurry of pre-publication interest, when Sterling sold first serial rights to several magazines, including *Sports Illustrated*, *Evergreen Review*, and the *Atlantic Monthly*. On February 6, the novel's critical reception ranged from ambivalent to savage, and was epitomized by *Time*'s schizophrenic reaction, in which the reviewer said it was Kerouac's "best book," and then complained that he was "far less talented" than Mailer. The reviewer also scorned the "dreadful indiscipline" of the writing. One of the few exceptions to the general drubbing came from the *Boston Globe*'s Gregory Mcdonald, who wrote, simply, "It's a good book." The *Christian Science Monitor* dismissed it with the quip, "Hit the space bar and GO!" In the daily *New York Times*, Thomas Lask called it the "road to nowhere." The *New York Times Book Review* was no better; Peter Sourian called Kerouac "infantile" and discounted *Vanity of Duluoz* as a "banal plea for the Good Old Days." In the *National Observer*, Kerouac's friend John Clellon Holmes commented, "Scott Fitzgerald . . . wrote that [his] two keenest regrets . . . were 'not . . . play[ing] football in college, and not getting overseas during the war.' *Vanity of Duluoz* is steeped in the keener knowledge of a writer who accomplished both these things, and it suggests that succeeding in such elementary endeavors prepares a young man for modern life no better than failing at them." Holmes concluded that *Vanity of Duluoz* was among "the most extraordinary, influential, maddening, and . . . prodigious achievements in recent literature." But when the novel came out in England, the *Times Literary Supplement* headlined its pan, "Be Your Age."[19]

At some point in 1967, Kerouac began to call me when he was obviously drunk. Out of nowhere one day, he said, "I know about you publishing boys on Madison Avenue. I'm gonna come down there and stick a pineapple up your ass." It was a swinish thing to say, and I hung up the phone. Stella called me later and said, "He's been drinking heavily. He's so lonely." Joe LeSueur and I shared the same office, and he asked me, "What's the matter?"

"I think Jack Kerouac just propositioned me," I said, and started laughing. I told Ann Sheldon not to put through any more calls from Kerouac unless he was sober. But soon he began to call me after work at my apartment. Sometimes he was completely unintelligible; often he was obscene. In 1996, agent Ron Bernstein recalled my story about Kerouac's "up your ass" threat. At other times, extraordinary tidbits emerged from Kerouac's maunderings. He said he'd "made it" with Montgomery Clift, who'd died in 1966 at the age of forty-five. Rock star Jim Morrison sought Kerouac out, but Mémêre wouldn't let him in "without a hairnet." Jack spoke of a strange trip to Canada in search of ancestral records, but he'd blacked out on cognac and beer and somehow ended up in Maine. He'd once had a tête-à-tête with Jacqueline Kennedy, who "loved to travel," he said, and who wanted to meet "the real Dean Moriarty."

I didn't believe him, but in the 1970s, when I was editor-in-chief of the Delacorte Press, and Jacqueline Kennedy Onassis was looking for a job in publishing following disagreements with Viking, her first employer, I took her to lunch at a hamburger joint on Second Avenue called Knickers. At one point, I told Onassis what Kerouac had said, and she smiled. "We asked many writers to the White House," she said, neither confirming nor denying Kerouac's claim. She was fascinated that I'd been Kerouac's editor, and asked me several questions about the editing of *Vanity of Duluoz*. In the notes I scribbled after our luncheon, I wrote, "Told Jackie O.: 'Query everything—it's the author's last chance to get it right.' She said, 'Oh, you're so oracular.'"

In 1995, when I was conducting interviews in St. Petersburg for this book, I was startled when Ron Lowe told me that Kerouac had had dinner in the Kennedy White House. "Isn't it odd," I asked, "that it doesn't appear in any of the Kennedy or Kerouac biographies?" Ron replied that Kerouac always liked to go out and eat after sitting in a bar all night and listening to Ron's band play, and he explained, "When we left the club and were talking about where we might go, Jack drew himself up and said, 'You know, Ronnie, I've eaten in the great restaurants of Europe, I've eaten in Tangier, I've even eaten in Jack Kennedy's White House. Do you know where the best chefs in the world are? It's those chefs who make those wonderful little hamburgers at White Castle.' "[20]

Strange things started happening to Kerouac in Lowell in 1967. He showed up at the high school one day to teach, and in a 1995 interview, Jack Lang, Kerouac's track teammate, recalled, "I was teaching high-school algebra and trig, and the substitute English teacher thought it would be a big hit to bring in the famous man to talk to the students. He brought in Mr. Kerouac, who was three sheets to the wind. He embarrassed himself, the teacher, and the kids. The headmaster called coach Raymond Riddick to escort Jack from the building. The substitute teacher was fired." According to other accounts, Kerouac enthralled the class when he improvised the story of *Moby-Dick*. The trouble occurred after class, when Kerouac squatted in the hallway, telling the coach, "I saved your school once against Lawrence, don't you remember that?"

The press interviews Kerouac granted in Lowell were becoming increasingly blowzy, but he was still capable of puncturing pretentious esthetic theories. A *Boston Globe* reporter asked him how he'd been able to complete so many books. He replied that he never finished a book; he just wrote until he got bored, at which point he stopped and called it a book. When he started writing again, it was a new book. "That's deep form," he said. Nick Sampas drove him to Montreal to appear on Canadian television, and he was at his best—pithy, original, and surprising. "Does anything in modern life make you sick?" the interviewer asked. "I'm sick of myself," Jack said, bringing down the house. Later, he and Nick Sampas hit fifteen jazz clubs in one night.

In October 1967, he wrote in his notebook that he was still mourning the death of Pitou the cat, and added that he'd fallen in love all over again with Stella, praising her as a perfect wife and the best friend his mother had ever had. He noted that he was overweight, tipping the bathroom scales at two hundred pounds.

Later that month, Jan Kerouac unexpectedly showed up in Lowell. In 1995, Doris Boisvert Kerouac, who was married to Harvey Kerouac, Jack's first cousin, recalled, "Jan came to me looking for Jack. Harvey and I took her to him. Jack asked Jan, 'Does your mother give you the money I send every month?' " At fifteen, Jan was pregnant, unmarried, had already been a prostitute and a heroin addict, had done a stint in Bellevue, and was now going to Mexico with her future husband, John Lash. When Jan first walked into Sanders Avenue that November night in 1967, Jack shrugged, smiled tentatively, and said, "Hi," she later wrote in *Baby Driver*, her first novel. Jack told her she could bring her boyfriend inside, but Mémère soon started yelling, "Is Caroline there? Foreigners! They're all foreigners," and they were asked to leave lest Mémère suffer another stroke. Kerouac said nothing to substantiate Jan's impression that she was his daughter, though according to Jan, he did tell her that she should write books and could use the Kerouac name. According to Joe Chaput, Kerouac said that he didn't believe Jan was his daughter. Kerouac claimed to be sterile, and explained that Joan had had sex with another man.

Approximately a month after Jan's visit to Lowell, poet Ted Berrigan saw her in Tompkins Square in New York. Kerouac later categorically told Berrigan, "She's not my daughter." Still pregnant, Jan left for Mexico, and her baby was stillborn in a Mexican jungle. She continued to receive "twelve dollars a week in support checks with the famous author's signature," she revealed at a press conference in 1994. "He was just a shy guy who drank too much," she told a *Washington Post* reporter. "Sure he wrote a lot of great stuff. But he wasn't a god."[21]

In 1967, the *Paris Review* interviewed Kerouac as part of its prestigious "Art of Fiction" series. The New Journalism, which stemmed from Kerouac's agitated, confessional style, was sweeping the literary world in scorching articles by Norman Mailer, Tom Wolfe, Jimmy Breslin, Jill Johnston, and many others. Even Philip Roth's *Portnoy's Complaint* seemed to have been influenced by Kerouac. "The consciousness of a writer *is* the protagonist," said Holmes in an interview. Kerouac was familiar with the *Paris Review* series, and regarded his inclusion in it as the most signal honor granted him in his lifetime. Sitting in the same kind of rocking chair President Kennedy used in the White House, Kerouac gave Ted Berrigan a remarkably honest account of his life, work, and homoerotic activities, admitting his penchant for sex with young males. At one point during the interview, drinks were served, and afterward a note of discontinuity entered the conversation. Then, Kerouac saw Berrigan taking pills, and said, "Give me one of those. What are they?" Berrigan told him they were Obertrols, and Kerouac helped himself to them, remembering aloud that Neal liked them.

Berrigan asked Kerouac's opinion of editors, and he replied that, once a sentence was written, nothing should be done "to defray its rhythmic thought impact." To Kerouac, thinking was more sacrosanct than writing. Thought was nature expressing itself like the flow of a river through the human mind. "The river flows over a rock once and for all and never returns and can never flow any other way in time," he said, trying to explain what he saw as the heresy of revision. It was it clear that the web of consciousness fascinated him perhaps even more than language, and that his aim was to reveal the human mind in the act of creation. As in a Pollock painting, every line was the record of an artist at work.

On the subject of Malcolm Cowley, Kerouac was characteristically cranky and contradictory, alternately praising the editor's flawless perception and accusing him of having disfigured the original version of *On the Road* with changes in content, grammar, and punctuation. Referring to his present editor, who at that point was me, he said he was grateful for help in discovering "logical errors, such as dates, names of places. For instance, in my last book I wrote 'Firth of Forth' then looked it up on the suggestion of my editor, and found that I'd really sailed off the Firth of Clyde. Things like that. Or I spelled Aleister Crowley 'Alisteir,' or he discovered little mistakes about the yardage in football games . . . and so forth." He still rated Neal the best writer of his generation, citing the "Joan Anderson Letter," but added that the "crown" of contemporary letters belonged to Genet, Burroughs, Ginsberg, and Corso. As the alcohol and Obertrols took effect, the interview degenerated into racism, recrimination, and sexual bluster. Though Stella was in the room, he talked about what a hot lover Esperanza had been. Aaram Saroyan and Duncan McNaughton, two young poets, had accompanied Berrigan, and at the conclusion of the interview, Kerouac told them, "So you boys are poets, hey? Well, let's hear some of your poetry." They stayed for another hour, reading their verse. Kerouac was delighted to be with the son of his idol William Saroyan, and he presented the young men with signed broadsides of a new poem.

Kerouac spent Christmas 1967 in Lowell, longing for the respect and recognition from his hometown that were certainly his due as one of America's best writers, but that were never forthcoming in his lifetime. He offered to pose nude if the city would erect a statue of him in front of City Hall, but it would take Lowell another twenty years to erect a monument to him, and by then it was a memorial. He fell into a depression, and his attorney, Jim Curtis, recalled, "When he wasn't putting down Johnny Walker scotch and chasing it down with beer, you could hardly get a word out of him." Tony Sampas felt it was because Lowell "was the one place in the world [where] he wanted to be respected . . . He didn't get that, and that made him sad."

Eager to secure his place in history, Kerouac granted an interview to author Bruce Cook for a book-length study of the Beats, *The Beat Generation*, later published, somewhat ironically, by Scribner's, the house that had turned down *The Town and the City*. Cook, who found Kerouac in a bar, later wrote that he was showing the effects of his alcoholism. Kerouac told Cook that he objected to the recent public pronouncements of Mailer and Ginsberg. "I wasn't trying to create any kind of new consciousness," he said, selling himself short and negating the visions and annunciations in works like *The Town and the City* and *The Dharma Bums*. "We were just a bunch of guys who were out trying to get laid." Puzzled, Cook subsequently asked Mailer why the Beats were reluctant to involve themselves in politics, and Mailer replied that Kerouac was a surrealist. "When Kerouac says, 'I like Eisenhower. I think he's a great man. I think he's our greatest president since Abraham Lincoln.' . . . It's a surrealistic remark," Mailer said. "He's mixing two ideas that have absolutely no relation to each other—one of them is greatness and the other is Eisenhower." Obviously, Mailer was unaware that Kerouac was completely sincere in his veneration of Ike. Mailer generously admitted that the Beats had been braver than he, and had fulfilled the primary purpose of literature, which was to cut through "layers of cultural junk" and come up with "a new view of man."[22]

In February 1968, Kerouac called me and said in a sane, sober, calm, almost amused, voice, "They're saying Neal Cassady's dead. I don't believe it. When Neal wants to skip out on a wife or something, he just disappears." I was jolted by this news, but Kerouac's interpretation of it had a certain logic, given the temper of the times. Earlier in the sixties, Sterling Lord had called me at the office one day to say that law-enforcement officials were asking him for Ken Kesey's address. He refused to disclose personal information about his client, and I agreed that he was right. Subsequently, I learned that Kesey, Cassady, and thirteen others had been arrested and charged with marijuana possession. Kesey faked his own death to escape imprisonment, abandoning his van on a bluff in Big Sur. He then fled to Mexico, where Neal joined him. "Neal will show up, mark my words," Kerouac said, laughing as he spoke, even though Carolyn herself had given him the news and had expressed no doubt as to its authenticity. Indeed, she was relieved that "the God within him had mercifully relieved Neal of a burden which was too great for him to carry or transcend," she wrote. Carolyn also called Ginsberg, who accepted Neal's death without question and thought, "Sir Spirit's now home in Spirit."

In recent months, all of Neal's friends had dropped him, though he had sent Jack a card and had begged Ginsberg to come to Mexico to "save" him. Neal was staying in San Miguel de Allende just north of Mexico City with Janice ("J. B.") Brown, a rich girl from Erie, Pennsylvania. On his arrival in Mexico City on February 2, he had boarded a train to Celaya, a mountain town near San Miguel de Allende. At Celaya, he checked most of his belongings at the station, deciding to return later for them, and took a cab to San Miguel, where J. B. greeted him. She felt sure he could recover from his drug addiction, but within a couple of days, they were fighting so badly that he stormed out of the house, speeding on "reds." According to William Plummer, Neal left J. B. at noon on February 3. He intended to walk the two-and-a-half miles to San Miguel, and then continue along the railroad tracks about fifteen miles to Celaya, where he would retrieve his "magic bag," containing his Bible and treasured mementos, such as letters from Kerouac and Ginsberg. J. B. was surprised to see him make the trip on foot, since he'd been complaining of pains in his feet, but he explained that he wanted to count the ties between the two train stations, something only a confirmed speed freak would do.

At the San Miguel station, around midafternoon, Neal fell in with a group of Mexican wedding revelers and drank a muddy alcoholic beverage known as *pulque*. He also dropped a handful of Seconal. Concocted from the fermented sap of the maguey plant, pulque had been considered a sacred drink by the Aztecs. Taken with barbiturates, it was as lethal as any other form of alcohol. In Carolyn's opinion, Neal knew that the combination of drugs and liquor would kill him. Setting out from San Miguel, he headed toward Celaya, walking along the railroad tracks, counting the ties. After a while, it began to rain, and his T-shirt and jeans provided little protection against the chill. He walked a quarter of a mile before collapsing beside the tracks.

Indians discovered his comatose body the following morning and rushed him to a hospital, but he died a few hours later. Though no autopsy was performed, Mexican authorities attributed his demise to "generalized congestion," while newspaper accounts cited "overexposure." In Ginsberg's moving "Elegy for Neal Cassady," composed on February 10, 1968, he recalled the touch of Neal's hands and begged forgiveness for having demanded selfish satisfaction from Neal's "beautiful body" during their epic hitchhike from Denver to New Waverly, Texas. In the poem's final lines, Ginsberg also expressed sorrow for Kerouac, who, except for Neal, was "lonelier than all."

A few days later, Kerouac called my office in tears. "I loved Neal more than anyone in the world," he said. "He inspired every word I wrote. Now there's nothing more to say or do." He sounded completely sober, and his voice, though full of grief, also had the supple, rich quality I'd first heard when we'd talked in 1964. He seemed like a very young man again. He was under the impression that Neal had been found "in the desert, against a fence, frozen," he said. Crying, he continued to speak of the depth of his love for Neal, and said that Neal had loved him too. "It's in a book I wrote," he said. "He told me, 'I love you, man, man you've got to dig that; boy, you've got to know.'" I expressed my sympathy and told him that he was fortunate to have loved and been loved in return. Then I inquired about Neal's funeral. "Funeral?" he asked, but he was crying again and never answered my question.

Neal's remains lay on a slab in a Mexican mortuary, and no one went to Mexico to bring his body home, but Kesey's lawyer at least paid for cremation. Possession of Neal's ashes, which J. B. brought to Carolyn in Los Gatos, was desired by three of his women, and Carolyn shared a spoonful with Diana Hansen, the mother of one of Neal's children. Perhaps Neal's greatest legacy was the love and respect of his son John Allen, who later called Neal "a very evolved soul."

Without Neal, Kerouac continued to see no reason for living, and he told Carolyn, "I'll be joining him soon. . . . It won't be long." She invited Jack to visit her, but he refused, giving her the excuse that he could hardly make it to the bathroom. She wasn't fooled, as she knew that he had no problem getting to the refrigerator for his next boilermaker.[23]

Not long afterward, I received a call that I wish Kerouac had never made, one that forever altered our relationship. We had survived the end of the "honeymoon" period between author and editor, those first days when both of us had dreamed of success. We had survived the commercial and critical failure of two of his novels. And we had even survived his obscene phone calls. But now he said something I found it impossible to forget, though it was not personal. He said he was going to Germany "to see the concentration camps, and dance on Jews' graves." The worst part of it was that he didn't even sound drunk. That cold, homicidal voice was crisp and chilling. As the

Merry Pranksters had said of Neal at the end, he burned out compassion. So did Kerouac. Even Carolyn gave up on him after he made sexual suggestions to her that she later deemed unprintable.

He sent a postcard to Billy Koumantzelis from Stuttgart, with a photo of the Munchen Hofbrauhaus on the front. He wrote that he, Tony, Nicky, and others in their party were enjoying themselves in Germany. Soon, however, he decided that Germans were boorish and coarse, and he told Joe Chaput they had no respect for freedom of speech or religion. Later, he claimed to a *Boston Globe* reporter that Germans were even still goose-stepping. After a lifetime of idolizing Germans from afar, once he finally saw them firsthand, he couldn't stand them, according to Joe. Kerouac told the *Globe* that he "came back to America saying 'the poor Jews.' "[24]

On his return to Sanders Avenue, Jack felt sexually drawn to Stella for the first time, and they had riotous and passionate sex. "She was a virgin and went to the hospital with a hemorrhage after Jack made love to her," Stella's sister, Helen Surprenant, recalled in 1995. Jack was so proud of the blood-stained sheets that he displayed them to visitors, and on one occasion, he even took out his penis, expressing awe it could cause such carnage. Though he once told Joe that he'd tricked Stella into marriage in order to acquire free maid service for Mémêre, all that eventually changed. According to Joe, Kerouac fell in love with Stella, and he told Joe that they had sexual intercourse.

Never satisfied anywhere, Mémêre finally nagged Jack to move back to Florida, and he put the Lowell house up for sale. On July 18, 1968, he wrote Joe that he'd disconnected the telephone because it was too pricey, and added that he and Mémêre were ready for the big move. His income was down to an average of sixty dollars a week, and he owed Sterling $157. He was beginning to talk about the devil, urinate in the street, and ask strangers what his next novel should be about. "You think I'm insane, don't you?" he told a reporter, adding, "I am insane."

As Kerouac's personal Walpurgisnacht played itself out in Lowell, the United States was in the midst of its most violent domestic conflict since the Civil War. Columbia University, Kerouac's alma mater, exploded in riots, touching off a worldwide chain reaction of campus protests against the Vietnam War. Radical leader Tom Hayden was at the barricades in Morningside Heights. He later said that Kerouac and Cassady had defined the "new frontier . . . To take risks and journey into an emotional and intellectual wilderness."

That summer, Kerouac's disintegration became public knowledge when he appeared drunk on William F. Buckley's nationally televised talk show, *Firing Line*. Shortly before the show, he called me. "I'm coming to New York," he said, sounding rather mischievous. "I want to get together with you." During the call, he was being interviewed by a reporter from the *Boston Globe*, who later wrote that Kerouac said to his editor, "Give me $5000 on *Compleat Visions of Cody* and $5000 on *Beat Spotlight* so I can get my mother to Florida and get to work on *Beat Spotlight*. Listen. Give me no money. Just publish *Compleat Visions of Cody*. Ginsberg says it's an important book."

According to my notes, Kerouac also said that *Visions of Cody* was "the source of everything I've written, and needs to be published because it's about Neal Cassady," but the novel was never submitted to me. I have no notes regarding *Beat Spotlight*, but I subsequently learned that its subject was Kerouac's life in the 1960s.

After Jack's call, I rang Sterling and said, "Kerouac wants to get together with me. He mentioned dinner. What should I do?"

"Ellis, he'll be swinging from the chandeliers at Johnny Nicholson's," Sterling said, referring to one of Kerouac's favorite New York restaurants. Fortunately, Kerouac didn't call me again about his New York trip.[25]

Several friends accompanied him to the city. Billy Koumantzelis said they drank Michelob and Teacher's Scotch on the drive down from Lowell and were "pretty well hammered by the time we got to the West End Bar, where about half the people recognized Jack." Later, at the Delmonico Hotel on Madison Avenue, some of them began smoking pot. Burroughs and Genet were at the same hotel, completing their *Esquire* articles on the 1968 Democratic National Convention in Chicago. Ginsberg, who had been instrumental in disrupting the convention, came to visit Kerouac. "Ginsberg, what are you hanging around with all those dirty Jew Communists for, anyway?" Kerouac asked, referring to Abbie Hoffman and Jerry Rubin, who had helped Ginsberg organize the historic Chicago "Festival of Life." Alternately feeling that Kerouac was "vaster of mind and heart than myself" and "full of shit," Ginsberg invariably made excuses for Jack's anti-Semitism, adopting an attitude of appeasement. Years later, at a party in Joe LeSueur's apartment on Second Avenue, Ginsberg told me that he had always managed to short-circuit Kerouac's anti-Semitism by saying, "Did your mother put you up to that? Well, tell her she's got a dirty cunt."

At Delmonico's, as Billy recalled, "They all came around to be with Jack—Ginsberg, Burroughs, Corso, Lucien. We spent at least five to seven hours rapping with Burroughs. They reminisced about Tangier, the Beat Generation. Burroughs looked like Mr. Peepers with his little thin glasses, and questioned me about being a prizefighter. He was great, like a pansy, a slap job. Burroughs reminded me of a sissy. Had fuckin' pajamas on—some guru. We were drinking pretty good and smoking pretty good. Burroughs didn't shoot his wife intentionally. 'I put a cocktail glass on her head,' he said. 'Done it a hundred times and never missed.'" (He'd never done it before, according to biographer Barry Miles.)

Burroughs could scarcely believe it when Jack, drunk and stoned, told him that he was about to appear on network television. When he asked Burroughs to accompany him to the studio, Burroughs said, "No, Jack, you're too drunk. I don't want to witness this outrage." Lest he be mistaken for a hippie, Jack demanded a haircut before appearing on camera. "I got some fuckin' scissors and said, 'I'll cut your hair,' " Billy recalled. "I put a fuckin' bowl on his head. I got a razor and cut his fuckin' ear. More blood. He had a fuckin' Humphrey Bogart haircut—like in *The Treasure of the Sierra Madre*—on the William Buckley show."

At the TV studio, Jack introduced Billy to Lucien. "Don't fuck around with me, Lucien," Jack said, according to Billy. "I've got my bodyguards from Lowell with me." Observing Jack and Lucien at close range, Billy realized that "Jack feared Lucien. Jack was afraid of him at that time. Maybe the correct word is: Jack was intimidated by him. But Lucien was just a slap job. He didn't deserve a right cross, just a slap." They saw Truman Capote in the makeup room; he was on another program, and Jack went up to him and scowled. "I don't care what you said about me, I still like ya," Jack said, according to Billy, who added that Kerouac "planted a kiss on Capote's cheek."

In 1968, *Firing Line* was still a fresh, exciting show. Buckley had started it after failing to get himself elected mayor of New York City, and he relished matching wits with conspicuous liberals on subjects such as "Youth Power," "Capital Punishment," "The Plight of the American Novelist," "Marijuana — How Harmful?" and "The Black Panthers." The pedantic, acerbic Buckley frequently attracted top guests, including James Michener, Norman Mailer, Ronald Reagan, Jorge Luis Borges, Rebecca West, and Clare Booth Luce. On the night Kerouac appeared, September 3, 1968, the subject was "The Hippies," and the other guests were progressive sociologist Lewis Yablonsky and Ed Sanders, publisher of *Fuck You: A Magazine of the Arts* and leader of the rock band, The Fugs. According to Joe Chaput, who drove Kerouac down from Lowell, Jack was "smashed to the gills." He'd also been gulping uppers all day, hoping to be alert at airtime.

As the show began, Buckley looked as cool and wholesome as an Ivy League soccer player, *vis à vis* the loaded, sagging Kerouac, who had poured himself into a blue polyester jacket that looked as if it were about to pop its buttons. "Now Jack, Mr. Kerouac, what I want to ask is this," Buckley said. "To what extent do you believe that the Beat Generation is related to the hippies?" Puffing a cigarette, Kerouac expounded at length, calling the hippies "good kids" and the beatniks communists. In the audience, Ginsberg watched tensely, concern and compassion for Jack written on his face. Jack rambled on, trying to make the point that he couldn't be a revolutionary, as the press maintained, because he was a good Catholic. Buckley stared at him in shock, and at the break he asked Ginsberg to replace Kerouac. Ginsberg refused, knowing it would hurt Kerouac. "Jack almost fell off the stage a couple of times," Billy recalled. "He was reaching down to get his coffee. Buckley may have been very rude. One of them called him an anti-Semite. They asked him about the Vietnam War. 'Oh, it's very simple,' Jack said. 'The only reason we're in Vietnam is to sell jeeps.' "

After the taping, Kerouac went to a bar with Ginsberg and Sanders, and seemed friendly and relaxed. This time, he was truly saying goodbye to his desolation angels. He never saw any of the Beats again.

"That night we went out to a jazz joint, almost got killed in a cab ride back," Billy said. According to another friend, Joe Chaput said that "Jack was writing the whole time and doing drugs the whole time. At one point, he had a guy blow him while he was wearing a black silk glove on his penis." A Negro prostitute took them to her hotel, but Joe later revealed that they were too full of liquor, and too tired, to have sex. They just talked to her and then left, making it back to the Delmonico around 5 A.M. "Next day, we went to some of his publishing houses," Billy said, "and they all discarded him like, didn't want to see him at all. [Kerouac did not come to Coward, McCann, as far as I have been able to determine.] We went to Sterling Lord's. I don't think we were welcome, because there was no response. We went to meet with Mr. Buckley at the Delmonico Hotel for lunch. We didn't get by the doorman. He wouldn't let us in. The doorman said, 'Let me check.' He went in and come back out with the attitude: See you later. We got throwed out by the bell captain. After that, we were coming home. We had twenty-two dollars on us and a full tank of gas." They stopped at a package store in the Bronx to pick up a six-pack of Michelob and a bottle of Galiano. "This trip is goin' down in print," Jack promised them, according to Billy.

Later, when the Buckley taping was aired, Jack invited the gang over to his house in Lowell to watch the show, including Billy and his wife, Nicky Sampas, Joe Chaput, Jim Curtis, and Charles Jarvis. Jack's friends realized the show was a disaster, but Stella dutifully told Jack he'd done a good job on television, and he leaned back with a sigh, commenting, "Now Bill Buckley, there's a guy that I admire. I know him from way back."[26]

At last, Jack, Mémère, and Stella were ready to leave for Florida. Jack had bought a house in St. Petersburg next door to the one he had owned in 1965. The reliable Joe Chaput drove them down to Florida, 1,390 miles in a borrowed station wagon, with the men sitting in front and Stella and Mémère in back on three layers of mattresses and blankets. Nipping from a bottle, Jack chattered all the way, and occasionally Stella told him to be quiet. Mémère remarked, "I've heard it before," but Joe, who relished Jack's eloquence, told them to let Jack continue. Jack said the only man he'd ever met who could outtalk him was Brendan Behan, author of Borstal Boy; Jack said that Behan had completely drowned him out. Jack and Joe discussed philosophy; Jack was reading Pascal, and Joe was reading Jacques Maritain.

When they arrived in St. Petersburg, Jack and Stella helped Mémère into their comfortable corner-lot home at 5169 Tenth Avenue North, and then Jack left to round up Betty Watley for a party. A few minutes later, at the Watley home, Betty's daughter came rushing in and said, "Mom, there's somebody on the lawn that's drunk, and he wants to see you." Betty went outside and saw Kerouac lying in the front yard. "Oh, my God, Jack, what are you doing here?" she asked. "I bought the Berles's house," he said. "Come over and see my mother and my wife. I've gotten married." Betty noticed at once that Stella "wasn't as glamorous as I thought Jack would have—you know—she was like a nice little Greek lady. Very nice." Stella bought a large bucket of Colonel Sanders' Kentucky fried chicken for supper. When asked in 1995 to describe Stella further, Betty said, "She was really the sister I never had. I always took her around in my car." According to John Sampas, "Betty Watley spent every day with Stella in Florida." Joe Chaput remained with them a couple of days, and then returned to his job in Lowell.[27]

In a November 13, 1968, letter to Joe, Jack wrote that Mémêre's doctors were worse than the Mafia, draining him of the nine thousand dollars he'd meant to use as a down payment on the house. Instead, Jack rented the place for a while and bought it later on. Some royalty money from Italy enabled him to build a five-foot fence around the backyard and pay the first month's rent. He established an office in his bedroom and described the setup as cushy. Evenings, he would step out of his room directly into tropical moon-beams and savor the fragrance of the pine trees on his property. Life seemed good and full and right. He'd once written a poem called "The Last Hotel," and he seemed to have found it on the Gulf of Mexico. He invited Joe to visit him in Florida, promising steaks prepared on the backyard grill and plenty of hooch. He planned to return to Lowell annually, and asked Joe to accompany him to Europe in the summer of 1969. Meanwhile, he was getting a suntan and hoping to start a new project. At Christmas, he sent Joe a card with an angelical salutation, and Stella appended a note inquiring whether Joe had heard from his son Phillip, who had run away from home at fifteen.

Kerouac's Christmas card to Billy Koumantzelis was full of curious references to Stella. Though Stella had a normal sex drive, he added that she was guided by Christ, who abstained from sexual activity; he seemed to be saying that she forgave Jack his sexual limitations. Betty Watley observed, "She really worshipped the ground that man walked on, whether he was mean or nasty to her. He wasn't a very nice man sometimes when he was drunk." But his January 16, 1969, letter to Philip Whalen revealed that he still considered Stella to be the ideal wife, dedicated and affectionate. Ron Lowe visited them, and he later objected to Kerouac's treatment of Stella, describing it as offensive. "Look at that," Jack said as Stella carried a bedpan from Mémêre's room. "Would you screw that?" In 1995, Ron commented, "I was embarrassed for her, him, and myself, because I was listening to it. It was almost like duplicity. . . . Mémêre and Jack would often speak in French. Not a whiff of that did Stella understand, which I think was the point. . . . Stella was a cook—stews, roasts. She was a wizard with baklava—the lightest flakes you ever saw. 'Beats any baklava I've ever eaten anywhere else,' Jack said. 'There's some baklava in the kitchen—get yourself some,' he'd tell me." Although Betty Watley never saw any signs of physical abuse, she too recalled that Kerouac was "very nasty with his mouth, but she just ignored that because she knew he was drunk."[28]

He observed his forty-seventh birthday on March 12, 1969. Ron remembered that Jack would shamble to his mailbox every day, hoping for a royalty check that never came. His income during the first half of 1969 was $1,770, and Stella had to take a job at $1.70 an hour. Betty recalled, "I'm telling you, I don't know what they lived on. . . . Stella never bought a new dress. She wore Jack's T-shirts until they were completely worn out. She would wear a sleeveless muumuu with the T-shirt sleeves hanging out. They had no car, and Stella walked to Forty-ninth Street and took the bus to Webb City, where she worked a sewing machine."

On certain nights, at the Collage, a USF student hangout, or at a coffeehouse in Pinellas Park called the Beaux Arts, Kerouac recovered some of his old brio and held the crowd spellbound as he recited his work by heart. As Ron Lowe noted, Kerouac used language the way a jazz sax soloist plays "notes, weaving around the melody." When *Easy Rider* played the Mustang Drive-in, Jack and Ron saw it, but Jack grumbled, "Neal and I had a hell of a good time, and we didn't hurt anybody. They're trying to make heroes out of those guys, and they're not heroes. They're criminals."

One day when Jack was visiting at Ron Lowe's house, he spotted a copy of Mickey Spillane's *Kiss Me Deadly*, which featured a sexy gun moll on the cover. "Aye, there she stands, looking like the last whore of heaven, looking for one last celestial lay," he remarked. Ron's mother, Anisi Khoury Lowe, turned around from the kitchen sink and said, "Mr. Kerouac, I don't care who you are, you're not going to talk that way in my house. Get out!" Though she was pointing toward the door, Jack didn't move. "You could see the rage on her face," Ron recalled, "and she took a step toward him. He jumped and scooted out the door." Afterward, Jack was rude to her when he telephoned and asked for Ron. "This is my home," she told Jack, "and if you want to use my phone to talk to my son, you can be polite and civil to me." In 1995, Ron said, "Those two things made a believer out of him as far as she was concerned. After that, she could do no wrong in his eyes." One afternoon, Jack arrived at the Lowe home with a carful of longhairs in a Volkswagen. As they tumbled out like circus clowns, "he ran ahead of them," Ron recalled, "and jumped up on the steps and turned toward them using the step as a soapbox and held his hand up and said, 'Listen up, you knaves. You are about to enter the home of a woman of royal Syrian parentage. So behave yourselves."

After the telephone was installed in Kerouac's house in late September, he started calling me again, describing a story he was working on called *Pic*. "That's short for 'Pictorial Review Jackson," he said. "It's about me and Cassady on the road." He read some passages to me, but I didn't like his black dialect, such as "Now I gotsa tell you 'bout ever-thing happened in New York," and warned him that those were fighting words in the age of growing black empowerment. Though I couldn't in good conscience be supportive of *Pic*, Kerouac was full of enthusiasm and love for it. Happy to be writing again, he sounded sober, confident, and hopeful.

The main reason for his upbeat attitude, no doubt, was that Sterling Lord, who was now running his own newspaper syndicate, had come through with an important assignment. The *Chicago Tribune* paid Kerouac fifteen hundred dollars for a nostalgia piece called "After Me the Deluge." It was the perfect swan song for a man with a divided nature, who now found himself "caught in the middle," torn between the radicals who claimed him as their hero, and the Nixon Republicans whose conservative values he endorsed, but whose authoritarian power he resented. At the end of the article, he cried out in bewilderment, "WHAT I NEED IS LESS PEOPLE TELLIN' ME WHAT I NEED!" With Sterling's syndicate aggressively promoting him, "After Me the Deluge" earned Kerouac a sorely needed three thousand dollars by late September. In addition to the *Tribune*, the article was serialized in the *Washington Post*, the *Boston Globe* (under the title "The Bippie in the Middle"), the *Los Angeles Times*, and the *Miami Herald*. In a sense, he scored a touchdown with his final piece of writing, making a clean sweep of most of the nation's major metropolitan dailies.[29]

Though Betty Watley had seen Kerouac in various stages of alcoholic decrepitude, the condition he showed up in "right before the end" in the early autumn of 1969 shocked even her.

> He had no incentive, nothing to look forward to, and pretty soon he got in with bad characters, and would come and go. It wasn't a good situation for anybody. He went to Tampa, got high on something, was gone for two or three days. There Stella is, alone with Mémère, and he's not there, not that he ever helped that much. . . . The worry of him being gone, who knows what she said to him. He got mad at her, and he said, "I'm going to go, and I'm going to change my will." He left everything to Mémère. Maybe Mémère was a little bit mad at Stella. Maybe she wanted Stella to say to Jack, 'Where have you been?' Anyway, that's what he was doing when he changed his will.

Betty added that when he returned from Tampa, "he was higher than a kite on something. He was talking real crazy, acting real crazy. He said something about LSD. It would have been very available to the people he was seeing." All Kerouac got out of his acid trip, he later told Ron Lowe, was a nightmarish hallucination of "pieces of bloody meat with hair growing out of it." Kerouac saw his lawyer on September 4 and drew up "The Last Will and Testament of Jean Kerouac, A/K/A Jack Kerouac," leaving everything to Mémère. As if he knew he was about to die, he started making inquiries about mortuaries and embalming techniques, expressing concern over how his body would be treated. "Then he got sick," Betty recalled, "and kept going out with these people and went in that bar and the end was very imminent." The bar was a hostile dive in St. Petersburg, called the Cactus, and Kerouac made the mistake of going there with a disabled air force veteran who was even more erotically demonstrative and affectionate with strangers than Kerouac was. They started talking with a jazz musician, and the airman casually put his arm around him. Assuming that he was being propositioned, the musician threw a punch at Jack's friend. "He's not queer!" Jack screamed, but the musician, who was also a boxer, said, "So you want it too?" Several black men dragged Kerouac into the parking lot, and he was "badly beaten up," according to an account in the *Detroit News* based on a letter Kerouac wrote to Edie. After the beating, he never fully recovered, dropping twenty pounds. Apparently his marriage to Stella was in trouble as well, if one can believe an October 20 letter Kerouac allegedly wrote to Nin's son. The authenticity of the letter has been contested by the Kerouac estate, however, and no final determination of the authorship has been handed down.[30]

On October 4, in a nostalgic mood, Kerouac typed a five-cent postcard to Charles Sampas, reminiscing about how Lou Little had refused to take Jack off the bench for the Columbia-Army game. As he replayed his football career for perhaps the millionth time, his past became a refuge from the unendurable present. Stella had been forced to give up her job in Webb City; Mémère needed her, as did Jack, whose alcoholism had reduced him to a vegetative stupor. "They only had Mémère's social security to live on," Betty recalled. Thus, Mémère, though paralyzed, once again became the breadwinner, and she kept Jack in booze to his last breath. "A boilermaker is a straight shot with a chaser of beer, and his shots were an ounce and a half," Betty said. Many old friends received incoherent calls in the last days of his life, including Holmes and Bob Burford. In his final call to me, I thanked him again for citing Stella and me on the dedication page of *Vanity of Duluoz*, and he said, "May the two of you sail into eternity, like hieroglyphs on my little obelisk of a book."[31]

Jack experienced trouble sleeping on the night of Sunday, October 19. Stella got up and sat with him as he read an old letter from Leo. At 4 A.M. on October 20, he went into Mémère's room and told her about another letter he'd discovered, which mentioned Leo and Spotlite Print. Mémère begged him to sit beside her and explain why God was punishing her. After a while, he went outside and lay on a cot, gazing at the stars. Around 9 A.M., Stella bathed and fed Mémère, and took out her bedpan. The heat was oppressive, and Hurricane Laurie was blowing in from the Gulf of Mexico, but Jack was "busy in thought and dreams," Stella recalled. He attempted to write a little on *The Beat Spotlite*, which was named after his father's shop and dealt with Jack's life after *On the Road*, but he soon gave up. At 10:30 A.M., Stella found him sitting in front of the TV set, drinking from a two-ounce medicine vial of whiskey, which had a white plastic top. She offered to prepare breakfast, but he told her to rest up after her labors with Mémère. "He opened a can of tunafish and was eating it right out of the can, out of a spoon," Stella later told Jay Pendergast. His notebook was on his lap, and he was working on an entry as "The Galloping Gourmet" TV program started. The host was a jolly Scottish chef named Graham Kerr, whose specialties included Mrs.

Enid Small's brandied prunes, suet pudding, and Tom Muir's kidney. Suddenly, Kerouac stood up and headed for the bathroom. "A couple of minutes later, I heard him crying out," Stella recalled. "I went in, and he was on his knees. 'Stella, I'm bleeding,' he said. 'I'm hurting, I'm bleeding. . . . Help me.'" She looked down at the toilet bowl. It was full of blood.

He told Stella he didn't want to go to the hospital and that the doctor should come to the house, but she went to the phone and rang for an ambulance. Jack then telephoned Ron Lowe, who recalled, "He told me he was throwing up blood. 'It's the goddamned tunafish,' Jack said. 'I'm going to the hospital.'" Later, Stella telephoned Ron from St. Anthony's Hospital in St. Petersburg. Ron's car was broken, but he borrowed one from a friend, and when he reached the hospital, Kerouac was still in the receiving area. "They asked me to help hold him down on the table," Ron said. "It was in the side room off the emergency room. So quick that the doctor was still wearing a yellow shirt and a regimental stripe tie, wasn't even in a gown. I was just trying to hold him down, and he kept trying to sit up. There was a lot of blood on the floor. I was wearing these Beatle boots, zipped up the side. When they were ready to move him, they asked me to leave, and I went to step aside, and my foot was stuck like suction to the floor. I looked down, and it was covered with blood; a good deal of it was not his, but blood that his body had refused to accept by transfusion."

At 6 P.M., Dr. E. H. Welch began to examine Kerouac. "He did not believe he was going to die at the last, in hospital," Stella said, according to Edie. By the time Betty arrived, after receiving a call from Stella, the scene at Kerouac's bedside was heartbreaking. When asked in 1995 what he'd looked like, Betty said, "Terrible. Screaming. And in pain. It seems to me Jack was curtained off, but I don't think he was in intensive care. He kind of burst or something. There was Stella. Jack was just screaming in agony. All I can remember is blood. I can see red. Stella was inconsolable."[32]

For the next fifteen hours, Kerouac paid many times over for whatever wrongs he'd ever done. Surgeons cut him open in a last-ditch effort to stop massive abdominal hemorrhaging. His transfusions, amounting to approximately thirty pints of blood, completely depleted the hospital's blood bank, and an urgent call was issued for Type A positive blood donors. "Ron Lowe gave him blood," Betty recalled. Anisi Lowe, Ron's mother, also rushed to the hospital. "There we sat—talk about a strange crew," Ron said. "My mother was Lebanese. Stella, myself, and this Nazi—I don't mean that as a descriptive term; I mean it literally—he claimed to be a member of the American Nazi Party. He had visited Jack one time at the house—Jack was lonely, and this guy came to see him—I was there—they chatted on and on. I had nothing to discuss with this creep. The banality of evil: as pleasant a chap as you could hope to meet, in his personal demeanor. He showed up at the hospital. You want to talk about a strange, premature wake."

After surgery, Kerouac never regained consciousness, but he tenaciously held onto life through the early morning hours of Tuesday, October 21. Family and friends were in the waiting room, but for some reason, he spent his last hours alone. Not even his physician was present at the end. "I attended the deceased from 6 P.M., 10/20/69, to 10/21/69 and last saw him alive on 10/20/69," Dr. Welch later wrote. At 5:15 A.M., October 21, 1969, at the age of forty-seven, Kerouac at last made his solitary journey to the end of the night. According to his death certificate, he died of "gastrointestinal hemorrhage, due to bleeding gastric varix from cirrhosis of liver, due to excessive ethanol intake many years."[33]

When Sterling called me with the news, the first thing I thought of was what Kerouac had said to me when Neal had died: that there was nothing more to do or say. Kerouac had killed himself with alcohol and drugs before reaching the age of fifty because he saw no reason to go on living. Middle-age lust, typified by his "pineapple up your ass" remark to me, had not been able to compensate for the love tragically deferred when proffered by Sammy in the 1930s and by Neal in the 1950s.

On the CBS evening news, Walter Cronkite, seated in front of giant blowups of Kerouac's face and On the Road's dust jacket, announced, "Jack Kerouac, the novelist who wrote On the Road, reached the end of it today. The forty-seven-year-old spokesman for the Beat Generation died of a massive hemorrhage in a St. Petersburg, Florida, hospital today. Kerouac's books, selling millions of copies, translated into eighteen languages, were regarded as a bridge between older bohemian movements and today's hippies."

Ginsberg was on his communal farm in upstate New York when New York Post reporter Al Aronowitz called. Corso answered the phone and cried, "Al! Jack died!" Taking the receiver, Ginsberg said, "He was very sweet. He was just unhappy." Then Ginsberg and Corso went for a walk in the snow and carved Kerouac's name on a tree.

In Los Gatos, Carolyn "felt strangely lonely and remote from his death at first, even resentful," she recalled. "I'd not been near Neal or Jack when either of them died. Other women had tended to the business of their passing, yet in my life I'd been closer to those two than anyone I'd known. It was right. Alive I knew them, and alive they would always be to me."

Lucien Carr was grieved for over a decade, and would tell Gifford and Lee in 1978, "He ain't dead to me by a long shot. What can a man do for love? Nothing. Nothing. . . . I should have done better by Jack than go to jail. . . . I should have saved his fucking ass."

In Lowell, Jack's boyhood friends, G. J., Scotcho Beaulieu, and Freddy Bertrand, drank all night in the Pawtucketville Social Club. The Sun ran Kerouac's obituary on page one, identifying him as "a former Lowell Sun sportswriter, and Columbia and Lowell High football star. . . . No other novelist ever wrote so much and so deeply about Lowell life."

Thirty miles away, at Harvard, the Crimson offered up a prayer: "God give us the strength to be as alive as Kerouac was. Send us more to help burn away the bullshit."[34]

In St. Petersburg, an open-casket service was held at the Rhodes funeral home, and *Esquire* later described Kerouac's "gray face" in an article entitled, "This Is How the Ride Ends." "I pushed his mother in a wheelchair to the funeral home, which was just a few blocks from the house," Ron Lowe recalled. Stella, who wore a black dress, took charge of Mémêre at the door, tightly gripping the handles of the wheelchair as she guided Mémêre into the parlor. At Jack's casket, Mémêre started "wailing, 'O my little boy. Isn't he pretty? . . . What will I do now?' "

According to Betty, "He left them destitute! There was no inheritance when Jack died." But Mémêre needn't have worried. Stella continued to care for her, and despite long periods when Jack's books earned no royalties, Mémêre would never want for anything, thanks to Stella and her family. Estimates of Jack's estate at the time of his death ranged from "all but worthless" (*USA Today*) and "under $10,000" (*Time Out New York*) to "less than $36,000" (*New York Post*) and "$53,280" (*Dharma Beat*). By the 1990s, it was worth two to three million dollars, according to John Sampas. On Mémêre's death in 1972, the estate went to Stella and, on Stella's death in 1990, to her family's trust. In the end, Kerouac more than repaid the loyalty of the precious few who stuck by him.[35]

After the funeral, Kerouac's remains were transported to Lowell by plane. "Stella and Gabrielle decided they wanted him to be buried here in Lowell, next to Sebastian," John Sampas said. Jack's body lay in the Archambault Funeral Parlor, just across the street from the Grotto, the religious shrine where Ti Jean and Gerard had once walked hand in hand on Sunday afternoons in the 1920s, pausing to pray before the stations of the cross.

As preparations were made for Jack's wake in Lowell, Ginsberg was in New Haven lecturing at Yale, and at the last minute he turned his address into a eulogy. Kerouac had been "the first to make a new crack in the consciousness," Ginsberg said. "He broke open the fantastic solidity in America, as solid as the Empire State Building, that turned out not to be solid at all." After the Yale program, Ginsberg, Holmes, Orlovsky, and Corso drove to Lowell, where the Sampas family put them up.

At the time of Kerouac's funeral rites in 1969, he was still in critical disrepute, and had never been singled out by the Pulitzer, National Book Award, or Nobel Prize committees. He was not, however, unloved or unhonored; approximately one hundred mourners attended his wake in Lowell, which began at 10 A.M. on Thursday, October 23, at Archambault's. In a gray casket, Kerouac had been laid out in a brown check sport jacket and a red bow tie. "Mémêre chose his clothes," John said. Across the hall from the room where Jack was laid out, a small boy named Jeffrey Levesque — Mémêre's family name — lay in a coffin, dressed entirely in white. "Shades of Gerard!" thought Spike Morissette, remembering Kerouac's description of his brother in white clothes, ascending to heaven in a wagon pulled by snowy lambs. Jack's casket was surrounded by floral wreaths, including a heart-shaped bouquet of red roses with a banner bearing the epitaph, "Guard the

Heart," and listing the names of Ginsberg, Orlovsky, Corso, Holmes, Burroughs, Carr, and Robert Creeley. Another wreath, which had a paperback copy of *Maggie Cassidy* attached to it with the message "Thank You," was almost certainly from Mary Carney, who had never moved from the house she was born in, 81 Billerica Street. She had married twice, and she told her daughter Judy, who was born September 23, 1945, that Jack was her father. Evidence from Jack's notebooks in the archive, however, indicate that he was elsewhere at the probable time of conception.

In a 1995 interview in Lowell, a man named Paul Dusamos recalled, "I went to the wake with my friend Chris Cyagos, and we were by the casket when Allen Ginsberg first came in. He went to the casket, looked down, and said, 'Jack, get up, you son of a bitch.' I swear on all that's holy. They thought of themselves not as of mother earth but as of mother universe, as infinite, not as mortals." At one point, Ginsberg, Corso, and Orlovsky linked arms and approached the casket together. Jack was "theatric-lit," Ginsberg later wrote Carolyn. "Touch him," Ginsberg said, talking to himself, and reached into the coffin. He lightly brushed a finger over Jack's brow and felt a "U-shaped wrinkled furrow." "There's really nothing inside," Ginsberg said, reflecting that Jack, like the Buddha, had come to earth to bring his message that all was illusion. Then, with a wink, he'd vanished, leaving nothing but a surprisingly thin-looking shell behind. It was exactly as Jack had predicted in *The Town and the City*: after heroic achievements, he'd simply disappear "in a mist of immolation . . . in the Valhalla of himself."

Under the curious stares of Lowell natives, Ginsberg read aloud from *Mexico City Blues*, including the resounding passage from the "211th Chorus," in which Kerouac said he wanted to be "safe in heaven dead." Corso was kneeling at Jack's coffin and sobbing. Ginsberg continued to pass his fingers gently over Jack's face; he later wrote that Jack was "large-headed, grim-lipped." He began to feel the chill on Jack's skin beneath the thick embalmer's makeup. Kerouac's hair was still black and soft, Ginsberg noted, but on closer inspection, a small bald spot was visible on top. A rosary lay entwined in his "wrinkled, hairy hands." Ginsberg's mind drifted back to Ozone Park in the 1940s, and he realized that Jack, in his middle-aged heaviness, had become a replica of Leo.

Suddenly, Edie Parker sailed in, ready to hold court in the middle of the room. No one recognized her. One of the Sampas brothers went up to her and inquired who she was. "I'm Mrs. Jack Kerouac!" she barked, though the real Mrs. Kerouac, Stella, was standing within earshot. Going over to Edie, Stella treated her with such kindness that Edie said Stella was entitled to everything that might have been left to her. Nevertheless, Edie subsequently attempted to lay claim to a portion of Jack's estate. Stella sat near the casket, greeting mourners. Jack had been "so lonely, so lonely," she said. Jack's boyhood friends, who'd "failed him," according to G. J., when he'd lived in Lowell in 1967, looked around nervously, realizing they "didn't know hardly anybody," G. J. added. When they discovered they weren't to be pallbearers, they left. According to Scotcho Beaulieu, they "didn't go to the burial because of all the crowds."

At one point, Stella confronted Corso and scolded him for having neglected Jack in recent years. Corso replied that he'd had no way of knowing Jack was "gonna die." Then, Stella turned on everyone, according to Holmes, and said, "All of you! Why didn't you come to Florida when he needed you?" For a moment, it looked as if Kerouac's funeral might turn into a sixties happening. Corso even considered dragging the corpse from the coffin and heaving it across the room to protest "people mourning something that ain't there." Everyone settled down, and Stella started kissing and embracing the Beats. The only original Beat not in attendance was Burroughs, who was at one of his low ebbs, living in London and paying a "Dilly boy," a Piccadilly Circus hustler, five pounds a day to live with him.[36]

Kerouac's funeral was held on Friday, October 24. Shortly before 11 A.M., the procession left Archambault's on Pawtucket Street and moved a short distance to St. Jean Baptiste, Jack's beloved slum cathedral, between Merrimack and Moody Streets. A group of priests had attempted to ban his body from any of the city's Catholic churches due to his "dope taking" and "free loving," according to Montgomery, but they were defeated by Spike Morissette, who officiated at a requiem high mass. Kerouac's career had always reminded Spike of the biblical story of the two disciples who encountered Jesus in the village of Emmaus near Jerusalem. The disciples walked with Jesus for a while, excitedly exchanging ideas, and then Jesus left them. One of the disciples turned to the other and said, "Wasn't it like a fire burning in us when He talked to us on the road?"

In the same church where twenty-five years previously Spike had encouraged Kerouac to become a champion athlete and an author, Spike now walked around Kerouac's coffin, swinging a censer. As the smoky incense rose, making spidery trails into the arches of the grand old cathedral, a ritual offering was made to God, a supplication for the soul of Jack Kerouac. Ironically, in view of Kerouac's anti-Semitism, a cross near the coffin bore the inscription "I.N.R.I.," proclaiming Jesus to be the king of the Jews. Spike begged, "O gentlest Heart of Jesus, ever present in the Blessed Sacrament, ever consumed with burning love for poor captive souls in Purgatory, have mercy on the soul of Thy departed servant." Then he delivered the heavenly salutation, "Hail, Mary, full of grace; the Lord is with thee: blessed art thou among women, and blessed is the fruit of thy womb, Jesus. Holy Mary, Mother of God, pray for us sinners, now and at the hour of our death. Amen."

Having scrupulously followed Kerouac's career and read all his books, Spike was able to present a eulogy of authority and ringing eloquence. "Champion of the forgotten and the forlorn and the free," Spike said, standing over Kerouac's bier, "in modern fashion Jack Kerouac expounded the beatitudes, and all about him there is the aura of a mystique. His talent was prodigious, and truly he became a master." Spike admitted that Kerouac had influenced him profoundly and made his ministry "more merciful." His key learning from Kerouac, he said, was "everybody's right to enjoy the whole universe, which is made possible by a person's willingness to share intelligently." According to the *Sun*, Spike said, "Blessed are the dead, they shall rest from their labors, for they shall take their works with them." He added, "Jack most excitedly felt he had something to tell the world, and he was determined to do it. . . . Our hope and our prayer is that Jack has now found complete liberation, sharing the visions of Gerard. Amen. Allelujia."[37]

A brisk wind buffeted the mourners as they emerged into the sunlight and started descending the wide, imposing steps of St. Jean Baptiste. Young Phil Chaput, who had come back home after months on the road, watched his father Joe and the other pallbearers as they bore Jack's coffin down the steps. Stella and Tony had selected the pallbearers, who included Joe, Tony, Billy, Harvey Kerouac, and Ginsberg. After helping slide Kerouac's coffin into the hearse, Ginsberg paused to answer reporters' questions. The procession headed out to the Edson Cemetery, about two miles from downtown Lowell on Gorham Street. The Sampas family's burial plot was deep in the graveyard, at the corner of Lincoln Avenue and Seventh Street near the large Eisentraut tombstone. Dean Contover, a young fan from western Massachusetts who'd once met Jack at the Highland Tap bar in Lowell, estimated the graveside crowd at fifty people. After a priest said final prayers, everyone took a rose from one of the wreaths and placed it on the coffin. Jack was buried next to Sammy. Ginsberg, Corso, and Holmes stood beside the open grave, and Ginsberg dropped in a handful of earth. Subsequently, Diana Hansen announced her intention to bury her portion of Neal's ashes in Jack's grave, and referred to "Neal being buried in Jack's heart."

In the following years, Stella wrote an epitaph for Jack. It was almost haiku-like in its simplicity: "He honored life." She arranged for Luz Brothers, stonemasons across from the cemetery, to engrave it on a flat stone, on which the only other decoration was a dove plunging earthward and surrounded by a glowing nimbus. "The engraving of the dove was my idea," John recalled. "Jack was into the Holy Ghost, he told me one time, when he saw that I was wearing a Holy Ghost medallion on a chain."

Official Catholic doctrine stipulates that when the dove is shown in a headlong dive from heaven, it "expresses innocence and purity. It signifies the Holy Spirit and the presence of God as hovering over the water at creation, and above Jesus at his baptism." The Holy Spirit is also the channel through which Christians communicate with God. There could not have been a more apt symbol for Jack, and yet when Ginsberg first saw the epitaph, he complained that it was corny. "He honored death, too," Ginsberg said.

But Stella's epitaph was closer to the essence of Jack. In *Big Sur* he'd said of Neal, "You can at least write on his grave someday 'He Lived, He Sweated'—No halfway house is Cody's house." Though Kerouac's achievement as an artist was complete, the fullness of life was something he only occasionally glimpsed, in the more open and honest lives he chronicled. Only in death, he once told me, would he stop vacillating between "wranglers and poets, and find wholeness at last."[38]

EPILOGUE

Sterling Lord and Jimmy Breslin drove up from New York to Lowell for Kerouac's funeral, but I stayed behind, feeling, like Carolyn Cassady, "strangely remote," perhaps because both Carolyn and I, two of the people closest to Kerouac in his final years, had been on the receiving end of more alcoholic abuse than we could tolerate. I remained grateful, however, that I had helped Jack earn some money, which in turn made his and Mémère's lives easier in the sixties and enabled them to live in nice houses. In many ways, Jack and I had been good for each other: a young editor struggling to gain a foothold in the slippery world of commercial publishing, and a great author fighting for a comeback. In *Desolation Angels*, he gave me the best novel I published in twenty-five years as a book editor.

After Sterling's call announcing Jack's death, I scrawled some lines on my desk calendar, recalling them from Trilling's Wordsworth class at Columbia: "We will grieve not, rather find strength in what remains behind." How literally our publishing company—which over the next three decades would evolve into an amalgam of Coward, Putnam, Viking, and Penguin—would find strength in what Kerouac left behind! The two novels I was responsible for, *Desolation Angels* and *Vanity of Duluoz*, proved to be incredibly durable, and the two that Viking published, *On the Road* and *The Dharma Bums*, eventually joined them under the same corporate umbrella. In 1998, Put-nam/Viking, now owned by Penguin, was still earning regular income from *Vanity of Duluoz*, in a Penguin trade paperback, and from *Desolation Angels*, in its Berkley Riverhead trade paperback edition, with a new introduction by Joyce Johnson. *On the Road* sales were up to three million copies. Most remarkable of all, a repentant literary establishment at last recognized Kerouac's genius.

The Sampas family provided the occasion for the long overdue critical revaluation of Kerouac with the dramatic release of his letters a quarter of a century after his death. On publication in 1995, the letters were greeted with overwhelming praise. Joyce Carol Oates compared Kerouac with Bryon and Shelley in the *New Yorker*, and noted that Kerouac "deserved to be treated better by the censorious 'literary' critics of his time." Defining "Kerouac's position in the literature of mid-twentieth-century America," Oates placed him alongside Salinger, Mailer, Nabokov, Ginsberg, Burroughs, Updike, and Paul Bowles. On the front page of the *New York Times Book Review*, Columbia professor Ann Douglas rated Kerouac "this country's most important critically unrecognized modern writer," and defined his achievement as "the most extensive experiment in language and literary form undertaken by an American writer of his generation." With "a dozen major novels" to his credit, Kerouac belonged, Douglas concluded, in the front rank of "mid-20th century" American writers, along with McCullers, Capote, Styron, Mailer, Salinger, Ginsberg, Burroughs, Robert Lowell, Saul Bellow, Tennessee Williams, James Baldwin, Arthur Miller, and Flannery O'Connor.

Perhaps the most moving accolade in the 1995 revaluation came from the *Village Voice*, in which Clark Coolidge wrote that Jack Kerouac is an author to "love and revere . . . with no reservation, no need to meddle or to judge . . . [to] take . . . seriously entire, as the magnificent artist that he will remain."

Two years later the Kerouac boom was still going strong, and the *New York Times* called me to see if I could account for a new generation that was chasing the spirit of the Beats. On December 11, 1997, reporter Doreen Carvajal wrote:

> Kerouac's former editor, Ellis Amburn . . . said Kerouac would not have been surprised that he is once again in vogue among young readers. . . . Kerouac thought it would take about 25 years to regain his popularity, said Amburn, who despaired himself when the writer's books slowed in sales during the 1960s. "He knew he had a message of enlightenment and freedom for people. Kerouac believed that people needed to be liberated from their anxieties and worries and connect with what he saw as the universal mind."

Kerouac liked the term "universal mind," but what he meant was God. When I was researching this book, I went to the Edson Cemetery and watched young people make pilgrimages to Jack's grave, leaving notes, prayers, joints, change, empty beer cans, and wine bottles. I thought of what psychologist Carl Jung once said: The Latin word for alcohol is *spiritus*. Whether in a drink or through prayer and meditation, it's the warmth of the spirit that people seek. As Kerouac made so clear in *Some of the Dharma*, his life was an ongoing quest for an authentic spiritual experience, that warm feeling of contentment everyone wants. "The two beers dont hit me right," Jack wrote in *Desolation Angels*, "I realize there's no need for alcohol whatever in your soul."[1]

ACKNOWLEDGMENTS

In 1995, Robert Weil, my editor at St. Martin's Press, commissioned *Subterranean Kerouac*. He stuck with it every step of the way, even flying up to Lowell, Massachusetts, and spending time with John Sampas and me at the Kerouac archive. In its later stages, this book had the benefit of both Bob's and Andrew Miller's brilliant editorial instincts. The executive team at St. Martin's—Bob Wallace, editor-in-chief; Sally Richardson, president and publisher; and John Sargent, Jr., CEO—have been constant and generous with both moral and material support. Jamie Brickhouse, head of publicity, is another invaluable ally at St. Martin's.

Al Lowman, my agent for the past twelve years, remains the indispensable miracle worker in my life, and I'm indebted to him not only for encouraging this book and placing it in the best possible hands, but for valuable and highly creative editorial guidance, and enduring friendship. Al's staff at Authors and Artists Group—B. G. Dilworth, Dean Williamson, Charlotte Patton, and Maggie Lang—invariably came up with the answers I needed.

I'm primarily grateful of course to Jack Kerouac for sharing his intimate thoughts with me from 1964 to 1969, and to the Sampas family of Lowell, Massachusetts, who administer his estate. Without them, the present volume would not have been possible. Nor would it have been possible without Cy

Egan, my best friend, and trusted first reader and adviser. The team that was in place at Coward-McCann when I was Kerouac's editor all talked to me and shared their memories for this book, including Betty A. Prashker, Joseph LeSueur, Sherry Arden, and Ann Sheldon.

Dick Epler, Jerry Montgomery, Mark Howell, and Nancy Coffey encouraged me when this work was little more than an idea. In London, Tony Palmer of the BBC and the *Observer* put me in touch with Mrs. Neal Cassady, with whom I subsequently corresponded and talked on the telephone. My thanks, also, to Angela Robertson for guiding me around Liverpool. In St. Petersburg, Florida, Ron Lowe gave me a beautiful and moving interview. Betty Watley, formerly of St. Petersburg, now of Hendersonville, North Carolina, shared powerful, poignant memories.

In Lowell, Joe Sorota breathed fresh life into Kerouac's glory days on the Lowell High football team. Phil Chaput, Janet Lambert-Moore, and R. Edward ("Bob") Roach provided the introductions essential for the writing of this book. Eleanor King put me in touch with Jack's relative Doris Boisvert Kerouac. Aida Panagiotakos, Jay Pendergast, Billy Koumantzelis, Tony Sampas, and Hunk Finneral filled in many gaps in Jack's story. Mary Sampas let everyone know I was in town, via her *Sun* column. John Sampas produced precious documents from the archive. Betty Sampas hosted a reunion at which I met the entire family of Stella Sampas Kerouac. One memorable night, Estelle Chaput served a roast turkey dinner for Jack's inner circle of sixties friends. Jim Sampas and his wife Dorothy, the U.S. ambassador to Mauritania, gave a dinner at La Boniche honoring the memory of Sebastian Sampas; one-time Promethean Connie Murphy was among the guests. In Nashua, New Hampshire, Reginald A. Ouellette helped me find the graves of Gerard, Leo, and Gabrielle, and took me on many tours of Lowell, as did Brian Foye and Hank Mulholland.

In Cazadero, California, Linda Gravenites reminisced about Kerouac in North Beach and Neal Cassady in the Haight Ashbury, and gave an insight into Neal's taste in women. In New York, Jerry Bauer contributed new information about Kerouac in Northport, Long Island, and Rome, Italy. During the course of my research, I spoke to over five hundred persons about Kerouac. I wish to acknowledge not only them, but also the people who helped me when I was Kerouac's editor, such as Sterling Lord; the scholars who interviewed me about Jack for their own articles and books; and various Good Samaritans. My special thanks to:

Allen Ginsberg, Richard Howard, Phyllis Jackson, Herbert Huncke, Bill Manville, John E. ("Jack") Lang, Mike McCoy, Tom Clark, Ron Bernstein, Sandy Friedman, Judy Feiffer, Frank O'Hara, Patsy Southgate Matthiessen, John Button, Scott Burton, Alvin Novak, Seymour Krim, Alan Barnard, Marc Jaffe, Clyde Taylor, Martha Mosher, Lena Wickman, Wendell Roos, Ben Aiello, Patricia B. Soliman, Connie Campbell, Catherine Wilson, Carol Sturm Smith, Toby Wherry, James Whitfield Ellison, Arabel Porter, Sherry Arden, Don Fine, Bernie Kurman, Helen Sampas Surprenant, Claire Sampas

Paicopolos, Spy Paicopolos, Paul Maher, Gertrude Maher, Elaine and David Markson, David H. Brow, Jacqueline Kennedy Onassis, Barbara Bannon, Roger Smith, Harriet Anderson, Dick Stuart, Tyler Hardeman, Barbara Miller, Sally Schinderman, Shelley Winters, Kim Novak, Janet Halverson, Roberta Pryor, Joan and Joseph Foley, Roger Brunelle, Gary Cheney, Larry Rivers, Mike Goldberg, Catherine Flomp, Dean Contover, Bill Taupier, Dave Desler, Rick Pierce, Chickie Pirello, Michael Gilday, Chauncey Moore, Meg Smith, Mark Hemenway, Shawn Kennedy, Beatrice Iams, Bernie Petrazziello, Jim Cook, Frank Makaiewicz, Bruce Lapore, Kathy Muldoon, Brendan Fleming, Marie Sweeney, Chuck Nicopolous, Dean Tavoularis, Jim Sheehan, Richard Marion, Truman Capote, Annie Cavanaugh, Kathy Davis, Mai Pho, Ed Davis, Linda Hart, Joan Schneider, Mary Keough, Peter Ascela, Martha Mayo, Denise Lefebvre, Carol Durand, Florence Marion, Kendall Wallace, Judy Caunter, Maureen Murphy Coimbra, Helen Weaver, James T. Curtis, Nick Natsios, Emile Dufour, Christine Sampas, Cassandra ("Cassie") Sampas, Amy Kopaczewski, Scot Castle, Rudolphe ("Red") Ouellette, Mary McLaughin, Anna Jabar, Kiki Theokas, Kathy McDonnell, Malcolm Gibson, Joyce Gibson, Nina M. Lepore, Timothy Leary, Warren Picower, Lionel Abel, Constance and George Murray, Greg Limperis, Brendan Sullivan, Jerry Charette, Carol McQuade, Dan McConnell, Don Hurd, Ann MacGibbon, Kathy O'Malley, Heather Holmes, Phil Coppola, Edwin E. Crusoe IV, Ed Wells, Timothy J. Fisher, Susan Scott, Attila Gyenis, David Scott, Jim Dee Dunleavy, and James Baldwin.

I owe my heartfelt thanks to the librarians who helped me with research and tracked down scores of hard-to-find books: Peter S. Alexis of the Pollard Memorial Library in Lowell, Massachusetts; Annette Choszczyk of the Glendale Public Library in Denver, Colorado; Sara Paulk, Laura Reeves, Bernice Bacon, Joan Newberry, and Deborah Moorman of the Tifton-Tift County Public Library; Gary F. Frizzell of the Coastal Plain Regional Library; and Marianne Duchardt and Charles Nundy of the Monroe County Public Library. Other research materials—rare tapes, books, CD-ROMs, and memorabilia—as well as illustrative matter were contributed by Billy Koumantzelis, David H. Brow, Jerry Bauer, Phil Chaput, Janet Lambert-Moore, John Sampas, Reginald Ouellette, Carolyn Cassady, Peter Alexis, Steve Ronan, Dana Moore, and Richard Weatherwax. At the Kerouac archives, the estate's right-hand man, Jim Sampas, son of Betty Sampas, extended many kindnesses, and arranged for copies to be made of documents. It was a privilege to listen to Kerouac nephews George Sampas and Tony Sampas talk about their uncle Sebastian's life and poetry during a symposium at the University of Massachusetts–Lowell, and to meet Larry Sampas.

With regard to primary sources not already acknowledged, Neal Cassady's *Grace Beats Karma: Letters From Prison 1958–60* and the Cassady-Ginsberg correspondence, *As Ever*, edited by Barry Gifford, were useful, as were the reminiscences of Gore Vidal, Lawrence R. Broer, Adele Mailer, Diane DiPrima, Joyce Johnson, Edie Parker, Robert Giroux, Michael McClure,

David Amram, Rev. Armand ("Spike") Morissette, Jan Kerouac, Gilbert Millstein, Paul Bowles, Steve Allen, Seymour Wyse, Charles E. Jarvis, John Clellon Holmes, Tennessee Williams, Donald Allen, Robert Creeley, and Hettie
Jones.

Everyone who writes about Kerouac should be grateful to the Beat Gen-
eration scholars who established chronologies and identities and interviewed
key figures. I wore out my copies of Barry Gifford and Lawrence Lee, Bernice
Lemire, Ann Charters, Barry Miles, Tom Clark, Dennis McNally, Steve
Turner, Peter Manso, William Plummer, Hilary Mills, Brad Gooch, Gerald
Nicosia, and Victor Bockris. I also relied on the collected issues of *Moody
Street Irregulars*, Joy Walsh's magnificent documentation of Kerouac, and on
the works of critics, scholars, journalists, editors, filmmakers, and interviewers
such as Colette Bachand Wood, Glenn Stout, Gregory Mcdonald, Alfred G.
Aronowitz, Val Duncan, Warren French, Ann Douglas, John Antonelli, Da-
vid Stanford, James T. Jones, Wolfgang Mohrhenn, Douglas Brinkley, Ted
Berrigan, Mike D'Orso, Jack McClintock, William Dunn, Jean-Pierre Geli-
nas, Jim Christy, Rebecca Solnit, Marc Charney, Paul Brouillette, John J.
Dorfner, Michael Schwartz and Neil Ortenberg, Alex Albright, Donald Mo-
tier, Maurice Poteet, Richard S. Sorrell, Brian F. Murphy, Maria Damon,
Dennis King, John Montgomery, Tom Hayden, Gregory Stephenson, Jim
Burns, Mona Lisa Saloy, Lisa Phillips, Dave Moore, Bruce Cook, Mike
McGrady, John G. Hanhardt, Daniel Pinchbeck, Doug Pizzi, Allen Young,
Bill McNiskin, Phyllis Raphael, Edward Manzi, Frank Moran, John Russell,
Clark Coolidge, Tim Madigan, Andy Darlington, John F. Kenney, David
Perry, Rev. Steve Edington, Brian Doyle, and Ken Kesey.

As always, I had the loving support of my family, Mr. and Mrs. W. E.
Bradbury of Fort Worth, Texas, and Bill and Joyce Amburn of Lake City and
High Springs, Florida. Steadfast friends encouraged me through many drafts
of *Subterranean Kerouac*. My thanks to Jean Egan of Tyron, North Carolina;
Joe Lambert of Lowell, Massachusetts; Fred Aanerud, Allston and Pepper
James, and Tim Hecht of San Francisco, California; Elaine Dundy of Los
Angeles, California; Violet and Jack Van Gundy, Judy Karshner, Charlotte
F. Johnson, and Mildred King of Tifton, Georgia; Cindy Langford of Sara-
sota, Florida; Woody Guyton of Richmond, Virginia; and Tim D'Este, Katie
Truax, Jim Thomas, Wendy Tucker, Sandford Birdsey, Ellie McConnell,
Chris O'Brien, Pete Peterson, Matt Dukes Jordan, June Keith, David Rhodes,
and Joanne Jacobson of Key West, Florida.

Without Guy Lefebvre's patient coaching, I wouldn't have been able to
master Clarisworks, Hewlett Packard Desk Writer 550C, or the Macintosh
Performa 578 on which this book was written. How Kerouac would have
loved the continuous scroll of a word processor!

Just before we went to press at St. Martin's, I benefited from the expertise of publicist John Murphy, production editor Naomi Shulman, and copy editor Patricia Phelan. Last but by no means least, attorney Celeste Phillips guided me through a legal reading of the manuscript with patience, wisdom, and a deep sensitivity to the themes and issues of Jack Kerouac's life.

NOTES

ABBREVIATIONS

AC: Ann Charters

ACBWJK: Ann Charters's *A Bibliography of Works by Jack Kerouac*

ACKB: Ann Charters's *Kerouac: A Biography*

AE: *As Ever: The Collected Correspondence of Allen Ginsberg and Neal Cassady*

AG: Allen Ginsberg

AGCP: Allen Ginsberg's *Collected Poems: 1947–1980*

AK: Alfred Kazin

ANEC: Author's notes from editorial conferences with Jack Kerouac

BB: Jack Kerouac's *Book of Blues*

BCBG: Bruce Cook, *The Beat Generation*

BD: *Jack Kerouac's Book of Dreams*

BDBC: Brian Doyle's "The Road Not Taken," *Boston College Magazine*

BL: Bernice Lemire's *Jack Kerouac: Early Influences*

BM: Barry Miles

BMG: Barry Miles's *Ginsberg: A Biography*

BMWB: Barry Miles's *William Burroughs, El Hombre Invisible: A Portrait*

BS: Jack Kerouac's *Big Sur*

CC: Carolyn Cassady

CCOR: Carolyn Cassady's *Off the Road: My Years with Cassady, Kerouac, and Ginsberg*

CGS: Charles G. Sampas

CKB: Carolyn ("Nin") Kerouac Blake

DA: Jack Kerouac's *Desolation Angels*

DB: Jack Kerouac's *The Dharma Bums*

DM: Dennis McNally's *Desolate Angel, A Biography: Jack Kerouac, the Beat Generation, and America*

DP: Doug Pizzi's "Creativity Encouraged, His Genius Realized," *Lowell Sun*, June 22, 1988.

DS: Jack Kerouac's *Dr. Sax*

EL: Elbert Lenrow

EW: Ed White

FEP: Frankie Edith ("Edie") Parker Kerouac

GB: Neal Cassady's *Grace Beats Karma: Letters from Prison (1958–60)*

GJA: George J. Apostolos

GK: Gabrielle Kerouac

GN: Gerald Nicosia's *Memory Babe: A Critical Biography of Jack Kerouac*

G&L: Barry Gifford and Lawrence Lee's *Jack's Book: An Oral Biography of Jack Kerouac*

GS: Gary Snyder

GVP: Gore Vidal's *Palimpsest*

H: Jack Kerouac's *Heaven and Other Poems*

HC: Hal Chase

JC: Joe Chaput

JCH: John Clellon Holmes

JCHG: John Clellon Holmes's *Go!*

JHK: Joan Haverty Kerouac

JJ: Joyce Johnson

JJMC: Joyce Johnson's *Minor Characters*

JK: Jack Kerouac

JM: John Montgomery

JMD: John MacDonald

JOE: Joe Sorota

JS: John Sampas

JTJ: James T. Jones's *A Map of Mexico City Blues, Jack Kerouac as Poet*

KALM: Kerouac archive, Lowell, Massachusetts

KAS: Glenn Stout, "Jack Kerouac—Athlete and Scholar," *Lowell Celebrates Kerouac!* 1996

KAWB: *Kerouac at the "Wild Boar"*

LC: Lucien Carr

LH: LuAnne Henderson

LCK: *Lowell Celebrates Kerouac!*

LS: *Lowell Sun*

LT: Jack Kerouac's *Lonesome Traveler*

MC: Jack Kerouac's *Maggie Cassidy*

MCB: Jack Kerouac's *Mexico City Blues*

MCE: Malcolm Cowley, editor

MM: Michael McClure

MSI: *Moody Street Irregulars*

NB: Norma Blickfelt

NC: Neal Cassady

OR: Jack Kerouac's *On the Road*

PBR: *The Portable Beat Reader*

PC: Phil Chaput

PJK: *The Portable Jack Kerouac*

PO: Peter Orlovsky

PR: Ted Berrigan's "Jack Kerouac: Writers at Work," *The Paris Review Interviews: Fourth Series*

PW: Philip Whalen

RG: Robert Giroux
RL: Ron Lowe
RO: Reginald Ouellette
SDE: Steve Edington
SHSI: Mike D'Orso's "Saturday's Hero," *Sports Illustrated*
SIP: Jack Kerouac's *Satori in Paris*
SL: Jack Kerouac's *Selected Letters 1940–1956*
SLA: Sterling Lord, agent
SM: Armand (Spike) Morissette's "A Catholic's View of Kerouac"
SS: Sammy Sampas
SSK: Stella Sampas Kerouac
SUB: Jack Kerouac's *The Subterraneans*
T&C: Jack Kerouac's *The Town and the City*
TCJK: Tom Clark's *Jack Kerouac: A Biography*
TJKC: *The Jack Kerouac Collection* (cassette album)
TRIS: Jack Kerouac's *Tristessa*
TT: Jack Kerouac, Lew Welch, and Albert Saijo's *Trip Trap*
TUVOTI: *the unspeakable visions of the individual*
ULKC: University of Massachusetts, Lowell Center for Lowell History, Oral 671 History Project, Kerouac Collection
VC: Jack Kerouac's *Visions of Cody*
VD: Jack Kerouac's *Vanity of Duluoz*
VG: Jack Kerouac's *Visions of Gerard*
VK: Charles E. Jarvis's *Visions of Kerouac*
WSB: William S. Burroughs
WPHG: William Plummer's *The Holy Goof: A Biography of Neal Cassady*
Note: Bibliographical details on articles, stories, videos, and films are given in the Notes. Full bibliographical details on most books are found in the Bibliography.

1: THE AGONIZED COCK OF THE MATTER

[1]JK's sex-charged childhood; the autobiographical nature of his work: DS, pp. 56, 61; JK to NC, December 28, 1950, SL, pp. 247, 251; MC, pp. 40, 42; JK to NC, January 10, 1951, SL, pp. 301–302, 305; DS, p. 60; ANEC, VD; BS, p. iii; ACKB, p. 404; G&L, pp. 322–332; GVP, p. 231; Dave Moore (Character Keys in MSI 9, 10, 16/17).

[2]JK's claims of noble ancestry: Colette Bachand Wood: "A Search of France for the Family's Castle," *Boston Sunday Globe*, February 4, 1990, pp. B 14–16; Richard Ellmann: *James Joyce*, p. 11.

[3]Cecile Plaud quoted in Joy Walsh: "Vision of Martin Eden as Jack Kerouac," Clarence Center, New York: Textile Bridge Press, 1984, p. 32.

[4]JK's parents—a background of survival, alcoholism, journalism, bisexuality, and Franco-American insularity: SDE: *Kerouac's Nashua Connection*, p. 14; SDE: "Kerouac's Family"; author interview with RO; TCJK, p. 6; VG, pp. 80, 86; MC, p. 107; T&C, p. 23; DS, p. 74; G&L, p. 184; VC, p. 62; VD, p. 29; JK to BL, October 1961, pp. 45, 50; JK to NC, January 10, 1951, SL, p. 305.

[5]JK's birth, baptism; erotic relationship to mother; family's constant moves: Author interviews with RO, Roger Brunelle, other Lowell neighbors; DS, p. 15; JK to NC, December 28, 1950, SL, pp. 249–250; VG, p. 74; ANEC, DA; JK to NC, December 28, 1950, SL, P. 249; certificate of baptism, Jean Louis Kirouac, made June 23, 1984, signed Rev. Roger N. Jacques, Associate Pastor; SDE: "Kerouac's Family"; VG, pp. 5, 102; DS, pp. 16, 167–168, 175, 269; JK to NC, January 3, 1951, SL, p. 269.

[6]JK's troubled relationship with Gerard: JK to NC, December 28, 1950, SL, pp. 251, 256, 259;

JK to NC, January 3, 1951, SL, p. 272; VG, pp. 16, 23, 37–38, 40–41, 51, 63, 101, 104–105, 107; T&C, pp. 35, 90–91; DS, pp. 31, 62; RL: "Satori in St. Petersburg," *Dharma Beat*, Fall 1993, No.1; author interview with RL; JK to NC, January 9, 1951, SL p. 285; SL, pp. 251–306; JK to NC, January 10, 1951, p. 305; VD, p. 89; *Alateen*, p. 8.

[7]Leo's early promise; effects of alcoholism on family; JK's ambivalence with regard to Gerard: The Lowell City Directory lists Leo "Keroach" as publisher of the *Lowell Spotlight* [sic] in 1923, as advertising manager of *L'Étoile* 1924–1925, and as owner, the Spotlight [sic] Print 1926–1929, courtesy RO; JK to NC, December 28, 1950, SL, pp. 250, 259; BD, pp. 11, 15; Maurice Poteet: "Two More for the Road," MSI, Spring/Summer 1982, No.11, p. 6; author interviews with RL, Rudolphe "Red" Ouellette, RO; VG, p. 46; *Alateen*, p. 8; MCB, p. 88; Donald Motier: *Gerard: The Influence of Jack Kerouac's Brother on His Life and Writing*, pp. 4–5.

[8]Death of Gerard: Motier: *Gerard*, p. 5; VG, pp. 6, 52, 66, 109; H, p. 39; death certificate, Gerard F. Keroack, June 2, 1926, No.760, 5 Ward, Commonwealth of Massachusetts; ANEC, VD; Lot No.151, St. Louis de Gonzague Cemetery records, SDE, *Kerouac's Nashua Connection*, pp. 26, 50, courtesy PC, RO.

[9]JK's disturbed childhood; sex explorations with Ovila and Robert; confession to NC: LT, p. iv; MC, p. 42; JK: MCB, p. 88; JK to NC, January 10, 1951, SL, pp. 302, 304–306.

[10]Early grade school; first communion; Leo's instability: BL, p. 51; BMG, p. 144; T&C, pp. 239–240; VD, pp. 16–17; MSI, Spring/Summer 1982, No.11, p. 1; VC, p. 487.

[11]JK's littleboy loves of puberty: JK referred to Gauthier as "Roland Bouthelier" in "In the "Ring," *Atlantic*, March 1968, and *Good Blonde*, p. 497 (see also TCJK, p. 16; DM, p. 13); ANEC, VD; DS, p. 56; Dave Moore: "*Book of Dreams*: A Name Index," MSI No.8, Summer/Fall 1980, p. 21; BL, p. 52; DS, pp. 51–53, 56, 61, 64, 134; MC, p. 40–42; BL, p. 61; BD, p. 123; BL, p. 26, GN, pp. 31–32; SM; BL, pp. 24–25, 41–42; BL, p. 52, demonstrates that St. Joseph's was run by Marist Brothers, not Jesuits, as JK wrote in DS and LT; TCJK, p. 18; MC, p. 42; author interview with RO; JK to BL, December 9, 1961, BL, p. 53, 65.

[12]Christmas 1932; JK's confirmation; Bartlett; Chandler; imaginary games: JK: "Home at Christmas: 1932": *Glamour*, PJK, p. 45; author interviews with RO and Cy Egan; BL, p. 58; DS, pp. 1, 13, 40–45, 65–66, ANEC, VD; GN, p. 35; G&L, p. 324 (Billy Chandler also appears as "Dicky Hampshire" in T&C and VD); KAS.

[13]JK emerges as a popular adolescent; homoerotic activity: DS, pp. 5, 32, 36, 49, 60–62; VD, pp. 15, 62; G&L, pp. 10, 11; SHSI; GN, p. 39; BL, p. 63; GN, p. 40; MC, pp. 5–13, 22–23, 40, 133; BL, p. 71; G&L, pp. 323, 331–332: both Omar Noel and Jean Fourchette are listed as the prototype for "Zaza Vauriselle" in MC, "Ali Zasa" in DS, and "Zouzou" in T&C.

[14]JK as sandlot sensation and junior-high writer; relationships with SS and SSK: VK, pp. 43, 54–55; SHSI; DS, pp. 6, 79; BL, pp. 58–59, 79; Nick Massey: "Recovering a Lost Poet: Sebastian Sampas," LCK 1995; LCK 1995: Miss Mansfield appears in DS, p. 153, as "Miss Wakefield"; LT, p. v; T&C, pp. 120, 131–132; VC, pp. 239, 349; ANEC, VD; author interview with BK; VC, p. 455 ("Like Rimbaud and his Verlaine, every rose's got a summer, Julien and his Dave, I had my Sebastian, Julien's Verlaine was murdered, my Verlaine was killed in a battle of war, Cody's Verlaine though is Irwin—or was." The code: Julien [Love] = LC, G&L, p. 324, and Dave Moore, who identified LC as Julien Love in BD, in "Book of Dreams: A Name Index," MSI, summer/fall, 1980, No.8, p. 21. Dave [Stroheim] = David Kammerer, G&L, p. 327. Sebastian [Savakis] = SS, G&L, p. 331. Cody [Pomeray] = NC, G&L, p. 324, and PJK, p. 620. Irwin [Garden] = AG, G&L, p. 326, and ACKB, p. 405); Warren French: *Jack Kerouac*, p. 124; in T&C, JK is the autobiographical character "Peter Martin," G&L, p. 331, while SS is "Alexander Panos"; JK to SS, March 15, 1943, SL, p. 47; JK to SS, February 1943, SL, p. 39; Odysseus Chiungos, LCK 1996, courtesy PC; "Odysseus Chiungos, Childhood Friend," LS, June 22, 1988; JK to SSK, November 9, 1955, SL, p. 529; Mary Rouses Karafelis: "Stella Sampas Kerouac: Unassailable Character and Unparalleled Friend," LS, December 11, 1995, P. 17; author interviews with Betty Sampas and JS, KALM; JK to SSK, October 12, 1955, SL, p. 527; author interview with Betty Watley.

[15]Flood of 1936; JK scorned as sissy; Spike's counsel: DS, pp. 150, 153, 155; author interview with Aida Panagiotakos; BL, p. 57; GN, p. 42; T&C, pp. 410, 412–413; VG, p. 248; G&L, pp. 327–328; SM; SHSI.

[16]JK's breakthrough in high-school football; conflicts with coaches: ANEC, VD; T&C, pp. 56–61; SHSI; KAS; Keady appears as "Tam Keating" in VD; VK, pp. 14–17; JK to CGS, October 4, 1969; PR, p. 370; KAS, courtesy PC and Janet Lambert-Moore; BDBC, p. 52; SHSI.

[17]JK's academic performance in high school; favorite teachers and authors: ANEC, VD; Dickinson: "14," "425," "435," Poems, The Heath Anthology of American Literature, Volume 1, Paul Lauter, editor, pp. 2845–2846, 2864; BL, p. 39; KAS; author interview with RO; SL: pp. 617, 619, 624, 628; VD, p. 27; MC, p. 57; JK to BL, June 1961, BL, p. 61; JK to AG, July 14, 1955, SL, p. 497.

[18]Beginning of interest in girls, swing, track; JK's rise to fame as climax runner: author interview with JOE; SHSI; ANEC, VD; VD, pp. 15–16; "This Group to Represent Lowell High Tomorrow: Statistics of Lowell High Squad," LS, November 24, 1938; BDBC; Bill McNiskin: "Keady Goes to Double Wing Back for Saturday: Brushes Up on Sunday Plays for Next Game," undated clipping, courtesy JOE; Unidentified 1938 Lowell-area sports stories, courtesy JOE; undated LS clipping, Pollard Memorial Library, courtesy Peter Alexis; BDBC; LCK 1996 T-shirt credits the Boston Post for "climax runner," but KAS attributed it to the Boston Herald, as did JK in VD, p. 19.

[19]JK's tentative behavior toward girls; relationship with Margaret Coffey; round-robin bisexual kiss: author interview with JOE; MC, pp. 99, 100–101, 142; BD, p. 19; T&C, p. 73; ANEC, VD; MC, p. 39–40, 137, 139; author interview with JOE; G&L, p. 324, GN, p. 53, and DM, p. 352, all agree that Margaret Coffey is "Pauline (Moe) Cole," and RO and JOE confirmed this; GVP, pp. 211–234; Jonathan Ned Katz: The Invention of Heterosexuality, p. 99; T&C, p. 410 (AG appears as "Leon Levinsky," and SS is "Alexander Panos," G&L, pp. 326, 331); KAS.

[20]Intensification of JK-SS relationship; flirtation with Communism: Edward Manzi: "Stella Kerouac Was Always There," reprinted in MSI, Spring/1991, No. 24–26, p. 47; George Constantinedes: "Recovering a Lost Poet: Sebastian Sampas," LCK 1995, ANEC, VD; VD, pp. 61–62; George Gordon, Lord Byron: "So We'll Go No More A-Roving," The Norton Anthology of English Literature, Fifth Edition, Volume 2, M. H. Abrams, editor, p. 512; JK to NB, July 15, 1942, and August 25, 1942, SL, pp. 24, 28; VK, pp. 58, 69–70; T&C, p. 280.

[21]JK's rise to star of team—Malden, Lynn Classical; romance in New Britain: Author interview with JOE; ANEC, VD; VD, pp. 20, 21; author interview with JOE; KAS; unidentified, undated clippings from JOE's scrapbook ("Lowell and Malden Both Gain"; "Malden Plans Air Attack"; Bill McNiskin: "Lowell Fans Sore"; Frank Moran: "Lowell Sharp for Malden Battle"; John F. Kenney: "The Lookout: Lowell vs. Lawrence"; Frank Moran: "Lynn Classical at Peak for Lowell"; "Defeat by Lynn Classical"; "Injured Lynn Player Recovers"; Bill McNiskin: "Team Now Prepares for Nutmeg Invasion"; Frank Moran: "Defeat by Lynn Classical Leaves Fandom Shocked"); KAS; T&C, p. 73.

[22]Nashua and Lawrence games; JK's drinking begins: Author interview with BK; ANEC, VD; VD, pp. 21, 22–23; GN, pp. 49, 50, 702; T&C, p. 73; the Nashua Telegraph, November 14, 1938, p. 8, SDE, Kerouac's Nashua Connection, p. 34, courtesy PC; CGS: That Was the Way It Was; BDBC; Frank Moran: "Red and Gray Conquers 8–0," LS, November 25, 1938; SHSI; McGuane: "Greats of Another L.H. Era," unidentified clipping, courtesy JOE; McGuane: "Roving Reporter at Stadium Probes Dispute," LS, November 25, 1938; T&C, pp. 74–76, 80–83; DM, p. 30; Moran: "Eleven Experienced Reserves"; LS, November 25, 1938; author interview with Ed Wells.

[23]Leo's firing; JK ambition to be world leader: BDBC; ANEC, VD; MC, p. 57; SHSI; T&C, p. 121; JK to NC, January 8, 1951, SL, p. 274.

[24]JK: "32nd Chorus," San Francisco Blues in Book of Blues, p. 33.

[25]JK's relationship with Mary Carney: Author interviews with JS, JOE, Jack Lang, RO; JK to JCH, October 12, 1952, SL, pp. 382–383; MC, pp. 29, 34, 58, 60, 89, 92–93, 150, 154, 160; G&L, pp. 324, 330; ANEC, VD; T&C, pp. 45, 47–48; Margaret Coffey appears as the young "Elizabeth Wilson" in T&C, but the mature Elizabeth Wilson is based on a girl from Grosse Point, Michigan (1962 JK interview with BL, pp. 73, 81, BL); JK to JMD, early April 1943, SL, p. 57; JK to SSK, October 12, 1955, SL, p. 526; JK to NC and CC, January 10, 1953, SL, p. 395; VK, pp. 45, 142; G&L, pp. 15–16; BL, p. 56.; JK to SS, after March 12, 1944, SL, p. 75; CC to author, April 10, 1996; JK to CC, CCOR, p. 206; BD p. 27; VC, p. 59; Some of the Dharma; Warren French: Jack Kerouac, p. 125.

[26]JK and SS relationship an emotional quagmire; graduation and difficulties with Columbia: T&C, published version, pp. 122, 278, 360; T&C, Northport Public Library draft, pp. 97–99; GN, p. 703; JK: "He went on the road, as Jack Kerouac says," Life, Volume 52, June 29, 1962, p. 22; DM p. 31; ANEC, VD; VD, p. 29.

2: MAD ABOUT THE BOY

[1]JK's arrival in New York; first heterosexual act; homoerotic inclinations; friends at Horace Mann; academic, athletic, and literary attainments: T&C, pp. 360, 364; VD, pp. 23, 31–35, 42–43, 45, 47, 52, 55; MC, pp. 173, 176–177, 188; ANEC, VD; DM, pp. 34–35; Allen Young: "The Life and Loves of Allen Ginsberg: An Interview," Real Paper, March 28, 1973, p. 8; VK, pp. 146, 245; PR, p. 378; LT, pp. iv, 7, 13; GN, pp. 61, 88; G&L, p. 331; Seymour Wyse: "My Really Best Friend," KAWB, pp. 79, 83; Andrew Turnbull: Scott Fitzgerald: A Biography, pp. 198, 126; JK to NC, December 27, 1950, SL, p. 242; SHSI; 1940 Horace Mann Yearbook; BDBC; JK notebook, courtesy JS, KALM.

[2]Impact of jazz on JK's style: JK: "Count Basie's Band Best in Land: Group Famous for 'Solid' Swing," Horace Mann Record, Volume 33, February 16, 1940, p. 3; G&L, p. 23; Wyse, pp. 23–24; VD, p. 52; JK: Horace Mann Record, Volume 33, March 15, 1940, p. 3 (Morton Maxwell shares the byline with JK); DM, p. 38; George T. Simon: Glenn Miller and His Orchestra, p. 272; JK: "The Beginning of Bop," PJK, pp. 555–557; Ross Russell: Bird Lives! The High Life and Hard Times of Charlie (Yardbird) Parker, p. 13; JK: "Belief and Technique for Modern Prose," PJK, p. 483; JK: "Essentials of Spontaneous Prose," PJK, p. 484–485; MCB, "239th Chorus," p. 241; Jim Christy: "Jack and Jazz: Woodsmoke and Trains," MSI No.8, Summer/Fall 1980, p. 10.

[3]Two early short stories: Horace Mann Quarterly, Fall 1939, pp. 11–13, and Summer 1940, pp. 16–19.

[4]JK's encounter with Cole Porter: VD, p. 51; ANEC, VD; George Eels: The Life That Late He Led: A Biography of Cole Porter, p. 173; Gerald Clarke: Capote: A Biography, p. 341; T&C, p. 128; MCB, "37th Chorus," p. 37; AG: Real Paper, in VK, p. 146; GV in G&L, pp. 183–184; GVP, p. 217.

[5]Return to Lowell exacerbates JK's sense of divided self: JK to AG, October 8, 1952, SL, p. 378; GN, pp. 72–74, 87; VD, p. 61–62; T&C, pp. 135, 137; ANEC, VD; JK to SS, May 5, 1941, SL, p. 11; SS symposium, LCK, 1995; author interview with Betty Watley; MC, p. 189; Frederick R. Karl: William Faulkner: American Writer, p. 871.

[6]JK's first days at Columbia and his admiration for Joyce: author conversation (Lowell 1995) with Tony Sampas, the son of Mike and Betty Sampas, who discovered that 209 was JK's room number at Livingston Hall; VD, pp. 64, 73; KAS; GN, p. 79; Ellmann: James Joyce, passim; James R. Mellow: Hemingway: A Life Without Consequences, p. 549; Clifton Daniel, editor, Chronicle of the 20th Century, p. 519; BD, p. 13.

[7]JK's leg injury; relations with FEP, NB, SS; Thomas Mann: SHSI; FEP: "Addenda," MSI, No.10, Fall/1981, p. 18; VD, pp. 78, 220: JK to SS, February 26, 1941, SL, pp. 7, 8; JK to SS, March 25, 1941, SL, p. 10; JK to NB, July 15, 1942, pp. 21, 24–25, and August 25, 1942, p. 27, SL; Anthony Heilbut: Thomas Mann: Eros and Literature, p. 433; JK to SS, April 15, 1941, p. 10, and May 5, 1941, SL, p. 11.

[8]JK's gay bashing; romance with Maria; misadventures in Lowell: SUB, pp. 7–8; GN, pp. 77, 79; VD, p. 59, 77–78, 84; Patrick Fenton: "The Jack I Knew: My Prom Date," Newsday Magazine, April 1, 1990, MSI, No.24, 25, & 26, Spring/1991, pp. 28–29; JK to Cornelius Murphy (undated), SL, p. 62; KALM, courtesy of JS; JK to Seymour Krim, February 13, 1965.

[9]George Sampas manslaughter case: "Stevens Street Man Held for Grand Jury; Evidence Shows Killer Bore Marks of Blows," LS, August 14, 1941, p. 1; "Says Gun Taken from Apostolakos," LS, August 1, 1941; "12–20 Years Sentence in Shooting Case; Stevens Street Man Pleads Guilty to Manslaughter," LS, p. 22, December 18, 1941; "Man Slain in Market St.," LS, July 31, 1941, p. 1; "D.A. Hears Police Report on Slaying," LS, undated clipping; "Killing Causes D.A. Gaming Check-Up Here; Lid Clamped Tight as a Local Vice Squad Also Is Enlarged," LS, August 4, 1941; "Sampatacacus Indicted," LS, September 4, 1941; LCK 1995; SS: "Summer in the Mill Town"; author interviews with BK, Brian Foye, and Aida Panagiotakos.

[10]JK at Bradley Point; rupture with Columbia; Washington misadventure; return home: author interview with JS, KALM; JK to CKB, late summer 1941, SL, pp. 13–14; VD, p. 91, 93–94; Newsday, December 17, 1961; JK: "Washington in 1941," Dharma Beat, No.6, Spring 1996, unpaged; JK to SS, midsummer 1941, SL, pp. 15–16; DB, p. 78; "Old Mike" was most likely Mike Fournier, his childhood friend—see VD, pp. 95, 100; JK to SS, October 1941, SL, p. 17; BL, pp. 35, 49; GN, p. 90; DS, pp. 51–53. JK in Connecticut: JK to NC, January 10, 1951, SL, pp. 296; JK to SS, late September 1941, SL, p. 17; Thomas Wolfe: Of Time and the River, pp. 2, 274–275, 332; VK, p. 131.

[11]First serious writing; sexual exploits in Connecticut: JK to NC, January 10, 1951, SL, p. 296; JK to SS, October 1941, SL, p. 17; author interview with JS; JK to SS, late September 1941, SL, pp. 17–18 (JK wrote from West Haven that he saw *Citizen Kane*, but in VD, p. 104, he sees *Citizen Kane* in Lowell at the Royal Theater on December 7, 1941); KALM; JK to NC, January 10, 1951, SL, pp. 296–300.

[12]Connecticut writing projects; Thanksgiving 1941; outbreak of war; brief journalistic career; Pentagon caper; Washington amours: author interview with JS; VD, pp. 96–97, 99, 105–106, 113, 179; JK to NC, January 10, 1951, SL, p. 296; VC, pp. 112, 151, 344; ANEC, VD; KALM indicates JK's address was 43 Crawford Street, but the 1942 Lowell City Directory lists 125 Crawford Street; "Jim Mayo," who hired JK at LS in VD, was identified as Frank Moran in Dave Moore: "*Vanity of Duluoz*: A Character Index," MSI, Winter/Spring 1981, p. 13; author interview with Brian Foye; LS, February 19, 1942; "Arch MacDougald" is the fictional name JK gave John MacDonald in VD and BD, according to Dave Moore's "*Book of Dreams*: A Name Index," MSI No.8, Summer/Fall 1980, p. 22; JK to Norma Blickfelt, July 15, 1942, SL, pp. 21–22; VK, p. 79; Allen Drury: *The Pentagon*, p. 8; JK to SS, September 26, 1942, SL, p. 28; GN, p. 97; JK to Norma Blickfelt, August 25, 1942, SL, p. 27.

[13]JK and FEP; flight from SS and past; the Scollay Square toilet episode; JK's pro-Nazi sympathies; homosexual experiences aboard the *Dorch*: ANEC, VD; FEP: "Remembering Mrs. William Seward Burroughs: Joan Vollmer Adams," KAWB, p. 100; JK to NB, July 15, 1942, SL, pp. 21–23; VD, p. 115, 127, 131–133, 124, 143–144; VK, pp. 83, 86–89, 91–92; PR, p. 370; author interviews with two Lowell men who were at the Spear when JK made his "buggery" statement (They requested anonymity. I also interviewed three people in Lowell who, though not at the Spear that night, heard of the incident); GN, p. 122; JK to SS, November 1942, SL, p. 31.

[14]Greenland; Nova Scotia bender; proposal to SS to live together; SS and GJA as symbols of JK's divided nature: Barrie Pitt: *The Battle of the Atlantic*, p. 151; T&C, p. 304; in VD, p. 135, "Wayne Duke" is Duke Ford, according to GN, p. 100; T&C, p. 304; JK to GJA, April 7, 1943, SL, p. 59; JK to SS, September 26, 1942, SL, p. 29; VD, p. 142; JK to GJA, April 7, 1943, SL, pp. 59–60; JK to SS, March 1943, SL, p. 43; JK–Alfred G. Aronowitz interview, January 1959.

[15]SS's training as a medic; *The Sea Is My Brother*; JK and Van Doren; clash with Lou Little; JK's tortured love for SS: JK to Bill Ryan, January 10, 1943, SL, pp. 35–36; JK to SS, February 1943, SL, pp. 39, 41–42; JK to SS, March 15, 1943, SL, p. 49; BD, p. 48; ANEC, VD; VD, pp. 143–145, 148; "Mark Van Doren, 78, Poet, Teacher, Dies," *New York Times*, December 12, 1972; GN, p. 139; Michael Mott: *Thomas Merton*, p. 112; Thomas Merton: *The Seven Storey Mountain*, p. 139; VK, pp. 95, 145; KAS; JK to NC, July 28, 1949, SL, p. 215; JK to GK, March 30, 1943, SL, p. 55; JK to SS, undated—early March 1943, SL, pp. 44–45; Thomas Wolfe: *Look Homeward, Angel*, p. 1; SS to JK, March 25, 1943, SL, p. 46; AK: *On Native Ground*, passim.

3: MACHO MANSLAUGHTER

[1]JK and the U.S. Navy; SS as medical trainee; JK's crack-up and 0-7 Sick Bay: VD, pp. 148 ff, 154, 159, 268; SL, p. 49; GK to JK, March 24, 1943, SL, p. 49; JK to GK, SL, March 30, 1943, pp. 54–55; author interview with Gertrude Maher (special thanks to Paul Maher); JK to SS, March 25, 1943, SL, pp. 52, 54; SS to JK, undated, 1943; T&C, p. 317; SS to Marjorie Semonian, October 2, 1943, Emerson College yearbook, 1944, p. 77; VK, p. 98; ANEC, VD; JK to JMD, early April 1943, SL, pp. 56–57, p. 61; JK to GJA, April 7, 1943, SL, p. 60; JK to Cornelius Murphy, Wednesday morning [undated], SL, pp. 61–63; T&C, p. 328; GK to JK, May 3, 1943, SL, pp. 63–64; SL, notes, pp. 63, 65; SS to JK, May 26, 1943, SL, pp. 65–70.

[2]JK's delusions; escape attempt; transfer to Bethesda; cock weather epiphany: VD, p. 161; GN, pp. 105–106; Andrew Jackson ("Big Slim") Holmes in VD, p. 156, was identified as William Holmes "Big Slim" Hubbard in JK's letter to NC, January 10, 1951, p. 307, SL, in which JK mentions that five guards accompanied them to Washington (he revised these details fifteen years later, in VD, writing that he and Big Slim were accompanied to Washington by two navy corpsmen); VD, pp. 161–164, 167–168; ANEC, VD; GN, p. 106, using JK's private character key to the *Duluoz Legend*, identified the psychiatrist as "Dr. Rosenberg" (ACKB, p. 373, refers to a "Doctor Rosenberger" JK mentioned when reliving his Bethesda experience during a 1961 psychedelic trip with AG and Timothy Leary); AGCP, "Howl"; VC, pp. 31, 63.

[3]JK in Queens and Asbury Park: FEP: "Addenda and Annotations," MSI, No.10, p. 18 (FEP

recalled JK's address as 133½ Cross Bay Boulevard, but I am using the address JS gave me at KALM; JK to Alan Harrington, April 23, 1949, SL, p. 188; GN, pp. 112–113, 124; JK to SS, April 15, 1941, SL, p. 10; *Chronicle of the Twentieth Century*, p. 552; VC, pp. 250, 252 (also see DM, p. 58); T&C., p. 312; G&L, p. 331; TCJK, p. 57; VD, p. 170; JK to FEP, September 18, 1943, SL, pp. 70–71.

⁴Aboard the *Weems*; Liverpool; London; JK and FEP's sexual connection: Pitt: *The Battle of the Atlantic*, p. 189; JK to FEP, September 18, 1943, SL, pp. 70–71; VD, pp. 175, 181, 188– 190, 192, 248; SL, note, p. 71; JK's sex list, KALM; VC, pp. 247, 381–383; FEP: "Remembering Mrs. William Seward Burroughs," KAWB, p. 99 (according to FEP, her abortion and taking possession of apartment No. 28 at 420 W. 119th Street occurred "just after Pearl Harbor," but GN, p. 126, interviewed FEP, and wrote that the abortion was performed after JK's voyage on the *Weems*); FEP: "Addenda and Annotations," MSI, No. 10, p. 18; G&L, p. 330, identify FEP as "Elly" in VD, but FEP in "Addenda" recalls that one of her names in Jack's books was "Ella"; ANEC, VD.

⁵The apartment; Joan Vollmer Adams's background and relationships with JK and Edie: author interview with JS; FEP: "Addenda," MSI, No.10, p. 18; BMG, pp. 43, 56; FEP: "Remembering," KAWB, pp. 99, 101, 105; GN, pp. 109, 111–112, 117, 142, 150, 456; VC, pp. 103, 246, 254, 379 ("June" in VD was based on Joan, according to G&L, p. 322, and she was also "June" in VC); MCB: "88th Chorus," p. 88; JK to NC, July 28, 1949, SL, p. 215; ANEC, VD; T&C, p. 388; Wilborn Hampton: "Allen Ginsberg, 70, Master of Beat Poets, Dies," *New York Times*, April 6, 1997, p. 1.

⁶LC brings together WSB, AG, and JK; JK's fatal attraction to LC: BMG, pp. 36, 40–42, 44– 45, 47, 49, 80, 541; Daniel Pinchbeck: "Children of the Beats," *New York Times Magazine*, November 5, 1995, p. 39; Laura Reynolds Adler: "On the Lower East Side with Caleb Carr, Talking About a Dark Obsession," *Bookpage*, October 1997, p. 5; G&L, p. 34–35, 37, 46, 326; BMWB, pp. 25, 29, 34–35; DM, pp. 64–65; GN, pp. 119, 121, 127, 550, 734 (JJ said JK was "in love" with LC); ANEC, VD; VD, pp. 195–196, 198, 204, 211–212, 250; ACKB, pp. 43, 51; KALM; AG: *Journals Mid-Fifties 1954–1958*, p. 14; JK to AG, October 1944, SL, p. 81; *Le Grand Jack Kerouac's Road*, H. Chiasson, producer, 1987; JK to NC, August 26, 1947, SL, p. 188; VK, pp. 103, 242; WSB: *The Wild Boys*, p. 90; G&L, p. 326; Dave Moore: "*Vanity of Duluoz*: A Character Index," MSI, Winter/Spring 1981, pp. 12–13; FEP: "Addenda," MSI, No.10, p. 18; JK: Diary entry for November 16, 1944, SL, p. 81; BD, p. 125 (FEP identified Celine Young as the Jeanne Desmarais of BD in "Addenda," p. 18); JK to AG, October 1944 and September 6, 1945, SL, pp. 81–82, 98.

⁷SS at Anzio; WSB's joke; SS's war verse and death: JK to CKB, March 14, 1945, SL, p. 89; Jones: WWII, pp. 88, 117, 125; author interview with JS, KALM. JS recited "Taste the Night-bane" to me on the telephone on June 21, 1996; SS: "Rhapsody in Red," *Puptent Poets of the Stars and Stripes*, quoted in full in DM, p. 60; JK to SSK, October 12, 1955, SL, p. 526; JK to AG, January 18, 1955, SL, p. 461; Percy Bysshe Shelley: "Adonais," *Norton Anthology of English Literature*, Volume 2, p. 741; GN, pp. 124, 707: In a letter to AG dated January 13, 1950, JK quoted SS's voice recording, which was mailed to JK from Italy shortly before SS's death; George Sampas: SS symposium, LCK 1995 (SS's message was received on March 12, 1944, after his death. The quotation is from Wolfe: *Look Homeward, Angel*, p. 1); Pyle: *Brave Men*, p. 202; JK to SS, "after March 12, 1944," SL, p. 75; JK to SSK, October 17, 1950, SL, pp. 234–235; JK to SSK, October 12, 1955, and December 10, 1952, SL, pp. 526, 390; VD, p. 160; ANEC, VD; A. E. Housman: "To an Athlete Dying Young" (1896), *Norton*, p. 1883; William Wordsworth: "Ode: Intimations of Immortality from Recollections of Early Child-hood," *Norton*, p. 214; TCJK, p. 7 (GK's half-Indian grandmother); B. H. Liddell Hart: *History of the Second World War*, p. 528.

⁸Complications among the early Beats leading to the Kammerer killing; criminal investigation and imprisonments; link to JK's marriage; Koestler on mankind's inherent insanity: JK to NC, September 13, 1947, SL, pp. 126–127; JK to NC, August 31, 1951, SL, p. 325; AG: *Allen Verbatim*, p. 103; JK to AG, January 2, 1948, SL, p. 139–140; JK to AG, October 8, 1952, SL, pp. 379–380; LC to JK, in JK to EL, June 28, 1949, SL, p. 207; VD, pp. 193–194, 214, 221– 222, 224, 228–233, 242–243, 248, 250; WSB to JK, April 3, 1952, SL, p. 340; Frank S. Adams: "Columbia Student Kills Friend and Sinks Body in Hudson River, *New York Times*, August 17, 1944; BMG, pp. 51, 53–54, 541; FEP: "Addenda," MSI, No.10, p. 18; G&L, pp. xxi, 43– 44, 324; JK wrote in VD, p. 221, that Kammerer was stabbed "twelve times," quoting Claude, the LC character (see G&L, p. 324), BMG, p. 51, wrote twice, ACKB, p. 48, wrote three times; G&L, p. 43, wrote twice; *New York Times* covered the crime on August 17 (p. 1), 18 (p. 14), 25 (p. 15), 31 (p. 19), September 16 (p. 15) and October 7 (p. 15), 1944; author interview with

JS; according to BMWB, p. 37, it took Lucien two days before he turned himself in—JK listed WSB's bail at five thousand dollars in VD, p. 229 (also see TCJK, p. 64, which lists it as five thousand dollars); ANEC, VD; AG to Eugene Brooks, October 1944; DM, p. 71; Harold Bloom: *Yeats*, p. 210; SL, note, p. 77; GK to JK, September 15, 1944, SL, p. 79; Steve Turner: *Angelheaded Hipster*, p. 70. Celine Young to JK, October 1 and 8, 1944; LC to AG, September 21 and 30, 1944, and August 13, 1944; AG to LC, 1944–1945 (undated); AG to Eugene Brooks, October and September 1944; JK to Mrs. Parker, September 1, 1944, SL, p. 76; JK to CKB, March 14, 1945, SL, p. 89; FEP: "Addenda and Annotations," MSI, No.10, p. 18; JK to CKB, March 14, 1945, SL, pp. 87–88; Arthur Koestler: *The Ghost in the Machine*, pp. xi, 239, 305.

[9]JK's amorous encounters with the bosun, Celine, and AG; Columbia scandal; Weaver's influence: JK: October–November 1944 notebooks, courtesy JS, KALM, VD, pp. 252–253, 256–257; VC, pp. 148, 267–268; KALM; AG: *Gay Sunshine Interview*, 1974, p. 4; in BMG, pp. 55, 56, 59, AG said he and JK had sex but not "for about half a year"; GN, pp. 139–140; ACKB, p. 382; Lionel Trilling: *Beyond Culture: Essays on Literature and Learning*, p. 9; BMG, p. 57; G&L, pp. 42–43, 280–281; AG: *Allen Verbatim*, p. 1; Diana Trilling: *The Beginning of the Journey*, pp. 280–281.

[10]Huncke and origin of "beat"; JK's homoerotic life with AG; WSB; collaboration: DM, p. 76; VD, pp. 259–260; WSB: *Queer*, pp. 98–99; WSB in PR and ACKB, p. 56; PBR, pp. 102, 104; JK: "Beatific: Origins of the Beat Generation," *Playboy*, June 6, 1959, PJK, pp. 568–570; JK to AG, January 2, 1948, SL, p. 140; JK to AG, September 6, 1945, SL, p. 97; BMG, p. 68; BMWB, pp. 27, 42; JK to CS, April 7, 1952, SL, pp. 341–342; G&L, pp. 17–19; DM, p. 77, ANEC, WSB: "Introduction," *The Naked Lunch*, p. ix; G&L, p. 132; PR, pp. 371.

[11]JK's relations with FEP and AG; his poetic influence on AG: JK: January 1945 notebook, courtesy JS, KALM. BMG, pp. 58, 62, 66, 68–69, 542; BMWB, p. 39; JK to AG, September 6, 1945, SL, p. 95; G&L, p. 57; JK to NC, August 26, 1947, SL, p. 119; AGCP: "Pull My Daisy," p. 24; MCB, "213th Chorus," p. 213; Timothy Leary, *Flashbacks*, p. 63; G&L, p. 58; AG in conversation with the author; AG: *Allen Verbatim*, p. 152.

[12]JK expands concept of Beat; Vicki Russell; drug addiction and early Beats; JK and the anti-Semitic tradition in French Canada and in modern literature; JK and Elie Wiesel compared: VD, pp. 259–260; AGCP, "Howl," p. 126; WSB: *Naked Lunch*, pp. 82–83. JK to NC, June 6, 1951, SL, p. 318; G&L, p. 330; VC, pp. 257, 261, 263, 281; BMG, p. 65. Simeon Margolis, M.D., and Hamilton Moses III, M.D., editors: *The Johns Hopkins Medical Handbook*, p. 303; ANEC, VD; GN, p. 163; Richard S. Sorrell: "Ti Jean and Papa Leo: Jack Kerouac's Relationship with His French-Canadian Father," *Moody Street Irregulars*, No.11, p. 10; John Gunther: *Inside U.S.A.*, p. xii; Wolfe: *The Notebooks*, Volume II, p. 829; *Ezra Pound Speaking*, Leonard A Doob, editor, p. 339; Tom Dardis: *Firebrand: The Life of Horace Liveright*, pp. 77, 79, 98; Frederick R. Karl: *William Faulkner: American Writer*, pp. 175, 201; Janis P. Stout: *Katherine Anne Porter: A Sense of the Times*, p. 178; Lyle Leverich: *Tom: The Unknown Tennessee Williams*, pp. 343, passim; Michael Shelden: *Graham Greene: The Enemy Within*, pp. 60–61, 123, 178; *All Rivers Run to the Sea: Memoirs*, p. 415.

[13]JK's burnout with WSB and drugs: JK: July 1945 notebook, courtesy JS, KALM. AC, editor: SL, pp. 95–97; VD, p. 261; ANEC, VD; AG to JK, October 29, 1958; JK to AG, November 13 and August 23, 1945, SL, pp. 92, 100; GN, p. 152.

[14]HC; Wolfeans and non-Wolfeans: ANEC, VD; VD, p. 259; JK to AG, November 13, 1945, SL, p. 100; GN, pp. 155–156 (GN interviewed HC in October 1978); BMG, p. 70; JK to AG, November 13, 1945, SL, pp. 100–101; VC, pp. 290–291, 445; Hal's fictional name is both "Val Hayes" and "Val King," according to G&L, p. 324.

[15]JK's lofty goals and delayed debut: JK to HC, April 19, 1947, SL, p. 107; JK to CKB, March 14, 1945, SL, p. 86–87; JK to MCE, November 21, 1953, SL, p. 402; GVP, p. 9; BMWB, p. 38.

[16]Effects of Benzedrine on Beats' writing and health: JK to AG, August 10, 1945; JK to AG, August 23, 1945, SL, p. 92; JK to CKB, March 14, 1945, SL, p. 86; BMWB, p. 40; ACKB, p. 61; VD, p. 262.

[17]T&C; AG as sounding board and sex partner; drug arrests; dissolution of the apartment; arrival of EW, NC, and LH on the Beat scene: author interview with RL; AG: *Allen Verbatim*, p. 152; T&C, p. 3; ACKB, pp. 58, 62, 64; G&L, pp. 46, 67, 100, 326 (LH appears as "Joanna Dawson" in VC; as Mary Lou in OR; and as Annie in SUB); CCOR, p. 26; transcript of a speech CC gave in London; BMWB, pp. 43–44, 78; WSB: "Dead on Arrival," *The Soft Machine*, p. 5; GN, pp. 58, 148, 176–177; VD, p. 260; OR, pp. 4, 6–8, 10, 131–132; BMG, pp. 79–80; SL, p. 116; JK to AG, May 18, 1952, and August 26, 1947, SL, pp. 356, 121; JK to HC, October 19, 1948, SL, p. 169; DM, p. 89; VC, pp. 77–78, 389, 445–449, 451–452, 478; FEP: "Ad-

denda," MSI, No.10, p. 18; WPHG, p. 64; ANEC, DA; GB, p. 15; Turner: *Angelheaded Hipster*, p. 79.

4: MUSCLES, MEAT, AND METAPHYSICS

[1]AG and NC's first sexual fling; LH: AGCP, "Many Loves," p. 156; BMG, p. 84; CC in interview with Gina Berriault, *Rolling Stone*, October 12, 1972, quoted in BMG, pp. 84, 85, 543; Ann Murphy quoted in WPHG, pp. 142–143; OR, p. 8 (AG appears as "Carlo Marx," G&L, p. 326, and NC as "Dean Moriarty," G&L, p. 324); JCHG, pp. 149–174; WPHG, p. 151; author interview with JS, KALM; FEP: "Addenda and Annotations," MSI, No.10, p. 18; VC, 418, G&L, p. 151.

[2]JK and NC in New York in 1947, NC's departure, New Year's 1947, and JK and AG's reconciliation: VC, p. 418; ANEC, DA; OR, p. 6; G&L, p. 67; T&C, pp. 498–499; BMG, p. 85; AE, p. iv; LC appears as "Julien Love" in VC, p. 264 (G&L, p. 324), and Vicki as herself (G&L, p. 330).

[3]JK's trip to North Carolina, the Beats' dispersal, and NC's influence on JK: Alex Albright: "Kerouac in Carolina," *Moody Street Irregulars*, No.16–17, Summer/1986, p. 37; Albright: "Satori in Rocky Mount," p. 36; JK to CKB and Paul Blake, March 20, 1947, SL, p. 105; JK to WSB, July 14, 1947, SL, p. 109; JB to FEP quoted by AC in SL, p. 108; NC to JK, March 7, 1947, PBR, pp. 191–192; GN, p. 186; ACKB, p. 76.

[4]AG's pursuits of JK and NC: BMG, pp. 95–98; NC to AG, March 30, 1947, AE, p. 11; NC to AG, April 10, 1947, AE, p. 16; NC to AG, quoted in CCOR, p. 18.

[5]AG and JK leave for Denver: BMG, p. 98; JK to WSB, July 14, 1947, SL, p. 108; AG to Mark Van Doren, June 1, 1948, ACKB, p. 377; JK to WSB, July 14, 1947, SL, p. 109; Tom Snyder: *Route 66: The Mother Road*, p. ix; OR, p. 15.

[6]JK with NC and CC in Denver: OR, p. 44; transcript of CC's London speech, "Of the Road," p. 26; VC, p. 242; CCOR, p. 28; Darlington: "Carolyn Cassady," MSI, No.24–25–26, p. 16; BS, pp. 136–137 (AC identifies CC as "Evelyn" in BS and BD and as "Camille" in OR, see PJK, pp. 619–620); ANEC, DA.

[7]JK forges a link with the West in Central City: OR, pp. 10, 41, 54; Gunther: p. 219; NC to AG, April 15, 1947, AE, p. 18; AG to JK, summer 1947, GN, p. 194; JK to AG, August 26, 1947, SL, p. 122.

[8]JK's jealousy of NC and AG, and negative first impression of San Francisco: JK to NC, August 26, 1947, SL, p. 115; OR, pp. 60–61; JK to CKB, September 25, 1947, SL, p. 131.

[9]Correspondence from San Francisco: NC as JK's mentor, and origins of Sal Paradise: JK to NC, August 26, 1947, SL, p. 118; AG: "Last Stanzas in Denver," ACKB, pp. 86, 377; JK to AG, August 26, 1947, SL, p. 120; AC, editor, SL, p. 120; JK to NC, September 13, 1947, SL, p. 126.

[10]Living with Cru, and gay bashing: JK to NC, August 26, September 13, 1947, SL, pp. 113, 127; JK to CKB, September 25, 1947, SL, pp. 130, 132.

[11]Screenplay attempts; homophobic attitude toward AG and NC; JK's hapless love life; Cru and his girl: JK to NC, August 26, 1947, SL, pp. 117–118; JK to EW, GN, p. 198 (also see OR, p. 63); JK to CKB, September 25, 1947, SL, p. 133; JK to AG, January 2, 1948; SL, p. 140; SL, p. 125; JK to NC, September 13, 1947, SL, p. 127–128.

[12]The scene on Burroughs's farm, summer 1947: VC, p. 180, 197–198; ANEC; BMWB, p. 45; DM, p. 99; Helen Hinkle in G&L, p. 134; BMWB, pp. 46–48; CCOR, p. 35; JCH in G&L, p. 128.

[13]Affair with Bea Franco: OR, pp. 81, 91; JK: "36th Chorus," *The San Francisco Blues*, p. 35; JK to NC, September 13, 1947, SL, p. 125.

[14]NC disappoints JK, AG, and CC, fall 1947: OR, pp. 106–107; BMWB, p. 49; CCOR, p. 44; NC to AG, December 30, 1947, CCOR, p. 49; NC to JK, December 1947, CCOR, p. 47; AG to NC, Fall 1947, AE, p. 27.

[15]NC's influence on T&C: JK to AG, January 2, May 18, 1948, SL, pp. 142, 152; JK: journal, in JCH to JK, November 30, 1948, *The Beat Diary*, TUVOTI 5, p. 117, TCJK, pp. 76, 230; NC to JK, October 5, 1947, SL, p. 133; NC to JK, CCOR, p. 50; NC, note, PBR, p. 189; JK to NC, May 7, 1948, SL, pp. 148–149.

[16]Relationships of JK, LC, AG, and NC in 1948, and finishing T&C: JK to AG, May 18, 1948,

SL, p. 152; JK to CKB, March 16, 1948, SL, p. 144; GN, pp. 204, 712; BMG, p. 95; JK to AG, January 2, 1948, SL, p. 140; WPHG, pp. 46, 48; NC to AG, September 1948, AE, BMG, p. 105; NC to AG, September 7, 1948, AE, pp. 50, 53; AG to NC, May 20, 1949, AE, p. 64; AG to JK, September 1948, GN, pp. 227, 713; JK to CGS, December 29, 1949; JK to AC, August 17, 1966, ACBWJK; JK to AG, April 1948, SL, p. 147; AG to NC, April 1948, AE, p. 34; NC to AG, May 1948, AE, p. 35; CCOR, p. 68.

[17]Maxwell Perkins, Scribner's, and T&C: JK to AG, April 1948, SL, p. 148; Clifton Daniel, editor: *Chronicle of the 20th Century*, p. 626; JK to AG, May 18, 1948, SL, p. 151; TCJK, p. 79; ACKB, p. 93.

[18]JK enters the Manhattan literary scene: BMG, p. 106; JCH: *Nothing More to Declare*, p. 48; JK to AG, November 17, 1948, SL, p. 171; JCHG, pp. xviii, 4, 18, 24, 27 ("The reader will have little trouble identifying the characters based on Jack Kerouac, Allen Ginsberg, Neal Cassady, Herbert Huncke. . . . Nor can I disclaim that Paul Hobbes bears a marked resemblance to the young man I was then. The character of Agatson was based on . . . Bill Cannastra"); Cannastra appears as "Finistra" in VC, and as himself in AG's "In Memoriam: William Cannastra, 1922–1950" and "Bayonne Entering NYC."

[19]Van Doren's support of T&C; JK's unrealistic expectations; plans for Beat ranch: JK to GK, June 15, 1948, SL, p. 153; JK to NC, June 27, 1948, SL, pp. 155–158; NC to JK, CCOR, p. 71; JK to NC and CC, July 10, 1948, SL, pp. 158–161; JK to HC, October 19, 1948, SL, p. 169; Charles A. Reich: *The Greening of America*, p. 4.

[20]Scribner's, Little, Brown reject T&C: JK to NC, September 5, 1948, SL, p. 162; TCJK, p. 79; DM, p. 103; JCHG, pp. 120–121; GN, p. 230; JK: "*On the Road* Journal," entries December 5, 6, 9, and 10, 1948, GN, pp. 233, 713; JK to NC, December 8, 1948, SL, p. 172.

[21]JK in Rocky Mount; relationship with Ann B.; denial of homosexuality: JK to NC, October 2 and 3, 1948, SL, pp. 165, 167–168; Ken Kesey: "Is There an End to Kerouac Highway?" in *50 Who Made the Difference*, p. 25.

[22]JK and Adele Mailer: Adele Mailer: *The Last Party: Scenes from My Life with Norman Mailer*, pp. 17–24, 34, 135, 209; Peter Manso: *Mailer: His Life and Times*, pp. 161, 163, 169; GN, p. 236.

[23]JK's New School courses: JK to AK, February 20, 1951, SL, p. 312; JM: "New School," KAWB, p. 51; JK to HC, October 19, 1948, SL, p. 170.

[24]NC leaves CC to be with JK: JK to NC, December 8, 1948, SL, p. 173; Brian F. Murphy: "Cross-Country Trip 'Like Driving Down the Street,'" LS, unpaged, undated clipping, Pollard Memorial Library; CCOR, pp. 75–77, 78–79; G&L, p. 123; JK to AG, December 15, 1948, SL, p. 177.

[25]NC's departure from the West Coast, and JK's last days in New York: JK to NC, December 8, 1948, SL, p. 175; WPHG; CCOR, p. 75; Brian Murphy: "Cross-Country Trip," LS, undated clipping, Pollard Memorial Library; JCHG, p. 122; JK to NC, December 15, 1948, SL, p. 179; JK to AG, December 15, 1948, SL, p. 179.

[26]The dumping of Helen Hinkle and NC's Denver detour: CCOR, pp. 108, 111; WPHG, p. 51; Murphy: "Cross-Country," LS; DM, p. 112; VC, p. 457; WPHG, pp. 50, 53; OR, p. 112.

[27]Christmas 1948 in Rocky Mount and NC's arrival: DA, p. 313; JS, KALM; SL, note, p. 164; John J. Dorfner: *Kerouac: Visions of Rocky Mount*, p. 9; Dorfner: "Kerouac Is Remembered in Rocky Mount," MSI No. 28, Fall/1994, p. 30. DB, p. 105; Albright: "Satori," p. 37; dust jacket, front, JJMC; GN, p. 339; OR, p. 110; VC, p. 457; G&L, p. 124.

[28]JK and NC on the road between North Carolina and New York; CC's plight in San Francisco: NC quoted by JK, ANEC, DA; "More from Alex Albright: Kerouac in Carolina," MSI No.16–17, p. 37; JK to NC, December 8, 1948, SL, p. 174; CCOR, pp. 80–81.

[29]New Year's 1949 and NC's attack on LH: NC to JK, January 7, 1948; GN, p. 246; OR, p. 126; JCHG, pp. 65, 115, 135, 176; NC to AG, March 15, 1949, AE, p. 54; CCOR, pp. 88, 177; NC to JK, CCOR, p. 100; AG to NC, May 1949, AE, p. 57.

[30]JK-NC 1949 New York–New Orleans–San Francisco cross-country trip: CCOR, pp. 112–114; NC to AG, March 15, 1949, AE, p. 55; G&L, p. 138; VC, p. 449; OR, p. 161; GN, p. 256, 260 (Alan Harrington appears as "Hingham" in OR).

[31]JK and LH adrift in San Francisco: G&L, pp. 140–141, 170; JK to NC, January 8, 1951, SL, p. 275; OR, pp. 139, 170, 171, 173.

³²JK and NC's bitter parting in San Francisco: CCOR, pp. 84–85, 87; AG to NC, May 1949, AE, p. 56; OR, pp. 171, 177–178.

5: SUCKING ASSES TO GET PUBLISHED

¹JK in early 1949 and T&C accepted for publication: JK to Mark Van Doren, March 9, 1949, SL p. 184; GN, p. 265; BMG, p. 110; PR, p. 386; JK to AG, June 29, 1955, SL, p. 490; "On the Road Journal," December 1, 1948, GN, pp. 228–229; David Diamond to AC, April 9 and May 3, 1973, ACKB, pp. 107, 379 (AC interviewed RG, October 18, 1972); JK to AK, March 1, 1951, SL, p. 314; RG: "Introduction," *500 Best American Films to Buy, Rent or Videotape*, p. xxv; RG: *The Education of an Editor*, pp. 29, 31–32; Michael Mott: *The Seven Mountains of Thomas Merton*, p. 99; Monica Furlong: *Merton: A Biography*, p. 153; JK to EW, May 29, 1949, SL, p. 185; JK to NC, December 8, 1948, SL, p. 172; JK: Journal entry, March 29, 1949, in AG and JK: *Take Care of My Ghost, Ghost*, unnumbered, TCJK, pp. 84, 231; JK to EW, March 29, 1949, SL, p. 186 (also quoted in *Street Magazine*, 2, No.4, 1978, p. 47, and in TCJK, pp. 84, 231); G&L, p. 144; *Variety*, David Halberstam: *The Fifties*, p. 186.

²Reactions of friends and teachers to T&C contract: NC to JK, CCOR, p. 94; BMG, pp. 110, 112 (JK and AG used the code name "Claude" to protect LC, who was on parole, G&L, p. 324); AG to NC, May 1949, AE, pp. 56–57, 60; Diana Trilling: *The Beginning*, p. 372; SL, note, p. 184; JK to AK, March 1, 1951, SL, p. 314.

³Relationship of JK and RG: G&L, pp. 78, 80; RG: *The Education*, pp. 13–14, 16; RG: "Introduction," *Bernard Malamud: The People and Uncollected Stories*, p. xv; JK to AG, July 26, 1949, SL, p. 209; JK to NC, July 28, 1949, SL, p. 214.

⁴JK and Gore Vidal: JK to AH, April 23, 1949, SL, p. 188. GVP, pp. 217–218, 233–234; ANEC, DA, VD; JK: *Some of The Dharma*, p. 402.

⁵JK in Denver; RG's visit; JK's attitude toward publishers; AG's arrest; Baldwin and Cleaver: JK to EW, March 29, 1949, SL, p. 186; JK to HC, May 15, 1949, SL, p. 190; JK to AG, June 10, 1949, SL, p. 191; Ivan Goldman: "Kerouac's Friend," *Denver Post*, January 1, 1965, p. 49, TCKB, pp. 85–87, 231; ANEC, DA; JK to JCH, June 24, 1949, SL, p. 196; G&L, pp. 79–80; ACKB, pp. 110, 379; JK to AG, July 26, 1949, SL, p. 210; Clarke: *Capote*, pp. 129, 135; JK to NC, July 28, 1949, SL, pp. 212–213, 215–216; JK to PW, March 6, 1956, SL, p. 565; BMG, pp. 109, 114, 121, 124; AG to NC, May 1949, AE, p. 58; "Wrong Way Turn Clears Up Robbery," *New York Times*, April 22, 1949, p. 1, ACKB, p. 108, and DM, p. 361; GN, p. 268; SL, note, p. 187; AG to JK, BMG, p. 119; JK to AG, June 10, 1949, SL, p. 191; AG to JCH, June 16, 1949, TUVOTI, No.10, p. 104, TCKB, pp. 85, 231; WSB to JK, BMG, p. 122; DM, p. 120; OR, p. 180; author (as editor-in-chief of the Delacorte Press) in conversation with James Baldwin, Dell Publishing Company luncheon, Paris; Eldridge Cleaver: *Soul on Ice*, p. 71, ACKB, pp. 379–380; ANEC.

⁶JK arrives Russian Hill, 1949, and JK and NC drive and hitchhike to New York: NC to JK, CCOR, p. 100; NC to AG, March 15, 1949, CCOR, p. 93; ACKB, pp. 111–112; OR, pp. 182, 189, 212, 241, 245; VC, pp. 462, 463, 473, 478, 481, 487; CCOR, p. 100; AC: "Introduction," VC, p. 11; ANEC (JK confirmed that he was jealous when NC had sex with the gay man, and this precipitated his fight with NC in the toilet); TCJK, p. 88.; WPHG, p. 64; JK to CKB, courtesy of JS, KALM (JS told me that JK's exact words were that Edie was a "head case").

⁷NC and Diana Hansen: G&L, pp. 149–150, 326; CCOR, p. 117; VC, p. 494; Daniel Pinchbeck: "Children of the Beats," p. 43; VC, p. 494; DM, p. 127; ANEC, DA; OR, pp. 230, 246, 250; JK to EL, September 28, 1949, SL, pp. 218–219.

⁸Friendship with RG; controversy over cuts; Mailer and his editor; dust jacket; CGS: G&L, p. 150; JK to EL, September 28, 1949, SL, pp. 218–219; GN, pp. 283–284, 300; RG to JK, November 1, 1949, DM, p. 123; H, p. 39; Manso: *Mailer*, pp. 107–108; JK to CGS, December 27, 1949, SL, pp. 220–221; JK: *Some of the Dharma*, p. 128.

⁹AG and "Pull My Daisy": In AGCP, AG printed "Fie My Fum" on p. 23 as his own poem, composed of seven verses. The longer "Pull My Daisy" appears on the following two pages and is attributed to AG, JK, and NC (New York, Spring-Fall 1949). Also see DM, p. 126; AGCP: "Author's Cover Writ," p. 813; BMG, pp. 124–125, 128.

¹⁰JK and Auden: BMG, p. 123; ANEC; Davenport-Hines: *Auden*, pp. 232, 241; JK to SSK, October 12, 1955, SL, p. 527.

¹¹JK and Adele Morales's affair: Adele Mailer: *The Last Party: Scenes from My Life with Norman Mailer*, pp. 34, 51–55 ff, 349; KALM, courtesy JS; ANEC, DA; JK to Ed White, November 30, 1948, GN, pp. 235–236, 714; Manso: *Mailer*, pp. 190–191, 271–272, 329; Hilary Mills in *Mailer: A Biography*, p. 129, writes of Adele, "Her limited education gave her a certain insecurity."

¹²Critical reception, T&C: ANEC, DA; John Brooks: "Of Growth and Decay," *New York Times Book Review*, March 5, 1950, p. 6; "War and Peace," *Newsweek*, March 13, 1950, p. 80; JK to Yvonne Le Maître, September 8, 1950, SL, p. 227–229; Howard Mumford Jones: "Back to Merrimack," *Saturday Review*, March 11, 1950, p. 18; "Briefly Noted," *New Yorker*, March 25, 1950, p. 115; Hugh F. Downey, "Books," LS, February 26, 1950; CGS: "Sampascoopies: And About a Lowell Novel That Will Make History," LS, January 4, 1950, p. 16; SM in film on JK, courtesy PC; JK to NC, December 3, 1950, SL, p. 239.

¹³Hustling; Latouche; Auden; Carr; Cannastra's loft; painting: TCJK, p. 88; PR, p. 373; Alan Ansen: journal entry, late February 1948, Davenport-Hines, pp. 246, 381; AG to NC, November 18, 1950, AE, p. 82 (LC is referred to as "Claude," which was the practice of his friends, to protect him from possible parole difficulties); AG: *Journals Mid-Fifties 1954–1958*, p. 24.

¹⁴JK, JHK, AG, and sex in Cannastra's loft: SL, note, p. 235; JK to NC, December 3, 1950, SL, p. 238; AG to NC, November 18, 1950, AE, pp. 81–82; PR, pp. 372–373; Alfred Aronowitz: "Jack Kerouac: Beyond the Road," *New York Post*, October 22, 1969, ACKB, pp. 121, 381; JCHG, p. 266; AGCP: "Howl," p. 129.

¹⁵Rivalry with LC over female colleague: JS, KALM; GN, p. 320; JK to AG, October 8, 1952, SL, p. 380.

¹⁶JK's Denver book-signing trip: TCJK, p. 91; CCOR, p. 119; OR, pp. 276, 284.

¹⁷JK and NC visit Burroughs in Mexico City: OR, pp. 280, 285, 301–302, 306, JK to Jim Sampas, August 1, 1950, DA, p. 274, BMWB, p. 51; WSB to Kells Elvins, BMWB, p. 51; BMG, p. 130; JK to JCH, July 11–12, 1950, DM, p. 129, and TCJK, p. 92.

¹⁸JK's search for his own voice; summer in Provincetown: JK journal entry, Fall 1950, note, SL, p. 230, and JK to NC, October 6, 1950, SL, pp. 232–233; GN, p. 327; Hilary Mills: *Mailer: A Biography*, p. 123; Manso: *Mailer*, p. 176; BMC, pp. 132 133.

¹⁹JCH supports early OR: Moore: KAWB, p. 82; DM, p. 130.

²⁰JK, Cannastra, et al. in bar fight: JCHG, pp. 265, 267; AG to NC, October 31, 1950, AE, p. 70; BM: *Greenwich Village*, Beard, editor, p. 172; JK to NC, December 3, 1950, p. 240–241.

²¹Cannastra's death and its impact on early Beats: AG to NC, October 31, November 18 and 25, 1950, AE, pp. 71–72, 81, 100; BM: *Greenwich Village*, Beard, editor, p. 172; ANEC, DA, VD; GN, p. 332; JCHG, pp. 302–303, 305–306; VC, pp. 271–272; AGCP: "Bayonne Entering NYC," p. 421, "In Memoriam: William Cannastra, 1922–1950," p. 57, "Howl," p. 129; Tennessee Williams: *Memoirs*, pp. 105–106; Donald Spoto: *The Kindness of Strangers: The Life of Tennessee Williams*, pp. 185–186; G&L, p. 154.

²²AG re Cannastra's loft, LC, GC, and Larry Rivers: AG to NC, Summer 1950, AE, p. 70 (see G&L, p. 324); AG to NC, January 1952, AE, p. 115 (according to BMG, p. 140, GC denied having sex with AG, saying, "That Ginzie, he'll say anything"); BMG, p. 134.

²³JK and JHK get married: G&L, p. 326; OR, p. 306; AG to NC, November 18, 1950, AE, pp. 81–82; JK to NC, November 21, 1950, SL, p. 236; JK to NC, December 3, 1950, SL, p. 238; JCH to AG, December 12, 1950, DM, pp. 131, 363; NC to AG, November 25, 1950, AE, pp. 85, 90; JK: VC; SL, note, p. 236; AG to NC, May 7, 1951, AE, p. 107.

²⁴JK's wedding night; early days of marriage: JK to NC, November 21, 1950, SL, p. 236; NC to JK, CCOR, p. 133; GN, pp. 334–335; JK to NC, December 3, 1950, SL, p. 238; JK and JCH to NC, December 14, 1950, CCOR, p. 135.

²⁵NC's pessimism re JK's marriage; NC and CC's sex issues: CCOR, p. 133; NC to AG, November 25, 1950, AE, pp. 88–89, 90; *Rolling Stone*, WPHG, p. 82; NC to AG, May 15, 1951, AE, p. 110; CC to NC, CCOR, p. 129; JK to SSK, December 10, 1952, SL, p. 391; JM: "Kerouac and the New School," KAWB, p. 53; CCOR, p. 152.

²⁶JK and JHK move in with Mémère: JK to NC, December 3, 1950, SL, pp. 237–238; JK journal, SL, note, p. 238; Halberstam: *The Fifties*, p. 69; GN, p. 339.

²⁷JK on Faulkner and Hemingway: JK to MCE, September 11, 1955, SL, p. 515; JK to JCH,

October 12, 1955, SL, p. 524; JK to PW, March 6, 1956, SL, p. 565; JK to NC, August 31, 1951, SL, p. 325; JK to NC, December 27, 1950, SL, p. 242.

[28]The "Joan Anderson Letter" and its influence: AC to NC, February or March 1951, AE, pp. 101–102, lists the date of the "Letter" as December 17, and in PBR, AC, p. 197, dates the letter as "Dec. 17 (?), 1950"; SL, note, p. 241; JK to NC, December 27, 1950, SL, pp. 242–244; JK to NC, October 6, 1950, SL, pp. 232–233; JK to NC, December 3, 1950, SL, p. 239; PR, pp. 364–365; JS, KALM; NC to JK, Dec. 17(?), 1950, "From 'Joan Anderson' letter to Jack Kerouac," PBR, pp. 202–203; PBR, p. 189; NC to AG, March 17, 1951, AE, p. 104; AG to NC, December 18, 1950, DM, p. 363.

[29]JHK moves out; JK and NC part in New York: JK to AK, February 20, 1951, SL, p. 312; JK to NC, January 10, 1951, SL, p. 307; JK to NC, December 3, 1950, SL, p. 238; NC to JK, CCOR, p. 133; VC, p. 522, 525–526; GN, p. 339–340; NC to CC, CCOR, p. 138.

[30]JK confides marital woes to AK and Seymour Wyse: JK to AK, February 20, 1951, SL, p. 312; GN, p. 350.

[31]JHK's, WSB's, and NC's impact on OR; some reactions to *Junky*: JK to NC, May 22, 1951, SL, p. 316; *Saturday Review*, September 28, 1957, ACKB, pp. 124, 381; GN, p. 343; PBR, p. 189; BMWB, p. 52; AG to NC, CCOR, p. 144; Norman Mailer: back ad blurb, WSB, *Naked Lunch*.

[32]Scroll version of OR: Dave Moore: "*On the Road*: The Scroll Revealed," *The Kerouac Connection* No. 10, April 1986; JK to NC, May 22, 1951, SL, p. 316; videotape, "Steve Allen Show," *On the Road with Jack Kerouac*; NC to JK, "April's Fool" 1951, CCOR, p. 141; JHK to JK, August 8, 1951, Eugene Brooks collection; JHK: "My Ex-Husband," *Confidential*, p. 56; DM, pp. 134, 363; G&L, pp. 156–157; BCBG, p. 74; ACKB, pp. 127–128; GN, p. 343; David Stanford: "About the Manuscript," *Some of the Dharma*, unpaged preface.

[33]Reactions to OR scroll: G&L, p. 157; JK to NC, June 10, 1951, SL, p. 318; AG to NC, May 7, 1951, AE, pp. 106–107; JK to AG, October 8, 1952, SL, p. 377; JK to NC, May 22, 1951, SL, p. 315; NC to JK, CCOR, p. 145; JK to NC, June 24, 1951, SL, p. 320; DM, p. 135.

[34]How RG lost OR: JK to NC, June 24, 1951, SL, p. 320; ACKB, p. 128 (AC interviewed RG, October 20, 1972, and also see SL, note, p. 320; Bruce Cook: *The Beat Generation*, p. 75; TCKB, p. 96); JK to AG, October 8, 1952, SL, pp. 377, 379; GN, p. 349; ACKB, p. 381; JK: "Beatific: On the Origins of the Beat Generation," *Playboy*, June 1959, PJK, p. 570; JK to NC, June 24, 1951, SL, p. 320; ACBWJK; JK to RG, late summer 1954, SL, p. 445.

[35]Passionate nature of JK and JHK's relationship; question of Jan Kerouac's paternity: JS, KALM (notebook entries used with the kind permission of JS); VC, p. 72; CCOR, p. 152; Paul Brouillette: "Interview with Joe Chaput," MSI, No.3, Winter/1979, p. 9

[36]Thrombophlebitis attack; AG's pursuit of LC: JK to NC, August 31, 1951, SL, p. 325.

[37]WSB kills Joan: DM, p. 157; SL, note, p. 340; WSB to AG, March 1962, BMWB, p. 56; WSB: *Queer*, pp. vii, xviii, xx, 21; BMG, pp. 136–138, 172, 174, 545; Associated Press: "Heir's Pistol Kills His Wife; He Denies Playing Wm. Tell," *New York Daily News*, September 8, 1951, p. 3; AG to NC, January 1952, AE, p. 115; CCOR, pp. 151–152; GN, p. 355. BMWB, pp. 52–53, 64, 71; VC, p. 73, 195, 247; JK to AG, May 10, 1952, quoted in ACKB, pp. 153, 384–385; G&L, p. 323; AGCP: "The Names," p. 177; AGCP: "Dream Record: June 8, 1955, p. 124.

[38]JK jailed: SL, note, p. 325; JK to NC, October 1, 1951, SL, p. 325; JK to SSK, August 30, 1951, SL, p. 323; author interview with JS; JK to Frank Morley, July 27, 1950, SL, p. 226; JK to NC, June 24, 1951, SL, p. 320; AG to JK and NC, early 1952, AE, p. 126.

[39]VC as "vertical" OR: SL, note, pp. 326–327; ACKB, p. 383; author interview with PC; VC, pp. 7,152; ANEC, DA.

[40]OR and *Junky* go to Ace: WSB: *Queer*, pp. xxii–xxiii; BMWB, pp. 54, 58; JK to James Laughlin, July 30, 1951, SL, p. 321; JK to James Laughlin, February 24, 1952, SL, p. 333.

[41]JK goes to live with the Cassadys: NC to JK, quoted in CCOR, pp. 145–147; JK: notebook entry, ACKB, p. 136; LT, p. 15; CC to JK, CCOR, p. 147; CCOR, pp. 159–160; JK to JCH, February 8, 1952, SL, p. 338.

[42]JK and CC's affair: CCOR, pp. 163, 166–167, 169; JK sexual intercourse list, courtesy JS, KALM.

[43]JK and NC create VC: CCOR, p. 161; JK: "Note," VC, 1959 New Directions edition; VC, 1980 Panther paperback edition, pp. 27, 175, 414; JK: "The First Word: Jack Kerouac Takes a Fresh Look at Jack Kerouac," *Escapade*, January 1, 1967, PJK, p. 482; PR, p. 376; Douglas

Brinkley: "Breakthrough: Thirteen Scholars and Critics Share Their Favorite Works," *Lingua Franca*, June/July 1997, p. 14.

44AG undercuts JK at Ace: JK to CS, December 27, 1951, SL, p. 328; TCKB, pp. 106, 108; SL, note, p. 333.

45JK and the Cassadys part company: WSB to JK, SL, note, p. 339; JK to AG, May 10, 1952, SL, pp. 348, 350; ANEC, DA.

46JK and WSB in Mexico City; *Dr. Sax*: JK to AG, May 10, 1952, SL, pp. 352–353; DM, p. 159; WSB: *Junky*, pp. 122, 133; JK to JCH, June 5, 1952, SL, p. 369; ACKB, p. 159; PR, p. 378; ACBWJK; WSB to AG, BMG, p. 148; author interview with PC; WSB: *Queer*, p. 12.

47Loan request; sex issues between AG, NC, and CC: JK to CC, CCOR, p. 188; NC to AG, May 20, 1952, AE (also quoted in CCOR, p. 183); AG to CC, CCOR, p. 185.

48JK completes *Dr. Sax*; reactions: Albright: "More from Alex Albright . . . Kerouac in Carolina," MSI, No.16–17, p. 37; JK to CC, June 3, 1952, SL, p. 363; Dorfner: "Kerouac Is Remembered in Rocky Mount," MSI, No.29, p. 30; JK: notebook entry, used with the kind permission of JS, KALM; JK to NC, July 28, 1949, SL, p. 212; JK to SSK, October 12, 1955, SL, p. 527; TCKB, p. 176; DM, pp. 160, 162; JK to HC, October 19, 1948, SL, p. 169; GN, p. 410; DS, pp. 5, 30, 53, 57, 215–216.

49AG denounces OR, VC, and DS: AG to JK, June 11, 1952, SL, p. 373; AG to NC, July 3, 1952, AE, p. 130; AG: "Introduction," VC, pp. 8, 13–14.

50JK's rage at AG and Ace for rejecting OR/VC: JK to SSK, December 10, 1952, SL, p. 390; JK to AG, October 8, 1952, SL, pp. 378–380; BMG, p. 134; JK to "Carl, Mr. Wyn, Miss James," August 5, 1952, SL, pp. 376–377; Mellow: *Hemingway: A Life Without Consequences*, pp. 92, 105; JK to CC, CCOR, p. 188 (also quoted in SL, note, p. 375).

51Reconciliation with JCH, reunion with the Cassadys: JK to JCH, SL, note, p. 375; WPHC, p. 91; CC to JK, CCOR, p. 192; JK to JCH, October 12, 1952, SL, p. 381, CCOR, pp. 193–194; NC to AG, June 29, 1953, AE, p. 151.

52JK and NC as railroad men: JK: "[October in] The Railroad Earth," *Lonesome Traveler*, pp. 39–40, 64; CCOR, p. 195; G&L, p. 164; NC to AG, October 4, 1952, AE, pp. 133–134.

53Failure of JK and the Cassadys' open-marriage experiment: CCOR, pp. 196–197; ANEC; DS, p. 50; NC to AG, October 4, 1952, AE, p. 133; JK to JCH, October 12, 1952, SL, p. 381; JK to AG, November 8, 1952, SL, p. 384.

54JK as a flophouse " 'bo"; meeting Billie Holiday: LT, p. 173; JK to JCH, October 12, 1952, SL, p. 382; JK to JCH, June 3, 1952, SL, p. 366.

55JK and CC as lovers; JK and NC go to Mexico City; JK settles there: JK to AG, November 8, 1952, SL, p. 384; CCOR, p. 198; JK to SSK, December 10, 1952, SL, pp. 389–390; CCOR, pp. 208, 210; BMG, p. 154; JK to JCH, December 9, 1952, SL, pp. 387–388; JK to NC and CC, December 9, 1952, SL, pp. 385–386; NC to CC, July 27, 1958, GB, pp. 30–31; ACKB, pp. 225–226; WSB: *Junky*, ACKB, p. 225; JK to NC and CC, January 10, 1953, SL, p. 395; JK to JCH, October 12, 1952, SL, p. 382; JK to JCH, June 5, 1952, SL, p. 371.

56JK unwittingly restores Cassady marriage: JK to NC and CC, December 9, 1952, SL, pp. 386–387; CCOR, pp. 203–204, 208.

57JK and JCH vie to launch "Beat Generation"; negative aspects of JK's relationships with JCH and AG: G&L, pp. 170–171; GN, p. 423; SL, note, p. 387; SSK to JK, quoted in JK to JCH, December 9, 1952, SL, p. 388; JK to SSK, December 30, 1952, SL, p. 391; author interview with Aida Panagiotakos; JK to SSK, December 10, 1952, SL, p. 390; JK to JCH, October 12, 1952, SL, p. 383; JK to AG, October 8, 1952, SL, pp. 377–379; JK to AG, November 8, 1952, SL, pp. 383–384; JK to JCH, June 3, 1952, SL, p. 368; AG to NC, January 1953, AE, p. 138 (also quoted in SL, note, p. 392); JCHG, p. xx.

58JK returns to Queens; finds old friends unattractive; visits Charles Van Doren; Mark Van Doren rejects *Dr. Sax*: GN: "Joe Chaput," MSI No.18–19, Fall/1987, p. 17; AG to NC, January 1953, AE, p. 137; JK to NC and CC, January 10, 1953, SL, p. 396; AG to NC, June 23, 1953, AE, p. 147; JK to AG, December 28, 1952, SL, p. 392; JK to AG, May 1954, SL, p. 414; Mark Van Doren quoted in JK to AG, May 1954, SL, p. 414.

59JK's Buddhism negated by alcoholism: AG to NC, May 14, 1953, AE, p. 141; AG to NC, January 1953, AE, p. 137; CCOR, p. 205.

60TCJK, p. 120.

61JK's continuing conflict with AG in 1953; MC completed; *Junky* published: JK to NC and

CC, CCOR, p. 206; CCOR, p. 207; GN, p. 427; JK to AG, February 21, 1953, SL, p. 398; JK to AG, February 21, 1953, DM, pp. 170, 367; G&L, p. 173; TCJK, p. 120.

[62]Phyllis Jackson establishes the crucial connection between MCE and OR; Canada trip: G&L, pp. 173, 187–188; Phyllis Jackson in conversation with the author, Coward-McCann, Inc.; JK to CC, SL, note, p. 397; SL, note, p. 430; JK to CC, SL, note, pp. 397, 430; JK to CC, CCOR, p. 209; JK to CC, December 3, 1953, SL, p. 403; JK to MCE quoted in JK to AG, May 20, 1955, SL, p. 482; BD, pp. 142, 76, 118, TCKB, p. 234; JK to AG, TCKB, p. 121.

[63]NC's injury, JK's railroad job in Santa Margarita, SS *William Carruth* voyage: NC to Father Harley, August 4, 1958, GB, p. 37; JK to GK, April 25, 1953, SL, p. 399; TCKB, p. 121; JK: "Slobs of the Kitchen Sea," LT, pp. 86–87, 90–91, 94, 102; AG to NC, June 23, 1953, AE, p. 146; CCOR, p. 214; AG: *Snapshot Poetics*, p. 28.

[64]AG resumes agenting JK; AG begins to build JK's career: G&L, pp. 187–188; MCE to AG, July 14, 1953, DM, p. 171; ACKB, p. 198.

6: ORGASM, BUDDHISM, AND THE ART OF WRITING

[1]"Subterranean" scenes at AG's and Mailer's apartments: JK to NC and CC, TCKB, p. 126; Manso, pp. 171–173; Adele Mailer: *The Last Party*, pp. 76, 79 ff; BMG, pp. 155–156.

[2]JK's affair with Alene Lee: BM: *Greenwich Village*, Beard, editor, p. 176 (BM refers to her as "Arlene Lee," but JK's sex list, KALM, lists her as "Alene Lee." According to JS, Alene Lee died in 1995. In SL, note, p. 408, AC, editor, refers to "Alene, the young woman he had called Mardou in *The Subterraneans*"); JK sex list, JS, KALM; SUB, pp. 2, 6, 36–38, 47, 49, 56, 62, 64, 72, 76; G&L, pp. 175–176, 182, 331–332.

[3]JK and GV have sex at the Chelsea: JK to SLA, October 7, 1956, SL, p. 590; G&L, p. 328; SUB, p. 54; GVP, pp. 228, 230–234, 262; ANEC, DA; JK to MCE, November 21, 1953, SL, p. 402; Mills: *Mailer*, p. 189.

[4]End of JK and Alene's affair: author interview with PC; JK to AG, May 1954, SL, p. 413; G&L, p. 176.

[5]SUB as prose innovation; MCE's campaign; JK's attack on GV; depression; departure for California: GN, "Catching Up with Kerouac," KAWB, p. 111; SUB, p. 67; G&L, p. 323–324, 326; JK to MCE, May 9, 1956, p. 576, and November 21, 1953, SL, p. 402; BD, p. 20; JK to CC, December 3, 1953, SL, p. 403.

[6]JK's Buddhism; NC's veneration for Cayce: JK to CC, CCOR, p. 239; JK to NC and CC, CCOR, p. 239; CCOR, p. 235; Edgar Cayce: *A Meditation Guide*, p. 4; Edgar Cayce: *The Edgar Cayce Handbook for Health*, pp. 129, 140; Edgar Evans Cayce and Hugh Lynn Cayce, editor: *Edgar Cayce on Atlantis*, passim; Ruth Montgomery: *Here and Hereafter*, pp. 187–188; Lynn Elwell Sparrow: *Reincarnation: An Edgar Cayce Guide*, passim; *Bhagavad-Gita (As It Is)*, translated by A. C. Bhaktivedanta Swami Prabhupada, passim; Ken Kesey: "Is There an End," *50 Who*, p. 24. JK to CC, April 15, 1955, SL, p. 477; DA, p. 229, also quoted in MSI, No.12, Fall/1982, p. 4; JK to AG, May 1954, SL, p. 416; *Los Angeles Times* quoted on back ad, ACKB.

[7]Deterioration of JK-NC-CC relationship; expulsion of AG: SL, notes, pp. 408, 442; TCKB, p. 132; JK to CC, August 26, 1954, SL, p. 443; JK to AG, GN, pp. 460, 725–726; CCOR, pp. 236, 245; CC journal entry, CCOR, p. 235; AGCP: "Love Poem on Theme by Whitman," p. 115; JK to CC, August 26, 1954, SL, p. 441 (also quoted in CCOR, p. 247); WSB to JK, BMG, p. 169 (AC attributes the same quotation to WSB to AG, SL, p. 442; ANEC, DA).

[8]JK writes *San Francisco Blues*: JTJ, pp. 8, 18; LT, p. v; JK: *San Francisco Blues*, Penguin 1995 edition, no page listed; JS: "A Note on Sources," *San Francisco Blues*, p. 81; JK to AG, May 1954, SL, p. 411; JK: *Pomes All Sizes*, pp. iv, vi; GN, p. 465.

[9]Exasperation with editors; continuing struggle to get published: ACKB, p. 195; JK to CC, April 22, 1954, SL, p. 408; NC to AG, April 23, 1954, AE, p. 178 (also quoted in TCJK, pp. 133, 235); JK to AG, May 1954, SL, p. 413; JK to CC, August 26, 1954, SL, p. 443; JK to CC, May 17, 1954, SL, p. 423; JK: *Some of the Dharma*, p. 18; OR, p. 309; JK to AG, August 23, 1954, SL, p. 434; JK to AG, TCKB, p. 133; AG to NC, November 14, 1953, AE, p. 157; JK to AG, August 23, 1954, SL, p. 434; JK to AG, August 23, 1954, SL, pp. 433–434; JK to SLA, August 14, 1954, SL, pp. 432, 436.

[10]Sterling Lord: ACKB, p. 217; TCJK, p. 134; JK to SLA, August 14, 1954, SL, p. 432; DM, pp. 187, 369.

¹¹Attitudes toward Buddhism, masturbation, and women: TCKB, p. 134; JK to AG, August 23, 1954, SL, p. 438; JK to AC, July 14, 1954, SL, p. 499.

¹²"cityCityCITY": JK to AG, July 14, 1955, SL, p. 495; JK to WSB, May 1955, SL, p. 480; JK to CC, August 26, 1954, SL, p. 442; Gregory Stephenson: "Kerouac's Dystopia: 'cityCity-CITY,'" MSI 13, Summer/1983, p. 8; JK: "Essentials of Spontaneous Prose," Evergreen Review, Summer/1958, pp. 72–73.

¹³JK to AK, October 27, 1954, SL, p. 449.

¹⁴Lowell visit; "beatific": JK to SSK, October 12, 1955, p. 527, and December 10, 1952, SL, pp. 389–390; JK to CGS, undated; VG, p. 48; JK: "Beatific: The Origins of the Beat Genera-tion," PJK, pp. 571–572; JK:"Lamb, No Lion," PJK, pp. 562–564; BL, p. 45; DA, p. 74; ANEC, DA; JK: Some of the Dharma, pp. 122, 142, 286.

¹⁵Comparison of JK and Mailer in the 1950s; encounters with Mailer; Cecil Taylor: DA, pp. 74–75; G&L, p. 328 (Adele Morales appears as "Estella"); Mills: Mailer, pp. 160, 186; Manso: Mailer, pp. 211, 218.

¹⁶1955 child-support litigation; Knopf and others decline OR; appearance of "Jazz of the Beat Generation": JK: journal entry, December 19, 1954, published as "Jack Kerouac Tells the Truth," Robert Lowry's Book USA, Fall/1958, no pagination, DM, p. 191; JK to AG, January 18, 1955, SL, pp. 457–458; GN, pp. 458, 462, 471; JK to SLA, January 23, 1955, SL, p. 466–468; Donald Allen quotation appeared in H, courtesy Pollard Memorial Library, Lowell; Robert Duncan, BMG, p. 183; JM: "Kerouac West Coast," KAWB; JK: Dharma, p. 221.

¹⁷JK in Rocky Mount; rattled instructions to agent; betrayal of CC and pursuit of NC: JK to NC, April 15, 1955, SL, pp. 471–472; JK to SLA, March 25, 1955, SL, p. 469; Albright: "More from Alex Albright," MSI, No.16–17, Summer/1986; DB, p. 116; JK to AG, July 14, 1955, SL, p. 494; CCOR, pp. 255, 257, 261; ACKB, pp. 17, 382; AG: Journals Mid-Fifties, p. 136; JTJ, p. 87; JK: Dharma, pp. 201, 268, 289, 297–298, 300, 418–419.

¹⁸Buddha Tells All and the crisis with SLA and RG: JK to AG, July 14, 1955, p. 498, May 20, 1955, p. 484, May 27, 1955, p. 485, SL; JM: "Kerouac West Coast"; SL, p. 488; JK: Dharma, p. 395.

¹⁹First-serial rights OR: ACKB, p. 390; GN, p. 474; JK to SLA, July 19, 1955, SL, p. 504; SL, p. 501; JK to MCE, July 19, 1955, SL, p. 502; SLA to JK, SL, note, p. 488; JK to MCE, July 4, 1955, SL, p. 493.

²⁰JK meets with MCE and Jennison in New York: GN, p. 476; JK to AG, June 29, 1955, SL, p. 490; JK to MCE, July 4, 1955, SL, p. 493; JK to AG, July 14, 1955, SL, p. 495; JK to MCE, July 19, 1955, SL, p. 502; TRIS, Avon back cover; JK to SLA, July 19, 1955, SL, p. 504; JK: Dharma, p. 331.

²¹JK keeps SLA busy circulating manuscripts: JK: Dharma, p. 308; JK to AG, June 29, 1955, SL, p. 492.

²²Suffering from ill health, JK begs MCE for money: JK to MCE, July 4, 1955, SL, p. 493 (also quoted in DM, p. 194).

²³JK goes to Mexico City; affair with Esperanza Villanueva: SL, note, p. 505; JK to MCE, July 19, 1955, SL, pp. 502–503; JK to AG, August 7, 1955, SL, pp. 505–506; GN, p. 476; JK sex list, KALM, courtesy JS; TCJK, p. 139; DM, pp. 195–196; G&L, p. 191; ACKB, pp. 225, 230; GN, p. 477; TRIS, pp. 7–8, 10, 12, 18, 28, 53, 58; BMG, p. 216; JK: Dharma, pp. 100, 114, 335–336.

²⁴JK's ministry; religious influence on AG; sex list: DB, pp. 6, 10; G&L, p. 215; BMG, p. 176; JK: Wake Up, Tricycle, No.4, Summer/1993, p. 17, courtesy JS; TCJK, p. 28; ANEC.

²⁵Writing MCB in Garver's room; plans for historical novel: JK to SLA, August 19, 1955, SL, p. 510; JK to MCE, May 9, 1956, SL, pp. 575–576; JK to AG, August 7, 1955, SL, p. 505; JK: "Note," MCB, cited in ACBWJK; JK, August 17, 1966, ACBWJK; MCE to JK, SL, note, p. 577.

²⁶End of affair with Esperanza; achievement of MCB: TRIS, pp. 93, 96; JK to AG, August 19, 1955, SL, p. 507; BMG, p. 237; MCB, pp. 19, 51, 211, 228–230, 241–243.

²⁷JK responds to "Howl": AG: "Howl," quoted in JK to AG, August 19, 1955, SL, p. 509; JK to AG, August 7, 1955, SL, p. 505; JK to AG, August 19, 1955, SL, p. 508; ACKB, pp. 234, 391; AG to AC, interview, April 20, 1973; AGCP: "Dedications to," p. 802; JK to AG, September 1–6, 1955, SL, p. 513; AG to JK, August 25, 1955, SL, note, p. 508; AG: Snapshot Poetics, p. 83.

²⁸"Good blonde" and "sweet presidents": JK: "Hitch Hiker," PJK, p. 467; JK to JCH, October

12, 1955, SL, p. 522; JK: "Good Blonde," *Playboy*, January 1965 (also see JK: *Good Blonde*, San Francisco: Grey Fox, 1993); DB, p. 10.

[29]Reunion with AG in San Francisco; legal issues OR; early meetings with GS, Natalie Jackson, and PO: ACKB, pp. 235, 236; JK to MCE, September 20, 1955, SL, pp. 518–519; MCE to JK, October 12, 1955, SL, note, p. 520; JK to SLA, November 10, 1955, SL, p. 530; GN, p. 495; SL, note, p. 518; JK to Keith Jennison, December 26, 1956, SL, note, p. 520; JK to SLA, note, SL, p. 521; AG: *Journals Mid 50s*, p. 136; JK to SLA, September 17, 1956, SL, p. 587; G&L, p. 192.

[30]JK's influence on GS and PW; yabyum party; JK as bodhisattva: G&L, pp. 202, 330–332, 326; DB, pp. 11, 12, 26; ACKB, p. 244; BMG, pp. 194, 199; JK to PW, November 22, 1955, SL, p. 531; AG: "Introduction," *Pomes All Sizes*, p. iv; GN and JM: "Catching Up with Kerouac," KAWB, p. 111; PBR, p. 307; AG: *Snapshot Poetics*, p. 92.

[31]The Six Gallery reading: DB, pp. 11–15; DM, pp. 203, 205, 217; BMG, p. 195–197; JK to JCH, October 12, 1955, SL, pp. 524–525; G&L, pp. 194–196, 199, 328, 330; PBR, note, p. 288; GN, KAWB, p. 49; Rebecca Solnit: "Heretical Constellations: Notes on California, 1946–61," *Beat Culture and the New America: 1950–1965*, p. 73; Josh Kun: "The Beat Goes On," *San Francisco Bay Guardian*, October 2, 1996, p. 59; MM: *Scratching*, PBR, pp. 273–275, 279–280, 282, 284; WPHG, p. 103; GN and JM: "Catching Up with Kerouac," KAWB, p. 111; ACKB, pp. 238, 241; JK to MCE, September 20, 1995, SL, p. 519; Robert Creeley: "Preface" to JK: *Good Blonde*, p. vii; Bob Donlin quoted in "Kerouac the Aspiring Writer Takes Refuge with a Bottle," LS, A4, undated clipping, courtesy Peter Alexis, Pollard Memorial Library, Lowell, Massachusetts; "Michael McClure, Poet," LS, June 22, 1988; Norman Mailer: "The White Negro," PBR, p. 596; JK to GS, January 15, 1956, SL, p. 539; Jack Goodwin to John Allen Ryan, Solnit: "Heretical," p. 73 (the letter was included in a 1988 booklet assembled by Goodwin for Solnit in 1988); JM: "Kerouac West Coast"; DA, p. 212; PBR, note, p. 288; GS: "A Berry Feast," *No Nature: New and Selected Poems*, p. 85; Turner: *Angelheaded Hipster*, p. 155.

[32]Visits with MM and Rexroth: MM: "The Artist as Endangered Species: Beat Ecology and Mutual Bio-Support," KAWB, pp. 47–48; "Michael McClure, Poet," LS, June 22, 1988; MM: *Scratching*, PBR, p. 275; JK to GS, January 16, 1956, SL, pp. 540–541; JK to PW, January 16, 1956, SL, p. 543; GN, p. 492; JK to GS, January 15, 1956, SL, p. 539; DB, p. 11.

[33]*Pull My Daisy* episode in Los Gatos; JK and CC make love: CCOR, pp. 261, 264–268; NC to CC, July 27, 1958, GB, p. 29; BMG, p. 199; G&L, p. 208; JK: *Dharma*, p. 7.

[34]Suicide of Natalie Jackson: NC to Father Harley, August 4, 1958, GB, p. 37; CCOR, pp. 271, 274; SL, note, p. 587; Maria Damon: "Victors of Catastrophe: Beat Occlusions," *Beat Culture and the New America: 1950–1965*, p. 147.

[35]Romance with SSK; mountain climbing with GS and JM; vision of rucksack revolution: JK to SSK, November 9, 1955, SL, p. 528; AGCP: "Sunflower Sutra," p. 138; DM, p. 210; DB, pp. 78, 90; JM: "Kerouac West Coast," KAWB; ANEC, DA; T&C, p. 121; JK: "An Excerpt From a Paraphrase of the Diamond Sutra: The Diamond Cutter of the Act of Wisdom," MSI No. 10, Fall/1981, p. 3. *New Testament*, Mark 9: 19, 31, Gideons International, p. 1042.

[36]JK leaves San Francisco; breach with AG: DB, pp. 90–91; CCOR, p. 275; JK to PW, February 7, 1956, p. 550, and January 5, 1956, SL, p. 537; JK to GS, January 16, 1956, SL, p. 541; JK: *Dharma*, pp. 342, 346, 350.

[37]1955 trip from Los Gatos to North Carolina; alcoholic despair, "Little Main Street Blues": CCOR, p. 275; JK to CC, December 30, 1955, SL, p. 532; JK to GS, January 15, 1956, SL, p. 538; JK to GS, February 14, 1956, SL, pp. 554, 557; DB, pp. 97–98; JK to GS, February 14, 1956, SL, p. 559; JK: *Dharma*, pp. 287, 360, 363, 365, 378–382.

[38]Christmas 1955; spread of Beat influence; Cayce; *Bridey Murphy*: JK to CC, CCOR, pp. 276–278. JK to GS, February 14, 1956, SL, p. 559. DB, pp. 109, 111; JK: *Dharma*, pp. 370, 399, 411; JK to PW, January 1958; Stanford, "About the Manuscript," *Dharma*, unpaged preface.

[39]Plans for 1956; daily life at CKB's: JK to PW, February 7, 1956, SL, pp. 547–548; JK to CC, March 2, 1956, SL, note, p. 571; JK: *Dharma*, p. 370.

[40]The writing of VG: JK to GS, January 17, 1956, SL, p. 545; JK to PW, February 7, 1956, SL, p. 549 (but in ACBWJK, JK wrote, "twelve nights"); JK to PW, January 5, 1956, SL, p. 536; JK: "Note," ACBWJK, also quoted in ACKB, p. 252; SL, note, p. 537; JK to GS, January 15, 1956, SL, p. 539; JK; *Dharma*, pp. 378, 381–382.

[41]JK trip to New York for relative's funeral; differences with AG: JK to GS, January 15, 1956,

SL, p. 539; JK to PW, February 7, 1956, SL, p. 546; DM, p. 214; JK to JCH, May 27, 1956, SL, p. 579; JK to LC, February 24, 1956, SL, pp. 562–563; JK to GS, January 16, 1956, SL, p. 541; JK to PW, January 16, 1956, SL, p. 543; JK to GS, March 8, 1956, SL, p. 567; JK: *Dharma*, pp. 375, 385–386, 414.

[42]JK and MCE fail to connect in New York: MCE to JK, October 12, 1955, SL, note, p. 520; JK to CC, CCOR, p. 276.

[43]Forest service job; dissatisfaction with representation: JK to PW, February 7, 1956, SL, p. 547; TCKB, p. 144; JK to CC, CCOR, p. 279; JK to SLA, February 24, 1956, SL, p. 561; JK to LC, February 24, 1956, SL, p. 562.

[44]JK "cures" Mémère: JK to CC, March 16, 1956, SL, pp. 571–573.

[45]Reincarnation; JK goes to San Francisco in 1956 and lives with CS; distressing news from MCE and GK; *Golden Eternity*: JK to CC, March 16, 1956, SL, p. 573; SL, note, p. 573; DB, pp. 118, 126, 149, 162, 164; GS: "Marin-An," *No Nature: New and Selected Poems*, p. 89; MM: "Jack's Old Angel Midnight" in JK: *Old Angel Midnight*, Donald Allen, editor, p. xiv; JK to JCH, May 27, 1956, SL, p. 580; G&L, pp. 205, 210, 218–219, 332; GS: "On Vulture Peak," *No Nature*, p. 329; GN, pp. 495, 515; GS: "Note on the Religious Tendencies," PBR, p. 306; GK to JK: April 1, 1956, SL, p. 574; ANEC, DA; TCKB, p. 150; JK to MCE, May 9, 1956, SL, p. 577; ACBWJK; JK: *The Scripture of the Golden Eternity*, PJK, pp. 592–593, 595–596; Robert Creeley: "Preface," *Good Blonde*, p. ix; JK: *Dharma*, 325, 390, 417, 419–420; ANEC; Ruth Montgomery: *Here and Hereafter*, p. 181.

[46]JK's relationship with Robert Creeley; conflict with Rexroth; failure to enlist GS as political ally: JK to JCH, May 27, 1956, SL, p. 579; AG: *Snapshot Poetics*, p. 89. Creeley: "Preface," *Good Blonde*, pp. viii, ix; JK to JCH, May 1956, SL, p. 582; GN, p. 526; ANEC, DA; JK to GS, March 8, May 1956, SL, pp. 569, 582; JK to PW, January 18, 1956, in Stanford: "About the Manuscript," *Dharma*.

[47]JK cooks in Marin-An; writes *Old Angel Midnight*: JK to GS, May 1956, SL, p. 581; JK to JCH, May 27, 1956, SL, p. 578; Creeley: "Preface," *Blonde*, p. x; DB, pp. 135–143; JK: *Old Angel Midnight*, PJK, pp. 544 545; Emily Dickinson: "I Heard a Fly Buzz," in Ruth Miller: *The Poetry of Emily Dickinson*, p. 32.

[48]Rapprochement between JK and AG; beautiful gold digger; JK threatens Viking: JK to CS, May 1956, SL, p. 582; JK to JCH, May 27, 1956, SL, p. 580; JK to GS, May 1956, SL, p. 583; JJMC, p. 155; ACKB, p. 11.

7: STARVATION RIDGE

[1]Trip to Desolation Peak: DB, pp. 170, 174–175; DA, pp. 99, 118; JM: "Letters," MSI, No.24–25–26, Spring/1991, p. 42.

[2]JK's sixty-three days on the mountain: DB, pp. 71, 185–188; JM: "Letters," MSI, No.24–25–26, p. 42.

[3]Relationship with Bob Kaufman: DA, pp. 145, 150; Jim Burns: "Bob Kaufman 1925–1986," KAWB, p. 13; Bob Kaufman: "Round About Midnight," PBR, p. 328; Mona Lisa Saloy: "Black Beats and Black Issues," *Beat Culture*, Whitney Museum, p. 163.

[4]The Beats at the height of the North Beach scene: Richard Eberhart: "West Coast Rhythms," *New York Times Magazine*, September 2, 1956, BMG, p. 211; author interview with Ed Crusoe; JK to SLA, September 17, 1956, SL, p. 586; DA, p. 156; G&L, pp. 224, 324.

[5]The Beats at a spiritual dead end in 1956; JK's plans for future: CCOR, pp. 279–281; JK to JM, November 6, 1956, SL, p. 590; JK to JM, November 6, 1956, SL, pp. 590–591; WSB to AG, October 13, 1956, SL, note, p. 591; LT, p. 181.

[6]Begins DA; paints; withdraws OR from Viking; homophobia: JK to JM, November 6, 1956, SL, p. 591; JK to SLA, October 7, 1956, SL, p. 589; JK to SLA, October 7, 1956, SL, p. 590; GN, p. 534; BMG, p. 216: "Some Mexican boys took Allen, Peter, and Jack home.... They ... had a gay orgy"; DA, p. 259; Mailer: "The White Negro," PBR, p. 597.

[7]*Evergreen* offer for SUB; Cowley as JK career architect: JK to SLA, October 7, 1956, SL, pp. 588–589.

[8]AG, GC, and the Orlovskys visit JK for sex and Beat strategies: AG to Robert LaVigne, BMG, p. 199; G&L, pp. 192, 330; BMG, pp. 199, 216, 222; DA, pp. 261–262, 280; WSB to AG, October 13, 1956, SL, note, p. 591; ANEC, DA.

⁹Beats' excruciating trip from Mexico to New York; JK and Helen Weaver: ANEC, DA; DA, pp. 284, 291, 294; GN, p. 342; JJMC, p. 124; author interview with Helen Weaver; author interview with JS, KALM; JK sex list, KALM.

¹⁰Richard Howard shelters the Beats: author interview with Richard Howard.

¹¹AG's promotional efforts; JK's veneration of LC: DA, pp. 302–303.

¹²MCE's editing of OR: ANEC, DA; ACBWJK, p. 5; ACKB, p. 223; GN, p. 537; G&L, p. 206; JK to JCH, June 23, 1957, *Beat Journey*, TUVOTI, 1978, p. 50; JCH: "Introduction," *The Beat Book*, p. 40; DA, p. 297; Dave Moore: "On the Road: The Scroll Revealed," *The Kerouac Connection* No. 10; AC: *Kerouac's Literary Method and Experiments: The Evidence of the Manuscript Notebooks in the Berg Collection*, passim.

¹³OR contractual matters: JK to JCH, December 19, 1956, SL, p. 592, GN, p. 541; SL, note, p. 597.

¹⁴The orgy at DiPrima's: AG and JK to CC, CCOR, p. 286; Diane DiPrima: "Three Laments," PBR, p. 360; DiPrima: "Brass Furnace Going Out: Song, After an Abortion," PBR, p. 363; BMG, p. 218; DiPrima: *Memoirs of a Beatnik*, pp. 101, 131–132.

¹⁵Verbal gay bashing; flirtation with Dalis: ANEC, DA; AG and JK to CC, CCOR, p. 287; BMG, p. 218; DA, p. 306.

¹⁶JK and GC visit Randall Jarrell: JK to AG, December 26, 1956, SL, pp. 594, 596; BMG, p. 544.

¹⁷JK loses his manuscripts; spends a boozy Christmas with family; writes a love letter to NC: DA, pp. 311, 313–316; JK to JCH, June 1952, SL, note, p. 375; JK and AG to NC, Early 1957, AE, p. 185; ACKB, p. 382.

¹⁸JK signs OR contract; the Beats visit Dr. Williams: DA, p. 319; William Carlos Williams to Theodore Roethke, BMG, p. 219.

¹⁹Affair with JJ, Mailer at the White Horse, contretemps with Weaver: DA, p. 321; JJMC: pp. 118, 124–125, 129, 132–135, 142; JJ: LCK 1995; ANEC, DA; Manso: *Mailer*, pp. 240, 243, 258–259; Adele Mailer: *The Last Party*, p. 175.

²⁰JK's life in WSB's set in Tangier: DA, pp. 330, 338, 341–346; LT, pp. 146, 150; BMWB, pp. 75–80; WSB to AG, BMWB, pp. 78–79; WSB to AG, BMWB, p. 77; JK to NC, CCOR, p. 288; JK to NC, CCOR, p. 289; BMG, p. 223; JJMC, p. 144.

²¹Brouhaha over SUB; AG and GC in Tangier; JK in France and England: JK to JCH, June 23, 1957, *The Beat Journey*, p. 48, and TCKB, pp. 154, 237; BMG, pp. 214, 224–225; DA, pp. 349, 351; LT, pp. 153–155, 158; AG to NC, April 24, 1957, AE, p. 186; Moore, KAWB, p. 83; Jim Burns: "The Day I Met Jack Kerouac," KAWB, p. 77.

²²JK leaves JJ in New York; resettles in Berkeley with GK; invites JJ west: JJMC, pp. 91, 147, 150, 153–154, 166–167, 174; DA, p. 364; G&L, p. 217; JK to JJ, JJMC, p. 156; author interview with Linda Gravenites.

²³Reactions to OR; JK's relationship with JJ; JK and GK return to Florida; JK plans Gary Snyder novel: ACBWJK; ANEC, DA; G&L, pp. 227–228; DA, pp. 324, 391–394, 407; CCOR, p. 291; JJMC, pp. 165, 178–179, 183; TCKB, p. 172; GK to Alfred G. Aronowitz: "The Beat Generation," *New York Post*, undated, spring 1959, ACKB, p. 308; JK to JJ, JJMC, pp. 178; JK: *Dharma*, p. 383.

8: TOUCHDOWN

¹JK on publication day OR: Gilbert Millstein in *On the Road with Jack Kerouac*, VHS 090, John Antonelli, producer, 1985. JK to AK, October 27, 1954, SL, p. 449; JK, sex list, JS, KALM; OR jacket copy, quoted in ACBWJK; JJMC, pp. 184–185; JK to EL, JM: "Kerouac and the New School," KAWB, p. 53; Charles Olson quoted in JM: KAWB, p. 111; Marty Gouveia in Pertinax: "On the Road with Marty and Jack," LS, October 2, 1962; PO in JM: "Kerouac and the New School," KAWB, p. 53; JK: *Dharma*, p. 18.

²The totality and pervasiveness of OR's impact: Ken Babbs: "A Cassady Rap," *On the Bus*, p. 91; *Esquire*, Phillip Moffitt, editor: *50 Who Made the Difference*, p. 23. Kevin Ring: "The Golden Juke Box," MSI, No.15, Spring/1985, p. 23; Alex Albright: "Van Morrison and Kerouac," MSI No. 15, p. 25; Robert Draper: *Rolling Stone Magazine: The Uncensored History*, p. 158; Paul Perry: *On the Bus*, p. 34; Jerry Hopkins and Danny Sugarman: *Nobody Here Gets Out Alive*, pp. 10–12; JK: "Beatific: The Origins of the Beat Generation," *Playboy*, June 6,

1959, PJK, p. 567; Hettie Jones: *How I Became Hettie Jones*, p. 42; Jim Christy: "What Kerouac Did for Me," in JM: KAWB p. 110; Arthur Ossterreicher, "*On the Road,*" *Village Voice,* September 18, 1957, p. 5, DM, pp. 241, 375, and ACKB, p. 396; JJMC, pp. 185–186; ANEC, DA; JK to EL, in JM: "Kerouac and the New School," KAWB, p. 53; Charles Olson in JM: KAWB, p. 111; GN, pp. 557, 732; TCJK, p. 164; JK to NC, October 29, 1957, *Beat Angels,* p. 60.

³Wallace and Wingate TV appearances: JK to NC, CCOR, p. 290; DM, p. 246; Hunter S. Thompson to Carey McWilliams, April 28, 1965, *The Proud Highway: The Fear and Loathing Letters, Volume I, Saga of a Desperate Southern Gentleman 1955–1967,* Douglas Brinkley, editor, p. 510; Thompson to Susan Haselden, March 18, 1958, *Proud Highway,* p. 110; "Tradewinds," *Saturday Review,* ACBWJK, p. 60, and DM, pp. 247, 376; JK to NC, October 29, 1957, *Beat Angels,* p. 60, TCJK, pp. 164, 237; ANEC; GN, p. 560; G&L, pp. 240–241; JJMC, p. 190; DM, p. 245; Gregory Mcdonald: *Boston Sunday Globe,* August 11, 1968.

⁴OR royalties and subsidiary rights; media issues; relationship with Millstein: Gregory Mcdonald: *The Boston Sunday Globe,* August 11, 1968; JK to NC, CCOR, p. 290; author interview with JS, KALM; AG to NC and CC, December 3, 1957, AE, p. 189; ACBWJK; JJMC, pp. 190–191; AG: "Prologue," Lisa Phillips, *Beat Culture,* pp. 18–19, revised version of "A Definition of the Beat Generation, *Friction,* No.1, Winter/1982, pp. 50–52; "Kerouac Depicts the Beat Generation," *Chronicle of the 20th Century,* December 1957, Clifton Daniel, editor, p. 808; G&L, p. 240; Gilbert Millstein: TJKC, liner notes, "Jack Kerouac/Steve Allen: Poetry for the Beat Generation," Rhino 4 70939-A.

⁵OR critical backlash: David Dempsey: "In Pursuit of 'Kicks,' " *New York Times Book Review,* September 8, 1957, p. 4; John Updike: "On the Sidewalk," *New Yorker,* February 21, 1959, p. 32, DM, pp. 256–257, and in TCJK, pp. 174, 29; Carlos Baker: "Itching Feet," *Saturday Review,* September 7, 1957, p. 19, DM, p. 375, and ACKB, p. 396; Benjamin DeMott: untitled, *Hudson Review,* Winter/1957–1958, p. 111, DM, p. 375, Gene Baro: "Restless Rebels," *New York Herald Tribune Book Review,* September 15, 1957, p. 4, R. W. Grandsden: "Adolescence and Maturity," *Encounter,* August 1958, p. 84; Phoebe Adams: "Ladder to Nirvana," *Atlantic,* October 1957, p. 180, DM, p. 375; *Time* quoted by Bill Randle: TJKC, "Readings by Jack Kerouac on the Beat Generation"; "The Ganser Syndrome," *Time,* September 16, 1957, CCOR, p. 291; ACKB, pp. 303, 396; Herbert Gold quoted in Bill Randle's liner notes for JK: "*Readings by Jack Kerouac on the Beat Generation,*" Rhino R4 70939-C; Gold: "Hip, Cool, and Frantic," *Nation,* November 16, 1957, p. 349, DM, p. 375, and GN, p. 557; Norman Podhoretz quoted in James Russell Huebel: *Jack Kerouac,* p. 316; Podhoretz: "The Know-Nothing Bohemians," *Partisan Review* 25, Spring/1958, pp. 307, 308, 317, DM, pp. 258, 378; Podhoretz: "Where Is the Beat Generation Going?" *Esquire,* December 1958, p. 316; Podhoretz: *Making It,* p. 253; Dennis King: "Norman Podhoretz's War on Kerouac," MSI, No.18–19, Fall/1987, p. 12; Bruce Cook: *The Beat Generation,* p. 96, TCKB, pp. 174, 239 (also quoted in DM, pp. 267, 379, cited in Janet Winn: "Capote, Mailer and Miss Parker," *New Republic,* February 9, 1959, p. 27); ACKB, pp. 295, 303; Pinchbeck: "Children of the Beats," *New York Times Magazine,* November 5, 1995, p. 39.

⁶JK and Robert Frank: John G. Hanhardt: "A Movement Toward the Real: *Pull My Daisy* and the American Independent Film, 1950–65," *Beat Culture and the New America: 1950–1965,* Lisa Phillips, editor, p. 223; Dave Marsh: *Glory Days,* p. 178; AG: *Snapshot Poetics,* p. 90.

⁷OR hits the best-seller list, but Viking fails to come up with a consistent publishing program for JK: CCOR, p. 290; AG: *Snapshot Poetics,* p. 91; JJMC, p. 204; BM: *Greenwich Village,* Beard, editor, p. 179; C&L, pp 242–243, 260; Thomas Wolfe to Maxwell Perkins, *Editor to Author: The Letters of Maxwell Perkins,* pp. 115–117, reprinted in Elizabeth Nowell's *Thomas Wolfe,* pp. 359, 362; Elizabeth Nowell: *Thomas Wolfe: A Biography,* pp. 215, 224; Maxwell Perkins to Thomas Wolfe, January 13, 1937, ibid., p. 265; AG to JK, BMG, p. 255; ACBWJK, p. 13; "Kerouac the Aspiring Writer," LS, July 19, 1987, p. A-4.

⁸JK's objections to Viking's handling of DB: GN, pp. 261, 562; JK: "Jack's Whereabouts Since 1951," JK document in KALM, courtesy JS; G&L, p. 243; David Herbert Donald: *Look Homeward,* p. 307.

⁹JJ's proposed visit to Florida: author interview with JS, KALM; Henri Cru: document in KALM, reprinted with permission of JS; JJMC, p. 220; JK to JJ, JJMC, p. 221; JK to CGS, undated; Lisa Phillips: *Beat Culture and the New America 1950–1965,* illustration, unpaged.

¹⁰JK as originator of New York jazz-poetry fusion movement: David Amram quoted in Uri Hertz: "David Amram on Jack Kerouac," KAWB, JM, editor, originally published in *Third Rail,* 1984, No.6, p. 16; Lisa Phillips: "Beat Culture: America Revisioned," *Beat Culture and the*

New America: 1950–1965, p. 33; WSB: "A Historic Memoir of America's Greatest Existentialist," TJKC, Rhino Records, Santa Monica, CA, 1990, p. 18.

[11]JK at the Vanguard: Lisa Phillips: "Beat Culture: America Revisioned," *Beat Culture*, p. 33; Val Duncan: "Kerouac Revisited," *Newsday*, July 18, 1964, KAWB, JM, editor, p. 40; Millstein: liner notes, "Jack Kerouac/Steve Allen: Poetry for the Beat Generation," TJKC; David Perry: "The Jack Kerouac Collection," album booklet, TJKC, p. 5; Steve Allen: "Kerouac was etc.," TJKC, p. 15; G&L, pp. 249, 251; Gregory Seese, GN, Dave Moore, David Perry, et al: "Sessionography," TJKC, p. 27; JK: *Heaven and Other Poems*, pp. 39–40, TCJK, pp. 167, 238; JM: "Kerouac West Coast," KAWB; Wolfgang Mohrhenn: "Interview mit David Amram und Jack Elliott am 16. und 19.9 1979," MSI, No.8 Summer/Fall/1980, p. 3; JJMC, pp. 220–221; JM: "Kerouac and the New School," KAWB, p. 54; Alfred G. Aronowitz: "The Beat Generation — Beaten," *Village Voice*, December 26, 1957, p. 10, DM, p. 245; Sheldon Harris: *Blues Who's Who*.

[12]OR as a film; NC's celebrity as Dean Moriarty; possible JK responsibility for bust: Bob Spitz: *Dylan*, p. 280; JK to NC, October 29, 1957, *Beat Angels*, p. 60, and in TCKB, pp. 167, 238; NC to Rev. Harley, August 4, 1958, GB, pp. 35–36; BMG, p. 250; WPHG, p. 105; DM, pp. 252, 377.

[13]NC's arrest and imprisonment: NC to CC, June 24, 1958, GB, p. 18; NC to CC, May 24, 1958, GB, p. 12; CCOR, p. 306; WPHG, p. 106; NC to CC, May 27, 1958, GB, p. 10; JK to AG, BMG, p. 250; NC to CC, August 10, 1958, GB, p. 40; JK to CC, CCOR, p. 326; NC to CC, August 20, 1958, GB, p. 315; NC to Rev. Harley, August 4, 1958, GB, pp. 35–36; GB, pp. 213–214; AG: *Snapshot Poetics*, p. 94.

[14]JK at his peak as a poetry reader: JJMC, p. 240; Uri Hertz: "David Amram on Jack Kerouac," KAWB, pp. 18, 21; G&L, pp. 250–251; Amram: *Vibrations*, pp. 295–296; AGCP, p. 802; William Butler Yeats: "The Poetry of Sir Samuel Ferguson," *Irish Fireside*, October 9, 1886, p. 220.

[15]SUB critical reception: Kenneth Rexroth: *Time*, February 24, 1958, p. 104, DM, p. 248; David Dempsey, "Diary of a Bohemian," *New York Times Book Review*, February 23, 1958, p. 4, DM, p. 248; Rexroth: "The Voice of the Beat Generation Has Some Square Delusions," "This World" section, *San Francisco Chronicle*, February 16, 1958, p. 3, DM, pp. 250, 377, and front and back covers, SUB Grove Weidenfeld paperback; Rexroth: "Revolt: True or False," *Nation*, April 26, 1958, pp. 378–387, DM, pp. 250, 377; Rexroth: "Daddy-O," *New Yorker*, May 3, 1958, pp. 29–30, DM, p. 250, 377; Henry Miller: Introduction to *The Subterraneans*, Parkinson, *Casebook*, p. 231, DM, p. 249; Uri Hertz: "David Amram on Jack Kerouac," KAWB, pp. 3, 19; JM: "Kerouac West Coast," KAWB; Mohrhenn, op.cit.

[16]JK's LP with Steve Allen: David Perry: TJKC, p. 5; Millstein: liner notes, *Jack Kerouac/Steve Allen: Poetry for the Beat Generation*, TJKC; Steve Allen: "Kerouac was etc.," TJKC, p. 15; Stephan Ronan: "Kerouac's Sound on Record," TJKC, p. 12.

[17]Reactions to JK's poetry readings: *On the Bus*, p. 88; Le Roi Jones: *The Autobiography of Le Roi Jones*, p. 153; Hertz: "David Amram," KAWB, p. 20; Mohrhenn: "Interview mit David Amram," MSI, No. 8, p. 3.

[18]JK brings Mémêre to Northport; JK's letter to Cru: JK to Henri Cru, 1958, KALM (permission to quote granted by JS, KALM); GN, p. 571; Robert Frank: TJKC, p. 20; DA, p. 397; BMG, p. 250; JJMC, p. 250.

[19]JK and GK in Northport: Mike McGrady: "Jack Kerouac, Beat Even in Northport," a series of two articles, *Newsday*, MSI, No.13, Summer/1983, p. 12; William Gargan: *The Kerouac We Knew*, compiled by JM, reviewed in MSI, No.13, Summer/1983, p. 12; Aronowitz: "Beat," *Post*, ACKB, p. 307; GK to AG, BMG, p. 250; WSB to AG, BMG, p. 250; JK to CC, April 17, 1959, *Dear Carolyn*, p. 22, quoted in TCJK, pp. 173, 239; Dorothy Kilgallen: "Broadway: Kerouac Buys $30,000 House," LS, December 1958, courtesy Peter Alexis, Pollard Public Library; TCKB, p. 173.

[20]JK's haiku LP with Zoot Sims and Al Cohn: Thiele: "The Last Time I Saw Jack," TJKC, p. 16; Joe Smith: *Off the Record*, p. 62; Barbara Ungar: "Jack Kerouac as Haiku Poet," KAWB, pp. 118, 123, 127; TJKC, p. 8; Michael Powell: "Kerouac the 'Endless' Poet, MSI No. 20–21, p. 1; PR, quoted in Ungar, pp. 127–128; G&L, pp. 211–212; AG:TJKC, p. 8.

[21]AG vies for leadership of Beat Generation; JK's alienation from friends; association with Northport gang; visit with Suzuki; DB critical reception: BD, p. 164; JK to GS, July 14, 1958, GN, pp. 574, 734; JK to EW, GN, p. 574; GN, pp. 566, 579; BMG, p. 251; GN: "Kerouac's Northport Gang," in JM: *The Kerouac We Knew: Unposed Portraits*, previewed by TC in "Book Reviews," MSI, No.11, Spring/Summer/1982, p. 17 (JK led the Northport boys "on minor

escapades," according to GN); DS, p. 60; G&L, p. 264; JK to Alfred G. Aronowitz, January 1959, DM, pp. 255, 378; AG to JK, BMG, p. 254; AG to JK, September 17, 1958, DM, pp. 255, 378; Nancy Wilson Ross: "Beat—and Buddhist," *New York Times Book Review*, October 5, 1958, pp. 5, 14, DM, pp. 256, 378; *Time*, October 6, 1958, p. 94, DM, pp. 255–256; Charles Poore: "Books of the Times," *New York Times*, October 2, 1958, p. 35; J. Donald Adams: "Speaking of Books," *New York Times*, October 26, 1958; ACBWJK; ACKB, p. 308; AG: "The Dharma Bums," *Village Voice*, November 12, 1958, pp. 3, 4, TCJK, p. 173; JK: "*Beatific*," PJK, p. 565; JK: "I Rang Mr. Suzuki's Door," *Berkeley Bussei*, 1960, MSI No. 10, Fall/1981, p. 4.

[22]JK and the Mailers; JK and Paul Bowles: ANEC, DA; Adele Mailer: *The Last Party*, p. 286; Manso: *Mailer*, pp. 245, 256–257, 262, 275; Mills, *Norman Mailer*, p. 159; Paul Bowles: *Without Stopping: An Autobiography*, p. 342; JK: *Dharma*, p. 402.

[23]Dody Muller; JK at the Cedar; JK in Steve Allen's apartment: DM, p. 261; Aronowitz: "The Beat Generation," *New York Post*, March 1959; GN, p. 590; Steve Allen: "Steve Allen Remembers Kerouac," MSI, No.8, Summer/Fall 1980, p. 23; TJKC, p. 15; JK sex list, KALM, courtesy JS; Allen: "Kerouac was etc.," TCJK, p. 15.

[24]JK's relations with Dody, Helen, Joyce, and Bob Lax: JK quoted in JJMC, p. 253; JJMC, p. 253; JK to RG, late summer 1954, SL, p. 444; JK to Robert Lax, October 26, 1954, SL, pp. 447–448; JK to AG, June 29, 1955, SL, pp. 491; BB, *Cerrada Medellin Blues*, "7th Chorus," "First Solo," p. 255; JK: *Dharma*, p. 396.

[25]Alfred Leslie and Robert Frank's visit to Northport: GN, pp. 582, 734. DM, pp. 261, 272; ACBWJK; Blaine Allan: "Oh Those Happy Pull My Daisy Days," MSI, No.22–23, Winter/1989/1990, p. 9.

[26]*Pull My Daisy*, the film: JK: "The Last Word," *Escapade*, October 1959, PJK, p. 587; DM, pp. 261, 268, ACBWJK; BMG, p. 258; Mohrhenn: "Interview mit David Amram," MSI, No.8, p. 3; GN, pp. 584–585, 735; PO to CC, January 10, 1959, AE, p. 194; Amram: *Vibrations*, pp. 313, 316; G&L, p. 262; Brad Gooch: *City Poet*, p. 205; "Notes on *Pull My Daisy*," MSI, Summer/Fall/1980, p. 8; John G. Hanhardt: *Beat Culture*, pp. 215, 223, 226; Jonas Mekas: "Appendix: The Independent Film Award," in P. Adams Sitney, ed., *Film Culture Reader*, 1970, p. 424, Robert C. Morgan: "Pull My Daisy, Fie My Fum—The everlasting underground film of the fifties," MSI No.22–23, p. 15; Larry Rivers: *What Did I Do?*, p. 173; Blaine Allan: "Oh, Those Happy *Pull My Daisy* Days," MSI No.22–23, Winter 1989–90, p. 4; JCH to Michael McCoy, March 29, 1953, MSI No.22–23, p. 3.

[27]DS, MCB, and MC ripped by critics: Ralph J. Gleason: "New Kerouac Effort Has Its Moments," *San Francisco Chronicle*, May 15, 1959, p. 37, TCJK, pp. 176, 239; Phoebe Adams: *Atlantic*, July 1959; *New York Times*, May 3, 1959, ACKB, pp. 311, 400, and TCJK, pp. 176, 239; Rexroth: "Discordant and Cool," *New York Times Book Review*, November 29, 1959, p. 14, DM, pp. 380–381; MM: *Scratching the Beat Surface*, 1982, p. 71; JTJ, p. 15; John Ciardi: *Saturday Review*, July 25, 1959, pp. 22–23, TCJK, pp. 178, 239; GN, p. 599; ACBWJK; Edward M. Cifelli: *John Ciardi*, pp. 283, 286.

[28]JK's early 1959 finances: Aronowitz: "The Beat Generation," *New York Post*, March 10, 1959, DM, pp. 266, 379; ACBWJK; TCJK, p. 173; GN, p. 586; DM, p. 272, 380; Wallis: *Route 66*, p. 227; "On the Road Back: An Interview of Jack Kerouac," *San Francisco Examiner*, October 5, 1958, p. 18.

[29]JK sells 34 Gilbert Street and buys 49 Earl Avenue: GN, p. 600; JK to Donald Allen, October 1, 1959, H, p. 50, and TCJK, pp. 178, 239; DM, p. 268; BMG, pp. 254–255; Donald Allen: "Introduction," H, p. 39.

[30]JK on *The Steve Allen Plymouth Show*: Steve Allen: *More Funny People*, p. 287; Steve Allen: "Steve Allen Remembers Kerouac," MSI, No.8, Summer/Fall 1980, p. 23; excerpts from NBC broadcast of *The Steve Allen Plymouth Show*, November 16, 1959, TJKC, and videotape *On the Road with Jack Kerouac*, VHS, Active Home Video, H090.

[31]Movie version of SUB, and JK at the San Francisco International Film Festival for *Pull My Daisy*: JCH to Michael McCoy, March 29, 1983, MSI, No.22–23, p. 3; MGM movie poster, TCKB, p. 188; DM, pp. 275, 278; James Powers: "Freed-MacDougall Pic Lacks Drama," *Hollywood Reporter*, June 21, 1960; *Time*, June 20, 1960; Hollis Alpert: *Saturday Review*, July 9, 1960; JK to NC, quoted in NC to CC, December 13, 1959, GB, p. 156; BS, p. 75; G&L, p. 327; JK's sex list, KALM, courtesy JS; CCOR, p. 338; "Notes on *Pull My Daisy*," New Yorker Films, MSI, No.8, Summer/Fall/1980, p. 8; TCJK, p. 178; GN, pp. 605, 736.

[32]JK reneges on promise to visit NC and lecture at San Quentin: BS, p. 69; NC to CC, October 25, 1959, GB, p. 140; CCOR, p. 336; NC to CC, quoted in CCOR, p. 335; NC to CC,

December 3, 1959, GB, p. 153; NC to CC, CCOR, p. 338; NC to CC, December 3, 1959, GB, pp. 153–154; NC to CC, CCOR, p. 335; NC to CC, May 19, 1958, GB, p. 10; NC to CC, June 24, 1958, GB, p. 19; NC to CC, July 25, 1958, GB, p. 28; CCOR, p. 345.

[33]JK on Route 66 with Welch and Saijo; Thanksgiving with Mémêre; yearning for wilderness: Saijo: "A Recollection," TT, pp. 4–5; G&L, pp. 283–284; CCOR, p. 346; TT, pp. 9, 33.; DM, p. 276; GN, p. 606; Michael Wallis: Route 66, pp. 2, 13; JK to PW, January 1958, quoted in David Stanford, "About the Manuscript," Dharma, unpaged preface; JK: Dharma, p. 418; PBR, p. 321; NC to CC, December 13, 1959, GB, p. 157.

[34]Pull My Daisy commercial release, critical reception: Dwight Macdonald: On Movies, pp. 310–311, DM, p. 379; Jonas Mekas: "Cinema of the New Generation," Film Culture, summer 1960, and "Movie Journal," Village Voice, November 18, 1959, p. 47; Peter Bogdanovich: "Movie Journal," Village Voice, January 5, 1961, p. 6; Tony Floyd: "Pull My Daisy: The Critical Reception," MSI No. 22–23, pp. 11–12.

[35]AG discourages VD; Ferlinghetti as JK publisher; flight from New York: BMG, p. 262; ACBWJK; BS, p. 5.

9: CRACK-UP

[1]JK and Mailer's crack-ups compared: JK to CC, October 17, 1961, Beat Journey, p. 90, TCJK, pp. 185, 240; Adele Mailer: The Last Party, pp. 209, 349; Manso: Mailer: pp. 311–318; the accuracy and attribution of the oft-reported remark re Mailer and Mickey Knox have been refuted in the letters column of the New York Times Book Review in 1997.

[2]JK's Big Sur misadventure: BS, pp. 106–107, 128, 151, 178, 331; JK to CC, CCOR, p. 360; G&L, p. 330; CCOR, pp. 177, 357; BB, p. 177; JK to Bob Kaufman, GN, pp. 618, 738; author interview with Linda Gravenites.

[3]JK returns east; crack-up continues: GK to JCH, G&L, p. 296; Bruce Cook: The Beat Generation, p. 83; BMG, pp. 269, 275.

[4]Beat obsolescence and the New Frontier: GN, p. 651; AG to JK, BMG, p. 275; DM, pp. 294, 382; JK to PW, April 10, 1961.

[5]JK's publishing woes and suicidal thoughts: JK to NC and CC, CCOR, p. 366; AG: Journals Early Fifties, Early Sixties, p. 178, TCJK, pp. 193, 240; AG to NC and CC, CCOR, p. 366.

[6]Archival material relating to paternity case: JK document, KALM; JK to NC and CC, CCOR, p. 367.

[7]Debasement of 49 Earl Avenue; JK's contentment on Alfred Drive, Orlando, turns to dissatisfaction: JK: "Jack's Whereabouts Since 1951," KALM, courtesy JS; TCJK, p. 194; JK to Donald Allen, June 10, 1961, H, p. 55, TCJK, pp. 194, 240; JK to CC and NC, CCOR, p. 368.

[8]JK writes Cerrada Medellin Blues; declines Grove's offer for DA; is robbed by boyfriend: JK: "Jack's Whereabouts Since 1951," KALM, courtesy JS; BB, p. 272; JK to CC, June 23, 1961, The Beat Book, p. 22 (also in Arthur and Glee Knight: Dear Carolyn, p. 24, TCJK, pp. 194, 240); BB, Cerrada Medellin Blues, pp. 252, 254, 258, 264–268; JK to CC, October 17, 1961, Dear Carolyn, p. 25, and TCJK, pp. 195, 240; ANEC, DA; GN, p. 625.

[9]JK's June 1961 meeting with Jan Kerouac, and his denial of her paternity: Joan Haverty: "My Ex-Husband Is an Ingrate," Confidential, August 1961, pp. 18–19, 53–54; JK to NC, April 3, 1961, Knight: The Beat Book: Volume 4, The Unspeakable Visions of the Individual, p. 9, and TCJK, pp. 194, 240; Albert Albelli: "Beat Bard Denies He's the Daddy-O," New York Daily News, March 14, 1961, DM, pp. 299, 383; Jan Kerouac: "Press Conference Speech," MSI, No. 28, Fall/1994, p. 14; GN, pp. 631, 738; Richard Gehr and Daniel Pinchbeck: "Dread Beat & Blood," The Village Voice, June 7, 1994; JJMC, pp. 136–137; Daniel Pinchbeck: "Children of the Beats," New York Times Magazine, November 5, 1995, p. 39.

[10]JK writes BS on Benzedrine: JK to Nanda Pivano, October 24, 1961, The Beat Book, p. 56, and TCKB, pp. 195, 240; ACKB, p. 401; JK to CC, October 17, 1961, Knight: Dear Carolyn, vol. 13, TUVOTI, p. 25, and TCJK, pp. 195, 240; ACBWJK (also see JK to CC, October 17, 1961, Dear Carolyn, p. 125, and TCJK, pp. 195, 240, and ACKB, p. 403).

[11]The writing, typing, selling, and critical reception of BS: JK to CC, January 7, 1962, Dear Carolyn, p. 26, TCKB, pp. 195, 240; GN, pp. 630, 632, 634, 738; author interview with JS; TCJK, p. 196; author conversation with SLA; Hunter S. Thompson to Paul Semonin, December 1, 1962, Proud Highway, p. 358; "Lions and Cubs," Time, September 14, 1962, p. 106,

DM, pp. 303, 384; Pertinax: "Kerouac in Lowell," LS, September 19, 1962, p. 7; Herbert Gold: "Squaring Off the Corners," *Saturday Review*, September 22, 1962, p. 29, DM, pp. 303, 384; William Wiegand: "A Turn in the Road for the King of the Beats," *New York Times Book Review*, September 16, 1962, pp. 4, 42, DM, pp. 303, 384; Ralph J. Gleason: "The Beatific Vision vs. the Beat Scene," *San Francisco Sunday Chronicle*, "This World Magazine," May 21, 1961, p. 28; JK to CC, October 21, 1962, DM, p. 384.

[12]JK's dissatisfaction in Florida; restless wanderings in Maine and Old Saybrook: JK to CC, October 21, 1962 (also see *Dear Carolyn*, p. 30, TCJK, pp. 196, 240); GN, p. 633, 635; G&L, pp. 296–297; JCH: *Visitor: Jack Kerouac in Old Saybrook*, vol. 11, TUVOTI (also see Richard Ardinger: "A Survivor on Survival: Two New Chapbooks by John Clellon Holmes," MSI, No. 12, Fall/1982, p. 22).

[13]JK in Lowell in the fall of 1962, with BK, SSK, Charles Jarvis, Huck Finneral, et al.: Pertinax: "Kerouac in Lowell," LS, September 19, 1962, p. 7; G&L, pp. 73, 304–305; Edward Manzi: "Stella Kerouac Was Always There," LS, February 14, 1991, MSI, No.24-25-26, Spring/1991, p. 47; author interviews with JS; Helen Sampas Surprenant, Betty Sampas, Aida Panagiotakos, Huck Finneral; VK, pp. 177, 236; DM, p. 303; TCJK, p. 198; JK to AG, October 4, 1962, *Street Magazine*, p. 51, and TCJK, pp. 198, 240; JK to Lawrence Ferlinghetti, in JK: "Among the Iroquois," *City Lights Journal* No. 1, 1963, p. 45, and in TCJK, pp. 198, 241; JK to EW, February 9, 1962, GN, pp. 629, 738; Pertinax: "On the Road with Marty and Jack," LS, October 2, 1962.

[14]Conflicts in Florida with Bourgeois and CKB's husband: JK to AG, October 4, 1952, *Street Magazine*, p. 51, and TCJK, pp. 198–199, 241; ACKB, p. 343; JK to LC, October 22, 1962, GN, pp. 640, 739; DM, p. 304; JK: *Notebook No. 38*, KALM.

[15]JK's move to No. 7 Judyann Court; SSK's visit; arguments with GC and GS: Val Duncan: "Kerouac Revisited." *Newsday*, July 18, 1964, KAWB, pp. 39–40; author interview with Betty Sampas; CCOR, p. 363; JK to CC, circa 1962, CCOR, p. 371; JK to CC, February 21, 1963, DM, pp. 309, 385; GC to AG, March 7, 1963, GN, p. 739; ACKB, p. 345; JK to GS, May 23, 1963, GN, p. 644.

[16]AG radicalized in sixties; JK's reactionary politics: BMG, p. 330; AG to JK, October 6, 1963, DM, p. 310; GN, pp. 654, 646, 740; G&L, p. 303; DM, pp. 308, 385.

[17]NC's July 1963 visit; JJ's *Esquire* remark and JK's slip: JK to CC, summer 1963, CCOR, pp. 371–372; CCOR, p. 378; JJ in *Esquire*, TCJK, p. 200; TCJK, pp. 200, 241; VG press release, 1963; G&L, p. 300.

[18]VG critical reception: *Newsweek*, September 9, 1963, p. 93, DM, p. 310; Saul Maloff: "A Yawping at the Grave," *New York Times Book Review*, September 8, 1963, pp. 4–5, DM, p. 310; Robert Phelps: *New York Herald Tribune*, September 8, 1963; JK to JCH, October 5, 1963, DM, pp. 310, 385.

[19]Perfunctory sex with AG and PO: AG and Allen Young: *Gay Sunshine Interview*, p. 8, TCJK, pp. 201, 246; DM, p. 312, 357 (privately circulated *Gay Sunshine* interview); G&L, p. 300; GN, pp. 651–652, 740.

[20]JK's relationship with Rev. Sweeney; Harvard fiasco; Val Duncan interview: Rev. Sweeney, SJ, to JK, May 1964, BDBC, p. 55; Val Duncan: "Kerouac Revisited," *Newsday*, July 18, 1964, KAWB, pp. 38–41; GN, pp. 648–651, 740.

[21]CKB's last days: author interview with Betty Watley; JK: notebook entry 1964, KALM.

[22]JK's relationships with Betty Watley, RL, Rev. Sweeney; CKB's death: author interviews with Betty Watley, RL; CKB: certificate of death; JK to Rev. Sweeney, BDBC, pp. 55–56.

10: A PERSONAL REMINISCENCE

[1]JK at Coward-McCann, Inc.: DA, p. 3; ACBWJK; TCJK, p. 202; ANEC, DA.

[2]Seymour Krim introduction to DA; JK's attitude toward post-Beat scene in New York: EA to JK, November 19, 1964, p. 1; ANEC, DA; Adele Mailer: *The Last Party*, passim; Phyllis Raphael, "Look at My Face," MSI, No.22–23, Winter/1989/1990, p. 34; author to JK, November 19, 1964; author in conversations with Frank O'Hara, JL, Truman Capote, Harriet Anderson, Lenny Gross.

[3]Author's editorial work on DA: ANEC, DA; author interview with Tony Sampas.

[4]Planning the physical package for DA; growing friendship between author and editor: EA to

JK, April 21, 1965; Mike McCoy: "Ellis Amburn: Editing the Final Words," MSI, No. 9, Winter/Spring/1981, p. 10; EA to JK, November 19, 1964, p. 2; ANEC, DA; Warren Tallman: "Kerouac's Sound," Thomas Parkinson: *A Casebook on the Beat*, DM, p. 383, and GN, pp. 447; EA to JK, November 27, 1964.

[5]Controversy over Krim intro to DA: ANEC, DA; JK to Seymour Krim, February 13, 1965, GN, pp. 658, 740; Seymour Krim in editorial conference with the author, Coward-McCann, Inc.; John Russell: "John Button's New York," *New York Times*, September 20, 1991, courtesy Alvin Novak; John Button in conversation with the author; DA, p. 13; EA to JK, February 18, 1965.

[6]Bantam paperback sale; DA; continuing Krim controversy: EA to JK, April 21, 1965; author conversation with Seymour Krim; EA to JK, April 21, 1965; both Mike McCoy in MSI No. 9 and TCJK mistakenly reported DA Bantam sale to be fifty thousand dollars after consulting me; JS corrected my memory when he showed me my letter to JK listing the amount at twenty thousand dollars.

[7]DA sales conference presentation; Biorkens: ANEC, DA; JK to J. G. Biorkens, May 3, 1965, MSI, No. 8, Summer/Fall/1980, p. 18.

[8]DA critical reception; ad campaign: Saul Maloff: "The Line Must Be Drawn," *New York Times Book Review*, May 2, 1965, p. 4; Charles Poore: "An Elegy for the Beat Syndicate of Writers," *New York Times*, May 4, 1965, p. 41; Nelson Algren: "His Ice-Cream Cone Runneth Over," *Book Week*, May 16, 1965; Hunter S. Thompson to Susan Haselden, November 12, 1958, *Proud Highway*, p. 140; EA to JK, May 7, 1965; Dan Wakefield: "Jack Kerouac Comes Home," *Atlantic*, July 1965, p. 69, DM, p. 317.

[9]JK, AG, and SSK in Europe; SIP: author's joint interview with JS and Betty Sampas; EA to JK, April 21, 1965; ANEC.

[10]Frequency of telephone contact between author and JK; JK's views on rock and roll: author interviews with Betty A. Prashker, JL, Ron Bernstein, and Ann Sheldon; ANEC; Bob Spitz: *Dylan*, pp. 329, 518; JK: *Kerouac—Kicks Joy Darkness*, RCD 10329, liner notes, Jim Sampas, producer; Ron Rosenbloom, "Interview With Bob Dylan," *Playboy*, March 1978.

[11]How VD came about: ANEC, VD; author letter to Mike McCoy, "Note from Ellis Amburn," MSI, No. 9, Winter/Spring 1981, p. 11; TCJK, p. 203; McCoy: "Ellis Amburn: Editing the Final Words," MSI, No. 9, Winter/Spring/1981, pp. 10–11.

[12]JK reads VD to the author; cavorts in Tampa; visits JCH; psychiatry; homoerotic life in Florida: ANEC, VD; VD, p. 11; Lawrence R. Broer: "Requiem for a Madman, Bum, and Angel," KAWB, pp. 11–14, and the University of South Florida publication, *Forum*; author interview with BK; DM, pp. 321–322, 386; GN, p. 665.

[13]JK's move to Hyannis; his July 4, 1966 arrest; AC's visit; GK's stroke: author interview with Betty Watley; ACKB, pp. 352, 354; Jerry Bauer in conversation with the author; author interviews with Tony Sampas and Jerry Bauer; ANEC, VD.

[14]JK's Italian promo trip for BS: ANEC, VD; JM: "Kerouac and Italy," KAWB, pp. 67–68, 94; Antonio Filiperti: *Kerouac*, in *Il Castoro 108*, La Nuova Italia, December 1975.

[15]JK's and SSK's wedding; life in Hyannis and Lowell: ANEC, VD; author interviews with JS and Helen Surprenant; G&L, p. 304; Rev. Armand "Spike" Morissette: "A Catholic View of Kerouac," MSI, No. 5, Fall/1979, p. 8; author interview with Aida Panagiotakos; author interview with BK; SSK in conversation with the author; TCJK, pp. 204, 206, 241; JK to Rev. Sweeney, early 1967, BDBC, p. 56; JK to Fabian Daly, February 1969, BDBC, p. 5; Robert Poole: "Nick Sampas at the Three Copper Men," "In Search of Kerouac in Lowell," KAWB, p. 61; author interview with Dennis and Ann Scannell; Alan Lavine and Jim Henderson: "Kerouac Aloud," MSI, No.13, Summer/1983, p. 24; author interview with Phil Coppola; Gregory Mcdonald: "Off the Road . . . The Celtic Twilight of Jack Kerouac," August 11, 1968; author interview with Guy Lefebvre; GN, 665, 741; "Stella Sampas, Unassailable Character and Unparalleled Friend," LS, p. 17, undated clipping, courtesy JS.

[16]JK and the psychedelic 1960s (episodes with Leary and Kesey, paranoia); Howard-Friedman party; Donald Droll dinner; O'Hara-Kerouac altercation: author interview with Linda Gravenites; ANEC, VD; BMG, pp. 276, 282; Timothy Leary: *Flashbacks*, p. 63; Timothy Leary in editorial conference with the author at William Morrow & Company; DM, pp. 314–315; Michael Schwartz and Neil Ortenberg, editors: *On the Bus: The Complete Guide to the Legendary Trip of Ken Kesey and the Merry Pranksters and the Birth of the Counterculture*, pp. xxi, 84, 86–89; CCOR, p. 386; Robert Stone quoted by Ruas, pp. 272–273.

[17]GK, JK, and AG in Lowell in 1967; NC as Prankster; JK's Lowell barroom style: JK: Note Book No. 91, courtesy JS, KALM; GN, p. 683; ANEC, VD; WPHG, pp. 146–147, 150; BMG, p. 410; author interviews with Gary Cheney, Jay Pendergast, and Maureen Murphy Coimbra; Jay Pendergast: "On Kerouac," MSI, No.6–7, Winter/Spring/1980, p. 19; JK to Nick Sampas, postcard, October 1969, in Robert Poole: "Nick Sampas at the Three Copper Men," in "In Search of Kerouac in Lowell," KAWB, p. 62; VD, p. 9; author interview with Linda Gravenites.

[18]VD delivered, accepted, and prepared for publication: EA to JK, July 17, 1967; AG to DM, "A Few Words on Kerouac's Merit," MSI, No. 2, Summer/1978, p. 12; Mike McCoy: "Ellis Amburn: Editing the Final Words," MSI, Winter/Spring 1981, p. 11; EA to JK, August 3, 1967; EA to JK, September 12, 1967; Ken Kesey: "Is There an End to Kerouac Highway?" 50 Who Made the Difference, editors of Esquire, p. 24.

[19]VD first-serial rights, critical reception: DM, p. 332; "Sanity of Kerouac," Time, February 23, 1968, p. 96; Gregory Mcdonald: "Off the Road . . . The Celtic Twilight of Jack Kerouac," Boston Sunday Globe, August 11, 1968, p. 12; Melvin Maddocks: Christian Science Monitor, March 21, 1968, p. 13; Thomas Lask: "Road to Nowhere," New York Times, February 17, 1968, p. 27; Peter Sourian: "One Dimensional Account," New York Times Book Review, February 18, 1968, pp. 4, 51; Times Literary Supplement, March 27, 1969, p. 317; JCH: "There's an Air of Finality in Kerouac's Latest," National Observer, February 5, 1968; cover of Penguin trade paperback; MSI, Winter/Spring/1981, pp. 8, 9.

[20]Editor-author relationship following failure of VD: Ron Bernstein to author, May 1, 1996; ANEC; author conversation with SSK; JC, home video, courtesy PC; Jacqueline Onassis in conversation with the author; notes, Jacqueline Onassis job interview conducted by author as editor-in-chief, Delacorte Press, Dell Publishing Company; author interview with RL.

[21]JK's decline in Lowell, 1967: high-school fiasco, Canadian television, Jan Kerouac's visit: Author interview with Jack Lang; DM, pp. 333, 388; Mcdonald: "Off the Road," Boston Sunday Globe, August 11, 1968, p. 16; Poole: "Nick Sampas at the 3 Copper Men," p. 61, JK: Note Book No.51, JS, KALM; author interview with Doris Boisvert Kerouac; Jan Kerouac: Baby Driver, in PBR, pp. 493–494; ULKC; TCJK, pp. 205, 206, 240; Jan Kerouac: "Press Conference Speech," MSI, No. 28, Fall/1994, p. 14; Washington Post, June 27, 1988, B4.

[22]JK's interviews with PR and Bruce Cook: Jim Curtis: DM, pp. 331, 388; ANEC, VD; PR, p. 362–364, 374–375, 378; GN, p. 685; Bruce Cook: The Beat Generation, pp. 89, 96–97; LS, June 22, 1988, p. 14; "Kerouac Gets What His Life Wouldn't Give," undated clipping, Pollard Memorial Library, LS, p. 14; ACKB, p. 363.

[23]The death of NC: ANEC; Hunter S. Thompson to Carey McWilliams, April 28, 1965, Proud Highway, p. 510; GN, p. 687; BMG, p. 411; WPHG, p. 158; AGCP: "Elegy for Neal Cassady," pp. 487, 489; VC, p. 432; CCOR, pp. 417, 422, 425; Pinchbeck: "Children of the Beats," New York Times Magazine, November 5, 1995, p. 43; NC card to JK in NC to AG, AE, p. 214.

[24]JK's anti-Semitic phone call to author; German trip: ANEC; WPHG, p. 151; JK to BK, 1968, courtesy BK; JC-GN interview, ULKC; DM, p. 335; GN, p. 688; Mcdonald: "Off the Road," Boston Sunday Globe, August 11, 1968, p. 11.

[25]JK and SSK's sexual breakthrough; JK's call to the author re New York trip; SLA's comment re JK's behavior at Nicholson's: VK, p. 203; Tom Hayden: Reunion: A Memoir, p. 19; GN, pp. 687, 743, JC-GN interview, ULKC; JK to JC, July 18, 1968, VK, p. 203; ANEC; Mcdonald: "Off the Road," Boston Sunday Globe, August 11, 1968, p. 16, TCJK, p. 214.

[26]JK goes to New York for Firing Line: author interview with BK; AG: "Literary History of the Beat Generation," BMG, pp. 422, 557; BMG, p. 422; AG in conversation with the author; John Antonelli video, On the Road with Jack Kerouac; TCJK, p. 213; Paul Brouillette: "Interview with Joseph Chaput," MSI No.3, Winter/1979, p. 8; author interview with PC; JC-GN interview, ULKC; VK, pp. 200–201; BMWB, p. 53.

[27]JC drives JK and his family to St. Petersburg: author interview with PC; JC home movie, courtesy PC; JC-GN interview, ULKC; author interview with Betty Watley.

[28]Daily life at 5169 Tenth Avenue North in late 1968 and 1969: JK to JC, November 13, 1968; JK and SSK to JC, Christmas 1968; author interview with PC; JK to BK, Christmas 1968; author interview with Betty Watley; JK to PW, courtesy JS, KALM; author interview with RL; JK: "The Last Hotel," Kerouac—Kicks Joy Darkness, CD liner notes.

[29]SSK saves JK and GK from poverty; JK on Easy Rider; Anisi Lowe confrontation; Pic; and "After Me the Deluge": author interviews with Betty Watley and RL; ANEC, Pic; TCJK, p. 214; DM, p. 342; RL: "Satori in St. Petersburg," Dharma Beat, No.1, Fall/1993; RL: "Kerouac: Cruising the Old Haunts and Hangouts," St. Petersburg Times, March 7, 1993, p. 4D; JK: Pic,

p. 174; PJK, p. 578; JK: "After Me, the Deluge," *Chicago Tribune,* September 28, 1969, Sunday magazine section, p. 3, PJK, p. 573.

[30]Events immediately preceding JK's death: author interviews with Betty Watley and RL; Richard Hill: "Jack Kerouac: Sad in the Sixties," *Knight,* Vol. 8, September 1970, GN, p. 697, 743 (Hill and Al Ellis visited JK with Jack McClintock, who wrote "Jack Kerouac Is Alive and Not-So-Well" for the *Miami Herald,* to accompany JK's syndicated "After Me the Deluge"); VK, p. 206; GN, p. 696; William Dunn: "A 'Beat' Era Love Story: She Recalls Marriage to Author Kerouac," *Detroit News,* August 19, 1979, p. 19A, in Jean-Pierre Gelinas: "The Death of Jack Kerouac," MSI, No. 11, Spring/Summer/1982, p. 21.

[31]JK's last correspondence with friends and final call to author: JK to CGS, October 4, 1969; author interview with Betty Watley; ANEC.

[32]JK's last night at home; fatal attack; agony in ER: author interviews with Jay Pendergast, RL, and Betty Watley; certificate of death, Florida, State Board of Health, Bureau of Vital Statistics, Pinellas County, John L. Kerouac, SSN 022-14-5342, 5:15 a.m., 10/21/69, copy made April 22, 1971, courtesy JS to EA, 9/23/96; FEP: "Addenda," MSI, No.10 p. 20; TCJK, pp. 216, 242; ACKB, p. 365–366; GN, p. 697; Al Aronowitz: "Jack Kerouac: Beyond the Road," *New York Post,* October 22, 1969; G&L, p. 313; DM, pp. 344, 390.

[33]Surgery and the death of JK: author interview with RL; JK's death certificate; Jean-Pierre Gelinas: "The Death of Jack Kerouac," MSI, No. 11, Spring/Summer/1982, p. 21; ACKB, p. 366; TCJK, p. 216.

[34]News of JK's death reaches friends and public: author in conversation with SLA; John Antonelli video, *On the Road with Jack Kerouac;* BMG, p. 425; Aronowitz: "Jack Kerouac: Beyond the Road," *New York Post,* October 22, 1969; TCJK, pp. 217, 242; CCOR, p. 424; G&L, p. 319; "Jack Kerouac, Lowell novelist, dies at 47," LS, October 21, 1969, p. 1; JCH: "Gone in October," *Playboy,* December 1972, p. 162, DM, pp. 345, 390.

[35]St. Petersburg funeral service; worth of estate: author interviews with Betty Watley, JS; Jack McClintock: "This Is How the Ride Ends," *Esquire,* March 1970, pp. 138–139; Ben Brown: "Kerouac's Back," *USA Today,* October 19, 1994, p. 1; Jean Nathan: "Eat to the Beats," *Time Out New York,* November 8–15, 1995, p. 7; "It's a Real Battle of Wills," *New York Post,* February 24, 1995, p. 7; "Kerouac Lawsuit," *Dharma Beat,* No. 3, Fall/1994, unpaged.

[36]Open-casket viewing of JK at Archambault Funeral Parlor: author interviews with Paul Dusamos, JS, KALM; Marc Charney, AP: "Jack Kerouac Remembered by Beat, Hip Generations," LS, October 23, 1969, p. 1; CCOR, p. 424; G&L, pp. 312, 314, 316; BMG, pp. 426–428; JK: "211th Chorus," MCB, p. 211; FEP to SLA, November 22, 1986, courtesy JS, KALM; David Perry: "Jack Kerouac's Daughter Drops Idea to Move His Grave," LS, April 1, 1996, pp. 1, 4; John Novack and Peter Ward: "Lowell Denies Daughter's Bid to Move Kerouac's Body to Nashua," LS, March 13, 1996, p. 4; Rev. Armand "Spike" Morissette: "A Catholic's View of Kerouac," MSI, No. 5, Fall/1979, p. 8; author interviews in Lowell; "Poets Join in Tribute to Kerouac," LS, October 24, 1969, p. 1; DM, p. 346; T&C, p. 121; Turner: *Angelheaded Hipster,* p. 76; ANEC; JK's notebook entries regarding whereabouts in 1944–45 (September 1944, October 1944, November 1944, January 1945, July 1945) courtesy JS, KALM; ACKB, pp. 336–337; JCH: "Gone in October," *Playboy,* December 1972, p. 158.

[37]JK's funeral at St. Jean Baptiste: Author interviews with JS, BK, PC; GN/JM: "Catching Up," KAWB, p. 112; Spike Morissette told *Washington Post* reporter Howard Mansfield that seventy five people attended Jack's funeral ("The Roots of 'The Road,'" June 27, 1988); BMG, p. 428, estimated the crowd at two hundred, but was not present; Spike Morissette: "A Catholic's View," MSI, No. 5, p. 8; Tim Madigan: "*Legacy: Biography of Rev. Armand Morissette OMI,*" MSI, Nos. 22–23, Winter/1989/1990, p. 37; ACKB, p. 367; Armand Chartier and Catherine Rivard Chartier: *Legacy,* Boston: Works-in-Progress Press, 1985.

[38]JK's burial in Edson Cemetery: author interviews with JS and BK; BMG, p. 428; "Poets Join," LS, October 24, 1969, p. 1; BMG, p. 428; CCOR, p. 428; Carroll E. Whittemore, editor: *Symbols of the Church,* p. 16; DM, pp. 346, 390; Andy Darlington: "Carolyn Cassady on and off the Road," MSI Nos. 24–26, p. 1; JK: "184th Chorus," MCB, p. 184; BS, p. 128; ANEC, VD; Dean Contover: "Safe in Heaven Dead," *Dharma Beat,* No. 3, Fall/1994.

EPILOGUE

[1]DM, p. 346; William Wordsworth: "Ode: Intimations of Immortality from Recollections of Early Childhood," *Norton Anthology of English Literature,* M. H. Abrams, editor, pp. 210, 213;

Joyce Carol Oates: "Down the Road," *New Yorker*, March 27, 1995, pp. 96, 100; Ann Douglas: "On the Road Again," *New York Times Book Review*, April 9, 1995, p. 1; Clark Coolidge: "Jack," *Village Voice Literary Supplement*, April 1995, p. 1, Doreen Carvajal: "A New Generation Chases the Spirit of the Beats," *New York Times*, December 11, 1997; DA, p. 124; C. J. Yung to Bill Wilson, January 30, 1961, in Bill W.: *The Language of the Heart*, p. 281.

BIBLIOGRAPHY

1. BOOKS BY JACK KEROUAC

1950 *The Town and the City*, New York: Harcourt, Brace and Company (edition consulted: Harvest/HBJ).

1957 *On the Road*, New York: Viking Press (edition consulted: Penguin Books).

1958 *The Subterraneans*, New York: Grove Press (edition consulted: Grove Weidenfeld).
The Dharma Bums, New York: Viking Press (edition consulted: Signet, 1959).

1959 *Dr. Sax*, New York: Grove Press (edition consulted: Ballantine, 1973).
Maggie Cassidy, New York: Avon Books (edition consulted: Penguin Books, 1993).
Mexico City Blues, New York: Grove Press (edition consulted: Grove Weidenfeld, 1990).
Visions of Cody, abridged edition, New York: New Directions.

1960 *The Scripture of the Golden Eternity*, New York: Totem/Corinth.
Tristessa, New York: Avon Books (edition consulted: Penguin Books, 1992).
Lonesome Traveler, New York: McGraw-Hill Book Company (edition consulted: Grove Weidenfeld, 1989).
Rimbaud, San Francisco: City Lights Books.

1961 *Book of Dreams*, San Francisco: City Lights Books.
Pull My Daisy, New York: Grove Press.

1962 *Big Sur*, New York: Farrar, Straus and Cudahy (edition consulted: Penguin, 1992).

1963 *Visions of Gerard*, New York: Farrar, Straus and Cudahy (edition consulted: Penguin Books, 1991).

1965 *Desolation Angels*, New York: Coward-McCann, Inc. (edition consulted: Paladin, London, 1990).

1966 *Satori in Paris*, New York: Grove Press (edition consulted: Grove Weidenfeld, 1988, also includes *Pic*).

1968 *Vanity of Duluoz*, New York: Coward-McCann, Inc. (edition consulted: Penguin Books, 1994).

1971 *Scattered Poems*, compiled by Ann Charters, San Francisco: City Lights Books.
     Pic, New York: Grove Press.

1973 *Visions of Cody*, New York: McGraw-Hill Book Company (edition consulted: Panther, London, 1980).
     Trip Trap: Haiku Along the Road from San Francisco to New York 1959 (with Albert Saijo and Lew Welch), Bolinas, California: Grey Fox Press.
     Two Early Stories, New York: Aloe Editions.

1977 *Heaven and Other Poems*, Don Allen, editor, Bolinas, California: Grey Fox Press.
     Take Care of My Ghost, Ghost, with Allen Ginsberg, New York: Ghost Press.

1992 *Pomes All Sizes*, San Francisco: City Lights Books.

1993 *Old Angel Midnight*, Donald Allen, editor, San Francisco: Grey Fox Press.
     Good Blonde & Others, San Francisco: Grey Fox Press.

1995 *Book of Blues*, New York: Penguin Books.
     The Portable Jack Kerouac, Ann Charters, editor, New York: Viking Press.
     San Francisco Blues, New York: Penguin Books.
     Selected Letters: 1940–1956, Ann Charters, editor, New York: Viking Press.

1997 *Some of the Dharma*, New York: Viking Press.

---

2. OTHER BOOKS

Allen, Steve: *More Funny People*, New York: Stein & Day, 1982.

Amram, David: *Vibrations: The Adventures and Musical Times*, Westport, Connecticut: Greenwood, 1968.

Auden, W. H.: *The Age of Anxiety*, New York: Random House, 1947.

Beard, Rick, and Leslie Cohen Berlowitz: *Greenwich Village*, New Brunswick: Rutgers University Press, 1993.

Bloom, Harold: *Yeats*, New York: Oxford University Press, 1970.

Bockris, Victor: *With William Burroughs*, New York: Seaver, 1981.

Bowles, Paul: *Without Stopping: An Autobiography*, New York: Putnam's, 1972.

Brando, Marlon, and Robert Lindsey: *Songs My Mother Taught Me*, New York: Random House, 1994.

Burroughs, William S.: *Naked Lunch*, New York: Grove Weidenfeld, 1959.

——: *The Wild Boys*, New York: Grove Press, 1969.

——: *Queer*, New York: Penguin, 1985.

Carr, Caleb: *The Angel of Darkness*, New York: Random House, 1997.

Cassady, Carolyn: *Off the Road: My Years With Cassady, Kerouac, and Ginsberg*, New York: William Morrow, 1990.

Cassady, Neal: *The First Third*, San Francisco: City Lights, 1971.

——: *Grace Beats Karma: Letters From Prison 1958–60*, New York: Blast Books, 1993.

Cayce, Edgar: *A Meditation Guide*, New York: St. Martin's Press, 1978.

Charters, Ann: *A Bibliography of Works by Jack Kerouac*, New York: Phoenix Bookshop, 1975.

——: *Kerouac: A Biography*, New York: St. Martin's Press, 1973.

——, editor: *The Portable Beat Reader*, New York: Penguin, 1992.

Clark, Tom: *Jack Kerouac: A Biography*, New York: Paragon, 1984.

Clarke, Gerald: *Capote: A Biography*, New York: Ballantine, 1988.

Cook, Bruce: *The Beat Generation*, New York: Scribner's, 1971.

Davenport-Hines, Richard: *Auden*, New York: Pantheon, 1995.

DiPrima, Diane: *Memoirs of a Beatnik*, San Francisco: Last Gasp, 1988.

Donald, David Herbert: *Look Homeward: A Life of Thomas Wolfe*, Boston: Little, Brown, 1987.

Dorfner, John J.: *Kerouac: Visions of Lowell*, Raleigh, North Carolina: Cooper Street Publications, 1993.

Drury, Allen: *The Pentagon*, Garden City: Doubleday, 1986.

Dupuy, R. Ernest: *WWII*, New York: Hawthorne, 1969.

Edington, Stephen D.: *Kerouac's Nashua Connection*, unpublished manuscript, 9 Vespa Lane, Nashua, New Hampshire, 1996.

Eells, George: *The Life That Late He Led: A Biography of Cole Porter*, New York: Putnam's, 1967.

Eisenhower, Dwight David: *Crusade in Europe*, Garden City: Doubleday, 1948.

Ellmann, Richard: *James Joyce*, New York: Oxford University Press, 1965.

Esquire, Phillip Moffitt, editor, *50 Who Made the Difference*, New York: Villard, 1984.

Foucault, Michel: *The Use of Pleasure*, volume 2, *The History of Sexuality*, New York: Pantheon, 1984.

French, Warren: *Jack Kerouac*, Boston: Twayne, 1986.

Furlong, Monica: *Merton: A Biography*, New York: Harper & Row, 1980.

Gifford, Barry, and Lawrence Lee: *Jack's Book: An Oral Biography of Jack Kerouac*, New York: St. Martin's Press, 1978.

Gilbert, Martin: *Winston S. Churchill*, Volume III, London: Heinemann, 1988.

———: *Winston S. Churchill: Road to Victory 1941–45*, Volume VII, Boston: Houghton Mifflin, 1986.

Gill, Brendan: *Cole*, Robert Kimball, editor, New York: Holt Rinehart & Winston, 1971.

Ginsberg, Allen: *Allen Verbatim: Lectures on Poetry, Politics, Consciousness*, Gordon Ball, editor, New York: McGraw-Hill, 1974.

———: *Collected Poems: 1947–1980*, New York: Harper & Row, 1984.

———: *Gay Sunshine Interview*, Bolinas, California: Grey Fox Press, 1974.

———: *Journals Mid-Fifties: 1954–1958*, Gordon Ball, editor, New York: HarperCollins, 1995.

———: *Snapshot Poetics*, San Francisco: Chronicle, 1993.

Ginsberg, Allen, and Neal Cassady: *As Ever: The Collected Correspondence of Allen Ginsberg and Neal Cassady*, Barry Gifford, editor, Berkeley, California: Creative Arts, 1977.

Giroux, Robert: *The Education of an Editor*, New York: R. R. Bowker, 1982.

Gooch, Brad: *City Poet: The Life and Times of Frank O'Hara*, New York: Knopf, 1993.

Gunther, John: *Inside U.S.A.*, New York: Harper, 1947.

Hamilton, Nigel: *Monty: Final Years of the Field-Marshal 1944–1976*, New York: McGraw-Hill, 1987.

Hart, B. H. Liddell: *History of the Second World War*, New York: Putnam's, 1970.

Hayden, Tom: *Reunion: A Memoir*, New York: Random House, 1988.

Heiferman, Ronald: *World War II*, Secacus, New Jersey: Derby, 1973.

Heilbut, Anthony: *Thomas Mann: Eros and Literature*, New York: Knopf, 1996.

Holmes, John Clellon: *Go!* New York: New American Library, 1980.

———: *Nothing More to Declare*, New York: Dutton, 1967.

Hunt, Tim: *Kerouac's Crooked Road: Development of a Fiction*, Hamden, Connecticut: Archon, 1981.

Jarvis, Charles E.: *Visions of Kerouac: A Biography*, Lowell, Massachusetts: Ithaca Press, 1974.

Johnson, Joyce: *Minor Characters*, Boston: Houghton Mifflin, 1983.

Jones, Hettie: *How I Became Hettie Jones*, New York: Dutton, 1990.

Jones, James: *WWII: A Chronicle of Soldiering*, New York: Ballantine, 1975.

Jones, James T.: *A Map of "Mexico City Blues," Jack Kerouac as Poet*, Carbondale, Illinois: Southern Illinois University Press, 1992.

Jones, LeRoi: *The Autobiography of LeRoi Jones*, New York: Freundlich, 1984.

Judis, John: *William F. Buckley: Patron Saint of the Conservatives*, New York: Simon and Schuster, 1988.

Karl, Frederick R.: *William Faulkner: American Writer*, New York: Weidenfeld & Nicholson, 1989.

Katz, Jonathan Ned: *The Invention of Heterosexuality*, New York: Dutton, 1995.

Kerouac, Jan: *Baby Driver: A Story About Myself*, New York: St. Martin's Press, 1981.

———: *Trainsong*, New York: Henry Holt, 1988.

Kerr, Graham: *The Graham Kerr Cookbook by the Galloping Gourmet*, Garden City: Doubleday, 1969.

Kesey, Ken: *The Further Inquiry*, New York: Viking, 1950.

Kinsey, Alfred C., Wardell B. Pomeroy, and Clyde E. Martin: *Sexual Behavior in the Human Male*, Philadelphia, Pennsylvania: W. B. Saunders, 1948.

Koestler, Arthur: *The Ghost in the Machine*, New York: Macmillan, 1967.

Kramer, Jane: *Ginsberg in America*, New York: Random House, 1969.

Lahr, John: *Coward: The Playwright*, New York: Avon, 1982.

Lauter, Paul, editor: *The Heath Anthology of American Literature*, Volume 1, Lexington, Massachusetts: D. C. Heath, 1990.

Lemire, Bernice M.: *Jack Kerouac: Early Influences*, unpublished manuscript, Boston College, Chestnut Hill, Massachusetts, May 1962.

Leverich, Lyle: *Tom: The Unknown Tennessee Williams*, New York: Crown, 1995.

Mailer, Adele: *The Last Party: Scenes From My Life With Norman Mailer*, New York: Barricade, 1997.

Manso, Peter: *Mailer: His Life and Times*, New York: Simon and Schuster, 1985.

Marcus, Phillip L.: *Yeats and the Beginning of the Irish Renaissance*, Syracuse University Press, 1987.

Margolis, Simeon, M D., and Hamilton Moses III, M. D., editors: *The Johns Hopkins Medical Handbook*, New York: Random House, 1992.

Mellow, James R.: *Hemingway: A Life Without Consequences*, New York: Addison-Wesley, 1992.

Merton, Thomas: *Contemplative Prayer*, New York: Image/Doubleday, 1969.

———: *Entering the Silence: Becoming a Monk and Writer*, Jonathan Montalde, editor, San Francisco: Harper, 1996.

———: *The Seven Storey Mountain*, New York: Harcourt Brace, 1948.

Miles, Barry: *Ginsberg: A Biography*, New York: Simon and Schuster, 1989.

———: *William Burroughs, El Hombre Invisible: A Portrait*, New York: Hyperion, 1993.

Miller, Edwin Haviland: *Melville*, New York: Braziller, 1975.

Millett, Kate: *Sexual Politics*, Garden City, New York: Doubleday, 1970.

Mills, Hilary: *Mailer: A Biography*, New York: Empire, 1982.

Montgomery, John: *Kerouac West Coast*, Palo Alto, California: Fels and Firn, 1976.

———: *Kerouac at the "Wild Boar,"* San Anselmo: Fels and Firn Press, 1986.

Morrison, Samuel Eliot: *The Two-Ocean War: A Short History of the U.S. Navy in the Second World War*, Boston: Atlantic Monthly Press, 1963.

Motier, Donald: *Gerard*, Harrisburg, Pennsylvania: Beaulieu Street Press, 1991.

Mott, Michael: *The Seven Mountains of Thomas Merton*, Boston: Houghton Mifflin, 1984.

McCarthy, Patrick: *Celine*, New York: Viking, 1975.

McClure, Michael: *Scratching the Beat Surface*, San Francisco: North Point, 1982.

McNally, Dennis: *Desolate Angel*, New York: Random House, 1979.

Nicosia, Gerald: *Memory Babe*, Berkeley: University of California Press, 1983.

Nowell, Elizabeth: *Thomas Wolfe: A Biography*, Garden City, New York: Doubleday, 1960.

Owens, Thomas: *Bebop*, New York: Oxford University Press, 1995.

Parker, Brad: *Kerouac: An Introduction*, Lowell Corporation for the Humanities, 1989.

Parkinson, Thomas: *A Casebook on the Beat*, New York: Thomas Y. Crowell, 1961.

Peirce, Neal R., and Jerry Hagstrom: *The Book of America: Inside 50 States Today*, New York: Norton, 1983.

Perry, Paul: *On the Bus: The Complete Guide to the Legendary Trip of Ken Kesey and the Merry Pranksters and the Birth of the Counterculture*, New York: Thunder's Mouth Press, 1990.

Phillips, Lisa: *Beat Culture and the New America: 1950–1965*, Paris-New York: Whitney Museum of American Art/Flammarion, 1995.

Pitt, Barrie: *The Battle of the Atlantic*, Alexandria, Virginia: Time-Life, 1977.

Plimpton, George, editor: *Writers at Work: The Paris Review Interviews*, Fourth Series, George Plimpton, editor, New York: Penguin, 1976.

Plummer, William: *The Holy Goof: A Biography of Neal Cassady*, Englewood Cliffs, New Jersey: Prentice Hall, 1981.

Podhoretz, Norman: *Making It*, New York: Random House, 1967.

Pound, Ezra: *Ezra Pound Speaking*, Leonard A. Doob, editor, Westport, Connecticut: Greenwood Press, 1978.

Pyle, Ernie: *Brave Men*, New York: Holt, 1944.

Reich, Charles A.: *The Greening of America*, New York: Random House, 1990.

Richardson, Joanna: *Verlaine*, New York: Viking, 1972.

Rimbaud: *Arthur Rimbaud: Complete Works*, translated by Paul Schmidt, New York: Perennial Library, 1967.

Rivers, Larry with Arnold Weinstein: *What Did I Do?* New York: HarperCollins, 1992.

Sampas, Charles G.: *That Was the Way It Was*, Marina Sampas, compiler, no city or publisher listed, 1986.

Shelden, Michael: *Graham Greene: The Enemy Within*, New York: Random House, 1994.

Simon, George T.: *The Big Bands*, New York: Macmillan, 1967.

———: *Glenn Miller and His Orchestra*, New York: Thomas Y. Crowell, 1974.

Snyder, Gary: *No Nature: New and Selected Poems*, New York: Pantheon, 1992.

Spoto, Donald: *The Kindness of Strangers: The Life of Tennessee Williams*, New York: Ballantine, 1985.

Stout, Janis P.: *Katherine Anne Porter: A Sense of the Times*, Charlottesville, Virginia: University Press of Virginia, 1995.

Tate, Allen: *Essays of Four Decades*, Chicago: Swallow, 1968.

Thompson, Hunter S.: *The Proud Highway: The Fear and Loathing Letters, Volume I, Saga of a Desperate Southern Gentleman, 1955–1967*, Douglas Brinkley, editor, New York: Villard.

Trilling, Diana: *The Beginning of the Journey: The Marriage of Diana and Lionel Trilling*, New York: Harcourt Brace, 1993.

——: *Claremont Essays*, New York: Harcourt Brace and World, 1964.

Trilling, Lionel: *Beyond Culture: Essays on Literature and Learning*, New York: Viking, 1965.

Truman, Harry S.: *Memoirs: Year of Decisions*, Volume One, Garden City, New York: Doubleday, 1955.

Turkus, Burton B., and Sid Feder: *Murder, Inc.: The Story of "the Syndicate,"* New York: Farrar, Straus and Young, 1951.

Turnbull, Andrew: *Scott Fitzgerald: A Biography*, New York: Scribner's, 1962.

Turner, Steve: *Angelheaded Hipster: A Life of Jack Kerouac*, New York: Viking, 1996.

Van Doren, Mark: *An Anthology of World Poetry*, New York: Harcourt Brace World, 1928.

Vidal, Gore: *The City and the Pillar Revised*, New York: Dutton, 1965.

——: *Palimpsest: A Memoir*, New York: Random House, 1995.

Wallis, Michael: *Route 66: The Mother Road*, New York: St. Martin's Press, 1990.

Walsh, Joy: "Vision of Martin Eden as Jack Kerouac," Clarence Center, New York: Textile Bridge Press, 1984.

Wertheim, Arthur: *The Rise and Fall of Milton Berle in American History, American Television*, New York: Times Books, 1978.

Wexler, Jerry, and David Ritz: *Rhythm and the Blues*, New York: Knopf, 1993.

White, Edmund: *Genet: A Biography*, New York: Knopf, 1993.

Whittemore, Carroll E., editor: *Symbols of the Church*, Abingdon Press, 1987.

Wiesel, Elie: *All Rivers Run to the Sea*, New York: Knopf, 1996.

Williams, Tennessee: *Memoirs*, New York: Bantam, 1972.

Wilson, Bill: *The Language of the Heart: Bill W's "Grapevine" Writings*, New York: AA Grapevine, 1988.

Wilson, James Q., and Richard J. Herrnstein: *Crime and Human Nature*, New York: Simon and Schuster, 1985.

Wolfe, Thomas: *Look Homeward, Angel*, New York: Scribner's, 1929.

——: *The Notebooks of Thomas Wolfe*, Volume 1, Richard S. Kennedy and Paschal Reeves, editors, Chapel Hill, North Carolina: University of North Carolina Press.

——: *Of Time and the River*, New York: Scribner's, 1935.

INDEX

Ellis Amburn grew up under wild West Texas skies. His mother and father were ranch hands, ran a gas station–grocery store, carried the mail, drove trucks, did anything to keep a family of five together during the Great Depression. Ellis won a writing prize that brought him to New York and a job at *Newsweek* at twenty. After studying at Columbia he got into book publishing, eventually becoming editor-in-chief of Delacorte Press and editorial director of G. P. Putnam's Sons.

Following Jack Kerouac's advice to take rock 'n' roll seriously, Amburn began his writing career with well-received biographies of the Texas pioneers of rock (Roy Orbison, Janis Joplin, and Buddy Holly). *Subterranean Kerouac* is the fourth book he has published since 1990. He lives in Key West, Florida, and Tifton, Georgia.